Standard Plate Number Catalog

EVALUATIONS
FOR SPECIFIC NUMBERS

Compiled and edited by
KIM D. JOHNSON
Assisted by
W. WALLACE CLELAND
JOHN L. LARSON

This catalog is a carefully prepared analysis forming an authoritative guide to the retail value of specific plate numbers and positions for all postal issues from 1851 as sheet stamps, coil stamps, and booklet panes including:

Commemoratives
Regular Postage
Air Mail
Postage Due
Parcel Post
Hunting Permit
Registration
Special Delivery
Special Handling
Certified Mail
Official
Postal Saving
Possessions
Newspaper

BUREAU ISSUES ASSOCIATION, Inc.
P.O. Box 2641 • Reston, VA 20195

This edition of the Durland Standard Plate Number Catalog is dedicated to the memory of George V. H. Godin who at the time of his death was editor of this work as well as Executive Secretary of the Bureau Issues Association.

Library of Congress Catalogue No. 55-22466
ISBN O-930412-24-9

Printed in the United States of America

INDEX

APPENDICES

GENERAL INFORMATION

POSITION ABBREVIATIONS

T = top	UL = upper left	CUL = center pane UL
L = left	UR = upper right	CUR = center pane UR
R = right	LL = lower left	CLL = center pane LL
B = bottom	LR = lower right	CLR = center pane LR

DATA SOURCES

The listing of early plate numbers does NOT guarantee that plate number blocks exist. The data used are based on the research by Mr. C.B. Durland and are supplemented by the plate number surveys conducted by the Bureau Issues Association and later research of the records at the Bureau of Engraving & Printing primarily by W. Wallace Cleland and others. Many of the reports were based on the plate number only and were not accompanied by a Scott Catalog number. The reports also did not list whether the basis was a plate single or a plate block. We have listed many numbers under various Scott Catalog numbers which could exist but have NOT been reported. These are shown with a †. We have delisted some previously listed plate numbers where erroneous entries had been made in past editions. Modern numbers are based on reports furnished to the Bureau Issues Association monthly publication, "The United States Specialist."

ABBREVIATIONS & SYMBOLS

c = used to indicate reported rare coil numbers that do not exist as coil waste.
* = a scarce plate number. (Not used when plate has been priced). See Appendix F for basis.
† = an unreported plate number or unreported position.
‡ = the position does NOT exist.
I = intermediate gauge plate without star.
N = read footnote.
o = the same plate number issued both tagged and untagged.
P = this number has only been reported as a Bureau Precancel.
s = wide gauge plate with star.
w = wide gauge plate without star, or coil with plate number farther from stamp.
Z = read footnote.

PRICING

The prices in this edition are based on plate blocks in *VERY FINE* condition. All commemoratives and regular rotary press issues use a format which lists the price followed by an appropriate numbers of blank □ for the positions. Flat plate commemoratives show a price for the top positions followed by □ and then another price followed by □ for the remaining positions. If the position has not been reported a † appears in the place of the □. If the position does not exist, a ‡ appears in the place of the □. If the price of a position is different, this is noted by a subscript number (example $□_3$ means 3 times the listed price) for that position. Multiply the listed price by the number shown in the subscript to obtain the price for the position.

The prices in this book are based for the greater part on a reasonable return for the cost, including labor, involved in the sale of one specific plate block to one customer.

We wish to point out very explicitly that a low quantity of impressions of any plate does not mean that the number is scarce. A specific example is Scott #803 plates 23445 & 23446 which had only 750 impressions (meaning that there are ONLY a total of 750 plate blocks of each position and of each number possible). One collector reportedly purchased the entire issue and his holdings have now been dispersed. The reverse is true of plate 25236 which had 192,577 impressions. This was a 3 cent Liberty issue plate that was sent to the post offices in time for Christmas mailings. It was used before many collectors even knew that it had been issued. The criterion is the number of copies that were saved and are available to collectors.

On any issue where a limited amount of information does not permit proper evaluation of the price, we have used a dash in place of a price. This does not mean that the price is necessarily higher or lower than the other plates in the issue. It does mean that there is a difference of opinion concerning the price.

MISCELLANEOUS

The listings of the plate numbers on rotary press coil stamps and booklet panes prior to 1981 are those that have been sent to the pressroom. They are listed for the benefit of collectors of partial plate numbers. An exception is made in the case of the product of the 9 color Huck where we list ONLY reported numbers for the coils. Up to about 1981, we list the actual plate number digits appearing in the selvage of the plate block. After the changeover to the new numbering system, we tabulate the single or multiple digits for each color in the order listed from left to right in the UL plate block.

Please read page 223 for additional information on the new plate numbering system.

ACKNOWLEDGEMENTS

We wish to acknowledge with our sincere thanks the cooperation and assistance given by: **P.R. Beutel, Jim Cochrane, Al Haake, Lewis Kaufman, Robert E. Kitson, Neal Lamb, Ken Lawrence, Joseph M. Napp, Jacques C. Schiff Jr., William O. Schuman, Clay Stabler, David Stiff, Stephen Wittig, Charles H. Yeager** and all of the reporters and traders listed in "The United States Specialist" monthly issues. In connection with compiling the pre-Bureau listings, we wish to thank **Bernard Biales, Richard Celler** and **Merritt Jenkins.** The following gave special help with the listings of Officials: **Alan Campbell, Rollin Huggins, Jr., Bob Merkovits** and **William Mooz.**

IMPRINTS

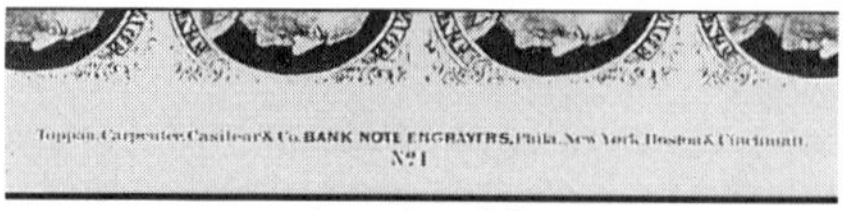

Imprint A1

"Toppan, Carpenter, Casilear & Co. BANK NOTE ENGRAVERS. Phila., New York, Boston & Cincinnati" on one line, with "No. ?" showing the plate number on a line underneath. The imprint is centered in the side margin, reading down in the left margin, and up in the right margin. The imprint and plate number are in the color of the stamp. Used for the plates of the imperforate 1851 issue.

Imprint A2

On later plates used only on the perforated issue of 1857, the word "Casilear" is deleted (although parts of it occasionally show, since it was left off by doing partial transfers from the original transfer roll). "P." occurs after the plate number, except on plates 10 and 11 of the 3c value.

Imprint A3

"TOPPAN CARPENTER & Co. PHILADELPHIA" in white on a colored tablet, with "No. ? P" in color on a line below the imprint. The imprint is centered in the side margin, reading down in the left margin, and up in the right margin. Used for 1c plates 11 and 12, 12c plate 3, 30c plate 1 and 90c plate 1.

Imprint B1

"ENGRAVED BY THE NATIONAL BANK NOTE COMPANY CITY OF NEW-YORK" on one line, with "No. ? Plate." underneath. The words "NATIONAL BANK NOTE COMPANY" are in white on a colored tablet, while the other words and plate number are in the color of the stamp. Imprint and plate number were centered in the bottom margin only. Used on the issues of 1861-6.

Imprint B2

"NATIONAL BANK NOTE Co. NEW YORK" in white letters on colored tablet. "No." followed by the plate number are in color and in italics, and follow the imprint in TL and BL positions, and precede it in TR and BR positions. The imprint and plate number are on the same line, although at various distances. The imprint was normally centered in the margin of the pane (i.e., in the center of 10 stamps), except that on the bicolored stamps of the 1869 series it was centered on each half pane (i.e., in the center of 5 stamps). Used on the issue of 1869, and the early plates of the 1870 issue.

Imprint B3

"ENGRAVED & PRINTED BY THE" on one line and "NATIONAL BANK NOTE CO. NEW YORK" on a line below it, with both in white letters on a colored tablet. Plate numbers and placements similar to imprint B2. This imprint is found on the same plate as imprint B2, but in different positions (on plate 44, the BL position is imprint B3 and the BR position imprint B2). Used on later plates of the 1870 issue.

Imprint E1

E1) "PRINTED BY THE" on one line, and "CONTINENTAL BANK NOTE CO. NEW YORK" on the line beneath it, with both in white letters on a colored tablet. The imprints on regular stamps and on 200 subject plates of Officials are centered in top or bottom margins of a pane of 100, with the plate number following the imprint in TL and BL positions, and preceding it in TR and BR positions. One 100 subject Official plates, the imprint is over stamps 2 and 3, or under 92 and 93, and the plate number follows the imprint, centered in the margin. The plate numbers are preceded by a large "No." in colored italics. The plate numbers themselves are solid block colored numbers about half the height as the "No.". Used on plates 2-193.

IMPRINTS

Imprint E2

The imprint is the same as E1, but the plate numbers are in large italics and the same size as "No." Used on plates 1 and 219-310 (except for Newspaper plates).

Imprint E3

"ENGRAVED AND PRINTED BY THE" on the top line, and "CONTINENTAL BANK NOTE CO. NEW YORK" on the second line, with both in white on a colored tablet. Imprint centered in top and bottom margins, but with no accompanying plate number. Used on Newspaper plates.

Imprint F

"AMERICAN BANK NOTE COMPANY." in colored letters with shading to the lower right. The imprint is centered in top or bottom margin and covers only two stamps. "No." followed by the plate number are in colored italics and similar in size to those of imprints B2 and B3, but smaller than those of imprint E2. The plate number follows the imprint in TL and BL positions, and precedes it in TR and BR positions, except on Special Delivery plates, where it always follows the imprint. Used on plates 311-481, plus 488, 489, 495, 496, 552 of the 1879 issues, plus plate numbers 21-25, 72, 73 of the 1890 issues. In addition, the bottom positions of plates between 483 and 723 with imprint F1 in the top margin are imprint F (i.e., the serial letter was placed in the top margin only on the banknote issues).

Imprint F1

Similar to imprint F, but with a serial letter or pair of letters in solid block color between the imprint and plate number. Used on the top positions of plates 483-7, 490-4 and 497-723 (except 552) of the 1879 issue, and on top and bottom positions of plates 1-20, 26-71, 74-269 of the 1890 issue.

Imprint F2

Similar to imprint F, but with a serial letter followed by an italic "1" of the same size as the numerals of the plate number on the opposite side of the imprint from the plate number. Used on all positions of plates 270-349 of the 1890 issue.

Imprint F3

Similar to imprint F, but with a serial letter or pair of letters on the opposite side of the imprint from the plate number. Used on all positions of the Columbian issue of 1893.

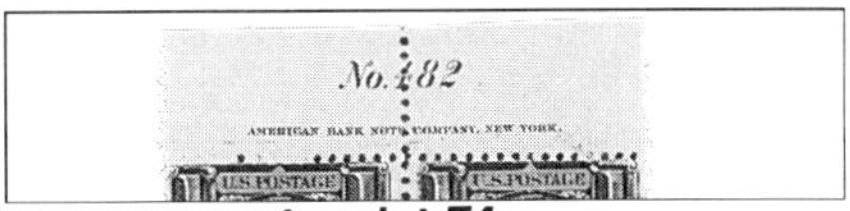

Imprint F4

"No. 482" in italics of the same size as imprint F, centered in the top margin, with "AMERICAN BANK NOTE COMPANY, NEW YORK" in very small print centered under the plate number. The same imprint was centered in the bottom margin, but with no plate number. Used only on Newspaper plate 482.

BUREAU IMPRINTS

Following the precedent established by the BANK NOTE COMPANIES in exhibiting their imprint on the margins of the sheets of Postage Stamps, the BUREAU OF ENGRAVING & PRINTING adopted the practice when awarded the contract in 1894. BUREAU IMPRINTS appeared, beginning with Plate #1 (approved June 19, 1894) until December, 1911 when it was discontinued for reasons of economy.

In the "PLATE NUMBER CHECKLIST" compiled and issued by the BUREAU ISSUES ASSOCIATION reference is made to the several types of imprint and Plate Number Combinations herein illustrated.

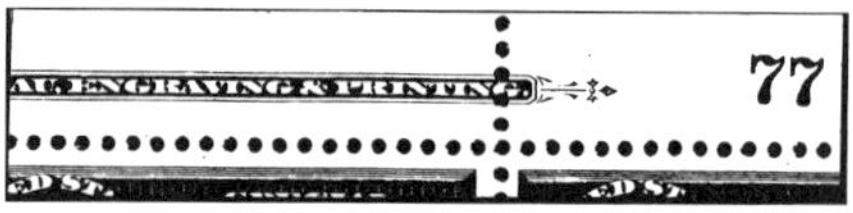

IMPRINT III

IMPRINT - Colorless, shaded capitals. Outer frame line. Ornate ends. Measurement - 56.75 mm. x 2 mm.

PLATE NUMBER - Shaded numerals - 3.2 mm.

Used on SPECIAL DELIVERY, NEWSPAPER & PERIODICAL stamp plates.

————INITIAL PLATE—#77.

IMPRINT I

IMPRINT - Colored rectangle with weak frame line. Colorless shaded letters - Measurement - 26.6 mm. x 1.7 mm.

PLATE NUMBER - Shaded numerals - 3.2 mm. high.

————INITIAL PLATE-#1.

IMPRINT IV

IMPRINT - Same as imprint II.

PLATE NUMBER - Heavily shaded numerals 2.7 mm. in height.

————INITIAL PLATE—#155.

IMPRINT II

IMPRINT - Outer frame line strong. Ends ornamented with rosettes and arrowheads - Meas. 37 mm. x 2 mm.

PLATE NUMBER - Shaded numerals as Imprint I - 3.2 mm.

Plate 74 was the first Imprint II plate assigned but 76 was the first one certified and used to print stamps.

————INITIAL PLATE—#76.

IMPRINT V

IMPRINT - Same as Type II.

PLATE NUMBER - Thin line numerals 2.7 mm. high.

Used generally, with modifications, on all subsequent plates.

————INITIAL PLATE—#255.

IMPRINT VI

IMPRINT - Same as Imprint III.

PLATE NUMBER - Same as Imprint IV.

Used - SPECIAL DELIVERY, NEWSPAPER & PERIODICAL stamp plates.

————INITIAL PLATE—#257.

BUREAU IMPRINTS

IMPRINT VII

IMPRINT - Same as imprint III.

PLATE NUMBER - Numerals same as Imprint V.

Used only on SPECIAL DELIVERY stamp plates.

————INITIAL PLATE—#381.

IMPRINT VIII

IMPRINT - Shaded colorless capitals in colored rectangle. Thin frame. Fork & Arrowhead ornaments at ends. 35.75 x 1.3 mm.

PLATE NUMBER - Numerals same as Imprint V.

Used - TRANS-MISSISSIPPI issue only.

————INITIAL PLATE—#590.

IMPRINT IX

IMPRINT - omitted.

PLATE NUMBER - Numerals same as Imprint V.

First Use - "STAMP BOOKLET" plates.

————INITIAL PLATE—#988.

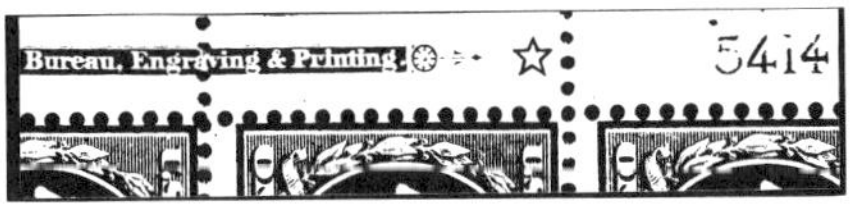

IMPRINT X

IMPRINT & PLATE NUMBER - similar to Imprint V with OPEN STAR 2.7 mm. high between.

Used on plates having varying gutter widths between the vertical rows of stamp subjects.

————INITIAL PLATE—#4968.

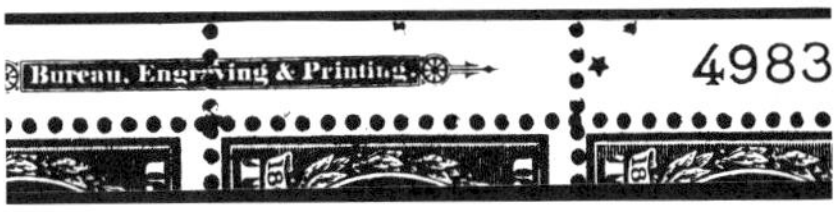

IMPRINT XI

IMPRINT & PLATE NUMBER - similar to Imprint X. Small solid star 1.3 mm. high substituted for open star.

Used similarly to Imprint X on plates of the LINCOLN COMMEMORATIVE and on 1¢ ordinary - #4980 & 2¢ ordinary-#4988

————INITIAL PLATE—#4976.

IMPRINT XII

IMPRINT & PLATE NUMBER - similar to Imprint V with capital "A" added between the imprint and number. "A" is 2.7 mm.

Used for plates having uniform horizontal spacing between rows of subjects, but wider than in those with Imprint V.

————INITIAL PLATE—#5557.

IMPRINT XIII

IMPRINT - omitted.

Used on plates having the same characteristics as Imprint XII.

————INITIAL PLATE—#5805.

IMPRINT XIV

PLATE NUMBER - together with the DENOMINATION in large capital letters 4.6 mm. high.

The VALUE was conspicuously displayed in the sheet margins that an error may not so easily occur due to all denominations being in the same color.

Used on PARCEL POST stamp plates - series, 1912.

————INITIAL PLATE—#6161.

IMPRINT XV- see pg. 298

2¢ TYPES 1894-1898 ISSUES

TYPE I

The horizontal lines of the ground work run across the double triangles and are of the same thickness. Plate numbers used are between 1 and 125 plus 144.

TYPE II

The horizontal lines of the groundwork run across the double triangles but are thinner within the triangles. Plate numbers used are 126, 131, 132, 133, 169 and part of 170.

TYPE III

The horizontal lines of the groundwork do not run across the double lines of the triangles. The lines inside the inner triangle are thin like type II.

Plate numbers used are 141, 142, 143, 145, 146, 148-158, 160, part of 170, and between 171 and 503.

TYPE IV

The corner triangles on Type IV are similar to those on Type III. In the center of the head are two prominent hair lines; on Type III the lower one extends farther left, while on Type IV the top one is longer and heavier. On Type III the toga button has a light line on the right side, while on Type IV this is a heavy line.

Plate numbers used are between 505 and 1493.

Types II-III

Except for triangles these two types are the same. Type III triangles are the same as Type IV.

Type IV

Arrows point to two major differences, viz.: central hairline extended to left and outline added to right side of toga button.

Pre-Bureau Issues

Plate blocks, strips or singles are very rare on early U.S. stamps. On Scott numbers 7-205 we use a dagger (†) to indicate plate numbers that have not been reported in the survey carried out by John C. Chapin ("A Census of United States Classic Plate Blocks 1851-1882", The Collectors Club, New York, 1982 and supplements from 1984 through 1990). On issues from Scott number 206-245 we use the † for all plates which we have not seen or had reported to us. Other plate numbers certainly exist; please report these. On many of these early issues, plate numbers exist more commonly on proofs than on issued stamps, and †np indicates a number "n" known on proofs only.

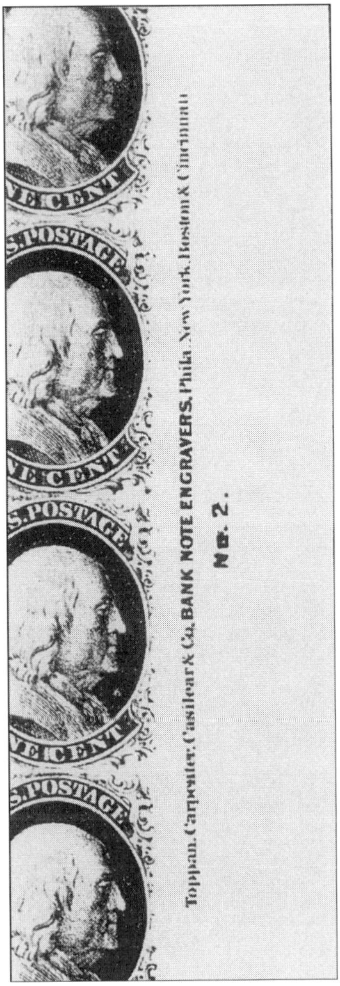

1851 ISSUE

Printed by Toppan, Carpenter, Casilear & Co.

Unwatermarked Imperforate

Imprint A1

#7 1¢ FRANKLIN, type II

Basic Price **L, R**

Imprint Block of 8 —

2 3

Plate 1(early) did not have an imprint or plate number; these were added when it was reentered and became Scott #9. Both side positions are known from plate 2, but only a single showing the top part of the "3" and part imprint is known from plate 3. L and R imprints are known from plate 3.

#8A 1¢ FRANKLIN, type IIIa

†4

#9 1¢ FRANKLIN, type IV

Price **L, R**

Imprint Strip of 4 —

Imprint Block of 8 —

1(late)

#10 3¢ WASHINGTON (orange brown)

Plates used were 1(early and Intermediate), 2(early), 5(early) and "0". None had plate numbers added, and 1(early) had no imprint.

#11 3¢ WASHINGTON (dull red)

Basic Price **L, R**

Imprint Strip of 4 $600

Imprint Block of 8 $2,500

1(late)	2(late)	3	4
5(late)	6	7	8

#12 5¢ JEFFERSON, type I

†1

#14,15 10¢ WASHINGTON, type II,III

1

Only plate singles and a pair are known.

#17 12¢ WASHINGTON

Plate 1 had only an imprint and no plate number.

1857 ISSUE

Printed by Toppan, Carpenter & Co.

Unwatermarked Perf. 15

#18, 20 1¢ FRANKLIN, type I,II

Imprint A3

12

A pair and strip of 3 are known.

#20 1¢ FRANKLIN, type II

Imprint A1

2

A part Imprint Strip of 3 and a part Imprint Block of 6 are known.

1857 ISSUE

#22 1¢ FRANKLIN, type IIIa

Imprint A1

4

A horizontal pair showing part imprint and top of the 4 is known.

Imprint A3

11

A part imprint pair is known.

#23 1¢ FRANKLIN, type IV

Imprint A1

†1 (late)

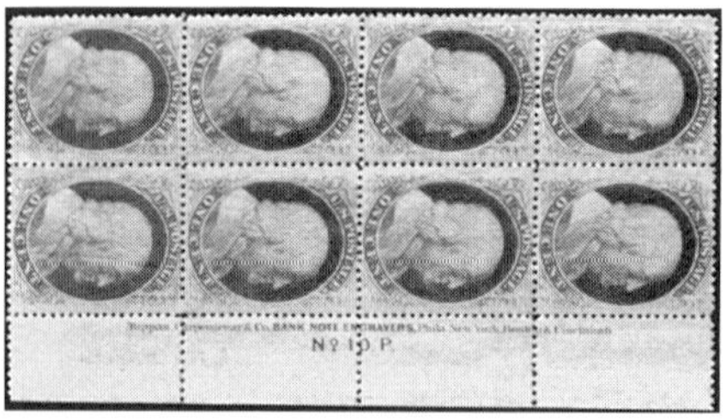

#24 1¢ FRANKLIN, type V

Basic Price	L, R	
Imprint Strip of 4		$800
Imprint Block of 8		$3,200

Imprint A2

5 7 8 9 10

The R position of plate 5 is type Va.

#25 3¢ WASHINGTON, type I

Imprint A1

†2(late) †3 †4 †5(late)
6 7 †8

Left position of plate 6 reported(size unknown)
An Imprint Strip of 3 of plate 7 is known.

#26 3¢ WASHINGTON, type II

Basic Price	L, R	
Imprint Strip of 4		$700
Imprint Block of 8		$2,800

Imprint A2

9	12	†13	14	15
16	17	18	19	20
21	22	23	24	25
26	27	28		

The plate numbers on 4L, 9L,R and the "4" of 14R are engraved in mirror image.

#26a 3¢ WASHINGTON, type IIa

Basic Price	L, R	
Imprint Strip of 4		—
Imprint Block of 8		—

Imprint A2

10 11

There is no "P" after the plate numbers on these plates.

#29 5¢ JEFFERSON (brown), type I

Imprint A1

1

A part Imprint Strip of 3 is known.

#30 5¢ JEFFERSON (orange brown), type II

Imprint A2

2

A part Imprint Block of 6 is known.

#30A 5¢ JEFFERSON (brown), type II

Imprint A2

2

A part Imprint Blocks of 9 and a part Imprint Strip of 3 are known.

#32,33 10¢ WASHINGTON, type II,III

Imprint A1

1

Only plate number pairs are known.

#35 10¢ WASHINGTON, type V

Price	L, R	
Imprint Strip of 4		$2,000
Imprint Block of 8		$8,000

Imprint A2

2

#36 12¢ WASHINGTON, type I

Imprint A1

There is no plate number

#36b 12¢ WASHINGTON

Price	(L),R	
Imprint Block of 8		—

Imprint A3

3

There is no "No." or "P" with the plate number.

1857 ISSUE

#37 24¢ WASHINGTON, type II

Price L,(R)

Imprint Block of 8 $25,000

Imprint A2

1

#38 30¢ FRANKLIN

Imprint A3

1

A part Imprint Block of 4 is known.

#39 90¢ WASHINGTON

Imprint A3

1

A part Imprint Block of 4 is known.

1875 REPRINT

#42 5¢ JEFFERSON

Price L,(R)

Imprint Strip of 4 $9,000

*Imprint A2**

2

1861 ISSUE

Printed by the National Bank Note Co.

Unwatermarked Perf 12

Imprint B1

#63-E11e (previously #55) 1¢

Price (B)

1

#65-E15h (previously #56) 3¢

Price B

Imprint Strip of 4 —

Imprint Block of 8 —

2

#67-E9e (previously #57) 5¢

†3p

#62B (previously #58) 10¢

Price B

Imprint Strip of 4 —

Part imprint block of 4 —

4

1861 ISSUE

#69-E6e (previously #59) 12¢

†5p

#72-E7h (previously #62) 90¢

†8

#63 1¢ FRANKLIN

Basic Price B

Imprint Strip of 4 $1,000

Imprint Block of 8 $4,000

9 10 †22 †25 27

#64 3¢ WASHINGTON (pink)

Price B

Imprint Block of 8 —

12

#64b 3¢ WASHINGTON (rose pink)

Price B

Part Imprint Block of 4 —

23

#65 3¢ WASHINGTON (rose)

Basic Price B

Imprint Strip of 4 $1,000

Imprint Block of 8 $4,000

*11	†12	13	14	19
†20	21	23	24	32
33	*34	35	36	37
†42	†43	†44p	†45	†46
†47	†48	†49	*52	†54
†55				

* also known imperforate

#66 3¢ WASHINGTON (lake)

Basic Price B

Imprint Strip of 4 —

Imprint Block of 8 —

34 *52 †55p

* known only imperforate

#67 5¢ JEFFERSON (buff)

Price B

Imprint Block of 8 —

17

1861 ISSUE

#68 10¢ WASHINGTON
Basic Price B
Imprint Block of 8 $5,000
15 †26p

#69 12¢ WASHINGTON
Price B
Imprint Strip of 4 —
16

#70 24¢ WASHINGTON (red lilac)
Price B
Part Imprint Block of 6 —
6

#71 30¢ FRANKLIN
Price B
Imprint Strip of 4 —
Imprint Block of 8 —
7

#72 90¢ WASHINGTON
Price B
Imprint Strip of 4 —
Imprint Block of 8 —
18

#73 2¢ JACKSON
Basic Price B
Imprint Strip of 4 $2,000
Imprint Block of 8 $8,000
28 29 30 31 50
51 53

#74 3¢ WASHINGTON (scarlet)
†19

#76 5¢ JEFFERSON (brown)
Price B
Imprint Strip of 4 —
17

#77 15¢ LINCOLN
Price B
Imprint Block of 8 —
41

#78 24¢ WASHINGTON (lilac)
Price B
Imprint Strip of 4 —
6

#79 3¢ WASHINGTON, A grill
Basic Price B
Imprint Block of 8 —
†11 52

#81 30¢ FRANKLIN, A grill
†7

#86 1¢ FRANKLIN, E grill
Price B
Imprint Block of 8 —
10

#87 2¢ JACKSON, E grill
Basic Price B
Imprint Strip of 4 —
29 51 53

#88 3¢ WASHINGTON, E grill
Basic Price B
Imprint Strip of 4 —
Imprint Block of 8 —
32 36 55

#92 1¢ FRANKLIN, F grill
Basic Price B
Part Imprint Block of 6 —
†10 †22 27

#93 2¢ JACKSON, F grill
Basic Price B
Imprint Strip of 4 —
Imprint Block of 8 —
†28 29 30 †50 51
53

#94 3¢ WASHINGTON, F grill
Basic Price B
Imprint Strip of 4 $600
Imprint Block of 8 $2,500
†11 14 32 †34 35
36 52

#95 5¢ JEFFERSON, F grill
Price B
Part Imprint Block of 6 —
17

#96 10¢ WASHINGTON, F grill
Basic Price B
Imprint Strip of 4 —
15 †26

1861 ISSUE

#97 12¢ WASHINGTON, F grill

Price B

Imprint Strip of 4 —

16

#98 15¢ LINCOLN, F grill

Price B

Imprint Block of 8 $25,000

41

#99 24¢ WASHINGTON, F grill

Price B

Imprint Block of 8 $36,000

6

#100 30¢ FRANKLIN, F grill

†7

1875 REISSUE

#102 1¢ FRANKLIN

†56p

#103 2¢ JACKSON

†57p

#105 5¢ JEFFERSON

†58p

#106 10¢ WASHINGTON

†59p

#107 12¢ WASHINGTON

†60p

1869 ISSUE

Plate numbers (preceded by "No.") are in top and bottom margins, with plate numbers following the imprint in TL and BL positions, and preceding it in TR and BR positions. On the 15c-90c values, the frame plate number is in the top margin, and the vignette plate number is in the bottom margin, but there are still TL, TR, BL, and BR positions. Plate numbers marked with †p are known only on proofs.

Printed by the National Bank Note Co.

Unwatermarked Perf. 12

Imprint B2

#112 1¢ FRANKLIN

Basic Price TL,(TR,BL,BR)

Block of 4 —

Imprint Block of 10 —

1 2

#113 2¢ POST HORSE and RIDER

Basic Price TL,TR,BL,BR

Imprint Strip of 5 —

Imprint Block of 10 —

3 4 5 †6 27
28

1869 ISSUE

#114 3¢ LOCOMOTIVE

Basic Price TL,TR,BL,BR

Imprint Strip of 5 $1,800

Imprint Block of 10 $7,000

7 8 9 10 11
12 †25 26 29 30

#115 6¢ WASHINGTON

Basic Price (TL,TR,BL,BR)

†13p 14

A plate number pair is known.

#116 10¢ SHIELD and EAGLE

†15 †16p

#117 12¢ S.S. ADRIATIC

†17p †18

#118 15¢ LANDING of COLUMBUS, type I

frame †19
vignette †19

#119 15¢ LANDING of COLUMBUS, type II

Basic Price (TL,TR),BL,BR

Imprint Block of 8 $20,000

frame 23 †31p
vignette 23

#120 24¢ DEC. of INDEPENDENCE

frame †20p
vignette †20p †24p

#121 30¢ SHIELD, EAGLE and FLAGS

Basic Price (TL,TR),BL,BR

Imprint Block of 8, no grill —

frame †21p
vignette 21

#122 90¢ LINCOLN

Basic Price (TL,TR,BL,BR)

frame 22
vignette 22

Proofs exist of the 15c-90c values with inverted centers. This puts the two imprints and plate numbers on top of each other.

1875 REPRINTS

#124 2¢ POST HORSE and RIDER

Price	TL,TR,BL,BR
Imprint Strip of 5	—
Block of 4	—

4

#129 15¢ LANDING of COLUMBUS,type III

frame †32p
vignette †23p

#132 90¢ LINCOLN

Basic Price	TL,TR,(BL,BR)
Imprint Block of 8	$100,000

frame 22
vignette †22

1880 REISSUE

#133 1¢ FRANKLIN

Price	TL,TR,BL,BR
Imprint Strip of 5	$4,000
Imprint Block of 10	$16,000

33

Plate 33 was produced by the American Bank Note Co., but the imprint on the plate reads "National Bank Note Co."

1870 ISSUE

Plate numbers (preceded by "No.") are in top or bottom margins, and follow the imprint in TL and BL positions, and precede it in TR and BR positions. The imprint is on one line (imprint B2) on plates up to 27, and on two lines (imprint B3) on higher plates, although the two types of imprint may occur on the same plate (such as 44). A number of these plate numbers are more common on proofs than on the issued stamps. Most of the issue is ungrilled.

Printed by the National Bank Note Co.

Unwatermarked Perf. 12

Imprint B2 or B3

On the grilled issue (#134-#144) only the following plate numbers are reported, other than for the higher values where only one plate was made. Other plates were certainly used.

#135 2¢ JACKSON

45

#136 3¢ WASHINGTON

Imprint Strip of 5	$1,500
Imprint Block of 10	$6,000

1 8 11 44 55

1870 ISSUE

#145 1¢ FRANKLIN

Basic Price	TL, TR, BL, BR
Imprint Strip of 5	—
Imprint Block of 10	—

16 17 50 †51 †52
†53

#146 2¢ JACKSON

Basic Price	TL, TR, BL, BR
Imprint Strip of 5	—
Imprint Block of 10	—

12 †13 †14 15 †28
†30 34 †35 †45 46

#147 3¢ WASHINGTON

Basic Price	TL, TR, BL, BR
Imprint Strip of 5	$500
Imprint Block of 10	$2,000

†1 †2 †3 †4 †5
6 7 †8 †9 †10
11 25 †29 †31 32
†36 †37 †38 †39 †40
†41 †42 †43 44 †54
†55

#148 6¢ LINCOLN

Basic Price	TL, TR, BL, BR
Imprint Strip of 5	—
Imprint Block of 10	—

26 27

#149 7¢ STANTON

Price	TL, TR, BL, BR
Imprint Strip of 5	—
Imprint Block of 10	—

33

#150 10¢ JEFFERSON

Basic Price	TL, TR, BL, BR
Imprint Strip of 5	—
Imprint Block of 10	—

18 †19 †48 †49

#151 12¢ CLAY

Price	TL, TR, BL, BR
Imprint Strip of 5	—
Imprint Block of 10	—

24

1870 ISSUE

#152 15¢ WEBSTER

Price **TL, TR, BL, BR**

Imprint Strip of 5 —

Imprint Block of 10 —

20

#153 24¢ SCOTT

Price **TL, TR, BL, BR**

Imprint Strip of 5 —

Imprint Block of 10 —

21

#154 30¢ HAMILTON

Price **TL, TR, BL, BR**

Imprint Strip of 5 —

Imprint Block of 10 —

22

#155 90¢ PERRY

Price **TL, TR, BL, BR**

Imprint Strip of 5 —

Imprint Block of 10 —

23

1873 ISSUE

The imprint is on two lines, but is wider than the NBNCo one, and thus a strip 6 or 7 stamps wide is needed to include it. Plate numbers follow the imprint in TL and BL positions, and precede it in TR and BR position. Numbers 2-193 were punched numerals, while 1 and 219-310 were large engraved script numerals. National Bank Note Co. plates were used for the 30c and 90c values.

Printed by the Continental Bank Note Co.

Unwatermarked Perf. 12

#156 1¢ FRANKLIN

Basic Price **TL, TR, BL, BR**

Imprint Strip of 6 $600

Imprint Strip of 7 $700

Imprint Block of 12 $2,500

Imprint Block of 14 $2,700

Imprint E1

12	13	16	26	125
126	†127	†128	†142	†143
†144	†146	147	†156	†157
†158	†159	†160	†181	182

Imprint E2

†229	230	294	†295	298
†299	†300	†301	307	†308

1873 ISSUE

#157 2¢ JACKSON (brown)

Basic Price **TL, TR, BL, BR**

Imprint Strip of 6 —

Imprint Strip of 7 —

Imprint Block of 12 —

Imprint Block of 14 —

Imprint E1

2	†3	4	†6	161
†162	163	164	†165	†166
†167	†168	†169		

Imprint E2

†234	241	242

#178 2¢ JACKSON (vermilion)

Basic Price **TL, TR, BL, BR**

Imprint Strip of 6 —

Imprint Strip of 7 —

Imprint Block of 12 —

Imprint Block of 14 —

Imprint E1

161	162	163	164	†165
†166	†167	†168	†169	

Imprint E2

†234	†241	242	245	†246
†296	†297			

#158 3¢ WASHINGTON

Basic Price **TL, TR, BL, BR**

Imprint Strip of 6 $700

Imprint Strip of 7 $750

Imprint Block of 12 $2,400

Imprint Block of 14 $2,800

Imprint E1

5	7	†8	9	†10
†11	14	†15	†17	†19
†20	†129	†130	†131	†132
†133	135	†136	138	†139
†148	†149	†150	†151	†152
†153	†154	†155	170	†171
†172	†173	†174	†175	176
177	†178	†179	†180	†183
†184	†185	†186	187	†188
†189	†190	†191	†192	†193

Imprint E2

†1	219	†220	†221	222
†223	†224	†225	†226	†227
†228	†231	†232	†235	†236
†237	†238	†239	240	250
251	252	†253	†254	†255
256	257	258	†259	†260
†261	†262	†263	†264	265
266	267	†268	†269	270
†271	†272	†273	†274	†275
†276	†277	†278	†279	†280
281	282	†283	†286	287
†288	†289	†290	†291	292
†293	†309	†310		

1873 ISSUE

#179 5¢ TAYLOR

Basic Price	TL, TR, BL, BR
Imprint Strip of 6	—
Imprint Strip of 7	—
Imprint Block of 12	—
Imprint Block of 14	—

Imprint E2

243 244 †247 †248 †284
†306

#159 6¢ LINCOLN

Basic Price	TL, TR, BL, BR
Imprint Strip of 6	$3,000
Imprint Block of 12	$12,000

Imprint E1

18 21

Imprint E2

†304 305

#160 7¢ STANTON

Price	TL, TR, BL, BR
Imprint Strip of 6	—
Imprint Block of 12	—

Imprint E1

22

#161 10¢ JEFFERSON

Basic Price	TL, TR, BL, BR
Imprint Strip of 6	$2,000
Imprint Block of 12	$8,000

Imprint E1

23 25

Imprint E2

†302 †303

#162 12¢ CLAY

Basic Price	TL, TR, BL, BR
Imprint Strip of 6	—
Imprint Block of 12	—

Imprint E1

†24 137

1873 ISSUE

#163 15¢ WEBSTER

Price	TL, TR, BL, BR
Imprint Strip of 6	—
Imprint Block of 12	—

Imprint E1

31

#165 30¢ HAMILTON

Price	TL, TR, BL, BR
Imprint Strip of 5	—
Imprint Block of 10	—

National Bank Note Co. plate

Imprint B2

22

#166 90¢ PERRY

Price	TL, TR, BL, BR
Imprint Strip of 5	—
Imprint Block of 10	—

National Bank Note Co. plate

Imprint B2

23

#178-#179
See page 7

1875 SPECIAL PRINTING

This printing was made for sale to collectors. Plate number strips of 4 used to exist, but have been broken into singles. The set of plate singles sold for $66,000 in 1983; the plate numbers and positions of these are:

#167	1c	127	bottom
#168	2c	161	bottom
#169	3c	1xx	bottom
	(last two digits not on stamp)		
#170	6c	18	top
#171	7c	22	top
#172	10c	25	bottom
#173	12c	137	bottom
	(half of 3 and all of 7 do not show)		
#174	15c	31	top
#175	24c	21	bottom
#176	30c	22	bottom
#177	90c	23	top

1879 ISSUE

At first plates made by the Continental Bank Note Co. were used, but later plates bear the one line imprint of the American Bank Note Co. Plate numbers follow the imprint in TL and BL positions, and precede it in TR and BL position.

Printed by the American Bank Note Co.
Unwatermarked Perf. 12

#182 1¢ FRANKLIN
Price **TL, TR, BL, BR**

Continental Bank Note Co. plate

Imprint E2

†301

American Bank Note Co. plates

Imprint Strip of 5	$800
Imprint Block of 10	$3,300

Imprint F

319 †320 †327 †328 336
†337 †344 †353 †354 355
†356

#183 2¢ JACKSON
Basic Price **TL, TR, BL, BR**

Continental Bank Note Co. plates

Imprint Strip of 6	$400
Imprint Block of 12	$1,750

Imprint E2

241**N** 242**N** 296 297

N May have been for a misidentified #178

American Bank Note Co. plates

Imprint Strip of 5	$350
Imprint Block of 10	$1,300

Imprint F

338 †339 391 392 393
†394 412 413

1879 ISSUE

#184 3¢ WASHINGTON
Basic Price **TL, TR, BL, BR**

Continental Bank Note Co. plates

Imprint Strip of 6	$300
Imprint Block of 12	$1,200

Imprint E2

256**N** 259**N** 267**N** 286**N** 291
292 †309 †310

N May have been for a misidentified #158

American Bank Note Co. plates

Imprint Strip of 5	$250
Imprint Block of 10	$1,000

Imprint F

†311 †312 †321 †322 †323
†324 329 †330 †334 †335
†340 †341 †341A †342 †343
†345 †346 347 348 †349
†350 †350A 351 †352 †357
†358

#185 5¢ TAYLOR
Basic Price **TL, TR, BL, BR**

Continental Bank Note Co. plate

Imprint E2

†306

American Bank Note Co. plates

Imprint Strip of 5	$1,200
Imprint Block of 10	$5,000

Imprint F

325 326 †379 †380

#186 6¢ LINCOLN
Basic Price **TL, TR, BL, BR**

Continental Bank Note Co. plates

Imprint Strip of 6	—
Imprint Block of 12	—

Imprint E2

†304 305

#187 10¢ JEFFERSON
American Bank Note Co. plates
(no secret mark)

Imprint F

†377 †378

#188 10¢ JEFFERSON
Continental Bank Note Co. plates
(with secret mark)

Imprint E2

†302 †303

1879 ISSUE

#189 15¢ WEBSTER
Price **TL, TR, BL, BR**
Continental Bank Note Co. plate

Imprint Strip of 6	$1,500
Imprint Block of 12	$6,000

Imprint E1

31

#190 30¢ HAMILTON (black)
Price **TL, TR, BL, BR**
American Bank Note Co. plate

Imprint Strip of 5	$2,500
Imprint Block of 10	$9,000

Imprint F

405

#191 90¢ PERRY (carmine)
Price **TL, TR, BL, BR**
National Bank Note Co. plate

Imprint Strip of 5	—
Imprint Block of 10	—

Imprint B2

23

1881-2 REENGRAVED DESIGNS

Printed by the American Bank Note Co.

A National Bank Note Co. plate was used for the 90c value. Imprints, plate numbers and positions are the same as for the preceding issue. Starting in 1885 serial letters were added to the top positions only of sets of plates that were to be used at the same time on the steam powered presses. Until midway through the 1890 issue they were placed between the imprint and the plate number.

#205 5¢ GARFIELD (yellow brown)
Basic Price **TL, TR, BL, BR**

Imprint Strip of 5	$900
Imprint Block of 10	$3,400

Imprint F

399	400	488	†489

Imprint F, F1

Imprint & Letter Strip of 5	T	$900
Imprint & Letter Block of 10	T	$3,500
Imprint Strip of 5	B	$800
Imprint Block of 10	B	$3,300

K	537	538	539	540	541

1881-2 REENGRAVED DESIGNS

On #206-213 and #219-220 we place a dagger in front of all plate numbers we have not seen or had reported to us. Many more exist; please report them to the editors for inclusion in the next edition.

#206 1¢ FRANKLIN
Basic Price **TL, TR, BL, BR**

Imprint Strip of 5	$325
Imprint Block of 10	$1,100

Imprint F

359	†360	361	362	†363
†364	†387	†388	389	†390
†401	402	†406	†407	†422
423	424	425	†475	

Imprint & Letter Strip of 5	T	$350
Imprint & Letter Block of 10	T	$1,200
Imprint Strip of 5	B	$300
Imprint Block of 10	B	$1,000

Imprint F, F1

C	†497	†498	†499	†500	†501
D	502	†503	504	505	†506
I	527	528	529	530	531

#207 3¢ WASHINGTON
Basic Price **TL, TR, BL, BR**

Imprint Strip of 5	$350
Imprint Block of 10	$1,200

Imprint F

†365	†366	367	†368	†369
370	†371	†372	†373	374
375	†376	†381	†382	†383
384	†385	†386	†395	396
†397	†398	408	†409	410
411	†414	†415	†416	417
418	†419	†420	421	

#208 6¢ LINCOLN
Basic Price **TL, TR, BL, BR**

Imprint Strip of 5	$1,600
Imprint Block of 10	—

Imprint F

426 427

1881-2 REENGRAVED DESIGNS

#209 10¢ JEFFERSON

Basic Price	**TL, TR, BL, BR**	
Imprint Strip of 5		$700
Imprint Block of 10		$1,800

Imprint F

403	†403A	†404p	†404A	†480
†481				

Imprint & Letter Strip of 5	**T**	$700
Imprint & Letter Block of 10	**T**	$1,800
Imprint Strip of 5	**B**	$600
Imprint Block of 10	**B**	$1,700

Imprint F, F1

M	547	548	549	550	551

1883 ISSUE

#210 2¢ WASHINGTON (red brown)

Basic Price	**TL, TR, BL, BR**	
Imprint Strip of 5		$250
Imprint Block of 10		$1,000

Imprint F

†430p	†431	†432	433	†434
†435	†436	†437	†438	†439
†440	†441	†442	443	†444
†445	†446	447	†448	†449
†450	†451	†452	†453	†454
†455	†458	†459	460	†461
†462	†463	†465	†466	†467
†468	†469	†470	471	†472
†473	474	†476	†477	†478
†479				

1883 ISSUE

#210 2c WASHINGTON (red brown)cont.

Imprint & Letter Strip of 5	**T**	$250
Imprint & Letter Block of 10	**T**	$1,000
Imprint Strip of 5	**B**	$200
Imprint Block of 10	**B**	$900

Imprint F, F1

A	†483	†484	†485	†486	487
B	†490	†491	†492	†493	†494
E	†507	†508	†509	510	†511
F	†512	513	514	†515	†516
G	†517	†518	†519	†520	†521
H	†522	†523	†524	525	526
J	†532	533	†534	†535	†536
N	†553	554	555	556	557
O	†558	†559	†560	561	562
P	†563	†564	†565	566	567
Q	568	†569	†570	†571	†572
U	†588	†589	†590	†591	592
V	†593	†594	†595	†596	†597

#211 4¢ JACKSON (blue green)

Basic Price	**TL, TR, BL, BR**	
Imprint Strip of 5		$1,200
Imprint Block of 10		$3,600

Imprint F

456	457

Imprint & Letter Strip of 5	**T**	$1,300
Imprint & Letter Block of 10	**T**	$3,600
Imprint Strip of 5	**B**	$1,100
Imprint Block of 10	**B**	$3,000

Imprint F, F1

L	542	543	†544	545	546

1887 ISSUE

#212 1¢ FRANKLIN

Basic Price	**TL, TR, BL, BR**	
Imprint & Letter Strip of 5	**T**	$500
Imprint & Letter Block of 10	**T**	$1,300
Imprint Strip of 5	**B**	$400
Imprint Block of 10	**B**	$1,200

Imprint F, F1

R	†573	574	575	576	577
S	†578	†579	†580	†581	†582
T	†583	584	†585	586	†587
FF	644	†645	†646	647	†648
GG	649	†650	651	652	653
JJ	664	665	666	667	668
PP	†694	695	†696	697	698
UU	719	720	721	722	723

1887 ISSUE

#213 2¢ WASHINGTON (green)

Basic Price	TL, TR, BL, BR		
Imprint & Letter Strip of 5		T	$225
Imprint & Letter Block of 10		T	$800
Imprint Strip of 5		B	$200
Imprint Block of 10		B	$700

Imprint F, F1

N	†553	†554	†555	†556	†557
O	558	†559	†560	†561	†562
P	†563	†564	†565	†566	567
Q	568	†569	†570	†571	†572
U	†588	589	†590	†591	†592
V	†593	†594	595	†596	†597
W	†598	†599	†600	†601	†602
X	†603	†604	605	†606	†607
Y	608	†609	†610	†611	†612
Y	†613(613 replaced 611,which was broken)				
Z	†614	†615	†616	617	618
AA	619	620	†621	622	†623
BB	†624	†625	†626	627	†628
CC	†629	†630	†631	†632	†633
DD	†634	†635	†636	†637	†638
EE	†639	†640	†641	†642	†643
HH	†654	655	656	†657	658
II	†659	660	661	662	†663
KK	†669	†670	†671	†672	†673
LL	674	†675	676	†677	†678
MM	†679	†680	†681	†682	683
NN	684	685	†686	†687	688
OO	689	690	†691	692	693
QQ	†699	700	†701	702	†703
RR	704	705	706	†707	708
SS	709	710	711	712	713
TT	714	715	716	717	718

#214 3¢ WASHINGTON (vermilion)

Price	TL, TR, BL, BR	
Imprint Strip of 5		$350
Imprint Block of 10		$1,100

Imprint F

421

#215 4¢ JACKSON (carmine)

Basic Price	TL, TR, BL, BR		
Imprint & Letter Strip of 5		T	$1,200
Imprint & Letter Block of 10		T	$3,600
Imprint Strip of 5		B	$1,000
Imprint Block of 10		B	$3,300

Imprint F, F1

L	542	543	544	545	546

#216 5¢ GARFIELD (indigo)

Basic Price	TL, TR, BL, BR		
Imprint & Letter Strip of 5		T	$1,200
Imprint & Letter Block of 10		T	$3,600
Imprint Strip of 5		B	$1,000
Imprint Block of 10		B	$3,300

Imprint F, F1

K	537	538	539	540	541

#217 30¢ HAMILTON (orange brown)

Price	TL, TR, BL, BR	
Imprint Strip of 5		$2,200
Imprint Block of 10		$6,500

Imprint F

405

#218 90¢ PERRY (purple)

Price	TL, TR, BL, BR	
National Bank Note Co. plate		
Imprint Strip of 5		$5,000
Imprint Block of 10		$20,000

Imprint C

23

1890 ISSUE

Printed by the American Bank Note Co. Plates for all 1c stamps and 2c stamp plates A-H, R, W, Y-Z, CC-HH, NN, QQ and SS-TT had 400 subjects, while the rest of the 2c plates and those for higher values had 200 subjects. Plate numbers (preceded by "No.") and imprints occur in top and bottom margins, with the plate number following the imprint in TL and BL positions, and preceding it in TR and BR positions. On all plates except those for 3c, 6c, 15c, 30c, and 90c values a letter or letters occurs with each set of 5 plates used together on the press. The letter(s) are in both top and bottom positions and were between the plate number and imprint on early 1c and 2c and all higher value plates, but were placed outside the imprint on 1c and 2c plates of sets A1-P1. With the early plates, a strip of 5 stamps includes the imprint and any letter(s), but for the sets A1-P1 a strip of 6 or 7 stamps is needed to include the full set of marginal markings.

#219 1¢ FRANKLIN

Basic Price **TL, TR, BL, BR**

Imprint & Letter Strip of 5	$140
Imprint & Letter Block of 10	$500

Imprint F1

C	11	†12	13	14	†15
G	†36	†37	†38	39	40
Q	89	90	91	92	93
BB	145	146	147	148	149
FF	165	166	167	168	169
UU	240	241	242	243	244

Imprint & Letter Strip of 6	$175
Imprint & Letter Strip of 7	$200
Imprint & Letter Block of 12	$650
Imprint & Letter Block of 14	$800

Imprint F2

C1	280	281	282	283	284
D1	285	286	287	288	289
F1	295	296	297	298	299

#219D 2¢ WASHINGTON (lake)

Basic Price **TL, TR, BL, BR**

Imprint & Letter Strip of 5	$900
Imprint & Letter Block of 10	$3,000

Imprint F1

A 1	A 2	A 3	B 6	B 7
B 8	B 9	B 10	D 17	D 18
D 19	F 31	F 32	F 34	K 59
L 62	OO 214	YY 263		

Other plates were certainly used.

#220 2¢ WASHINGTON (carmine)

Basic Price **TL, TR, BL, BR**

Imprint & Letter Strip of 5	$130
Imprint & Letter Block of 10	$500

Imprint F1

A	1	†2	3	4	†5
B	6	7	8	9	10
B	†71 (plate 71 replaced a damaged plate)				
D	†16	†17	18	19	†20
F	†31	†32	†33	34	†35
H	†41	†42	†43	†44	†45
K	56	†57	†58	†59	60
L	†61	†62	†63	†64	†65
M	†66	†67	†68	†69	†70
M	†99 (plate 99 replaced a damaged plate)				
N	†74	†75	†76	†77	†78
O	†79	†80	†81	†82	†83
P	†84	†85	†86	87	†88
R	†94	†95	†96	†97	†98
S	†100	†101	†102	†103	†104
T	†105	†106	†107	†108	†109
U	†110	†111	†112	†113	†114
V	†115	†116	†117	†118	†119
W	120	†121	†122	†123	†124
X	†125	†126	†127	†128	129
Y	†130	†131	†132	†133	†134
Z	†135	†136	†137	†138	†139
AA	†140	†141	142	143	144
CC	†150	†151	†152	†153	154
DD	†155	†156	†157	†158	†159
EE	†160	161	162	†163	†164
GG	170	†171	†172	†173	†174
HH	†175	†176	†177	†178	†179
II	180	†181	†182	†183	†184
JJ	185	†186	†187	188	189
KK	190	†191	†192	193	†194
LL	†195	196	197	198	199
NN	†205	206	207	†208	209
OO	†210	†211	212	213	214
PP	†215	†216	†217	†218	†219
QQ	220	†221	222	†223	†224
RR	†225	226	227	†228	†229
SS	†230	†231	232	233	†234
TT	235	236	237	238	239
VV	245	246	†247	248	†249
WW	†250	251	†252	†253	254
XX	†255	256	†257	258	259
YY	260	†261	262	263	264

1890 ISSUE

#220 2¢ WASHINGTON (carmine) cont.

Imprint F2

Imprint & Letter strip of 6	$160
Imprint & Letter Strip of 7	$175
Imprint & Letter Block of 12	$600
Imprint & Letter Block of 14	$750

A1	270	†271	272	273	274
B1	†275	†276	277	278	279
E1	290	†291	†292	293	294
G1	†300	†301	302	†303	†304
H1	305	306	307	308	309
I1	310	311	312	313	314
J1	315	†316	317	318	319
K1	320	321	322	323	324
L1	325	326	327	328	329
M1	330	331	†332	†333	†334
N1	335	336	337	338	339
O1	340	341	342	343	344
P1	†345	346	347	†348	349

#221 3¢ JACKSON

Basic Price	TL, TR, BL, BR
Imprint Strip of 5	$350
Imprint Block of 10	$1,800

Imprint F

21 72

#222 4¢ LINCOLN

Basic Price	TL, TR, BL, BR
Imprint & Letter Strip of 5	$375
Imprint & Letter Block of 10	$2,000

Imprint F1

J	51	52	53	54	55
MM	200	201	202	203	204

#223 5¢ GRANT

Basic Price	TL, TR, BL, BR
Imprint & Letter Strip of 5	$375
Imprint & Letter Block of 10	$2,000

Imprint F1

I	46	47	48	49	50

#224 6¢ GARFIELD

Price	TL, TR, BL, BR
Imprint Strip of 5	$375
Imprint Block of 10	$2,000

Imprint F

23

#225 8¢ SHERMAN

Basic Price	TL, TR, BL, BR
Imprint & Letter Strip of 5	$300
Imprint & Letter Block of 10	$1,300

Imprint F1

ZZ	265	266	267	268	269

#226 10¢ WEBSTER

Basic Price	TL, TR, BL, BR
Imprint & Letter Strip of 5	$800
Imprint & Letter Block of 10	$3,200

Imprint F1

E	26	27	28	29	30

#227 15¢ CLAY

Price	TL, TR, BL, BR
Imprint Strip of 5	$1,000
Imprint Block of 10	$5,500

Imprint F

22

#228 30¢ JEFFERSON

Price	TL, TR, BL, BR
Imprint Strip of 5	$1,500
Imprint Block of 10	$9,000

Imprint F

24

#229 90¢ PERRY

Price	TL, TR, BL, BR
Imprint Strip of 5	$2,500
Imprint Block of 10	$20,000

Imprint F

25

1893 COLUMBIAN ISSUE

Printed by the American Bank Note Co. Plates for the 1c and many of the 2c had 200 subjects, and were separated into panes of 100 with top or bottom straight edges. Plates for the higher values had 100 subjects. Imprints and plate numbers were in top and bottom margins only, with imprints only in the side margins. Plate numbers in TL and BL position follow the imprint, while in TR and BR position they precede it. A letter or letters are on the opposite side of the imprint from the plate number. Because panes of 100 were issued, one can obtain full top or bottom marginal strips showing two sets of letters, imprints, and plate numbers. We price strips of 4 or blocks of 8 with letter, imprint and plate number. Strips of 3 without letter sell for 70-80% of these prices, while blocks of 6 sell for 50-75%.

Imprint F3

#230 1¢ COLUMBIAN

Basic Price **TL, TR, BL, BR**

Imprint & Letter Strip of 4 $110

Imprint & Letter Block of 8 $500

J	46	47	48	49	50
K	51	52	53	54	55
P	65	66	67	68	69
MM	149	150	151	152	153
OO	159	160	161	162	163
VV	194	195	196	197	198

#231 2¢ COLUMBIAN

Basic Price **TL, TR, BL, BR**

Imprint & Letter Strip of 4 $100

Imprint & Letter Block of 8 $450

All plates had 200 subjects, except those marked s, which had 100 subjects.

A	1	2	3	4	5
C	11	12	13	14	15
E	21	22	23	24	25
sF	26	27	28	29	30
sG	31	32	33	34	35
sH	36	37	38	39	40
sI	41	42	43	44	45
sO	60	61	62	63	64
sQ	70	71	72	73	74
T	78	79	80	81	82
sU	83	84	85	86	87
V	88	89	90	91	92
sX	94	95	96	97	98
EE	109	110	111	112	113
FF	114	115	116	117	†118
sGG	119	120	121	122	123
HH	124	†125	126	127	128
JJ	134	135	136	137	138
KK	139	140	141	142	143
LL	144	145	146	147	148
NN	154	155	156	157	158
PP	164	165	166	167	168
QQ	169	170	171	172	173
RR	174	175	176	177	178
SS	179	180	181	182	183
TT	184	185	186	187	188
UU	189	190	191	192	193

1893 COLUMBIAN ISSUE

#232 3¢ COLUMBIAN
Basic Price **TL, TR, BL, BR**
Imprint & Letter Strip of 4 $275
Imprint & Letter Block of 8 $1,000

L 56 57
R 75 76

#233 4¢ COLUMBIAN
Basic Price **TL, TR, BL, BR**
Imprint & Letter Strip of 4 $400
Imprint & Letter Block of 8 $1,800

D 16 17 18 19 20

#234 5¢ COLUMBIAN
Basic Price **TL, TR, BL, BR**
Imprint & Letter Strip of 4 $500
Imprint & Letter Block of 8 $2,300

B 6 7 8 9 10

#235 6¢ COLUMBIAN
Price **TL, TR, BL, BR**
Imprint & Letter Strip of 4 $400
Imprint & Letter Block of 8 $,2000

Z 104

#236 8¢ COLUMBIAN
Basic Price **TL, TR, BL, BR**
Imprint & Letter Strip of 4 $350
Imprint & Letter Block of 8 $1,300

II 129 130 131 132 133

#237 10¢ COLUMBIAN
Basic Price **TL, TR, BL, BR**
Imprint & Letter Strip of 4 $600
Imprint & Letter Block of 8 $4,400

Y 99 100 101 102 103

#238 15¢ COLUMBIAN
Price **TL, TR, BL, BR**
Imprint & Letter Strip of 4 $1,000
Imprint & Letter Block of 8 $5,000

M 58

#239 30¢ COLUMBIAN
Price **TL, TR, BL, BR**
Imprint & Letter Strip of 4 $1,500
Imprint & Letter Block of 8 $10,000

N 59

#240 50¢ COLUMBIAN
Price **TL, TR, BL, BR**
Imprint & Letter Strip of 4 $2,500
Imprint & Letter Block of 8 $15,000

S 77

#241 $1 COLUMBIAN
Price **TL, TR, BL, BR**
Imprint & Letter Strip of 4 $6,500
Imprint & Letter Block of 8 $50,000

W 93

#242 $2 COLUMBIAN
Price **TL, TR, BL, BR**
Imprint & Letter Strip of 4 $7,000
Imprint & Letter Block of 8 $60,000

AA 105

#243 $3 COLUMBIAN
Price **TL, TR, BL, BR**
Imprint & Letter Strip of 4 $12,000
Imprint & Letter Block of 8 $75,000

BB 106

#244 $4 COLUMBIAN
Price **TL, TR, BL, BR**
Imprint & Letter Strip of 4 $16,000
Imprint & Letter Block of 8 $200,000

CC 107

#245 $5 COLUMBIAN
Price **TL, TR, BL, BR**
Imprint & Letter Strip of 4 $18,000
Imprint & Letter Block of 8 $180,000

DD 108

1894 REGULAR ISSUE

Printed by the Bureau of Engraving and Printing

When the Bureau of Engraving and Printing took over the printing of United States postage stamps from private contractors in 1894 there was considerable interest in the collecting of the new plate numbers.

These were usually collected in strips of three stamps showing the plate number and the imprint so imprint blocks of six are very difficult to find on many plates.

As the seemingly endless plate numbers climbed higher and higher few collectors kept up their interest and so many of the later plates are considerably more difficult to find.

No records of impressions per plate are available so there is no way of being certain but we have marked with an asterisk those plates which we have found to be difficult to find based on the B.I.A. plate number survey. See Appendix F for basis.

Unwatermarked Perf.12

FLAT PRESS

#246 1¢ FRANKLIN (ultramarine) **12 Plates**

Basic Price **T, L, R, B**

Imprint Strip of 3 .... $90

Imprint Block of 6 .... $300

Imprint I

2	6	15	17	18
21	24	27	29	31
33	35			

#247 1¢ FRANKLIN (blue) **16 Plates**

Basic Price **T, L, R, B**

Imprint Strip of 3 .... $225

Imprint Block of 6 .... $600

Imprint I

*18	*21	24	*27	29
*31	33	35		

Imprint II

98	99	101	102	*119
*120	*121	122		

#248 2¢ WASHINGTON (pink) **20 Plates**

Basic Price **T, L, R, B** **Type I**

Imprint Strip of 3 .... $80

Imprint Block of 6 .... $225

Imprint I

1	3	4	5	7
8	9	10	11	12
13	16	19	20	22
23	25	26	30	32

#249 2¢ WASHINGTON (carmine lake)
30 Plates

Basic Price **T, L, R, B** **Type I**

Imprint Strip of 3 .... $500

Imprint Block of 6 .... $1,300

Imprint I

1	3	4	5	7
8	9	10	11	12
13	16	19	20	22
23	25	26	30	32

Imprint II

78	79	80	82	88
*89	96	97	110	111

#250 2¢ WASHINGTON (carmine)
39 Plates

Basic Price **T, L, R, B** **Type I**

Imprint Strip of 3 .... $90

Imprint Block of 6 .... $275

Imprint I

1	3	4	5	*7
8	9	*10	11	12
13	16	19	20	22
23	25	26	30	32

Imprint II

78	79	80	82	88
*89	96	97	110	111
112	113	114	115	116
*117	124	125	144	

#251 2¢ WASHINGTON (carmine)
4 Plates

Basic Price **T, L, R, B** **Type II**

Imprint Strip of 3 .... $700

Imprint Block of 6 .... $2,200

Imprint II

126	131	132	133

#252 2¢ WASHINGTON (carmine)
16 Plates

Basic Price **T, L, R, B** **Type III**

Imprint Strip of 3 .... $400

Imprint Block of 6 .... $1,200

Imprint II

141	142	143	145	146
148	149	150	151	152
153	154			

Imprint IV

155	156	157	158

1894 REGULAR ISSUE

#253 3¢ JACKSON 8 Plates
Basic Price **T, L, R, B**
Imprint Strip of 3 $325
Imprint Block of 6 .... $1,000

Imprint I

44 46 47 48

The following have no side plate numbers.
Basic Price **T, B**
Imprint Strip of 3 .... $325
Imprint Block of 6 .... $1,000

Imprint II

91 95 103 107

#254 4¢ LINCOLN (dark brown) 8 Plates
Basic Price **T, L, R, B**
Imprint Strip of 3 .... $450
Imprint Block of 6 .... $1,250

Imprint I

45 50 51 59

The following have no side plate numbers.
Basic Price **T, B**
Imprint Strip of 3 .... $450
Imprint Block of 6 .... $1,250

Imprint II

92 94 *104 106

#255 5¢ GRANT (chocolate) 12 Plates
Basic Price **T, L, R, B**
Imprint Strip of 3 .... $300
Imprint Block of 6 .... $875

Imprint I

*49 *53 *54 *56

The following have no side plate numbers.
Basic Price **T, B**
Imprint Strip of 3 .... $300
Imprint Block of 6 .... $875

Imprint II

128 129 130 134

Imprint IV

161 162 163 164

#256 6¢ GARFIELD (dull brown) 1 Plate
Price **T, B only**
Imprint Strip of 3 .... $550
Imprint Block of 6 .... $1,900

Imprint I

28

#257 8¢ SHERMAN 1 Plate
Price **T, B only**
Imprint Strip of 3 .... $500
Imprint Block of 6 .... $1,250

Imprint I

58

#258 10¢ WEBSTER (green) 4 Plates
Basic Price **T, L, R, B**
Imprint Strip of 3 .... $775
Imprint Block of 6 .... $2,200

Imprint I

55 62 63 64

#259 15¢ CLAY (dark blue) 1 Plate
Price **T, B only**
Imprint Strip of 3 .... $1,100
Imprint Block of 6 .... $3,500

Imprint I

52

#260 50¢ JEFFERSON 1 Plate
Price **T, B only**
Imprint Strip of 3 .... $1,700
Imprint Block of 6 .... $6,000

Imprint I

75

#261 $1 PERRY 1 Plate
On plate number 76, a two hundred subject plate, the top and bottom plate blocks from the right pane will contain two stamps of Type I and four of Type II. The strip of three will have one copy of Type I and two of Type II.
Price **BL only** **Type I**
Imprint Strip of 3 .... $3,500
Imprint Block of 6 .... $16,500

Imprint II

76

#261A $1 PERRY 1 Plate
Price **BR only Type I and Type II**
Imprint Strip of 3 .... $6,000
Imprint Block of 6 .... $27,500

Imprint II

76

1894 REGULAR ISSUE

#262 $2 MADISON 1 Plate
Price **B only**
Imprint Strip of 3 .... $10,500
Imprint Block of 6 .... $35,000

Imprint II

84

#263 $5 MARSHALL 1 Plate
Price **B only**
Imprint Strip of 3 .... $17,000
Imprint Block of 6 .... $87,500

Imprint II

85

No top positions of the $1, $2, or $5 have been reported.

1895-98 REGULAR ISSUE

Double Line Wmk. Perf. 12

FLAT PRESS

#264 1¢ FRANKLIN (blue) **77 Plates**
Basic Price **T, L, R, B**
Imprint Strip of 3 .... $25
Imprint Block of 6 .... $175

Imprint I

*24	*29	*33	*35	

Imprint II

98	99	101	102	119
120	121	122		

Imprint IV

165	166	167	168	177
178	179	180	234	237
240	245	276	277	278
280	294	295	296	297
298	299	300	301	304
308	310	313	314	

Imprint V

333	334	335	336	344
345	346	347	348	350
352	355	360	362	365
366	367	369	370	371
439	440	441	442	443
444	445	446	452	453
454	455	493	494	495
496				

#265 2¢ WASHINGTON (carmine)
17 Plates
Basic Price **T, L, R, B** **Type I**
Imprint Strip of 3 .... $100
Imprint Block of 6 .... $325

Imprint II

78	79	80	82	88
96	97	111	112	113
114	115	*116	117	124
125	144			

1895-98 REGULAR ISSUE

#266 2¢ WASHINGTON (carmine)
6 Plates
Basic Price **T, L, R, B** **Type II**
Imprint Strip of 3 .... $115
Imprint Block of 6 .... $350

Imprint II

126	131	132	133

Imprint IV

169	170**N**

Numerous shades occur on Scott #267 and #279B, and color cannot be used to distinguish them. We list Type III stamps as #267 and Type IV stamps as #279B.

#267 2¢ WASHINGTON (carmine)
207 Plates
Basic Price **T, L, R, B** **Type III**
Imprint Strip of 3 .... $20
Imprint Block of 6 .... $135

Imprint II

141	142	143	145	146
148	149	150	151	152
153	154			

Imprint IV

155	156	157	158	160
170**N**	171	172	173	174
175	176	181	182	183
185	186	187	188	191
198	199	201	202	203
204	205	206	207	209
210	211	212	213	214
215	216	217	218	219
220	221	222	223	224
225	226	227	228	229
230	231	232	233	235
236	238	239	241	242
243	244	274	275	279
281	282	283	290	291
292	293	307	311	312
315	316	317	318	319
320	321	322	323	324
325	326	327		

N The first three rows of the left of plate 170 are triangle II so the block and strip from the left side positions will be Type II's. All other positions will show triangle III stamps only.

Imprint V

328	329	330	331	332
337	338	339	340	341
342	343	349	354	356
358	361	363	364	368
372	374	376	379	382
383	384	385	387	388
393	394	395	396	397
398	399	400	401	402
403	404	405	406	411
412	413	414	415	416

1895-98 REGULAR ISSUE

#267 2¢ WASHINGTON Cont.

417	418	419	420	421
422	423	424	425	426
*427	*428	*429	*430	431
432	433	434	435	436
437	438	464	465	466
467	468	469	470	471
472	473	474	475	476
477	478	479	480	481
482	483	484	485	486
487	488	489	490	491
497	498	499	500	501
502	503			

#268 3¢ JACKSON 12 Plates

Basic Price **T, B only**

Imprint Strip of 3 .... $135
Imprint Block of 6 .... $500

Imprint II

91 95 103 107

Imprint V

447 448 449 450 *1213
*1214 *1215 *1216

#269 4¢ LINCOLN (dark brown) **16 Plates**

Basic Price **T, B only**

Imprint Strip of 3 .... $135
Imprint Block of 6 .... $525

Imprint II

92 94 104 106

Imprint IV

194 195 196 197

Imprint V

456 457 458 459 460
461 462 463

#270 5¢ GRANT (chocolate) **24 Plates**

Basic Price **T, B only**

Imprint Strip of 3 .... $135
Imprint Block of 6 .... $525

Imprint II

128 129 130 134

Imprint IV

161 162 163 164 189
190 192 193 250 251
252 253

Imprint V

*351 *353 *357 *359 389
390 391 392

#271 6¢ GARFIELD (dull brown) **6 Plates**

Basic Price **T, B only**

Imprint Strip of 3 .... $300
Imprint Block of 6 .... $1,250

Imprint I

28

Imprint IV

184 *248

Imprint V

373 386 451

#272 8¢ SHERMAN 11 Plates

Basic Price **T, B only**

Imprint Strip of 3 .... $200
Imprint Block of 6 .... $650

Imprint I

58

Imprint IV

249

Imprint V

555 928 *929 *930 *931
*1094 *1095 *1096 *1097

#273 10¢ WEBSTER (green) **8 Plates**

Basic Price **T, L, R, B**

Imprint Strip of 3 .... $275
Imprint Block of 6 .... $1,100

Imprint I

55 62 63 64

Imprint IV

302 303 305 306

#274 15¢ CLAY (dark blue) **2 Plates**

Basic Price **T, B only**

Imprint Strip of 3 .... $800
Imprint Block of 6 .... $2,800

Imprint I

52

Imprint IV

264

#275 50¢ JEFFERSON 1 Plate

Price **T, B only**

Imprint Strip of 3 .... $1,150
Imprint Block of 6 .... $5,000

Imprint I

75

1895-98 REGULAR ISSUE

#276 $1 PERRY 1 Plate

On plate number 76, a two hundred subject plate, the top and bottom plate blocks from the right pane will contain two stamps of Type I and four of Type II. The strip of three will have one copy of Type I and two of Type II.

Price **TL, BL** **Type I**

Imprint Strip of 3 .... $2,500

Imprint Block of 6 .... $10,000

Imprint II

76

#276A $1 PERRY 1 Plate

Price **TR, BR** **Type I and Type II**

Imprint Strip of 3 .... $4,500

Imprint Block of 6 .... $20,000

Imprint II

76

#277 $2 MADISON 1 Plate

Price **T, B only**

Imprint Strip of 3 .... $4,000

Imprint Block of 6 .... $17,000

Imprint II

84

1895-98 REGULAR ISSUE

#278 $5 MARSHALL 1 Plate

Price **T, B only**

Imprint Strip of 3 .... $8,000

Imprint Block of 6 .... $60,000

Imprint II

85

(For plate 288 see page 345)

1898 REGULAR ISSUE

Double Line Wmk. Perf. 12

FLAT PRESS

#279 1¢ FRANKLIN (green) **273 Plates**

Basic Price **T, L, R, B**

Imprint Strip of 3 .... $40

Imprint Block of 6 .... $175

Imprint V

439	440	*441	446	452
493	494	495	496	526
527	528	529	534	535
536	537	538	539	540
541	542	543	544	545
546	547	548	549	564
565	566	567	572	573
574	575	766	767	768
769	770	771	772	773
794	795	796	797	810
811	812	813	818	819
820	821	822	823	824
825	826	827	828	829
830	831	832	833	846
847	848	849	862	863
864	865	936	937	938
939	940	941	942	943
944	945	946	947	952
953	954	955	956	957
958	959	960	961	962
963	964	*965	*966	967
*968	969	*970	971	972
*973	*974	975	976	977
978	979	984	985	986
987	992	993	994	995
1000	1001	1002	1003	1004
1005	1006	1007	1012	1013
1014	1015	1016	1017	1018
1019	1020	1021	1022	1023
1028	1029	1030	1031	1042

1898 REGULAR ISSUE

#279 1¢ FRANKLIN Cont.

1043	1044	1045	1050	1051
1052	1053	1058	1059	1060
1061	1062	1063	1064	1065
1130	1131	1132	1133	1146
1147	1148	1149	1157	1158
1159	1160	1161	1162	1163
1164	1183	1184	1185	1186
1188	*1189	1190	1191	1204
1205	1206	1207	1209	1210
1211	1212	1287	1288	1289
1290	1303	1304	1305	*1306
1315	1316	1317	1318	1328
1329	1330	1331	1340	1341
1342	1343	1376	1377	1378
1379	1392	1393	1394	1395
1396	1397	1398	*1399	1400
*1401	1402	1403	1404	1405
1406	1407	1408	1409	1410
1411**Z**	1420	*1421	1422	1423
1424	1425	*1426	1427	1453
1454	*1455	1456	*1457	*1458
*1459	*1460	1469	1470	*1471
*1472	1485	1486	1487	*1488
*1501	1502	*1503	*1504	1505
1506	1507	1508		

Z On plate 1411 the plate number on the bottom of the LL pane precedes the imprint.

#279B 2¢ WASHINGTON (red)
309 Plates

Basic Price	T, L, R, B	Type IV
Imprint Strip of 3		$35
Imprint Block of 6		$175

Imprint V

505	506	507	508	509
510	511	512	513	514
515	516	517	522	523
524	525	550	551	552
553	556	557	558	559
560	561	562	563	568
569	570	571	593	594
595	596	745	746	747
748	753	754	755	756
758	759	760	761	762
763	764	765	774	775
776	777	778	779	780
781	782	783	784	785
786	787	788	789	798

#279B 2¢ WASHINGTON Cont.

799	800	801	802**N**	803
804	805	806	807	808
809	814	815	816	817
838	839	840	841	842
843	844	845	850	851
852	853	854	855	856
857	858	859	860	861
866	867	869	870	875
876	877	878	885	886
887	888	895	896	897
898	904	905	906	907
909	910	911	912	913
914	915	916	917	918
919	920	921	926	927
1024	1025	1026	1027	1032
1033	1034	1035	1038	1039
1040	1041	1046	1047	1048
1049	1054	1055	1056	1057
1066	1067	1068	1069	1070
1071	1072	1073	1074	*1075
1076	1077	1080	1081	1082
1083	1088	1089	1090	1091
1104	1105	1106	1107	1108
1109	1110	1111	1152	1153
1154	1155	*1251	1252	1265
1266	1267	1268	1269	1270
1275	1276	1277	1278	1279
1280	1281	1282	1283	1284
1285	1286	1291	1292	1293
*1294	1295	1296	1297	1298
*1299	1300	1301	1302	1307
1308	1309	1310	1311	1312
1313	1314	*1319	*1320	*1321
*1322	1344	1345	1346	1347
1348	1349	1350	1351	1352
1353	1354	1355	1356	1357
1358	1359	1360	1361	1362
1363	1364	1365	1366	1367
1372	1373	1374	1375	1380
1381	1382	1383	1384	1385
1386	1387	1412	1413	1414
1415	1416	1417	1418	1419
1428	1429	1430	1431	*1433
1434	*1435	*1436	*1437	1438
*1439	1440	1441	1442	1443
1444	*1449	*1450	*1451	*1452
1461	1462	1463	1464	*1465
*1466	*1467	*1468	*1493	

N The top right imprint and plate number on plate 802 are spread out so that a strip of four or a block of eight stamps are required. See US Specialist, July 1988.

1898 REGULAR ISSUE

#280 4¢ LINCOLN (rose brown) **20 Plates**

Basic Price **T, B only**

Imprint Strip of 3 .... $125

Imprint Block of 6 .... $600

Imprint V

460	461	462	463	530
531	532	533	790	791
792	793	1100	1101	*1102
*1103	*1332	*1333	*1334	*1335

#281 5¢ GRANT (dark blue) **32 Plates**

Basic Price **T, B only**

Imprint Strip of 3 .... $155

Imprint Block of 6 .... $600

Imprint V

389	390	391	392	407
408	409	410	834	835
836	837	948	949	950
951	*980	*981	*982	*983
*1084	*1085	*1086	*1087	1199
1200	*1201	*1202	*1217	*1218
*1219	*1220			

#282 6¢ GARFIELD (lake) **5 Plates**

Basic Price **T, B only**

Imprint Strip of 3 .... $180

Imprint Block of 6 .... $800

Imprint V

554	922	923	924	925

#282C 10¢ WEBSTER (brown) **9 Plates**

Basic Price **T, L, R, B** **Type I**

Imprint Strip of 3 .... $700

Imprint Block of 6 .... $2,200

Imprint IV

302	303	305	306

Imprint V

518	*519	*520	521	*932 **N**

#283 10¢ WEBSTER (brown) **12 Plates**

Basic Price **T, B, R, B** **Type II**

Imprint Strip of 3 .... $425

Imprint Block of 6 .... $1,200

Imprint V

*932 **N**	*933	*934	*935	996
997	998	999		

N On plate 932 all stamps are Type I except 7 entries of Type II. Since one of these is position 86 of the lower left pane, the bottom plate block contains one Type II example.

#283 10¢ WEBSTER Cont.

The following have no side plate numbers.

Basic Price **T, B only** **Type II**

Imprint Strip of 3.................................... $750

Imprint Block of 6.................................... $3,250

*1336	*1337	*1338	*1339

#284 15¢ CLAY (olive green) **1 Plate**

Price **T, B only**

Imprint Strip of 3.................................... $500

Imprint Block of 6.................................... $2,000

Imprint IV

264

BOOKLET PANES
PANES OF 6

#279e 2¢ WASHINGTON (red) **20 Plates**

Basic Price **T** $900

Imprint IX

360 Subjects

988	989	990	991	*1008
*1009	*1010	*1011		

180 Subjects

1324	1325	1326	1327	*1368
*1369	1370	1371	1489	1490
1491	1492			

Plates 988-991 are more common with the "Specimen" overprint.

1898 COMMEMORATIVES

Double Line Wmk. Perf. 12
FLAT PRESS **Positions T, B**

Imprint VIII

#285 1¢ TRANS-MISSISSIPPI

Basic Price **14 Plates**
Imprint Pair $70
Imprint Block of 4 .... $225

	T	B		T	B		T	B
590	☐	☐	591	☐	☐	592	☐	☐
598	☐	☐	600	☐	☐	601	☐	☐
*605	☐	☐	607	☐	☐	612	☐	☐
635	☐	☐	*709	☐	☐	710	☐	☐
711	☐	☐	712	☐	☐			

#286 2¢ TRANS-MISSISSIPPI

Basic Price **121 Plates**
Imprint Pair $55
Imprint Block of 4 .... $200

597	☐	☐	608	☐	☐	610	☐	☐
611	☐	☐	615	☐	☐	616	☐	☐
619	☐	☐	621	☐	☐	622	☐	☐
623	☐	☐	624	☐	☐	625	☐	☐
626	☐	☐	627	☐	☐	628	☐	☐
629	☐	☐	630	☐	☐	631	☐	☐
632	☐	☐	633	☐	☐	638	☐	☐
639	☐	☐	640	☐	☐	641	☐	☐
642	☐	☐	644	☐	☐	645	☐	☐
646	☐	☐	647	☐	☐	648	☐	☐
649	☐	☐	650	☐	☐	651	☐	☐
652	☐	☐	653	☐	☐	654	☐	☐
655	☐	☐	656	☐	☐	657	☐	☐
658	☐	☐	659	☐	☐	660	☐	☐
661	☐	☐	662	☐	☐	663	☐	☐
664	☐	☐	665	☐	☐	666	☐	☐
*667	☐	☐	668	☐	☐	669	☐	☐
670	☐	☐	*671	☐	☐	672	☐	☐
673	☐	☐	674	☐	☐	*675	☐	☐
676	☐	☐	677	☐	☐	678	☐	☐
679	☐	☐	680	☐	☐	681	☐	☐
683	☐	☐	684	☐	☐	*685	☐	☐
686	☐	☐	687	☐	☐	688	☐	☐
689	☐	☐	690	☐	☐	*691	☐	☐
692	☐	☐	693	☐	☐	694	☐	☐
695	☐	☐	696	☐	☐	697	☐	☐
698	☐	☐	699	☐	☐	700	☐	☐
701	☐	☐	702	☐	☐	703	☐	☐
704	☐	☐	705	☐	☐	706	☐	☐
707	☐	☐	708	☐	☐	713	☐	☐
714	☐	☐	715	☐	☐	716	☐	☐
717	☐	☐	718	☐	☐	719	☐	☐
720	☐	☐	721	☐	☐	722	☐	☐
724	☐	☐	725	☐	☐	726	☐	☐
727	☐	☐	728	☐	☐	729	☐	☐
732	☐	☐	733	☐	☐	734	☐	☐
735	☐	☐	737	☐	☐	738	☐	☐
739	☐	☐	740	☐	☐	741	☐	☐
742	☐	☐	743	☐	☐	744	☐	☐
749	☐	☐	750	☐	☐	751	☐	☐
752	☐	☐						

#287 4¢ TRANS-MISSISSIPPI

Basic Price **3 Plates**
Imprint Pair $300
Imprint Block of 4 .... $875

599	☐	☐	634	☐	☐	*636	☐	☐

#288 5¢ TRANS-MISSISSIPPI

Basic Price **3 Plates**
Imprint Pair $275
Imprint Block of 4 .... $825

602	☐	☐	614	☐	☐	618	☐	☐

#289 8¢ TRANS-MISSISSIPPI

Basic Price **2 Plates**
Imprint Pair $350
Imprint Block of 4 .... $1,750

609	☐	☐	643	☐	☐

#290 10¢ TRANS-MISSISSIPPI

Basic Price **3 Plates**
Imprint Pair $375
Imprint Block of 4 .... $1,900

604	☐	☐	617	☐	☐	620	☐	☐

#291 50¢ TRANS-MISSISSIPPI

Price **1 Plate**
Imprint Pair $1,500
Imprint Block of 4 .... $12,000

603	☐	☐

#292 $1 TRANS-MISSISSIPPI

Price **1 Plate**
Imprint Pair $3,200
Imprint Block of 4 .... $35,000

606	☐	☐

#293 $2 TRANS-MISSISSIPPI

Price **1 Plate**
Imprint Pair $5,000
Imprint Block of 4 .... $75,000

613	☐	☐

1901 COMMEMORATIVES

These plates are collected in top and bottom strips of three and blocks of six with the frame plate number only or in bottom strips of five or blocks of ten showing both frame and vignette plate numbers. This combination comes from the bottom left position of the sheet. Some of the 1¢ and 2¢ combinations are very scarce.

Double Line Wmk. Perf. 12

FLAT PRESS

#294 1¢ PAN-AMERICAN

Basic Price:
Imprint Strip of 3, **T, B** $75
Imprint Block of 6, **T, B** $250
Imprint Strip of 5, **B** $150
Imprint Block of 10, **B** $500

8 Frame Plates ***Imprint V***

	T	B		T	B		T	B
1112	☐	☐	1116	☐	☐	1123	☐	☐
1139	☐	☐	1172	☐	☐	1175	☐	☐
1179	☐	☐	*1181	☐	☐			

20 Vignette Plates ***Imprint IX***

	B		B		B		B
1113	☐	1117	☐	1125	☐	1136	☐
1156	☐	1168	☐	1170	☐	1177	☐
1180	☐	1194	☐	1196	☐	1225	☐
*1226	☐	1227	☐	1228	☐	*1233	☐
*1234	☐	*1235	☐	*1236	☐	*1248	☐

#295 2¢ PAN-AMERICAN

Basic Price:
Imprint Strip of 3, **T, B** $70
Imprint Block of 6, **T, B** $275
Imprint Strip of 5, **B** $150
Imprint Block of 10, **B** $500

12 Frame Plates ***Imprint V***

1078	☐	☐	1092	☐	☐	1098	☐	☐
1114	☐	☐	1119	☐	☐	1122	☐	☐
1126	☐	☐	1129	☐	☐	*1165	☐	☐
1167	☐	☐	*1169	☐	☐	1176	☐	☐

36 Vignette Plates ***Imprint IX***

1079	☐	1093	☐	1115	☐	1118	☐
1124	☐	1127	☐	1128	☐	*1134	☐
1135	☐	1137	☐	1138	☐	1166	☐
1171	☐	*1173	☐	1174	☐	1178	☐
1182	☐	1187	☐	1192	☐	1193	☐
*1195	☐	*1197	☐	1198	☐	1208	☐
1221	☐	1222	☐	1223	☐	1224	☐
1229	☐	*1230	☐	*1231	☐	*1232	☐
*1238	☐	1239	☐	*1240	☐	*1241	☐

#296 4¢ PAN-AMERICAN

Basic Price:
Imprint Strip of 3, **T, B** $400
Imprint Block of 6, **T, B** $2,600
Imprint Strip of 5, **B** $675
Imprint Block of 10, **B** $5,000

1 Frame Plate ***Imprint V***
1145 ☐ ☐

1 Vignette Plate ***Imprint IX***
1142 ☐

#297 5¢ PAN-AMERICAN

Basic Price:
Imprint Strip of 3, **T, B** $450
Imprint Block of 6, **T, B** $3,000
Imprint Strip of 5, **B** $750
Imprint Block of 10, **B** $5,500

1 Frame Plate ***Imprint V***
1140 ☐ ☐

1 Vignette Plate ***Imprint IX***
1141 ☐

#298 8¢ PAN-AMERICAN

Basic Price:
Imprint Strip of 3, **T, B** $550
Imprint Block of 6, **T, B** $5,000
Imprint Strip of 5, **B** $900
Imprint Block of 10, **B** $8,000

1 Frame Plate ***Imprint V***
1150 ☐ ☐

1 Vignette Plate ***Imprint IX***
1143 ☐

#299 10¢ PAN-AMERICAN

Basic Price:
Imprint Strip of 3, **T, B** $800
Imprint Block of 6, **T, B** $7,500
Imprint Strip of 5, **B** $1,300
Imprint Block of 10, **B** $11,500

1 Frame Plate ***Imprint V***
1151 ☐ ☐

1 Vignette Plate ***Imprint IX***
1144 ☐

1902-03 REGULAR ISSUE

Double Line Wmk. Perf. 12

FLAT PRESS

Imprint V

#300 1¢ FRANKLIN 823 Plates

Basic Price **T, L, R, B**

Imprint Strip of 3 .... $30

Imprint Block of 6 .... $175

1541	1542	1543	1544	1545
1546	1547	1548	1549	1550
1551	1552	1578	1579	1580
1581	1608	1609	1610	1611
1625	1626	1627	1628	1634
1635	*1636	1637	1638	1639
1640	1641	1651	1652	1653
1654	1655	1656	1657	1658
1659	1660	1661	1662	1680
1681	1682	1683	1700	1701
1702	1703	1720	1721	1722
1723	1725	1726	1727	1728
1733	1734	1735	1736	1737
1738	1739	1740	1793	1794
1795	1796	1801	1802	1803
1804	1821	1822	1823	1824
1865	1866	1867	1868	1869
1870	*1871	1872	1873	1874
*1875	*1876	1881	*1882	1883
1884	*1897	1898	1899	1900
1945	*1946	*1947	1948	1953
*1954	1955	1956	1957	1958
*1959	*1960	1973	1974	1975
1976	1977	1978	1979	1980
1981	1982	1983	1984	1985
1986	1987	1988	2029	2030
2031	2032	*2037	2038	2039
2048	*2053	2054	2055	2056
2061	2062	2063	2064	2077
2078	2079	2080	2085	2086
2087	2088	2089	2090	2091
2092	2141	2142	2143	2144
2173	2174	2175	2176	2181
2186	2187	2188	2193	2194
2195	2196	2257	2258	2259
2260	2273	2274	2275	2276
2281	2282	2283	2284	2285
2286	2287	2288	2310	2311
2312	2313	2391	2392	2393
2394	2407	2408	2409	2410
2415	2416	2417	2418	2451
2452	2453	2454	2468	2469
2470	2471	2484	2485	2486
2487	2492	2493	2494	2495
2500	2501	2502	2503	2552
2553	2554	2555	2560	2561
2562	2563	*2580	2581	2582
2583	2584	2585	2586	2587
2645	2646	2647	2648	2675
2676	2677	2678	2693	2694
2695	2696	2697	2698	2699
2700	2733	2734	2735	2736
2737	2738	2739	2740	2745
2746	2747	2748	2749	*2750

#300 1¢ FRANKLIN Cont.

2751	2752	2753	2754	2755
2756	2757	2758	2759	2760
2761	2762	2763	2764	*2789
2790	2791	2792	2797	2798
2799	2800	2801	2818	2819
2820	2821	2822	2823	*2824
2825	2907	2908	2909	2910
2911	2912	2913	2914	2915
2916	2917	2918	2919	2920
2921	2922	2927	2928	2929
2930	2935	2936	2937	2938
2939	2940	2941	2942	2943
2944	2945	2946	2947	2948
2949	2950	2991	2992	2993
*2994	2995	2996	2997	2998
2999	3000	3001	3002	3015
3016	3017	3018	3024	3026
3029	3034	3035	3037	3038
3039	3040	3041	3043	3082
3095	3096	3103	*3104	3119
3120	3121	3122	3123	3124
3125	3126	3127	3128	3129
3130	3131	3132	3133	3134
3178	3182	3186	3189	3194
3201	3203	3207	3214	3217
3220	3223	3224	3225	3226
3227	3228	3229	3230	3231
3232	3233	3234	3239	3243
3244	3245	3246	3247	3252
3261	3266	3283	3284	3285
3286	3287	3290	3293	3320
3364	3365	3366	3367	3370
3371	3373	3374	3377	3378
3379	3380	3381	3382	3383
3384	3385	3386	3391	3392
3393	3394	3396	3400	3401
3402	3404	3407	3476	3477
3482	3483	3485	3489	*3492
*3494	3495	3499	3500	3506
3509	3515	3518	3529	3530
3535	3558	3567	3588	*3590
3596	3598	*3599	3692	3696
3704	3710	3714	3719	3725
3726	3731	*3738	3741	3742
3746	3747	3748	3749	3750
3751	3752	3757	3760	3761
3764	3768	3769	3771	3772
3776	3777	3778	3781	3782
*3783	3785	*3786	*3788	*3789
*3790	*3791	*3793	*3794	*3795
3797	3798	3800	3803	3805

1902-03 REGULAR ISSUE

#300 1¢ FRANKLIN Cont.

*3809	3813	3815	3818	3874
3875	3880	3881	3882	3885
3887	3889	*3890	3891	3893
3894	*3898	3900	3901	3905
*3907	*3909	3910	3914	3917
3919	3921	3922	3926	3930
3933	3936	3937	3938	3942
3943	3944	3947	3949	3950
3951	3952	3953	3957	3958
3959	3960	3961	3965	3966
3967	3968	3971	3972	3973
3974	3976	3977	3978	3979
3980	3982	3983	3984	3986
3987	3988	3990	3991	*3992
3993	3994	3995	3996	4130
4131	4134	4135	4136	4137
4138	4139	4142	*4143	4144
4147	4148	4149	4150	4151
4154	4155	4156	*4157	4160
4161	4162	4163	4164	4165
4168	4169	4170	4171	4172
4176	4177	4178	4179	4181
4183	*4191	4192	4193	4198
4199	4201	4216	4221	*4228
*4229	4232	4233	*4234	4236
4237	4240	4241	4246	4252
4253	4257	*4258	4259	4265
4266	4270	4273	4274	4278
4281	4282	4287	*4288	*4290
*4293	*4294	4295	4296	4297
*4301	4302	*4303	*4304	*4305
4309	4310	4311	4314	4319
4324	*4325	*4328	*4334	4340
4341	4347	4348	4349	4354
4355	4356	4362	4366	4370
4371	4376	4386	4387	4392
4397	4403	4412	4413	4421
4422	4427	4428	4432	4436
4440	4450	4453	4455	4458
4462	4466	*4467	4472	4473
4474	4478	4479	4480	4484
4485	4486	4491	4492	4493
*4494	4498	4499	4504	4505
4506	4511	4517	4529	4533
4539	4547	4554	4559	4562
4565	*4566	*4567	4571	*4573
4574	4578	4582	4585	4586
4591	4592	4597	4600	4601
4603	4605	4606	4608	4609
4610	4618	4619	4620	4621
4622	4623	4626	4629	4630
4633	4637	4640	4641	4645
4656	4673	4674	4675	4679
4680	4681	4682	4688	*4691
*4694	4698	4699	4700	*4702
4705	4706	4710	4712	4713
4717	4719	4722	4723	4724
4727	4729	4733	4734	4737
4738	4742	4744	4748	4752
4753	*4757	4758		

#301 2¢ WASHINGTON (FLAG)

Basic Price **T, L, R, B** **145 Plates**

Imprint Strip of 3 .... $45

Imprint Block of 6 .... $200

1513	1514	1515	1516	1517
1518	1519	1520	1521	1522
1523	1524	1525	1526	1527
1528	1529	1530	1531	1532
1533	1534	1535	1536	1553
1554	1555	1556	1557	1559
1560	1561	1562	1563	1564
1565	1566	1567	1568	1569
1570	1571	1572	1573	*1574
*1575	1576	1577	1603	1604

1605	1606	1612	1613	1614
1615	1616	1617	1618	1619
1621	1622	1623	1624	*1643
1644	1645	1646	1647	1648
1649	1650	1668	1669	1670
1671	*1672	1673	1674	1675
1676	1677	1678	1679	1684
1685	1686	1687	1692	1693
1694	1695	1696	1697	1698
1699	1704	1705	1706	1707
1708	1709	1710	1711	1712
1713	1714	1715	1716	1717
1718	1719	1724	1729	1730
1731	1732	1741	*1742	1743
1744	*1745	*1746	*1747	*1748
1749	*1750	*1751	*1752	*1753
*1754	*1755	*1756	1757	*1758
*1759	*1760	1761	1762	*1763
1764	*1765	*1766	*1767	*1768

#302 3¢ JACKSON 16 Plates

Basic Price **T, L, R, B**

Imprint Strip of 3 .... $200

Imprint Block of 6 .... $650

1586	1587	1588	1589	*2516
*2517	*2518	*2519	2806	2807
2808	2809	*3511	3523	*3527
3536				

1902-03 REGULAR ISSUE

#303 4¢ GRANT 24 Plates

Basic Price **T, L, R, B**

Imprint Strip of 3 .... $220
Imprint Block of 6 .... $675

1477	1478	1479	1480	1797
1798	1799	1800	2298	2299
2300	2301	4214	4255	4264
*4271	4501	4512	4520	4527
*4747	4754	4759	*4761	

#304 5¢ LINCOLN 34 Plates

Basic Price **T, L, R, B**

Imprint Strip of 3 .... $230
Imprint Block of 6 .... $700

1537	1538	1539	1540	1663
1885	*1886	1887	1888	2225
2226	2227	2297	2951	*2952
*2953	2954	3147	3153	3157
*3158	3159	*3484	*3488	3493
3498	*4073	*4074	*4075	*4076
4190	4194	4203	4209	

#305 6¢ GARFIELD 8 Plates

Basic Price **T, L, R, B**

Imprint Strip of 3 .... $250
Imprint Block of 6 .... $800

1598	1599	1600	1601	*4658
*4660	*4664	*4666		

#306 8¢ MARTHA WASHINGTON

Basic Price **T, L, R, B** **12 Plates**

Imprint Strip of 3 .... $150
Imprint Block of 6 .... $600

1497	1498	1499	1500	2802
2803	2804	2805	3557	3565
3570	3576			

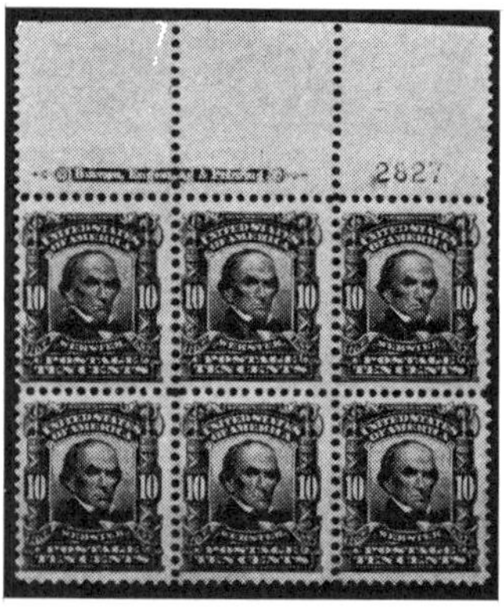

#307 10¢ WEBSTER 12 Plates

Basic Price **T, L, R, B**

Imprint Strip of 3 .... $250
Imprint Block of 6 .... $850

1590	1591	1592	1593	2289
2290	2291	2292	2826	2827
2828	2829			

#308 13¢ HARRISON 8 Plates

Basic Price **T, L, R, B**

Imprint Strip of 3 .... $150
Imprint Block of 6 .... $550

1473	1474	1475	1476	3827
3831	3835	3840		

#309 15¢ CLAY 6 Plates

Basic Price **T, B**

Imprint Strip of 3 .... $600
Imprint Block of 6 .... $2,600

1607	2330

Basic Price **T, L, R, B**

Imprint Strip of 3 .... $600
Imprint Block of 6 .... $2,600

3202	3206	3208	3209

1902-03 REGULAR ISSUE

#310 50¢ JEFFERSON 1 Plate
Price **T, B**

Imprint Strip of 3 .... $1,800
Imprint Block of 6 .... $6,500

1602

#311 $1 FARRAGUT 1 Plate
Price **T, B**

Imprint Strip of 3 .... $2,500
Imprint Block of 6 .... $13,000

1629

#312 $2 MADISON 1 Plate
Price **T, B**

Imprint Strip of 3 .... $3,600
Imprint Block of 6 .... $22,000

1630

#313 $5 MARSHALL 1 Plate
Price **T, B**

Imprint Strip of 3 .... $10,000
Imprint Block of 6 .... $55,000

1620

BOOKLET PANES
PANES OF 6
Imprint IX

#300b 1¢ FRANKLIN 20 Plates
Basic Price T $1,000

*3339	*3340	*3341	*3342	*3468
*3469	*3471	*3472 N	†3474	†3475
†3479	*3480	3503	3508	3510
3514	†4544	*4550	*4553	*4557

N Plate number over left stamp

BOOKLET PANES

#301c 2¢ WASHINGTON(FLAG) 20 Plates
Basic Price T $1,200

1582	1583	*1584	*1585	*1594
*1595	*1596	1597	1664	*1665
1666	*1667	*1688	*1689	*1690
1691	*1769	1770	*1771	*1772

IMPERFORATE

For listing of the vending and affixing machine coil stamps, please see APPENDIX A

Blocks of 6
Imprint V

#314 1¢ FRANKLIN 38 Plates
Basic Price **T, L, R, B**

Imprint Block of 6 .... $200

3119	3120	3121	3122	3227
3228	3230	3231	3364	3365
3366	3367	3373	3374	*4147
4149	4296	*4324	*4354	4370
4371	4376	4386	4474	4493
4498	4499	4505	4559	4562
*4605	4608	4681	4682	4688
*4712	4713	*4734		

#314A 4¢ GRANT 1 Plate
4255

Imperforate stamp was issued but all known examples have Schermack perforations Type III.

#314H 1¢ FRANKLIN 1 Plate
4324

#315 5¢ LINCOLN 6 Plates
Basic Price **T, L, R, B**

Imprint Block of 6 .... $3,200

2951	2952	2953	2954	4073
4075				

END COIL

#317 5¢ LINCOLN 1 Plate

2952

1902-03 REGULAR ISSUE

#319 2¢ WASHINGTON (SHIELD) (DIE 1) 1450 Plates

Double Line Wmk. Perf. 12

FLAT PRESS

Imprint V

Basic Price **T, L, R, B**

Imprint Strip of 3 .... $20

Imprint Block of 6 .... $85

1805	1806	1807	1808	1809
1810	1811	1812	1813	1814
1815	1816	1817	1818	1819
1820	1825	1826	1827	1828
1829	1830	1831	1832	1833
1834	1835	1836	1837	1838
1839	1840	1841	1842	1843
1844	*1849	1850	*1851	1852
1853	1854	1855	1856	1857
1858	*1860	1861	1862	1863
1864	1877	1878	1879	1880
1893	1894	1895	1896	1901
1902	1903	1904	1905	1906
1907	1908	*1909	1910	1911
1913	1914	1915	1916	1917
1918	1919	1920	1921	1922
1923	1924	1925	1926	*1927
*1928	1929	*1930	1931	1932
1933	1934	1935	1936	1937
1938	1940	1941	1942	1943
1944	1961	1962	1963	1964
1965	1966	1967	*1968	*1969
1970	1971	1972	1989	1990
1991	1992	1993	1994	1995
1996	1997	1998	1999	2000
2001	2002	2003	2004	2005
*2006	2007	2008	2013	2014
2015	2016	2017	2018	2019
2020	2021	2022	2023	2024
2025	2026	2027	2028	2033
2034	2035	2036	2040	2041
2042	2043	2044	2045	2046
2047	2049	2051	2052	2057
2058	2059	2060	2065	2066
2067	2068	2073	2074	2075
2076	2133	2134	2135	2136
2169	2170	2171	2172	2189
2191	2192	2201	2202	2203
2204	2205	2206	2207	2208
2209	2210	2111	2212	2213
2214	2215	2216	2217	2218
2219	2220	2221	2222	2223
2224	2229	2230	2231	2232
2237	2238	2239	2240	2241
2242	2243	2244	2245	2246
2247	2248	2249	2250	2251
2252	2253	2254	2255	2256
2261	2262	2263	*2264	2265
2266	2267	2268	2269	2270
2271	2272	2277	2278	2279
2280	2293	2294	2295	2296
2306	*2307	2308	2309	2314
2315	2316	2317	2318	2319
2320	2321	2322	2323	2324
2325	2326	2327	2328	2329
2331	2332	2333	2334	2335
2336	2337	2338	2339	2340
2341	2342	2343	2344	2345
2346	2347	2348	2349	2350
2351	2352	2353	2354	2355
2356	2357	2358	2359	2360
2361	2362	2363	2364	2365
2366	2367	2368	2369	2370
2379	2380	2381	2382	2383
2384	2385	2386	2387	2388
2389	2390	2395	2396	2397
2398	2399	2400	2401	2402
2403	2404	2405	2406	2419
2420	2421	2422	2423	2424
2425	2426	2427	2428	2429
2430	2431	2432	2433	2434
2435	*2436	2437	2438	2439
2440	2441	2442	2443	2444
2445	2446	2447	2448	2449
2450	2455	2456	2457	2458
2459	2460	2461	2462	2463
2464	2465	2466	2472	2473
2474	2475	2476	2477	2478
2479	2480	2481	2482	2483
2488	2489	2490	2491	2508
2509	2510	2511	2512	2513
2514	2515	2520	2521	2522
2523	2524	2525	2526	2527
2528	2529	2530	2531	2532
2533	2534	2535	2536	2537
2538	2539	2540	2541	2542
2543	2544	2545	2546	2547
2556	2557	2558	2559	2564
2565	2566	2567	2568	2569
2570	2571	2572	2573	2574
2575	2576	2577	2578	2579
2588	2589	2590	2591	2592
2593	2594	2595	2596	2597
2598	2599	2608	2609	2610
2611	2612	2613	2614	2615
2616	2617	2618	2619	2620
2621	2622	2623	2624	2625
2626	2627	2628	2629	2630
2631	2632	2633	2634	2635
2636	2637	2638	2639	2640
2641	2642	2643	2644	2649
2650	2651	2652	2653	2654
2655	2656	2657	2658	2659
2660	2661	2662	2663	2664
2665	2666	2667	2668	2669
2670	2671	2672	2673	2674
2679	2680	2681	2682	2683
2684	2685	2686	2687	2688
2689	2690	2691	2692	2701
2702	2703	2704	2705	2706
2707	2708	2709	2710	2711
2712	2717	2718	2719	2720
2721	2722	2723	2724	2725
2726	2727	2728	2729	2730
2731	2732	2741	2742	2743
2744	2765	2766	2767	2768
2773	2774	2775	2776	2777
2778	2779	2785	2786	2787

1902-03 REGULAR ISSUE

#319 2¢ WASHINGTON (SHIELD) (DIE 1) Continued

2788	2793	2794	*2795	2796
2810	2811	2812	2813	2814
2815	2816	2817	2830	2831
2832	2833	2834	2835	2836
2837	2838	2839	2840	2841
2842	2843	2844	2845	2846
2847	2848	2849	2850	2851
2852	2853	2854	2855	2856
2857	2858	2859	2860	2861
2862	2863	2864	2865	2866
2867	2868	2869	2870	2871
2872	2873	2874	2875	2876
2877	2878	2883	2884	2885
2886	2887	2888	2889	2890
2891	2892	2893	2894	2895
2896	2897	2898	2899	2900
2901	2902	2903	2904	2905
2906	2959	2960	2961	2962
2963	2964	2965	2966	2967
2968	2969	2970	2971	2972
2973	2974	2975	2976	2977
2978	2979	*2980	*2981	2982
2983	2984	2985	2986	2987
2988	*2989	2990	3003	3004
3005	3006	3007	3008	3009
3010	3036	3042	3044	3045
3046	3047	3048	3049	3050
3051	3052	3053	3054	3055
3056	3057	3058	3059	3060
3061	3062	3063	3064	3065
3066	3067	3068	3069	3070
3071	3072	3073	3074	3075
3076	3077	3078	3079	3080
3081	3083	3084	3085	3086
3087	3088	3089	3090	3091
3092	3093	3094	3097	3098
3099	3100	3101	3102	3105
3106	3107	3108	3109	3110
3111	3112	3113	3114	3115
3116	3117	3118	3135	3136
3137	3138	3139	3140	3141
3142	3143	*3144	3145	3146
3148	3149	3150	3151	3152
3154	3155	3156	3160	3161
3162	3163	3164	3166	3167
3168	3169	3170	3171	3172
3173	3174	3175	3176	3179
3180	3183	3184	3185	3187
3188	3190	3191	3193	*3200
3204	3205	3210	3211	3212
*3213	3218	3222	3248	3249
3250	3251	*3253	3254	3255
3256	3257	3258	3259	3260
3262	3263	3264	*3265	3267
3268	3269	3270	3271	3272
3273	3274	3275	3276	3277
3278	3279	3280	3281	3282
3288	3289	3291	3292	3294
3295	3296	3297	3298	3301
3304	3305	3306	3309	3310
3313	3314	3315	3316	3317

3318	3319	3321	3322	3323
3324	3325	3326	3327	3328
3329	3330	3331	3332	3333
3334	3335	3336	3337	3338
3343	3344	3345	3346	3347
3348	3349	3350	3351	3352
3353	3356	3357	3358	3361
3362	3363	3368	3369	3372
*3375	3376	3389	*3390	3395
3399	3403	3408	3411	3412
3415	3416	3417	3418	3419
3420	3423	3424	3425	3426
3427	3428	3429	3430	3431
3432	3433	3434	3435	3438
3439	3440	3441	3442	*3445
3446	3447	3448	3451	3452
3453	3454	3455	3456	3457
3458	3461	3462	3463	*3465
3466	3467	3470	3473	3478
3481	3486	3487	*3490	3491
3496	3497	3501	3502	3507
3516	3519	3528	3533	3534
3537	3539	3547	3548	3551
3552	3555	*3559	3562	3563
3564	3566	*3568	3569	3571
3572	*3573	*3574	*3575	3581
3582	3584	3586	3587	3589
3600	3605	3606	3607	3608
3609	3611	3612	3614	3615
3616	3617	3620	3621	3622
*3623	3624	3625	3626	3627
3628	3629	3630	*3631	3632
3633	3634	3635	3640	3641
3642	3643	3644	3649	3650
3651	3652	3653	3654	3659
3660	3663	3665	3668	3674
3675	3676	3679	*3680	3681
3682	3683	3684	3685	3686
3687	3688	3689	3690	*3691
3693	3694	3695	3697	3698
*3699	*3700	*3701	*3702	3703
*3705	*3706	*3707	*3708	*3709
3711	3712	3713	3715	*3716
3717	*3718	3721	3722	*3723
3724	3727	*3728	*3729	*3730
*3732	*3735	*3736	3737	3743
*3744	3745	*3758	3759	3765
*3767	3773	*3774	3779	3784
*3792	*3796	*3801	*3806	*3808
*3811	*3812	*3816	3820	*3821
3823	*3824	3825	*3826	3828
3829	3830	3832	3833	3834
3836	3837	3838	3839	3841
3842	3843	3844	3845	3846
3847	3848	*3849	*3850	3851
3852	3853	3854	3855	3856
3857	*3858	3859	3860	*3861
3862	3863	3864	3865	3866
3867	3868	*3869	3870	3871
3872	3873	3876	3877	3878
3879	3883	*3884	3886	3888

1902-03 REGULAR ISSUE

#319 2¢ WASHINGTON (SHIELD) (DIE I) Continued

3892	3895	3896	3897	3899
3902	3903	3904	3906	3908
3911	3912	3913	3915	3916
3918	3920	3925	3929	3931
3932	3934	3935	3939	3940
3941	3945	3946	3948	3954
3955	3956	3962	3963	3964
3969	3970	3975	3981	3985
*3989	3998	4000	4005	4006
4009	4010	4011	4012	4013
4014	4015	4016	4017	4018
4019	4020	4021	4022	4023
4024	4025	4026	4027	4028
4029	4030	4031	4032	*4033
4034	*4035	4036	4037	4038
4039	4040	4041	*4042	4043
4044	4045	4046	4047	*4048
4049	4050	*4051	4053	*4054
*4055	4056	*4058	4059	4060
4063	4064	4065	4066	4067
*4068	*4069	4070	4071	4072
4077	4078	4079	4080	4081
*4082	4083	4084	4085	4086
*4087	4088	4089	4090	4091
4092	4093	4094	*4095	4096
4097	4098	4099	4100	4101
4102	4103	4104	4105	4110
4111	4112	4113	4116	4117
4119	4122	*4123	4124	*4125
*4126	*4127	*4128	4129	4132
4133	4140	4141	4145	4146
4152	4153	4158	4159	4166
4167	4173	4174	4175	*4180
*4182	*4184	4185	4186	*4187
4188	*4189	4195	4196	4197
4200	4202	*4204	*4205	4206
*4207	4208	4210	4211	4212
*4213	*4215	4217	*4218	*4219
*4220	*4222	*4224	4225	4226
4227	4238	4243	4244	4245
4249	4250	4251	4254	4256
4260	4261	4262	4263	4267
4268	4269	4272	4276	4277
4280	4284	4285	4286	4291
4292	4298	4299	4300	*4306
4307	4308	4312	*4313	4315
*4316	4317	4318	4320	4321
4322	4323	4326	4327	4329
4330	4331	4332	4333	4335
4336	4337	4338	*4342	4345

#319f 2¢ WASHINGTON (SHIELD) (DIE II) 225 Plates

Basic Price **T, L, R, B**

Imprint Strip of 3 .... $27

Imprint Block of 6 .... $150

4339	4343	4344	4346	4350
4351	4352	4353	4359	4360
4361	4365	4369	4372	4373
4377	4378	*4380	4381	4383
4384	4385	4388	4389	4390
4391	4393	4394	4395	4396
4398	4399	4400	4401	4402
4404	4405	4406	4407	4408
4409	4410	4411	4414	4415
4416	4417	4419	4420	4424
4425	4426	4429	4431	4433
4434	4437	4438	4447	4448
4449	4452	4454	4456	4459
4460	4461	4463	4465	4468
4469	4470	4471	4475	4476
4477	4481	4482	4483	4487
4488	4489	4490	4495	4496
4497	4500	4502	4503	4507
4508	4509	4510	4513	4514
4515	4516	4518	4519	4521
4522	4523	4524	4525	4526
4528	4530	4531	4532	4534
4535	4536	4537	4538	4540
4541	4542	4543	4545	4546
4548	4549	4552	4555	4556
4560	4561	4569	4575	4581
4587	4588	4595	4596	4599
4604	4611	4612	4615	4616
4617	4624	4625	4627	4628
4631	4632	4634	4635	4636
4638	4639	4642	4643	4644
4646	4647	4648	4649	4650
4651	*4652	*4653	4654	4655
4657	4659	4661	4662	4663
4665	4667	4668	4669	4670
4671	4672	4676	4677	4678
4683	4684	4685	4686	4687
4689	4690	4692	4693	4695
4696	4697	4701	4703	4704
4707	4708	4709	4711	4714
4715	4716	4718	4720	4721
4725	4726	4728	4730	4731
4732	4735	4736	4739	4740
4741	4743	4745	*4746	*4750
4756	4764	4769	4772	4776

1902-03 REGULAR ISSUE

BOOKLET PANES

PANES OF 6

Imprint IX

#319g 2¢ WASHINGTON (SHIELD)
(DIE I) 232 Plates

Basic Price T $275

*1845	†1846	†1847	†1848	*1889
1890	1891	1892	*1949	*1950
1951	*1952	*2009	*2010	*2011
*2012	*2109	2110	2111	2112
*2121	*2122	*2123	*2124	*2233
†2234	2235	2236	*2302	2303
*2304	2305	*2371	*2372	*2373
*2374	2375	*2376	2377	2378
*2411	*2412	*2413	*2414	2467
*2496	*2497	*2498	*2499	*2504
2505	*2506	2507	2548	2549
2550	2551	2600	*2601	*2602
*2603	*2604	†2605	*2606	*2607
2713	2714	2715	2716	2769
2770	2771	2772	2781	2782
*2783	*2784	*2879	2880	2881
2882	*2923	*2924	2925	*2926
*2931	*2932	2933	*2934	*2955
2956	2957	*2958	*3011	*3012
*3013	*3014	*3019	3020	3021
*3022	3023	*3025	*3027	*3028
3030	3031	*3032	*3033	*3196
3197	3198	3199	†3215	†3216
*3219	*3221	†3235	†3236	†3237
*3238	†3240	*3241	*3242	3299
3300	3302	*3303	*3307	*3308
*3311	*3312	3354	*3355	3359
*3360	3387	3388	*3397	*3398
†3405	†3406	3409	*3410	†3413
†3414	†3421	†3422	*3436	*3437
*3443	*3444	*3449	†3450	*3459
*3460	†3464	*3521	3525	3526
†3531	*3532	3549	*3550	3553

#319g 2¢ WASHINGTON (SHIELD) Cont.

*3636	†3637	†3638	†3639	*3645
*3646	*3647	*3648	*3661	3662
*3664	†3666	†3667	*3669	†3670
3673	*3733	*3734	*3739	3740
*3753	3754	*3755	†3756	3762
3763	3766	3810	3814	3817
3819	3822	*3923	3924	3928
*3997	3999	4001	*4002	†4003
†4004	†4007	†4008	*4052	†4057
*4061	†4062	4106	†4107	4108
†4109	*4114	4115	*4118	*4120
†4223	*4230	*4231	*4235	*4239
*4242	*4247	*4248	†4275	*4279
*4283	*4289	†4357	4358	4363
*4364	4367	4368	*4374	*4375
*4379	4382	4418	4423	4430
*4435	*4439	4443	4445	4451
4457	4464			

#319h 2¢ WASHINGTON (SHIELD)
(DIE II) 20 Plates

Basic Price T $400

4441	4442	*4444	4446	4551
4558	4564	*4570	*4577	*4580
4584	4590	4594	*4598	4602
*4607	4749	4751	4755	4760

IMPERFORATE

For listing of the vending and affixing machine coil stamps, please see APPENDIX A

Blocks of 6

Imprint V

#320 2¢ WASHINGTON (SHIELD)
(DIE I) 37 Plates

Basic Price **T, L, R, B**

Imprint Block of 6 .... $250

*3136	3160	3161	3162	3164
3222	3248	3249	3250	3251
*3295	*3298	*3301	3305	3399
3451	3452	3453	3454	*3706
*3709	4146	4152	4153	*4204
*4218	*4219	4227	4243	4245
4250	4262	4268	4269	*4277
4315	4323			

#320a 2¢ WASHINGTON (SHIELD)
(DIE II) 6 Plates

Basic Price **T, L, R, B**

Imprint Block of 6 .... $800

*4617	4651	4671	4701	4704
4718				

1904 COMMEMORATIVES

Double Line Wmk. Perf. 12

FLAT PRESS

Imprint V

#323 1¢ LOUISIANA PURCHASE

Basic Price: **24 Plates**

Imprint Pair $70

Imprint Block of 4 .... $165

	T	B		T	B		T	B
2113	□	□	2114	□	□	2115	□	□
2116	□	□	2117	□	□	2118	□	□
2119	□	□	2120	□	□	2129	□	□
2130	□	□	2131	□	□	2132	□	□
2137	□	□	2138	□	□	2139	□	□
2140	□	□	*2149	□	□	2150	□	□
2151	□	□	2152	□	□	2161	□	□
2162	□	□	2163	□	□	2164	□	□

#324 2¢ LOUISIANA PURCHASE

Basic Price: **40 Plates**

Imprint Pair $65

Imprint Block of 4 .... $175

2069	□	□	2070	□	□	2071	□	□
2072	□	□	2081	□	□	2082	□	□
2083	□	□	2084	□	□	2093	□	□
2094	□	□	2095	□	□	2096	□	□
2125	□	□	2126	□	□	2127	□	□
2128	□	□	2145	□	□	2146	□	□
2147	□	□	2148	□	□	2153	□	□
*2154	□	□	2155	□	□	2156	□	□
2157	□	□	2158	□	□	2159	□	□
2160	□	□	*2165	□	□	2166	□	□
2167	□	□	2168	□	□	*2177	□	□
2178	□	□	2179	□	□	2180	□	□
*2182	□	□	2183	□	□	*2184	□	□
2185	□	□						

#325 3¢ LOUISIANA PURCHASE

Basic Price: **4 Plates**

Imprint Pair $200

Imprint Block of 4 .... $600

2101	□	□	2102	□	□	2103	□	□
2104	□	□						

#326 5¢ LOUISIANA PURCHASE

Basic Price: **4 Plates**

Imprint Pair $225

Imprint Block of 4 .... $650

	T	B		T	B		T	B
2097	□	□	2098	□	□	2099	□	□
2100	□	□						

#327 10¢ LOUISIANA PURCHASE

Basic Price: **4 Plates**

Imprint Pair $425

Imprint Block of 4 .... $1,300

2105	□	□	2106	□	□	2107	□	□
2108	□	□						

1907 COMMEMORATIVES

Double Line Wmk. Perf. 12

FLAT PRESS

Imprint V

#328 1¢ JAMESTOWN 9 Plates

Basic Price:

Imprint Strip of 3 .... $85

Imprint Block of 6 .... $250

	T	B		T	B		T	B
3538	□	□	3540	□	□	3541	□	□
3542	□	□	3543	□	□	3544	□	□
3545	□	□	3546	□	□	*3799	□	□

#329 2¢ JAMESTOWN 32 Plates

Basic Price:

Imprint Strip of 3 .... $100

Imprint Block of 6 .... $325

3504	□	□	3505	□	□	3512	□	□
3513	□	□	3517	□	□	3520	□	□
3522	□	□	3524	□	□	3577	□	□
3578	□	□	3579	□	□	3580	□	□
3592	□	□	3593	□	□	*3594	□	□
*3595	□	□	3601	□	□	3602	□	□
3603	□	□	3604	□	□	3610	□	□
3613	□	□	3618	□	□	3619	□	□
*3655	□	□	*3656	□	□	3657	□	□
*3658	□	□	3671	□	□	3672	□	□
3677	□	□	3678	□	□			

#330 5¢ JAMESTOWN 4 Plates

Basic Price:

Imprint Strip of 3 .... $400

Imprint Block of 6 .... $2,000

3554	□	□	3556	□	□	3560	□	□
3561	□	□						

1908-09 REGULAR ISSUE

Double Line Wmk. Perf. 12

FLAT PRESS

#331 1¢ FRANKLIN 161 Plates

Imprint V

Basic Price **T** $75

Basic Price **L, R, B** $70

4874	4875	4880	*4881	4882
4885	4886	4888	4889	4890
4891	4892	4894	*4895	4897
4898	4899	*4900	4901	4902
4903	4904	4906	*4907	4908
4909	4910	4911	*4912	4913
4914	4915	*4960	4962	4966
*4967	4971	4972	4974	4975

Imprint XI

Basic Price **T** $1300

Basic Price **L, R, B** $1250

4980

Imprint X

Basic Price **T** $70

Basic Price **L, R, B** $65

4985	4986	4989	4991	4993
4994	4995	4997	4998	4999
5000	5001	5002	5003	5004
5005	5006	5007	5008	5009
5010	5011	5012	5013	5014
*5023	*5024	*5076	5077	5078
5079	*5080	5081	*5082	5083
5084	5085	*5086	*5087	5089
5091	5093	5097	5098	5100
5101	5103	5111	5118	5124
5137	5152	5153	5159	5162
5166	5169	5179	5180	5186
5187	5192	5193	5198	5206
5216	5223	5227	5232	5234
5242	5255	5259	5279	5287
5294	5301	5313	5320	5322
5330	5333	5336	5340	5345
5352	5359	5360	5373	5378
5380	5382	5383	†5384	5385
5386	5387	5401	5402	5403
5404	5413	5414	5416	5418
5420	5429	5432	5435	5438
5441	5444	5474	5476	5488
5489	5490	5491	*5494	*5495

#332 2¢ WASHINGTON 266 Plates

Imprint V

Basic Price **T** $65

Basic Price **L, R, B** $60

4807	4809	4810	4811	4812
4813	4814	4815	4816	4817
4818	4819	4820	4821	4822
4823	4824	4825	4827	4828
4829	4830	4831	4833	4834
4835	4837	*4838	4839	4840
4841	4842	4843	4844	4845
4846	*4847	4848	4849	4850
4851	4852	4853	4854	4855
4856	4857	4858	4859	4860
4861	4862	4863	4864	4865
4866	4868	4871	4872	4873

#332 2¢ WASHINGTON Cont.

4876	4878	4879	4883	4884
4887	4893	4896	4905	

Imprint XI

Basic Price **T** $1600

Basic Price **L, R, B** $1500

4988

Imprint X

Basic Price **T** $70

Basic Price **L, R, B** $65

4968	4969	4987	4990	*4992
4996	5015	5016	5017	5018
5019	5020	5021	5022	5025
5026	5027	5028	5031	5032
5033	5036	5039	5044	5045
5046	5049	5050	5051	5052
5053	5054	5055	5056	5057
5058	5059	5060	5061	5062
5063	5064	5065	5066	5067
5068	5069	5070	5071	5072
*5073	5074	5075	5092	5094
5102	5105	5107	5109	5110
5114	5115	5116	5117	5119
5120	5122	5123	5125	5127
5128	5129	5133	5134	5135
5140	5141	5147	5148	5149
5150	5151	5155	5156	5157
5160	5161	5163	5164	5165
5167	5168	5174	5175	5176
5177	5178	5181	5182	5183
5184	5185	5188	5189	5190
5191	5194	5195	5196	5197
5256	5258	5260	5265	5269
5270	5271	5272	5273	5274
5275	5276	5277	5278	5280
5281	5282	5283	5284	5285
5286	5288	5289	5290	5291
5292	5293	5295	5296	5297
5298	5299	5300	5302	5303
5304	5305	5306	5307	5308
5309	5310	5311	5312	5314
5315	5316	5317	5318	5319
5321	5323	5324	5325	5326
5327	5328	5329	5331	5332
5334	5335	5337	5338	5339
5342	5343	5346	5347	5348
5349	5351	5361	5362	5363
*5364	5365	5366	5367	5368
5369	5371	5374	5375	5377
5381				

1908-09 REGULAR ISSUE

#333 3¢ WASHINGTON Type I

Imprint V **8 Plates**

Basic Price **T** $325
Basic Price **L, R, B** $275

4918 4925 4926 4927

Imprint X

Basic Price **T** $350
Basic Price **L, R, B** $300

5121 5126 5131 5136

#334 4¢ WASHINGTON 20 Plates

Imprint V

Basic Price **T** $400
Basic Price **L, R, B** $350

4932 4933 4934 4935

Imprint X

Basic Price **T** $400
Basic Price **L, R, B** $350

5132 5138 5146 *5158 5199
5212 5217 5226 5405 5406
5407 5408 5415 5417 5422
*5426

#335 5¢ WASHINGTON 12 Plates

Imprint V

Basic Price **T** $500
Basic Price **L, R, B** $450

4928 4929 4930 4931 4958
4959 4961 4973

Imprint X

Basic Price **T** $525
Basic Price **L, R, B** $475

5341 5376 5379 5396

#336 6¢ WASHINGTON 4 Plates

Imprint V

Basic Price **T** $725
Basic Price **L, R, B** $675

4936 4937 4938 4939

#337 8¢ WASHINGTON 4 Plates

Imprint V

Basic Price **T** $450
Basic Price **L, R, B** $400

4919 4922 4923 4924

#338 10¢ WASHINGTON 4 Plates

Imprint V

Basic Price **T** $750
Basic Price **L, R, B** $700

4940 4941 4943 4944

#339 13¢ WASHINGTON 4 Plates

Imprint V

Basic Price **T** $475
Basic Price **L, R, B** $425

4942 4945 4946 4948

#340 15¢ WASHINGTON 4 Plates

Imprint V

Basic Price **T** $600
Basic Price **L, R, B** $550

4949 4951 4952 4954

#341 50¢ WASHINGTON 1 Plate

Imprint V

Price **T** $6,000
Price **B** $5,500

4956

#342 $1 WASHINGTON 1 Plate

Imprint V

Price **T** $12,000
Price **B** $10,000

4957

1908-09 REGULAR ISSUE

BOOKLET PANES

PANES OF 6

Imprint IX

#331a 1¢ FRANKLIN 16 Plates

Basic Price T $250

180 Subject Plates

*4867	*4869	*4870	*4877	5029
5030	5034	5035	5037	5038
5040	5041			

360 Subject Plates

5263	5264	5267	5268

#332a 2¢ WASHINGTON 44 Plates

Basic Price T $175

180 Subject Plates

*4803	*4804	*4805	*4806	*4808
*4826	*4832	*4836	4947	4950
4953	4955	4963	4964	4965
4970	5042	5043	5047	5048
5088	5090	5095	5096	5099
5104	5106	5108	5112	5113
5139	5154			

360 Subject Plates

5130	5261	5262	5266	5445
5446	5448	5450	5451	5456
5458	5459			

IMPERFORATE

Blocks of 6

#343 1¢ FRANKLIN 85 Plates

Imprint V

Basic Price T $65

Basic Price L, R, B $60

4874	4875	4880	*4881	4882
4889	4890	4892	4894	*4895
4899	*4900	*4902	4903	4908
*4962	4971	4972	4974	4975

Imprint XI

Price T $700

Price L, R, B $650

4980

Imprint X

Basic Price T $75

Basic Price L, R, B $70

4985	4989	4991	*4994	4997
*5001	5002	*5003	5004	*5005
*5006	*5009	5011	*5014	*5023
*5024	5084	*5085	5089	5091
5093	5103	5152	5159	5162
5166	*5169	5179	5180	5186
5193	5198	5206	5227	5232

#343 1¢ FRANKLIN Cont.

5234	5242	5259	5279	5287
5294	5301	5313	5320	5322
5330	5333	5336	5345	5352
5359	5360	5373	5378	5380
5387	5413	5414	5416	5435
5488	*5490	5491	*5495	

#344 2¢ WASHINGTON 117 Plates

Imprint V

Basic Price T $120

Basic Price L, R, B $100

4812	4813	*4814	4815	4816
4817	4818	4820	4821	4824
4829	4830	4831	4833	4848
4849	4856	4858	4859	4862
4864	4865	4866	4868	4872
4873	4876	4878	4879	4883
4884	4887	4893	4896	4905

Imprint X

Basic Price T $110

Basic Price L, R, B $90

*4987	*4992	4996	*5015	5017
5020	5021	5031	5032	5033
5036	*5059	5068	5075	5092
5114	5117	5119	5122	5123
5129	5133	5134	5135	5141
5150	5151	5155	5156	5157
5167	5168	5178	5181	*5182
5183	5188	5189	5256	5258
5260	5273	5280	*5283	5284
5285	5286	5292	5293	5295
5296	5297	5298	5299	5300
*5303	5305	5306	*5307	5308
5309	5310	5311	5312	5314
5321	5323	5326	5327	5344
5347	5349	5361	5363	5365
5366	5367	5368	5371	5375
5377	5381			

#345 3¢ WASHINGTON Type I

Imprint V **4 Plates**

Basic Price T $200

Basic Price L, R, B $175

4918	4925	4926	4927

1908-09 REGULAR ISSUE

IMPERFORATE

#346 4¢ WASHINGTON 14 Plates

Imprint V

Basic Price	T	$225
Basic Price	L, R, B	$200

4932 4933 4934 4935

Imprint X

Basic Price	T	$300
Basic Price	L, R, B	$250

5199 5212 5217 5226 5405
5406 5407 5408 5415 5417

#347 5¢ WASHINGTON 8 Plates

Imprint V

Basic Price	T	$400
Basic Price	L, R, B	$350

4928 4929 4930 4931 4958
4959 4961 4973

IMPERFORATE COILS

For listing of the vending and affixing machine coil stamps, please see APPENDIX A

#343V 1¢ FRANKLIN

Imprint X

5313 5320 5352 5373 5380
5386 5387 5413 5414 5416

#343H 1¢ FRANKLIN

none reported

#344V 2¢ WASHINGTON

Imprint X

5033 5115 5120 5122 5260
5273 5274 5283 5293 5295
5296 5297 5298 5299 5302
5303 5305 5306 5309 5317

#344H 2¢ WASHINGTON

Imprint V

4873

Imprint X

5189 5256 5258 5260 5273
5280 5296 5299

#346V 4¢ WASHINGTON

Imprint X

5199 5217

#347V 5¢ WASHINGTON

Imprint V

4928 4929 4958 4959 4961
4973

Other plate numbers may exist on these imperforate coils with fake perforations to represent the more expensive perforated coil stamps.

END COILS

Perf. 12 Horizontally

#348 1¢ FRANKLIN

Imprint V

4903 4974

Imprint X

5159 5186 5198 5255 5352
5383 5387 5403 5404 5418
5420 5429 5432 5474 5487
5489 5496 5497 5498

#349 2¢ WASHINGTON

Imprint X

5115 5116 5119 5120 5122
5177 5260 5273 5295 5296
5298 5299 5302 5305 5306
5307 5315 5316 5319 5321

#350 4¢ WASHINGTON

Imprint X

5212 5415 5417 5422 5426

#351 5¢ WASHINGTON

Imprint V

4928 4929 4930 4973

1908-09 REGULAR ISSUE

SIDE COILS

Perf. 12 Vertically

#352 1¢ FRANKLIN

Imprint V

4972 4975

Imprint X

5169 5179 5180 5255 5382

#353 2¢ WASHINGTON

Imprint V

4858

Imprint X

5160 *5174 5177 5183 5184
5194 5256 5272 5273 5332
5334 5348 5367 5369

#354 4¢ WASHINGTON

Imprint V

4932 4935

#355 5¢ WASHINGTON

Imprint V

4929 4958 4959 4961 4973

#356 10¢ WASHINGTON

Imprint V

4944

CLAY PAPER

X-ray diffraction studies show that stamps once considered to be printed on "Clay Paper" in fact contain no clay, and thus we have deleted these listings. See American Philatelist, March 1996, p 218.

SHEET STAMPS

BLUISH PAPER

Double Line Wmk. Perf. 12

FLAT PRESS

#357 1¢ FRANKLIN (BLUISH)

Imprint V **7 Plates**

Basic Price **T** $1,100
Basic Price **L, R, B** $1,000
4889 4890 4892 4894 4899

Imprint X

Basic Price **T** $3,500
Basic Price **L, R, B** $3,250
4994 4997

#358 2¢ WASHINGTON (BLUISH)

Imprint V **8 Plates**

Basic Price **T** $1,200
Basic Price **L, R, B** $1,000
4837 *4860 4861 4863

Imprint X

Basic Price **T** $1,700
Basic Price **L, R, B** $1,500
4996 5015 5016 *5017

BLUISH PAPER Cont.

#359 3¢ WASHINGTON Type I (BLUISH) **4 Plates**

Imprint V

Basic Price **T** $16,000
Basic Price **L, R, B** $14,000
4918 4925 4926 4927

#360 4¢ WASHINGTON (BLUISH)

Imprint V **1 Plate**

No plate blocks exist
Imprint Strip of 3 $75,000
4934

#361 5¢ WASHINGTON (BLUISH)

Imprint V **2 Plates**

Basic Price **T** $32,000
Basic Price **L, R, B** --
4928 4931

#362 6¢ WASHINGTON (BLUISH)

Imprint V **4 Plates**

Basic Price **T** $15,000
Basic Price **L, R, B** $13,000
4936 4937 4938 4939

#363 8¢ WASHINGTON (BLUISH)

Imprint V **1 Plate**

No plate blocks exist
Imprint Strip of 3 $75,000
4922

#364 10¢ WASHINGTON (BLUISH)

Imprint V **3 Plates**

Basic Price **T**
Basic Price **L, R, B** $16,000
4940 4943 4944

#365 13¢ WASHINGTON (BLUISH)

Imprint V **3 Plates**

Basic Price **T** $18,000
Basic Price **L, R, B**
4942 4945 4948

#366 15¢ WASHINGTON (BLUISH)

Imprint V **4 Plates**

Basic Price **T** $10,000
Basic Price **L, R, B** $9,500
4949 4951 4952 4954

1909 COMMEMORATIVES

Double Line Wmk. Perf. 12
FLAT PRESS Imprint Block of 6

#367 2¢ LINCOLN 8 Plates
Imprint XI

	T		L		R	B
4976	$135	☐	$125	☐	☐	☐
4977	$135	☐	$125	☐	☐	☐
4978	$135	☐	$125	☐	☐	☐
4979	$135	☐	$125	☐	☐	☐
4981	$135	☐	$125	☐	☐	☐
4982	$135	☐	$125	☐	☐	☐
4983	$135	☐	$125	☐	☐	☐
4984	$135	☐	$125	☐	☐	☐

#368 2¢ LINCOLN IMPERFORATE
Imprint XI **8 Plates**

4976	$200	☐	$175	☐	☐	☐
4977	$200	☐	$175	☐	☐	☐
4978	$200	☐	$175	☐	☐	☐
4979	$200	☐	$175	☐	☐	☐
4981	$200	☐	$175	☐	☐	☐
4982	$200	☐	$175	☐	☐	☐
4983	$200	☐	$175	☐	☐	☐
4984	$200	☐	$175	☐	☐	☐

#369 2¢ LINCOLN BLUISH PAPER
Imprint XI **4 Plates**

4976	$2,800	☐	$2,500	☐	☐	☐
4977	$2,800	☐	$2,500	☐	☐	☐
4978	$2,800	☐	$2,500	☐	☐	☐
4979	$2,800	☐	$2,500	☐	☐	☐

#370 2¢ ALASKA-YUKON 20 Plates
Imprint V

5142	$225	☐	$200	☐	☐	☐
5143	$225	☐	$200	☐	☐	☐
5144	$225	☐	$200	☐	☐	☐
5145	$225	☐	$200	☐	☐	☐
5170	$225	☐	$200	☐	☐	☐
5171	$225	☐	$200	☐	☐	☐
5172	$225	☐	$200	☐	☐	☐
5173	$225	☐	$200	☐	☐	☐
5208	$225	☐	$200	☐	☐	☐
5209	$225	☐	$200	☐	☐	☐

#370 2¢ ALASKA YUKON Cont.

	T		L		R	B
*5210	$225	☐	$200	☐	☐	☐
*5211	$225	☐	$200	☐	☐	☐
*5235	$325	☐	$300	☐	☐	☐
5236	$225	☐	$200	☐	☐	☐
5237	$225	☐	$200	☐	☐	☐
*5241	$325	☐	$300	☐	☐	☐
5249	$225	☐	$200	☐	☐	☐
5225	$225	☐	$200	☐	☐	☐
5251	$225	☐	$200	☐	☐	☐
5257	$225	☐	$200	☐	☐	☐

#371 2¢ ALASKA-YUKON IMPERF.
Imprint V **9 Plates**

5209	$350	☐	$300	☐	☐	☐
5235	$350	☐	$300	☐	☐	☐
5236	$200	☐	$200	☐	☐	☐
5237	$225	☐	$200	☐	☐	☐
5241	$350	☐	$300	☐	☐	☐
5249	$225	☐	$200	☐	☐	☐
5250	$225	☐	$200	☐	☐	☐
5251	$225	☐	$200	☐	☐	☐
5257	$225	☐	$200	☐	☐	☐

#372 2¢ HUDSON-FULTON
Imprint V **8 Plates**

5388	$300	☐	$275	☐	☐	☐
5389	$300	☐	$275	☐	☐	☐
5390	$300	☐	$275	☐	☐	☐
5391	$300	☐	$275	☐	☐	☐
5392	$300	☐	$275	☐	☐	☐
5393	$300	☐	$275	☐	☐	☐
5394	$300	☐	$275	☐	☐	☐
5395	$300	☐	$275	☐	☐	☐

#373 2¢ HUDSON-FULTON IMPERF.
Imprint V **8 Plates**

5388	$275	☐	$250	☐	☐	☐
5389	$275	☐	$250	☐	☐	☐
5390	$275	☐	$250	☐	☐	☐
5391	$275	☐	$250	☐	☐	☐
5392	$275	☐	$250	☐	☐	☐
5393	$275	☐	$250	☐	☐	☐
5394	$275	☐	$250	☐	☐	☐
5395	$275	☐	$250	☐	☐	☐

1910-11 REGULAR ISSUE

Single Line Wmk. Perf. 12

FLAT PRESS

#374 1¢ FRANKLIN 113 Plates

Imprint X

Basic Price **T** $75
Basic Price **L, R, B** $70

5159	5232	5255	*5313	5322
5345	5352	5359	5360	5382
5383	*5384	5385	*5387	5401
5402	5403	5404	5413	5414
5416	5418	5420	5429	5432
5435	5438	5441	5444	5473
5474	5475	5476	5477	5478
5479	5480	5481	5482	5483
5484	5485	5486	5487	5488
5489	5490	5491	5493	5494
5495	5496	5497	5498	5499
5591	5592	5595	5596	5598
5599	5600	5601	5602	5603
5604	5605	5607	5620	5622
5631	5632	5633	5634	5637
5639	5640	5643	5644	5647
5651	5672	5673	*5794	*5799

Imprint XII

Basic Price **T** $85
Basic Price **L, R, B** $80

5566	5567	5572	5573	5656
5657	5658	5659	5663	5664
5665	5666	5677	5678	5679
5682	5699	5705	5706	5707
5708	5709	5710	5712	5713
5714	5715	5716		

See Appendix B for panes of 60

#375 2¢ WASHINGTON 146 Plates

Imprint X

Basic Price **T** $80
Basic Price **L, R, B** $75

5092	5274	5276	5280	5281
5282	5283	5284	5293	5296
5297	5298	5299	5300	5303
5305	5306	5307	5308	5309
5310	5311	5312	5314	5317
5318	5319	5321	5323	5324
5325	*5326	5327	5328	5329
5331	5332	5334	5335	5337
5338	5339	5342	5343	*5344
5346	5347	5348	5349	5351
5353	5358	5362	5369	5370
5375	5508	5509	5512	5515
5516	5517	5518	5528	5542
5543	5544	5545	5546	5547
5548	5549	5550	5551	5552
5553	5554	5555	5556	5578
5581	5585	5589	5590	5606
5608	5609	5610	5611	5612
5616	5617	5618	5619	5621
5623	5624	5625	5626	5627
5628	5629	5630	5635	5636
5642	5645	5648	5650	*5652
5654	5655	5671	*5795	*5796

#375 2¢ WASHINGTON Cont.

Imprint XII

Basic Price **T** $90
Basic Price **L, R, B** $85

5557	5558	5559	5560	5561
5562	5563	5564	5565	5660
5661	*5662	5667	5668	5669
5670	5674	5683	5684	*5685
5686	5687	5688	5689	5690
5693	5694	5711	5717	*5797
*5798				

#376 3¢ WASHINGTON Type I 12 Plates

Imprint X

Basic Price **T** $175
Basic Price **L, R, B** $150

5121	5126	5131	5136	5421
5424	5428	5433		

Imprint IX

Basic Price **T** $200
Basic Price **L, R, B** $175

6044	6048	6050	6052

#377 4¢ WASHINGTON 12 Plates

Imprint X

Basic Price **T** $225
Basic Price **L, R, B** $200

5568	5569	5570	5571	5574
5575	5576	5577		

Imprint IX

Basic Price **T** $250
Basic Price **L, R, B** $225

6002	6004	6010	6025

#378 5¢ WASHINGTON 24 Plates

Imprint V

Basic Price **T** $250
Basic Price **L, R, B** $225

4958	4959	4961	4973

Imprint X

Basic Price **T** $250
Basic Price **L, R, B** $225

5341	5376	5379	5396	5638
5641	5649	5653		

Imprint XIII

Basic Price **T** $300
Basic Price **L, R, B** $250

5894	5898	5902	5906

Imprint IX

Basic Price **T** $300
Basic Price **L, R, B** $250

6348	6349	6352	6353	6733
6734	6736	6739		

1910-11 REGULAR ISSUE

#379 6¢ WASHINGTON 12 Plates

Imprint V

Basic Price	T	$425
Basic Price	L, R, B	$400

4936 4937 4938 4939

Imprint X

Basic Price	T	$400
Basic Price	L, R, B	$375

5203 5215 5222 5231 5419
5423 5425 5430

#380 8¢ WASHINGTON 8 Plates

Imprint V

Basic Price	T	$1,100
Basic Price	L, R, B	$1,000

4919 4922 4923 4924

Imprint X

Basic Price	T	$1,600
Basic Price	L, R, B	$1,400

5204 5214 5233 5238

#381 10¢ WASHINGTON 8 Plates

Imprint V

Basic Price	T	$1,100
Basic Price	L, R, B	$1,000

4940 4941 4943 4944

Imprint X

Basic Price	T	$1,100
Basic Price	L, R, B	$1,000

5200 5213 5220 5239

#382 15¢ WASHINGTON 4 Plates

Imprint V

Basic Price	T	$2,250
Basic Price	L, R, B	$2,000

4949 4951 4952 4954

BOOKLET PANES
PANES OF 6

Imprint IX

#374a 1¢ FRANKLIN 12 Plates

Basic Price	T	$185

5263 5264 5267 5268 5447
5449 5452 5454 †5455 †5457
*5460 *5463

#375a 2¢ WASHINGTON 17 Plates

Basic Price	T	$150

5130 5261 5266 5445 5446
5448 5450 5451 5456 5459
5461 5462 5464 5466 5467
†5469 *5472

IMPERFORATE
Blocks of 6

#383 1¢ FRANKLIN 85 Plates

Imprint X

Basic Price	T	$50
Basic Price	L, R, B	$40

*5232 5322 5359 5360 5378
5380 5383 *5384 5385 5401
5402 5403 5404 5418 5420
5429 5432 5438 5473 5475
5477 5478 5479 5480 5481
5482 5483 5484 5485 5486
5488 5489 5490 5491 5494
5495 5496 5497 5498 5592
5596 5598 5599 5600 5601
5603 5604 5605 5607 5620
5622 5631 5632 5633 5634
5637 5639 5640 5643 5644
5647 5651 5672 5673 *5794
*5799

Imprint XII

Basic Price	T	$90
Basic Price	L, R, B	$70

5566 5567 *5572 5573 5656
5657 5658 5659 5664 5665
*5666 *5677 *5679 5709 5712
5713 5714 5715 5716

See Appendix B for panes of 160

#384 2¢ WASHINGTON 96 Plates

Imprint X

Basic Price	T	$150
Basic Price	L, R, B	$125

5092 5134 5151 5280 5282
5283 5284 5296 5297 5298
5299 5300 5303 5307 *5308
*5309 *5311 5312 5314 5318
*5321 *5323 5325 *5327 5328
5329 5332 5337 5342 5348
5353 5358 *5362 5370 5375
5509 5512 5516 5517 5518
5528 5542 5549 5551 *5552
5553 *5554 5585 5589 5590
5608 5609 5611 *5612 *5616
5618 5619 *5623 5624 *5625
5627 *5628 *5635 5636 5642
5645 5648 5654 5655

Imprint XII

Basic Price	T	$175
Basic Price	L, R, B	$150

5557 5558 5559 5560 5561
5562 5563 5564 5565 5660
5661 *5662 5667 *5668 5669
*5685 5686 5687 5688 *5689
5690 5693 5694 5711 5717
*5797 *5798

1910-11 REGULAR ISSUE

IMPERFORATE COILS

#368V 2¢ LINCOLN

Imprint XI

4983

For listing of the vending and affixing machine coil stamps, please see APPENDIX A

#383V 1¢ FRANKLIN

Imprint X

5322	5360	5378	5383	5401
5402	5403	5404	5416	5418
5420	5429	5432	5438	5473
5475	5480	5481	5599	5639
5643	5644	5673		

Imprint XII

*5566	5567	5572	5573	5656
5657	5658	5659	*5677	*5678
*5679				

#383H 1¢ FRANKLIN

Imprint XII

5573	5656	5657	5658	5659

#384V 2¢ WASHINGTON

Imprint X

5283	5307	5308	5309	5311
5312	*5616	*5635		

Imprint XII

5557	5558	5559	5560	5561
5562	*5563	5564	*5565	5660
5661	5662	5667	5668	5669
5689				

#384H 2¢ WASHINGTON

Imprint X

5518

Imprint XII

5557	5558	5561	5661

Other plate numbers may exist on these imperforate coils with fake perforations to represent the more expensive perforated coil stamps.

END COILS

Perf. 12 Horizontally

#385 1¢ FRANKLIN

Imprint X

5159	5179	5255	5322	5352
5359	*5378	*5383	5387	5403
5414	5416	5418	5420	5429
5432	5435	*5438	5441	*5444
5474	5475	*5476	5479	5489
5496	5497	5498		

Imprint XII

See footnote

#386 2¢ WASHINGTON

Imprint X

5116	5281	5307	*5309	*5311
5321	*5331			

Imprint XII

See footnote

SIDE COILS

Perf. 12 Vertically

#387 1¢ FRANKLIN

none reported

#388 2¢ WASHINGTON

Imprint X

5334 5351

Imprint XII

See footnote

#389 3¢ WASHINGTON

Imprint X

5126

END COILS

Perf. 8 1/2 Horizontally

#390 1¢ FRANKLIN

Imprint X

See footnote

Imprint XII

5566	5567	5572	5573	5656
5657	5658	5659	5666	5677
5678	5679	5699	5705	5709
5714	5715	5716		

#391 2¢ WASHINGTON

Imprint X

See footnote

Imprint XII

5557	5558	5559	5560	5561
5562	5563	5564	*5565	5661
*5667	*5668	5674	5686	5687
5688	5690			

SIDE COILS

Perf. 8 1/2 Vertically

#392 1¢ FRANKLIN

Imprint X

See footnote

Imprint XII

5566	5567	5572	5573	5656
5657	5658	5659	5682	5699
5705	5706	5709	*5715	5716

Note: Plate number examples with fake perforations exist on imperforate (sheet or coil) stamps made to represent the more expensive coils.

1910-11 REGULAR ISSUE

SIDE COILS

Perf. 8 1/2 Vertically

#393 2¢ WASHINGTON

Imprint X

All examples are probably fake perforated versions of #384H.

Imprint XII

5557	5558	5559	5560	5561
5562	5563	5667	5668	*5669
5670	5674	5688	5795	5798

#394 3¢ WASHINGTON

Imprint X

5121	5126	5131	5136	5421
5424	5428	5433	6044	*6050
6052				

#395 4¢ WASHINGTON

Imprint X

5574 5575 5576 5577

Imprint IX

6002

#396 5¢ WASHINGTON

Imprint XIII

5894 5898 5902 5906

1912-15 COMMEMORATIVES

Single Line Wmk. Perf. 12

FLAT PRESS Block of 6

Imprint IX

#397 1¢ PANAMA-PACIFIC 12 Plates

		T		L	R	B
6127	$175	☐	$150	☐	☐	☐
6128	$175	☐	$150	☐	☐	☐
6131	$175	☐	$150	☐	☐	☐
6132	$175	☐	$150	☐	☐	☐
6144	$175	☐	$150	☐	☐	☐
6146	$175	☐	$150	☐	☐	☐
6147	$175	☐	$150	☐	☐	☐
6148	$175	☐	$150	☐	☐	☐
6548	$175	☐	$150	☐	☐	☐
6549	$175	☐	$150	☐	☐	☐
6550	$175	☐	$150	☐	☐	☐
6551	$175	☐	$150	☐	☐	☐

1912-15 COMMEMORATIVES

#398 2¢ PANAMA-PACIFIC 23 Plates

		T		L	R	B
6306	$250	☐	$225	☐	☐	☐
6307	$250	☐	$225	☐	☐	☐
6308	$250	☐	$225	☐	☐	☐
6309	$250	☐	$225	☐	☐	☐
6310	$250	☐	$225	☐	☐	☐
6311	$250	☐	$225	☐	☐	☐
6312	$250	☐	$225	☐	☐	☐
6313	$250	☐	$225	☐	☐	☐
6314	$250	☐	$225	☐	☐	☐
6315	$250	☐	$225	☐	☐	☐
6316	$250	☐	$225	☐	☐	☐
6317	$250	☐	$225	☐	☐	☐
6320	$250	☐	$225	☐	☐	☐
6321	$250	☐	$225	☐	☐	☐
6322	$250	☐	$225	☐	☐	☐
6323	$250	☐	$225	☐	☐	☐
6432	$250	☐	$225	☐	☐	☐
6442	$250	☐	$225	☐	☐	☐
6447	$250	☐	$225	☐	☐	☐
6647	$250	☐	$225	☐	☐	☐
6648	$250	☐	$225	☐	☐	☐
6649	$250	☐	$225	☐	☐	☐
6650	$250	☐	$225	☐	☐	☐

#399 5¢ PANAMA-PACIFIC 4 Plates

6129	$2,000	☐	$1,750	☐	☐	☐
6133	$2,000	☐	$1,750	☐	☐	☐
6134	$2,000	☐	$1,750	☐	☐	☐
6138	$2,000	☐	$1,750	☐	☐	☐

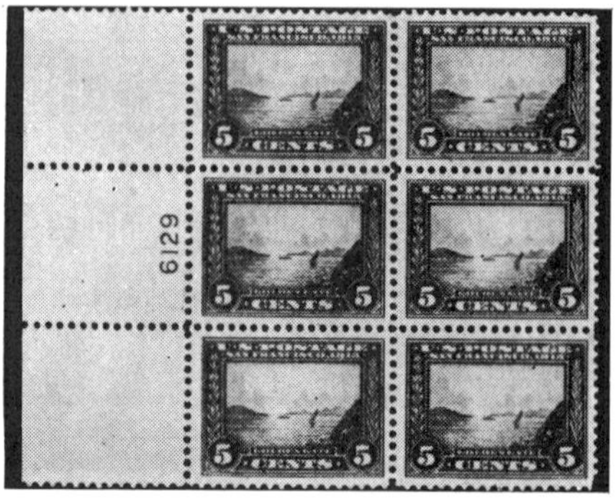

1912-15 COMMEMORATIVES

#400 10¢ PANAMA-PACIFIC 4 Plates

Plate		T		L	R	B
6130	$2,500	☐	$2,250	☐	☐	☐
6135	$2,500	☐	$2,250	☐	☐	☐
6139	$2,500	☐	$2,250	☐	☐	☐
6143	$2,500	☐	$2,250	☐	☐	☐

#400A 10¢ PANAMA-PACIFIC 4 Plates

6130	$14,000	☐	$12,500	☐	☐	☐
6135	$14,000	☐	$12,500	☐	☐	☐
6139	$14,000	☐	$12,500	☐	☐	☐
6143	$14,000	☐	$12,500	☐	☐	☐

Single Line Wmk. Perf. 10

Imprint IX

#401 1¢ PANAMA-PACIFIC 8 Plates

6548	$350	☐	$325	☐	☐	☐
6549	$350	☐	$325	☐	☐	☐
6550	$350	☐	$325	☐	☐	☐
6551	$350	☐	$325	☐	☐	☐
6875	$350	☐	$325	☐	☐	☐
6880	$350	☐	$325	☐	☐	☐
6891	$350	☐	$325	☐	☐	☐
6944	$350	☐	$325	☐	☐	☐

#402 2¢ PANAMA-PACIFIC13 Plates

6322	$2,500	☐	$2,200	☐	☐	☐
†6323	—	☐	—	☐	☐	☐
6432	$2,500	☐	$2,200	☐	☐	☐
6442	$2,500	☐	$2,200	☐	☐	☐
6447	$1,750	☐	$1,500	☐	☐	☐
6647	$1,750	☐	$1,500	☐	☐	☐
6648	$1,750	☐	$1,500	☐	☐	☐
6649	$1,750	☐	$1,500	☐	☐	☐
6650	$1,750	☐	$1,500	☐	☐	☐
7034	$1,750	☐	$1,500	☐	☐	☐
7035	$1,750	☐	$1,500	☐	☐	☐
7038	$1,750	☐	$1,500	☐	☐	☐
7039	$1,750	☐	$1,500	☐	☐	☐

1912-15 COMMEMORATIVES

#403 5¢ PANAMA-PACIFIC 4 Plates

Plate		T		L	R	B
6129	$3,800	☐	$3,500	☐	☐	☐
6133	$3,800	☐	$3,500	☐	☐	☐
6134	$3,800	☐	$3,500	☐	☐	☐
6138	$3,800	☐	$3,500	☐	☐	☐

#404 10¢ PANAMA-PACIFIC 4 Plates

6130	$12,500	☐	$11,000	☐	☐	☐
6135	$12,500	☐	$11,000	☐	☐	☐
6139	$12,500	☐	$11,000	☐	☐	☐
6143	$12,500	☐	$11,000	☐	☐	☐

1912-14 REGULAR ISSUE

Single Line Wmk. Perf. 12

FLAT PRESS Block of 6

#405 1¢ WASHINGTON 289 Plates

Imprint XII

Basic Price **T** $85

Basic Price **L, R, B** $80

5727	5728	5730	5731	5732
5733	5734	5735	5736	*5737
5738	5739	5781	5787	5801

Imprint XIII

Basic Price **T** $85

Basic Price **L, R, B** $80

5806	5807	5822	5828	5831
5833	5834	5837	5840	5843
5849	5853	5855	5858	5859
5862	5864	5867	5870	5873
5874	5878	5880	5881	5882
5884	5885	5886	5887	5891
5892	5893	5895	5897	5900
5901	5903	5905	5910	5913
5915	5916	5918		

Imprint IX

Basic Price **T** $80

Basic Price **L, R, B** $75

5921	5924	5930	6005	6006
6007	6008	6009	6011	6012

1912-14 REGULAR ISSUE

#405 1¢ WASHINGTON Cont.

Imprint IX

6013	6014	6015	6016	6017
6018	6019	6020	6026	6027
6028	6029	6030	6031	6032
6033	6034	6035	6036	6037
6038	6039	6040	6041	6042
6045	6114	6115	6117	6118
6120	6121	6122	6150	6154
6272	6273	6282	6283	6301
6305	6327	6328	6342	6344
6354	6373	6437	6443	6450
6455	6465	*6468	6472	6473
6474	6475	6476	6477	6478
6479	6480	6481	6482	6483
6484	6485	6486	6487	6488
6521	6528	6532	6533	6534
6535	6539	6540	6541	6542
6543	6544	6545	6546	6547
6574	6575	6576	6577	6578
6588	6600	6601	6606	6607
6608	6609	6610	6611	6612
6613	6614	6615	6616	6617
*6618	6619	6621	6623	6624
6628	6631	6632	6634	6636
6676	*6678	*6680	6681	6682
*6683	6688	6691	6713	6718
6719	6720	6721	6722	6723
6724	6725	6726	6727	6775
6776	6777	6778	6781	6782
6783	6785	6787	6788	6789
6792	6793	6798	6804	6805
6808	6810	6811	6812	6814
6816	6820	6821	6823	6824
6826	6829	6831	6832	6834
6835	6836	6837	6841	6844
6845	6849	6851	6854	6858
6861	6937	6940	6941	6942
6945	6946	6947	6948	6949
6953	6954	6955	6958	6959
6961	6962	6967	6968	6970
6974	6975	6981	6982	6983
6987	6989	6990	6996	7001
7003	7008	7010	7012	7017
7023	7027	7030	7032	7103
7106	7142	7144	7149	7151
7153				

#406 2¢ WASHINGTON 568 Plates

Imprint XII

Basic Price	T	$110
Basic Price	L, R, B	$100

5740	5743	5754	5759	5763
5769	5777	5779	5785	5788
5789	5790	*5791	5792	5800
5802	5803			

Imprint XIII

Basic Price	T	$100
Basic Price	L, R, B	$90

5805	5808	5809	5810	5811
5812	5813	5814	5815	5816

#406 2¢ WASHINGTON Cont.

Imprint XIII

5817	5818	5819	5820	5821
5823	5824	5825	5826	5827
5830	5832	5835	5836	5838
5839	5841	5842	5845	5851
5856	5861	5865	5866	5868
5869	5872	5876	5877	5883
5888	5889	5890	5896	5899
5904	5907	5908	5909	5911
5912	5914	5917		

Imprint IX

Basic Price	T	$90
Basic Price	L, R, B	$85

5919	5920	5922	5923	5925
5926	5927	5928	5929	5931
5932	5933	5934	5935	5936
5940	5944	5945	5946	5948
5949	5950	5951	5952	5953
5954	5955	5956	5959	5960
5961	5962	5963	5964	5965
5966	5967	5968	5969	5970
5971	5972	5973	5974	5975
5976	5977	5978	5979	5980
5981	5982	5983	5984	5985
5986	5987	5988	5989	5991
5992	5993	5994	5995	5996
5997	5998	5999	6000	6001
6003	6024	6051	6054	6055
6058	6059	6062	6063	6064
6065	6066	6067	6068	6069
6070	6071	6072	6073	6074
6075	6077	6078	6080	6081
6082	6083	6084	6085	6087
6088	6089	6090	6091	6092
6093	6094	6095	6096	6097
6098	6099	6100	6101	6102
6103	6104	6105	6106	6107
6108	6109	6110	6111	6151
6153	6155	6157	6158	6159
6190	6223	6267	6268	6269
6270	6271	6278	6281	6284
6285	6286	6289	6290	6291
6292	6293	6294	6295	6297
6298	6300	6302	6303	6304
6318	6319	6324	6325	6326
6329	6343	6358	6362	6368
6372	6387	6398	6403	6406
6413	6414	6415	6419	6422
6429	6430	6436	6438	6440
6444	6445	6446	6451	6452
6453	6454	6456	6457	6459
6460	6461	6462	6464	6466
6467	6469	6471	6489	6490
6491	6492	6493	6494	6495
6496	6497	6498	6499	6500
6501	6502	6503	6504	6505
6506	6507	6508	6509	6510
6511	6512	6513	6514	6515
6516	6517	6518	6519	6520
6522	6523	6524	6525	6526

1912-14 REGULAR ISSUE

#406 2¢ WASHINGTON Cont.

Imprint IX

6527	6529	6530	6531	6536
6537	6538	6620	6622	6625
6626	6627	6629	6630	6633
6635	6637	6638	6639	6640
6641	6642	6643	6644	6645
6646	6651	6652	6653	6654
6655	6656	6657	6658	6659
6660	6661	6662	6663	6664
6665	6666	6667	6668	6669
6670	6671	6672	6673	6674
6675	6677	*6679	6684	6685
6686	6687	6689	6690	6692
6693	6694	6698	6699	6700
6715	6716	6717	6731	6737
6738	6740	6741	6743	6744
6746	*6747	6748	6750	6753
6754	6756	6757	6758	6759
6760	6761	6762	6764	6765
6766	6767	6768	*6769	6770
6771	6772	6773	6774	6779
6780	6784	6786	6790	6791
6794	6795	*6796	6797	6799
6800	6802	6806	6807	6815
6817	6818	6827	6828	6830
6838	6839	6840	6842	6843
6846	6847	6848	6850	6852
6853	6855	6859	6860	6862
6866	6867	6870	6871	6873
6874	6876	6877	6881	6883
6886	6887	6888	6889	6890
6893	6894	6895	6896	6897
6898	6912	6939	6943	6950
6951	6952	6956	6960	6963
6969	6971	6972	6976	6977
6978	6979	6980	6984	6985
6986	6988	6991	6992	6993
6994	6995	6997	6998	6999
7000	7002	7004	7005	7006
7007	7009	7011	7013	7014
7015	7019	7020	7024	7025
7026	7028	7029	7031	7041
7043	7044	7045	7046	7047
7048	7050	7051	7052	7053
7054	7055	7056	7058	7059
7060	7061	7062	7063	7064
7065	7066	7067	7068	7069
7070	7071	7072	7074	7075
7076	7077	7078	7079	7080
7081	7082	7083	7084	7085
7086	7087	7088	7094	7099
7100	*7112	7115	7117	7120
*7124	7125	7128	7150	7158
7177	7178			

Electrolytic Plate

Price	T	$1,200
Price	L, R, B	$1,100

6023

#407 7¢ WASHINGTON 4 Plates

Imprint IX

Basic Price	T	$1,150
Basic Price	L, R, B	$1,000

6903 6904 6916 6919

BOOKLET PANES

PANES OF 6

Imprint IX

#405b 1¢ WASHINGTON 16 Plates

Basic Price T $85

5741	5744	5748	5750	5753
5757	5762	5768	5776	6076
6079	6086	6355	6363	6364
6369				

#406a 2¢ WASHINGTON 32 Plates

Basic Price T $80

5756	5761	5767	5772	5778
*5783	5786	5793	5844	5937
5938	5939	5941	5942	5943
5947	6047	6053	6057	6061
6112	6113	6116	6119	6554
6559	6560	6561	6562	6563
*6564	6565			

IMPERFORATE

Block of 6

#408 1¢ WASHINGTON 212 Plates

Imprint XII

Basic Price	T	$55
Basic Price	L, B	$50
Basic Price	R	$400

5727	5728	5730	5732	5733
5735	*5737	5739	5781	5787

Imprint XIII

Basic Price	T	$30
Basic Price	L, R, B	$27

5806	5807	5828	5831	5833
5834	5837	5840	5843	5849
5858	5859	5862	5864	5867

1912-14 REGULAR ISSUE

#408 1¢ WASHINGTON Cont.

Imprint XIII

5873	5874	5878	5880	5881
5882	*5885	5886	5887	5891
5892	5895	5897	5900	5901
5903	5905	5915	5918	

Imprint IX

Basic Price **T** $22
Basic Price **L, R, B** $20

6006	6007	6008	6009	6011
6012	6013	6014	*6016	6018
6020	*6032	6038	6041	6114
6150	6154	6282	6283	6301
*6327	*6472	6474	6475	6476
6477	6478	6485	6486	6487
6488	6528	6532	6533	6534
6542	6543	6544	6545	6546
6547	6606	6607	6608	6609
6610	6611	6612	6613	6614
6615	6616	6617	6619	6628
*6631	6632	6681	6713	6720
6721	6722	6723	6724	6725
6775	6776	6777	6778	6782
*6785	*6787	6789	6793	6798
6804	*6805	6811	6812	6814
*6816	6820	6821	*6823	6829
6831	*6832	*6841	*6845	*6851
*6854	6861	6940	6941	6942
6945	6955	6958	6970	6974
6975	6982	*6983	6987	7017
7023	7027	7030	7032	7106
7107	7108	7110	7113	7114
7116	7118	7119	7148	7149
7153	7281	*7282	7283	7284
7285	7288	7289	7290	7291
7292	7293	7294	7299	7300
7301	7302	7312	7320	7326
7329	*7361	7363	7364	7375
*7382	7464	7485	*7493	7500
7514	7515	7516	7517	7518
7519	7520	7525	7533	7534
*7535	*7536	7546	*7547	*7549
7671	7674			

#409 2¢ WASHINGTON 353 Plates

Imprint XII

Basic Price **T** $60
Basic Price **L, R, B** $55

5754	5785	5789	5792	5802

Imprint XIII

Basic Price **T** $55
Basic Price **L, R, B** $50

5811	5814	5815	5818	5819
*5824	5827	5830	5832	5835
5836	5838	5839	5841	5842
5845	5851	5856	5861	5866
5868	5869	5872	5876	5877
5888	5889	5890	5896	5899
5904	5907	5908	5911	*5912
5917				

For "Kansas City Roulettes" on #408-409 see Appendix H.

#409 2¢ WASHINGTON Cont.

Imprint IX

Basic Price **T** $40
Basic Price **L, R, B** $35

5919	5920	5923	*5925	*5928
5929	5932	5940	5960	5962
*5963	5964	5965	5966	*5968
5969	*5972	5975	5976	5978
*5979	5980	5981	5982	5983
5985	5986	5987	5988	5991
5992	5993	5994	5995	5996
5998	*6000	6001	6003	*6024
6051	6054	6055	6058	6059
6063	6064	6065	6067	6070
6071	6072	6073	6077	6082
6089	*6090	6091	6093	6094
6095	6096	6097	6098	6099
6111	6151	6157	6159	6190
*6269	6286	*6289	6294	*6297
6300	6302	6303	6319	6329
6343	6358	*6362	6436	6445
6446	6451	6452	6453	6454
6456	6461	6464	*6466	*6467
*6469	6489	6490	6491	6492
6493	6494	6495	6496	6497
6498	6499	6501	*6502	6503
*6505	*6506	6507	6508	6509
6510	6511	*6513	6522	*6524
6536	6537	6620	*6622	6629
6630	6633	6639	6641	6643
6645	6646	6651	6654	6670
6671	6672	6673	6757	6758
6761	6765	6770	6771	6772
6773	6774	6780	6784	6794
*6796	6799	6815	6817	6818
6827	6839	6842	6867	6873
6877	6886	6943	6950	6951
6952	6956	6963	6969	6971
6978	6979	6980	*6984	6985
6988	6991	6992	*7005	*7006
7043	7044	*7045	7046	7048
7052	7054	7058	7059	7060
7067	*7068	7075	7076	7077
7078	7080	*7081	7082	7088
*7091	7115	7117	7120	7124
*7158	7178	7184	7185	7186
7187	7197	*7206	*7222	7223
7224	7225	7226	7227	*7245
7259	7261	7265	7311	7313
7314	7315	*7318	*7319	7322
7328	*7334	7336	7337	7340
7342	7347	7349	7350	7352
7356	7368	7373	7376	7377
7386	7388	7389	7390	7391
7392	7393	7394	7395	7396
*7399	7400	7401	7402	*7403
7404	7416	7420	7421	7424
7451	7454	7455	7459	7472
*7473	*7476	*7477	7478	7481
7486	7487	*7494	7495	7501

1912-14 REGULAR ISSUE

#409 2¢ WASHINGTON Cont.

Imprint IX

7568 7569 7571 7572 7573
7574 7575 7576 7578 7579
7580 7582 7583 7589 7590
7591 7593 7594 7609 7610
7611 7612 *7614 *7639 7701
*7703 *7708 *7714 7724 7732
7735 *7737

IMPERFORATE COILS

For listing of the vending and affixing machine coil stamps, please see APPENDIX A

#408V 1¢ WASHINGTON

Imprint XII

5787 5801

Imprint XIII

5831 5833 5834 5837 5843
5862 5881 5882

Imprint IX

6007 6031 6475 6477 6478
6479 6485 6486 6487 6528
6535

#408H 1¢ WASHINGTON

Imprint XIII

5837 5840 5843

Imprint IX

6154 6282 6283 6465 6528
6546

#409V 2¢ WASHINGTON

Imprint XIII

5836 5839 5841 5845 5856
5861 5866 5876

Imprint IX

5920 5962 5964 5965 5979
5981 6024 6055 6063 6286
6300 6436 6444 6445 6446
6451 6452 6453 6460 6461
6462 6466 6467 6469 6489
6491 6492 6493 6494 6495
6496 6497 6498 6501

#409H 2¢ WASHINGTON

Imprint XIII

5896

Imprint IX

5919 5920 5923 *6499 6505
*6506 6515 *7487

Other plate numbers may exist on these imperforate coils with fake perforations to represent the more expensive perforated coil stamps.

END COILS

Perf. 8 1/2 Horizontally

#410 1¢ WASHINGTON

Imprint XII

5727

Imprint XIII

5828 5853 5880 5887 5891
5892 5893 5897 5900 5905

Imprint IX

6005 6006 6008 6014 6117
6305 6327 6328 6344 6437
6455 6472 6473 6474 6475
6476 6477 6478 6479 6480
6485 6486 6487 6488 6535
6539 6540 6541

#411 2¢ WASHINGTON

Imprint XII

5740 5754

Imprint XIII

5820 5821 *5904 5907 *5912
*5914

Imprint IX

5925 5927 5933 5955 5960
5972 5978 5981 5995 5998
6051 6054 6055 6058 6059
6063 6070 6071 6075 6083
6302 6326 6329 6403 6436
6451 6452 6453 6454 6459

SPECIAL END COIL PLATES

The items listed below are from special plates for end coils that had plate numbers only in the side margin. The plate numbers were normally trimmed off during coiling, but partial plate numbers may occur on off-center coils. Please report any examples from either the 1¢ or 2¢ special end coil plates.

#410 1¢ WASHINGTON

6581 6582 †6585 †6589

#411 2¢ WASHINGTON

†6566 †6567 †6569 †6570 †6571
†6572 †6573

Note: See #424-5 for these numbers used as coil waste.

1912-14 REGULAR ISSUE

SIDE COILS

Perf. 8 ° Vertically

#412 1¢ WASHINGTON

Imprint XIII

5807 5828 5831 5840 5859
5862 5864 5867 5870

Imprint IX

6009 6014 6015 6034 6035
6037 *6040 6114 6117 *6154
6282 6301 6327 6437 *6450
6477 6480 6521 6535 6545
*6546 6547 *6613 6615 6616
6617 *6719 *6775 *6776 *6777
*6778 6811 6812 6814 6820
*6821 6831 6832 6837 6841
6844 *6851 6858 6937

#413 2¢ WASHINGTON

Imprint XII

All examples are probably fake perforated versions of #409H

Imprint XIII

5815 5827 5830 5838 5839
5872 5888 5907

Imprint IX

5920 5955 5960 5988 5989
5991 5992 5995 5996 6063
6065 6069 6070 6072 6075
6090 6091 6094 6158 6267
6270 6278 6294 6326 6362
6372 6444 6454 6457 6493
6498 6513 6522 6530 6531
6536 6626 6629 6630 6637
6639 6640 6641 6642 6646
6651 6664 6666 6677 6753
6784 6786 6795 6799 6800
6802 6806 6807 6828 6830
6839 6840 6871 6874 6883
6943 6951 6960 6971 6972
6976 6995

SHEET STAMPS

#414 8¢ FRANKLIN 4 Plates

Imprint XII

Basic Price T $425
Basic Price L, R, B $375
5718 5719 5721 5722

1912-14 REGULAR ISSUE

#415 9¢ FRANKLIN 4 Plates

Imprint IX

Basic Price T $700
Basic Price L, R, B $650
6901 6905 6907 6915

#416 10¢ FRANKLIN 8 Plates

Imprint XII

Basic Price T $500
Basic Price L, R, B $450
5745 5751 5764 5770 5773
5784

Imprint XIII

Basic Price T $550
Basic Price L, R, B $500
5847 5852

#417 12¢ FRANKLIN 4 Plates

Imprint IX

Basic Price T $475
Basic Price L, R, B $425
6900 6902 6910 6913

#418 15¢ FRANKLIN 12 Plates

Imprint XII

Basic Price T $700
Basic Price L, R, B $650
5747 5755 5760 5766 5771
5775 5780

Imprint XIII

Basic Price T $1,350
Basic Price L, R, B $1,275
5850

Imprint IX

Basic Price T $1,700
Basic Price L, R, B $1,600
6809 6819 6825 6833

#419 20¢ FRANKLIN 4 Plates

Imprint IX

Basic Price T $1,850
Basic Price L, R, B $1,750
6908 6909 6920 6926

#420 30¢ FRANKLIN 4 Plates

Imprint IX

Basic Price T $1,600
Basic Price L, R, B $1,500
6899 6911 6914 6917

#421 50¢ FRANKLIN 4 Plates

Imprint IX

Basic Price T $8,000
Basic Price L, R, B $7,500
7040 7042 7049 7057

1912 REGULAR ISSUE

Double Line Wmk. Perf. 12

#422 50¢ FRANKLIN 1 Plate

Imprint XII

Price	T	$4,500
Price	B	$4,000

5749

#423 $1 FRANKLIN 1 Plate

Imprint XII

Price	T	$10,000
Price	B	$9,000

5782

1914-15 REGULAR ISSUE

Single Line Wmk. Perf. 10

FLAT PRESS Block of 6

#424 1¢ WASHINGTON 182 Plates

Imprint IX

Basic Price	T	$45
Basic Price	L, R, B	$40

6845	6942	6946	6947	6948
6949	6953	*6954	6955	6958
6959	6961	6962	6967	6968
6970	6974	6975	6981	6982
6983	6987	6989	6990	6996
7001	7003	7008	7010	7012
7017	7023	7027	7030	7032
7103	7106	7107	7108	7110
7113	7114	7116	7118	7119
7142	7144	7145	7146	7148
7149	7151	7153	7156	7157
7159	7161	7164	7165	7167
7169	7173	7281	7282	7283
7284	7285	7288	7289	7290
7291	7292	7293	7294	7295
7296	7297	7298	7299	7300
7301	7302	7303	7304	7305
7306	7307	7308	7309	7310
7312	7320	7326	7329	7332
7338	7351	7359	7361	7363
7364	7365	7370	7371	7374
7375	7380	7381	7382	7384
7464	7485	7493	7500	7514
7515	7516	7517	7518	7519
7520	7525	7526	7527	7528
7529	7530	7531	7532	7533
7534	7535	7536	7537	7538
7539	7540	7541	7542	7543
7544	7545	7546	7547	7549
7570	7577	7585	7592	7596
7602	7644	7645	7646	7647
7649	7650	7651	7652	7654
7655	7656	7657	7658	7659
7660	7663	7664	7665	7666
7667	7668	7669	7670	7671
7674	7725	7736		

1914-15 REGULAR ISSUE

#424 1¢ WASHINGTON Cont.

COIL PLATES

Side plate numbers only Block of 10

Basic Price	UR, LL	$150

6581 6582 6585 6589

These were flat plates prepared for endwise coils. When rotary press plates replaced them the excess stock was perforated and sold as sheet stamps.

The words 'COIL STAMPS' do not appear with the UL and LR plate numbers. These positions would be collected in blocks of six. The only example known is an UL pane of 100 of 6581. Please report any other positions and plate numbers.

424b 1¢ WASHINGTON

Perf. 10 x 12

7142

#425 2¢ WASHINGTON Block of 6

Imprint IX **351 Plates**

Basic Price	T	$32
Basic Price	L, R, B	$30

6806	6815	6852	*6896	6971
6972	6993	6994	6995	6997
6998	6999	7000	7002	7013
7014	7015	7019	7024	7026
7028	7029	7044	7045	7046
7047	7048	7050	7051	7052
7053	*7054	7055	*7056	7058
7059	7060	7061	7062	7063
7064	7065	7066	7067	7068
7069	7070	7071	7072	7074

1914-15 REGULAR ISSUE

#425 2¢ WASHINGTON Cont.

Imprint IX

7075	7076	7077	7078	7079
7080	7081	7082	7083	7084
7085	7086	7087	7088	7090
7091	7092	7094	7097	7099
7100	7101	7102	7104	7105
7109	7111	7112	7115	7117
7120	7124	7125	7128	7150
7152	7154	7155	7158	7162
7168	7177	7178	7184	7185
7186	7187	7188	7189	7190
7191	7192	7193	7194	7195
7196	7197	7198	7199	7200
7201	7202	7203	7206	7207
7208	7209	7210	7211	7212
7214	7216	7217	7218	7219
7220	7221	7222	7223	7224
7225	7226	7227	7228	7229
7232	7233	7234	7244	7245
7246	7248	7251	7252	7255
7257	7259	7261	7264	7265
7311	7313	7314	7315	7316
7317	7318	7319	7321	7322
7323	7324	7327	7328	7330
7333	7334	7335	7336	7337
7339	7340	7341	7342	7343
7344	7345	7346	7347	7349
7350	7352	7353	7354	7355
7356	7357	7360	7366	7367
7368	7373	7376	7377	7378
7383	7386	7387	7388	7389
7390	7391	7392	7393	7394
7395	7396	7397	7398	7399
7400	7401	7402	7403	7404
7405	7406	7407	7410	7416
7420	7421	7424	7447	7448
7450	7451	7454	7455	7456
7459	7460	7461	7465	7466
7471	7472	7473	7475	7476
7477	7478	7479	7481	7486
7487	7488	7491	7492	7494
7495	7501	7568	7569	7571
7572	7573	7574	7575	7576
7578	7579	7580	7581	7582
7583	7584	7586	7587	7588
7589	7590	7591	7593	7594
7595	7597	7601	7603	7604
7605	7607	7608	7609	7610
7611	7612	7613	7614	7615
7618	7620	7638	7639	7640
7641	7681	7682	7683	7684
7685	7692	7693	7694	7695
7696	7697	7698	7699	7700
7701	7702	7703	7704	7705
7706	7707	7708	7709	7710
7711	7712	7713	7714	7715
7716	7717	7721	7722	7724
7728	7729	7730	7732	7735
7737	7760	7762	*7769	*7770
*7771	*7773	7774	*7775	7776
7777	7778			

COIL PLATES

Side plate numbers only Block of 10

Basic Price **UR, LL** $150

6568 6570 6571 6572

These were flat plates prepared for endwise coils. When rotary press plates replaced them the excess stock was perforated and sold as sheet stamps.

The words 'COIL STAMPS' do not appear with the UL and LR plate numbers. These positions would be collected in blocks of six. No examples are known.

Blocks of 6

#426 3¢ WASHINGTON Type I
16 Plates

Imprint IX

Basic Price **T** $175
Basic Price **L, R, B** $150

6044	6048	6050	6052	6749
6751	6755	6763	6863	6868
6878	6882	7253	7254	7258
7267				

#427 4¢ WASHINGTON 16 Plates

Imprint IX

Basic Price **T** $525
Basic Price **L, R, B** $475

6002	6004	6010	6025	6728
6729	6730	6732	7263	7269
7273	7276	*7331	†7348	*7362
†7372				

#428 5¢ WASHINGTON 20 Plates

Imprint IX

Basic Price **T** $400
Basic Price **L, R, B** $350

6733	6734	6736	6739	7016
7018	7021	7022	7235	7236
7237	7238	7239	7240	7241
7242	7622	7623	7632	7633

#429 6¢ WASHINGTON 12 Plates

Imprint X

Basic Price **T** $450
Basic Price **L, R, B** $400

5203	5215	5222	5231	5419
5423	5425	5430		

Imprint IX

Basic Price **T** $500
Basic Price **L, R, B** $450

7136 7137 7138 7139

1914-15 REGULAR ISSUE

#430 7¢ WASHINGTON 12 Plates

Imprint IX

Basic Price T $1,000
Basic Price L, R, B $900

6903 6904 6916 6919 6923
6929 6932 6936 7718 7719
7720 7723

#431 8¢ FRANKLIN 8 Plates

Imprint XII

Basic Price T $500
Basic Price L, R, B $475

5718 5719 5721 5722 5724
5725 5804

Imprint XIII

Basic Price T $550
Basic Price L, R, B $525

5846

#432 9¢ FRANKLIN 4 Plates

Imprint IX

Basic Price T $800
Basic Price L, R, B $700

6901 6905 6907 6915

#433 10¢ FRANKLIN 12 Plates

Imprint XII

Basic Price T $700
Basic Price L, R, B $650

5770 5773

Imprint XIII

Basic Price T $1,250
Basic Price L, R, B $1,100

5847 5852

Imprint IX

Basic Price T $700
Basic Price L, R, B $650

6735 6742 6745 6752 7204
7205 7213 7215

#434 11¢ FRANKLIN 4 Plates

Imprint IX

Basic Price T $275
Basic Price L, R, B $250

7498 7499 7504 7505

#435 12¢ FRANKLIN 4 Plates

Imprint IX

Basic Price T $300
Basic Price L, R, B $275

6900 6902 6910 6913

#437 15¢ FRANKLIN 8 Plates

Imprint XII

Basic Price T $1,100
Basic Price L, R, B $1,000

5771 5775 5780

Imprint XIII

Basic Price T $1,300
Basic Price L, R, B $1,100

5850

Imprint IX

Basic Price T $1,100
Basic Price L, R, B $1,000

6809 6819 6825 6833

1914-15 REGULAR ISSUE

#438 20¢ FRANKLIN 4 Plates

Imprint IX

Basic Price	T	$3,200
Basic Price	L, R, B	$3,000

6908 6909 6920 6926

#439 30¢ FRANKLIN 4 Plates

Imprint IX

Basic Price	T	$4,500
Basic Price	L, R, B	$4,000

6899 6911 6914 6917

#440 50¢ FRANKLIN 4 Plates

Imprint IX

Basic Price	T	$12,500
Basic Price	L, R, B	$11,000

7040 7042 7049 7057

BOOKLET PANES

PANES OF 6

#424d 1¢ WASHINGTON 32 Plates

Basic Price T $12

6355	6363	6364	6369	6695
6697	6707	6710	6864	6865
6869	6872	6879	6884	6885
6892	*7160	*7163	*7166	*7172
7176	7179	7180	7181	7268
7275	7277	7278	†7449	7474
7480	7484			

#425e 2¢ WASHINGTON 48 Plates

Basic Price T $35

6562	6563	*6564	6565	6696
6701	6702	6708	6709	6711
6712	6714	6801	6803	6813
6822	6964	6965	6966	6973
7089	7093	7095	7096	7098
7123	7127	7131	7133	7135
7140	7143	7147	7243	7247
7249	7250	7256	7260	7325
7548	7550	7551	7554	7555
7556	7557	7560		

END COILS

Perf. 10 Horizontally

Imprint IX

#441 1¢ WASHINGTON

†6581 †6582 †6585 †6589

#442 2¢ WASHINGTON

†6566 †6567 †6568 †6569 †6570
†6571 †6572 †6573

SIDE COILS

Perf. 10 Vertically

Imprint IX

#443 1¢ WASHINGTON 39 Plates

6821	6824	6826	6831	6834
6835	6837	6845	6849	6854
6861	6937	6946	6947	6948
6949	6954	6958	6959	6961
*6962	6967	*6968	*6970	*6974
*6975	6989	6990	6996	7001
7003	*7008	7010	7023	7030
7032	*7103	7106	7291	

#444 2¢ WASHINGTON 73 Plates

6513	6786	6800	6847	6852
6859	*6876	6889	*6893	6895
6896	6897	6898	6912	*6939
6956	6976	6984	6985	6986
*6994	6995	*6997	6998	7000
*7002	*7015	7019	7024	7026
7028	7029	7047	7048	7051
7053	7059	7060	*7061	7062
7063	*7064	*7067	7079	7080
7081	7082	7083	7084	7085
7086	7087	7090	7091	7092
*7120	7124	7125	7128	7150
*7155	7178	*7194	7200	7202
7207	7224	*7487		

#445 3¢ WASHINGTON 4 Plates

6044 6048 6050 6052

#446 4¢ WASHINGTON 8 Plates

6002 6004 6010 6025 6728
6729 *6730 6732

#447 5¢ WASHINGTON 4 Plates

6733 6734 6736 6739

1914-16 REGULAR ISSUE

ROTARY PRESS COILS

On rotary press coils the plate numbers were usually located in the left margins of endwise coils or the top margin of sidewise coils(see Appendix D) and were trimmed off during the coiling process. Partial plate numbers do occur, rarely, on mis-slit coils. We use a large star to indicate reported plate numbers. Please send the editor a clear xerox with the report of any examples you have of unreported plate numbers.

ROTARY PRESS Single Line Wmk.

END COILS

Perf. 10 Horizontally

#448 1¢ WASHINGTON

7433 7434

#449 2¢ WASHINGTON Type I

6279 6280

#450 2¢ WASHINGTON Type III

7561 7562

SIDE COILS

Perf. 10 Vertically

#452 1¢ WASHINGTON

7170	☆7171	☆7182	7183	7552
7553	7558	7559	7565	7566
7567	7619	7626	7627	7690
7691				

#453 2¢ WASHINGTON Type I

6856	6857	7174	7175	7230
7231	7270	7271	7408	7409
7417	7418	7422	7423	

#454 2¢ WASHINGTON Type II

☆7425	☆7426	☆7427	7428	7429
☆7430	7437	7438	7443	7444
7457	7458	7462**N**	7463**N**	7467
7468	☆7469	☆7470	7482	7483
7489	7490	7496	7497	7502
7503				

N These plate numbers also occur on sheet stamps issued as coil waste (see #539)

#455 2¢ WASHINGTON Type III

7510	7511	☆7512	7513	7421
☆7522	☆7523	7524	☆7617	7621
7624	7625	7630	7631	7636
7637	7661	7662	7672	7673
☆7677	☆7678	7679	7680	7686
7687	7688	7689	7782	

#456 3¢ WASHINGTON Type I

7441 7442

#457 4¢ WASHINGTON

7440 7452

#458 5¢ WASHINGTON

7435 7436

IMPERFORATE

#459 2¢ WASHINGTON Type I

6856 6857

1915 REGULAR ISSUE

Double Line Wmk. Perf. 10

FLAT PRESS Block of 6

#460 $1 FRANKLIN 1 Plate

Imprint XII

Price	T	$12,500
Price	B	$12,000

5782

Single Line Wmk. Perf. 11

FLAT PRESS Block of 6

#461 2¢ WASHINGTON 4 Plates

Imprint IX

Basic Price	T	$1,000
Basic Price	L, R, B	$950

7259 7261 7264 7265

1916-17 REGULAR ISSUE

Unwatermarked Perf. 10

FLAT PRESS Block of 6

#462 1¢ WASHINGTON 86 Plates

Imprint IX

Basic Price	T	$150
Basic Price	L, R, B	$140

6953	*7532	*7533	*7535	7647
7649	7650	7651	7652	7654
7655	7656	*7658	7659	*7660
*7663	7664	7665	7666	7667
7668	7669	7670	7671	7674
7725	7726	7727	7731	7733
7736	7741	7743	7749	7750
7753	7754	7755	7756	7757
7758	7759	7761	7764	7765
7831	7832	7838	7850	7862
7863	7864	7865	7874	7875
7876	7877	7878	7879	7883
7884	7886	7888	7889	7890
7891	7892	7893	7894	7895
7896	7897	7898	7899	7900
*7901	7902	7903	7904	7905
7906	7907	7908	7938	*8003
*8008				

1916-17 REGULAR ISSUE

#463 2¢ WASHINGTON 159 Plates

Imprint IX

Basic Price **T** $125
Basic Price **L, R, B** $115

7225	7322	*7398	*7401	7405
7406	7407	7410	7456	7475
7495	7501	7569	7581	*7583
7589	7590	7594	7638	7639
7640	7641	7682	7698	7699
*7701	*7703	7705	7706	7707
7708	7709	7710	7711	7712
*7713	*7714	*7715	7716	*7717
*7721	7722	7724	7728	7729
7730	7732	7735	7737	7760
7762	7768	7769	7770	7771
7772	7773	7774	7775	7776
7777	7778	7779	7780	7781
7783	7784	7792	7793	7794
7795	7796	7797	7798	7799
7800	7801	7802	7805	7806
7807	7808	7809	7810	7811
7812	7815	7816	7817	7818
7819	7820	7821	7823	7824
7825	7833	7839	7840	7842
7843	7844	7845	7846	7847
7848	7849	7851	7854	7855
7856	7857	7858	7859	7866
7867	7868	7869	7870	7871
7872	7873	7921	7922	7923
7930	7931	7932	*7934	7935
7936	7941	*7942**N**	7944	7945
7946	7947	7948	7949	7951
7952	7955	7982	7983	7985
7986	7987	7988	7989	7995
7996	8000	8001	8002	8004
8005	8006	8009	8010	

N Plate 7942 is not scarce but it is the sheet on which the 5¢ errors are found and, for that reason, the plates bring a substantial premium. *The errors do not appear in any of the plate blocks.* See #467

#464 3¢ WASHINGTON Type I

Imprint IX **8 Plates**

Basic Price **T** $1,500
Basic Price **L, R, B** $1,300

7253 7254 7258 7262 7266
7267 7272 7274

#465 4¢ WASHINGTON 8 Plates

Imprint IX

Basic Price **T** $800
Basic Price **L, R, B** $750

7331 7348 7362 7372 7598
7599 †7600 7606

#466 5¢ WASHINGTON 8 Plates

Imprint IX

Basic Price **T** $950
Basic Price **L, R, B** $900

7622 7623 7632 7633 7787
7788 7789 7790

#467 5¢ ERROR PLATE

Price **T** $150
Price **L, R, B** $140

7942**N**

N The 2¢ stamp plate 7942 is not scarce but it is the sheet on which the 5¢ errors are found. The errors are located at stamps #74 and #84 of the upper left pane and stamp #18 in the lower right pane of plate 7942. *The errors, therefore, do not appear in any of the plate blocks.* See #463

#468 6¢ WASHINGTON 4 Plates

Imprint IX

Basic Price **T** $1,350
Basic Price **L, R, B** $1,250

7136 7137 7138 7139

#469 7¢ WASHINGTON 8 Plates

Imprint IX

Basic Price **T** $1,500
Basic Price **L, R, B** $1,400

7718 7719 7720 7723 7919
7920 7924 7925

#470 8¢ FRANKLIN 4 Plates

Imprint XII

Basic Price **T** $625
Basic Price **L, R, B** $600

5724 5725 5804

Imprint XIII

Basic Price **T** $700
Basic Price **L, R, B** $650

5846

#471 9¢ FRANKLIN 4 Plates

Imprint IX

Basic Price **T** $900
Basic Price **L, R, B** $800

6901 6905 6907 6915

#472 10¢ FRANKLIN 8 Plates

Imprint IX

Basic Price **T** $1,500
Basic Price **L, R, B** $1,350

7204 *7205 7213 7215 7358
7369 7379 7385

1916-17 REGULAR ISSUE

#473 11¢ FRANKLIN 4 Plates

Imprint IX

Basic Price T $400
Basic Price L, R, B $350

7498 7499 7504 7505

#474 12¢ FRANKLIN 4 Plates

Imprint IX

Basic Price T $675
Basic Price L, R, B $600

6900 6902 6910 6913

#475 15¢ FRANKLIN 8 Plates

Imprint XII

Basic Price $7,500

5771 †5775 5780

Imprint XIII

†5850

A top plate block of 5780 and a bottom one of 5771 are the only recorded examples.

Imprint IX

Basic Price T $3,000
Basic Price L, R, B $2,800

6809 6819 6825 6833

#476 20¢ FRANKLIN 4 Plates

Imprint IX

Basic Price T $3,700
Basic Price L, R, B $3,500

6908 6909 6920 6926

#476A 30¢ FRANKLIN 4 Plates

Imprint IX

Basic Price T $30,000
Basic Price L, R, B $30,000

†6899 6911 6914 6917

#477 50¢ FRANKLIN 4 Plates

Imprint IX

Basic Price T $45,000
Basic Price L, R, B $37,500

7040 7042 7049 7057

#478 $1 FRANKLIN 1 Plate

Imprint XII

Price T $13,500
Price B $12,500

5782

#479 $2 MADISON 1 Plate

Imprint IX

Price T $4,800
Price L, R, B $4,000

8015

#480 $5 MARSHALL 1 Plate

Imprint IX

Price T $3,300
Price L, R, B $3,000

8016

BOOKLET PANES

PANES OF 6

#462a 1¢ WASHINGTON 12 Plates

Basic Price T $25

7179	7275	7277	7278	7449
7474	7480	7484	7785	7786
7791	7880			

#463a 2¢ WASHINGTON 12 Plates

Basic Price T $125

7555	7556	7557	7560	7881
7882	7885	7887	7968	7969
7970	7971			

IMPERFORATE

Blocks of 6

#481 1¢ WASHINGTON 155 Plates

Imprint IX

Basic Price T $15
Basic Price L, R, B $13

7535	7669	7671	7674	7725
7736	7741	7743	7749	7750
7753	7754	7755	*7756	7757
7850	7862	7863	7865	7875
7877	7878	7879	*7889	*7890
7894	7898	7899	7900	7901
7902	7905	7907	7908	8038
8039	8040	8042	8045	8046

1916-17 REGULAR ISSUE

#481 1¢ WASHINGTON Cont.

Imprint IX

8068	8115	8116	8117	8168
*8259	8372	8373	8374	8377
8378	8387	8388	8389	8390
8397	8398	*8431	8457	8915
*8931	9477	*9478	9479	9480
9481	10073	10075	10076	10083
10084	10085	10091	10092	10110
10112	10113	10195	10197	10232
*10248	10258	10260	10264	10265
10278	10279	10280	10281	10282
10284	10285	10290	*10291	10292
10293	10298	*10299	10344	10351
10365	*10369	*10599	*10600	*10659
10682	*10757	*10783	10799	*10800
11728	11806	*11807	12493	*12494
*12501	12504	*12505	12548	12611
12616	12617	12924	*13199	*13267
13301	13303	13304	13306	13308
13316	13317	13319	*13320	13332
13337	13338	13339	13340	13349
13350	*13356	13359	13361	13363
*13366	13368	13370	13371	*13378
13379	13380	13381		

Electrolytic Plates

Basic Price	T	$300
Basic Price	L, R, B	$250

13376 13377

#482 2¢ WASHINGTON Type I

Imprint IX **159 Plates**

Basic Price	T	$25
Basic Price	L, R, B	$22

7322	7393	*7583	7639	7699
7701	7714	7729	7730	7760
7762	7771	7780	7781	7783
7784	7792	7800	7801	7802
7805	7806	7807	7808	7809
7816	7817	7818	7819	7820
7821	7824	*7867	*7930	7935
*7936	7942**N**	7944	7945	7946

N The 2¢ stamp plate 7942 is the plate on which the 5¢ errors are found. See #485.

#482 2¢ WASHINGTON Cont.

Imprint IX

7947	7985	7986	7987	7995
*8009	*8010	8011	8012	8014
8018	8022	8023	8024	8025
8026	8067	8069	8070	8501
*8522	8535	8536	8537	*8539
*8541	8548	8550	8870	8871
8886	*9119	*9163	*9166	9168
9169	9172	9173	9191	9192
*9221	*9224	9231	9238	9239
9411	9420	*9421	*9425	*9434
9443	9445	9448	9455	9456
*10236	10240	10267	10272	10304
10305	10313	10314	10354	*10378
10379	10392	10393	10398	10419
10424	10425	10426	10427	10428
10429	*10554	*10560	*10569	10577
*10578	10579	10585	10593	10594
*12960	12963	*12964	12977	12978
12979	12980	12981	12993	*12994
*12996	13207	13208	13209	13227
*13246	*13298	*13454	*13480	*13495
*13524	*13550	13669	13670	13671
13672	13683	13728	13729	*13869
13884	13885	13886	13887	

#482A 2¢ WASHINGTON Type Ia

10208 10209

All of the stamps on these two plates are Type Ia except for two entries on the lower left pane of plate 10208.

Imperforate Type Ia was issued but all known examples have Schermack perf. Type III.

#483 3¢ WASHINGTON Type I

Imprint IX **36 Plates**

Basic Price	T	$150
Basic Price	L, R, B	$125

7272	8091	*8092	8120	8121
8123	8126	8128	8129	8130
8131	8132	8134	8135	8137
8138	8139	8140	8141	8142
8143	8144	8146	8161	8192
*8193	8195	8196	8197	8204
*8206	8209	8230	8232	*8235
*8236				

#484 3¢ WASHINGTON Type II

Imprint IX **26 Plates**

Basic Price	T	$125
Basic Price	L, R, B	$100

8308	*8310	*8316	*8317	*8319
*8320	8325	8330	8338	8351
8352	8354	8355	8356	8357
8358	8362	8364	8365	8366
8371	8386	8456	8462	8473
8476				

1916-17 REGULAR ISSUE

#485 5¢ ERROR PLATE

Price T $165

Price L, R, B $135

7942N

N The 2¢ plate 7942 is the plate on which the 5¢ errors are found.

The errors are located at stamps #74 and #84 of the upper left pane and stamp #18 in the lower right pane of plate 7942.

The errors, therefore, do not appear in any of the plate blocks. See #482

ROTARY COILS

Partial plate numbers occur on mis-slit coils. We indicate those known to us with a "c". Many of the plates used for #490-94 exist as sheet stamps issued as coil waste (see #538-541 & 545, 546). Please send clear xerox to the editor with the report of any examples you have that are unreported.

1916-22 REGULAR ISSUE

END COILS

Unwatermarked Perf. 10 Horizontally

#486 1¢ WASHINGTON

7433	7434	7563	7564	8079
8080	10081	c10082	10408	10409
c10410	10411	13928	c13929	

#487 2¢ WASHINGTON Type II

7431 7432

#488 2¢ WASHINGTON Type III

7628	7629	8077	8078	10767
10768	13629	13630	13631	13632

#489 3¢ WASHINGTON Type I

7634 7635 8111 8112

SIDE COILS

Unwatermarked Perf. 10 Vertically

#490 1¢ WASHINGTON

7506	7507	7508	7690	7691
7744	7745	7763	7766	7767
7957	7958	7963	7964	7978
7979	8081	8082	8336	8337
8339	8340	9099	9111	9112
9113	9114	9141	9142	9151
9152	9450	9451	9452	9453
9463	9464	9467	9468	10087
10088	10089	10090	10103	10104
10184	10185	c10202	10203	10345
10346	10347	10348	10349	10350
10361	10640	10641	10643	10686
10687	10688	10689	10690	10691
10692	10693	10694	10695	11740
11741	11742	11743	11764	11765
11766	11767	13312	13313	13314
13315	13445	13446	13447	13448
13491	13492	13575	13576	13611
13612	13615	13616	13810	13811
13812	13813	13820	13821	c13826

1916-22 REGULAR ISSUE

#490 1¢ WASHINGTON Cont.

c13827	13856	13857	c13872	13873
13896	c13897	c13906	c13907	13910
13911	13930	13931	13942	13943
13968	13969	13976	14104	

#491 2¢ WASHINGTON Type II

7445 7446 7462 7463

#492 2¢ WASHINGTON Type III

7661	7662	7672	7673	7686
7738	7739	7746	7747	7751
7752	7782	7803	7804	7813
7814	7826	7827	7829	7830
7835	7836	7852	7853	7909
7910	7915	7916	7939	7940
7953	7961	7962	7965	7967
7976	8049	8050	8051	8052
8056	8057	8061	8062	8071
8072	8073	8074	8075	8076
8169	8170	8171	8172	8326
8327	8328	8329	8928	8939
8940	9103	9104	c9105	9106
9153	9154	9233	9234	9235
9236	9237	9457	9458	9465
9466	9469	9470	10097	10098
10115	10116	10175	10176	10177
10178	10183	10295	10296	10297
10306	10307	10308	10315	10316
10317	10318	10384	10386	10387
10388	10389	10444	10445	10446
10447	10448	10449	10450	10451
10452	10453	10466	10467	10468
10469	10470	10471	10478	10479
10480	10485	10486	10487	10488
10489	10491	10492	10648	10649
10650	10651	10652	10670	10671
10680	10681	10723	10724	10725
10726	10727	10728	10729	10730
10731	10732	10733	10738	10739
10740	10741	10750	11718	11719
11724	11725	11726	11727	11730
11731	11732	11733	11734	11735
11736	11737	11769	11770	11771
11772	11797	11798	11799	11800
11808	11809	11810	11811	12464
12465	12466	12469	12470	12471
12472	12473	12474	12475	12476
12483	12484	12485	12486	12513
12514	12515	12516	12517	12518
12519	12520	12529	12530	12531
12532	12601	12602	12603	12604
12918	12919	12920	12921	12922
12927	12928	12929	12970	12971
12972	12973	13002	13004	13005
13239	13240	13253	13254	13286
13287	13288	13289	13290	13291
13292	13293	13294	13295	13386
13387	13388	13397	13398	13399
13400	13401	13402	13413	13414

1916-22 REGULAR ISSUE

W#492 2¢ WASHINGTON Type III Cont.

13417	13418	13425	13426	13427
13428	13505	13506	13507	13508
13509	13510	13511	13512	13514
13536	13537	13538	13539	13583
13584	13585	13586	13595	13596
13597	13598	13599	13600	13601
13602	13603	13604	13605	13606
13607	13608	13637	13638	13641
13642	13647	13648	13651	13652
13657	13658	13677	13678	13692
13693	13694	13695	13718	13719
13720	13721	13740	13741	c13742
13743	13764	13765	13766	13767
13776	13777	13778	c13779	13786
c13787	c13788	13789	13800	c13801
c13802	13803	13804	13805	13807
13809	13814	13815	13830	13831
13840	13841	c13842	c13843	13874
13875	13894	13895	13938	c13939
c13958	c13959	13960	13961	13970
13971	13984	13985	14030	c14031
c14032	14033	c14038	c14039	c14040
14041	14050	14051	14052	c14053
c14054	14055	c14056	14057	

#493 3¢ WASHINGTON Type I

7441	7442	8107	8108	8109
8110	8124	8125	8151	8152
8153	8154	8155	8201	8202
8203	c8216	8218	8219	8226
c8227	8228	8229	8233	c8234
8237	8238	8239	8240	8244
8245	8247	8248	8250	8251

#494 3¢ WASHINGTON Type II

8269	8270	8275	8276	c8281
c8282	8402	8408	8409	8428
8429	8442	8454	8455	8458
8459	8464	8467	8468	8469
8470	8471	8472	c8474	8475
8482	8483	8923	8924	8949
8950	8951	9107	9108	9109
9110	9133	9134	9135	9136
9143	9144	9145	9146	9181
9182				

#495 4¢ WASHINGTON

7440	c7452	7675	7676

#496 5¢ WASHINGTON

7435	7436	13633	13634

#497 10¢ FRANKLIN

13625	13626

Starting with plate 8377, most flat plates had an "F" added to indicate that the plate was hardened. The usual position was next to the TR plate number, but other positions occur. See U.S. Specialist, April 1990, p.217 and June 1990, p.321.

1917-19 REGULAR ISSUE

All Imprint IX except as noted.

Unwatermarked. Perf. 11

FLAT PRESS Block of 6

#498 1¢ WASHINGTON 662 Plates

Basic Price **T** $20

Basic Price **L, R, B** $16

7532	7533	7535	7647	7651
7655	7656	7658	7659	7668
7669	7670	7671	7674	7726
7727	*7731	7733	7741	7743
7750	7754	7755	*7756	7757
*7758	7759	7761	7764	7765
7831	7832	*7863	*7876	7889
7890	7891	7892	*7894	7895
7896	7897	*7898	*7899	*7900
7901	7902	7903	7904	*7905
7906	*7907	*7908	7911	7912
7913	*7914	7933	7937	7938
7943	7950	7956	7959	7999
8003	8007	8008	8013	8034
8035	8036	8037	8038	8039
8040	8042	8043	8044	8045
8046	8047	8048	8054	8060
8068	8115	8116	8117	8164
8165	8166	8167	8168	8173
8174	8175	8176	8257	8258
*8259	8260	8261	8335	8341
*8342	*8343	8344	8345	*8346
*8347	8348	8349	8350	8360
8361	8368	8369	8372	8373
8374	8377	8378	8387	8388
8389	8390	8391	8392	8393
8394	8395	8396	8397	8398
8399	8400	8401	8404	8405
8406	8407	8422	8423	8424
8425	8426	8427	8430	8431
8432	8433	8434	8439	8440
8443	8444	8445	8446	8447
8450	8453	8457	8461	8465
8510	8511	8512	8513	8526
8527	8528	8529	8884	8885
8907	8908	8909	8910	8911
8912	8913	8914	8915	8916
8917	8918	8919	8920	8921
8922	8925	8926	8927	8929
8930	8931	8932	8933	8934

1917-19 REGULAR ISSUE

#498 1¢ WASHINGTON Cont.

8935	8937	8941	8942	8944
9477	9478	9479	9480	9481
10073	10074	10075	10076	10083
10084	10085	10086	10091	10092
10099	10100	10101	10102	10105
10106	10107	10108	10109	10110
10111	10112	10113	10114	10117
10118	10119	10120	10121	10122
10123	10124	10125	10126	10127
10128	10129	10130	10131	10132
10133	10134	10153	10154	10155
10156	*10157	10158	10159	10160
10161	*10162	10163	10164	10165
10166	10167	10168	10173	10174
10186	10187	10188	10189	10194
10195	10196	10197	10230	10231
10232	10233	10242	10243	*10244
*10245	10246	10247	*10248	*10249
10258	*10259	10260	10261	10262
*10263	10264	10265	10278	10279
10280	10281	10282	10283	10284
10285	10290	10291	10292	10293
10298	10299	10343	10344	10351
10352	10357	10358	10359	10360
10362	10363	10364	10365	10366
10367	10368	10369	10370	10371
10374	10375	10376	10377	10380
10381	10382	10383	10390	10391
10394	10395	10396	10397	10414
10415	10417	10420	10421	10422
10423	10440	10441	10454	10455
10472	10473	10529	10530	10539
10540	10557	10558	10565	10566
10567	10568	10571	10572	10573
10574	10575	10576	10580	10583
10584	10586	10587	10588	10591
10592	10595	10596	10599	10600
10601	10602	10603	10604	10613
10614	10615	10616	10625	10626
10644	10645	10646	10647	10654
10656	10657	10658	10659	10660
10661	10662	10663	10664	10665
10676	10677	10678	10679	10682
10683	10684	10685	10696	10697
10698	10699	10701	10702	10703
10708	10709	10710	10711	10712
10713	10742	10743	10744	10745
10746	10747	10748	10749	10751
10752	10753	10754	10755	10756
10757	10758	10759	10760	10761
10762	10769	10770	10771	10772
10773	10774	10779	10780	10781
10782	10783	10784	10789	10790
10799	10800	10801	10802	10803
10804	10805	10806	10807	10808
10809	10810	10811	10812	10814
10815	10816	*11720	11721	11722
11723	11728	11729	11786	11787
11788	11789	11790	11791	11792
11802	11803	11804	11805	11806
11807	11812	11813	12491	12492

#498 1¢ WASHINGTON Cont.

12493	12494	12497	12498	12499
12500	12501	12502	12503	12504
12505	12506	12507	12508	12521
12522	12523	12524	12525	12527
12528	12533	12534	12535	12536
12537	12538	12539	12540	12541
12542	12543	12544	12545	12546
12547	12548	12609	12610	12611
12612	12613	12614	12615	12616
12617	12923	12924	12925	12926
13198	13199	13200	13201	13214
13216	13217	13219	13220	13221
13222	13223	13224	13225	13226
13231	13232	13233	13234	13249
13250	13251	13252	13256	13257
13258	13259	13265	13266	13267
13300	13301	13302	13303	13304
13305	13306	*13307	13308	13309
13310	13311	13316	13317	13318
13319	13320	13321	13322	13323
13324	*13325	*13326	*13327	*13328
13329	13330	13331	13332	13333
13334	13335	13336	13337	13338
13339	13340	13341	13342	13343
13344	13345	13346	13347	13348
13349	13350	13351	*13356	13357
13358	13359	13360	13361	*13362
13363	13364	13365	13366	13367
13368	13369	13370	13371	*13378
13379	13380	13381	*13544	*13545
13546	13547			

Electrolytic Plates

Basic Price	T	$500
Basic Price	L, R, B	$450

13376	13377	13389	†13390

#499 2¢ WASHINGTON 837 Plates

Basic Price	T	$20
Basic Price	L, R, B	$17

5990	*7322	7393	*7398	7456
7495	7501	7569	7581	7589
7590	7640	7641	7682	7698
7699	7701	7703	7705	7707
*7708	7709	7710	7711	7713
7714	†7715	7716	†7721	*7722
7724	7728	7730	7732	7737
*7773	7792	7795	7797	7801
7802	*7808	7809	7816	7817
7818	7819	7823	7839	7840
7841	7842	7843	*7844	7845
7847	*7848	7854	7855	7856
7857	7858	7859	7866	7867
7868	7869	7870	7871	*7872
*7873	7921	7922	7923	7930
7931	*7932	7934	7935	7936
7941	7942**N**	7944	7945	7946

N Plate 7942 is not scarce but it is the sheet on which the 5¢ errors are found. The plates bring a substantial premium. *The errors do not appear in any of the plate blocks.* See #505

1917-19 REGULAR ISSUE

#499 2¢ WASHINGTON Cont.

7947	7948	7949	7951	7952
7955	7982	7983	7985	7986
7987	7988	7989	7995	7996
8000	8001	8002	8004	8005
8006	8009	8010	8011	8012
8014	8017	8018	8019	8020
8021	8022	8023	8024	8025
8026	8027	8028	8029	8030
8031	8032	8033	8041	8053
8055	8058	8059	8063	8064
8065	8066	8067	8069	8070
8083	8084	8085	8086	8087
8088	8089	8090	8180	8181
8182	8498	8499	8500	8501
8502	8503	8504	8505	8514
8515	8516	8517	8518	8519
8520	8521	8522	8523	8524
8525	8531	8532	8533	8534
8535	8536	8537	8538	8539
8540	8541	8542	8546	8547
8548	8549	8550	8551	8552
8553	8870	8871	8872	8874
8875	8876	8877	8886	8887
8952	8953	8954	9098	9100
9101	9102	9119	9120	9121
9122	9123	9124	9125	9126
9127	9128	9131	9132	9139
9140	9156	9157	9158	9159
9160	9161	9162	9163	9165
9166	9167	9168	9169	9170
9171	9172	9173	9174	9175
9176	9183	9184	9185	9186
9187	9188	9189	9190	9191
9192	9197	9198	9199	9200
9201	9202	9203	9204	9205
9206	9207	9208	9209	9210
9211	9212	9213	9214	9215
9216	9217	9218	9219	9220
9221	9222	9223	9224	9225
9226	9227	9228	9229	9230
9231	9232	9238	9239	9240
9241	9410	9411	9420	9421
9422	9423	9424	9425	9434
9435	9436	9437	9438	9439
9440	9441	9442	9443	9444
9445	9446	9447	9448	9449
9454	9455	9456	9459	9460
9461	9462	10190	10191	10192
10193	10198	10199	10200	10201
10204	10205	10206	10207	*10208 **Z**
10210	10211	10212	10213	10214
10215	10216	10217	10226	10227
10228	10229	10234	10235	10236
10237	10238	10239	10240	10241
10266	10267	10268	10269	10270
10271	10272	10273	10286	10287
10288	10289	10304	10305	10313
10314	10319	10320	10321	10322
10323	10324	10333	10334	10339
10340	10341	10342	*10353	10354
10355	10356	10372	10373	10378

Z See #500 Type Ia

#499 2¢ WASHINGTON Cont.

10379	10392	10393	10398	10399
10412	10413	10418	10419	10424
10425	10426	10427	10428	10429
10434	10435	10442	10443	10456
10457	10462	10463	10464	10465
10481	10482	10483	10484	10493
10495	10496	10497	10498	10499
10500	10505	10506	10507	10508
10515	10516	10517	10518	10519
10520	10521	10522	10523	10524
10531	10532	10533	10534	10535
10536	10537	*10538	*10545	*10546
10547	10548	*10549	*10550	10551
*10552	*10553	10554	10555	10556
10559	10560	10561	10562	10563
10564	10569	10570	10577	10578
10579	10581	10582	10585	10589
10590	10593	10594	10597	10598
12938	12939	12940	12941	12942
12943	12944	12945	12946	12947
12948	12949	12950	12951	12952
12953	12954	12955	12956	12957
12958	12959	12960	12961	12962
12963	12964	12965	12966	12967
12968	12969	12974	12975	12976
12977	12978	12979	12980	12981
12982	12983	12984	12985	12986
12987	12988	12989	12990	12991
12993	12994	12995	12996	12997
12998	12999	13000	13001	13006
13007	13008	13009	13014	13015
13016	13017	13194	13195	13196
13197	13202	13203	13204	13205
13206	13207	13208	13209	13227
13228	13229	13230	13235	13236
13237	13238	13241	13242	13243
13244	13245	13246	13247	13248
13260	13261	13262	13263	13296
13297	13298	13299	13433	13434
13435	13436	13437	13438	13439
13440	13441	13442	13451	13452
13453	13454	13455	13456	13457
13458	13475	13476	13477	13478
13479	13480	13481	13482	13483
13484	13485	13486	13487	13488
13489	13490	13493	13494	13495
13496	13518	13519	13520	13521
13524	13525	13526	13527	13532
13533	13534	13535	13540	13541
13542	13543	13548	13549	13550
13551	13560	13561	13562	13563
13564	13565	13566	13567	13587
13588	13589	13590	13591	13592
13593	13594	13659	13660	13661
13662	13663	13664	13665	13666
13667	13668	13669	13670	13671
13672	13673	13674	13679	13680
13681	13682	13683	13684	13685
13686	13687	13689	13690	13691
13698	13699	13700	13701	13702
13703	13704	13705	13706	13707

1917-19 REGULAR ISSUE

#499 2¢ WASHINGTON Cont.

13708	13709	13710	13711	13712
13713	13714	13715	13716	13717
13724	13725	13726	13727	13728
13729	13730	13731	13732	13733
13734	13735	13736	13737	13738
13739	13746	13747	13748	13749
13758	13759	13760	13761	13768
13769	13770	13771	13772	13773
13774	13775	13780	13781	13782
13783	13792	13793	13794	13795
13848	13849	13850	13851	13864
13865	13866	13867	13868	13869
13870	13871	13878	13879	13880
13881	13882	13883	13884	13885
13886	13887	13888	13889	13898
13899	13900	13901	13902	13903
13904	13905	13912	13913	13914
13915	13924	13925	13926	13927
13932	13933	13934	13935	13944
13945	13946	13947	13954	13955
13956	13957	13972	13973	13974
13975	13978	13979	13980	13981
13986	13987	13988	13989	13992
13993	13994	13995	13996	13997
13998	13999	14002	14003	14004
14005	14008	14009	14010	*14011
14014	14015	14016	14017	*14018
14019	14020	14021	14022	14023
14024	14025			

#500 2¢ WASHINGTON Type Ia

Basic Price	T	$2,400
Basic Price	L, R, B	$2,200

10208 10209

All of the stamps on these two plates are Type Ia except tor two entries on the lower left pane 10208. A bottom plate block of this pane shows the combination of Type I and Type Ia. These are quite scarce.

This block is valued at: $7,500

#501 3¢ WASHINGTON Type I

90 Plates

Basic Price	T	$120
Basic Price	L, R, B	$100

7253	7254	7258	7262	7266
7267	7272	7274	8091	8092
8093	8094	8099	8100	8101
8102	8103	8104	8105	8106
8118	8119	8120	8121	8122
8123	8126	8127	8128	8129
8130	8131	8132	8133	8134
8135	8136	8137	8138	8139
8140	8141	8142	8143	8144
8145	8146	8147	8148	*8149
8156	*8157	8158	8159	8160
8161	8163	8192	8193	8195
8196	8197	8198	8199	8204
8206	8207	8208	8209	8210
8215	8221	8222	8223	8224
8225	8230	8232	8235	8236
8241	8242	8243	8246	8249
8252	8253	8254	8255	8256

#502 3¢ WASHINGTON Type II

85 Plates

Basic Price	T	$160
Basic Price	L, R, B	$140

8262	8263	8264	8265	8266
8267	8268	8271	8273	8274
8277	8278	8279	8280	8283
8284	8285	8286	*8287	8288
*8289	8290	8291	8292	8293
*8294	8295	8296	*8297	8298
*8299	8300	8305	8306	8307
8308	*8309	*8310	8311	8312
8313	8314	*8315	*8316	*8317
*8318	*8319	8320	*8321	8322
8323	8324	8325	8330	8338
8351	8352	8353	8354	8355
8356	8357	8358	8359	8362
8363	8364	8365	8366	8367
8371	8386	8456	8462	8473
8476	*8481	†8866	†8867	*8868
*8869	†8903	*8904	*8905	8906

#503 4¢ WASHINGTON 35 Plates

Basic Price	T	$160
Basic Price	L, R, B	$140

7331	*7362	*7372	7598	7599
7600	7606	7972	7973	7974
7975	8494	8495	8496	8497
8880	8881	8888	8889	10474
10475	10476	10477	12549	12550
12551	12552	13556	13557	13558
13559	13569	13570	13571	13572

1917-19 REGULAR ISSUE

#504 5¢ WASHINGTON 88 Plates

Basic Price	**T**	$130
Basic Price	**L, R, B**	$125

7622	7623	7632	7633	7787
7788	7789	7790	7993	7994
7997	7998	8200	8205	8220
8231	8484	8485	8486	8487
8882	8883	8901	8902	9115
9116	9117	9118	10139	10140
10141	10142	10222	10223	10224
10225	10309	10310	10311	10312
10458	10459	10460	10461	10541
10542	10543	10544	10666	10667
10668	10669	10704	10705	10706
10707	11748	11749	11750	11751
12479	12480	12481	12482	12509
12510	12511	12512	12553	12554
12555	12556	13272	13273	13274
13275	13463	13464	13465	13466
13497	13498	13499	13500	13822
13823	13824	*13825		

#505 5¢ ERROR PLATE

Price	**T**	$30
Price	**L, R, B**	$25

7942**N**

N The 2¢ stamp plate 7942 is not scarce but it is the sheet on which the 5¢ errors are found.The errors are located at stamps #74 and #84 of the upper left pane and stamp #18 In the lower right pane of plate 7942. *The errors, therefore, do not appear in any of the plate blocks.* See #499

#506 6¢ WASHINGTON 24 Plates

Basic Price	**T**	$175
Basic Price	**L, R, B**	$165

7136	7137	7138	7139	7822
7828	7834	7837	10093	10094
10095	10096	10763	10764	10765
10766	12557	12558	12559	12560
13372	13373	13374	13375	

#507 7¢ WASHINGTON 56 Plates

Basic Price	**T**	$275
Basic Price	**L, R, B**	$250

7718	7719	†7720	†7723	7919
7920	7924	7925	8488	8489
8490	8491	8897	8898	8899
8943	*10169	*10170	*10171	*10172
10300	10301	10302	10303	*10511
10512	*10513	10514	10636	10637
10638	10639	10795	10796	10797
10798	11752	11753	11754	11755
12561	12562	12563	12564	13276
13277	13278	13279	13750	13751
13752	13753	13950	13951	13952
13953				

#508 8¢ FRANKLIN 24 Plates

Imprint XII

Basic Price	**T**	$200
Basic Price	**L, R, B**	$175

5724 5725 5804

Imprint XIII

Price	**T**	$300
Price	**L, R, B**	$250

5846

Imprint IX

Basic Price	**T**	$175
Basic Price	**L, R, B**	$150

7734	7740	7742	7748	10785
10786	10787	10788	12565	12566
12567	12568	13382	13383	13384
13385	13852	13853	13854	13855

#509 9¢ FRANKLIN 17 Plates

Basic Price	**T**	$175
Basic Price	**L, R, B**	$150

6901	6905	6907	6915	6918
6922	6925	6930	11773	11774
11775	11776	12569	12570	12571
12572	*13754			

#510 10¢ FRANKLIN 65 Plates

Imprint XIII

Price	**T**	$400
Price	**L, R, B**	$360

5847

Imprint IX

Basic Price	**T**	$225
Basic Price	**L, R, B**	$200

7204	7205	7213	7215	7358
7369	7379	7385	8301	8302
8303	8304	8435	8436	8437
8438	10143	10144	10145	10146
10254	10255	10256	10257	10525
10526	*10527	10528	10605	10606
10607	10608	10627	10628	10629
10630	10734	10735	10736	10737

1917-19 REGULAR ISSUE

#510 10¢ FRANKLIN Cont.

11744 11745 11746 11747 12573
12574 12575 12576 12605 12606
12607 12608 13403 13404 13405
13406 13501 13502 13503 13504
13796 13797 13798 13799

#511 11¢ FRANKLIN 12 Plates

Basic Price T $140
Basic Price L, R, B $130

7498 7499 7504 7505 12577
12578 12579 12580 *13467 *13468
*13469 *13470

#512 12¢ FRANKLIN 16 Plates

Basic Price T $130
Basic Price L, R, B $120

6900 6902 6910 6913 6931
6934 7036 7037 10621 10622
10623 10624 12581 12582 12583
12584

#513 13¢ FRANKLIN 8 Plates

Basic Price T $140
Basic Price L, R, B $130

9147 9148 9149 9150 12585
12586 12587 12588

#514 15¢ FRANKLIN 36 Plates

Basic Price T $575
Basic Price L, R, B $525

*6809 *6819 *6825 *6833 7926
7927 7928 7929 8878 8879
8890 8891 10179 10180 10181
10182 10501 *10502 10503 10504
10617 10618 10619 10620 12589
12590 12591 12592 13280 13281
13282 13283 *13860 *13861 *13862
*13863

#515 20¢ FRANKLIN 32 Plates

Basic Price T $650
Basic Price L, R, B $600

6908 6909 6920 6926 6933
6935 6938 7033 10135 10136
10137 10138 10325 10326 10327
10328 11793 11795 11796 11801
12593 12594 12595 12596 13471
13472 13473 13474 13836 13837
13838 13839

#516 30¢ FRANKLIN 8 Plates

Basic Price T $625
Basic Price L, R, B $575

6899 6911 6914 6917 6921
6924 6927 6928

#517 50¢ FRANKLIN 6 Plates

Basic Price T $1,750
Basic Price L, R, B $1,650

7040 7042 7049 7057 13653
13654 13655 13656

#518 $1 FRANKLIN 1 Plate

Imprint XII

Price T $1,300
Price B $1,200

5782

BOOKLET PANES

PANES OF 6

#498e 1¢ WASHINGTON 73 Plates

Basic Price T $6

6885 7179 7275 7277 7278
7449 7474 7480 7484 7785
7786 7791 7880 7980 7981
7990 7991 8183 8184 8185
8186 8187 8188 8189 8194
8945 8946 8947 8948 9177
9178 9179 9180 10077 10078
10079 10080 10250 10251 *10252
10253 10430 10431 10432 10433
10714 10715 10716 10717 11756
11757 11758 11759 11761 11762
11763 11768 13268 13269 13270
13271 13421 13422 13423 13424
13429 13430 13431 13432 13459
13460 13461 13462

1917-19 REGULAR ISSUE

#499e 2¢ WASHINGTON 100 Plates

Basic Price T $7.50

7881	7882	7885	7887	7968
7969	7970	7971	8191	8893
8894	8895	9471	9472	9473
9474	10147	10148	10149	10150
10218	10219	10220	10221	10329
10330	10331	10332	*10400	*10401
*10402	10403	10404	10405	*10406
10407	10609	10610	10611	10612
10672	10673	10674	*10675	10718
10719	10720	10721	10775	*10776
*10777	10778	10791	10792	10793
10794	11777	11778	11779	11780
11781	11782	11783	11784	12487
12488	12489	12490	12930	12931
12932	12933	12934	12935	12936
12937	13010	13011	13012	13013
13210	13211	13212	13213	13528
13529	13530	13531	13617	13618
13619	13620	13621	13622	13623
13624	13964	13965	13966	13967

#501b 3¢ WASHINGTON Type I 4 Plates

Basic Price T $100

8095	8096	8097	8098

#502b 3¢ WASHINGTON Tp. II 12 Plates

Basic Price T $75

8331	8332	8333	8334	8448
8449	8452	8460	9129	9130
9137	9138			

PANES OF 30

#498f 1¢ WASHINGTON

No plate number reported to date

#499f 2¢ WASHINGTON

No plate number reported to date

1917 REGULAR ISSUE

Double Line Wmk. Perf. 11

FLAT PRESS Block of 6

#519 2¢ WASHINGTON 8 Plates

Imprint V

Basic Price T $2,500

Basic Price L, R, B $2,400

4818	4848	4856	4864	4865
4866	4868	4905		

Some early imperforate sheets of Scott's #344 were returned to the Bureau and perforated with the 11 gauge.

1918 REGULAR ISSUE

Unwatermarked Perf. 11

FLAT PRESS Block of 8

#523 $2 FRANKLIN

Price T $13,000

Frame Plate 8177

Vignette Plate 8179

#547 $2 FRANKLIN

see page 75

#524 $5 FRANKLIN

Price T $4,500

Frame Plate 8178

Vignette Plate 8179

OFFSET PRINTING

Early in 1918 the Bureau of Engraving and Printing began producing the lower values of the current issue of postage stamps by the offset printing method. The stamps were much inferior to the engraved work and as soon as the volume of work in the Bureau would permit, the engraving of postage stamp plates was resumed. Collectors, in general, were not greatly interested in these stamps and the printing method is such that the stamps abound in major and minor defects and varieties. Both of these factors make the issue a very rewarding field for study today.

Many varieties appear on the plate blocks of this issue and two of the most popular are the CRNTS and 'OAM' varieties. These are priced under Scott #528, #528A, and #534.

1918-20 REGULAR ISSUE

OFFSET PRESS

#525 1¢ WASHINGTON 260 Plates

Basic Price T $22

Basic Price L, R, B $20

*9095	*9096	9242	9245	9247
9248	9249	9250	9257	9258
9259	9260	9261	9266	9267
9283	9284	9285	9290	9291
9306	9307	9308	9318	9320
9321	9322	9328	9399	9402
9403	9486	9487	9488	9489
9496	*9497	*9498	9499	9508
9509	9510	9511	9515	9516
9517	9518	9519	9521	9522
9523	9524	9525	9526	9527
9539	9540	*9541	9555	9556
9557	9558	9640	9641	9643
9661	9662	9672	9673	9674
9675	9676	*9677	*9678	9679
*9680	*9681	*9682	*9685	9692
9693	*9694	9698	*9699	9700
9703	9710	*9711	9712	9713
9714	9715	*9716	9717	†9718
†9720	9721	9723	9724	9725
9753	9754	9755	9756	9763
9764	9765	9766	9767	9768
9772	9773	*9774	*9779	9780
9781	9782	9787	*9788	9789
9790	†9791	9792	*9802	*9803
9804	9805	*9806	*9807	*9808
9809	9810	9811	9812	9817
9818	9819	*9820	9821	9822
9824	9825	9828	9829	9830
9837	*9838	9839	†9840	*9841
*9842	9843	*9844	*9859	9860
9861	9870	*9871	9874	9876
9878	*9879	9893	9894	9895
9896	9897	*9906	*9907	9909
9916	9917	9918	9920	9949
*9950	9951	*9952	9953	9954
9965	9966	9967	*9968	9969
9970	9971	9972	*9973	9974
9975	*9976	9977	*9978	†9979
9980	*9981	9982	*9983	*9984
9985	*9986	9987	*9988	9989
*9990	*9991	†9992	9993	9995
*9996	9997	*9998	9999	10000
10001	10002	10003	10005	10006
10007	10008	10009	10010	10011
10012	10013	10014	10015	10016
10017	10020	*10021	10022	10023
10024	10025	10026	10027	10028
10029	10030	†10031	10032	10033
*10034	10035	10036	10037	10038
10041	10042	10043	10044	*10045
10049	*10050	10052	10053	*10054

1918-20 REGULAR ISSUE

#526 2¢ WASHINGTON Tp. IV 95 Plates

Basic Price T $230

Basic Price L, R, B $200

*10818	*10819	10820	10821	10822
10823	10824	10825	10826	10827
10828	10829	10830	10831	10832
*10833	10834	*10835	10836	10837
10839	10840	10841	10842	*10843
10844	10845	10852	10853	10854
10855	10856	10857	10858	*10859
10860	*10861	10862	10863	10864
10866	10871	*10872	10873	*10874
10876	10878	*10879	10880	10881
10882	10883	10884	10885	10886
10887	10888	10890	10892	10893
10894	10895	10896	10897	10898
10899	*10900	10901	*10902	10904
10905	*10906	10907	10908	10909
10910	10912	10913	10914	10915
10916	10917	10918	*10919	10921
*10922	10923	10927	10928	10929
10931	10932	*10933	10934	*10935

#527 2¢ WASHINGTON Tp. V 302 Plates

Basic Price T $175

Basic Price L, R, B $150

†10924	*10936	10948	10949	10950
*10951	*10953	10954	10955	10956
10957	*10958	10959	*10960	10961
*10962	*10965	*10968	10969	*10970
10971	10972	*10973	*10974	*10975
10976	10977	†10978	†10981	*10982
10983	*10984	10986	*10987	*10988
*10989	10990	10991	*10992	10993
*10994	*10995	*10996	*10997	*10998
10999	11000	11001	*11002	*11003
11004	11005	11006	11007	11008
11009	11010	11011	*11012	*11013
*11014	*11015	*11016	*11017	11018
11019	11020	11021	11022	11023
11024	11025	*11026	11027	11028
11029	*11031	11032	11033	11034
*11035	11036	11037	11038	*11039
11040	11041	*11042	11043	11044
11045	11046	11047	*11048	11050
†11051	11052	*11053	*11054	*11057
*11058	11059	*11060	*11061	*11062
11063	*11064	11065	11066	11067
11069	11070	11071	*11072	*11073
*11074	11075	*11076	11077	11078
*11079	11080	11081	11082	11083
11084	11085	11086	11087	11088
11090	11091	*11092	*11093	*11094
11095	*11097	*11098	11099	*11100
11101	*11102	11103	11104	*11105
11106	*11107	11109	*11110	11111
*11112	11114	11115	*11116	11120
11121	11122	11124	11125	11126
11127	11128	11129	*11130	11131
11132	11133	11134	11135	11136

1918-1920 REGULAR ISSUE

#527 2¢ WASHINGTON Type V Cont.

*11137	11139	11140	11142	11143
11144	†11145	11146	*11147	11149
11150	11151	11152	*11153	11154
11155	11156	11157	11159	11160
11161	11162	*11164	11165	11166
11168	11169	11170	*11171	11172
11173	11174	11175	11176	*11177
*11178	11179	11180	11181	11182
11183	*11184	11185	11186	11187
*11188	*11189	*11190	11191	11193
*11196	11197	11198	11199	*11200
11202	11203	11204	11205	11206
11209	11210	11211	11212	*11213
11214	11215	*11216	11218	11219
*11220	†11221	11222	11223	*11224
11226	*11227	11229	11230	11231
*11232	11233	11234	11235	11236
11237	11238	11241	*11242	11243
*11245	11246	*11247	11248	11249
11250	11251	11252	11253	11254
11256	*11257	11260	11261	11262
11263	†11264	*11265	*11272	11273
11274	11275	*11276	11277	11278
11279	*11281	11282	11283	11284
11386	11878	11879	11883	11892
11893	11894	11895	11896	11934
11936	11937			

#528 2¢ WASHINGTON Tp. Va 548 Plates

Basic Price	**T**	$80
Basic Price	**L, R, B**	$75

The plate numbers initials O A M are found on the plate number blocks of at least 19 plates.
These blocks are valued at......................$100

A defective "E" in CENTS that causes the word to look almost as though it was spelled C R NTS occurs on the stamp directly below the top plate number on many plates.
These blocks are valued at......................$80

*11266	11267	11285	*11286	11287
*11288	*11289	11290	11291	11292
11293	11294	*11295	*11299	11300
11301	*11302	*11303	11304	11305
11306	11307	*11308	11309	†11310
11311	11312	11313	11315	11316
11317	11318	*11319	*11320	*11321
*11323	11324	*11325	11326	11327
11328	11329	11330	11331	*11332
11333	11335	*11336	*11337	*11338
11339	11340	11341	11342	11343
11344	*11345	*11346	11347	11348
11349	11350	*11351	*11353	11354
*11355	11356	*11358	11359	11360
11361	*11362	11363	*11364	11365
*11366	11367	11368	11369	*11370
11371	11373	*11374	*11375	*11376
11378	11379	11380	11381	11382
11383	11384	11385	11388	*11389
11390	11391	11392	11393	11395

#528 2¢ WASHINGTON Type Va Cont.

11397	11398	11399	*11400	11402
11403	11404	*11405	11406	11407
11408	11409	11410	11411	11412
11413	11414	11415	11416	11417
11418	11419	*11420	11421	11422
11423	*11424	11425	11426	11427
11428	11429	11430	11431	11433
11434	11435	11436	11439	11440
11441	*11443	11444	*11445	11446
11447	*11448	*11449	11450	*11451
*11452	11453	11455	11456	11457
11458	*11459	*11460	11461	*11462
11463	11464	11466	*11467	11468
11469	11470	11472	11473	*11474
11475	11476	*11477	11478	*11479
†11480	11481	11482	11483	*11485
11487	11488	11489	11490	*11491
11492	*11493	*11494	11495	11497
11498	*11499	†11500	*11501	11503
11504	11505	11506	11507	11508
11509	11510	11511	11512	11513
11514	11515	11516	11517	11518
11519	11520	*11521	11522	*11523
11524	11525	11526	11527	11528
11529	11530	11531	11532	11533
11535	11536	11537	11538	*11539
11540	*11541	*11542	*11543	11544
11545	11546	11547	11548	11549
11550	11551	11552	*11553	*11555
11556	*11558	11559	11560	11561
†11563	11564	*11565	11566	11567
*11570	11571	11572	11573	11574
11575	*11576	11577	11578	*11579
11580	11581	11582	11583	11591
11592	*11593	11594	11595	*11596
11597	11823	*11824	*11825	11826
11827	11828	*11829	11831	11832
11835	11836	*11837	11838	11839
11840	†11841	11842	*11843	11845
11846	11847	11848	11849	11850
11851	11852	11853	11854	11855
11856	*11857	*11858	11859	11860
*11861	11862	11863	11864	11865
11866	11867	11868	11869	11870
11871	11872	11873	11874	11875
11876	11887	11888	†11889	11890
11891	11897	11898	11899	11900
11901	11902	11903	11904	11905
11906	11908	11909	11910	11911
11912	11913	11914	11915	11916
*11917	11918	11920	11921	†11922
11924	11925	11926	11927	11928
*11929	11930	11931	11932	11933
11938	*11939	11944	11945	11946
11947	11948	11949	11950	11952
11957	11958	11959	11962	11964
11965	11967	11968	11969	*11970
11971	11972	11973	*11974	11975
*11976	11977	11979	11980	11981
11982	11983	11984	11985	11986
11987	11988	11989	11990	11991

1918-1920 REGULAR ISSUE

#528 2¢ WASHINGTON Type Va Cont.

11992	11993	*11994	11996	11997
11998	12000	*12001	12002	12003
12004	12005	12007	12011	12012
12013	12014	12015	*12017	12018
12019	12020	12021	*12022	12023
12024	12025	12026	12027	12028
12029	12030	12031	12032	12033
12034	12035	12036	12037	12038
12039	12040	12041	12042	12043
12044	12047	12048	12049	12050
12051	12052	12053	*12054	12056
12057	12058	12059	12060	12061
12062	12063	12064	12066	12067
12068	*12069	12070	12071	12072
12073	12074	12075	*12076	*12077
*12078	12079	12081	12082	*12084
*12085	12086	*12089	12090	12091
12092	12093	*12094	12095	12096
12097	12099	12100	12101	*12102
12103	12104	12105	12106	12107
12108	12109	12110	12111	12112
*12114	12115	12117	12118	12119
12120	12121	*12122	12123	12124
*12125	12126	†12127	12128	12129
12130	12132	*12133	12134	12135
12136	12137	12138	12140	12141
12142	12143	12144	12145	†12148
†12149	12155	12838	12850	*12851
*12852	*12854	12855		

#528A 2¢ WASHINGTON Type VI
103 Plates

Basic Price	T	$430
Basic Price	L, R, B	$400

The plate printers initials O A M are found on the plate number block of 11590 top.
This block is valued at..........................$500

†11562	*11585	*11586	11587	11588
11590	11599	11600	11601	11603
11604	11605	11606	11607	11608
11609	11611	11612	*11613	11615
11616	*11617	*11618	11620	11624
11629	11630	11631	11632	11633
*11634	*11635	11636	11637	11638
11639	11641	11642	11643	*11646
11647	11648	11649	11650	11651
11652	*11653	11654	11655	11656
11657	11658	*11659	11660	*11661
11662	11663	11664	11665	11666
11667	11668	*11669	11670	11671
11673	11674	11675	11676	11677
11678	11679	11680	11681	11682
11683	11684	11685	11686	11688
†11690	11691	11692	11693	11694
11695	11696	11697	11698	11699
11700	11703	11706	†11707	11708
11709	11710	11712	11713	11717
11818	11819	11820		

#528B 2¢ WASHINGTON Type VII
604 Plates

Basic Price	T	$175
Basic Price	L, R, B	$150

12151	12152	12153	12157	*12158
12159	12160	†12161	12162	12164
12165	12166	12167	12168	12169
12170	12171	12172	12173	12174
12175	12176	12177	12178	*12179
12180	12182	12183	12184	12185
12186	12187	†12188	12189	12190
12191	*12192	12193	12194	12195
12197	12198	12199	12200	12201
12202	12203	12205	*12207	12208
12209	12210	12212	12213	12215
12217	12219	12220	12221	12222
12223	12224	12225	12226	12227
12228	*12229	12230	12239	†12240
12241	12242	12243	12244	12245
12246	12247	12248	*12249	12250
*12251	12252	*12253	12254	12255
12256	12257	*12258	12259	12260
12262	12263	12264	12265	12266
12267	12268	12269	12270	12271
12272	12274	12275	12276	12277
12278	12279	12280	12281	12282
12283	12284	12285	12286	12287
12288	12289	12290	12291	12292
12293	*12294	12295	12296	12297
12298	12299	12301	12302	12303
12304	12305	12306	12307	12308
12309	12310	12311	12312	12313
12314	12315	12316	12318	*12319
12320	12321	12324	*12325	12326
12327	12328	12329	12330	12331
12332	12333	12334	12335	12336
12338	12339	12340	*12341	12342
12343	†12344	12345	12346	12347
†12348	*12349	12350	12351	12352
12353	12354	*12355	12356	12357
*12358	12359	*12360	†12361	12362
12363	*12364	12365	*12367	12368
12370	12371	12372	*12373	12374
*12375	12376	*12377	12378	*12379
12380	12381	*12391	12393	12394
12396	†12397	12398	12399	*12402
12403	12404	†12405	12406	12407
12408	12409	12410	12411	12412
12413	12415	12416	12417	12618
12619	12620	12621	12623	*12624
12625	†12626	12627	*12629	*12630
12631	*12633	*12634	12635	12636
12637	12638	12640	12641	12642
12643	12644	12645	†12646	*12647
*12648	12649	12650	12651	12652
12653	12654	12655	†12656	12657
12658	12659	12660	12661	12662
12663	*12664	*12665	*12666	12667
12668	12669	12670	12671	12672
12673	12674	12675	12677	*12678
12679	12680	12682	12683	*12684
12685	12686	12687	*12688	*12689
12690	12691	12692	12693	12694
12695	12696	12697	12698	12699

1918-20 REGULAR ISSUE

#528B 2¢ WASHINGTON Type VII Cont.

†12700	12701	12702	12703	12704
12705	12706	12707	12709	12710
12711	12712	12713	*12714	12715
12716	12717	12718	12719	12720
12721	12722	12723	*12724	*12725
12726	12727	12728	12729	*12730
†12731	*12732	12733	12734	*12735
12736	†12738	12739	12740	12741
12742	*12743	12744	12745	12746
12747	12748	12749	12750	12751
12752	*12754	12756	12758	*12762
12764	12765	12767	12768	12769
†12770	*12771	12772	*12773	12774
12776	*12777	*12778	*12779	12780
12781	*12782	12785	12786	12789
*12790	*12791	12792	†12794	†12795
†12796	12797	12798	12799	12800
12801	12803	†12804	*12805	12806
12807	*12808	12809	12810	12811
12812	*12813	12814	12815	12816
*12817	12818	12819	12821	12822
12823	12824	12825	12826	12827
12828	12829	12830	*12831	12832
12833	12834	12835	12840	*12841
*12843	*12844	12845	12846	12847
†12848	*12858	12859	12860	12861
12862	12863	*12864	12868	*12869
12870	*12871	12872	12873	12874
12875	12876	12877	12879	12880
12881	12882	12883	12884	12885
12886	12887	*12888	*12889	12890
12891	12892	12893	12894	12895
12896	*12897	12898	12899	12900
*12903	12904	12905	*12907	*12908
*12909	12910	12911	12912	12913
*12914	*12915	12916	12917	13018
13019	13020	13021	13022	13023
13024	13025	13026	13027	13028
*13029	13030	*13031	13032	13033
*13034	13035	*13037	*13038	*13039
13040	*13041	13042	*13043	13044
*13045	*13046	*13047	*13048	13049
13050	*13051	13052	13053	13054
*13055	*13056	13057	13058	*13059
13060	13061	13062	*13063	*13064
13066	*13067	13069	13070	13071
13072	13073	13075	13076	13077
13078	13079	13080	*13081	*13082
13083	13084	*13085	13086	13087
*13088	13089	13090	13091	13092
13093	*13095	13096	13097	13098
13099	13100	13101	13102	13103
13106	13107	13108	13109	13110
13111	13112	*13113	*13114	13115
*13116	*13117	*13118	13119	*13120
*13121	13122	*13123	13124	13125
13126	13127	13128	13129	13130
13131	13132	13133	*13134	13136
13137	13139	13141	13142	*13143
*13145	*13157	13158	*13159	13160
13161	†13162	*13163	13164	

#529 3¢ WASHINGTON Tp. III 127 Plates

Basic Price	T	$55
Basic Price	L, R, B	$50

*8370	8375	8379	*8380	8381
8382	8383	8384	8385	8411
8412	8413	*8414	8415	8417
8418	8420	8421	8554	8556
8557	8558	*8559	8560	8561
*8562	8563	*8564	*8565	8567
8568	8569	8572	8573	*8574
8578	8579	8580	8581	8582
*8583	8584	8585	*8586	8587
8588	*8589	*8590	*8591	8592
*8593	8596	8597	8598	*8599
8600	8601	8602	8604	8605
8606	*8607	8608	8609	8610
*8611	8612	*8613	8614	8615
8616	†8617	*8618	*8619	*8620
*8621	*8622	8625	8626	8627
8628	8629	8630	8631	8632
8633	8634	8635	8636	8637
8639	8640	8641	8642	8643
8644	8645	8646	*8647	8648
8649	8650	8651	8652	8653
8654	8655	8656	8657	8658
*8659	*8660	*8661	8662	8663
8664	8665	8666	8667	8668
8669	*8670	*8671	8672	8674
*8700	†8717			

#530 3¢ WASHINGTON Tp. IV 566 Plates

Basic Price	T	$18
Basic Price	L, R, B	$15

†8720	*8721	*8722	*8723	8724
†8725	8726	8728	*8730	8731
8732	8733	8734	8735	8736
8737	8738	8739	8740	8741
8742	8743	8744	8745	8746
8747	8748	8749	*8750	8751
8752	8754	8755	8756	8757
8759	8760	8761	8762	*8763
8764	8765	8766	8769	8772
8773	8774	8775	8776	*8777
8778	8779	8780	8781	8782
8784	8785	8786	8787	8788
8789	8790	8791	8792	8793
8794	8795	8796	8797	8798
8799	8800	8801	8802	8803
8804	8805	8808	8809	8810
8811	8812	8813	†8814	8815
8816	8817	8818	8819	8820
8821	8824	8825	*8828	8329
8830	8831	8832	8833	8834
8835	8836	8837	8838	8839
8840	8841	8842	8844	8845
8846	8848	8852	8853	*8854
8855	*8856	*8857	8859	8860
8861	8862	*8863	8955	*8956
*8958	8959	8961	8962	8963
8965	8966	8967	8968	†8969
8970	8971	8972	8973	*8974
*8975	8976	8977	8978	8979
8980	8981	8982	8983	8985

1918-20 REGULAR ISSUE

#530 3¢ WASHINGTON Type IV Cont.

*8986	8987	8988	*8989	8990
8991	8992	8995	8996	8997
8998	8999	9000	9001	9002
9003	9004	9005	9006	9007
9008	9009	9010	9011	9012
*9013	9014	*9015	9016	9017
9018	9019	9020	9021	9023
9024	*9026	9027	9028	9029
*9030	*9033	*9034	9035	*9036
*9037	9038	*9039	*9042	*9044
*9045	9046	*9047	*9048	9050
*9051	9052	9055	9056	9057
9058	9059	9061	9062	9063
9064	*9065	9066	9069	*9071
9072	9073	9074	9075	9077
9078	9079	9080	*9081	9082
9083	9084	9085	9086	9087
9088	9089	9090	9091	9092
9093	9094	9251	9252	9253
9254	9255	9256	9263	9265
*9268	9270	9274	9275	*9278
9279	9280	9281	9286	9287
9288	9289	9292	9293	9294
9295	9296	*9297	9298	9300
9301	9302	9303	9304	9305
9309	9310	9311	9312	9313
9314	9323	9324	9325	9326
9327	9330	9331	9332	9333
9334	*9335	9336	9337	9338
9339	*9340	9341	*9342	9343
9344	9346	9347	9348	9349
9350	9351	9352	9353	9354
9355	9356	9357	9358	9359
9360	9361	9362	9363	*9365
9366	*9367	9368	9369	9371
9372	9373	9374	9375	9376
9377	9378	9379	9380	*9381
9382	9383	9384	9385	9386
*9388	9389	*9390	9391	*9392
9393	9394	*9395	9396	9398
9405	9406	*9407	9408	9482
9483	9484	*9485	9490	9491
9492	9493	9494	9495	9500
9501	9502	9503	9504	9505
9506	9507	9512	9513	9514
9529	9530	9531	9532	9533
9534	9535	9536	9537	9538
9543	9544	9545	*9546	9547
*9548	9549	9550	9553	9554
9559	9561	9562	*9566	9572
9573	9574	9575	9576	9577
9578	9579	9580	9581	9583
9585	9586	9587	9588	9589
9590	9591	9592	9593	9594
9595	9596	9597	*9598	9599
9600	*9601	9602	9603	9604
*9605	*9606	*9607	9608	*9609
*9611	9612	9613	9614	9615
*9616	9617	9618	9619	9620
9621	*9622	*9623	9624	9625

#530 3¢ WASHINGTON Type IV Cont.

9626	9627	9628	9629	9630
9631	9632	*9633	9634	9635
9636	*9637	9638	9639	9646
*9647	9648	9649	*9650	9651
9652	*9653	9654	9655	*9656
9657	9658	9659	*9660	9666
*9667	9668	9669	9670	*9671
9686	*9687	*9688	*9689	*9690
9691	9695	9696	9697	9704
9705	9706	9707	*9708	*9709
*9726	*9727	9728	9729	9730
9731	9732	9733	9784	*9785
9786	9799	*9800	9801	*9813
9814	9815	9816	9832	9845
9846	9847	9848	9849	*9850
9851	9852	9853	9854	9855
9856	9857	9858	9863	9864
9865	9866	9867	9868	9882
9883	9884	9885	9886	9887
9888	9889	9898	*9899	9900
*9901	9903	*9904	9905	9910
*9911	*9912	*9913	9922	9923
9924	9925	9926	*9927	9930
*9933				

IMPERFORATE

#531 1¢ WASHINGTON 22 Plates

Basic Price T $90

Basic Price L, R, B $80

9402	9509	9521	9523	9527
9540	9558	9789	*9808	9817
9818	9819	9828	*9830	*9906
*9920	9951	*9952	*9954	*9965
*9967				

#532 2¢ WASHINGTON Type IV 7 Plates

Basic Price T $350

Basic Price L, R, B $300

10864	10881	*10892	10896	10915
10918	*10919			

#533 2¢ WASHINGTON Type V 4 Plates

Basic Price T $1,700

Basic Price L, R, B $1,600

11260	11893	11895	11896

#534 2¢ WASHINGTON Tp. Va 35 Plates

Basic Price T $110

Basic Price L, R, B $95

11356	11373	11380	11384	11390
*11398	11403**N**	11410	11412	11414
11415	11422	11425	11428	11431
11433	11434**N**	11439	*11443	*11493
11853	11854	11855	*11860	11862
11864	11865	11866	11887	*12002
12007	*12025	12028	12109	12119

N (O A M) blocks are valued at $200

1918-1920 REGULAR ISSUE

#534A 2¢ WASHINGTON Tp. VI 12 Plates

Basic Price T $350
Basic Price L, R, B $325

*11629 11641 11654 11667 11668
*11669 11673 11688 11696 *11699
11703 11710

#534B 2¢ WASHINGTON Tp. VII 8 Plates

Basic Price T $12,000
Basic Price L, R, B $11,000

12252 12274 12275 12280 12288
12305 12778 12809

#535 3¢ WASHINGTON Tp. IV 29 Plates

Basic Price T $75
Basic Price L, R, B $65

8781 8787 8979 9004 9019
9023 9024 *9048 9050 *9055
9252 9255 9256 9323 9324
9331 9332 9333 9334 9384
9385 9386 9391 9393 9394
9408 *9637 9926 *9930

#536 1¢ WASHINGTON 7 Plates
"ROSSBACK" Perf. 12°

Basic Price T $160
Basic Price L, R, B $150

9985 9993 10001 10025 10032
10033 10052

1919 COMMEMORATIVE

Unwatermarked Perf. 11
FLAT PRESS Block of 6

#537 3¢ VICTORY 16 Plates

		TL	TR	L	R	B
9412	$100	☐	☐	☐	☐	☐
9413	$100	☐	☐	☐	☐	☐
9414	$100	☐	☐	☐	☐	☐
9415	$100	☐	☐	☐	☐	☐
9416	$100	☐	☐	☐	☐	☐
9417	$100	☐	☐	☐	☐	☐
9418	$100	☐	☐	☐	☐	☐
9419	$100	☐	☐	☐	☐	☐
9426	$100	☐	☐	☐	☐	☐
9427	$100	☐	☐	☐	☐	☐
9428	$100	☐	☐	☐	☐	☐
9429	$100	☐	☐	☐	☐	☐
9430	$100	☐	☐	☐	☐	☐
9431	$100	☐	☐	☐	☐	☐
9432	$100	☐	☐	☐	☐	☐
9433	$100	☐	☐	☐	☐	☐

1919-22 REGULAR ISSUE

COIL WASTE

Unwatermarked Perf. 11x10
ROTARY PRESS Block of 4

Please refer to Appendix D for description of marginal markings

#538 1¢ WASHINGTON 88 Plates

Arrangement #10

Basic Price T $100

8336 8839 8340 9099 9111
9112 9113 9114 9141 9142
9151 9152 *9450 *9451 9452
9453 9463 9464 9467 9468
*10087 *10089 10090 10103 10104
10184 10185 10202 *10203 10347
10348 10350 10361 10640 *10641
*10643 *10686 10687 *10688 *10689
10690 10691 10692 10693 10694
10695 *11740 *11741 11742 11743
11764 11765 11766 11767 13312
13313 13314 13315

Arrangement #8

Basic Price T $100

13445 13446 *13447 *13448 13575
13576 13611 13612 *13615

Arrangement #11

Basic Price T $100

*13810 13811 13812 13813 *13820
13826 13827 13856 13857 13872
13873 13896 13897 13910 *13911
13930 13942 13943 13968 13976
14104

#539 2¢ WASHINGTON Type III 2 Plates
Arrangement #3 **Blocks of 4**

Basic Price T $17,500

7462 7463

1919-22 REGULAR ISSUE

#540 2¢ WASHINGTON Type III

Arrangement #10 **271 Plates**

Basic Price T $100

8171	8172	8327	*8328	8329
8928	8939	8940	9103	9104
9105	9106	9153	9154	*9233
9234	9235	9236	9237	*9458
*9465	9466	9469	9470	*10097
*10098	10115	*10116	*10175	*10176
*10177	10178	10183	10295	*10296
10297	10306	10307	*10308	*10315
*10316	10317	*10318	10384	*10386
*10387	10388	10389	10444	10445
10446	*10447	10448	10449	10450
10451	10452	10453	*10466	*10467
*10468	10469	*10470	10478	10479
10480	10485	10486	*10488	10489
*10491	*10492	*10648	*10649	10650
10651	10652	10670	10671	10680
10681	10723	10724	10725	10726
10727	*10728	*10729	10730	10731
10732	*10733	10738	10739	10740
10741	*10750	*11724	*11726	*11727
*11730	11731	11732	*11733	11734
11735	11736	11737	11769	11770
11771	11772	*11797	*11798	*11799
*11800	*11808	*11809	*11810	*11811
*12464	*12465	*12466	12469	12470
12471	12472	*12473	12474	12475
12476	12483	12484	12485	12486
*12513	12514	12515	12516	12517
12518	12519	12520	12529	12530
12531	12532	12601	12602	12603
12604	12918	12919	*12920	12921
12922	*12927	*12928	12929	*12970
*12971	*12972	*12973	13002	13004
13005	13239	13240	13253	13254
13286	13287	13288	*13289	13290
13291	13292	13293	*13294	13295
13386	13387	13388	13536	13537
13538	13539			

Arrangement #10 ***S 30 inverted***

Price T $500

10471

Arrangement #8

Basic Price T $100

13397	13398	13399	13400	*13414
*13418	*13511	13512	*13514	13583
13584	13585	13586	13595	13596
13597	13598	13599	13600	13601
13602	13603	13604	*13647	*13648
13651	13652	*13657	*13658	13677
13678	13692	13693	13694	13695
13718	13719	13720	*13721	13740
*13764				

#540 2¢ WASHINGTON Type III Cont.

Arrangement #11

Basic Price T $100

13741	13742	13743	*13765	13766
13767	*13777	13778	*13779	13786
*13788	*13789	13802	*13803	13807
13809	13814	13815	*13831	13840
13938	13939	13958	*13959	13984
13985	14030	14031	14032	*14033
14038	14039	14040	14041	*14050
14051	14052	14053	14054	14055
14056	14057			

#541 3¢ WASHINGTON Type II 20 Plates

Arrangement #8

Basic Price T $350

8454	8482	8483	8923	8924
8949	8950	8951	9107	9108
9109	9110	9133	9134	9135
9136	*9143	*9144	9145	9146

1922 SPECIAL PRINTINGS

COIL WASTE

ROTARY PRESS

PERF. 10 VERT. IMPERF. HOR.

#538a 1¢ WASHINGTON 2 Plates

Arrangement #8

Basic Price T $1,000

13611 13612

#540a 2¢ WASHINGTON Type III

Arrangement #8

Price T $1,000

13740

Arrangement #11

Price T $1,000

13741

A sealed package of 100 panes of 170 of each denomination was obtained by E. C. Worden (probably from the Philatelic Agency in Washington), and consigned to the Scott Stamp & Coin Co. in New York, which sold them as "errors" for 50¢ per stamp in July 1922. Thus fifty plate blocks of each plate number potentially exist. Johl says that this issue was produced as the result of a misunderstood order for stamps imperforate in top and bottom margins only, which were available later that summer through the Philatelic Agency. See the U.S. Specialist, August 1986, p345.

PERF. 11x10, EXCEPT IMPERF. IN THE TOP MARGIN

We list below those plates known to exist on 538 and 540 with imperforate top margins. Most of these come from the Philatelic Agency stock that was imperforate in both top and bottom margins, but some may have resulted from regularly issued coil waste that had only imperforate top margins. Please report any other plate blocks with imperf top margins.

#538 1¢ WASHINGTON 4 Plates

Basic Price T $150

Arrangement #8

13611 13612

Arrangement #11

13812 13813

#540 2¢ WASHINGTON Type III 4 Plates

Basic Price T $150

Arrangement #11

13778 13779 13786 13840

1919-22 REGULAR ISSUE

ROTARY PRESS Perf. 10 x 11

Block of 6

#542 1¢ WASHINGTON 12 Plates

Side plate numbers only

Basic Price **L, R** $150

10151 10152 10436 10437 10439
10509 10510 10635 11738 11739
12467 12468

ROTARY PRESS Perf. 10

#543 1¢ WASHINGTON 64 Plates

Block of 6

Side plate numbers only

Basic Price **L, R** $40

12467 12468 12495 12496 12597
12598 12599 12600 13284 13285
13352 13353 13354 13355 13419
13420 13522 13523 13573 13574
13609 13610 13613 13614 13649
13650 13675 13676

Block of 4

With corner plate numbers

Basic Price **UL, UR, LL, LR** $15

13744 13745 13762 13763 13784
13785 13790 13791 13858 13859
13876 13877 13890 13891 13892
13893 13908 13909 13937 13940
13941 13948 13949 13962 13963
13982 13983 13990 13991 14000
14001 14006 14007 14012 14013
14293

ROTARY PRESS Perf.11

#544 1¢ WASHINGTON

No plate number reported to date.

COIL WASTE

Please refer to Appendix D for a description of marginal markings.

ROTARY PRESS Perf.11

#545 1¢ WASHINGTON 38 Plates

Arrangement #10

Basic Price T $1,000

10090 *10640 *10686 10687 11764
*11765 11766 *11767 13314 13315

Arrangement #8

Basic Price T $1,000

13445 13446 *13447 *13448 13491
13492 13575 13576 13611 13612
*13615 13616

Arrangement #11

Basic Price T $1,000

*13812 13813 *13826 13827 13856
13857 13872 13873 13896 13897
13906 13907 13910 13931 13969
13976

1919-22 REGULAR ISSUE

#546 2¢ WASHINGTON 80 Plates

Arrangement #10

Basic Price		T		$750
10651	*10670	10671	*10750	*11726
*11727	11730	11731	11732	11734
*12465	*12466	12470	*12473	*12474
12483	12484	12485	12486	*12513
12514	12515	*12516	12517	*12518
*12519	*12529	12918	12919	*12920
12922	12929	*13292	*13293	*13386
*13387	*13388			

Arrangement #8

Basic Price		T		$750
*13397	*13398	*13508	*13511	*13512
13583	13584	13595	13596	*13647
*13648	13651	13652	*13657	*13658
13677	13678	13692	13693	13694
13718	13719			

Arrangement #11

Basic Price		T		$750
13807	13814	13815	*13840	*13841
*13842	13843	13874	13875	*13894
*13895	13938	13939	13958	*13959
*13960	*13970	*13971	14031	14040
14041				

All issues after this point are on unwatermarked paper unless otherwise noted.

Flat plate stamps from here on have F in TR position unless otherwise noted.

1920 COMMEMORATIVES

FLAT PRESS Perf. 11

Block of 6

#548 1¢ PILGRIM 12 Plates

		TL	TR	L	R	B
12418	$50	☐	☐	☐	☐	☐
12419	$50	☐	☐	☐	☐	☐
12420	$50	☐	☐	☐	☐	☐
12421	$50	☐	☐N	☐	☐	☐
12428	$50	☐	☐N	☐	☐	☐
12429	$50	☐	☐	☐	☐	☐
12431	$50	☐Z	☐	☐	☐	☐
12436	$50	☐	☐	☐	☐	☐
12437	$50	☐	☐	☐	☐	☐
12438	$50	☐	☐	☐	☐	☐
12439	$50	☐Z	☐	☐	☐	☐
12448	$50	☐	☐	☐	☐	☐

N The letter F is on the left bottom position and is inverted in relation to the plate number. The right bottom has only the plate number. The TR position has no letter F.

Z F in TL position

#547 $2 FRANKLIN

Price Block of 8 $5,000

Frame Plate 8177 **Vignette Plate** 8179

1920 COMMEMORATIVES

#549 2¢ PILGRIM 20 Plates

		TL	TR	L	R	B
12422	$60	□	□	□	□	□
12423	$60	□ Z	□	□	□	□
12424	$60	□	□	□	□	□
12425	$60	□	□	□	□	□
12432	$60	□	□	□	□	□
12433	$60	□	□	□	□	□
12434	$60	□	□	□	□	□
12435	$60	□	□	□	□	□
12440	$60	□	□	□	□	□
12441	$60	□	□	□	□	□
12442	$60	□	□	□	□	□
12443	$60	□	□	□	□	□
12444	$60	□ N	□ N	□	□	□
12445	$60	□	□	□	□	□
12446	$60	□	□	□	□	□
12447	$60	□	□	□	□	□
12452	$60	□	□	□	□	□
12453	$60	□	□	□	□	□
12454	$60	□	□	□	□	□
12455	$60	□	□	□	□	□

Z F in TL position instead of TR
N F in Both positions

#550 5¢ PILGRIM 2 Plates

12426	$500	□	□	□	□	□
12427	$500	□	□	□	□	□

1922-25 REGULAR ISSUE

The first plates used for the Series of 1922 were the "A" plates with the uniform 2 3/4mm vertical gutters. On the lower denominations which were arranged vertically, the plates measured 21.6cm (8.5 inches) from the center vertical guideline to the edge of the last printed stamps. On the higher denominations arranged horizontally, this measurement is in the vertical direction. These are called "narrow gauge" plates. In 1925 the Bureau began to make plates with wider spacing. After an initial trial with an intermediate spacing, 21.85cm, the spacing adopted was 22.0cm, and these are called "wide gauge" plates. After the first such set, most wide gauge plates were marked with a star to indicate the wider spacing (indicated by the symbol S). Except on one plate, the stars were large ones (5mm) and were placed at first to the left of the TR plate number. Later they were placed below the side plate number on the UR pane. At first both 5 and 6 point stars were used, but later only 5 point ones were used. We list star plate blocks separately, but we will also indicate wide gauge plates without stars by the symbol W after the plate number, except on the 1/2 and 1 1/2 denominations, all plates of which were wide gauge.

FLAT PRESS Perf. 11
Block of 6

#551 .5¢ NATHAN HALE 49 Plates
Basic Price **TL, TR, L, R, B** $7

17017	17018	17019	17020	17029
17030	17031	17032	17033	17034
17035	17036	17037	17038	17039
17040	17041	17042	17043	17044
17045	17046	17047	17048	17049
17050	17051	17052	17054	17055
17056	17057	17058	17071	17072
17073	17074	17075	17076	17077
17078	17079	17080	17081	17082
17083	17084	17085	17086	

#552 1¢ FRANKLIN 255 Plates
Basic Price **TL, TR, L, R, B** $28

14157	14158	14159	14160	14191
14192	14193	14194	14215	14216
14217	14218	14243	14244	14245
14246	14254	14255	14256	14257
14281	14283	14284	*14975	*14976
14977	*14978	*15021	15022	15023
15024	*15043	15044	15045	15046
15047	15048	15049	15050	15069
15070	15071	15072	15073	15074
15075	15076	15093	15094	15095
15096	15105	15106	15107	15108
15133	*15134	15135	15136	15143
15144	15145	15146	15159	15160

1922-25 REGULAR ISSUE

#552 1¢ FRANKLIN Cont.

15161	15162	15185	15186	15187
15188	15215	15216	15217	15218
15267	15268	15269	15270	15285
15286	15287	15288	15292	15293
*15294	15295	15296	*15297	15298
15299	*15300	*15301	*15302	15303
15310	*15311	*15312	15313	15314
*15315	15316	15317	15318	15319
15320	15321	15328	15329	15330
15331	15332	15333	15334	15335
15342	15343	15344	15345	15358
15359	15360	15361	15366	15367
15368	15369	15372	15373	15374
15375	15380	15381	15382	15383
15384	15385	15386	15387	15398
15399	15400	15401	15408	15409
15410	15411	15420	15421	15422
15423	15429	15430	15431	15432
15437	15438	15439	15440	15453
15454	15455	15456	15489	15490
15491	15492	15584	15585	15586
15587	15953	15954	15955	15956
15979	15980	15981	15982	15983
15984	15985	15986	15987	15988
15989	15990	15991	15992	15993
15994	15995	15996	15997	15998
15999	16000	16001	16002	16003
16004	16005	16006	16007	16008
16009	16010	16017	16018	16019
16020	16023	16024	16025	16026
16027	16028	16029	16030	16031
16032	16033	16034	16035	16036
16037	16038	16041	16042	16043
16044	16049	16050	16051	16052
16055	16056	16057	16058	16061
16062	16556	16557	16558	16559
16560	16561	†16562	*16563	16564
16565	16568	16569	16570	*16571

#553 1.5¢ HARDING(PROFILE) 66 Plates

Basic Price **TL, TR, L, R, B** $32

16829	16830	16831	16832	16837
16838	16839	16840	16841	16842
16843	16844	16845	16846	16847
16848	16861	16862	16863	16864
16865	16866	16867	16868	16869
16870	16871	16872	16873	16874
16875	16876	16877	16878	16879
16880	16910	16911	16912	16913
16914	16915	16916	16917	16930
16931	*16932	16933	16934	16935
16936	*16937	16938	16939	16940
16941	*16968	16970	16971	16972
16973	16974	16975	16982	*16983
*16984				

#554 2¢ WASHINGTON 1363 Plates

Except as noted, plates prior to 17000 are narrow gauge.

Basic Price **TL, TR, L, R, B** $25

14074	14075	14076	14077	14082

#554 2¢ WASHINGTON Cont.

14083	14084	14085	14086	14087
14088	14089	14090	14091	14092
14093	14100	14101	14102	14103
14105	14106	14107	14108	14113
14114	14115	14116	14119	14120
14121	14122	14127	14128	14129
14130	14139	14140	14141	14142
14143	14144	14145	14146	14151
14152	14153	14154	14161	14162
14163	14164	14165	14166	14167
14168	14177	14178	14179	14180
14185	14186	14187	14188	14195
14196	14197	14198	14211	14212
14213	14214	14225	14226	14227
14228	14258	14259	14260	14261
*14277	14278	14279	14280	14300
14301	14302	14303	14307	14308
14309	14310	14313	14314	14315
14316	14317	14318	14319	14320
14322	14323	14324	14325	14332
14333	14334	14335	14336	14337
14338	14339	14344	14345	14346
14347	14350	14351	14352	14353
14354	14355	14356	14357	14360
14361	14362	14363	14364	14365
14366	14367	14374	14375	14376
14377	14378	14379	14380	14381
14386	14387	14388	14389	14390
14391	14392	14393	14396	14397
14398	14399	14400	14401	14402
14403	14408	14409	14410	14411
14412	14413	14414	14415	14422
14423	14424	14425	14426	14427
14428	14429	14430	14431	14432
14433	14440	14441	14442	14443
14444	14445	14446	14447	14448
14449	14450	14451	14452	14453
14454	14455	14458	14459	14460
14461	14466	14467	14468	14469
14470	14471	14472	14473	14474
14475	14496	14497	14498	14500
14501	14502	14503	14504	14505
14506	14507	14508	14509	14510
14511	14518	14519	14520	14521
14522	14523	14524	14525	14529
14530	14531	14532	14533	14534
14535	14536	14539	14540	14541
14542	14543	14544	14545	14546
14555	*14556	14557	14558	14575
14576	14577	14578	14620	14621
14622	14623	14626	14627	14628
14629	14636	14637	14638	14639
14644	14645	14646	14647	14656
14657	14658	14668	14669	14670
14671	14672	14673	14674	14675
14676	14677	14678	14679	14684
14685	14686	14687	14688	14689
14690	14691	14692	14693	14694
14695	14696	14697	14698	14699
14700	14701	14702	14703	14708
14709	14710	14711	14712	14713

1922-25 REGULAR ISSUE

#554 2¢ WASHINGTON Cont.

14714	14715	14716	14717	14718
14719	14722	14723	14724	14725
14726	14727	14729	14738	14739
14740	14741	14742	14743	14744
14745	14746	14747	14748	14749
14750	14751	14752	*14753	*14758
14759	14760	14761	14762	14763
14764	14765	14768	14769	14770
14771	14772	14773	14774	14775
14778	14779	14780	14781	14782
14783	14784	14785	14786	14787
14788	14789	14790	14791	14792
14793	14800	14801	14802	14803
14804	14805	14806	14807	14820
14821	14822	14823	14832	14833
14834	14835	14836	14837	14838
14839	14922	14923	14924	14925
15247	15248	15249	15250	15281
15282	15283	15284	15306	15307
15308	15309	*15324	15325	15326
15327	15336	15337	15338	15339
15354	15355	15356	15357	15362
15363	15364	15365	15376	15377
15378	15379	15388	15389	15390
15391	15394	15395	15396	15397
15402	15403	15404	15405	15424
15425	15426	15427	†15433	15434
15435	15436	15445	15446	15447
15448	15457	*15458	15459	15460
15465	15466	15467	15468	15469
15470	15471	15472	15481	15482
15483	15484	15493	15494	15495
15496	15501	15502	15503	15504
15514	15515	15516	15517	15592
15593	15594	15595	15596	15597
15598	15599	15602	15603	15604
15605	15606	15607	15608	15609
15612	15613	15614	15615	15622
15623	15624	15625	15626	15627
15628	15629	15630	15631	15632
15633	15634	15635	15636	15637
15640	15641	15642	15643	15644
15645	15646	15647	15648	15649
15650	15651	15656	15657	15658
15659	15660	15661	15662	15663
15668	15669	15670	15671	15672
15673	15674	15675	15680	15681
15682	15683	15684	15685	15686
15687	15688	15689	15690	15691
15696	15697	15698	15699	15700
15701	15702	15703	15708	15709
15710	15711	15712	15713	15714
15715	15716	15717	15718	15719
15726	15727	15728	15729	15736
15737	15738	15739	15748	15749
15750	15751	15770	15771	15772
15773	15812	15813	15814	15815
15816	15817	15818	15819	15834
15835	15836	15837	15842	15843
15844	15845	15850	15851	15852
15853	15864	15865	15866	15867
15872	15873	15874	15875	15878

#554 2¢ WASHINGTON Cont.

15879	15880	15881	15882	15883
15884	15885	15896	15897	15898
15899	15904	15905	15906	15907
15912	15913	15914	15915	15932
15933	15934	15935	15969	15970
15971	15972	16095	16096	16097
16098	16099	16100	16101	16102
16103	16104	16105	16106	16111
16112	16113	16114	16115	16116
16117	16118	16123	16124	16125
16126	16127	16128	16129	16130
*16131	16132	16133	16134	16140
16141	16142	16143	16148	16149
16150	16151	*16152	16153	*16154
16155	16157	16158	16159	16160
16165	16166	16167	16168	16179
16180	16181	16182	16183	16184
16185	16186	16187	16188	16189
16190	16197	16198	16199	16200
16205	16206	16207	16208	16221
16222	16223	16224	16225	16226
16227	16228	16231	16232	16233
16234	16235	16236	16237	16238
16239	16240	16241	16242	16253
16254	16255	16256	16258	16259
16260	16261	16266	16267	16268
16269	16272	16273	16274	16275
16280	16281	16282	16283	16292
16293	16294	16295	16296	16297
16298	16299	16314	16315	16316
16317	16322	16323	16324	16325
16343	16344	16345	16346	16347
16348	16349	16350	16351	16352
16353	16354	16371	16372	16373
16374	16383	16384	16385	16386
16407	16408	16409	16410	16417
16418	16419	16420	16427	16428
16429	16430	16431	16432	16433
16434	16439	16440	16441	16442
16487	16488	16489	16490	16491
16492	16493	16494	16497	16498
16499	16500	16501	16502	16503
16504	16505i	16506i	16507i	16508i
16518	16519	16520	16521	16526
16527	16528	16529	16530	16531
16532	16533	16534	16535	16536
16537	16538	16539	16540	16541
16546	16547	16548	16549	16550
16551	16552	16553	16580	16581
16582	16583	16630	16631	16632
16633	16634	16635	16636	16637
16638	16639	16640	16641	16642
16643	16644	16645	16650	16651
16652	16653	16656w	16657w	16658w
16659w	16697	16698	16699	16700
16713	16714	16715	16716	16717
16718	16719	16720	16721	16722
16723	16724	16737	*16738	16739
16740	16741s	16742	16743	16744
16745	16746	16747	16748	16753
16754	16755	16756	16757	16758s
16759	16760	16761s	16762w	16763s

1922-25 REGULAR ISSUE

#554 2¢ WASHINGTON Cont.

16764s	16785s	16786s	16787s	16788s
*16789	16790s	16791s	16792s	17107s
17108s	17109s	17110s	17111w	17112s
17113s	17114s	17115s	17116s	17117s
17118w	17119s	17120s	17121s	17122s
17123s	17124s	17125s	17126s	17147s
17148s	17149s	17150w	17151s	17152s

All 2¢ plates from here to end are wide gauge star plates.

17153	17154	17163	17164	17165
17166	17179	17180	17181	17182
17187	17188	17189	17190	17195
17196	17197	17198	17207	*17209
17210	17215	17216	17217	17218
17219	17220	17221	17222	17243
17244	17245	17246	17255	*17256
17257	17258	17263	17264	17265
17266	17267	17268	17269	17270
17286	17287	17288	17289	17292
17293	17294	17295	17296	17297
17298	17299	17300	17301	17302
17303	17308	17309	17310	17311
17312	17313	17314	17315	17317
17318	17319	17320	17325	17326
17327	17328	17329	17330	17331
17332	17333	17334	17335	17336
17337	*17338	17339	17340	17341
17342	17343	17344	17345	17346
17347	17348	17349	17350	17351
17352	17357	17358	17359	17360
17361	17362	17363	17364	17367
17368	17369	17370	17371	17372
17373	17374	17375	*17376	17377
17378	17380	17381	17382	17383
17384	17385	17386	17387	17388
*17389	17390	*17391	17392	17393
*17394	*17395	17396	*17397	*17398
*17399	17402	17403	17404	*17405
17489	17490	17491	17492	17534
17535	17536	17537	17538	17539
17540	17541	*17550	17551	17552
17553	17554	*17555	*17556	17557
17576	17577	17578	17579	17580
17581	*17582	17583	17592	17593
*17594	17595	*17596	*17597	17598
*17599	17602	17603	*17604	*17605
*17606	17607	17608	17609	17629
17630	17631	17632	17645	17646
17647	17648	17654	17655	17656
17657	17658	*17659	17660	17661
17666	17667	17668	17669	17670
17671	17672	17673	17676	17677
17678	17679	17687	17688	17689
17690	17695	17696	17697	17698
17699	17700	17701	17702	17705
17706	17707	17708	17709	17710
17711	17712	17717	17718	17719
17720	17721	17722	17723	17724
17726	17727	17728	17730	17731
17732	17733	17734	17735	17736
17737	17740	17741	17742	17743

#554 2¢ WASHINGTON Cont.

17744	17745	17746	17747	17748
17749	17750	17751	17752	17753
17754	17755	*17756	*17757	17758
*17759	17764	17765	17766	17767
17768	*17769	17770	*17771	17778
17779	17780	17781	17782	*17783
17784	17785	17788	17789	17790
17791	17794	17795	17796	17797
17802	17803	17804	17805	17808
17809	17810	17811	17812	17813
17814	17815	17818	17819	17820
17821	17828	17829	17830	17831
17834	17835	17836	17837	17838
17839	17840	17841	17842	17843
17844	17845	17848	17849	17850
17851	17860	17861	17862	17863
17864	17865	17866	17867	17868
17869	17870	17871	17874	17875
17876	17877	17890	17891	17892
17893	17894	17895	17896	17897
18167	18168	18169	18170	18175
18176	18177	18178	18197	18198
18199	18200	18203	18204	18205
18206	18207	18208	18209	*18210
18211	18212	18213	18214	18215
18216	18217	18218	18219	18220
18221	18222	18223	18224	18225
18226	18227	18228		

i Intermediate Gauge (21.85cm); no star
w Wide Gauge (22.0cm); no star
s Wide Gauge (22.0cm); with star

Star Plates

Small five pointed star at left of top plate number of upper right pane.

Price TR $400

16758

Six pointed star at left of top plate number of upper right pane.

Basic Price TR $600

16741	16761	16787	17107	17109
17117	17124	17179	17187	17188
17190				

1922-25 REGULAR ISSUE

#554 2¢ WASHINGTON Cont.

Star Plates

Six pointed star below side plate number of upper right pane.

Price R $850

17196

Large five pointed star at left of top plate number of upper right pane.

Basic Price R $400

16763	16764	16785	16786	16790
16791	16792	17108	17110	17112
17113	17114	17115	17116	17119
17120	17121	17122	17123	17125
17126	17147	17148	17149	17151
17152	17153	17154	17163	17164
17165	17166	17180	17181	17182
17195	17198			

Large five pointed star below side plate number of upper right pane.

Basic Price R $70

16788	17189	17197	17207	*17209
17210	17215	17216	17217	17218
17219	17220	17221	17222	17243
17244	17245	17246	17255	*17256
17257	17258	17263	17264	17265
17266	17267	17268	17269	17270
17286	17287	17288	17289	17292
17293	17294	17295	17296	17297
17298	17299	17300	17301	17302
17303	17308	17309	17310	17311
17312	17313	17314	17315	17317
17318	17319	17320	17325	17326
17327	17328	17329	17330	17331
17332	17333	17334	17335	17336
17337	*17338	17339	17340	17341
17342	17343	17344	17345	17346
17347	17348	17349	17350	17351
17352	17357	17358	17359	17360
17361	17362	17363	17364	17367
17368	17369	17370	17371	17372
17373	17374	17375	*17376	17377
17378	17380	17381	17382	17383
17384	17385	17386	17387	17388
*17389	17390	*17391	17392	17393
*17394	*17395	17396	*17397	*17398
*17399	17402	17403	17404	*17405
17489	17490	17491	17492	17534
17535	17536	17537	17538	17539
17540	17541	*17550	17551	17552
17553	17554	*17555	*17556	17557
17576	17577	17578	17579	17580
17581	*17582	17583	17592	17593
*17594	17595	*17596	*17597	17598
*17599	17602	17603	*17604	*17605
*17606	17607	17608	17609	17629
17630	17631	17632	17645	17646
17647	17648	17654	17655	17656
17657	17658	*17659	17660	17661
17666	17667	17668	17669	17670

#554 2¢ WASHINGTON Cont.

Star Plates

17671	17672	17673	17676	17677
17678	17679	17687	17688	17689
17690	17695	17696	17697	17698
17699	17700	17701	17702	17705
17706	17707	17708	17709	17710
17711	17712	17717	17718	17719
17720	17721	17722	17723	17724
17726	17727	17728	17730	17731
17732	17733	17734	17735	17736
17737	17740	17741	17742	17743
17744	17745	17746	17747	17748
17749	17750	17751	17752	17753
17754	17755	*17756	*17757	17758
*17759	17764	17765	17766	17767
17768	*17769	17770	*17771	17778
17779	17780	17781	17782	*17783
17784	17785	17788	17789	17790
17791	17794	17795	17796	17797
17802	17803	17804	17805	17808
17809	17810	17811	17812	17813
17814	17815	17818	17819	17820
17821	17828	17829	17830	17831
17834	17835	17836	17837	17838
17839	17840	17841	17842	17843
17844	17845	17848	17849	17850
17851	17860	17861	17862	17863
17864	17865	17866	17867	17868
17869	17870	17871	17874	17875
17876	17877	17890	17891	17892
17893	17894	17895	17896	17897
18167	18168	18169	18170	18175
18176	18177	18178	18197	18198
18199	18200	18203	18204	18205
18206	18207	18208	18209	*18210
18211	18212	18213	18214	18215
18216	18217	18218	18219	18220
18221	18222	18223	18224	18225
18226	18227	18228		

#555 3¢ LINCOLN 44 Plates

Basic Price **TL, TR, L, R, B** $175

14296	14297	14298	14299	14734
14735	14736	14737	15171	15172
15173	15174	15550	15551	15552

1922-25 REGULAR ISSUE

#555 3¢ LINCOLN Cont.

15553 15725 16399 16400 16401
16402 16473 16474 16475 16476
16666 16667 16668 16669 16709
16710 16711 16712 16769 16770
*17921 17922 17923 17924 17925
18120 18121 *18122 *18123

#556 4¢ MARTHA WASHINGTON
36 Plates
Basic Price **TL, TR, L, R, B** $175

14094 14095 14096 14097 14796
14797 14798 14799 15085 *15086
15087 15088 15219 15220 15221
15222 15251 15252 15253 15254
15526 15527 15528 15529 16211
16212 16213 16214 16335 16336
16337 16338 16367 16368 *16369
16370

#557 5¢ THEODORE ROOSEVELT
75 Plates
Basic Price **TL, TR, L, R, B** $200

14066 14067 14068 14069**N**14078
14079 14080 14081 14285 14286
14287 14288 14549 14550 14551
14552 14565 14566 14567 14568
14602 14603 14604 14605 14848
14849 14850 14851 14880 14881
14882 14883 14916 14917 14918
14919 14930 14931 14932 14933
15147 15148 15149 15150 15203
15204 15205 15206 15227 15228
15229 15230 15544 15545 15546
15547 15568 15569 15570 15571
15952 16330 16331 16332 16333
16363 16364 16365 16366 16391
*16392 16393 16394 *18035 *18060

N F above LR-R plate number

#557a 5¢ THEODORE ROOSEVELT IMPERFORATE

Only one sheet known, now broken. Bottom plate block realized $6,500 at auction in April 1983.

15568

#558 6¢ GARFIELD 22 Plates
Basic Price **TL, TR, L, R, B** $400

14169 14170 14171 14172 14962
14963 14964 14973 15892 15893
15894 15895 16045 16046 16047
16048 16243 16334 16469 16470
16471 16472

#559 7¢ McKINLEY 61 Plates
Basic Price **TL, TR, L, R, B** $75

14584 14585 14586 14587 14812
14813 14814 14815 14950 14951
14952 14953 15181 15182 15183
15184 15211 15212 15213 15214

#559 7¢ McKINLEY Cont.

15271 15272 15273 15274 15794
16135 16136 16137 16138 16139
16156 16247 16248 *16249 16250
16251 16252 16453 16454 16455
16456 16662 16663 16664 16665
17452 17453 17454 17455 17621
17622 17623 17624 18116 18117
18118 18119 18163 18164 18165
18166

#560 8¢ GRANT 54 Plates
Basic Price **TL, TR, L, R, B** $600

14569 14570 14571 14572 15223
15224 15225 15226 15263 15264
15265 15266 15477 15478 15479
15480 15946 15947 15948 15949
16011 16012 16013 16014 16169
16170 16171 16172 16175 16176
16177 16178 16215 16216 16217
16218 16449 16450 16451 16452
16701 16702 16703 16704 16765
16768 16795 *16796s 17467 17916
17917 17918 17919 17920

Star Plate
Six pointed star at left of top plate number of upper right pane

†16796

Only two TL plate singles are known from this plate.

1922-25 REGULAR ISSUE

#561 9¢ JEFFERSON 16 Plates

Basic Price **TL, TR, L, R, B** $160

14239 14240 14241 14242 15235
15236 15237 15238 15259 15260
15261 15262 17521 *17522 *17523
*17524

#562 10¢ MONROE 103 Plates

Basic Price **TL, TR, L, R, B** $200

14229 14230 14231 14232 14233
14234 14235 14236 14492 14493
14494 14495 14580 14581 14582
14583 14606 14607 14608 14609
14610 14611 14612 14613 14808
14809 14810 14811 14816 14817
14818 14819 14844 14845 14846
14847 15125 15126 15127 15128
15199 15200 15201 15202 15275
15276 15277 15278 15346 15347
15348 15349 15509 *15510 *15511
15512 *15513 15554 15555 15556
15557 15734 15735 15924 15925
15926 15927 15940 15941 15942
15943 16069 16070 16071 16072
16075 16076 16077 16078 16355
16356 16357 16358 16359 16360
16361 16362 16375 16376 16377
16378 16379 16380 16381 16382
16387 16388 16389 16390 *17468
*17469 *18033 *18034

#562a 10¢ MONROE IMPERFORATE

14818 (only Lower Left reported)

#563 11¢ HAYES 28 Plates

Basic Price **TL, TR, L, R, B** $30

14058**N** 14059 14060**Z** 14061 15798
15799 15800 15801 16445 16446
16447 16448 17414w 17415w 17416w
17417w 17456 17457 17458 17459
17617 17618 17619 17620 19135w
19136w 19137w 19138w

N The "F" was originally above the LR-R plate #, but was later moved to the TR position.

Z The "F" was originally below the UL-L plate #, but was later moved to the TR position.

#564 12¢ CLEVELAND 35 Plates

Basic Price **TL, TR, L, R, B** $75

14404 14405 14406 14407 15350
15351 15352 15692 15693 15694
15695 16257 16404 16405 16406
16515 17418s 17419s 17420s 17421s
17470 17471 17472 18031 18032
18398s 18399 18424 18921w 18922w
18923w 19161w 19162w 19163w 19442w

w Wide Gauge (22.0cm); no star
s Wide Gauge (22.0cm); with star

Star Plates

Large five pointed star below side plate number of upper right pane.

Basic Price **R** $125

17418 17419 17420 18398

Six pointed star below side plate number of upper right pane.

Price **R** $250

17421

#622 13¢ HARRISON

See page 92

#565 14¢ AMERICAN INDIAN 20 Plates

Basic Price **TL, TR, L, R, B** $60

14512 14513 14514 14515 14526
15795 15796 15797 16625 17464
17465 17466 19417w 19418w 19419w
19420w 19438w 19439w 19440w 19441w

#566 15¢ STATUE OF LIBERTY 41 Plates

Basic Price **TL, TR, L, R, B** $275

14070 14071 14072 14073 14910
14911 14912 14913 17422s 17423s
17424s 17425s 17430s 17431s 17432s
17433s 17460 17461 17462 17463
17525 17526 17527 17528 *17529
17931 17932 17933 17934 18928w
18929w 18930w 19139w 19140w 19141w
19142w 19462w *19463w

The following have no side plate numbers

*20180w *20181w *20182w

Star Plates

Large five pointed star below side plate number of the upper right pane.

Basic Price **R** $475

17422 17423 17424 17425 17430
17431 17432 17433

#623 17¢ WILSON

See page 92

1922-25 REGULAR ISSUE

#567 20¢ GOLDEN GATE 76 Plates

Basic Price **TL, TR, L, R, B** $250

14559 14560 14561 14562 14966
14967 14968 14969 15536 15537
15538 15539 15572 15573 15574
15575 16646 16647 16648 *16649
17227s 17228s 17229s 17230s 17426s
17427s 17428s 17429s 17530 17531
17532 17533 17682 17683 17684
17685 17686 18377 18668s 18669s
18670s 18671s 18672s 18673s 18674s
18675s 18688s 18689s 18690s 18691s
18925w 18926w 18927w 19131w *19132w
19133w 19134w 19468w 19646w 19647w
19648w 19649w 19872w *20033w *20034w
20037w *20038w

The following have no side plate numbers.

*17725w *20195w *20196w *20197w *20198w
*20271w *20272w *20273w *20274w

Star Plates

Large five pointed star below side plate number of the upper right pane.

Basic Price **R** $500

17227 17228 17229 17230 17426
17427 17428 17429 18668 18669
18670 18671 18672 18673 18674
18675 18688 18689 18690 18691

#568 25¢ NIAGARA FALLS 12 Plates

Basic Price **TL, TR, L, R, B** $225

14062 14063 14064 14065 16626
16627 16628 16629 17442w 17443w
17444w 17445w

w Wide Gauge (22.0cm); no star
s Wide Gauge (22.0cm); with star

#569 30¢ BISON 24 Plates

Basic Price **TL, TR, L, R, B** $250

14436 14437 14438 14439 16065
16066 16067 16068 16465 16466
16467 16468 17446w 17447w 17448w
17449w 17558 17559 17560 17561

The following plates have no side numbers.

*20191w *20192w *20193w *20194w

#570 50¢ AMPHITHEATER 16 Plates

Basic Price **TL, TR, L, R, B** $650

14042 14043 14044 14045Z 15151
15152 15153 15154 17479 17480
17481 17482 19143w 19144w 19145w
19146w

Z F above LR-R plate number

#571 $1 LINCOLN MEMORIAL 5 Plates

Basic Price **TL, TR, B** $425

14268 18642 18680 18681 18682

#572 $2 U.S. CAPITOL 1 Plate

Price **TL, TR, B** $850

14306

#573 $5 AMERICA 1 Combination

Price **T** Block of 8 $2,500

Frame Plate 14327
Vignette Plate 14326

1922-25 REGULAR ISSUE

BOOKLET PANES

PANES OF 6

#552a 1¢ FRANKLIN 20 Plates

Basic Price T $12

14221	14222	14223	14224	14250
14251	14252	1w4253	14269	14270
14271	14272	15961	15962	15963
15964	15965	15966	15967	15968

#554c 2¢ WASHINGTON 194 Plates

Basic Price T $15

14181	14182	14183	14184	14199
14200	14201	14202	14207	14208
*14209	14210	14418	14419	14420
14421	14462	14463	14464	14465
14476	14477	14478	14479	14480
14481	14482	14483	14484	14485
14486	14487	14488	14489	14490
14491	14934	14935	14937	14974
14983	14984	14985	14986	15255
15256	15257	15258	15289	15414
15415	15416	15417	15505	15506
15507	15508	15522	15523	15524
15525	15558	15559	15560	15561
15576	15577	15578	15579	15724
15730	15731	*15732	15733	15790
15791	15792	15793	15804	*15805
15806	15807	16085	16086	16087
16088	16146	16147	16193	16194
16195	16196	16288	16290	16291
16306	16307	16308	16309	16318
16319	16320	16321	16326	16327
16328	16329	16592	16593	16594
16595	16600	16601	16602	16603
16613	16614	16615	16616	16617
16618	16619	*16620	*16621	*16622
16623	16624	16705	16706	16707
16708	16773	*16774	16775	16776
17475	17476	17477	17478	17483
17484	17485	17486	17494	17495
17496	17497	17880	17881	17882
17883	17886	17887	17888	17889
17910	17911	17912	17913	17927
17928	17929	17930	*17941	*17942
17943	*17944	17951	17952	*17953
*17954	*17955	17956	17957	*17958
18259	*18260	*18261	18262	*18297
18298	18299	18300	18373	18374
18383	*18384	18385	18386	18400
*18401	*18408	*18409	18521	

IMPERFORATE

#575 1¢ FRANKLIN 47 Plates

Basic Price TL, TR, L, R, B $85

14157	14158	14159	14160	14217
14244	14245	15045	15069	15106

#575 1¢ FRANKLIN Cont.

15136	15146	15268	15269	15328
15331	15344	15366	15372	15385
15398	15399	15400	15401	15408
*15410	15422	15432	15440	15456
15489	15490	15954	15991	16043
16049	16050	16061	16062	16556
16557	16558	16559	16560	16561
16568	16569			

#576 1.5¢ HARDING (PROFILE) 40 Plates

Basic Price TL, TR, L, R, B $25

16829	16830	16831	16832	16837
16838	16839	16840	16841	16842
16843	16845	16846	16847	16848
16861	16862	16863	16864	16865
16866	16867	16868	16869	16870
16872	16873	16911	16917	*16932
16933	16936	16938	16939	16940
16971	16972	16973	16974	16982

#577 2¢ WASHINGTON 117 Plates

Basic Price TL, TR, L, R, B $30

14091	14093	14177	14178	14179
14180	14195	14196	14197	14198
14323	14325	14332	14334	14449
14455	14536	14555	14577	14691
14759	14760	14761	14763	14764
14771	14781	14788	14820	14821
14822	14823	15640	15642	15686
15690	15699	15739	15835	15836
15843	15881	15970	15971	16096
16097	16098	16099	16101	16104
16105	16130	16151	16190	16208
16235	16520	16580	16645	16651
16714	16722	16724	16739	16743
16755				

All plates from 17122 on are star plates, wide gauge.

17122	17222	*17357	17490	17492
17608	17671	*17677	17679	17696
*17701	17706	17708	17709	17710
17721	17724	17727	17728	17731
17740	17741	17742	17743	17745
17746	17747	17748	17874	17875
17876	17877	17891	18197	18198
18199	18200	18206	18207	18208
18217	18219	*18220	*18221	18222
18223	18224	18225	18226	18227
18228				

Star Plate

Large five pointed star at left of top plate number of upper right pane.

†17122

1922-25 REGULAR ISSUE

#577 2¢ WASHINGTON Cont.

Star Plates

Large five pointed star below side plate number of upper right pane.

Basic Price R $70

17222	†17357	17490	17492	17608
17671	*17677	17679	17696	†17701
17706	17708	17709	17710	17721
17724	17727	17728	17731	17740
17741	17742	17743	17745	17746
17747	17748	17874	17875	17876
17877	17891	18197	18198	18199
18200	18206	18207	18208	18217
18219	*18220	18221	18222	18223
18224	18225	18226	18227	18228

1923-26 REGULAR ISSUE

COIL WASTE

ROTARY PRESS Perf.11x10

Blocks of 4

Please refer to Appendix D for description of marginal markings.

#578 1¢ FRANKLIN 25 Plates

Arrangement #11

Basic Price T $700

14563	14564	14573	14574	14588
14589	14590	14591	*14600	14601
14618	14619	14633	*14655	14661
*15290	*15291	15304	*15323	15370
15428	15721	*15723	15743	15810

#579 2¢ WASHINGTON 181 Plates

Arrangement #11

Basic Price T $500

14098	*14099	*14109	14110	*14111
14112	14117	*14118	14123	14124
14125	14126	14131	14132	14133
*14134	14135	14136	14138	14147
14148	14149	14150	14173	14174
14175	14176	14203	14204	14219
14220	14237	14238	14247	14248
14249	14266	14267	14289	14290
14291	*14292	14304	14305	14311
14312	14340	14341	14342	*14343
14358	14359	14368	14369	14372
14373	14384	14385	*14416	14417
14434	14435	14456	14457	14517
14537	14538	14547	14548	14553
14554	14664	14665	14666	14667

1923-26 REGULAR ISSUE

#579 2¢ WASHINGTON Cont.

14680	14681	14682	14683	14704
14705	14706	14707	14730	14731
14732	14733	14754	14755	14756
14757	14766	14767	14776	14777
14794	14795	14864	14865	14914
14915	14920	14921	14926	14927
14928	14929	14944	14945	14958
14959	*14970	14971	14979	†14980
15003	15004	15015	*15016	15033
15034	15051	*15052	15142	15392
15393	*15419	*15441	15449	*15451
*15461	*15462	15463	*15464	*15473
*15474	*15475	15476	*15485	15486
15487	*15488	15497	15498	15499
15500	15531	15532	*15533	15540
15542	15564	15566	*15567	15580
15582	15583	*15588	*15589	*15600
15601	15616	15619	15639	15664
*15667	15840	15841	15847	15848
15849	15868	15869	15888	15889
15890	15891	15910	15919	15920
15921				

SHEET STAMPS

ROTARY PRESS Perf. 10

Blocks of 4

#581 1¢ FRANKLIN 56 Plates

Basic Price **UL, UR, LL, LR** $100

14205	14206	14348	14349	14370
14371	14382	*14383	14394	14395
*14527	14528	14624	14625	14630
*14631	14642	14643	14651	*14652
14653	14662	14663	*14960	14961
*14981	14982	15548	15549	15652
*15653	*15655	*15944	*15945	15950
15951	15957	15958	15959	15960
15977	15978	16173	16174	*16191
16192	*16201	16209	16210	*16751
*16752	16811	16812	18730	18731
18732				

#582 1.5¢ HARDING (PROFILE)

37 Plates

Basic Price **UL, UR, LL, LR** $35

16825	16826	16849	16850	16851
16852	16885	16886	16887	*16888
16905	*16906	*16948	16949	16950
16951	17008	*17022	17023	*17024
*17487	*17488	*18235	18357	18358
18359	18360	18412	18413	18482
18483	18488	18489	18693	18699
18701	18702			

#583 2¢ WASHINGTON 284 Plates

Basic Price **UL, UR, LL, LR** $30

15412	15413	15518	15519	15534
15535	*15562	*15563	15610	15611
15620	15621	15764	15765	15802
15803	15820	15821	15822	15823
15900	15901	15902	15903	16262
16263	16270	16271	16286	16287
16304	*16305	*16413	*16414	*16415

1923-26 REGULAR ISSUE

#583 2¢ WASHINGTON Cont.

*16416	*16463	16464	*16749	* 16750
17273	*17274	†17284	*17285	17305
17321	17322	*17365	17366	17400
17401	17473	17474	17498	17499
17500	17501	*17507	17508	*17856
17857	17914	17915	17935	17936
17949	17950	17959	17960	17965
17966	17969	17970	17971	17972
17977	17978	17979	17980	17993
17994	18005	18006	18007	18008
18009	18010	18011	18012	18042
18043	18044	18045	18056	18057
18061	18062	18063	18064	18065
18066	18092	18093	18094	18095
†18124	†18125	18139	18140	18161
18162	18231	18232	18233	18234
18240	18241	18242	18243	18251
18252	18273	18274	18283	18284
18289	18290	18295	18296	18301
18302	*18317	*18318	18329	18330
18337	18338	18343	18344	*18351
*18352	18355	18356	18363	*18364
18368	18369	18517	18518	18519
18520	18525	18526	18527	18528
18529	18530	18531	18534	18535
18537	18548	*18549	18584	18585
18586	18587	18588	18589	18590
18591	18592	18593	18602	18603
18604	18605	18610	18611	18616
18617	18620	18621	18628	18629
18630	18631	18632	18633	18654
18655	18656	18657	18658	*18659
18660	18661	18763	18764	18779
18780	18781	18782	18783	18784
18787	18788	18795	18796	18797
18798	18801	18802	18809	18810
18811	18812	18813	18814	18815
18816	18826	18827	18828	18829
18834	18835	18836	18837	18852
18853	18856	18857	18858	*18859
18862	18863	18864	18865	18868
18869	18870	18871	18872	18873
18874	18875	18876	18877	18878
18879	18880	18881	18882	18883
18884	18885	18886	18887	18888
18889	18895	18896	18901	18902
18931	18932	18933	18934	18935
18936	18937	*18938	18939	18940
18941	18943	18944	18945	18946
18947	*18948	*18951	*18952	

#584 3¢ LINCOLN 22 Plates

Basic Price **UL, UR, LL, LR** $225

*17155	*17156	17161	17162	*17511
*17512	17568	17569	17616	17653
17898	17899	17900	*17901	18114
18115	18379	18380	18439	18440
18445	18446			

#585 4¢ MARTHA WASHINGTON
12 Plates

Basic Price **UL, UR, LL, LR** $175

16079	16080	16660	16661	17436
17437	17739	17760	17761	17989
17990	18365			

#586 5¢ THEODORE ROOSEVELT
36 Plates

Basic Price **UL, UR, LL, LR** $165

16089	16090	16495	16566	*16567
16608	16654	16670	16671	17493
17519	17520	17586	17587	17651
17652	17762	17763	17772	17773
18157	18158	18159	18160	18394
18395	18418	18419	18441	18442
18459	18460	*18789	*18790	*18850
*18854				

#587 6¢ GARFIELD 10 Plates

Basic Price **UL, UR, LL, LR** $70

16083	16084	*17584	*17585	17588
17589	17967	17968	18036	18421

#588 7¢ McKINLEY 8 Plates

Basic Price **UL, UR, LL, LR** $90

17786	17787	17798	17799	18179
18180	18195	18196		

#589 8¢ GRANT 8 Plates

Basic Price **UL, UR, LL, LR** $225

17816	17817	17832	17833	18189
18190	18775	18777		

#590 9¢ JEFFERSON 4 Plates

Basic Price **UL, UR, LL, LR** $50

17854	17855	18193	18194

#591 10¢ MONROE 28 Plates

Basic Price **UL, UR, LL, LR** $500

16107	16108	*17440	17441	17590
17591	17614	17615	17649	*17650
17693	17694	18135	18136	*18137
18138	18387	18388	18414	18415
18532	18533	18538	18539	18614
18615	18622	18623		

BOOKLET PANES

PANES OF 6

The price for miscut panes showing part or all of the plate number depends on the percentage of the number showing. See Appendix G for the maximum reported percentage for each plate number and position.

#583a 2¢ WASHINGTON 14 Plates

17450	17451	18550	18551	18662
18663	†18695	*18696	18697	18698
18705	18706	18708	18710	

1923-26 REGULAR ISSUE

COIL WASTE

ROTARY PRESS Perf.11

Blocks of 4

#594 1¢ FRANKLIN

No plate number reported to date

Please refer to Appendix D for description of marginal markings.

#595 2¢ WASHINGTON 96 Plates

Arrangement #11

Basic Price T $1,000

14098	*14099	*14109	14110	*14111
14112	14117	*14118	14123	14124
14125	14126	14131	14132	14133
*14134	14135	14136	14138	14147
14148	14149	14150	14173	14174
14175	14176	14203	14204	14219
14220	14237	14238	14247	14248
14249	14266	14267	14289	14290
14291	*14292	14304	14305	14311
14340	14341	14342	*14343	14358
14359	14368	14369	14372	14373
14384	*14416	14417	14434	14435
14456	14457	14517	14538	14547
14548	14553	14554	14664	14665
14666	14667	14680	14681	14682
14683	14704	14705	14706	14707
14730	14731	14733	14754	14756
14766	14767	14776	14794	14795
14864	14914	14915	14920	14921
14926				

SHEET STAMP

ROTARY PRESS Perf. 11

#596 1¢ FRANKLIN

No plate number reported to date. This issue is from rotary press SHEET production.

1923-29 REGULAR ISSUE

SIDE COILS

ROTARY PRESS Perf. 10 VERTICALLY

#597 1¢ FRANKLIN 104 Plates

Many of the earlier plates were issued as coil waste (#578) and are not known on coils. We mark those that have been reported as coils with a "c". Since the original survey did not differentiate where more than one Scott number was represented by one plate number, we use a † where we have no later report confirming the existence as a coil. The symbol * is used to indicate the scarcer plate numbers where coil waste does not exist.

Top plate number only

†14563	c14564	c14573	c14574	c14588
c14589	c14590	c14591	†14600	c14601
c14618	c14619	c14633	*14640	*14641
*14648	*14649	*14654	†14655	†14660
†14661	†15290	†15291	c15304	†15322
c15323	†15340	15341	c15370	†15371
c15428	15676	15677	*15678	15679
*15704	*15705	†15706	†15707	*15720
c15721	*15722	†15723	15741	15742
c15743	15774	15775	*15776	*15777
†15808	*15809	c15810	15811	†15973
†15975	*15976	†16015	†16022	†16039
*16053	†16054	†16063	*16064	*16074
16081	16082	†16109	†16110	*16777
†16779	16780	16827	†19356	19581
19582	19583	19584		

Top and bottom plate numbers

19756	19757	19758	19759	19860
19861	19862	19863	19864	19865
19868	19869	19870	19871	20043
20044	20045	20046	20051	20052
20073	20074	20093	20094	*20102
*20103				

#598 1.5¢ HARDING (PROFILE)

Top plate number only **62 Plates**

*16828	*16853	†16854	*16855	*16856
16881	16882	†16883	*16884	*16907
*16908	*16909	*16942	*16943	*16944
†16945	*16946	*16947	16976	*16977
*16994	†16995	16996	*16997	†16998
16999	17025	*17026	*17067	*17068
†17069	18478	18479	*18492	*18513
†18514	*18515	*18516	18643	18644
18645	18713	18714	*18715	*18759
*18760	*18761	*18762	*18817	18818
18821	18822	18823	18824	19320
19321	19322	19323	19324	19325
19326	*19327			

1923-29 REGULAR ISSUE

#599 2¢ WASHINGTON(DIE I) 685 Plates

Many of the earlier plates were issued as coil waste (#579 & #595) and are not known on coils. We indicate those that have been reported as coils with a "c". Since the original survey did not differentiate where more than one Scott number was represented by one plate number, we use a single dagger where we have no later report confirming the existence of the number as a coil. The symbol (*) is used to indicate the scarcer plate numbers where coil waste does not exist.

Top plate number only

†14098 †14099 †14109 †14110 †14111
†14112 †14117 c14118 †14123 †14124
†14125 †14126 c14131 †14132 †14133
†14134 †14135 c14136 †14138 †14147
†14148 †14149 †14150 †14173 †14174
c14175 †14176 †14203 †14204 †14219
†14220 †14237 †14238 †14247 †14248
†14249 †14266 †14267 †14289 †14290
†14291 †14292 †14304 †14305 †14311
c14312 †14340 †14341 †14342 †14343

†14358 †14359 †14368 †14369 †14372
†14373 †14384 †14385 †14416 †14417
†14434 †14435 †14456 †14457 †14517
†14537 †14538 †14547 †14548 †14553
†14554 †14664 †14665 †14666 †14667
†14680 c14681 †14682 †14683 †14704
c14705 †14706 †14707 †14730 †14731
†14732 †14733 c14754 c14755 †14756
†14757 †14766 †14767 †14776 †14777
†14794 c14795 †14864 †14865 †14914

c14915 c14920 †14921 †14926 †14927
c14928 †14929 †14944 †14945 †14958
†14959 †14970 †14971 †14979 †14980
†15003 †15004 †15015 †15016 †15033
†15034 †15051 †15052 *15141 †15142
†15392 †15393 †15406 †15407 †15418
†15419 †15441 †15442 *15443 †15444
†15449 †15450 †15451 †15461 †15462
†15463 †15464 †15473 †15474 †15475
c15476 c15485 †15486 †15487 †15488

†15497 †15498 †15499 †15500 †15521
*15530 c15531 †15532 †15533 †15540
†15541 †15542 †15543 †15564 †15565
†15566 †15567 †15580 *15581 †15582
†15583 †15588 c15589 †15590 *15591
c15600 †15601 c15616 †15617 †15618
†15619 †15638 †15639 †15664 †15665
†15666 †15667 †15824 †15825 *15826
*15827 †15838 †15839 †15840 †15841
†15846 †15847 †15848 c15849 †15868

†15869 †15870 *15871 †15888 †15889
†15890 †15891 *15908 †15909 c15910
*15911 †15916 *15917 †15918 c15919
†15920 †15921 *15922 *15923 †15928
†15929 †15930 †15931 †15936 †15937

#599 2¢ WASHINGTON(DIE I) Cont.

†15938 †15939 †16161 †16162 *16163
†16164 *16203 †16204 *16219 †16220
*16230 *16264 †16265 †16284 †16285
*16300 *16301 *16302 *16303 *16395
†16396 †16397 *16398 *16411 *16412
*16421 †16422 †16423 †16424 †16435
†16436 †16437 *16438 †16457 †16458
†16459 *16460 †16461 †16462 *16479
†16480 †16481 †16482 †16483 *16484
†16485 †16486 †16509 †16510 *16511

†16512 †16513 *16514 †16516 †16517
†16522 †16523 †16524 †16525 †16542
†16543 †16544 †16545 †16676 *16677
*16682 †16683 *16684 †16685 *16695
†16696 *16725 *16726 *16727 *16728
†16729 †16730 †16731 *16732 *16733
*16734 *16735 †16736 †16809 †16810
*16821 †16822 *16823 †17271 †17272
†17275 †17276 †17277 †17278 †17279
†17280 †17281 †17282 †17283 †17290

*17291 †17306 †17307 *17316 †17323
†17324 †17502 †17503 †17504 †17505
†17510 †17517 †17518 *17562 †17563
†17574 †17575 †17600 *17601 †17633
*17634 †17635 †17636 †17662 †17663
†17664 †17665 †17674 †17675 †17691
*17692 †17703 †17713 *17714 †17715
*17716 †17774 †17775 †17776 †17777
*17792 †17800 †17801 †17806 †17807
*17822 †17823 †17824 †17825 †17826

†17827 †17846 †17847 *17852 17853
*17858 †17859 †17872 †17873 *17878
†17879 †17902 †17903 †17904 †17905
†17973 †17974 *17975 †17976 †17981
†17982 †17985 *17986 *17987 *17988
†17991 †17992 *17995 †17996 *17997
*17998 †17999 18000 *18001 18002
*18004 *18013 †18014 †18015 *18016
*18017 *18018 18019 18020 *18040
*18041 †18046 *18047 †18048 †18049

†18050 †18051 †18052 †18053 *18055
†18067 *18068 †18069 *18070 †18071
*18072 †18073 †18074 †18075 18076
†18077 †18078 *18088 *18089 †18090
*18091 †18100 †18101 †18102 *18103
*18104 *18105 †18128 †18129 *18141
*18142 †18147 *18148 *18171 *18172
*18173 †18174 18244 18245 *18253
†18254 †18271 18272 *18291 *18292
†18293 *18294 *18303 18304 *18305

†18306 †18315 *18316 †18324 †18339
*18340 18341 18342 †18353 †18354
†18366 18367 *18392 †18393 18402
*18403 *18404 *18405 *18416 *18417
*18426 †18427 †18447 †18448 *19049
19050 *19051 †19052 19090 *19091
19092 *19093 *19102 19103 †19177
†19178 †19179 †19180 †19219 *19220
*19223 †19224 *19229 *19230 19231

1923-29 REGULAR ISSUE

#599 2¢ WASHINGTON (DIE I) Cont.

19306 19307 *19308 *19309 19310
*19311 19312 *19313 †19367 *19368
*19369 *19370 †19386 *19387 *19388
*19389 *19394 19395 *19396 *19397
†19450 19451 19460 19461 †19471
*19472 *19473 *19474 *19483 *19484
*19485 *19486 †19491 †19492 †19499
*19512 *19513 *19514 19515 †19516
*19517 †19524 †19533 *19534 †19535
†19536 *19539 19540

Top and bottom plate numbers

*19752 *19753 19754 *19755 *19765
*19766 19767 *19768 19769 19770
19771 19772 *19773 *19774 19814
19815 19816 †19817 *19818 *19819
19820 19821 19822 19823 19833
19836 19837 19842 19843 19885
19886 19887 19888 19889 19890
19891 19892 19893 19894 19899
19900 19901 19902 19909 19910
19913 19914 19917 19918 19923
19924 19939 19940 19960 19961
19970 19971 19974 19975 19982
19983 19984 19985 19992 19993
19996 19997 20002 20003 20006
20007 20017 20018 20021 20022
20023 20024 20118 20119 20120
20121 20122 20123 20166 20167
20176 20177 20183 20184 20199
20200 20207 20208 20223 20224
20301 20302 20315 20316 20329
20330 20339 20349 20350 20353
20354 *20363 *20777 20778 20779
20780 20785 20786 20787 20788
20797 20798 20799

#599A 2¢ WASHINGTON (DIE II) 9 Plates

Top plate number only

*19682 †19683 †19684 *19685 19686

Top and bottom plate numbers

19748 *19749 19750 †19751

Joint line pairs or strips showing plate number 19748 or plate number 19515 may be the combination die I and die II pieces.

#600 3¢ LINCOLN 20 Plates

Top plate number only

*14720 †14721 †16425 *16426 †17434
†17435 17906 †17907 *17908 *17909
*18799 *18800 18807 18808 18838
18839 18840 18841

Top and bottom plate numbers.

20376 20377

#601 4¢ MARTHA WASHINGTON

Top plate number only **8 Plates**

*14189 *14190 *14294 *14321 17937
17938 17939 17940

#602 5¢ THEODORE ROOSEVELT

Top plate number only **10 Plates**

*15279 †15280 16443 *16444 *16477
16478 17945 17946 17947 17948

1923-29 REGULAR ISSUE

#723 6¢ GARFIELD 2 Plates

Top and bottom plate numbers

20968 20969

#603 10¢ MONROE 9 Plates

Top plate number only

†16339 †16340 16341 16342 *17610
*17961 17962 †17963 17964

END COILS

ROTARY PRESS Perf.10 HORIZONTALLY

#604 1¢ FRANKLIN 8 Plates

Position L only

*15179 15180 15239 *15240

Position L, R

20355 20356 20357 20358

#605 1.5¢ HARDING (PROFILE) 2 Plates

Position R only

†17027 †17028

#606 2¢ WASHINGTON (DIE I) 12 Plates

Position L only

†14155 †14156 15193 15194 *15243
†15244 18755 18756 18757 18758
19287 *19289

Position R only **6 Plates**

15245 15246 *17570 †17571 *17572
†17573

1923 COMMEMORATIVES

FLAT PRESS Perf.11

#610 2¢ HARDING 166 Plates

		TL	TR	L	R	B
14852	$20	☐	☐	☐	☐	☐
14853	$20	☐	☐	☐	☐	☐
14854	$20	☐	☐	☐	☐	☐
14855	$20	☐	☐	☐	☐	☐
14856	$20	☐	☐	☐	☐	☐
14857	$20	☐	☐	☐	☐	☐
14858	$20	☐	☐	☐	☐	☐
14859	$20	☐	☐	☐	☐	☐
14860	$20	☐	☐	☐	☐	☐
14861	$20	☐	☐	☐	☐	☐
14862	$20	☐	☐	☐	☐	☐
14863	$20	☐	☐	☐	☐	☐
14868	$20	☐	☐	☐	☐	☐
14869	$20	☐	☐	☐	☐	☐
14870	$20	☐	☐	☐	☐	☐
14871	$20	☐	☐	☐	☐	☐
14872	$20	☐	☐	☐	☐	☐
14873	$20	☐	☐	☐	☐	☐
14874	$20	☐	☐	☐	☐	☐
14875	$20	☐	☐	☐	☐	☐
14876	$20	☐	☐	☐	☐	☐
14877	$20	☐	☐	☐	☐	☐
14878	$20	☐	☐	☐	☐	☐
14879	$20	☐	☐	☐	☐	☐
14884	$20	☐	☐	☐	☐	☐
14885	$20	☐	☐	☐	☐	☐
14886	$20	☐	☐	☐	☐	☐
14887	$20	☐	☐	☐	☐	☐
14888	$20	☐	☐	☐	☐	☐
14889	$20	☐	☐	☐	☐	☐

1923 COMMEMORATIVES

#610 2¢ HARDING Continued

Plate	Price	TL	TR	L	R	B
14890	$20	☐	☐	☐	☐	☐
14891	$20	☐	☐	☐	☐	☐
14892	$20	☐	☐	☐	☐	☐
14893	$20	☐	☐	☐	☐	☐
14894	$20	☐	☐	☐	☐	☐
14895	$20	☐	☐	☐	☐	☐
14896	$20	☐	☐	☐	☐	☐
14897	$20	☐	☐	☐	☐	☐
14898	$20	☐	☐	☐	☐	☐
14899	$20	☐	☐	☐	☐	☐
14902	$20	☐	☐	☐	☐	☐
14903	$20	☐	☐	☐	☐	☐
14904	$20	☐	☐	☐	☐	☐
14905	$20	☐	☐	☐	☐	☐
14906	$20	☐	☐	☐	☐	☐
14907	$20	☐	☐	☐	☐	☐
14908	$20	☐	☐	☐	☐	☐
14909	$20	☐	☐	☐	☐	☐
14940	$20	☐	☐	☐	☐	☐
14941	$20	☐	☐	☐	☐	☐
14942	$20	☐	☐	☐	☐	☐
14943	$20	☐	☐	☐	☐	☐
14946	$20	☐	☐	☐	☐	☐
14947	$20	☐	☐	☐	☐	☐
14948	$20	☐	☐	☐	☐	☐
14949	$20	☐	☐	☐	☐	☐
14954	$20	☐	☐	☐	☐	☐
14955	$20	☐	☐	☐	☐	☐
14956	$20	☐	☐	☐	☐	☐
14972	$20	☐	☐	☐	☐	☐
14987	$20	☐	☐	☐	☐	☐
14988**N**	$20	☐	☐	☐	☐	☐
14989	$20	☐	☐	☐	☐	☐
14990	$20	☐	☐	☐	☐	☐
14991	$20	☐	☐	☐	☐	☐
14992	$20	☐	☐	☐	☐	☐
14993	$20	☐	☐	☐	☐	☐
14994	$20	☐	☐	☐	☐	☐
14997	$20	☐	☐	☐	☐	☐
14998	$20	☐	☐	☐	☐	☐
14999	$30	☐	☐	☐	☐	☐
15000	$35	☐	☐	☐	☐	☐
15005	$20	☐	☐	☐	☐	☐
15006	$30	☐	☐	☐	☐	☐
15007	$20	☐	☐	☐	☐	☐
15008	$20	☐	☐	☐	☐	☐
15009	$20	☐	☐	☐	☐	☐
15010	$35	☐	☐	☐	☐	☐
15011	$50	☐	☐	☐	☐	☐
15012	$20	☐	☐	☐	☐	☐
15017	$45	☐	☐	☐	☐	☐
15018	$20	☐	☐	☐	☐	☐
15019	$20	☐	☐	☐	☐	☐
15020	$30	☐	☐	☐	☐	☐
15025	$20	☐	☐	☐	☐	☐
15026	$20	☐	☐	☐	☐	☐
15027	$20	☐	☐	☐	☐	☐
15028	$20	☐	☐	☐	☐	☐
15029	$35	☐	☐	☐	☐	☐
15030	$25	☐	☐	☐	☐	☐

N extra "8" in LR-B plate number

#610 2¢ HARDING Continued

Plate	Price	TL	TR	L	R	B
15031	$30	☐	☐	☐	☐	☐
15032	$20	☐	☐	☐	☐	☐
15035	$20	☐	☐	☐	☐	☐
15036	$20	☐	☐	☐	☐	☐
15037	$20	☐	☐	☐	☐	☐
15038	$20	☐	☐	☐	☐	☐
15039	$20	☐	☐	☐	☐	☐
15040	$20	☐	☐	☐	☐	☐
15041	$45	☐	☐	☐	☐	☐
15042	$20	☐	☐	☐	☐	☐
15053	$20	☐	☐	☐	☐	☐
15054	$30	☐	☐	☐	☐	☐
15055	$20	☐	☐	☐	☐	☐
15056	$20	☐	☐	☐	☐	☐
15057	$20	☐	☐	☐	☐	☐
15058	$20	☐	☐	☐	☐	☐
15059	$20	☐	☐	☐	☐	☐
15060	$30	☐	☐	☐	☐	☐
15061	$20	☐	☐	☐	☐	☐
15062	$20	☐	☐	☐	☐	☐
15063	$20	☐	☐	☐	☐	☐
15064	$20	☐	☐	☐	☐	☐
15065	$20	☐	☐	☐	☐	☐
15066	$20	☐	☐	☐	☐	☐
15067	$20	☐	☐	☐	☐	☐
15068	$30	☐	☐	☐	☐	☐
15077	$20	☐	☐	☐	☐	☐
15078	$20	☐	☐	☐	☐	☐
15079	$20	☐	☐	☐	☐	☐
15080	$20	☐	☐	☐	☐	☐
15081	$20	☐	☐	☐	☐	☐
15082	$20	☐	☐	☐	☐	☐
15083	$20	☐	☐	☐	☐	☐
15084	$20	☐	☐	☐	☐	☐
15089	$20	☐	☐	☐	☐	☐
15090	$20	☐	☐	☐	☐	☐
15091	$20	☐	☐	☐	☐	☐
15092	$20	☐	☐	☐	☐	☐
15097	$20	☐	☐	☐	☐	☐
15098	$20	☐	☐	☐	☐	☐
15099	$20	☐	☐	☐	☐	☐
15100	$20	☐	☐	☐	☐	☐
15109	$20	☐	☐	☐	☐	☐
15110	$20	☐	☐	☐	☐	☐
15111	$20	☐	☐	☐	☐	☐
15112	$20	☐	☐	☐	☐	☐
15113	$20	☐	☐	☐	☐	☐
15114	$20	☐	☐	☐	☐	☐
15115	$30	☐	☐	☐	☐	☐
15116	$20	☐	☐	☐	☐	☐
15117	$20	☐	☐	☐	☐	☐
15118	$20	☐	☐	☐	☐	☐
15119	$20	☐	☐	☐	☐	☐
15120	$20	☐	☐	☐	☐	☐
15121	$20	☐	☐	☐	☐	☐
15122	$20	☐	☐	☐	☐	☐
15129	$20	☐	☐	☐	☐	☐
15130	$20	☐	☐	☐	☐	☐
15131	$20	☐	☐	☐	☐	☐
15132	$20	☐	☐	☐	☐	☐

1923 COMMEMORATIVES

#610 2¢ HARDING Continued

		TL	TR	L	R	B
15137	$20	□	□	□	□	□
15138	$20	□	□	□	□	□
15139	$20	□	□	□	□	□
15155	$20	□	□	□	□	□
15156	$40	□	□	□	□	□
15157	$20	□	□	□	□	□
15158	$20	□	□	□	□	□
15163	$20	□	□	□	□	□
15164	$20	□	□	□	□	□
15165	$35	□	□	□	□	□
15167	$30	□	□	□	□	□
15177	$20	□	□	□	□	□
15178	$40	□	□	□	□	□
15191	$30	□	□	□	□	□
15192	$50	□	□	□	□	□
15195	$100	□	□	□	□	□

IMPERFORATE ERROR

Tentative valuation $5,000

Plate 14870 **Position TL, L**

This plate was never used for the #611 Imperforate printings. A single Upper Left pane of the Imperforate error was discovered in an otherwise normal package of **perforated** sheets **before** the stamp was **issued** in **imperforate** form. Therefore the pane was a #610 unperforated error. Through the later release of the regularly issued imperforates, the plain copies in the error pane lost their identity.

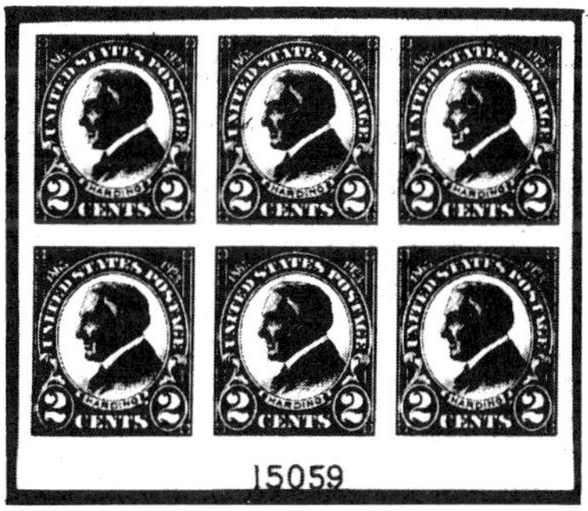

1923 COMMEMORATIVES

#611 2¢ HARDING 6 Plates

FLAT PRESS IMPERFORATE

		TL	TR	L	R	B
15019	$90	□	□	□	□	□
15025	$90	□	□	□	□	□
15027	$90	□	□	□	□	□
15028	$90	□	□	□	□	□
15054	$2,200	□	□	□	□	□
15059	$1,350	†	†	□	□	□

(See 14870 under #610)

#612 2¢ HARDING 8 Plates

ROTARY PRESS Perf. 10

This is a poorly centered issue. The basic price is for reasonably fine condition.

		UL	UR	LL	LR
14866	$275	□	□	□	□
14867	$275	□	□	□	□
14900	$275	□	□	□	□
14901	$275	□	□	□	□
14938	$275	□	□	□	□
14939	$275	□	□	□	□
14995	$275	□	□	□	□
14996	$275	□	□	□	□

#613 2¢ HARDING

ROTARY PRESS Perf. 11

No plate number reported to date. This issue is from rotary press SHEET production.

1924 COMMEMORATIVES

FLAT PRESS Perf. 11

#614 1¢ HUGUENOT-WALLOON

12 Plates		TL	TR	L	R	B
15756	$40	□	□	□	□	□
15757	$40	□	□	□	□	□
15758	$40	□	□	□	□	□
15759	$40	□	□	□	□	□
15778	$40	□	□	□	□	□
15779	$40	□	□	□	□	□
15780	$40	□	□	□	□	□
15781	$40	□	□	□	□	□
15782	$40	□	□	□	□	□
15783	$40	□	□	□	□	□
15784	$40	□	□	□	□	□
15785	$40	□	□	□	□	□

1924 COMMEMORATIVES

#615 2¢ HUGUENOT-WALLOON

16 Plates		**TL**	**TR**	**L**	**R**	**B**
15744	$75	☐	☐	☐	☐	☐
15745	$75	☐	☐	☐	☐	☐
15746	$75	☐	☐	☐	☐	☐
15747	$75	☐	☐	☐	☐	☐
15760	$75	☐	☐	☐	☐	☐
15761	$75	☐	☐	☐	☐	☐
15762	$75	☐	☐	☐	☐	☐
15763	$75	☐	☐	☐	☐	☐
15766	$75	☐	☐	☐	☐	☐
15767	$75	☐	☐	☐	☐	☐
15768	$75	☐	☐	☐	☐	☐
15769	$75	☐	☐	☐	☐	☐
15786	$75	☐	☐	☐	☐	☐
15787	$75	☐	☐	☐	☐	☐
15788	$75	☐	☐	☐	☐	☐
15789	$75	☐	☐	☐	☐	☐

#616 5¢ HUGUENOT WALLOON

15752	$350	☐	☐	☐	☐	☐
15753	$350	☐	☐	☐	☐	☐
15754	$350	☐	☐	☐	☐	☐
15755	$350	☐	☐	☐	☐	☐

TR plate blocks of 15754 contain three examples of the "broken-circle" variety and are worth about 20% more than normal blocks.

1925 COMMEMORATIVES

#617 1¢ LEXINGTON-CONCORD

16797	$50	☐	☐	☐	☐	☐
16798	$50	☐	☐	☐	☐	☐
16799	$50	☐	☐	☐	☐	☐
16800	$50	☐	☐	☐	☐	☐

#618 2¢ LEXINGTON-CONCORD

16801	$80	☐	☐	☐	☐	☐
16803	$80	☐	☐	☐	☐	☐
16804	$80	☐	☐	☐	☐	☐
16813	$80	☐	☐	☐	☐	☐
16814	$80	☐	☐	☐	☐	☐
16815	$80	☐	☐	☐	☐	☐
16816	$80	☐	☐	☐	☐	☐
17004	$80	☐	☐	☐	☐	☐

#619 5¢ LEXINGTON-CONCORD

16805	$300	☐	☐	☐	☐	☐
16806	$300	☐	☐	☐	☐	☐
16807	$300	☐	☐	☐	☐	☐
16808	$300	☐	☐	☐	☐	☐

1925 COMMEMORATIVES

BICOLORED

#620 2¢ NORSE-AMERICAN

Blocks of 8, with Arrow and Plate Number combination.

Basic Price **Top only** $200

8 Vignette Plates

4 Frame Plates	16687	16688	16689	16960	17353	17355	17356	17379
16694					*		*	
16924								
16958						*		
16959								

All 32 Number combinations exist

#621 5¢ NORSE-AMERICAN

Blocks of 8, with Arrow and Plate Number combination.

Basic Price **Top only** $650

4 Vignette Plates

4 Frame Plates	16927	16928	16929	16957
16925				
16926				
16961				
16963				*

All 16 Number combinations exist

1925-29 REGULAR ISSUE

FLAT PRESS Perf. 11

#622 13¢ HARRISON 15 Plates

Basic Price **TL, TR, L, R, B** $200

18106w 18107w 18108w 18109s 18110w
18111w 18112w 18113s 18924w 19104w
19105w 19119w 19120w 19121w 19122w

s Wide Gauge (22.0cm); with star
w Wide Gauge (22.0cm); no star

Star Plates

Large five pointed star below side plate number of the upper right pane.

Basic Price **R** $2,000

18109 †18113

#623 17¢ WILSON 8 Plates

Basic Price **TL, TR, L, R, B** $180

18021 18022 18023 18024 18025
18026 18027 18028

1926 COMMEMORATIVES

#627 2¢ SESQUICENTENNIAL EXPO. (LIBERTY BELL) 60 Plates

		TL	TR	L	R	B
18540	$40	☐	☐	☐	☐	☐
18541	$40	☐	☐	☐	☐	☐
18542	$40	☐	☐	☐	☐	☐
18543	$40	☐	☐	☐	☐	☐
18544	$40	☐	☐	☐	☐	☐
18545	$40	☐	☐	☐	☐	☐
18546	$40	☐	☐	☐	☐	☐
18547	$40	☐	☐	☐	☐	☐
18552	$40	☐	☐	☐	☐	☐
18553	$40	☐	☐	☐	☐	☐
18554	$40	☐	☐	☐	☐	☐
18555	$40	☐	☐	☐	☐	☐
18556	$40	☐	☐	☐	☐	☐
18557	$40	☐	☐	☐	☐	☐
18558	$40	☐	☐	☐	☐	☐
18559	$40	☐	☐	☐	☐	☐
18560	$40	☐	☐	☐	☐	☐
18561	$40	☐	☐	☐	☐	☐
18562	$40	☐	☐	☐	☐	☐
18563	$40	☐	☐	☐	☐	☐
18564	$40	☐	☐	☐	☐	☐
18565	$40	☐	☐	☐	☐	☐
18566	$40	☐	☐	☐	☐	☐
18567	$40	☐	☐	☐	☐	☐
18568	$40	☐	☐	☐	☐	☐
18569	$40	☐	☐	☐	☐	☐
18570	$40	☐	☐	☐	☐	☐
18571	$40	☐	☐	☐	☐	☐
18572	$40	☐	☐	☐	☐	☐
18573	$40	☐	☐	☐	☐	☐
18574	$40	☐	☐	☐	☐	☐
18575	$40	☐	☐	☐	☐	☐
18576	$40	☐	☐	☐	☐	☐
18577	$40	☐	☐	☐	☐	☐
18578	$40	☐	☐	☐	☐	☐
18579	$40	☐	☐	☐	☐	☐
18580	$40	☐	☐	☐	☐	☐
18581	$40	☐	☐	☐	☐	☐
18582	$40	☐	☐	☐	☐	☐
18583	$40	☐	☐	☐	☐	☐
18634	$40	☐	☐	☐	☐	☐
18635	$40	☐	☐	☐	☐	☐
18636	$40	☐	☐	☐	☐	☐
18637	$40	☐	☐	☐	☐	☐
18638	$40	☐	☐	☐	☐	☐
18639	$40	☐	☐	☐	☐	☐
18640	$40	☐	☐	☐	☐	☐
18641	$40	☐	☐	☐	☐	☐
18646	$40	☐	☐	☐	☐	☐
18647	$40	☐	☐	☐	☐	☐
18648	$40	☐	☐	☐	☐	☐
18649	$40	☐	☐	☐	☐	☐
18650	$40	☐	☐	☐	☐	☐
18651	$40	☐	☐	☐	☐	☐
18652	$40	☐	☐	☐	☐	☐
18653	$40	☐	☐	☐	☐	☐
18664	$40	☐	☐	☐	☐	☐
18665	$40	☐	☐	☐	☐	☐
18666	$40	☐	☐	☐	☐	☐
18667	$40	☐	☐	☐	☐	☐

1926 COMMEMORATIVES

#628 5¢ ERICSSON MEMORIAL

12 Plates		TL	TR	L	R	B
18595	$90	☐	☐	☐	☐	☐
18597	$90	☐	☐	☐	☐	☐
18598	$90	☐	☐	☐	☐	☐
18599	$90	☐	☐	☐	☐	☐
18600	$90	☐	☐	☐	☐	☐
18601	$90	☐	☐	☐	☐	☐
18606	$90	☐	☐	☐	☐	☐
18607	$90	☐	☐	☐	☐	☐
18608	$90	☐	☐	☐	☐	☐
18609	$90	☐	☐	☐	☐	☐
18612	$90	☐	☐	☐	☐	☐
18613	$90	☐	☐	☐	☐	☐

#629 2¢ WHITE PLAINS 5 Plates

18765	$45	☐	☐	☐	☐	☐
18766	$45	☐	☐	☐	☐	☐
18767	$45	☐	☐	☐	☐	☐
18768	$45	☐	☐	☐	☐	☐
18769	$45	☐	☐	☐	☐	☐

#630 2¢ WHITE PLAINS SOUVENIR SHEET

Each pane has the plate number at top, left, right and bottom. The positions listed below are for panes of 25.

		UL	UR	LL	LR
18770	$400	☐	☐	☐	☐
18771	$400	☐	☐	☐	☐
18773	$400	☐	☐	☐	☐
18774	$400	☐	☐	☐	☐

1926-29 REGULAR ISSUE

Condition and centering are very important factors in the valuation of the scarce plate numbers of this issue. These were produced during the Depression years and this may account for the small supply of well centered plate number blocks that are available. *Plate number singles are more plentiful and some of the better plates are available in quantity as plate singles.*

ROTARY PRESS IMPERFORATE

#631 1.5¢ HARDING (PROFILE)

2 Plates		UL	UR	LL	LR
18360	$60	☐	☐	☐	☐
18413	$60	☐	☐	☐	☐

ROTARY PRESS Perf. 11 x 10˚

#653 .5¢ NATHAN HALE 12 Plates

19650	$1.60	☐	☐	☐	☐
19651	$1.60	☐	☐	☐	☐
19652	$1.60	☐	☐	☐	☐
19653	$1.60	☐	☐	☐	☐

1926-29 REGULAR ISSUE

#653 .5¢ NATHAN HALE Cont.

		UL	UR	LL	LR
20370	$1.60	□	□	□	□
20371	$1.60	□	□	□	□
20408	$1.60	□	□	□	□
20409	$1.60	□	□	□	□
20922	$1.60	□	□	□	□
20923	$1.60	□	□	□	□
20924	$1.60	□	□	□	□
20925	$1.60	□	□	□	□

#632 1¢ FRANKLIN 133 Plates

15549	$2.50	□	□	□	□
16811	$6.00	□	□	□	□
16812	$2.50	□	□	□	□
18730	$2.50	□	□	□	□
18731	$3.00	□	□2	□	□
18732	$2.50	□	□	□	□
18955	$2.50	□	□	□	□
18956	$2.50	□	□	□	□
18957	$2.50	□	□	□	□
18958	$2.50	□	□	□	□
19215	$2.50	□	□2	□	□2
19216	$2.50	□	□	□	□
19217	$2.50	□	□2	□	□
19218	$6.00	□	□	□	□
19264	$12.00	□	□	□	□
19265	$2.50	□	□	□	□
19266	$2.50	□2	□	□2	□2
19267	$3.00	□2	□	□2	□
19300	$5.00	□	□	□	□
19301	$4.00	□	□	□	□
19302	$2.50	□	□	□	□
19303	$2.50	□	□	□	□
19336	$2.50	□	□	□	□
19337	$3.00	□2	□	□	□2
19338	$2.50	□	□	□	□
19339	$2.50	□	□	□	□
19537	$2.50	□2	□2	□	□2
19538	$2.50	□	□	□	□
19593	$8.00	□2	□	□	□2
19594	$2.50	□	□	□	□
19595	$2.50	□	□	□	□
19596	$2.50	□	□	□	□
19601	$2.50	□	□	□	□
19602	$2.50	□	□	□	□
19603	$2.50	□	□	□	□

#632 1¢ FRANKLIN Cont.

		UL	UR	LL	LR
19604	$30.00	□	□	□	□
19852	$2.50	□	□	□	□
19853	$2.50	□	□	□	□
19854	$2.50	□	□	□	□
19855	$2.50	□	□	□	□
19873	$2.50	□	□	□	□
19874	$2.50	□	□	□	□
19875	$2.50	□	□	□	□
19876	$2.50	□	□	□	□
20027	$3.00	□	□	□2	□2
20028	$4.00	□	□	□2	□2
20029	$2.50	□	□	□	□
20030	$2.50	□	□	□	□
20031	$2.50	□	□	□	□
20032	$3.00	□	□	□	□
20039	$2.50	□	□	□	□
20040	$3.00	□2	□2	□	□
20047	$2.50	□	□	□	□
20048	$5.00	□	□2	□2	□
20049	$2.50	□	□	□	□
20050	$2.50	□	□	□	□
20075	$2.50	□	□	□	□
20076	$2.50	□	□	□	□
20081	$2.50	□	□	□	□
20082	$2.50	□	□	□	□
20083	$3.00	□	□	□	□
20084	$2.50	□	□	□	□
20098	$2.50	□	□	□	□
20099	$3.00	□	□	□	□
20104	$2.50	□	□	□	□
20105	$2.50	□	□	□2	□2
20114	$2.50	□	□	□	□
20115	$2.50	□	□	□	□
20126	$25.00	□	□	□	□
20127	$10.00	□	□	□	□
20138	$2.50	□	□	□	□
20139	$2.50	□	□	□	□
20144	$5.00	□	□	□	□
20145	$3.00	□3	□2	□	□
20148	$2.50	□	□	□	□
20149	$2.50	□	□	□	□
20152	$30.00	□	□	□	□
20153	$50.00	□	□	□	□
20156	$6.00	□	□	□	□
20157	$6.00	□	□	□	□
21220	$6.00	□	□	□	□
21221	$2.50	□	□	□	□
21226	$4.00	□	□	□	□
21227	$2.50	□	□	□	□
21228	$2.50	□	□	□	□
21229	$2.50	□	□	□	□
21230	$2.50	□	□	□	□
21232	$2.50	□	□	□	□
21233	$2.50	□	□	□	□
21270	$2.50	□	□	□	□
21271	$2.50	□	□	□	□
21272	$2.50	□	□	□	□

1926-29 REGULAR ISSUE

#632 1¢ FRANKLIN Cont.

Plate	Price	UL	UR	LL	LR
21273	$2.50	☐	☐	☐	☐
21286	$2.50	☐	☐	☐	☐
21287	$2.50	☐	☐	☐	☐
21288	$2.50	☐	☐	☐	☐
21289	$2.50	☐	☐	☐	☐
21292	$2.50	☐	☐	☐	☐
21293	$2.50	☐	☐	☐	☐
21294	$2.50	☐	☐	☐	☐
21295	$2.50	☐	☐	☐	☐
21296	$2.50	☐	☐	☐	☐
21297	$2.50	☐	☐	☐	☐
21304	$2.50	☐	☐	☐	☐
21305	$2.50	☐	☐	☐	☐
21306	$2.50	☐	☐	☐	☐
21307	$2.50	☐	☐	☐	☐
21343	$2.50	☐	☐	☐	☐
21344	$2.50	☐	☐	☐	☐
21345	$2.50	☐	☐	☐	☐
21346	$2.50	☐	☐	☐	☐
21371	$2.50	☐	☐	☐	☐
21372	$2.50	☐	☐	☐	☐
21379	$2.50	☐	☐	☐	☐
21380	$2.50	☐	☐	☐	☐
21387	$2.50	☐	☐	☐	☐
21388	$2.50	☐	☐	☐	☐
21412	$2.50	☐	☐	☐	☐
21413	$2.50	☐	☐	☐	☐
21414	$2.50	☐	☐	☐	☐
21415	$2.50	☐	☐	☐	☐
21433	$2.50	☐	☐	☐	☐
21434	$2.50	☐	☐	☐	☐
21435	$2.50	☐	☐	☐	☐
21436	$2.50	☐	☐	☐	☐
21568	$2.50	☐	☐	☐	☐
21569	$2.50	☐	☐	☐	☐
21572	$2.50	☐	☐	☐	☐
21573	$2.50	☐	☐	☐	☐
21594	$9.00	☐	☐	☐	☐
21595	$9.00	☐	☐	☐	☐
21620	$2.50	☐	☐	☐	☐
21621	$3.00	☐	☐	☐	☐

#633 1.5¢ HARDING(PROFILE) 40 Plates

Plate	Price	UL	UR	LL	LR
18358	$60	☐	☐	☐	☐
18359	$60	☐	☐	☐	☐
18360	$150	☐	☐	☐	☐
18412	$60	☐	☐	☐	☐
18413	$150	☐	☐	☐	☐
18488	$60	☐	☐	☐	☐
18489	$60	☐	☐	☐	☐
18694	$150	☐	☐	☐	☐
18700	$250	☐	☐	☐	☐
18701	$60	☐	☐	☐	☐
18702	$60	☐	☐	☐	☐
18703	$60	☐	☐	☐	☐
18704	$60	☐	☐	☐	☐
18722	$60	☐	☐	☐	☐
18723	$60	☐	☐	☐	☐
18728	$120	☐	☐	☐	☐
18729	$60	☐	☐	☐	☐
18737	$60	☐	☐	☐	☐
18738	$60	☐	☐	☐	☐
18825	$60	☐	☐	☐	☐
19047	$60	☐	☐	☐	☐
19048	$150	☐	☐	☐	☐
19057	$120	☐	☐	☐	☐
19058	$100	☐	☐	☐	☐
19072	$60	☐	☐	☐	☐
19073	$100	☐	☐	☐	☐
19125	$60	☐	☐	☐	☐
19126	$60	☐	☐	☐	☐
19181	$60	☐	☐	☐	☐
19182	$60	☐	☐	☐	☐
19191	$60	☐	☐	☐	☐
19192	$60	☐	☐	☐	☐
19201	$60	☐	☐	☐	☐
19202	$60	☐	☐	☐	☐
19213	$60	☐	☐	☐	☐
19214	$60	☐	☐	☐	☐
19290	$60	☐	☐	☐	☐
19291	$60	☐	☐	☐	☐
19292	$150	☐	☐	☐	☐
19293	$150	☐	☐	☐	☐

#634 2¢ WASHINGTON (DIE I) 480 Plates

Plate	Price	UL	UR	LL	LR
18043	$7.50	☐	☐	☐	☐
18061	$10.00	☐	☐	☐	☐
18095	$10.00	☐	☐	☐	☐
18139	$10.00	☐	☐	☐	☐
18231	$10.00	☐	☐	☐	☐
18234	$20.00	☐	☐	☐	☐
18243	$20.00	☐	☐	☐	☐
18284	$50.00	☐	☐	☐	†
18368	$10.00	☐	☐	☐	☐
18369	$5.00	☐	☐	☐	☐
18517	$10.00	☐	☐	☐	☐
18520	$2.00	☐2	☐3	☐	☐
18529	$3.50	☐	☐	☐	☐
18586	$7.50	☐	☐	☐	☐
18588	$15.00	☐	☐	☐	☐
18589	$6.00	☐	☐	☐2	☐2

1926-29 REGULAR ISSUE

#634 2¢ WASHINGTON (DIE I) Cont.

		UL	UR	LL	LR
18605	$7.50	□4	□4	□4	□
18610	$7.50	□	□	□	□
18611	$50.00	†	†	□	†
18616	$3.00	□2	□2	□2	□
18617	$50.00	†	†	†	□
18620	$1.50	□8	□4	□8	□
18621	$50.00	†	□	†	†
18628	$1.50	□3	□6	□6	□
18630	—	†	†	†	†
18655	$10.00	□	□	□	□
18657	$35.00	□	□	□	□
18658	$50.00	□	†	□	†
18659	$50.00	†	†	□	□
18660	$7.50	□	□	□	□
18661	$7.50	□	□	□	□
18763	$5.00	□	□	□	□
18764	$35.00	□	□	□	□
18779	$4.00	□	□	□	□
18780	$4.00	□	□	□	□
18781	$10.00	□	□	□	□
18782	$7.50	□	□	□	□
18783	$10.00	□	□	□	□
18784	$2.00	□2	□	□2	□
18787	$30.00	□	□	□	□
18788	$15.00	□	□	□	□
18795	$3.75	□	□2	□2	□2
18796	$3.75	□	□	□	□
18797	$15.00	□	□	□	□
18798	$7.50	□	□2	□2	□2
18801	$50.00	□	□	□	□
18802	$50.00	□	□	□	□
18809	$3.75	□	□	□	□
18810	$35.00	□	□	□	□
18811	$3.75	□2	□	□	□
18812	$3.75	□2	□2	□	□
18813	$2.50	□3	□3	□	□3
18814	$3.75	□	□2	□2	□
18815	$3.75	□	□	□	□2
18816	$35.00	□	□	□	□
18826	$3.00	□2	□	□	□
18827	$3.00	□	□	□	□
18828	$3.75	□2	□2	□	□
18829	$3.75	□2	□2	□	□
18834	$4.00	□2	□2	□	□2
18835	$7.50	□	□	□	□

#634 2¢ WASHINGTON (DIE I) Cont.

		UL	UR	LL	LR
18836	$1.50	□	□2	□5	□5
18837	$3.00	□	□2	□2	□
18852	$3.00	□	□	□	□
18853	$1.50	□6	□	□3	□2
18856	$5.00	□2	□2	□	□2
18857	$5.00	□	□2	□2	□2
18858	$1.50	□	□3	□	□3
18859	$1.50	□	□3	□2	□3
18862	$25.00	□	□	□	□
18863	$25.00	□	□	□	□
18864	$5.00	□	□	□	□
18865	$3.00	□	□	□	□
18868	$3.75	□	□2	□	□2
18869	$3.75	□	□2	□	□
18870	$12.50	□	□	□	□
18871	$3.00	□	□	□	□
18872	$10.00	□	□	□	□
18873	$4.00	□2	□	□	□
18874	$3.00	□	□	□	□
18875	$5.00	□2	□2	□	□
18876	$5.00	□2	□2	□	□
18877	$10.00	□	□	□	□
18878	$7.50	□2	□2	□	□2
18879	$12.50	□	□	□	□
18880	$15.00	□	□	□	□
18881	$35.00	□	□	□	□
18882	$35.00	□	□	□	□
18883	$50.00	□	□	□	□
18884	$12.50	□	□	□	□
18885	$2.50	□4	□	□4	□4
18886	$12.50	□	□	□	□
18887	$15.00	□	□	□	□
18888	$3.75	□	□	□	□
18889	$20.00	□	□	□	□
18895	$10.00	□	□	□	□
18896	$5.00	□2	□2	□	□
18901	$7.50	□2	□2	□	□2
18902	$25.00	□	□	□	□
18931	$3.00	□	□	□	□
18932	$3.00	□	□	□	□
18933	$3.00	□	□	□	□
18934	$3.00	□	□	□	□
18935	$2.50	□	□	□	□
18936	$3.00	□	□	□	□
18937	$1.50	□2	□3	□2	□
18938	$1.50	□	□	□	□
18939	$3.00	□	□	□	□
18940	$1.50	□	□	□	□
18941	$2.50	□	□	□	□
18942	$1.50	□	□	□	□
18943	$3.00	□	□	□	□
18944	$3.00	□	□	□	□
18945	$2.50	□	□	□	□
18946	$2.50	□	□	□	□
18947	$2.50	□	□	□	□
18948	$3.00	□	□	□	□
18949	$1.50	□3	□	□	□
18950	$1.50	□	□	□	□
18951	$3.50	□	□	□	□
18952	$3.50	□	□	□	□

1926-29 REGULAR ISSUE

#634 2¢ WASHINGTON (DIE I) Cont.

		UL	UR	LL	LR
18953	$1.50	□	□2	□	□
18954	$1.50	□	□	□	□
18959	$1.50	□2	□	□	□4
18962	$3.00	□	□	□	□
18963	$1.50	□2	□	□	□3
18964	$1.50	□	□2	□	□3
18965	$4.00	□	□	□	□
18966	$10.00	□	□	□	□
18967	$1.50	□2	□	□	□2
18968	$1.50	□	□	□	□2
18969	$2.00	□	□	□	□
18970	$2.00	□	□	□2	□
18971	$35.00	□	□	□	□
18972	$25.00	□	□	□	□
18973	$2.00	□	□	□	□
18974	$2.00	□	□	□	□
18975	$2.00	□	□2	□	□
18976	$4.00	□2	□2	□	□
18977	$1.50	□	□	□	□
18978	$1.50	□	□	□	□
18979	$7.00	□2	□	□2	□2
18980	$1.50	□	□	□	□
18981	$1.50	□	□	□	□
18982	$1.50	□	□	□	□
18983	$1.50	□2	□3	□	□3
18984	$1.50	□	□	□	□
18985	$1.50	□	□2	□	□
18986	$1.50	□	□	□	□2
18987	$1.50	□	□2	□3	□3
18988	$1.50	□	□2	□3	□3
18989	$1.50	□2	□	□	□
18990	$1.50	□3	□	□3	□2
18991	$1.50	□	□2	□2	□2
18992	$1.50	□	□	□	□
18993	$1.50	□	□	□	□
18994	$1.50	□	□	□	□
18995	$1.50	□	□	□	□
18996	$1.50	□	□	□	□
19009	$1.50	□	□	□	□
19010	$1.50	□	□	□	□
19011	$7.00	□	□	□	□
19017	$10.00	□	□	□	□
19018	$1.50	□	□	□	□
19019	$1.50	□	□	□	□
19020	$1.50	□	□	□	□
19021	$1.50	□	□	□	□

#634 2¢ WASHINGTON (DIE I) Cont.

		UL	UR	LL	LR
19022	$1.50	□	□	□	□
19023	$1.50	□	□	□	□
19024	$1.50	□	□	□	□
19025	$1.50	□	□	□	□
19026	$1.50	□	□	□	□
19027	$1.50	□	□	□	□
19028	$4.00	□	□	□	□
19029	$10.00	□	□	□	□
19030	$1.50	□	□	□	□
19031	$1.50	□	□	□	□
19032	$1.50	□	□	□	□
19033	$1.50	□	□	□	□
19034	$1.50	□	□	□	□
19043	$1.50	□	□	□	□
19044	$1.50	□	□	□	□
19045	$1.50	□	□	□	□
19046	$1.50	□	□	□	□
19053	$1.50	□	□	□	□
19054	$1.50	□	□	□	□
19055	$1.50	□	□	□	□
19056	$1.50	□	□	□	□
19059	$1.50	□	□	□	□
19060	$1.50	□	□	□	□
19070	$1.50	□	□	□	□
19071	$1.50	□	□	□	□
19074	$1.50	□	□	□	□
19075	$1.50	□	□	□	□
19080	$1.50	□	□	□	□
19081	$1.50	□	□	□	□
19086	$1.50	□	□	□	□
19087	$1.50	□	□	□	□
19094	$1.50	□2	□	□2	□2
19095	$1.50	□	□	□	□
19107	$1.50	□	□	□	□
19108	$1.50	□	□	□	□
19109	$1.50	□	□	□	□
19110	$1.50	□	□	□	□
19115	$1.50	□	□	□	□
19116	$1.50	□	□	□	□
19117	$1.50	□	□	□	□
19118	$1.50	□	□	□	□
19123	$1.50	□	□	□	□
19124	$1.50	□	□	□	□
19149	$1.50	□2	□	□	□
19150	$2.00	□	□	□	□
19151	$1.50	□	□	□	□
19152	$1.50	□	□	□	□
19153	$1.50	□	□	□	□
19154	$4.00	□2	□	□2	□2
19157	$2.00	□	□	□	□
19158	$1.50	□	□	□	□
19159	$1.50	□	□	□	□
19160	$15.00	□	□	□	□
19165	$20.00	□	□	□	□
19166	$4.00	□	□	□	□
19167	$1.50	□	□	□	□
19168	$1.50	□	□	□	□
19171	$2.00	□	□	□	□
19172	$1.50	□	□	□	□

1926-29 REGULAR ISSUE

#634 2¢ WASHINGTON (DIE I) Cont.

		UL	UR	LL	LR
19173	$1.50	□	□	□	□
19174	$1.50	□	□	□	□
19175	$1.50	□	□	□	□
19176	$2.00	□	□	□	□
19185	$1.50	□	□	□	□
19186	$1.50	□	□	□	□
19187	$30.00	□	□	□	□
19188	$20.00	□	□	□	□
19189	$25.00	□	□	□	□
19190	$1.50	□	□	□	□
19195	$3.00	□2	□	□	□2
19196	$1.50	□	□	□	□
19197	$30.00	□	□	□	□
19198	$20.00	□	□	□	□
19203	$20.00	□	□	□	□
19204	$1.50	□	□	□	□
19205	$1.50	□	□	□	□
19206	$20.00	□2	□	□	□2
19209	$30.00	□2	□	□	□2
19210	$1.50	□	□	□	□
19211	$1.50	□	□	□	□
19212	$1.50	□	□	□	□
19221	$3.00	□2	□	□2	□2
19222	$1.50	□	□	□	□
19227	$1.50	□	□	□	□
19228	$25.00	□	□	□	□
19232	$20.00	□	□	□	□
19233	$1.50	□	□	□	□
19240	$10.00	†	□	□	□
19241	$30.00	□	□	□	□
19242	$2.00	□	□	□	□
19243	$1.50	□	□	□	□
19244	$3.00	□	□2	□2	□
19245	$1.50	□	□	□	□
19250	$5.00	□	□	□	□
19251	$10.00	□	□	□	□
19252	$15.00	□	□	□	□2
19253	$25.00	□	□	□	□

		UL	UR	LL	LR
19258	$1.50	□	□	□	□
19259	$1.50	□	□	□	□
19268	$5.00	□	□	□	□
19269	$4.00	□	□	□	□
19270	$1.50	□	□	□	□
19271	$4.00	□	□	□	□
19272	$1.50	□2	□2	□	□
19273	$1.50	□	□	□	□
19284	$1.50	□	□	□	□

#634 2¢ WASHINGTON (DIE I) Cont.

		UL	UR	LL	LR
19285	$1.50	□	□	□	□
19304	$1.50	□	□	□	□
19305	$1.50	□	□	□	□
19318	$1.50	□	□	□	□
19319	$1.50	□	□	□	□
19328	$1.50	□	□	□	□
19329	$5.00	□2	□2	□2	□
19330	$1.50	□	□	□	□
19331	$5.00	□2	□2	□	□2
19332	$1.50	□	□	□	□
19333	$1.50	□	□	□	□
19334	$1.50	□	□	□	□
19335	$1.50	□	□	□	□
19340	$1.50	□	□	□	□
19341	$1.50	□	□	□	□
19342	$1.50	□	□	□	□
19343	$3.00	□	□	□	□
19344	$3.00	□	□	□	□
19345	$4.00	□	□	□	□
19346	$1.50	□	□	□	□
19347	$1.50	□	□	□	□
19348	$5.00	□	□	□	□
19349	$1.50	□	□	□	□
19378	$1.50	□	□	□	□
19379	$1.50	□	□	□	□
19380	$1.50	□	□	□	□
19381	$1.50	□	□	□	□
19382	$1.50	□	□	□	□
19383	$1.50	□3	□3	□	□
19384	$1.50	□	□	□	□
19385	$1.50	□	□	□	□
19398	$1.50	□	□2	□	□
19399	$1.50	□	□	□	□
19400	$1.50	□	□	□	□
19401	$1.50	□	□	□	□
19402	$1.50	□	□	□	□
19403	$1.50	□	□4	□4	□
19415	$2.00	□	□	□	□
19416	$2.00	□	□2	□2	□2
19421	$1.50	□	□	□	□
19422	$1.50	□	□	□	□
19424	$50.00	□	□	□	□
19428	$1.50	□	□	□	□
19429	$1.50	□	□	□	□
19430	$1.50	□	□	□	□
19431	$1.50	□	□	□	□
19432	$1.50	□	□	□	□
19433	$1.50	□	□	□	□
19434	$3.00	□	□	□	□
19435	$1.50	□	□	□	□
19436	$1.50	□	□	□	□
19437	$1.50	□	□	□	□
19446	$1.50	□	□	□	□
19447	$2.00	□	□	□	□
19448	$1.50	□	□	□	□
19449	$7.00	□	□	□	□
19453	$1.50	□	□	□	□
19454	$1.50	□	□	□	□
19455	$1.50	□	□	□	□

1926-29 REGULAR ISSUE

#634 2¢ WASHINGTON (DIE I) Cont.

		UL	UR	LL	LR
19456	$1.50	☐	☐	☐	☐
19457	$1.50	☐	☐	☐	☐
19458	$1.50	☐	☐	☐	☐
19459	$1.50	☐	☐	☐	☐
19475	$1.50	☐	☐	☐	☐
19476	$1.50	☐	☐	☐	☐
19477	$3.00	☐	☐	☐	☐
19478	$1.50	☐	☐	☐	☐
19479	$5.00	☐[2]	☐[2]	☐[2]	☐
19480	$15.00	☐	☐	☐	☐
19481	$4.00	☐	☐	☐	☐
19482	$1.50	☐	☐	☐	☐
19518	$1.50	☐	☐	☐	☐
19519	$1.50	☐	☐	☐	☐
19792	$1.50	☐	☐	☐	☐
19793	$15.00	☐	☐	☐	☐
19810	$1.50	☐	☐	☐	☐
19811	$1.50	☐	☐	☐	☐
19812	$1.50	☐	☐	☐	☐
19813	$1.50	☐[2]	☐	☐	☐
19856	$1.50	☐	☐	☐	☐
19857	$1.50	☐	☐	☐	☐
19858	$1.50	☐	☐	☐	☐
19859	$1.50	☐	☐	☐	☐
19866	$1.50	☐	☐	☐	☐
19867	$1.50	☐	☐	☐	☐
19895	$1.50	☐	☐	☐	☐
19896	$1.50	☐	☐	☐	☐
19897	$1.50	☐	☐	☐	☐
19898	$1.50	☐	☐	☐	☐
19903	$1.50	☐	☐	☐	☐
19904	$1.50	☐	☐	☐	☐
19905	$1.50	☐	☐	☐	☐
19906	$1.50	☐	☐	☐	☐
19907	$1.50	☐	☐	☐	☐
19908	$1.50	☐	☐	☐	☐
19911	$1.50	☐	☐	☐	☐
19912	$1.50	☐	☐	☐	☐
19915	$1.50	☐	☐	☐	☐
19916	$1.50	☐	☐	☐	☐
19919	$1.50	☐	☐	☐	☐
19920	$1.50	☐	☐	☐	☐
19925	$1.50	☐	☐	☐	☐
19926	$1.50	☐	☐	☐	☐
19927	$1.50	☐	☐	☐	☐
19928	$1.50	☐	☐	☐	☐
19929	$1.50	☐	☐	☐	☐
19930	$1.50	☐	☐	☐	☐
19931	$1.50	☐	☐	☐	☐
19932	$1.50	☐	☐	☐	☐
19937	$1.50	☐	☐	☐	☐
19938	$1.50	☐	☐	☐	☐
19949	$1.50	☐	☐	☐	☐
19950	$1.50	☐	☐	☐	☐
19951	$1.50	☐	☐	☐	☐
19952	$1.50	☐	☐	☐	☐
19955	$1.50	☐	☐	☐	☐
19956	$1.50	☐	☐	☐	☐
19958	$1.50	☐	☐	☐	☐
19959	$1.50	☐	☐	☐	☐
19964	$1.50	☐[3]	☐[3]	☐	☐[2]

#634 2¢ WASHINGTON (DIE I) Cont.

		UL	UR	LL	LR
19965	$1.50	☐	☐	☐	☐
19966	$1.50	☐	☐	☐	☐
19967	$1.50	☐	☐	☐	☐
19968	$1.50	☐	☐	☐	☐
19969	$1.50	☐	☐	☐	☐
19976	$1.50	☐	☐	☐	☐
19977	$1.50	☐	☐	☐	☐
19978	$1.50	☐	☐	☐	☐
19979	$1.50	☐	☐	☐	☐
19980	$1.50	☐	☐	☐	☐
19981	$1.50	☐	☐	☐	☐
19986	$1.50	☐	☐	☐	☐
19987	$1.50	☐	☐	☐	☐
19988	$1.50	☐	☐	☐	☐
19989	$1.50	☐	☐	☐	☐
19994	$1.50	☐	☐	☐	☐
19995	$1.50	☐	☐	☐	☐
19998	$1.50	☐	☐	☐	☐
19999	$1.50	☐	☐	☐	☐
20000	$1.50	☐	☐	☐	☐
20001	$1.50	☐	☐	☐	☐
20011	$1.50	☐	☐	☐	☐
20012	$1.50	☐	☐	☐	☐
20013	$1.50	☐	☐	☐	☐
20014	$1.50	☐	☐	☐	☐
20015	$35.00	☐	☐	☐	☐
20016	$1.50	☐	☐	☐	☐
20019	$4.00	☐	☐	☐	☐
20020	$1.50	☐	☐	☐	☐
20025	$4.00	☐	☐	☐	☐
20026	$15.00	☐	☐	☐	☐
20146	$5.00	☐	☐	☐	☐
20147	$5.00	☐	☐	☐	☐
20150	$1.50	☐	☐	☐	☐
20151	$2.00	☐	☐	☐	☐
20154	$4.00	☐	☐	☐	☐
20155	$2.00	☐	☐	☐	☐
20178	$3.00	☐	☐	☐	☐
20179	$7.00	☐	☐	☐	☐
20185	$1.50	☐	☐	☐	☐
20186	$1.50	☐	☐	☐	☐
20201	$1.50	☐	☐	☐	☐
20202	$25.00	☐	☐	☐	☐
20205	$25.00	☐	☐	☐	☐
20206	$10.00	☐	☐	☐	☐
20221	$1.50	☐	☐	☐[2]	☐[2]
20222	$1.50	☐	☐	☐[2]	☐[2]
20233	$1.50	☐	☐	☐	☐
20234	$1.50	☐	☐	☐	☐
20243	$1.50	☐	☐	☐	☐
20244	$1.50	☐	☐	☐[2]	☐
20255	$1.50	☐	☐	☐	☐
20256	$1.50	☐	☐	☐	☐
20285	$25.00	☐	☐	☐	☐
20286	$1.50	☐	☐	☐	☐
20295	$25.00	☐	☐	☐	☐
20296	$10.00	☐	☐	☐	☐
20297	$30.00	☐	☐	☐	☐
20298	$10.00	☐	☐	☐	☐
20303	$7.00	☐	☐	☐	☐

1926-29 REGULAR ISSUE

#634 2¢ WASHINGTON (DIE I) Cont.

		UL	UR	LL	LR
20304	$1.50	☐	☐	☐	☐
20321	$1.50	☐	☐	☐	☐
20322	$1.50	☐	☐	☐	☐
20331	$4.00	☐2	☐	☐	☐2
20332	$1.50	☐	☐	☐	☐
20341	$1.50	☐	☐	☐	☐
20342	$1.50	☐	☐	☐	☐
20347	$1.50	☐	☐	☐	☐
20348	$7.00	☐2	☐2	☐2	☐
20351	$1.50	☐	☐	☐	☐
20352	$1.50	☐	☐	☐	☐
20382	$15.00	☐	☐	☐	☐
20383	$1.50	☐	☐	☐	☐
20529	$1.50	☐	☐	☐	☐
20530	$1.50	☐	☐	☐	☐
20531	$1.50	☐	☐	☐	☐
20532	$15.00	☐	☐	☐	☐
20541	$1.50	☐	☐	☐	☐
20542	$1.50	☐	☐	☐	☐
21147	$1.50	☐	☐	☐	☐
21148	$1.50	☐	☐	☐	☐
21377	$1.50	☐	☐	☐	☐
21378	$1.50	☐	☐	☐	☐
21383	$5.00	☐	☐	☐	☐
21384	$4.00	☐	☐	☐	☐
21555	$1.50	☐	☐	☐	☐
21556	$1.50	☐	☐	☐	☐

EXPERIMENTAL-EYE PLATES

The first two of these plates made their appearance early in February 1935; the others went to press between March 1935 and January 1938. By June 1940 all had been cancelled.

This issue has special importance since it is Eye Printing No. 1, the forerunner of all Electric-Eye issues. Because of the unusual position for a rotary-press plate number (3-up or 3-down from the corner of the sheet), collectors were at a loss to know what size pieces to take.

Today, position collectors want to show the corner sheet margins. In order to do this, a block of 6 is the minimum requirement. This size has a chopped-off appearance and is not popular, but a vertical corner block of 10 is well balanced and desirable in every respect.

#634 Experimental Eye Plates 28 Plates
Corner Vertical Blocks of 10

21149	$5.00	☐	☐	☐	☐
21150	$5.00	☐	☐	☐	☐
21367	$5.00	☐	☐	☐	☐
21368	$5.00	☐	☐	☐	☐
21399	$5.00	☐	☐	☐	☐
21402	$5.00	☐	☐	☐	☐
21411	$5.00	☐	☐	☐	☐

#634 Experimental-Eye Plates Cont.

		UL	UR	LL	LR
21416	$5.00	☐	☐	☐	☐
21417	$5.00	☐	☐	☐	☐
21418	$5.00	☐	☐	☐	☐
21419	$5.00	☐	☐	☐	☐
21420	$5.00	☐	☐	☐	☐
21421	$5.00	☐	☐	☐	☐
21422	$5.00	☐	☐	☐	☐
21423	$5.00	☐	☐	☐	☐
21424	$5.00	☐	☐	☐	☐
21437	$5.00	☐	☐	☐	☐
21438	$5.00	☐	☐	☐	☐
21441	$5.00	☐	☐	☐	☐
21442	$5.00	☐	☐	☐	☐
21447	$7.00	☐	☐	☐	☐
21448	$7.00	☐	☐	☐	☐
21676	$15.00	☐	☐	☐	☐
21677	$15.00	☐	☐	☐	☐
21678	$15.00	☐	☐	☐	☐
21679	$15.00	☐	☐	☐	☐
21688	$15.00	☐	☐	☐	☐
21689	$15.00	☐	☐	☐	☐

1926-29 REGULAR ISSUE

#634A 2¢ WASHINGTON (DIE II) 6 Plates

Plate blocks of this scarce die are usually off center. Prices vary greatly according to condition.

	Blocks of 4	UL	UR	LL	LR
19644	$2,000	☐	☐	☐	☐
19645	$2,500	☐	☐	☐	☐
19744	$2,000	☐	☐	☐	☐
19745	$2,500	☐	☐	☐	☐
19746	$2,000	☐	☐	☐	☐
19747	$2,000	☐	☐	☐	☐

#635 3¢ LINCOLN 30 Plates

18114	$30	☐	☐	☐	☐
18115	$45	☐	☐	☐	☐
18126	$8	☐	☐	☐	☐
18127	$8	☐	☐	☐	☐
18379	$12	☐	☐	☐	☐
18380	$15	☐	☐	☐	☐
18439	$15	☐	☐	☐	☐
18440	$15	☐	☐	☐	☐
18445	$9	☐	☐	☐	☐
18446	$8	☐	☐	☐	☐
18457	$8	☐	☐	☐	☐
18458	$8	☐	☐	☐	☐
18791	$13	☐	☐	☐	☐
18792	$18	☐	☐	☐	☐
18803	$8	☐	☐	☐	☐
18804	$12	☐	☐	☐	☐
18830	$8	☐	☐	☐	☐
18831	$8	☐	☐	☐	☐
18832	$8	☐	☐	☐	☐
18833	$8	☐	☐	☐	☐
19096	$12	☐	☐	☐	☐
19097	$10	☐	☐	☐	☐
19098	$20	☐	☐	☐	☐
19099	$13	☐	☐	☐	☐
19111	$8	☐	☐	☐	☐
19112	$8	☐	☐	☐	☐
20432	$10	☐	☐	☐	☐
20433	$10	☐	☐	☐	☐

#635a 3¢ LINCOLN REISSUE (1934)

21185	$3.50	☐	☐	☐	☐
21186	$3.50	☐	☐	☐	☐

#636 4¢ MARTHA WASHINGTON

8 Plates		UL	UR	LL	LR
17761	$75	☐	☐	☐	☐
17989	$75	☐	☐	☐	☐
17990	$75	☐	☐	☐	☐
18038	$75	☐	☐	☐	☐
18039	$75	☐	☐	☐	☐
18082	$75	☐	☐	☐	☐
18083	$75	☐	☐	☐	☐
18365	$75	☐	☐	☐	☐

#637 5¢ THEODORE ROOSEVELT
21 plates

18394	$17.50	☐	☐	☐	☐
18441	$17.50	☐	☐	☐	☐
18459	$40.00	☐	☐	☐	☐
18460	$40.00	☐	☐	☐	☐
18785	$17.50	☐	☐	☐	☐
18850	$55.00	☐	☐	☐	☐
18851	$30.00	☐	☐	☐	☐
18854	$55.00	☐	☐	☐	☐
18855	$30.00	☐	☐	☐	☐
18907	$22.50	☐	☐	☐	☐
18908	$17.50	☐	☐	☐	☐
18909	$17.50	☐	☐	☐	☐
18910	$17.50	☐	☐	☐	☐
18911	$17.50	☐	☐	☐	☐
18912	$17.50	☐	☐	☐	☐
18913	$17.50	☐	☐	☐	☐
18914	$17.50	☐	☐	☐	☐
19088	$17.50	☐	☐	☐	☐
19089	$17.50	☐	☐	☐	☐
19100	$17.50	☐	☐	☐	☐
19101	$17.50	☐	☐	☐	☐

#638 6¢ GARFIELD 12 Plates

18029	$17.50	☐	☐	☐	☐
18030	$17.50	☐	☐	☐	☐
18036	$17.50	☐	☐	☐	☐
18037	$17.50	☐	☐	☐	☐
18396	$35.00	☐	☐	☐	☐
18397	$17.50	☐	☐	☐	☐
18420	$17.50	☐	☐	☐	☐
18421	$17.50	☐	☐	☐	☐
18860	$17.50	☐	☐	☐	☐
18861	$17.50	☐	☐	☐	☐
18866	$17.50	☐	☐	☐	☐
18867	$17.50	☐	☐	☐	☐

1926-29 REGULAR ISSUE

#639 7¢ MCKINLEY 10 Plates

Plate	Price	UL	UR	LL	LR
18195	$17.50	☐	☐	☐	☐2
18196	$17.50	☐	☐	☐	☐2
18735	$25.00	☐	☐	☐	☐
18736	$17.50	☐	☐	☐	☐
18739	$25.00	☐	☐	☐	☐
18740	$17.50	☐	☐	☐	☐
19236	$17.50	☐	☐	☐	☐
19237	$17.50	☐	☐	☐	☐
19238	$17.50	☐	☐	☐	☐
19239	$17.50	☐	☐	☐	☐

#640 8¢ GRANT 26 Plates

Plate	Price	UL	UR	LL	LR
18189	—	†	†	†	†
18190	$100.00	☐	☐	☐	☐
18191	$17.50	☐	☐	☐	☐
18192	$17.50	☐	☐	☐	☐
18733	$17.50	☐	☐	☐	☐
18734	$25.00	☐	☐	☐	☐
18753	$25.00	☐	☐	☐	☐
18754	$25.00	☐	☐	☐	☐
18775	$25.00	☐	☐	☐	☐
18776	$50.00	☐	☐	☐	☐
18777	$25.00	☐	☐	☐	☐
18778	$30.00	☐	☐	☐	☐
19246	$35.00	☐	☐	☐2	☐
19247	$27.50	☐2	☐2	☐	☐
19262	$17.50	☐	☐	☐	☐
19263	$17.50	☐	☐	☐	☐
19372	$50.00	☐	☐	☐	☐
19373	$35.00	☐	☐	☐	☐
19374	$17.50	☐	☐	☐	☐
19375	$17.50	☐	☐	☐	☐
19376	$17.50	☐	☐	☐	☐
19377	$17.50	☐	☐	☐	☐
20128	$17.50	☐	☐	☐	☐
20129	$17.50	☐	☐	☐	☐
20364	$50.00	☐	☐	☐	☐
20365	$40.00	☐	☐	☐	☐

#641 9¢ JEFFERSON 16 Plates

Plate	Price	UL	UR	LL	LR
17884	$35.00	☐	☐	☐	☐
17885	$35.00	☐	☐	☐	☐
18193	$27.50	☐	☐	☐2	☐
18194	$17.50	☐	☐	☐	☐
18201	$17.50	☐	☐	☐	☐
18202	$17.50	☐	☐	☐	☐
18741	$25.00	☐	☐	☐	☐
18742	$17.50	☐	☐	☐	☐
18743	$25.00	☐	☐	☐	☐
18744	$17.50	☐	☐	☐	☐
19350	$17.50	☐	☐	☐	☐
19351	$20.00	☐	☐	☐	☐
19352	$17.50	☐	☐	☐	☐
19353	$17.50	☐	☐	☐	☐
19354	$17.50	☐	☐	☐	☐
19355	$17.50	☐	☐	☐	☐

#642 10¢ MONROE 26 Plates

Plate	Price	UL	UR	LL	LR
18532P	$100.00	☐	☐	☐	☐
18533	$100.00	†	†	†	☐
18538P	$100.00	†	☐	†	†
18539	$100.00	☐	†	†	☐
18614	$30	☐	☐	☐	☐
18615	$30	☐	☐	☐	☐
18622	$30	☐	☐	☐	☐
18623	$30	☐	☐	☐	☐
18626	$45	☐	☐	☐	☐
18627	$40	☐	☐	☐	☐
18846	$35	☐	☐	☐	☐
18847	$30	☐	☐	☐	☐
18848	$30	☐	☐	☐	☐
18849	$35	☐	☐	☐	☐
19234	$30	☐	☐	☐	☐
19235	$30	☐	☐	☐	☐
19254	$30	☐	☐	☐	☐
19255	$30	☐	☐	☐	☐
19256	$30	☐	☐	☐	☐
19257	$30	☐	☐	☐	☐
19489	$30	☐	☐	☐	☐
19490	$30	☐	☐	☐	☐
19504	$30	☐	☐	☐	☐
19505	$30	☐	☐	☐	☐
19506	$30	☐	☐	☐	☐
19507	$30	☐	☐	☐	☐

#692-701

See pages 107-108

1926-29 REGULAR ISSUE

BOOKLET PANES

PANES OF 6

#632a 1¢ FRANKLIN 14 Plates

18915	18916	18917	18918	*19529
*19530	19531	19532	19561	19562
19563	19564	19921	*19922	

#634d 2¢ WASHINGTON 78 Plates

*18662	*18663	18697	18698	18705
18706	*18707	*18708	*18709	18710
†18711	*18712	*18716	*18717	18718
*18719	18720	18721	18842	18843
18844	*18845	*19183	*19184	19193
19194	19199	*19200	19274	19275
*19276	*19277	19278	19279	19314
19315	*19316	*19317	19357	19358
*19359	*19360	19361	19362	*19404
*19405	19406	*19407	19408	19409
19760	19761	*19762	19763	19834
19835	19844	19845	19846	19847
19848	19849	19850	19851	19962
19963	*19972	19973	19990	19991
20041	20042	20096	20097	20100
20101	20106	20107		

See appendix G for largest reported plate number percentage by position.

Between #643 & #1843
Flat press stamps are perf. 11
Rotary press stamps are 10˚ x 11 or 11 x 10˚ depending upon orientation of stamp unless otherwise specified.

1927 COMMEMORATIVES

FLAT PRESS

#643 2¢ VERMONT SESQUICENTENNIAL

		TL	TR	L	R	B
19035	$40	☐	☐	☐	☐	☐
19036	$40	☐	☐	☐	☐	☐
19037	$40	☐	☐	☐	☐	☐
19038	$40	☐	☐	☐	☐	☐
19039	$40	☐	☐	☐	☐	☐
19040	$40	☐	☐	☐	☐	☐
19041	$40	☐	☐	☐	☐	☐
19042	$40	☐	☐	☐	☐	☐

#644 2¢ BURGOYNE

19061	$37.50	☐	☐	☐	☐	☐
19062	$37.50	☐	☐	☐	☐	☐
19063	$37.50	☐	☐	☐	☐	☐
19064	$37.50	☐	☐	☐	☐	☐
19065	$37.50	☐	☐	☐	☐	☐
19066	$37.50	☐	☐	☐	☐	☐
19067	$37.50	☐	☐	☐	☐	☐
19068	$37.50	☐	☐	☐	☐	☐
19069	$37.50	☐	☐	☐	☐	☐
19106	$37.50	☐	☐	☐	☐	☐

1927 COMMEMORATIVES

#645 2¢ VALLEY FORGE

		TL	TR	L	R	B
19493	$30	☐	☐	☐	☐	☐
19494	$30	☐	☐	☐	☐	☐
19495	$30	☐	☐	☐	☐	☐
19496	$30	☐	☐	☐	☐	☐
19497	$30	☐	☐	☐	☐	☐
19500	$30	☐	☐	☐	☐	☐
19501	$30	☐	☐	☐	☐	☐
19502	$30	☐	☐	☐	☐	☐

1928 COMMEMORATIVES

ROTARY PRESS

OVERPRINTS

#646 2¢ MOLLY PITCHER (on #634)

		UL	UR	LL	LR
19070	$35	☐	☐	☐	☐
19071	$35	☐	☐	☐	☐

#647 2¢ HAWAII (on #634)

18983	$110	☐	☐	☐	☐
18984	$110	☐	☐	☐	☐
19054	$110	☐	☐	☐	☐
19055	$110	☐	☐	☐	☐

#648 5¢ HAWAII (on #637)

18907	$275	☐	☐	☐	☐
18908	$275	☐	☐	☐	☐

FLAT PRESS

#649 2¢ AERONAUTICS

		TL	TR	L	R	B
19654	$15	☐	☐	☐	☐	☐
19655	$15	☐	☐	☐	☐	☐
19656	$15	☐	☐	☐	☐	☐
19657	$15	☐	☐	☐	☐	☐
19662	$15	☐	☐	☐	☐	☐
19663	$15	☐	☐	☐	☐	☐
19664	$15	☐	☐	☐	☐	☐
19665	$15	☐	☐	☐	☐	☐
19678	$15	☐	☐	☐	☐	☐
19679	$15	☐	☐	☐	☐	☐
19680	$15	☐	☐	☐	☐	☐
19681	$15	☐	☐	☐	☐	☐
19708	$15	☐	☐	☐	☐	☐
19709	$15	☐	☐	☐	☐	☐
19710	$15	☐	☐	☐	☐	☐
19711	$15	☐	☐	☐	☐	☐

#650 5¢ AERONAUTICS

19658	$60	☐	☐	☐	☐	☐
19659	$60	☐	☐	☐	☐	☐
19660	$60	☐	☐	☐	☐	☐
19661	$60	☐	☐	☐	☐	☐

12 Frame Plates

12 Vignette Plates	19720		19721		19722		19723		19724		19725		19726		19727		19740		19741		19742		19743	
	L	R	L	R	L	R	L	R	L	R	L	R	L	R	L	R	L	R	L	R	L	R	L	R
19728																								
19729																								
19730																								
19731																								
19732																								
19733																								
19734																								
19735																								
19736																								
19737																								
19738																								
19739																								

Position Chart for #651

1929 COMMEMORATIVES

FLAT PRESS

#651 2¢ CLARK (BICOLORED)
Only Two Positions, TL, TR

TL Blocks of six:
Red plate, Black plate, Red TOP

TR Blocks of six:
Black TOP, Black F plate, Red F plate

Basic Price $12.50

Every red (frame) plate exists in combination with every black (vignette) plate. Thus, a complete collection of left and right pane combinations has 288 blocks. (See chart above) Although there are no rare combinations, completion is difficult and mixed centering is to be expected.

1926-29 REGULAR ISSUE

#653 .5¢ NATHAN HALE
See page 93

1929 COMMEMORATIVES

FLAT PRESS

#654 2¢ EDISON

		TL	TR	L	R	B
19775	$32.50	☐	☐	☐	☐	☐
19776	$32.50	☐	☐	☐	☐	☐
19777	$32.50	☐	☐	☐	☐	☐
19778	$32.50	☐	☐	☐	☐	☐

ROTARY PRESS

#655 2¢ EDISON

		UL	UR	LL	LR
19779	$40	☐	☐	☐	☐
19780	$40	☐	☐	☐	☐
19796	$40	☐	☐	☐	☐
19797	$40	☐	☐	☐	☐

1929 COMMEMORATIVES

#655 2¢ EDISON Cont.

		UL	UR	LL	LR
19806	$70	☐	☐	☐	☐
19807	$80	☐	☐	☐	☐
19808	$80	☐	☐	☐	☐
19809	$70	☐	☐	☐	☐

SIDE COILS

ROTARY PRESS Perf.10 VERTICALLY

#656 2¢ EDISON 8 Plates

19781 19782 19794 19795 19802
*19803 *19804 *19805

SHEET STAMPS

FLAT PRESS

#657 2¢ SULLIVAN

		TL	TR	L	R	B
19783	$30	☐	☐	☐	☐	☐
19784	$30	☐	☐	☐	☐	☐
19785	$30	☐	☐	☐	☐	☐
19786	$30	☐	☐	☐	☐	☐

1929 KANSAS NEBRASKA STATE OVERPRINTS

Completion of these in matched sets is rarely accomplished. The 2¢ Kansas plates are the biggest obstacle, for at least half of the numbers are troublesome when one is searching for missing positions. There is no general agreement as to which are the scarest plates, and the positions show up so infrequently that there is no established market value. To a lesser degree the 2¢ Nebraska plates present the same problem.

1¢ Kansas 18957 and 19302 are often referred to as much harder than the other two 1¢ Kansas plates, but their scarcity does not approach that of the difficult 2¢ numbers. 3¢ Kansas 18804 is definitely scarce. Among the higher denominations we have found the 9¢ and 10¢ Nebraska plates about the hardest to locate in fine condition, but centering is a problem on most of the State Overprints, and we do not know of one complete collection that is fine throughout.

ROTARY PRESS

			UL	UR	LL	LR
#658	**1¢**	**KANSAS (ON #632)**				
18957		$45	☐	☐	☐	☐
19302		$45	☐	☐	☐	☐
19338		$35	☐	☐	☐	☐
19339		$35	☐	☐	☐	☐
#659	**1.5¢**	**KANSAS (ON #633)**				
19181		$45	☐	☐	☐	☐
19191		$45	☐	☐	☐	☐
#660	**2¢**	**KANSAS (ON #634)**				
19174		$40	☐	☐	☐	☐
19175		$40	☐	☐	☐	☐
19273		$75	☐	☐	☐	☐
19379		$40	☐	☐	☐	☐
19383		$40	☐	☐	☐	☐
19384		$40	☐	☐	☐	☐
19385		$40	☐	☐	☐	☐
19398		$40	☐	☐	☐	☐
19430		$65	☐	☐	☐	☐
19431		$65	☐	☐	☐	☐
19436		$65	☐	☐	☐	☐
19447		$65	☐	☐	☐	☐
#661	**3¢**	**KANSAS (ON #635)**				
18126		$175	☐	☐	☐	☐
18803		$175	☐	☐	☐	☐
18804		$200	☐	☐	☐	☐
#662	**4¢**	**KANSAS (ON #636)**				
18038		$175	☐	☐	☐	☐
18082		$175	☐	☐	☐	☐

			UL	UR	LL	LR
#663	**5¢**	**KANSAS (ON #637)**				
18907		$140	☐	☐	☐	☐
18908		$140	☐	☐	☐	☐
#664	**6¢**	**KANSAS (ON #638)**				
18030		$400	☐	☐	☐	☐
18037		$400	☐	☐	☐	☐
#665	**7¢**	**KANSAS (ON #639)**				
18736		$450	☐	☐	☐	☐
18740		$450	☐	☐	☐	☐

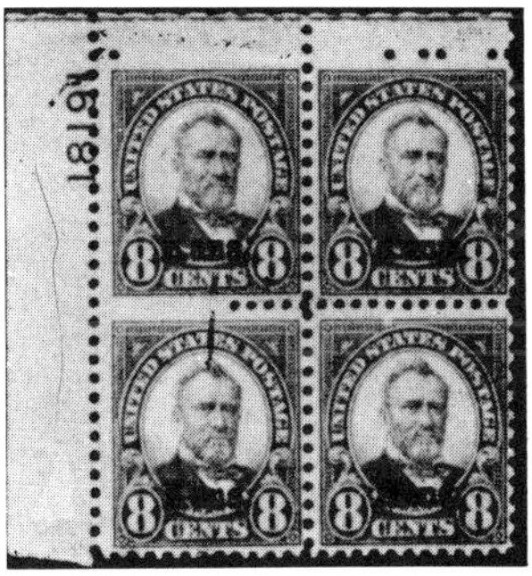

#666	**8¢**	**KANSAS (ON #640)**				
18191		$750	☐	☐	☐	☐
18192		$750	☐	☐	☐	☐
#667	**9¢**	**KANSAS (ON #641)**				
18742		$175	☐	☐	☐	☐
18744		$175	☐	☐	☐	☐
#668	**10¢**	**KANSAS (ON #642)**				
19234		$300	☐	☐	☐	☐
19235		$300	☐	☐	☐	☐
#669	**1¢**	**NEBRASKA (ON #632)**				
19338		$40	☐	☐	☐	☐
19339		$40	☐	☐	☐	☐
#670	**1.5¢**	**NEBRASKA (ON #633)**				
19182		$45	☐	☐	☐	☐
19192		$45	☐	☐	☐	☐
#671	**2¢**	**NEBRASKA (ON #634)**				
18989		$35	☐	☐	☐	☐
18990		$35	☐	☐	☐	☐
19059		$35	☐	☐	☐	☐
19204		$35	☐	☐	☐	☐
19205		$35	☐	☐	☐	☐
19233		$35	☐	☐	☐	☐
19378		$35	☐	☐	☐	☐
19430		$35	☐	☐	☐	☐
19431		$35	☐	☐	☐	☐

1929 KANSAS NEBRASKA OVERPRINTS

#672	**3¢**	**NEBRASKA (ON #635)**				
			UL	**UR**	**LL**	**LR**
18803		$150	☐	☐	☐	☐
18804		$150	☐	☐	☐	☐
#673	**4¢**	**NEBRASKA (ON #636)**				
18038		$225	☐	☐	☐	☐
18082		$225	☐	☐	☐	☐
#674	**5¢**	**NEBRASKA (ON #637)**				
18907		$225	☐	☐	☐	☐
18908		$225	☐	☐	☐	☐
#675	**6¢**	**NEBRASKA (ON #638)**				
18030		$450	☐	☐	☐	☐
18037		$450	☐	☐	☐	☐
#676	**7¢**	**NEBRASKA (ON #639)**				
18736		$275	☐	☐	☐	☐
18740		$275	☐	☐	☐	☐
#677	**8¢**	**NEBRASKA (ON #640)**				
18191		$400	☐	☐	☐	☐
18192		$400	☐	☐	☐	☐
#678	**9¢**	**NEBRASKA (ON #641)**				
18742		$500	☐	☐	☐	☐
18744		$500	☐	☐	☐	☐

#679	**10¢**	**NEBRASKA (ON #642)**				
19234		$1,000	☐	☐	☐	☐
19235		$1,000	☐	☐	☐	☐

1929 COMMEMORATIVES

FLAT PRESS

#680	**2¢**	**FALLEN TIMBERS**					
			TL	**TR**	**L**	**R**	**B**
19824		$40	☐	☐	☐	☐	☐
19825		$25	☐	☐	☐	☐	☐
19826		$40	☐	☐	☐	☐	☐
19827		$25	☐	☐	☐	☐	☐
19828		$40	☐	☐	☐	☐	☐
19829		$25	☐	☐	☐	☐	☐
19830		$25	☐	☐	☐	☐	☐
19831		$40	☐	☐	☐	☐	☐

1929 COMMEMORATIVES

#681	**2¢**	**OHIO RIVER CANALIZATION**					
			TL	**TR**	**L**	**R**	**B**
19838		$20	☐	☐	☐	☐	☐
19839		$20	☐	☐	☐	☐	☐
19840		$20	☐	☐	☐	☐	☐
19841		$20	☐	☐	☐	☐	☐
20005		$20	☐	☐	☐	☐	☐

1930 COMMEMORATIVES

#682	**2¢**	**MASS. BAY COLONY**					
20053		$25	☐	☐	‡	‡	☐
20054		$25	☐	☐	‡	‡	☐
20055		$25	☐	☐	‡	‡	☐
20056		$25	☐	☐	‡	‡	☐
20057		$25	☐	☐	‡	‡	☐
20058		$25	☐	☐	‡	‡	☐
20059		$25	☐	☐	‡	‡	☐
20060		$25	☐	☐	‡	‡	☐
#683	**2¢**	**CAROLINA-CHARLESTON**					
20061		$45	☐	☐	‡	‡	☐
20062		$45	☐	☐	‡	‡	☐
20063		$45	☐	☐	‡	‡	☐
20064		$45	☐	☐	‡	‡	☐

#684-87

See page 107

#688	**2¢**	**BRADDOCK**					
20168		$35	☐	☐	‡	‡	☐
20169		$35	☐	☐	‡	‡	☐
20170		$35	☐	☐	‡	‡	☐
20171		$35	☐	☐	‡	‡	☐
#689	**2¢**	**VON STEUBEN**					
20267		$25	☐	☐	‡	‡	☐
20268		$25	☐	☐	‡	‡	☐
20269		$25	☐	☐	‡	‡	☐
20270		$25	☐	☐	‡	‡	☐
20281		$25	☐	☐	‡	‡	☐
20282		$25	☐	☐	‡	‡	☐
20283		$25	☐	☐	‡	‡	☐
20284		$25	☐	☐	‡	‡	☐

1931 COMMEMORATIVES

#690	**2¢**	**PULASKI**					
20416		$15	☐	☐	‡	‡	☐
20417		$15	☐	☐	‡	‡	☐
20418		$15	☐	☐	‡	‡	☐
20419		$15	☐	☐	‡	‡	☐
20420		$15	☐	☐	‡	‡	☐
20421		$15	☐	☐	‡	‡	☐
20422		$15	☐	☐	‡	‡	☐
20423		$15	☐	☐	‡	‡	☐
20424		$15	☐	☐	‡	‡	☐
20425		$15	☐	☐	‡	‡	☐
20426		$15	☐	☐	‡	‡	☐
20427		$15	☐	☐	‡	‡	☐

1930 REGULAR ISSUE

ROTARY PRESS

#684 1.5¢ HARDING (FULL FACE)

52 Plates

		UL	UR	LL	LR
20259	$2	☐	☐	☐	☐
20260	$2	☐	☐	☐	☐
20265	$2	☐	☐	☐	☐
20266	$8	☐	☐	☐	☐
20390	$2	☐	☐	☐	☐
20391	$2	☐	☐	☐	☐
20394	$2	☐	☐	☐	☐
20395	$2	☐	☐	☐	☐
20398	$2	☐	☐	☐	☐
20399	$2	☐	☐	☐	☐
20412	$2	☐	☐	☐	☐
20413	$2	☐	☐	☐	☐
20414	$2	☐	☐	☐	☐
20415	$2	☐	☐	☐	☐
20430	$2	☐	☐	☐	☐
20431	$2	☐	☐	☐	☐
21080	$2	☐	☐	☐	☐
21081	$2	☐	☐	☐	☐
21082	$2	☐	☐	☐	☐
21083	$2	☐	☐	☐	☐
21088	$2	☐	☐	☐	☐
21089	$2	☐	☐	☐	☐
21090	$4	☐	☐	☐	☐
21091	$2	☐	☐	☐	☐
21092	$2	☐	☐	☐	☐
21093	$2	☐	☐	☐	☐
21094	$25	☐	☐	☐	☐
21095	$2	☐	☐	☐	☐
21381	$2	☐	☐	☐	☐
21382	$2	☐	☐	☐	☐

		UL	UR	LL	LR
21389	$2	☐	☐	☐	☐
21390	$2	☐	☐	☐	☐
21503	$3	☐	☐	☐	☐
21504	$4	☐	☐	☐	☐
21549	$2	☐	☐	☐	☐
21550	$2	☐	☐	☐	☐
21551	$5	☐	☐	☐	☐
21552	$2	☐	☐	☐	☐
21570	$6	☐	☐	☐	☐
21571	$2	☐	☐	☐	☐
21584	$2	☐	☐	☐	☐
21585	$9	☐	☐	☐	☐
21586	$2	☐	☐	☐	☐
21587	$2	☐	☐	☐	☐

1930 REGULAR ISSUE

#684 1.5 HARDING (FULL FACE) Cont.

		UL	UR	LL	LR
21744	$9	☐	☐	☐	☐
21745	$6	☐	☐	☐	☐
21749	$5	☐	☐	☐	☐
21750	$4	☐	☐	☐	☐
21752	$5	☐	☐	☐	☐
21753	$4	☐	☐	☐	☐
21758	$2	☐	☐	☐	☐
21759	$2	☐	☐	☐	☐

#685 4¢ TAFT

20136	$10	☐	☐	☐	☐
20137	$10	☐	☐	☐	☐
20140	$10	☐	☐	☐	☐
20141	$10	☐	☐	☐	☐
20172	$10	☐	☐	☐	☐
20173	$10	☐	☐	☐	☐
20174	$10	☐	☐	☐	☐
20175	$12	☐	☐	☐	☐
20203	$11	☐	☐	☐	☐
20204	$11	☐	☐	☐	☐

SIDE COILS

Perf.10 VERTICALLY

Positions T,B

#686 1.5¢ HARDING (FULL FACE)

20 Plates

20261	20262	20263	20264	20388
20389	20392	20393	20396	20397
20402	20403	20410	20411	21112
21113	21487	21488	21511	21512

#687 4¢ TAFT 4 Plates

20134 20135 20142 20143

#688-90

See page 106

1931 REGULAR ISSUE

ROTARY PRESS

#692 11¢ HAYES

		UL	UR	LL	LR
20533	$15.00	☐	☐	☐	☐
20534	$17.50	☐	☐	☐	☐
20617	$15.00	☐	☐	☐	☐
20618	$15.00	☐	☐	☐	☐
21078	$17.50	☐	☐	☐	☐

1931 REGULAR ISSUE

#693 12¢ CLEVELAND

		UL	UR	LL	LR
20543	$25	☐	☐	☐	☐
20614	$25	☐	☐	☐	☐
20708	$25	☐	☐	☐	☐
20709	$25	☐	☐	☐	☐
21179**N**	$500	☐	†	†	†
21180**N**	$500	☐	†	†	†

N Rare in mint condition. All positions exist precancelled and are less difficult.

#694 13¢ HARRISON

20545	$15	☐	☐	☐	☐
20546	$15	☐	☐	☐	☐
20712	$15	☐	☐	☐	☐
20713	$15	☐	☐	☐	☐
21079	$15	☐	☐	☐	☐

#695 14¢ AMERICAN INDIAN

20549	$20	☐	☐	☐	☐
20550	$20	☐	☐	☐	☐

#696 15¢ STATUE OF LIBERTY

20547	$40	☐	☐	☐	☐
20548	$40	☐	☐	☐	☐
20722	$50	☐	☐	☐	☐
20723	$50	☐	☐	☐	☐
21181**N**	$100	☐	☐	☐	☐
21182**N**	$100	☐	☐	☐	☐

N Very scarce in mint condition. All positions also exist precancelled and are less difficult.

#697 17¢ WILSON

20535	$22.50	☐	☐	☐	☐
20536	$22.50	☐	☐	☐	☐

#698 20¢ GOLDEN GATE

20537	$45	☐	☐	☐	☐
20538	$45	☐	☐	☐	☐
20688	$45	☐	☐	☐	☐
20689	$45	☐	☐	☐	☐

#699 25¢ NIAGARA FALLS

		UL	UR	LL	LR
20539	$45	☐	☐	☐	☐
20540	$45	☐	☐	☐	☐
20729	$45	☐	☐	☐	☐
20730	$45	☐	☐	☐	☐

#700 30¢ BISON

20551	$70	☐	☐	☐	☐
20552	$70	☐	☐	☐	☐
20743	$150	☐	☐	☐	☐
20744	$150	☐	☐	☐	☐

#701 50¢ AMPHITHEATER

20553	$225	☐	☐	☐	☐
20554	$225	☐	☐	☐	☐

1931 COMMEMORATIVES

FLAT PRESS

#702 2¢ RED CROSS BICOLORED

Plate Combination Block of 4

Basic Price $2.50

The last 4 frame plates had short runs and are comparatively scarce. We place a tentative valuation of $7.50 on combination blocks containing 20514, 20515, 20516 and 20525.

TL - BLACK NO.- RED NO.
TR - RED NO. -F BLACK NO.
BL - BLACK NO.- RED NO.
BR - RED NO.- BLACK NO.

20 Vignette Plates

24 Frame Plates		20445		20446		20447		20448		20449		20489		20490		20491		20492		20493		20494		20495		20496		20497		20498		20499		20500		20501		20502		20503	
		L	R	L	R	L	R	L	R	L	R	L	R	L	R	L	R	L	R	L	R	L	R	L	R	L	R	L	R	L	R	L	R	L	R	L	R	L	R	L	R
20434	T																																								
	B																																								
20435	T																																								
	B																																								
20436	T																																								
	B																																								
20437	T																																								
	B																																								
20438	T																																								
	B																																								
20439	T																																								
	B																																								
20440	T																																								
	B																																								
20441	T																																								
	B																																								
20450	T																																								
	B																																								
20451	T																																								
	B																																								
20452	T																																								
	B																																								
20453	T																																								
	B																																								
20454	T																																								
	B																																								
20455	T																																								
	B																																								
20456	T																																								
	B																																								
20457	T																																								
	B																																								
20466	T																																								
	B																																								
20467	T																																								
	B																																								
20468	T																																								
	B																																								
20469	T																																								
	B																																								
20514	T																																								
	B																																								
20515	T																																								
	B																																								
20516	T																																								
	B																																								
20525	T																																								
	B																																								

1931 COMMEMORATIVES

#703 2¢ YORKTOWN BICOLORED
FIRST LAYOUT WITHOUT ARROW

Plate Combination Block of 4
Basic Price **TL, TR, BL, BR** $2.50

In the first layout every red (frame) plate exists in combination with every black (vignette) plate. There are 352 number combinations.

Printed from 100-subject plates divided into left and right panes.

16 Frame Plates

22 Vignette Plates

		20461		20462		20463		20464		20465		20478		20479		20480		20481		20482		20483		20484		20485		20486		20487		20488	
		L	R	L	R	L	R	L	R	L	R	L	R	L	R	L	R	L	R	L	R	L	R	L	R	L	R	L	R	L	R	L	R
20470	T																																
	B																																
20472	T																																
	B																																
* 20473	T																																
	B																																
20474	T																																
	B																																
20475	T																																
	B																																
20476	T																																
	B																																
20477	T																																
	B																																
20504	T																																
	B																																
20505	T																																
	B																																
20506	T																																
	B																																
20507	T																																
	B																																
20508	T																																
	B																																
20509	T																																
	B																																
20510	T																																
	B																																
20511	T																																
	B																																
20512	T																																
	B																																
*20597	T																																
	B																																
*20598	T																																
	B																																
*20599	T																																
	B																																
*20600	T																																
	B																																
*20601	T																																
	B																																
*20602	T																																
	B																																

SECOND LAYOUT WITH ARROW

Plate Combination Block of 6

Black #-Red #-Black TOP

Basic Price **TL, TR, B** $4.00

While the frame plates for the second layout still contained 100 subjects, the vignette plates contained only 50 subjects, so there are no identifiable left and right vignette panes. Every vignette number exists in combination with every frame plate. There are 128 number combinations. Most of the vignette plates were used with only one side of the frame plates; that is left or right panes only. Therefore on these there are only two positions, top & bottom. A few of the vignette numbers were used with both left and right sides of some frame plates. In these cases the bottom position can be identified in strips of 10 by the difference in selvage, with wider left selvage identifying the left side and wider right selvage identifying the right side.

8 Frame Plates / **16 Vignette Plates**

		20646		20647		20648		20649		20668		20669		20670		20671	
		L	R	L	R	L	R	L	R	L	R	L	R	L	R	L	R
20650	T	s	c	s	c	s	c	s	c		c		c		c		c
	B	s	c	s	c	s	c	s	c		c		c		c		c
20651	T	c	s	c	s	c	s	c	s	c		c		c		c	
	B	c	s	c	s	c	s	c	s	c		c		c		c	
20652	T		c	s	c	s	c	s	c		c		c		c		c
	B		c	s	c	s	c	s	c		c		c		c		c
20653	T	s	c	s	c	s	c	s	c		c		c		c		c
	B	s	c	s	c	s	c	s	c		c		c		c		c
20656	T	c	s	c	s	c	s	c	s	c		c		c		c	
	B	c	s	c	s	c	s	c	s	c		c		c		c	
20657	T	c		c		c		c		c	s	c		c		c	
	B	c		c		c		c		c	s	c		c		c	
20658	T	c		c		c		c		c	s	c		c		c	
	B	c		c		c		c		c	s	c		c		c	
20659	T	s	c	s	c	s	c	s	c		c		c		c		c
	B	s	c	s	c	s	c	s	c		c		c		c		c
20660	T	c		c		c		c		c		c		c	s	c	
	B	c		c		c		c		c		c		c	s	c	
20661	T		c		c		c		c		c		c		c		c
	B		c		c		c		c		c		c		c		c
20662	T		c		c		c		c	s	c		c		c		c
	B		c		c		c		c	s	c		c		c		c
20663	T	c		c		c		c		c		c		c		c	
	B	c		c		c		c		c		c		c		c	
20664	T		c		c		c		c		c		c		c		c
	B		c		c		c		c		c		c		c		c
20665	T	c		c		c		c		c		c		c		c	
	B	c		c		c		c		c		c		c		c	
20666	T	c		c		c		c		c		c		c		c	
	B	c		c		c		c		c		c		c		c	
20667	T		c		c		c		c		c		c		c		c
	B		c		c		c		c		c		c		c		c

c = common s = scarce

Identifying plate block positions

FIRST LAYOUT

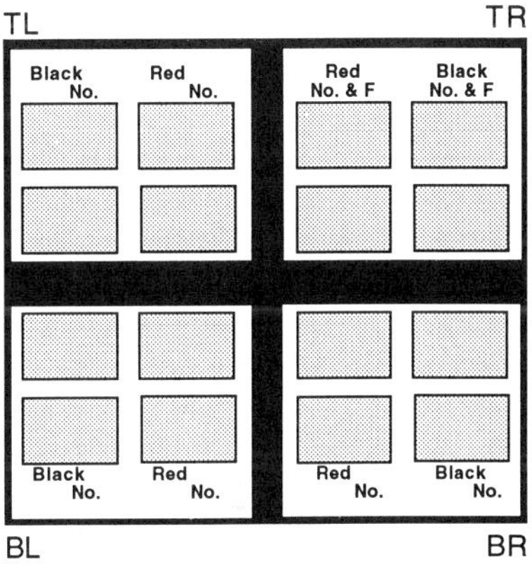

SECOND LAYOUT

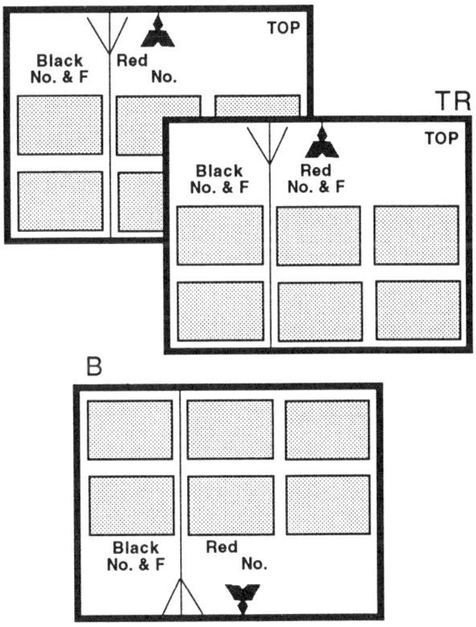

1932 WASHINGTON BICENTENNIAL ISSUE

ROTARY PRESS

#704 .5¢ BICENTENNIAL 6 Plates

		UL	UR	LL	LR
20559	$5	☐	☐	☐	☐
20560	$5	☐	☐	☐	☐
20605	$5	☐	☐	☐	☐
20629	$5	☐	☐	☐	☐
20698	$8	☐	☐	☐	☐
20699	$8	☐	☐	☐	☐

#705 1¢ BICENTENNIAL 28 Plates

20561	$4.50	☐	☐	☐	☐
20562	$4.50	☐	☐	☐	☐
20573	$4.50	☐	☐	☐	☐
20574	$4.50	☐	☐	☐	☐
20654	$4.50	☐	☐	☐	☐
20655	$4.50	☐	☐	☐	☐
20690	$4.50	☐	☐	☐	☐
20691	$4.50	☐	☐	☐	☐
20692	$4.50	☐	☐	☐	☐
20693	$4.50	☐	☐	☐	☐
20714	$4.50	☐	☐	☐	☐
20715	$4.50	☐	☐	☐	☐
20739	$4.50	☐	☐	☐	☐
20740	$4.50	☐	☐	☐	☐
20741	$4.50	☐	☐	☐	☐
20742	$4.50	☐	☐	☐	☐
20747	$4.50	☐	☐	☐	☐
20766	$4.50	☐	☐	☐	☐
20775	$4.50	☐	☐	☐	☐
20776	$4.50	☐	☐	☐	☐
20831	$4.50	☐	☐	☐	☐
20832	$4.50	☐	☐	☐	☐
20835	$4.50	☐	☐	☐	☐
20836	$4.50	☐	☐	☐	☐
20839	$4.50	☐	☐	☐	☐
20840	$4.50	☐	☐	☐	☐
20843	$4.50	☐	☐	☐	☐
20844	$4.50	☐	☐	☐	☐

#706 1.5¢ BICENTENNIAL 8 Plates

20632	$17.50	☐	☐	☐	☐
20633	$17.50	☐	☐	☐	☐
20634	$17.50	☐	☐	☐	☐
20635	$17.50	☐	☐	☐	☐
20678	$17.50	☐	☐	☐	☐
20679	$17.50	☐	☐	☐	☐
20680	$17.50	☐	☐	☐	☐
20681	$17.50	☐	☐	☐	☐

#707 2¢ BICENTENNIAL 60 Plates

		UL	UR	LL	LR
20555	$1.75	☐	☐	☐	☐
20556	$1.75	☐	☐	☐	☐
20577	$1.75	☐	☐	☐	☐
20578	$1.75	☐	☐	☐	☐
20583	$1.75	☐	☐	☐	☐
20584	$1.75	☐	☐	☐	☐
20630	$1.75	☐	☐	☐	☐
20631	$1.75	☐	☐	☐	☐
20644	$1.75	☐	☐	☐	☐
20645	$1.75	☐	☐	☐	☐
20684	$1.75	☐	☐	☐	☐
20685	$1.75	☐	☐	☐	☐
20696	$1.75	☐	☐	☐	☐
20697	$1.75	☐	☐	☐	☐
20706	$1.75	☐	☐	☐	☐
20707	$1.75	☐	☐	☐	☐
20716	$1.75	☐	☐	☐	☐
20717	$1.75	☐	☐	☐	☐
20726	$1.75	☐	☐	☐	☐
20727	$1.75	☐	☐	☐	☐
20733	$1.75	☐	☐	☐	☐
20734	$1.75	☐	☐	☐	☐
20749	$1.75	☐	☐	☐	☐
20750	$1.75	☐	☐	☐	☐
20751	$1.75	☐	☐	☐	☐
20752	$1.75	☐	☐	☐	☐
20753	$1.75	☐	☐	☐	☐
20754	$1.75	☐	☐	☐	☐
20755	$1.75	☐	☐	☐	☐
20756	$1.75	☐	☐	☐	☐
20759	$1.75	☐	☐	☐	☐
20760	$1.75	☐	☐	☐	☐
20761	$1.75	☐	☐	☐	☐
20762	$1.75	☐	☐	☐	☐
20763	$1.75	☐	☐	☐	☐
20764	$1.75	☐	☐	☐	☐
20767	$1.75	☐	☐	☐	☐
20768	$1.75	☐	☐	☐	☐
20771	$1.75	☐	☐	☐	☐
20772	$1.75	☐	☐	☐	☐
20773	$1.75	☐	☐	☐	☐
20774	$1.75	☐	☐	☐	☐
20781	$1.75	☐	☐	☐	☐
20782	$1.75	☐	☐	☐	☐
20783	$1.75	☐	☐	☐	☐
20784	$1.75	☐	☐	☐	☐
20789	$1.75	☐	☐	☐	☐
20790	$1.75	☐	☐	☐	☐
20791	$1.75	☐	☐	☐	☐
20792	$1.75	☐	☐	☐	☐
20793	$1.75	☐	☐	☐	☐
20794	$1.75	☐	☐	☐	☐
20795	$1.75	☐	☐	☐	☐
20796	$1.75	☐	☐	☐	☐
20801	$1.75	☐	☐	☐	☐
20802	$10.00	☐	☐	☐	☐
20803	$10.00	☐	☐	☐	☐
20804	$1.75	☐	☐	☐	☐
20805	$1.75	☐	☐	☐	☐
20806	$1.75	☐	☐	☐	☐

1932 WASHINGTON BICENTENNIAL ISSUE

#708	3¢	BICENTENNIAL 12 Plates			
		UL	UR	LL	LR
20557	$15.00	☐	☐	☐	☐
20558	$15.00	☐	☐	☐	☐
20694	$15.00	☐	☐	☐	☐
20695	$15.00	☐	☐	☐	☐
20847	$17.50	☐	☐	☐	☐
20848	$17.50	☐	☐	☐	☐
21014	$15.00	☐	☐	☐	☐
21015	$15.00	☐	☐	☐	☐
21042	$17.50	☐	☐	☐	☐
21043	$17.50	☐	☐	☐	☐
21044	$17.50	☐	☐	☐	☐
21045	$17.50	☐	☐	☐	☐

#709	4¢	BICENTENNIAL 4 Plates			
20567	$6	☐	☐	☐	☐
20568	$6	☐	☐	☐	☐
20593	$6	☐	☐	☐	☐
20594	$6	☐	☐	☐	☐

#710	5¢	BICENTENNIAL 4 Plates			
20636	$19	☐	☐	☐	☐
20637	$19	☐	☐	☐	☐
20638	$20	☐	☐	☐	☐
20639	$20	☐	☐	☐	☐

#711	6¢	BICENTENNIAL 2 Plates			
20569	$60	☐	☐	☐	☐
20570	$60	☐	☐	☐	☐

#712	7¢	BICENTENNIAL 4 Plates			
20563	$7	☐	☐	☐	☐
20564	$7	☐	☐	☐	☐
20731	$10	☐	☐	☐	☐
20732	$10	☐	☐	☐	☐

#713	8¢	BICENTENNIAL 2 Plates			
20565	$60	☐	☐	☐	☐
20566	$60	☐	☐	☐	☐

1932 WASHINGTON BICENTENNIAL ISSUE

#714	9¢	BICENTENNIAL 2 Plates			
		UL	UR	LL	LR
20640	$40	☐	☐	☐	☐
20641	$40	☐	☐	☐	☐

#715	10¢	BICENTENNIAL 4 Plates			
20642	$110	☐	☐	☐	☐
20643	$110	☐	☐	☐	☐
20686	$150	☐	☐	☐	☐
20687	$150	☐	☐	☐	☐

1932 COMMEMORATIVES

FLAT PRESS

#716	2¢	OLYMPIC LAKE PLACID				
		TL	TR	L	R	B
20815	$15	☐	☐	‡	‡	☐
20816	$15	☐	☐	‡	‡	☐
20817	$15	☐	☐	‡	‡	☐
20818	$15	☐	☐	‡	‡	☐
20819	$15	☐	☐	‡	‡	☐
20820	$15	☐	☐	‡	‡	☐
20821	$15	☐	☐	‡	‡	☐
20822	$15	☐	☐	‡	‡	☐
20823	$15	☐	☐	‡	‡	☐
20824	$15	☐	☐	‡	‡	☐
20825	$15	☐	☐	‡	‡	☐
20826	$15	☐	☐	‡	‡	☐

ROTARY PRESS

#717	2¢	ARBOR DAY			
		UL	UR	LL	LR
20872	$8	☐	☐	☐	☐
20873	$8	☐	☐	☐	☐
20874	$8	☐	☐	☐	☐
20875	$8	☐	☐	☐	☐
20876	$8	☐	☐	☐	☐
20877	$8	☐	☐	☐	☐

#718	3¢	OLYMPIC RUNNER			
20864	$12	☐	☐	☐	☐
20865	$12	☐	☐	☐	☐
20906	$12	☐	☐	☐	☐
20907	$12	☐	☐	☐	☐
20908	$12	☐	☐	☐	☐
20909	$12	☐	☐	☐	☐

#719	5¢	DISCUS THROWER			
20868	$22	☐	☐	☐	☐
20869	$22	☐	☐	☐	☐
20870	$22	☐	☐	☐	☐
20871	$22	☐	☐	☐	☐

1932 REGULAR ISSUE

ROTARY PRESS

#720 3¢ "STUART" WASHINGTON

This stamp is very popular with collectors who enjoy tackling a long run of plate numbers. There are 206 plates for a total of 824 pieces if one is to go for all 4 positions. Although the stamp is common and the majority of the plates are not classed as difficult, it is quite an achievment to complete even the easier numbers in all positions. Beyond that the struggle begins, for the scarce to rare plates offer a stout challenge.

The issue is not noted for very fine centering. Although it is possible to obtain many of the blocks in fine or better condition, anyone starting a "Stuart" collection with the idea of being super-fussy should be warned at the beginning that there is no such thing as an importatnt showing of the plates except in mixed condition. Even the best possible "Stuart" collection will contain a percentage of less-than-fine specimens. Nevertheless, the condition on the whole should be reasonably attractive to warrant our evaluations.

206 Plates		UL	UR	LL	LR
20878	$1.50	□	□	□	□
20879	$1.50	□	□	□	□
20880	$7.00	□	□	□	□
20881	$3.00	□	□	□	□
20884	$1.50	□	□	□	□
20885	$1.50	□	□	□	□
20886	$1.50	□	□	□	□
20887	$1.50	□	□	□	□
20888	$2.50	□	□2	□	□
20889	$2.00	□	□5	□2	□2
20890	$1.50	□	□	□	□
20891	$1.50	□	□	□	□
20892	$1.50	□	□	□	□
20893	$1.50	□	□	□	□
20894	$1.50	□	□	□	□
20895	$1.75	□	□	□	□
20910	$1.50	□	□	□	□
20911	$1.50	□	□	□	□
20912	$1.50	□	□	□	□
20913	$1.50	□	□	□	□
20914	$5.00	□2	□3	□	□2
20915	$1.50	□	□	□	□

#720 3¢ "STUART" WASHINGTON

Continued		UL	UR	LL	LR
20920	$1.50	□	□	□	□
20921	$1.50	□	□	□	□
20932	$1.50	□	□	□	□
20933	$1.50	□	□	□	□
20934	$1.50	□	□	□	□
20935	$1.50	□	□	□	□
20950	$1.50	□	□	□	□
20951	$1.50	□	□	□	□
20952	$1.50	□	□	□	□
20953	$1.50	□	□	□	□
20954	$1.50	□	□	□	□
20955	$1.50	□	□	□	□
20956	$1.50	□2	□2	□	□2
20957	$1.50	□	□	□	□
20958	$1.50	□	□	□	□
20959	$1.50	□	□	□	□
20960	$1.50	□	□	□	□
20961	$30.00	□	□2	□	□
20962	$3.00	□	□2	□2	□2
20963	$1.50	□	□	□	□
20964	$1.50	□	□	□	□
20965	$1.50	□	□	□	□
20966	$1.50	□	□	□	□
20967	$1.50	□	□	□	□
20970	$1.50	□	□	□	□
20971	$1.50	□	□	□	□
20972	$1.50	□	□	□	□
20973	$1.50	□	□	□	□
20974	$1.50	□	□	□	□
20975	$1.50	□	□	□	□
20980	$3.00	□	□	□	□
20981	$30.00	□	□	□	□
20982	$1.50	□	□	□	□
20983	$1.50	□	□	□	□
20984	$25.00	□	□	□	□
20985	$1.50	□	□	□	□
20986	$1.50	□	□	□	□
20987	$1.50	□	□	□	□
20988	$1.50	□	□	□	□
20989	$1.50	□	□	□	□
20990	$1.50	□	□	□	□
20991	$1.50	□	□	□	□
20992	$1.50	□	□	□	□
20993	$1.50	□	□	□	□
20996	$1.50	□	□	□	□
20997	$1.50	□	□	□	□
20998	$1.50	□	□	□	□
20999	$1.50	□	□	□	□
21000	$1.75	□	□	□	□
21001	$1.50	□	□	□	□
21004	$1.50	□	□	□	□
21005	$1.50	□	□	□	□
21006	$1.50	□	□	□	□
21007	$1.50	□	□	□	□
21008	$1.50	□	□	□	□
21009	$1.50	□	□	□	□
21018	$1.75	□	□	□	□
21019	$1.75	□	□	□	□

1932 REGULAR ISSUE

#720 3¢ "STUART" WASHINGTON Cont.

		UL	UR	LL	LR
21022	$1.75	☐	☐	☐	☐
21023	$1.50	☐	☐	☐	☐
21024	$2.00	☐	☐	☐	☐
21025	$4.00	☐	☐	☐	☐
21114	$1.50	☐	☐	☐	☐
21115	$2.00	☐	☐	☐	☐
21116	$1.50	☐	☐	☐	☐
21117	$1.75	☐	☐	☐	☐2
21224	$1.50	☐	☐	☐	☐
21225	$1.50	☐	☐	☐2	☐
21266	$1.50	☐	☐	☐	☐
21267	$1.50	☐	☐	☐2	☐
21268	$1.50	☐	☐	☐	☐
21269	$1.50	☐	☐	☐	☐
21282	$1.50	☐	☐	☐	☐
21283	$1.50	☐	☐	☐	☐
21284	$1.50	☐	☐	☐	☐
21285	$1.50	☐	☐	☐	☐
21290	$1.50	☐	☐	☐	☐
21291	$1.50	☐	☐	☐	☐
21298	$1.50	☐	☐	☐	☐
21299	$1.50	☐	☐	☐	☐
21300	$1.50	☐	☐	☐	☐
21301	$1.50	☐	☐	☐	☐
21308	$1.50	☐	☐	☐	☐
21309	$1.50	☐	☐	☐	☐
21310	$1.50	☐	☐	☐	☐
21311	$1.50	☐	☐	☐	☐
21347	$1.50	☐	☐	☐	☐
21348	$1.50	☐	☐	☐	☐
21349	$1.50	☐	☐	☐	☐
21350	$1.50	☐	☐	☐	☐
21351	$1.50	☐	☐	☐	☐
21352	$1.50	☐	☐3	☐	☐
21353	$1.50	☐	☐	☐	☐
21354	$1.50	☐	☐	☐	☐
21355	$1.50	☐	☐	☐	☐
21356	$1.50	☐	☐	☐	☐
21357	$1.50	☐	☐	☐	☐
21358	$1.50	☐	☐2	☐	☐
21359	$1.50	☐	☐	☐	☐
21360	$1.50	☐	☐	☐	☐
21361	$1.50	☐	☐	☐	☐
21362	$1.50	☐	☐	☐	☐
21363	$1.50	☐	☐	☐	☐
21364	$1.50	☐	☐	☐	☐
21365	$1.50	☐	☐	☐	☐
21366	$1.50	☐	☐	☐	☐
21369	$1.50	☐	☐	☐	☐
21370	$1.50	☐	☐	☐	☐
21373	$1.50	☐	☐	☐	☐
21374	$1.50	☐	☐	☐	☐
21375	$1.50	☐	☐	☐	☐
21376	$1.50	☐	☐	☐	☐
21385	$1.50	☐	☐	☐	☐
21386	$1.50	☐	☐	☐	☐
21397	$1.50	☐	☐	☐	☐
21398	$1.50	☐	☐	☐	☐
21400	$1.50	☐	☐	☐	☐
21401	$1.50	☐	☐	☐	☐

#720 3¢ "STUART" WASHINGTON Cont.

		UL	UR	LL	LR
21403	$1.50	☐	☐	☐	☐
21404	$1.50	☐	☐	☐	☐
21425	$1.50	☐	☐	☐	☐
21426	$1.50	☐	☐	☐	☐
21427	$1.50	☐	☐	☐	☐
21428	$1.50	☐	☐	☐	☐
21429	$1.50	☐	☐	☐	☐
21430	$1.50	☐	☐	☐	☐
21431	$1.50	☐	☐	☐	☐
21432	$1.50	☐	☐	☐	☐
21439	$1.50	☐	☐	☐	☐
21440	$1.50	☐	☐	☐	☐
21449	$1.50	☐	☐	☐	☐
21450	$1.50	☐	☐	☐	☐
21451	$1.50	☐	☐	☐	☐
21452	$1.50	☐	☐	☐	☐
21453	$1.50	☐	☐	☐	☐
21454	$1.50	☐	☐	☐	☐
21521	$1.50	☐	☐	☐	☐
21522	$1.50	☐	☐	☐	☐
21523	$1.50	☐	☐	☐	☐
21524	$1.50	☐	☐	☐	☐
21525	$1.50	☐	☐	☐	☐
21526	$1.50	☐	☐	☐	☐
21529	$1.50	☐	☐	☐	☐
21530	$1.50	☐	☐	☐	☐
21545	$1.50	☐	☐	☐	☐
21546	$1.50	☐	☐	☐	☐
21547	$1.50	☐	☐	☐	☐
21548	$1.50	☐	☐	☐	☐
21574	$1.50	☐	☐	☐	☐
21575	$1.50	☐	☐	☐	☐
21580	$1.50	☐	☐	☐	☐
21581	$1.50	☐	☐	☐	☐
21582	$1.50	☐	☐	☐	☐
21583	$1.50	☐	☐	☐	☐
21616	$1.50	☐	☐	☐	☐
21617	$1.50	☐	☐	☐	☐
21618	$1.50	☐	☐	☐	☐
21619	$1.50	☐	☐	☐	☐
21649	$1.50	☐	☐	☐	☐
21650	$1.50	☐	☐	☐	☐
21659	$1.50	☐	☐	☐	☐
21660	$1.50	☐	☐	☐	☐
21661	$1.50	☐	☐	☐	☐
21662	$1.50	☐	☐	☐	☐
21667	$1.50	☐	☐	☐	☐
21668	$1.50	☐	☐	☐	☐
21669	$4.00	☐	☐2	☐2	☐2
21670	$1.75	☐	☐	☐	☐
21672	$1.50	☐	☐	☐	☐
21673	$3.00	☐	☐	☐	☐3
21718	$2.00	☐	☐2	☐	☐
21748	$1.75	☐	☐2	☐	☐
21754	$1.50	☐	☐	☐	☐
21755	$1.50	☐	☐	☐	☐
21762	$1.75	☐	☐	☐	☐
21763	$2.00	☐	☐	☐	☐
21764	$2.00	☐	☐	☐	☐
21765	$1.75	☐	☐	☐	☐

1932 REGULAR ISSUE

#720 3¢ "STUART" WASHINGTON Cont.

		UL	UR	LL	LR
21766	$2.00	□	□	□	□
21767	$1.50	□	□	□	□
21768	$1.50	□2	□	□2	□
21769	$1.75	□2	□	□	□
21772	$10.00	□	□4	□2	□
21773	$12.00	□	□4	□2	□

COILS and BOOKLET PANES

When rotary-press coils and booklet panes are perfectly cut, the plate numbers are removed, but off-center and/or widely cut specimens show part of the number, the percentage visible depending, of course, on the width of the margin containing the number. It follows that the bigger the percentage, the greater the desirability. It is possible to obtain 100% complete numbers on several booklet-pane plates, but, although seen infrequently, their scarcity does not compare with that of 100% coil numbers. Any complete coil-plate number is **rare**.

It is possible to reconstruct numerous coil-plate numbers by joining partial plates.

The full numbers seen on booklet panes are invariably upper- or lower-left positions. The cutting is never as wide on upper and lower rights, and booklet-pane specialists are usually satisfied when right-pane plate number percentages are large enough to be identified.

BOOKLET PANES

ROTARY PRESS

PANES OF 6

#720b 3¢ "STUART"WASHINGTON

20900 20901 *20902 20903 20904
20905 21010 21011 21012 21013
21489 21490 21515 21516 21519
21520

See appendix G for largest reported plate number percentage by position.

SIDE COILS

Perf.10 VERTICALLY

#721 3¢ "STUART" WASHINGTON

Positions T, B **88 Plates**

20916 *20917 *20918 *20919 20936
20937 20938 20939 20940 20941
20942 20943 20944 20945 20946
20947 20948 20949 20976 20977
20978 20979 20994 20995 *21002
21003 21016 21017 *21020 21021

1932 REGULAR ISSUE

#721 3¢"STUART" WASHINGTON Cont.

*21026 *21027 21050 21051 *21052
21053 *21060 21061 *21062 *21063
21076 21077 21084 21085 21086
21087 21222 21223 21477 21478
21479 21480 21481 21482 21483
21484 21513 21514 21541 21542
21543 21544 21553 21554

Numbers through 21554 were entered approximately 1/16 inch from the stamp design. Those that follow were wide spaced, about 1/8 inch from the design. Because of the wide spacing, very few of the numbers are known to exist.

†21592 †21593 †21596 †21597 †21639
†21640 †21641 †21642 †21643 †21644
†21646 †21647 *21648 *21675 †21702
†21703 †21704 *21790 †21791 †21792
*21799 †21800 †21803 †21804

END COILS

Perf. 10 HORIZONTALLY

#722 3¢ "STUART" WASHINGTON

Positions L, R **2 Plates**

20930 20931

SIDE COILS

#723 6¢ GARFIELD

See page 89

1932 COMMEMORATIVES

FLAT PRESS

#724 3¢ PENN

		TL	TR	L	R	B
21064	$10	□	□	‡	‡	□
21065	$10	□	□	‡	‡	□
21066	$10	□	□	‡	‡	□
21067	$10	□	□	‡	‡	□
21068	$10	□	□	‡	‡	□
21069	$10	□	□	‡	‡	□
21070	$10	□	□	‡	‡	□
21071	$10	□	□	‡	‡	□
21072	$10	□	□	‡	‡	□
21073	$10	□	□	‡	‡	□
21074	$10	□	□	‡	‡	□
21075	$10	□	□	‡	‡	□

#725 3¢ WEBSTER

21034	$20	□	□	‡	‡	□
21035	$20	□	□	‡	‡	□
21036	$20	□	□	‡	‡	□
21037	$20	□	□	‡	‡	□

1932 COMMEMORATIVES

#725 3¢ WEBSTER Cont.

		TL	TR	L	R	B
21038	$20	☐	☐	‡	‡	☐
21039	$20	☐	☐	‡	‡	☐
21040	$20	☐	☐	‡	‡	☐
21041	$20	☐	☐	‡	‡	☐
21046	$20	☐	☐	‡	‡	☐
21047	$20	☐	☐	‡	‡	☐
21048	$20	☐	☐	‡	‡	☐
21049	$20	☐	☐	‡	‡	☐

1933 COMMEMORATIVES

#726 3¢ OGLETHORPE

There are no F numbers on Oglethorpe plates. Instead, the initials C.S., indicating chromed steel, appear in the top margin over the stamp second to the left of the plate-number copy. The inscription is entered on right panes only. Since Blocks of 6 stamps may be from either pane, we list them as T (Top).

Top blocks of 10 showing the C. S., or its absence, sell for 1.5 times the basic price.

		T	CS	L	R	B
21096	$12	☐	☐	‡	‡	☐
21097	$12	☐	☐	‡	‡	☐
21098	$12	☐	☐	‡	‡	☐
21099	$12	☐	☐	‡	‡	☐
21100	$12	☐	☐	‡	‡	☐
21101	$12	☐	☐	‡	‡	☐
21102	$12	☐	☐	‡	‡	☐
21103	$12	☐	☐	‡	‡	☐
21104	$12	☐	☐	‡	‡	☐
21105	$12	☐	☐	‡	‡	☐
21106	$12	☐	☐	‡	‡	☐
21107	$12	☐	☐	‡	‡	☐
21108	$12	☐	☐	‡	‡	☐
21109	$12	☐	☐	‡	‡	☐
21110	$12	☐	☐	‡	‡	☐
21111	$12	☐	☐	‡	‡	☐

1933 COMMEMORATIVES

ROTARY PRESS

#727 3¢ NEWBURGH

		UL	UR	LL	LR
21118**N**	$5	☐	☐	☐	☐
21119**N**	$5	☐	☐	☐	☐
21120	$5	☐	☐	☐	☐
21121	$5	☐	☐	☐	☐
21123	$5	☐	☐	☐	☐
21124	$5	☐	☐	☐	☐

N These plates also used for #752 but issued without gum.

#728 1¢ CENTURY OF PROGRESS

21131	$3	☐	☐	☐	☐
21132	$3	☐	☐	☐	☐
21133	$3	☐	☐	☐	☐
21134	$3	☐	☐	☐	☐
21135	$3	☐	☐	☐	☐
21136	$3	☐	☐	☐	☐
21139	$6	☐	☐	☐	☐
21140	$6	☐	☐	☐	☐
21141	$20	☐	☐	☐	☐
21142	$20	☐	☐	☐	☐

#729 3¢ CENTURY OF PROGRESS

21125	$3	☐	☐	☐	☐
21126	$3	☐	☐	☐	☐
21127	$3	☐	☐	☐	☐
21128	$3	☐	☐	☐	☐
21129	$3	☐	☐	☐	☐
21130	$3	☐	☐	☐	☐
21137	$4.50	☐	☐	☐	☐
21138	$4.50	☐	☐	☐	☐

1933 CENTURY OF PROGRESS SOUVENIR SHEETS

IMPERFORATE PANES OF 25

FLAT PRESS Issued WIthout Gum

#730 1¢

		B
21145	$30	☐
21159	$30	☐

#731 3¢

21146	$25	☐
21160	$25	☐

SHEET STAMPS

ROTARY PRESS

#732 3¢ N. R. A.

		UL	UR	LL	LR
21151	$2	☐	☐	☐	☐
21152	$2	☐	☐	☐	☐
21153	$2	☐	☐	☐	☐
21154	$2	☐	☐	☐	☐
21155	$2	☐	☐	☐	☐
21156	$2	☐	☐	☐	☐
21157	$2	☐	☐	☐	☐
21158	$2	☐	☐	☐	☐

1933 COMMEMORATIVES

#732 3¢ N. R. A. Cont.

		UL	UR	LL	LR
21161	$2	□	□	□	□
21162	$5	□	□	□	□
21163	$2	□	□	□	□
21164	$2	□	□	□	□
21165	$2	□	□	□	□
21166	$2	□	□	□	□

FLAT PRESS

#733 3¢ BYRD

		TL	TR	L	R	B
21167	$20	□	Z	‡	‡	□
21168	$20	□	Z	‡	‡	□
21169	$20	□	Z	‡	‡	□
21170	$20	□	Z	‡	‡	□

Same plates used for #753 but issued without gum.

#734 5¢ KOSCIUSZKO

		TL	TR	L	R	B
21173	$30	□	Z	‡	‡	□
21174	$30	□	Z	‡	‡	□
21175	$30	□	Z	‡	‡	□
21176	$30	□	Z	‡	‡	□

Z no F in top right position

1934 COMMEMORATIVES

SOUVENIR SHEET

IMPERFORATE PANE OF 6

FLAT PRESS Issued Without Gum

#735 BYRD

		B
21184	$15	□

SHEET STAMPS

FLAT PRESS

#736 3¢ MARYLAND

		TL	TR	L	R	B
21188	$10	□	□	‡	‡	□
21189	$10	□	□	‡	‡	□
21190	$10	□	□	‡	‡	□
21191	$10	□	□	‡	‡	□
21196	$10	□	□	‡	‡	□
21197	$10	□	□	‡	‡	□
21198	$10	□	□	‡	‡	□
21199	$10	□	□	‡	‡	□

ROTARY PRESS

#737 3¢ MOTHER'S DAY

		UL	UR	LL	LR
21210	$2	□	□	□	□
21211	$2	□	□	□	□
21212	$2	□	□	□	□
21213	$2	□	□	□	□
21214	$2	□	□	□	□
21215	$2	□	□	□	□
21216	$2	□	□	□	□
21217	$2	□	□	□	□
21218	$2	□	□	□	□
21219	$2	□	□	□	□

1934 COMMEMORATIVES

FLAT PRESS

#738 3¢ MOTHER'S DAY

		TL	TR	L	R	B
21202	$5	□	□	‡	‡	□
21203	$5	□	□	‡	‡	□
21204	$5	□	Z	‡	‡	□
21205	$5	□	□	‡	‡	□

Z no F in top right position

#739 3¢ WISCONSIN

		TL	TR	L	R	B
21238	$4	□	□	‡	‡	□
21239	$4	□	□	‡	‡	□
21240	$4	□	□	‡	‡	□
21241	$4	□	□	‡	‡	□
21242	$4	□	□	‡	‡	□
21243	$4	□	□	‡	‡	□
21244	$4	□	□	‡	‡	□
21245	$4	□	□	‡	‡	□

1934 NATIONAL PARKS

#740 1¢ YOSEMITE

		TL	TR	L	R	B
21246	$1.50	□	□	‡	‡	□
21247	$1.50	□	□	‡	‡	□
21248	$1.50	□	□	‡	‡	□
21249	$1.50	□	□	‡	‡	□
21250	$1.50	□	□	‡	‡	□
21251	$1.50	□	□	‡	‡	□
21252	$1.50	□	□	‡	‡	□
21253	$1.50	□	□	‡	‡	□

#741 2¢ GRAND CANYON

		TL	TR	L	R	B
21254	$1.50	□	□	‡	‡	□
21255	$1.50	□	□	‡	‡	□
21256	$1.50	□	□	‡	‡	□
21257	$1.50	□	□	‡	‡	□
21258	$1.50	□	□	‡	‡	□
21259	$1.50	□	□	‡	‡	□
21260	$1.50	□	□	‡	‡	□
21261	$1.50	□	□	‡	‡	□

#742 3¢ MT. RAINIER

		TL	TR	L	R	B
21262	$2.25	□	□	‡	‡	□
21263	$2.25	□	□	‡	‡	□
21264	$2.25	□	□	‡	‡	□
21265	$2.25	□	□	‡	‡	□
21274	$2.25	□	□	‡	‡	□
21275	$2.25	□	□	‡	‡	□
21276	$2.25	□	□	‡	‡	□
21277	$2.25	□	□	‡	‡	□
21332	$2.75	□	□	‡	‡	□

#743 4¢ MESA VERDE

		TL	TR	L	R	B
21328	$8	□	□	‡	‡	□
21329	$8	□	□	‡	‡	□
21330	$8	□	□	‡	‡	□
21331	$8	□	□	‡	‡	□

1934 NATIONAL PARKS

#744 5¢ OLD FAITHFUL

		TL	TR	L	R	B
21278	$10	☐	☐	‡	‡	☐
21279	$10	☐	☐	‡	‡	☐
21280	$10	☐	☐	‡	‡	☐
21281	$10	☐	☐	‡	‡	☐

#745 6¢ CRATER LAKE

21320	$18	☐	☐	‡	‡	☐
21321	$18	☐	☐	‡	‡	☐
21322	$18	☐	☐	‡	‡	☐
21323	$18	☐	☐	‡	‡	☐

#746 7¢ ACADIA

21333	$12	☐	☐	‡	‡	☐
21334	$12	☐	☐	‡	‡	☐
21335	$12	☐	☐	‡	‡	☐
21336	$12	☐	☐	‡	‡	☐

#747 8¢ ZION PARK

21324	$20	☐	☐	‡	‡	☐
21325	$20	☐	☐	‡	‡	☐
21326	$20	☐	☐	‡	‡	☐
21327	$20	☐	☐	‡	‡	☐

#748 9¢ GLACIER PARK

21316	$20	☐	☐	‡	‡	☐
21317	$20	☐	☐	‡	‡	☐
21318	$20	☐	☐	‡	‡	☐
21319	$20	☐	☐	‡	‡	☐

#749 10¢ GREAT SMOKY MOUNTAINS

21337	$30	☐	☐	‡	‡	☐
21339	$30	☐	☐	‡	‡	☐
21340	$30	☐	☐	‡	‡	☐
21342	$30	☐	☐	‡	‡	☐

SOUVENIR SHEET

IMPERFORATE PANES OF 6

Issued With Gum

#750 3¢ MT. RAINIER

		B
21303	$32.50	☐

#751 1¢ YOSEMITE

21341	$15	☐

1935 "FARLEY" REPRINTS SPECIAL PRINTINGS

Issued Without Gum

ROTARY PRESS

#752 3¢ NEWBURGH

		UL	UR	LL	LR
21118	$15	☐	☐	☐	☐
21119	$15	☐	☐	☐	☐

Same plates used for #727 but issued with gum.

FLAT PRESS

#753 3¢ BYRD

		TL	TR	L	R	B
21167	$20	☐	Z	‡	‡	☐
21168	$20	☐	Z	‡	‡	☐
21169	$20	☐	Z	‡	‡	☐
21170	$20	☐	Z	‡	‡	☐

Same plates used for #733 but issued with gum.

FLAT PRESS IMPERFORATE

#754 3¢ MOTHER'S DAY

21202	$18	☐	☐	‡	‡	☐
21203	$18	☐	☐	‡	‡	☐
21204	$18	☐	Z	‡	‡	☐
21205	$18	☐	☐	‡	‡	☐

Z no "F" in top right position

#755 3¢ WISCONSIN

21238	$18	☐	☐	‡	‡	☐
21239	$18	☐	☐	‡	‡	☐
21240	$18	☐	☐	‡	‡	☐
21241	$18	☐	☐	‡	‡	☐

#756 1¢ YOSEMITE

21246	$5	☐	☐	‡	‡	☐
21247	$5	☐	☐	‡	‡	☐
21248	$5	☐	☐	‡	‡	☐
21249	$5	☐	☐	‡	‡	☐

#757 2¢ GRAND CANYON

21254	$6	☐	☐	‡	‡	☐
21255	$6	☐	☐	‡	‡	☐
21256	$6	☐	☐	‡	‡	☐
21257	$6	☐	☐	‡	‡	☐

#758 3¢ MT. RAINIER

21262	$15	☐	☐	‡	‡	☐
21263	$15	☐	☐	‡	‡	☐
21264	$15	☐	☐	‡	‡	☐
21265	$15	☐	☐	‡	‡	☐

#759 4¢ MESA VERDE

21328	$19	☐	☐	‡	‡	☐
21329	$19	☐	☐	‡	‡	☐
21330	$19	☐	☐	‡	‡	☐
21331	$19	☐	☐	‡	‡	☐

#760 5¢ OLD FAITHFUL

21278	$24	☐	☐	‡	‡	☐
21279	$24	☐	☐	‡	‡	☐
21280	$24	☐	☐	‡	‡	☐
21281	$24	☐	☐	‡	‡	☐

1935 "FARLEY" REPRINTS SPECIAL PRINTINGS

#761 6¢ CRATER LAKE

		TL	TR	L	R	B
21320	$35	□	□	‡	‡	□
21321	$35	□	□	‡	‡	□
21322	$35	□	□	‡	‡	□
21323	$35	□	□	‡	‡	□

#762 7¢ ACADIA

21333	$32.50	□	□	‡	‡	□
21334	$32.50	□	□	‡	‡	□
21335	$32.50	□	□	‡	‡	□
21336	$32.50	□	□	‡	‡	□

#763 8¢ ZION PARK

21324	$36	□	□	‡	‡	□
21325	$36	□	□	‡	‡	□
21326	$36	□	□	‡	‡	□
21327	$36	□	□	‡	‡	□

#764 9¢ GLACIER PARK

21316	$40	□	□	‡	‡	□
21317	$40	□	□	‡	‡	□
21318	$40	□	□	‡	‡	□
21319	$40	□	□	‡	‡	□

#765 10¢ GREAT SMOKY MOUNTAINS

21337	$50	□	□	‡	‡	□
21339	$50	□	□	‡	‡	□
21340	$50	□	□	‡	‡	□
21342	$50	□	□	‡	‡	□

IMPERFORATE SOUVENIR SHEETS

Blocks of 50 containing 2 complete panes of 25 stamps.

#766 1¢ CENTURY OF PROGRESS

		B
21145	$80	□
21159	$80	□

#767 3¢ CENTURY OF PROGRESS

21146	$75	□
21160	$75	□

Blocks of 12 containing 2 complete panes of 6 stamps.

#768 3¢ BYRD

21184	$50	□

#769 1¢ YOSEMITE

21341	$30	□

#770 3¢ MT. RAINIER

21303	$75	□

#771 16¢ SPECIAL DELIVERY AIR MAIL

		TL	TR	L	R	B
21312	$60	□	□	‡	‡	□
21313	$60	□	□	‡	‡	□
21314	$60	□	□	‡	‡	□
21315	$60	□	□	‡	‡	□

1935 COMMEMORATIVES

ROTARY PRESS

#772 3¢ CONNECTICUT

		UL	UR	LL	LR
21391	$1.75	□	□	□	□
21392	$1.75	□	□	□	□
21393	$1.75	□	□	□	□
21394	$1.75	□	□	□	□
21395	$1.75	□	□	□	□
21396	$1.75	□	□	□	□

#773 3¢ SAN DIEGO

21405	$1.50	□	□	□	□
21406	$1.50	□	□	□	□
21407	$1.50	□	□	□	□
21408	$1.50	□	□	□	□
21409	$1.50	□	□	□	□
21410	$1.50	□	□	□	□

FLAT PRESS

#774 3¢ BOULDER DAM

		TL	TR	L	R	B
21455	$2.00	□	□	‡	‡	□
21456	$2.00	□	□	‡	‡	□
21457	$2.00	□	□	‡	‡	□
21458	$2.00	□	□	‡	‡	□
21459	$2.00	□	□	‡	‡	□
21460	$2.00	□	□	‡	‡	□
21461	$2.00	□	□	‡	‡	□
21462	$2.00	□	□	‡	‡	□
21463	$2.00	□	□	‡	‡	□
21464	$2.00	□	□	‡	‡	□
21465	$2.00	□	□	‡	‡	□
21466	$2.00	□	□	‡	‡	□

ROTARY PRESS

#775 3¢ MICHIGAN

		UL	UR	LL	LR
21467	$1.75	□	□	□	□
21469	$1.75	□	□	□	□
21470	$1.75	□	□	□	□
21471	$1.75	□	□	□	□

1936 COMMEMORATIVES

#776 3¢ TEXAS

21537	$1.75	□	□	□	□
21538	$1.75	□	□	□	□
21539	$1.75	□	□	□	□
21540	$1.75	□	□	□	□

#777 3¢ RHODE ISLAND

21559	$1.75	□	□	□	□
21560	$1.75	□	□	□	□
21561	$1.75	□	□	□	□
21562	$1.75	□	□	□	□

1936 COMMEMORATIVES

#778 TIPEX SOUVENIR SHEET

FLAT PRESS IMPERFORATE

PANE OF 4		B
21557	$2.50	☐
21558	$2.50	☐

ROTARY PRESS

		UL	UR	LL	LR
#782	**3¢ ARKANSAS**				
21564	$1.50	☐	☐	☐	☐
21565	$1.50	☐	☐	☐	☐
21566	$1.50	☐	☐	☐	☐
21567	$1.50	☐	☐	☐	☐
#783	**3¢ OREGON**				
21576	$1.25	☐	☐	☐	☐
21577	$1.25	☐	☐	☐	☐
21578	$1.25	☐	☐	☐	☐
21579	$1.25	☐	☐	☐	☐
#784	**3¢ SUSAN ANTHONY**				
21588	$1	☐	☐	☐	☐
21589	$1	☐	☐	☐	☐
21590	$1	☐	☐	☐	☐
21591	$1	☐	☐	☐	☐

1936-37 COMMEMORATIVES

ARMY and NAVY ISSUES

ROTARY PRESS

		UL	UR	LL	LR
#785	**1¢ ARMY**				
21600	$1	☐	☐	☐	☐
21601	$1	☐	☐	☐	☐
21602	$1	☐	☐	☐	☐
21603	$1	☐	☐	☐	☐
#786	**2¢ ARMY**				
21608	$1	☐	☐	☐	☐
21609	$1	☐	☐	☐	☐
21610	$1	☐	☐	☐	☐
21611	$1	☐	☐	☐	☐
#787	**3¢ ARMY**				
21634	$1.50	☐	☐	☐	☐
21636	$1.50	☐	☐	☐	☐
21637	$1.50	☐	☐	☐	☐
21638	$1.50	☐	☐	☐	☐
#788	**4¢ ARMY**				
21651	$10	☐	☐	☐	☐
21652	$10	☐	☐	☐	☐
21653	$10	☐	☐	☐	☐
21654	$10	☐	☐	☐	☐
#789	**5¢ ARMY**				
21680	$10	☐	☐	☐	☐
21681	$10	☐	☐	☐	☐
21682	$10	☐	☐	☐	☐
21683	$10	☐	☐	☐	☐
#790	**1¢ NAVY**				
21604	$1	☐	☐	☐	☐
21605	$1	☐	☐	☐	☐
21606	$1	☐	☐	☐	☐
21607	$1	☐	☐	☐	☐
#791	**2¢ NAVY**				
21612	$1	☐	☐	☐	☐
21613	$1	☐	☐	☐	☐
21614	$1	☐	☐	☐	☐
21615	$1	☐	☐	☐	☐
#792	**3¢ NAVY**				
21630	$1.50	☐	☐	☐	☐
21631	$1.50	☐	☐	☐	☐
21632	$1.50	☐	☐	☐	☐
21633	$1.50	☐	☐	☐	☐
#793	**4¢ NAVY**				
21655	$10	☐	☐	☐	☐
21656	$10	☐	☐	☐	☐
21657	$10	☐	☐	☐	☐
21658	$10	☐	☐	☐	☐
#794	**5¢ NAVY**				
21684	$10	☐	☐	☐	☐
21685	$10	☐	☐	☐	☐
21686	$10	☐	☐	☐	☐
21687	$10	☐	☐	☐	☐

1936-37 COMMEMORATIVES

ROTARY PRESS

#795 3¢ ORDINANCE

		UL	UR	LL	LR
21691	$1.25	☐	☐	☐	☐
21692	$1.25	☐	☐	☐	☐
21693	$1.25	☐	☐	☐	☐
21694	$1.25	☐	☐	☐	☐

FLAT PRESS

#796 5¢ VIRGINIA DARE

		T	L	R	B
21697	$7.50	☐	‡	‡	☐
21698	$7.50	☐	‡	‡	☐
21699	$7.50	☐	‡	‡	☐
21700	$7.50	☐	‡	‡	☐

#797 10¢ S.P.A. EXPOSITION SHEET

IMPERFORATE		B
21695	$.70	☐
21696	$.70	☐

ROTARY PRESS

#798 3¢ CONSTITUTION

		UL	UR	LL	LR
21705	$1.25	☐	☐	☐	☐
21706	$1.25	☐	☐	☐	☐
21707	$1.25	☐	☐	☐	☐
21708	$1.25	☐	☐	☐	☐
#799 3¢ HAWAII					
21710	$1.50	☐	☐	☐	☐
21711	$1.50	☐	☐	☐	☐
21712	$1.50	☐	☐	☐	☐
21713	$1.50	☐	☐	☐	☐
#800 3¢ ALASKA					
21714	$1.50	☐	☐	☐	☐
21715	$1.50	☐	☐	☐	☐
21716	$1.50	☐	☐	☐	☐
21717	$1.50	☐	☐	☐	☐
#801 3¢ PUERTO RICO					
21721	$1.50	☐	☐	☐	☐
21722	$1.50	☐	☐	☐	☐
21723	$1.50	☐	☐	☐	☐
21724	$1.50	☐	☐	☐	☐
#802 3¢ VIRGIN ISLANDS					
21730	$1.50	☐	☐	☐	☐
21731	$1.50	☐	☐	☐	☐
21732	$1.50	☐	☐	☐	☐
21733	$1.50	☐	☐	☐	☐

1938 REGULAR ISSUE

The 1938 regular issue is also known as the Presidential Series.

CONDITION IMPORTANT: There are no plates in the Presidential Series which cannot be found in very fine condition, and our evaluations are based on "Generally Very Fine." While centering requirements for the very scarce to rare plates may be considered somewhat less exacting, most of them, including the scarcest positions, exist in attractive condition, and our evaluations are based accordingly.

The plates of the Presidential Series have great popular appeal, for the issue marks an important milestone in philatelic history — the conversion from "ordinary" to electronic perforation control. All denominations from the 1/2¢ to 50¢ show the change from "Pre-Eye", to "Eye" plates, and the 2¢ and 3¢ give us examples of the Experimental-Eye printings with plate numbers 3-up or 3-down from the corner stamps of the sheets.

ROTARY PRESS

#803 .5¢ FRANKLIN 6 Plates

Pre-Eye Plates		UL	UR	LL	LR
21885	$.50	☐	☐	☐	☐
21887	$.50	☐	☐	☐	☐
21888	$.50	☐	☐	☐	☐
21889	$.50	☐	☐	☐	☐
21899	$.50	☐	☐	☐	☐
21900	$.50	☐	☐	☐	☐

#803 .5¢ FRANKLIN 10 Plates

Eye Plates					
22406	$.40	☐	☐	☐	☐
22407	$.40	☐	☐	☐	☐
22470	$.40	☐	☐	☐	☐
22471	$.40	☐	☐	☐	☐
22898	$.40	☐	☐	☐	☐
22899	$.40	☐	☐	☐	☐
23408	$.40	☐	☐	☐	☐
23409	$.40	☐	☐	☐	☐
23445**P**	$2.00	☐	☐	☐	☐
23446**P**	$2.00	☐	☐	☐	☐

P These plate numbers have been reported only on precancelled stamps.

#804 1¢ WASHINGTON 55 Plates

Pre-Eye Plates					
21823	$.30	☐	☐	☐	☐
21824	$.30	☐	☐	☐	☐
21825	$.30	☐	☐	☐	☐
21826	$.30	☐	☐	☐2	☐
21828	$.30	☐	☐	☐	☐
21829	$.30	☐	☐	☐	☐
21830	$.50	☐	☐	☐	☐
21831	$.30	☐	☐	☐	☐

1938 REGULAR ISSUE

#804 1¢ WASHINGTON Cont.

Pre-Eye Plates		UL	UR	LL	LR
21832	$.30	□	□	□	□
21833	$.30	□	□	□	□
21834	$600.00	□	□	□	□
21859	$3.00	□	□	□	□
21860	$.30	□	□	□	□
21861	$1.00	□	□	□	□
21862	$.30	□	□	□	□
21863	$1.00	□	□	□	□
21864	$400.00	□	□	□	□
21865	$2.00	□	□	□	□

21866	$2.50	□	□	□	□
21867	$3.00	□	□	□	□
21868	$750.00	□	□	□	□
21869	$3.00	□	□	□	□
21870	$3.00	□	□	□	□
22150	$3.50	□	□	□	□
22151	$4.00	□	□	□	□
22152	$3.00	□	□	□	□
22153	$4.50	□	□	□	□
22240	$1.50	□	□	□	□
22241	$.75	□	□	□	□
22242	$3.00	□	□	□	□
22243	$3.00	□	□	□	□
22244	$2.50	□	□	□	□
22245	$1.50	□	□	□	□
22246	$2.50	□	□	□	□
22247	$2.00	□	□	□	□
22253	$.75	□	□	□	□
22254	$1.00	□	□	□	□
22255	$15.00	□ 2	□ 2	□	□

#804 1¢ WASHINGTON
Pre-Eye Plates Cont.

		UL	UR	LL	LR
22256	$2.00	□	□	□	□
22261	$3.00	□	□	□	□
22262	$3.00	□	□	□	□
22263	$3.00	□	□	□	□
22264	$2.00	□	□	□	□
22265	$4.50	□ 2	□	□	□ 3
22266	$7.00	□ 3	□	□	□ 4
22267	$12.00	□	□	□	□
22268	$15.00	□	□	□	□
22275	$10.00	□	□ 2	□	□
22276	$10.00	□	□ 2	□	□
22277	$10.00	□	□	□	□ 2
22278	$6.00	□	□	□	□ 2
22279	$7.00	□	□ 3	□ 2	□
22280	$10.00	□	□	□	□
22281	$8.00	□	□	□	□
22282	$9.00	□	□	□	□

#804 1¢ WASHINGTON 72 Plates

Eye Plates					
22337	$.25	□	□	□	□
22338	$.25	□	□	□	□
22359	$.25	□	□	□	□
22360	$.25	□	□	□	□
22408	$.25	□	□	□	□
22409	$.25	□	□	□	□
22410	$.25	□	□	□	□
22411	$.25	□	□	□	□
22430	$.25	□	□	□	□
22431	$.25	□	□	□	□
22904	$.25	□	□	□	□
22905	$.25	□	□	□	□
22906	$.25	□	□	□	□
22907	$.25	□	□	□	□
23101	$.25	□	□	□	□
23107	$.25	□	□	□	□
23108	$.25	□	□	□	□
23139	$.25	□	□	□	□
23228	$.25	□	□	□	□
23229	$.25	□	□	□	□

1938 REGULAR ISSUE

#804 1¢ WASHINGTON Cont.

Eye Plates		UL	UR	LL	LR
23303	$.25	☐	☐	☐	☐
23304	$.25	☐	☐	☐	☐
23330	$.25	☐	☐	☐	☐
23331	$.25	☐	☐	☐	☐
23332	$.25	☐	☐	☐	☐
23333	$.25	☐	☐	☐	☐
23406	$.25	☐	☐	☐	☐
23407	$.25	☐	☐	☐	☐
23414	$.25	☐	☐	☐	☐
23415	$.25	☐	☐	☐	☐
23433	$.25	☐	☐	☐	☐
23434	$.25	☐	☐	☐	☐
23436	$.25	☐	☐	☐	☐
23437	$.25	☐	☐	☐	☐
23451	$.25	☐	☐	☐	☐
23452	$.25	☐	☐	☐	☐
23455	$.25	☐	☐	☐	☐
23456	$.25	☐	☐	☐	☐
23529	$.25	☐	☐	☐	☐
23530	$.25	☐	☐	☐	☐
23650	$.25	☐	☐	☐	☐
23651	$.25	☐	☐	☐	☐
23679	$.25	☐	☐	☐	☐
23680	$.25	☐	☐	☐	☐
23746	$.25	☐	☐	☐	☐
23747	$.25	☐	☐	☐	☐
23748	$.25	☐	☐	☐	☐
23749	$.25	☐	☐	☐	☐
23754	$.25	☐	☐	☐	☐
23755	$.25	☐	☐	☐	☐
23782	$.25	☐	☐	☐	☐
23783	$.25	☐	☐	☐	☐
23837	$.25	☐	☐	☐	☐
23838	$.25	☐	☐	☐	☐
24003	$.25	☐	☐	☐	☐
24004	$.25	☐	☐	☐	☐
24007	$.25	☐	☐	☐	☐
24008	$.25	☐	☐	☐	☐
24009	$.25	☐	☐	☐	☐
24010	$.25	☐	☐	☐	☐
24015	$.25	☐	☐	☐	☐
24016	$.25	☐	☐	☐	☐
24023	$.25	☐	☐	☐	☐
24024	$.25	☐	☐	☐	☐
24131	$.25	☐	☐	☐	☐
24132	$.25	☐	☐	☐	☐
24276	$.25	☐	☐	☐	☐
24277	$.25	☐	☐	☐	☐
24282	$.25	☐	☐	☐	☐
24288	$.25	☐	☐	☐	☐
24289	$3.50	☐	☐	☐	☐
24290	$3.50	☐	☐	☐	☐

#805 1.5¢ MARTHA WASHINGTON

Pre-Eye Plates 31 Plates

		UL	UR	LL	LR
21873	$.50	☐	☐	☐	☐
21874	$.50	☐	☐	☐	☐
21876	$2.00	☐	☐	☐	☐

#805 1.5¢ MARTHA WASHINGTON Cont.

		UL	UR	LL	LR
21877	$3.00	☐	☐	☐	☐
21878	$.30	☐	☐	☐	☐
21879	$.30	☐	☐	☐	☐
21880	$100.00	☐	☐	☐	☐
21881	$1.00	☐	☐	☐	☐
21882	$2.50	☐	☐	☐	☐
21883	$1.50	☐	☐	☐	☐
21884	$3.00	☐	☐	☐	☐
21934	$4.00	☐	☐	☐	☐
21935	$3.50	☐	☐	☐	☐
21936	$2.50	☐	☐	☐	☐
21937	$1.00	☐	☐	☐	☐

		UL	UR	LL	LR
22077	$1.50	☐	☐	☐	☐
22078	$1.00	☐	☐	☐	☐
22079	$.75	☐	☐	☐	☐
22080	$2.50	☐	☐	☐	☐2
22154	$100.00	☐	☐	☐	☐
22155	$3.00	☐	☐	☐	☐
22172	$4.00	☐	☐	☐	☐
22173	$.75	☐	☐	☐	☐
22174	$.30	☐	☐	☐	☐
22175	$2.50	☐	☐	☐	☐
22315	$2.50	☐	☐	☐	☐
22316	$4.00	☐	☐	☐	☐
22317	$3.00	☐	☐	☐	☐
22318	$5.00	☐	☐	☐	☐
22339	$2.50	☐	☐	☐	☐
22340	$1.50	☐	☐	☐	☐

#805 1.5¢ MARTHA WASHINGTON

Eye Plates 66 Plates

		UL	UR	LL	LR
22412	$.30	☐	☐	☐	☐
22413	$.30	☐	☐	☐	☐
22414	$.30	☐	☐	☐	☐
22415	$.30	☐	☐	☐	☐
22432	$.30	☐	☐	☐	☐
22433	$.30	☐	☐	☐	☐

1938 REGULAR ISSUE

#805 1.5¢ MARTHA WASHINGTON
Eye Plates **Cont.**

		UL	UR	LL	LR
22464	$.30	☐	☐	☐	☐
22465	$2.50	☐	☐	☐	☐
22466	$.30	☐	☐	☐	☐
22467	$2.00	☐2	☐	☐	☐
22472	$.30	☐	☐	☐	☐
22473	$.30	☐	☐	☐	☐
22645	$.30	☐	☐	☐	☐
22646	$.30	☐	☐	☐	☐
22876	$.30	☐	☐	☐	☐
22877	$.30	☐	☐	☐	☐
22880**N**	$2.00	☐	☐	☐	☐
22881	$.30	☐	☐	☐	☐
22916	$.30	☐	☐	☐	☐
22917	$.30	☐	☐	☐	☐
22918	$.30	☐	☐	☐	☐
22919	$.30	☐	☐	☐	☐
23083	$.30	☐	☐	☐	☐
23084	$.30	☐	☐	☐	☐
23085	$.30	☐	☐	☐	☐
23086	$.30	☐	☐	☐	☐
23087	$.30	☐	☐	☐	☐
23088	$.30	☐	☐	☐	☐
23089	$.30	☐	☐	☐	☐
23090	$.30	☐	☐	☐	☐
23203	$.30	☐	☐	☐	☐
23204	$.30	☐	☐	☐	☐
23205	$.30	☐	☐	☐	☐
23206	$.30	☐	☐	☐	☐
23209	$.30	☐	☐	☐	☐
23210	$.30	☐	☐	☐	☐
23289	$.30	☐	☐	☐	☐
23290	$.30	☐	☐	☐	☐
23371	$.30	☐	☐	☐	☐
23372	$.30	☐	☐	☐	☐
23373	$.30	☐	☐	☐	☐
23374	$.30	☐	☐	☐	☐
23379	$.30	☐	☐	☐	☐
23380	$.30	☐	☐	☐	☐
23453	$.30	☐	☐	☐	☐
23454	$.30	☐	☐	☐	☐
23697	$1.00	☐	☐3	☐3	☐
23698	$.50	☐	☐3	☐3	☐
23730	$.30	☐	☐	☐	☐
23731	$.30	☐	☐	☐	☐
23734	$1.00	☐	☐	☐	☐
23735	$3.00	☐	☐	☐	☐
23742	$2.00	☐	☐	☐	☐
23743	$1.50	☐	☐	☐	☐
23756	$3.00	☐	☐	☐	☐
23757	$4.00	☐	☐	☐	☐

N This plate, although not scarce, is of special interest because the second 8 is inverted.

#805 1.5¢ MARTHA WASHINGTON
Eye Plates **Cont.**

		UL	UR	LL	LR
23764	$1.50	☐	☐	☐	☐
23765	$.50	☐	☐	☐	☐
23766	$3.50	☐	☐	☐	☐
23767	$4.00	☐	☐	☐	☐
23778	$1.50	☐	☐	☐	☐
23779	$2.00	☐	☐	☐	☐
23823	$.75	☐	☐	☐	☐
23824	$2.00	☐	☐	☐	☐
23870	$3.50	☐	☐	☐	☐
23871	$3.00	☐	☐	☐	☐

#806 2¢ JOHN ADAMS 12 Plates
Pre-Eye Plates

21891	$.35	☐	☐	☐	☐
21892	$.35	☐	☐	☐	☐
21893	$.35	☐	☐	☐	☐
21894	$.35	☐	☐	☐	☐
22283	$2.75	☐	☐	☐	☐
22284	$1.50	☐	☐	☐	☐
22285	$4.25	☐	☐	☐	☐
22286	$3.50	☐	☐	☐	☐
22297	$6.25	☐	☐	☐	☐
22298	$4.25	☐	☐	☐	☐
22299	$2.00	☐	☐	☐	☐
22300	$2.00	☐	☐	☐	☐

#806 2¢ JOHN ADAMS
EXPERIMENTAL EYE PLATES
Corner Vertical Blocks of 10 6 Plates

21895	$8.00	☐	☐	☐	☐
21896	$4.00	☐	☐	☐	☐
21897	$5.00	☐	☐	☐	☐
21898	$4.00	☐	☐	☐	☐
22000	$5.00	☐	☐	☐	☐
22001	$6.00	☐	☐	☐	☐

#806 2¢ JOHN ADAMS
Eye Plates Blocks of 4 92 Plates

21999	$.70	☐	☐	☐	☐
22002	$.35	☐	☐	☐	☐
22051	$.35	☐	☐	☐	☐
22052	$2.00	☐	☐	☐	☐
22053	$4.25	☐	☐	☐	☐
22054	$4.25	☐	☐	☐	☐
22156	$2.00	☐	☐	☐	☐
22157	$.70	☐	☐	☐	☐
22158	$4.25	☐	☐	☐	☐
22159	$4.25	☐	☐	☐	☐
22319	$1.00	☐	☐	☐	☐
22320	$.35	☐	☐	☐	☐
22420	$2.75	☐2	☐	☐	☐2
22421	$.35	☐	☐	☐	☐
22424	$.35	☐	☐	☐	☐
22425	$.35	☐	☐	☐	☐
22444	$.35	☐	☐	☐	☐
22445	$.35	☐	☐	☐	☐

1938 REGULAR ISSUE

#806 2¢ JOHN ADAMS Cont.
Eye Plates

		UL	UR	LL	LR
22453	$.35	☐	☐	☐	☐
22454	$.35	☐	☐	☐	☐
22468	$.35	☐	☐	☐	☐
22469	$.35	☐	☐	☐	☐
22647	$.35	☐	☐	☐	☐
22648	$.35	☐	☐	☐	☐
22649	$.35	☐	☐	☐	☐
22650	$.35	☐	☐	☐	☐
23796	$.35	☐	☐	☐	☐
23797	$.35	☐	☐	☐	☐
23981	$.35	☐	☐	☐	☐
23982	$.35	☐	☐	☐	☐
23983	$.35	☐	☐	☐	☐
23984	$.70	☐	☐	☐	☐
23987	$1.00	☐	☐	☐	☐
23988	$.70	☐	☐	☐	☐
23989	$1.00	☐	☐	☐	☐
23990	$.35	☐	☐	☐	☐
23991	$.70	☐	☐	☐	☐
23992	$.35	☐	☐	☐	☐
23993	$.35	☐	☐	☐	☐
23994	$.35	☐	☐	☐	☐
23995	$2.75	☐	☐	☐	☐
23996	$.35	☐	☐	☐	☐
23997	$.35	☐	☐	☐	☐
23998	$.35	☐	☐	☐	☐
23999	$.35	☐	☐	☐	☐
24000	$.70	☐	☐	☐	☐
24112	$2.75	☐	☐	☐	☐
24113	$.35	☐	☐	☐	☐
24127	$.70	☐	☐	☐	☐
24128	$1.50	☐	☐	☐	☐
24300	$3.50	☐	☐	☐	☐
24301	$2.00	☐	☐	☐	☐
24304	$1.00	☐	☐	☐	☐
24305	$1.50	☐	☐	☐	☐
24306	$4.25	☐	☐	☐	☐
24307	$3.50	☐	☐	☐	☐
24316	$2.75	☐	☐	☐	☐
24319	$6.25	☐	☐	☐	☐
24324	$2.00	☐	☐	☐	☐
24325	$3.50	☐	☐	☐	☐
24330	$2.75	☐	☐	☐	☐
24331	$.35	☐	☐	☐	☐
24346	$1.00	☐	☐	☐	☐
24347	$5.00	☐	☐	☐	☐
24372	$2.00	☐	☐	☐	☐
24373	$2.75	☐	☐	☐	☐
24378	$2.75	☐	☐	☐	☐
24379	$2.75	☐	☐	☐	☐
24382	$2.75	☐	☐	☐	☐
24383	$5.75	☐	☐	☐	☐
24483	$8.50	☐	☐	☐	☐
24484	$2.75	☐	☐	☐	☐
24540	$.70	☐	☐	☐	☐

#806 2¢ JOHN ADAMS Cont.
Eye Plates

		UL	UR	LL	LR
24541	$.70	☐	☐	☐	☐
24566	$3.50	☐	☐	☐	☐
24567	$4.25	☐	☐	☐	☐
24601	$4.25	☐	☐	☐	☐
24602	$.35	☐	☐	☐	☐
24711	$2.00	☐	☐	☐	☐
24712	$1.50	☐	☐	☐	☐
24713	$.35	☐	☐	☐	☐
24714	$.70	☐	☐	☐	☐
24721	$2.00	☐	☐	☐	☐
24722	$1.50	☐	☐	☐	☐
24723	$1.00	☐	☐	☐	☐
24724	$3.50	☐	☐	☐	☐
24741	$2.75	☐	☐	☐	☐
24742	$7.75	☐	☐	☐	☐
24811	$4.25	☐	☐	☐	☐
24812	$3.50	☐	☐	☐	☐
24910	$.35	☐	☐	☐	☐
24911	$1.00	☐	☐	☐	☐

#807 3¢ JEFFERSON 48 Plates
Pre-Eye Plates

21925	$.35	☐	☐	☐	☐
21926	$4.25	☐	☐	☐	☐
21927	$.70	☐	☐	☐	☐
21928	$.35	☐	☐	☐	☐
21929	$.70	☐	☐	☐	☐
21930	$1.00	☐	☐	☐	☐
21931	$1.00	☐	☐	☐	☐
21932	$.35	☐	☐	☐	☐
21938	$.35	☐	☐	☐	☐
21939	$.35	☐	☐	☐	☐
21940	$2.00	☐	☐	☐	☐
21941	$.70	☐	☐	☐	☐
21942	$.35	☐	☐	☐	☐
21943	$1.50	☐	☐	☐	☐
21944	$2.00	☐	☐	☐	☐
21945	$.35	☐	☐	☐	☐
22055	$.70	☐	☐	☐	☐
22056	$1.00	☐	☐	☐	☐
22057	$6.25	☐	☐	☐	☐
22058	$1.00	☐	☐	☐	☐
22059	$.70	☐	☐	☐	☐
22060	$2.00	☐	☐	☐	☐
22061	$1.50	☐	☐	☐	☐
22062	$2.00	☐	☐	☐	☐
22063	$3.50	☐	☐	☐	☐
22064	$2.75	☐	☐	☐	☐
22065	$1.50	☐	☐	☐	☐
22066	$3.50	☐	☐	☐	☐
22067	$5.00	☐	☐	☐	☐
22068	$.35	☐	☐	☐	☐
22069	$3.50	☐	☐	☐	☐
22070	$1.00	☐	☐	☐	☐
22104	$2.75	☐	☐	☐	☐
22105	$1.00	☐	☐	☐	☐
22106	$1.50	☐	☐	☐	☐
22107	$3.50	☐	☐	☐	☐
22131	$4.25	☐	☐	☐	☐
22132	$6.75	☐	☐	☐	☐

1938 REGULAR ISSUE

#807 3¢ JEFFERSON
Pre-Eye Plates **Cont.**

		UL	UR	LL	LR
22133	$2.75	☐	☐	☐	☐
22134	$8.00	☐	☐	☐	☐
22137	$6.25	☐	☐	☐	☐
22138	$4.25	☐	☐	☐	☐
22139	$7.00	☐	☐	☐	☐
22140	$6.25	☐	☐	☐	☐
22141	$15.00	☐	☐	☐	☐
22142	$25.00	☐	☐	☐	☐
22160	$7.00	☐	☐	☐	☐
22161	$10.00	☐	☐	☐	☐

#807 3¢ JEFFERSON 6 Plates
EXPERIMENTAL-EYE PLATES
Corner Vertical Blocks of 10

22301	$20.00	☐	☐	☐	☐
22302	$20.00	☐	☐	☐	☐
22355	$25.00	☐	☐	☐	☐
22356	$20.00	☐	☐	☐	☐
22357	$25.00	☐	☐	☐	☐
22358	$25.00	☐	☐	☐	☐

#807 3¢ JEFFERSON
Eye Plates **Blocks of 4** **302 Plates**

22361	$.35	☐	☐	☐	☐
22362	$.35	☐	☐	☐	☐
22363	$.35	☐	☐	☐	☐
22364	$.35	☐	☐	☐	☐
22422	$.35	☐	☐	☐	☐
22423	$.35	☐	☐	☐	☐
22426	$.35	☐	☐	☐	☐
22427	$2.75	☐	☐	☐	☐
22446	$.35	☐	☐	☐	☐
22447	$2.00	☐	☐	☐	☐
22455	$2.75	☐	☐	☐	☐
22456	$5.75	☐	☐	☐	☐
22462	$1.50	☐	☐	☐	☐
22463	$1.50	☐	☐	☐	☐
22651	$1.00	☐	☐	☐	☐
22652	$.35	☐	☐	☐	☐

#807 3¢ JEFFERSON
Eye Plates **Cont.**

		UL	UR	LL	LR
22653	$.35	☐	☐	☐	☐
22654	$.35	☐	☐	☐	☐
22655	$.35	☐	☐	☐	☐
22656	$.35	☐	☐	☐	☐
22920	$.35	☐	☐	☐	☐
22921	$.35	☐	☐	☐	☐
22928	$1.00	☐	☐	☐	☐
22929	$.35	☐	☐	☐	☐
22936	$.35	☐	☐	☐	☐
22937	$.35	☐	☐	☐	☐
23056	$.35	☐	☐	☐	☐
23057	$.35	☐	☐	☐	☐
23066	$.35	☐	☐	☐	☐
23067	$.35	☐	☐	☐	☐
23091	$.35	☐	☐	☐	☐
23092	$.35	☐	☐	☐	☐
23095	$.35	☐	☐	☐	☐
23096	$.35	☐	☐	☐	☐
23193	$.35	☐	☐	☐	☐
23194	$.35	☐	☐	☐	☐
23199	$4.00	☐	☐	☐	☐2
23200	$5.75	☐	☐	☐2	☐2
23201	$.35	☐	☐	☐	☐
23202	$.35	☐	☐	☐	☐
23250	$1.00	☐	☐	☐	☐
23251	$.70	☐	☐	☐	☐
23254	$1.00	☐	☐	☐	☐
23255	$.35	☐	☐	☐	☐
23316	$.35	☐	☐	☐	☐
23317	$.35	☐	☐	☐	☐
23318	$.35	☐	☐	☐	☐
23319	$.35	☐	☐	☐	☐
23320	$.35	☐	☐	☐	☐
23321	$.35	☐	☐	☐	☐
23322	$.35	☐	☐	☐	☐
23323	$.35	☐	☐	☐	☐
23359	$.35	☐	☐	☐	☐
23360	$.35	☐	☐	☐	☐
23363	$.35	☐	☐	☐	☐
23364	$.35	☐	☐	☐	☐
23384	$.35	☐	☐	☐	☐
23385	$.35	☐	☐	☐	☐
23386	$.35	☐	☐	☐	☐
23387	$.35	☐	☐	☐	☐
23390	$.35	☐	☐	☐	☐
23391	$.35	☐	☐	☐	☐
23396	$.35	☐	☐	☐	☐
23397	$.35	☐	☐	☐	☐
23401	$.35	☐	☐	☐	☐
23402	$.35	☐	☐	☐	☐
23403	$.35	☐	☐	☐	☐

1938 REGULAR ISSUE

#807 3¢ JEFFERSON
Eye Plates **Cont.**

		UL	UR	LL	LR
23404	$.35	☐	☐	☐	☐
23418	$.35	☐	☐	☐	☐
23419	$.35	☐	☐	☐	☐
23424	$.35	☐	☐	☐	☐
23425	$.35	☐	☐	☐	☐
23426	$.35	☐	☐	☐	☐
23427	$.35	☐	☐	☐	☐
23443	$.35	☐	☐	☐	☐
23444	$1.50	☐	☐	☐	☐
23457	$.35	☐	☐	☐	☐
23458	$.35	☐	☐	☐	☐
23527	$.35	☐	☐	☐	☐
23528	$.35	☐	☐	☐	☐
23539	$.35	☐	☐	☐	☐
23540	$.35	☐	☐	☐	☐
23541	$.35	☐	☐	☐	☐
23542	$.35	☐	☐	☐	☐
23543	$.35	☐	☐	☐	☐
23544	$.35	☐	☐	☐	☐
23545	$.35	☐	☐	☐	☐
23546	$.70	☐	☐	☐	☐
23547	$.35	☐	☐	☐	☐
23548	$.70	☐	☐	☐	☐
23550	$.35	☐	☐	☐	☐
23551	$.35	☐	☐	☐	☐
23552	$.35	☐	☐	☐	☐
23554	$.35	☐	☐	☐	☐
23555	$.35	☐	☐	☐	☐
23556	$.35	☐	☐	☐	☐
23557	$.35	☐	☐	☐	☐
23565	$.35	☐	☐	☐	☐
23566	$.35	☐	☐	☐	☐
23569	$.70	☐	☐	☐	☐
23570	$12.00	☐	☐	☐	☐
23571	$.35	☐	☐	☐	☐
23572	$.35	☐	☐	☐	☐
23575	$.35	☐	☐	☐	☐
23646	$.35	☐	☐	☐	☐
23647	$5.00	☐	☐	☐	☐3
23675	$.35	☐	☐	☐	☐
23676	$.70	☐	☐	☐	☐
23677	$.35	☐	☐	☐	☐
23678**N**	$.35	☐	☐	☐	☐
23695	$.35	☐	☐	☐	☐
23696	$.35	☐	☐	☐	☐
23699	$.35	☐	☐	☐	☐
23700	$.35	☐	☐	☐	☐
23701	$.35	☐	☐	☐	☐
23702	$.35	☐	☐	☐	☐
23703	$.35	☐	☐	☐	☐
23704	$.35	☐	☐	☐	☐

N Common plate but of interest because of number entry about 1/8" from design like pre-eye and experimental-eye plates of the series. All other Presidential eye numbers were entered about 1/16" from design.

#807 3¢ JEFFERSON
Eye Plates **Cont.**

		UL	UR	LL	LR
23705	$.35	☐	☐	☐	☐
23706	$1.00	☐	☐	☐	☐
23724	$.35	☐	☐	☐	☐

		UL	UR	LL	LR
23725	$.35	☐	☐	☐	☐
23726	$.35	☐	☐	☐	☐
23727	$1.50	☐	☐	☐	☐
23728	$.35	☐	☐	☐	☐
23729	$.35	☐	☐	☐	☐
23732	$.35	☐	☐	☐	☐
23733	$.35	☐	☐	☐	☐
23760	$25.00	☐	☐	☐	☐
23761	$.35	☐	☐	☐	☐
23790	$.35	☐	☐	☐	☐
23791	$.35	☐	☐	☐	☐
23794	$.35	☐	☐	☐	☐
23795	$.70	☐	☐	☐	☐
23827	$.35	☐	☐	☐	☐
23828	$.35	☐	☐	☐	☐
23862	$.35	☐	☐	☐	☐
23863	$.35	☐	☐	☐	☐
23868	$.35	☐	☐	☐	☐
23869	$.35	☐	☐	☐	☐
23886	$.35	☐	☐	☐	☐
23887	$ 35	☐	☐	☐	☐
23894	$.35	☐	☐	☐	☐
23895	$.35	☐	☐	☐	☐
23914	$.35	☐	☐	☐	☐
23915	$.35	☐	☐	☐	☐
23951	$.35	☐	☐	☐	☐
23952	$.35	☐	☐	☐	☐
23959	$.35	☐	☐	☐	☐
23960	$.35	☐	☐	☐	☐
23971	$.35	☐	☐	☐	☐
23972	$.35	☐	☐	☐	☐
24001	$.35	☐	☐	☐	☐
24002	$.35	☐	☐	☐	☐
24005	$.70	☐	☐	☐	☐
24006	$.35	☐	☐	☐	☐
24011	$.35	☐	☐	☐	☐
24012	$2.00	☐	☐	☐	☐

1938 REGULAR ISSUE

#807 3¢ JEFFERSON
Eye Plates

Plate	Price	UL	UR	LL	LR
24013	$.70	☐	☐	☐	☐
24014	$.35	☐	☐	☐	☐
24017	$.35	☐	☐	☐	☐
24018	$1.00	☐	☐	☐	☐
24044	$.35	☐	☐	☐	☐
24045	$.35	☐	☐	☐	☐
24054	$.35	☐	☐	☐	☐
24055	$.35	☐	☐	☐	☐
24056	$.35	☐	☐	☐	☐
24057	$.70	☐	☐	☐	☐

Plate	Price	UL	UR	LL	LR
24071	$1.50	☐	☐	☐	☐
24072	$.35	☐	☐	☐	☐
24105	$1.00	☐	☐	☐	☐
24106	$.35	☐	☐	☐	☐
24109	$.70	☐	☐	☐	☐
24110	$.70	☐	☐	☐	☐
24111	$.35	☐	☐	☐	☐
24114	$.70	☐	☐	☐	☐
24115	$.35	☐	☐	☐	☐
24124	$1.50	☐	☐	☐	☐
24125	$.70	☐	☐	☐	☐
24133	$.70	☐	☐	☐	☐
24170	$.35	☐	☐	☐	☐
24171	$50.00	☐	☐	☐	☐
24172	$.35	☐	☐	☐	☐
24173	$1.00	☐	☐	☐	☐
24197	$2.75	☐	☐	☐	☐
24198	$2.75	☐	☐	☐	☐
24201	$3.50	☐	☐	☐	☐
24202	$2.00	☐	☐	☐	☐
24213	$1.50	☐	☐	☐	☐
24214	$.70	☐	☐	☐	☐
24220	$5.75	☐	☐	☐	☐
24221	$5.75	☐	☐	☐	☐
24241	$4.25	☐	☐	☐	☐
24242	$2.00	☐	☐	☐	☐
24249	$2.75	☐	☐	☐	☐
24250	$1.50	☐	☐	☐	☐
24251	$7.00	☐3	☐	☐	☐3
24252	$8.00	☐3	☐	☐	☐3

#807 3¢ JEFFERSON
Eye Plates Cont.

Plate	Price	UL	UR	LL	LR
24265	$.35	☐	☐	☐	☐
24266	$1.00	☐	☐	☐	☐
24267	$2.75	☐	☐	☐	☐
24268	$2.00	☐	☐	☐	☐
24294	$2.00	☐	☐	☐	☐
24295	$2.00	☐	☐	☐	☐
24314	$.35	☐	☐	☐	☐
24315	$2.00	☐	☐	☐	☐
24320	$1.50	☐	☐	☐	☐
24321	$.35	☐	☐	☐	☐
24322	$.35	☐	☐	☐	☐
24323	$.70	☐	☐	☐	☐
24326	$1.00	☐	☐	☐	☐
24327	$2.00	☐	☐	☐	☐
24334	$1.00	☐	☐	☐	☐
24335	$1.50	☐	☐	☐	☐
24336	$1.00	☐	☐	☐	☐
24337	$.70	☐	☐	☐	☐
24338	$.70	☐	☐	☐	☐
24339	$1.00	☐	☐	☐	☐
24340	$1.50	☐	☐	☐	☐
24345	$1.50	☐	☐	☐	☐
24350	$1.00	☐	☐	☐	☐
24351	$1.50	☐	☐	☐	☐
24352	$1.50	☐	☐	☐	☐
24353	$4.25	☐	☐	☐	☐
24354	$1.50	☐	☐	☐	☐
24355	$2.75	☐	☐	☐	☐
24356	$3.50	☐	☐	☐	☐
24357	$2.00	☐	☐	☐	☐
24358	$2.00	☐	☐	☐	☐
24359	$1.00	☐	☐	☐	☐
24452	$3.50	☐	☐	☐	☐
24453	$1.50	☐	☐	☐	☐
24469	$1.50	☐	☐	☐	☐
24470	$.70	☐	☐	☐	☐
24485	$1.00	☐	☐	☐	☐
24486	$2.75	☐	☐	☐	☐
24488	$1.00	☐	☐	☐	☐
24489	$2.00	☐	☐	☐	☐
24490	$2.75	☐	☐	☐	☐
24542	$2.00	☐	☐	☐	☐
24543	$.35	☐	☐	☐	☐
24544	$1.00	☐	☐	☐	☐
24545	$.35	☐	☐	☐	☐
24546	$.35	☐	☐	☐	☐
24547	$2.00	☐	☐	☐	☐
24568	$3.50	☐	☐	☐	☐
24569	$1.50	☐	☐	☐	☐
24570	$1.00	☐	☐	☐	☐
24586	$.70	☐	☐	☐	☐
24587	$.35	☐	☐	☐	☐
24588	$1.00	☐	☐	☐	☐
24590	$1.50	☐	☐	☐	☐
24591	$.35	☐	☐	☐	☐

1938 REGULAR ISSUE

#807 3¢ JEFFERSON
Eye Plates **Cont.**

		UL	UR	LL	LR
24617	$1.50	☐	☐	☐	☐
24618	$.70	☐	☐	☐	☐
24619	$4.25	☐	☐	☐	☐
24620	$2.75	☐	☐	☐	☐
24621	$2.00	☐	☐	☐	☐
24622	$.70	☐	☐	☐	☐
24623	$.35	☐	☐	☐	☐
24624	$.35	☐	☐	☐	☐
24625	$.35	☐	☐	☐	☐
24626	$2.00	☐	☐	☐	☐
24659	$.70	☐	☐	☐	☐
24660	$1.00	☐	☐	☐	☐
24731	$2.75	☐	☐	☐	☐
24732	$1.50	☐	☐	☐	☐
24737	$6.25	☐	☐	☐	☐
24738	$.70	☐	☐	☐	☐
24765	$1.00	☐	☐	☐	☐
24766	$.70	☐	☐	☐	☐
24773	$.35	☐	☐	☐	☐
24774	$2.75	☐	☐	☐	☐
24775	$2.00	☐	☐	☐	☐
24776	$.70	☐	☐	☐	☐
24777	$.70	☐	☐	☐	☐
24778	$1.50	☐	☐	☐	☐
24779	$1.50	☐	☐	☐	☐
24780	$2.75	☐	☐	☐	☐
24787	$1.50	☐	☐	☐	☐
24788	$.35	☐	☐	☐	☐
24789	$3.50	☐	☐	☐	☐
24790	$2.00	☐	☐	☐	☐
24791	$.70	☐	☐	☐	☐
24792	$1.50	☐	☐	☐	☐
24795	$3.50	☐	☐	☐	☐
24796	$2.00	☐	☐	☐	☐
24799	$2.75	☐	☐	☐	☐
24800	$5.00	☐	☐	☐	☐
24807	$5.00	☐	☐	☐	☐
24808	$5.75	☐	☐	☐	☐
24817	$5.00	☐	☐	☐	☐
24818	$3.50	☐	☐	☐	☐
24821	$2.75	☐	☐	☐	☐
24822	$5.00	☐	☐	☐	☐
24823	$3.50	☐	☐	☐	☐
24824	$4.25	☐	☐	☐	☐
24837	$6.25	☐	☐	☐	☐
24838	$4.25	☐	☐	☐	☐
24839	$2.75	☐	☐	☐	☐
24840	$5.75	☐	☐	☐	☐
24841	$5.00	☐	☐	☐	☐

#808 4¢ MADISON
Pre-Eye Plates **2 Plates**

21960	$5	☐	☐	☐	☐
21961	$5	☐	☐	☐	☐

#808 4¢ MADISON
Eye Plates **12 Plates**

		UL	UR	LL	LR
22341	$4	☐	☐	☐	☐
22342	$4	☐	☐	☐	☐
22819	$6	☐	☐	☐	☐
22820	$6	☐	☐	☐	☐
24501	$4	☐	☐	☐	☐
24502	$4	☐	☐	☐	☐
24506	$16	☐	☐	☐	☐
24507	$16	☐	☐	☐	☐
24508	$10	☐	☐	☐	☐
24509	$7	☐	☐	☐	☐
24510	$7	☐	☐	☐	☐
24511	$8	☐	☐	☐	☐

#809 4.5¢ WHITE HOUSE
Pre-Eye Plates **2 Plates**

21972	$1.75	☐	☐	☐	☐
21973	$1.75	☐	☐	☐	☐

#809 4.5¢ WHITE HOUSE
Eye Plates **4 Plates**

22343	$1.75	☐	☐	☐	☐
22344	$1.75	☐	☐	☐	☐
22843**P**	$20.00	☐	☐	☐	☐
24073**P**	$20.00	☐	☐	☐	☐

P These plates numbers have been reported only on precancelled stamps.

#810 5¢ MONROE
Pre-Eye Plates **4 Plates**

22003	$1.00	☐	☐	☐	☐
22004	$1.00	☐	☐	☐	☐
22005	$4.50	☐	☐	☐	☐
22006	$4.50	☐	☐	☐	☐

#810 5¢ MONROE
Eye Plates **12 Plates**

22345	$1	☐	☐	☐	☐
22346	$1	☐	☐	☐	☐
22835	$1	☐	☐	☐	☐
22836	$1	☐	☐	☐	☐
22837	$1	☐	☐	☐	☐
22838	$1	☐	☐	☐	☐
23784	$1	☐	☐	☐	☐
23785	$1	☐	☐	☐	☐
24269	$1	☐	☐	☐	☐
24270	$1	☐	☐	☐	☐
24562	$4	☐	☐	☐	☐
24563	$4	☐	☐	☐	☐

#811 6¢ JOHN QUINCY ADAMS
Pre-Eye Plates **4 Plates**

21964	$2	☐	☐	☐	☐
21965	$2	☐	☐	☐	☐
21966	$2	☐	☐	☐	☐
21967	$2	☐	☐	☐	☐

1938 REGULAR ISSUE

#811 6¢ JOHN QUINCY ADAMS
Eye Plates 14 Plates

		UL	UR	LL	LR
22347	$2	☐	☐	☐	☐
22348	$2	☐	☐	☐	☐
22745	$2	☐	☐	☐	☐
22800	$2	☐	☐	☐	☐
23531	$2	☐	☐	☐	☐
23532	$2	☐	☐	☐	☐
23880	$2	☐	☐	☐	☐
23881	$2	☐	☐	☐	☐
24074	$2	☐	☐	☐	☐
24075	$2	☐	☐	☐	☐
24475	$2	☐	☐	☐	☐
24476	$2	☐	☐	☐	☐
24847	$2	☐	☐	☐	☐
24848	$2	☐	☐	☐	☐

#812 7¢ JACKSON
Pre-Eye Plates 2 Plates

22031	$2.50	☐	☐	☐	☐
22033	$2.50	☐	☐	☐	☐

#812 7¢ JACKSON
Eye Plates 6 Plates

22796	$1.50	☐	☐	☐	☐
22797	$1.50	☐	☐	☐	☐
22801	$3.00	☐	☐	☐	☐
22802	$3.00	☐	☐	☐	☐
24845	$3.00	☐	☐	☐	☐
24846	$3.00	☐	☐	☐	☐

#813 8¢ VAN BUREN
Pre-Eye Plates 4 Plates

21968	$2.25	☐	☐	☐	☐
21969	$10.00	☐	☐	☐	☐
21970	$2.25	☐	☐	☐	☐
21971	$10.00	☐	☐	☐	☐

#813 8¢ VAN BUREN
Eye Plates 12 Plates

22349	$4.00	☐	☐	☐	☐
22350	$5.00	☐	☐	☐	☐
22839	$2.25	☐	☐	☐	☐
22840	$2.25	☐	☐	☐	☐
22844	$2.25	☐	☐	☐	☐
23167	$2.25	☐	☐	☐	☐
23780	$2.25	☐	☐	☐	☐
23781	$2.25	☐	☐	☐	☐
24076	$10.00	☐	☐	☐	☐
24107	$10.00	☐	☐	☐	☐
24302	$2.25	☐	☐	☐	☐
24303	$2.25	☐	☐	☐	☐

#814 9¢ WILLIAM HARRISON 2 Plates
Pre-Eye Plates

22035	$3.50	☐	☐	☐	☐
22036	$3.50	☐	☐	☐	☐

#814 9¢ WILLIAM HARRISON
Eye Plates 8 Plates

		UL	UR	LL	LR
22798	$3.00	☐	☐	☐	☐
22799	$2.00	☐	☐	☐	☐
22803	$3.00	☐	☐	☐	☐
22804	$2.00	☐	☐	☐	☐
23788	$2.00	☐	☐	☐	☐
23789	$2.00	☐	☐	☐	☐
24310	$2.00	☐	☐	☐	☐
24311	$3.00	☐	☐	☐	☐

#815 10¢ TYLER
Pre-Eye Plates 4 Plates

22039	$3.00	☐	☐	☐	☐
22040	$5.00	☐	☐	☐	☐
22041	$7.50	☐	☐	☐	☐
22042	$5.00	☐	☐	☐	☐

#815 10¢ TYLER
Eye Plates 14 Plates

22351	$1.75	☐	☐	☐	☐
22352	$1.75	☐	☐	☐	☐
22448	$1.75	☐	☐	☐	☐
22449	$1.75	☐	☐	☐	☐
22983	$1.75	☐	☐	☐	☐
22984	$1.75	☐	☐	☐	☐
23634	$1.75	☐	☐	☐	☐
23635	$1.75	☐	☐	☐	☐
23876	$1.75	☐	☐	☐	☐
23877	$1.75	☐	☐	☐	☐
24077	$10.00	☐	☐	☐	☐
24126	$10.00	☐	☐	☐	☐
24471	$3.00	☐	☐	☐	☐
24472	$3.00	☐	☐	☐	☐

#816 11¢ POLK
Pre-Eye Plates 2 Plates

22043	$5	☐	☐	☐	☐
22044	$5	☐	☐	☐	☐

#816 11¢ POLK
Eye Plates 3 Plates

22045	$3.75	☐	☐	☐	☐
22046	$3.75	☐	☐	☐	☐
22845	$3.75	☐	☐	☐	☐

#817 12¢ TAYLOR
Pre-Eye Plates 2 Plates

22047	$9	☐	☐	☐	☐
22049	$9	☐	☐	☐	☐

#817 12¢ TAYLOR
Eye Plates 6 Plates

22048	$6	☐	☐	☐	☐
22050	$6	☐	☐	☐	☐
22846	$12	☐	☐	☐	☐
23910	$12	☐	☐	☐	☐
24757	$25	☐	☐	☐	☐
24758	$25	☐	☐	☐	☐

1938 REGULAR ISSUE

#818 13¢ FILLMORE
Pre-Eye Plates **2 Plates**

		UL	UR	LL	LR
22073	$12	☐	☐	☐	☐
22074	$12	☐	☐	☐	☐

#818 13¢ FILLMORE
Eye Plates **4 Plates**

		UL	UR	LL	LR
22075	$7.50	☐	☐	☐	☐
22076	$7.50	☐	☐	☐	☐
22847	$15.00	☐	☐	☐	☐
23911	$15.00	☐	☐	☐	☐

#819 14¢ PIERCE
Pre-Eye Plates **2 Plates**

		UL	UR	LL	LR
22087	$9	☐	☐	☐	☐
22090	$9	☐	☐	☐	☐

#819 14¢ PIERCE
Eye Plates **4 Plates**

		UL	UR	LL	LR
22088	$5	☐	☐	☐	☐
22089	$5	☐	☐	☐	☐
22848	$35	☐2	☐	☐	☐
23928	$35	☐2	☐	☐	☐

#820 15¢ BUCHANAN
Pre-Eye Plates **2 Plates**

		UL	UR	LL	LR
22124	$4.25	☐	☐	☐	☐
22125	$4.25	☐	☐	☐	☐

#820 15¢ BUCHANAN
Eye Plates **17 Plates**

		UL	UR	LL	LR
22126	$2.50	☐	☐	☐	☐
22127	$2.50	☐	☐	☐	☐
22922	$2.50	☐	☐	☐	☐
22923	$2.50	☐	☐	☐	☐
22924	$2.50	☐	☐	☐	☐
23223	$2.50	☐	☐	☐	☐
23707	$2.50	☐	☐	☐	☐
23786	$4.00	☐	☐	☐	☐
23787	$17.50	☐	☐	☐	☐
24312	$2.50	☐	☐	☐	☐
24313	$2.50	☐	☐	☐	☐
24727	$7.00	☐	☐	☐	☐
24728	$7.00	☐	☐	☐	☐
24733	$2.50	☐	☐	☐	☐
24734	$2.50	☐	☐	☐	☐
24735	$6.00	☐	☐	☐	☐
24736	$6.00	☐	☐	☐	☐

#821 16¢ LINCOLN
Pre-Eye Plates **2 Plates**

		UL	UR	LL	LR
22129	$10	☐	☐	☐	☐
22130	$10	☐	☐	☐	☐

#821 16¢ LINCOLN
Eye Plates **4 Plates**

		UL	UR	LL	LR
22815	$6	☐	☐	☐	☐
22816	$6	☐	☐	☐	☐
23037	$15	☐	☐	☐	☐
23929	$15	☐	☐	☐	☐

#822 17¢ JOHNSON
Pre-Eye Plates **2 Plates**

		UL	UR	LL	LR
22108	$9	☐	☐	☐	☐
22110	$9	☐	☐	☐	☐

#822 17¢ JOHNSON
Eye Plates **4 Plates**

		UL	UR	LL	LR
22109	$6	☐	☐	☐	☐
22111	$6	☐	☐	☐	☐
22985	$9	☐	☐	☐	☐
23930	$9	☐	☐	☐	☐

#823 18¢ GRANT
Pre-Eye Plates **2 Plates**

		UL	UR	LL	LR
22143	$18	☐	☐	☐	☐
22144	$18	☐	☐	☐	☐

#823 18¢ GRANT
Eye Plates **4 Plates**

		UL	UR	LL	LR
22817	$10	☐	☐	☐	☐
22818	$10	☐	☐	☐	☐
23931	$16	☐	☐	☐	☐
24078	$16	☐	☐	☐	☐

#824 19¢ HAYES
Pre-Eye Plates **2 Plates**

		UL	UR	LL	LR
22135	$13.50	☐	☐	☐	☐
22136	$13.50	☐	☐	☐	☐

#824 19¢ HAYES
Eye Plates **5 Plates**

		UL	UR	LL	LR
22823	$8.00	☐	☐	☐	☐
22824	$8.00	☐	☐	☐	☐
23045**P**	$150.00	☐	☐	†	†
23932	$13.50	☐	☐	☐	☐
24079	$13.50	☐	☐	☐	☐

P This plate number has been reported only on precancelled stamps.

1938 REGULAR ISSUE

#825 20¢ GARFIELD

Pre-Eye Plates **2 Plates**

		UL	UR	LL	LR
22145	$7.50	☐	☐	☐	☐
22146	$7.50	☐	☐	☐	☐

#825 20¢ GARFIELD

Eye Plates **11 Plates**

22176	$3500	☐	☐	☐	☐
22183	$4	☐	☐	☐	☐
22184	$4	☐	☐	☐	☐
22855	$4	☐	☐	☐	☐
23549	$4	☐	☐	☐	☐
23558	$4	☐	☐	☐	☐
23904	$4	☐	☐	☐	☐
24060	$4	☐	☐	☐	☐
24061	$4	☐	☐	☐	☐
24572	$4	☐	☐	☐	☐
24573	$4	☐	☐	☐	☐

#826 21¢ ARTHUR

Pre-Eye Plates **2 plates**

22112	$13	☐	☐	☐	☐
22113	$13	☐	☐	☐	☐

#826 21¢ ARTHUR

Eye Plates **4 Plates**

22114	$10	☐	☐	☐	☐
22115	$10	☐	☐	☐	☐
23053**P**	$50	†	☐2	☐	†
23933**P**	$50	†	☐3	☐	†

P These plate numbers have been reported only on precancelled stamps.

#827 22¢ CLEVELAND

Pre-Eye Plates **2 Plates**

22147	$20	☐	☐	☐	☐
22148	$20	☐	☐	☐	☐

#827 22¢ CLEVELAND

Eye Plates **4 Plates**

22825	$12	☐	☐	☐	☐
22826	$12	☐	☐	☐	☐
23934	$20	☐	☐	☐	☐
24081	$20	☐	☐	☐	☐

#828 24¢ BENJAMIN HARRISON

Pre-Eye Plates **2 Plates**

22162	$30	☐	☐	☐	☐
22163	$30	☐	☐	☐	☐

#828 24¢ BENJAMIN HARRISON

Eye Plates **2 Plates**

22827	$20	☐	☐	☐	☐
22828	$20	☐	☐	☐	☐

#829 25¢ MCKINLEY

Pre-Eye Plates **2 Plates**

		UL	UR	LL	LR
22116	$12	☐	☐	☐	☐
22117	$12	☐	☐	☐	☐

#829 25¢ MCKINLEY

Eye Plates **10 Plates**

22118	$4	☐	☐	☐	☐
22119	$4	☐	☐	☐	☐
23115	$4	☐	☐	☐	☐
23878	$4	☐	☐	☐	☐
23879	$4	☐	☐	☐	☐
24082	$4	☐	☐	☐	☐
24699	$4	☐	☐	☐	☐
24700	$4	☐	☐	☐	☐
24959	$4	☐	☐	☐	☐
24960	$4	☐	☐	☐	☐

#830 30¢ THEODORE ROOSEVELT

Pre-Eye Plates **2 Plates**

22164	$42.50	☐	☐	☐	☐
22165	$42.50	☐	☐	☐	☐

#830 30¢ THEODORE ROOSEVELT

Eye Plates **4 Plates**

22833	$25	☐	☐	☐	☐
22834	$25	☐	☐	☐	☐
23116	$25	☐	☐	☐	☐
23906	$25	☐	☐	☐	☐

#831 50¢ TAFT

Pre-Eye Plates **2 Plates**

22207	$60	☐	☐	☐	☐
22212	$60	☐	☐	☐	☐

#831 50¢ TAFT

Eye Plates **4 Plates**

22205	$35	☐	☐	☐	☐
22206	$35	☐	☐	☐	☐
22353	$45	☐	☐	☐	☐
22354	$45	☐	☐	☐	☐

$1, $2, $5 BICOLORED

FLAT PRESS

All first printings of these denominations were in the 22,000 series, and all were with arrow. Later printings of the 22,000 series are without arrow. All number combinations of this series exist both with and without arrow. There are no arrows on any combinations containing vignette or frame plates of the 23,000 or 24,000 series.

1938 REGULAR ISSUE

#832 $1 WILSON With Arrow
16 Plate Combination Blocks of 4

Vignette-Frame		T
22096-22085	$40	☐
22096-22086	$40	☐
22096-22094	$40	☐
22096-22095	$40	☐
22097-22085	$40	☐
22097-22086	$40	☐
22097-22094	$40	☐
22097-22095	$40	☐
22098-22085	$40	☐
22098 22086	$40	☐
22098-22094	$40	☐
22098-22095	$40	☐
22099-22085	$40	☐
22099-22086	$40	☐
22099-22094	$40	☐
22099-22095	$40	☐

#832 $1 WILSON Without Arrow
57 Plate Combination Blocks of 4

Vignette-Frame		T
22096-22085	$45	☐
22096-22086	$45	☐
22096 22094	$45	☐
22096-22095	$45	☐
22097 22085	$45	☐
22097-22086	$45	☐
22097-22094	$45	☐
22097-22095	$45	☐
22098-22085	$45	☐
22098-22086	$45	☐
22098-22094	$45	☐
22098-22095	$45	☐
22099-22085	$45	☐
22099-22086	$45	☐
22099-22094	$45	☐
22099-22095	$45	☐
24477-22085	$45	☐
24477-22086	$110	☐
24477-22094	$45	☐
24477-22095	$45	☐
24477-24478	$45	☐
24477-24497	$45	☐
24477-24498	$45	☐
24477-24499	$45	☐
24477-24500	$45	☐
24493-22085	$45	☐
24493-22086	$110	☐
24493-22094	$110	☐
24493-22095	$110	☐
24493-24478	$45	☐
24493-24497	$45	☐
24493-24498	$45	☐
24493-24499	$45	☐
24493-24500	$45	☐

#832 $1 WILSON Without Arrow
Cont.

		T
24494-22085	$110	☐
24494-22086	$45	☐
24494-22094	$110	☐
24494-22095	$45	☐
24494-24478	$45	☐
24494-24497	$45	☐
24494-24498	$45	☐
24494-24499	$45	☐
24494-24500	$45	☐
24495-22085	$140	☐
24495-22086	$125	☐
24495-22094	$45	☐
24495-22095	$110	☐
24495-24478	$45	☐
24495-24497	$45	☐
24495-24498	$45	☐
24495-24499	$45	☐
24495-24500	$45	☐
24496-24478	$45	☐
24496-24497	$45	☐
24496-24498	$45	☐
24496-24499	$45	☐
24496-24500	$45	☐

#832b $1 WILSON Without Arrow
16 Plate Combination Blocks of 4
On USIR Watermarked Paper

Vignette-Frame		
22096-22085	$2,000	☐
22096-22086	—	†
22096-22094	$2,000	☐
22096-22095	$2,000	☐
22097-22085	$2,000	☐
22097-22086	$2,000	☐
22097-22094	$2,000	☐
22097-22095	$2,000	☐
22098-22085	—	†
22098-22086	$2,000	☐
22098-22094	$2,000	☐
22098-22095	$2,000	☐
22099-22085	$2,000	☐
22099-22086	$2,000	☐
22099-22094	$2,000	☐
22099-22095	$2,000	☐

In 1953 several sheets of the $1 Presidential were discovered printed in error on watermarked paper intended for revenue stamps. The quantity printed must have been large, for cancelled copies have been reported with postmarks from coast to coast. The period during which the watermarked stamps were printed and distributed is not known, but it is certain that they were not early printings. We surmise that they may have been printed between 1950-51 or perhaps earlier. The watermarked error will be found on without-arrow blocks only, and occurs only in the 22000 series combinations.

1938 REGULAR ISSUE

#832C $1 WILSON WIthout Arrow

1954 New Printing on Dry Paper. Printed from 400 subject sheets wlth top and bottom plate number entries.Left pane and right pane plate combinations are alike.

25 Plate Combination Blocks of 4

Vignette-Frame		T	B
25017-24836	$35	☐	☐
25017-25015	$35	☐	☐
25017-25016	$35	☐	☐
25017-25026	$35	☐	☐
25017 25027	$35	☐	☐
25018-24836	$35	☐	☐
25018-25015	$35	☐	☐
25018-25016	$35	☐	☐
25018-25026	$35	☐	☐
25018-25027	$35	☐	☐
25019-24836	$35	☐	☐
25019-25015	$35	☐	☐
25019-25016	$35	☐	☐
25019-25026	$35	☐	☐
25019-25027	$35	☐	☐
25020-24836	$35	☐	☐
25020-25015	$35	☐	☐
25020-25016	$35	☐	☐
25020-25026	$35	☐	☐
25020-25027	$35	☐	☐
25025-24836	$300	☐	☐
25025-25015	$35	☐	☐
25025-25016	$35	☐	☐
25025-25026	$35	☐	☐
25025-25027	$35	☐	☐

#833 $2 HARDING WIth Arrow

4 Plate Combination Blocks of 4

Vignette -Frame		T
22120-22122	$125	☐
22120-22123	$125	☐
22121-22122	$125	☐
22121-22123	$125	☐

#833 $2 HARDING WIthout Arrow

20 Plate Combination Blocks of 4

Vignette-Frame		
22120-22122	$175	☐
22120-22123	$175	☐
22120-23477	$175	☐
22120-23478	$175	☐
22120-24480	$175	☐
22121-22122	$175	☐
22121-22123	$175	☐
22121-23477	$175	☐
22121-23478	$175	☐
22121-24480	$175	☐

#833 $2 HARDINGWIthout Arrow Cont.

Vignette-Frame		T
23479-22122	$200	☐
23479-22123	$200	☐
23479-23477	$200	☐
23479-23478	$200	☐
23479-24480	$200	☐
23480-22122	$200	☐
23480-22123	$200	☐
23480-23477	$200	☐
23480-23478	$200	☐
23480-24480	$200	☐

#834 $5 COOLIDGE WIth Arrow

4 Plate Combination Blocks of 4

Vignette-Frame		
22166-22168	$485	☐
22166-22169	$485	☐
22167-22168	$485	☐
22167-22169	$485	☐

With Arrow

#834 $5 COOLIDGE WIthout Arrow

25 Plate Combination Blocks of 4

Vignette-Frame		
22166-22168	$465	☐
22166-22169	$465	☐
22166-23475	$465	☐

1938 REGULAR ISSUE

#834 $5 COOLIDGE WIthout Arrow Cont.

Vignette-Frame		T
22166-23476	$465	☐
22166-24482	$1,100	☐
22167-22168	$465	☐
22167-22169	$465	☐
22167-23475	$465	☐
22167-23476	$465	☐
22167-24482	$465	☐
23481-22168	$465	☐
23481-22169	$465	☐
23481-23475	$465	☐
23481-23476	$465	☐
23481-24482	$465	☐
23482-22168	$465	☐
23482-22169	$465	☐
23482-23475	$465	☐
23482 23476	$465	☐
23482-24482	$465	☐
24481-22168	$1,100	☐
24481-22169	$750	☐
24481-23475	$750	☐
24481-23476	$1,000	☐
24481-24482	$750	☐

#834a $5 COOLIDGE With Arrow

22166-22168	$12,000	☐
22166-22169	$12,000	☐
22167-22168	$12,000	☐
22167-22169	$12,000	☐

#835-38

See page 138

BOOKLET PANES

ROTARY PRESS **PANES OF 6**

Most of the Presidential Booklet Pane plates can be found with good percentages (65% or more) of the number showing in the UL and LL positions. Right pane positions are seen infrequently and the percentages are often too small for plate number identification.

See appendix G for largest reported plate number percentage by position.

#804b 1¢ WASHINGTON 6 Plates
Pre-Eye Plates (3mm vert. gutter)

*22007 *22008 22009 22010 22234
22235

8 Plates
Eye Plates (2°mm vert. gutter)

22389 22390 22402 22403 22930
22931 22977 22978

#806b 2¢ JOHN ADAMS 2 Plates
Pre-Eye Plates (3mm vert. gutter)

22011 22012

6 Plates
Eye Plates (2°mm vert. gutter)

22392 22404 22405 22461 *24298
*24299

#807a 3¢ JEFFERSON 6 Plates
Pre-Eye Plates (3mm vert. gutter)

21995 21996 21997 21998 22170
22171

57 Plates
Eye Plates (2°mm vert. gutter)

22434	22435	22436	22437	22886
22887	22932	22933	22973	22974
22975	22976	23158	23159	23160
23161	23283	23284	23291	23292
23412	23413	23422	23423	23573
23574	23594	23595	23758	23759
23770	23771	*23847	*23848	24089
24090	24255	24256	24257	24258
24412	24413	24418	24419	24420
24421	*24422	24423	24424	24425
24426	24427	*24428	*24429	24443
†24739	†24740			

1938 REGULAR ISSUE

SIDE COILS

170 Subject Plates STRIPS OF 5
Positions T, B

Most of the 1¢ to 3¢ Presidential side coils exist with plate number percentages exceeding 50%. The end coils and the 4¢, 4½¢, 5¢, 10¢ side coils rarely show as much as 50%. Almost complete numbers are very scarce and full 100% plates are rare. Reconstructed 100% numbers are usually difficult, and frequently impossible, to complete even on plates that can be found with 50% or more of the number. One of the positions, top or bottom, may not have been miscut wide enough to show more than a small percentage of the number.

#839 1¢ WASHINGTON 52 Plates

21871	21978	†21979	21980	21981
21982	22219	22220	22225	22226
22236	22237	22248	22249	22250
22251	22900	22901	22902	22903
23081	23082	23117	23118	23119
23120	23301	23302	23388	23389
23392	23393	23461	23462	23632
23633	23762	23763	23792	23793
23817	23818	23839	23840	24025
24026	24099	24100	*24274	*24275
*24384	*24385			

#840 1.5¢ MARTHA WASHINGTON 24 Plates

21983	21984	21985	21986	22221
22222	22227	22228	22238	22239
22311	22312	23207	23208	*23567
*23568	*23578	*23579	*23768	*23769
*25164	*25165	*25166	†25167	

#841 2¢ JOHN ADAMS 36 Plates

21987	21988	21989	21990	22203
22204	22257	22258	22259	22260
22269	22270	22271	22272	22313
22314	22325	22326	22882	22883
22884	22885	22892	22893	22894
22895	22896	22897	*23058	*23059
*23068	*23069	*24390	*24391	*24398
*24399				

#842 3¢ JEFFERSON 224 Plates

21991	21992	21993	21994	22213
22214	22215	22216	†22223	†22224
22287	22288	22307	22308	22309
22310	22321	22322	22323	22324
22327	22328	22329	22330	22335
22428	22429	22638	22908	22909
22910	22911	22912	22913	22914
22915	23060	23061	23064	23065
23133	23215	23216	23217	23218
23221	23222	23232	23233	23234
23235	23236	23240	23241	23242
23243	23248	23249	23344	23345
23346	23347	23361	23362	23369
23370	23375	23376	23377	23378
†23394	23395	23410	23411	23416
23417	23420	23421	23440	23459
23460	23537	23538	23576	23577
23584	23585	23613	23614	23615
23616	23648	23649	23662	23663
23673	23674	23708	23709	23740
23741	23750	23751	23752	23753
23808	23809	23810	23811	23849
*23850	23916	23917	*23926	23927
24019	*24020	24021	24022	24046
24047	24048	24049	24050	24051
24101	24102	24104	24129	24130
24174	24175	24176	24177	24178
24179	24180	24181	24189	24190
24199	24200	24215	24216	24222
24223	24231	24232	24272	24273
24278	*24279	*24280	24281	24286
24287	24292	*24293	24296	24297
24308	24309	24332	24333	24360
24361	24362	*24363	*24364	24365
24404	24405	24406	24407	24408
24409	24434	24435	24458	24459
24460	24461	24462	24467	24468
24491	24492	24597	24598	24599
24600	24609	24610	24653	24654
24655	24656	24667	24668	24707
24708	24709	24710	24715	24716
24717	24718	24743	24744	24793
24794	24797	24798	24801	24802
24813	24815	24816	24819	24820
24855	24856	*24873	*24874	

1938 REGULAR ISSUE

SIDE COILS

#843 4¢ MADISON 8 Plates
22015 22016 22017 22018 †24052
*24053 *24512 *24513

#844 4.5¢ WHITE HOUSE 2 Plates
22081 22082

#845 5¢ MONROE 6 Plates
22019 22020 22021 22022 *23722
*23723

#846 6¢ JOHN QUINCY ADAMS6 Plates
22023 22024 22025 22026 24857
24858

#847 10¢ TYLER 4 Plates
22100 22101 *22102 †22103

END COILS

150 Subject Plates STRIPS OF 5
Positions L, R

#848 1¢ WASHINGTON 2 Plates
22179 22180

#849 1.5¢ MARTHA WASHINGTON
4 Plates
22193 22194 †22208 †22209

#850 2¢ JOHN ADAMS 2 Plates
22210 22211

#851 3¢ JEFFERSON 2 Plates
22189 22190

1938 COMMEMORATIVES

ROTARY PRESS

#835 3¢ RATIFICATION

		UL	UR	LL	LR
21905	$4	☐	☐	☐	☐
21906	$4	☐	☐	☐	☐
21907	$4	☐	☐	☐	☐
21908	$4	☐	☐	☐	☐

FLAT PRESS

#836 3¢ DELAWARE

		TL	TR	L	R	B
21952	$3	☐	☐	‡	‡	☐
21953	$3	☐	☐	‡	‡	☐
21954	$3	☐	☐	‡	‡	☐
21955	$3	☐	☐	‡	‡	☐
21956	$3	☐	☐	‡	‡	☐
21957	$3	☐	☐	‡	‡	☐
21958	$3	☐	☐	‡	‡	☐
21959	$3	☐	☐	‡	‡	☐

ROTARY PRESS

#837 3¢ SECOND NORTHWEST

		UL	UR	LL	LR
22027	$8	☐	☐	☐	☐
22028	$8	☐	☐	☐	☐
22029	$8	☐	☐	☐	☐
22030	$8	☐	☐	☐	☐

#838 3¢ IOWA

22091	$6	☐	☐	☐	☐
22092	$6	☐	☐	☐	☐

#839-42

See page 137

1939 COMMEMORATIVES

#852 3¢ GOLDEN GATE

		UL	UR	LL	LR
22289	$1.50	☐	☐	☐	☐
22290	$1.50	☐	☐	☐	☐
22291	$1.50	☐	☐	☐	☐
22292	$1.50	☐	☐	☐	☐

#853 3¢ NEW YORK

22293	$2	☐	☐	☐	☐
22294	$2	☐	☐	☐	☐
22295	$2	☐	☐	☐	☐
22296	$2	☐	☐	☐	☐

FLAT PRESS

#854 3¢ INAUGURATION

		TL	TR	L	R	B
22365	$5	☐	☐	‡	‡	☐
22366	$4	☐	☐	‡	‡	☐
22367	$4	☐	☐	‡	‡	☐
22368	$4	☐	☐	‡	‡	☐
22369	$4	☐	☐	‡	‡	☐
22370	$4	☐	☐ N	‡	‡	☐
22371	$4	☐	☐	‡	‡	☐
22372	$6	☐	☐	‡	‡	☐
22373	$4	☐	☐	‡	‡	☐

N Has no F but 3 in plate number has 2 dots.

ROTARY PRESS

#855 3¢ BASEBALL

		UL	UR	LL	LR
22385	$7	☐	☐	☐	☐
22386	$7	☐	☐	☐	☐
22387	$7	☐	☐	☐	☐
22388	$7	☐	☐	☐	☐

FLAT PRESS

#856 3¢ PANAMA CANAL

		TL	TR	L	R	B
22394	$4	☐	☐	‡	‡	☐
22395	$4	☐	☐	‡	‡	☐
22396	$4	☐	☐	‡	‡	☐
22397	$4	☐	☐	‡	‡	☐
22398	$4	☐	☐	‡	‡	☐
22399	$4	☐	☐	‡	‡	☐
22400	$4	☐	☐	‡	‡	☐
22401	$4	☐	☐	‡	‡	☐

ROTARY PRESS

#857 3¢ PRINTING PRESS

		UL	UR	LL	LR
22438	$1.25	☐	☐	☐	☐
22439	$1.25	☐	☐	☐	☐
22440	$1.25	☐	☐	☐	☐
22450	$1.25	☐	☐	☐	☐

1939 COMMEMORATIVES

#858 3¢ FOUR STATES

		UL	UR	LL	LR
22457	$1.50	☐	☐	☐	☐
22458	$1.50	☐	☐	☐	☐
22459	$1.50	☐	☐	☐	☐
22460	$1.50	☐	☐	☐	☐

1940 FAMOUS AMERICANS

AUTHORS

#859 1¢ IRVING

22474	$1	☐	☐	☐	☐
22475	$1	☐	☐	☐	☐

#860 2¢ COOPER

22477	$1.25	☐	☐	☐	☐
22478	$1.25	☐	☐	☐	☐
22479	$1.25	☐	☐	☐	☐
22490	$1.25	☐	☐	☐	☐

#861 3¢ EMERSON

22480	$1.50	☐	☐	☐	☐
22481	$1.50	☐	☐	☐	☐
22482	$1.50	☐	☐	☐	☐
22491	$1.50	☐	☐	☐	☐

#862 5¢ ALCOTT

22483	$10	☐	☐	☐	☐
22484	$10	☐	☐	☐	☐

#863 10¢ CLEMENS

22486	$40	☐	☐	☐	☐
22488	$40	☐	☐	☐	☐

POETS

#864 1¢ LONGFELLOW

22502	$1.75	☐	☐	☐	☐
22503	$1.75	☐	☐	☐	☐

#865 2¢ WHITTIER

22505	$2	☐	☐	☐	☐
22506	$2	☐	☐	☐	☐

#866 3¢ LOWELL

22508	$3	☐	☐	☐	☐
22510	$3	☐	☐	☐	☐

#867 5¢ WHITMAN

22511	$10	☐	☐	☐	☐
22512	$10	☐	☐	☐	☐

#868 10¢ RILEY

22514	$35	☐	☐	☐	☐
22515	$35	☐	☐	☐	☐

EDUCATORS

#869 1¢ MANN

22521	$2	☐	☐	☐	☐
22522	$2	☐	☐	☐	☐

1940 FAMOUS AMERICANS

EDUCATORS Cont.

#870 2¢ HOPKINS

		UL	UR	LL	LR
22524	$1.50	☐	☐	☐	☐
22525	$1.50	☐	☐	☐	☐

#871 3¢ ELIOT

22527	$3	☐	☐	☐	☐
22528	$3	☐	☐	☐	☐

#872 5¢ WILLARD

22530	$11	☐	☐	☐	☐
22532	$11	☐	☐	☐	☐

#873 10¢ BOOKER WASHINGTON

22533	$30	☐	☐	☐	☐
22535	$30	☐	☐	☐	☐

SCIENTISTS

#874 1¢ AUDUBON

22546	$1	☐	☐	☐	☐
22547	$1	☐	☐	☐	☐

#875 2¢ LONG

22549	$1	☐	☐	☐	☐
22550	$1	☐	☐	☐	☐

#876 3¢ BURBANK

22552	$1.25	☐	☐	☐	☐
22553	$1.25	☐	☐	☐	☐

#877 5¢ REED

22555	$7.50	☐	☐	☐	☐
22556	$7.50	☐	☐	☐	☐

#878 10¢ ADDAMS

22558	$25	☐	☐	☐	☐
22560	$25	☐	☐	☐	☐

MUSICIANS

#879 1¢ FOSTER

22564	$1	☐	☐	☐	☐
22565	$1	☐	☐	☐	☐

#880 2¢ SOUSA

22567	$1	☐	☐	☐	☐
22568	$1	☐	☐	☐	☐

#881 3¢ HERBERT

22570	$1.50	☐	☐	☐	☐
22571	$1.50	☐	☐	☐	☐

#882 5¢ MacDOWELL

22574	$10	☐	☐	☐	☐
22575	$10	☐	☐	☐	☐

1940 FAMOUS AMERICANS

MUSICIANS Cont.

#883 10¢ NEVIN

		UL	UR	LL	LR
22576	$35	☐	☐	☐	☐
22577	$35	☐	☐	☐	☐

ARTISTS

#884 1¢ STUART

22587	$1	☐	☐	☐	☐
22588	$1	☐	☐	☐	☐

#885 2¢ WHISTLER

22602	$1	☐	☐	☐	☐
22603	$1	☐	☐	☐	☐

#886 3¢ SAINT-GAUDENS

22593	$1	☐	☐	☐	☐
22594	$1	☐	☐	☐	☐

#887 5¢ FRENCH

22596	$10	☐	☐	☐	☐
22597	$10	☐	☐	☐	☐

#888 10¢ REMINGTON

22599	$30	☐	☐	☐	☐
22600	$30	☐	☐	☐	☐

INVENTORS

#889 1¢ WHITNEY

22619	$2.25	☐	☐	☐	☐
22620	$2.25	☐	☐	☐	☐

#890 2¢ MORSE

22622	$1.25	☐	☐	☐	☐
22624	$1.25	☐	☐	☐	☐

#891 3¢ MCCORMICK

22625	$2	☐	☐	☐	☐
22626	$2	☐	☐	☐	☐

#892 5¢ HOWE

22628	$15	☐	☐	☐	☐
22629	$15	☐	☐	☐	☐

#893 10¢ BELL

22631	$80	☐	☐	☐	☐
22632	$80	☐	☐	☐	☐

1940 COMMEMORATIVES

#894 3¢ PONY EXPRESS

22579	$4	☐	☐	☐	☐
22580	$4	☐	☐	☐	☐
22581	$4	☐	☐	☐	☐
22582	$4	☐	☐	☐	☐

#895 3¢ PAN AMERICAN UNION

22561	$3.50	☐	☐	☐	☐
22562	$3.50	☐	☐	☐	☐

1940 COMMEMORATIVES

#896 3¢ IDAHO

		UL	UR	LL	LR
22615	$2.50	☐	☐	☐	☐
22616	$2.50	☐	☐	☐	☐
22617	$2.50	☐	☐	☐	☐
22618	$2.50	☐	☐	☐	☐

#897 3¢ WYOMING

22583	$2	☐	☐	☐	☐
22584	$2	☐	☐	☐	☐
22585	$2	☐	☐	☐	☐
22586	$2	☐	☐	☐	☐

#898 3¢ CORONADO

22634	$2	☐	☐	☐	☐
22635	$2	☐	☐	☐	☐
22636	$2	☐	☐	☐	☐
22637	$2	☐	☐	☐	☐

#899 1¢ DEFENSE 28 Plates

22661	$.50	☐	☐	☐	☐
22662	$.50	☐	☐	☐	☐
22663	$.50	☐	☐	☐	☐
22664	$.50	☐	☐	☐	☐
22673	$.50	☐	☐	☐	☐
22674	$.50	☐	☐	☐	☐
22679	$.50	☐	☐	☐	☐
22684	$.50	☐	☐	☐	☐
22685	$.50	☐	☐	☐	☐
22698	$.50	☐	☐	☐	☐
22699	$.50	☐	☐	☐	☐
22709	$.50	☐	☐	☐	☐
22746	$.50	☐	☐	☐	☐
22747	$.50	☐	☐	☐	☐
22768	$.50	☐	☐	☐	☐
22769	$.50	☐	☐	☐	☐
22782	$.50	☐	☐	☐	☐
22783	$.50	☐	☐	☐	☐
22790	$.50	☐	☐	☐	☐
22791	$.50	☐	☐	☐	☐
22849	$2	☐	☐	☐	☐
22850	$2	☐	☐	☐	☐
22856	$12	☐	☐	☐	☐
22857	$12	☐	☐	☐	☐
22862	$3	☐	☐	☐	☐
22863	$3	☐	☐	☐	☐
22868	$5	☐	☐	☐	☐
22869	$5	☐	☐	☐	☐

#900 2¢ DEFENSE 28 Plates

22665	$.60	☐	☐	☐	☐
22666	$.60	☐	☐	☐	☐
22667	$.60	☐	☐	☐	☐
22668	$.60	☐	☐	☐	☐
22675	$.60	☐	☐	☐	☐
22676	$.60	☐	☐	☐	☐
22686	$.60	☐	☐	☐	☐
22687	$1.50	☐	☐	☐	☐

#900 2¢ DEFENSE Cont.

		UL	UR	LL	LR
22700	$.60	☐	☐	☐	☐
22701	$.60	☐	☐	☐	☐
22710	$.60	☐	☐	☐	☐
22711	$.60	☐	☐	☐	☐
22748	$.60	☐	☐	☐	☐
22749	$.60	☐	☐	☐	☐
22770	$.60	☐	☐	☐	☐
22771	$.60	☐	☐	☐	☐
22784	$.60	☐	☐	☐	☐
22785	$.60	☐	☐	☐	☐
22792	$.60	☐	☐	☐	☐
22793	$.60	☐	☐	☐	☐
22851	$1.00	☐	☐	☐	☐
22852	$1.00	☐	☐	☐	☐
22858	$1.50	☐	☐	☐	☐
22859	$1.50	☐	☐	☐	☐
22864	$.75	☐	☐	☐	☐
22865	$.75	☐	☐	☐	☐
22870	$1.50	☐	☐	☐	☐
22871	$1.50	☐	☐	☐	☐

#901 3¢ DEFENSE 44 Plates

22669	$.75	☐	☐	☐	☐
22670	$.75	☐	☐	☐	☐
22671	$.75	☐	☐	☐	☐
22672	$.75	☐	☐	☐	☐
22677	$.75	☐	☐	☐	☐
22678	$.75	☐	☐	☐	☐
22688	$.75	☐	☐	☐	☐
22689	$.75	☐	☐	☐	☐
22690	$.75	☐	☐	☐	☐
22691	$.75	☐	☐	☐	☐
22692	$.75	☐	☐	☐	☐
22693	$.75	☐	☐	☐	☐
22694	$.75	☐	☐	☐	☐
22695	$.75	☐	☐	☐	☐
22696	$.75	☐	☐	☐	☐
22697	$.75	☐	☐	☐	☐
22702	$.75	☐	☐	☐	☐
22703	$.75	☐	☐	☐	☐
22704	$.75	☐	☐	☐	☐
22705	$.75	☐	☐	☐	☐

1940 COMMEMORATIVES

#901 3¢ DEFENSE Cont.

		UL	UR	LL	LR
22712	$.75	☐	☐	☐	☐
22713	$.75	☐	☐	☐	☐
22750	$1	☐	☐	☐	☐
22751	$1	☐	☐	☐	☐
22772	$.75	☐	☐	☐	☐
22773	$.75	☐	☐	☐	☐
22786	$2	☐	☐	☐	☐
22787	$.75	☐	☐	☐	☐
22788	$1	☐	☐	☐	☐
22789	$1	☐	☐	☐	☐
22794	$1	☐	☐	☐	☐
22795	$2	☐	☐	☐	☐
22853	$3	☐	☐	☐	☐
22854	$3	☐	☐	☐	☐
22860	$4	☐	☐	☐	☐
22861	$1.50	☐	☐	☐	☐
22866	$8	☐	☐	☐	☐
22867	$8	☐	☐	☐	☐
22872	$35	☐	☐	☐	☐
22873	$35	☐	☐	☐	☐
22874	$25	☐2	☐	☐	☐
22875	$12	☐2	☐	☐	☐
22878	$6	☐2	☐	☐	☐
22879	$6	☐2	☐	☐	☐

#902 3¢ EMANCIPATION

22680	$4	☐	☐	☐	☐
22681	$4	☐	☐	☐	☐
22682	$4	☐	☐	☐	☐
22683	$4	☐	☐	☐	☐

1941 COMMEMORATIVE

#903 3¢ VERMONT

22706	$2	☐	☐	☐	☐
22707	$2	☐	☐	☐	☐

1942 COMMEMORATIVES

#904 3¢ KENTUCKY

22925	$1.75	☐	☐	☐	☐
22926	$1.75	☐	☐	☐	☐

#905 3¢ WIN THE WAR 86 Plates

22938	$.50	☐	☐	☐	☐
22939	$.50	☐	☐	☐	☐
22940	$.50	☐	☐	☐	☐
22941	$.50	☐	☐	☐	☐
22942	$.50	☐	☐	☐	☐
22943	$.50	☐	☐	☐	☐
22944	$.50	☐	☐	☐	☐
22945	$.50	☐	☐	☐	☐
22946	$.50	☐	☐	☐	☐
22947	$.50	☐	☐	☐	☐
22948	$.50	☐	☐	☐	☐
22949	$.50	☐	☐	☐	☐

1942 COMMEMORATIVES

#905 3¢ WIN THE WAR Cont.

		UL	UR	LL	LR
22950	$.50	☐	☐	☐	☐
22951	$.50	☐	☐	☐	☐
22952	$.50	☐	☐	☐	☐
22953	$.50	☐	☐	☐	☐
22957	$.50	☐	☐	☐	☐
22958	$.50	☐	☐	☐	☐
22959	$.50	☐	☐	☐	☐
22960	$.50	☐	☐	☐	☐
22961	$.50	☐	☐	☐	☐
22962	$.50	☐	☐	☐	☐
22965	$.50	☐	☐	☐	☐
22966	$.50	☐	☐	☐	☐
22967	$.50	☐	☐	☐	☐
22968	$.50	☐	☐	☐	☐
22969	$.50	☐	☐	☐	☐
22970	$.50	☐	☐	☐	☐
22971	$.50	☐	☐	☐	☐
22972	$.50	☐	☐	☐	☐
23030	$.50	☐	☐	☐	☐
23031	$.50	☐	☐	☐	☐
23032	$.50	☐	☐	☐	☐
23036	$.50	☐	☐	☐	☐
23039	$.50	☐	☐	☐	☐
23040	$.50	☐	☐	☐	☐
23041	$.50	☐	☐	☐	☐
23042	$.50	☐	☐	☐	☐
23046	$.50	☐	☐	☐	☐
23047	$.50	☐	☐	☐	☐
23050	$.50	☐	☐	☐	☐
23051	$.50	☐	☐	☐	☐
23062	$.50	☐	☐	☐	☐
23063	$.50	☐	☐	☐	☐
23073	$.50	☐	☐	☐	☐
23074	$.50	☐	☐	☐	☐
23075	$.50	☐	☐	☐	☐
23076	$.50	☐	☐	☐	☐
23077	$.50	☐	☐	☐	☐
23078	$.50	☐	☐	☐	☐
23079	$.50	☐	☐	☐	☐
23080	$.50	☐	☐	☐	☐
23093	$1.00	☐	☐	☐	☐
23094	$.50	☐	☐	☐	☐
23097	$.50	☐	☐	☐	☐
23098	$.50	☐	☐	☐	☐
23099	$.50	☐	☐	☐	☐
23100	$.50	☐	☐	☐	☐
23154	$.50	☐	☐	☐	☐
23155	$.50	☐	☐	☐	☐
23176	$.50	☐	☐	☐	☐
23177	$.50	☐	☐	☐	☐
23178	$.50	☐	☐	☐	☐
23183	$.50	☐	☐	☐	☐
23184	$.50	☐	☐	☐	☐
23185	$.50	☐	☐	☐	☐
23186	$.50	☐	☐	☐	☐
23187	$.50	☐	☐	☐	☐
23188	$.50	☐	☐	☐	☐
23189	$1.00	☐	☐	☐	☐

1942 COMMEMORATIVES

#905 3¢ WIN THE WAR Cont.

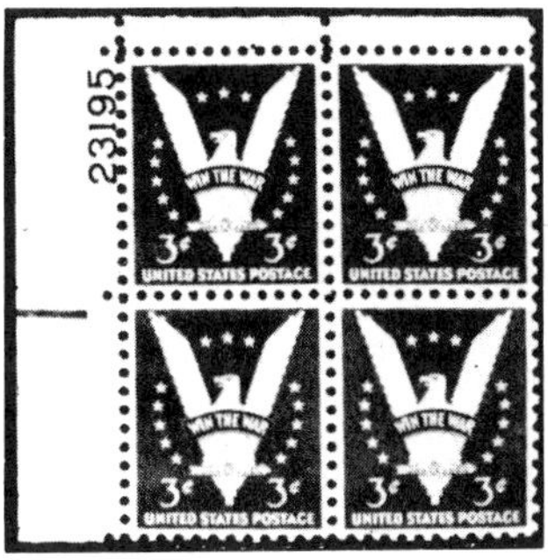

		UL	UR	LL	LR
23191	$1.00	☐	☐	☐3	☐
23192	$1.00	☐	☐	☐3	☐
23195	$150.00	☐2	☐	☐	☐
23196	$150.00	☐2	☐	☐	☐
23198	$5.00	☐	☐	☐	☐
23213	$2.50	☐	☐	☐	☐
23214	$4.00	☐	☐	☐	☐
23219	$3.00	☐	☐	☐	☐
23224	$1.50	☐	☐	☐	☐
23225	$2.50	☐	☐	☐	☐
23226	$2.00	☐	☐	☐	☐
23227	$2.50	☐	☐	☐	☐
23244	$10.00	☐	☐	☐	☐
23245	$10.00	☐	☐	☐	☐
23246	$15.00	☐	☐	☐	☐
23247	$8.00	☐	☐	☐	☐

#906 5¢ CHINA

22954	$10.00	☐	☐	☐	☐
22955	$10.00	☐	☐	☐	☐

1943 COMMEMORATIVES

#907 2¢ ALLIED NATIONS

22986	$.40	☐	☐	☐	☐
22987	$.40	☐	☐	☐	☐
22988	$.40	☐	☐	☐	☐
22989	$.40	☐	☐	☐	☐
22990	$.40	☐	☐	☐	☐
22991	$.40	☐	☐	☐	☐
22992	$.40	☐	☐	☐	☐
22993	$.40	☐	☐	☐	☐
22994	$1.00	☐	☐	☐	☐
22995	$1.00	☐	☐	☐	☐
22996	$3.00	☐	☐	☐	☐
22997	$2.00	☐	☐	☐	☐
22998	$2.00	☐	☐	☐	☐
22999	$1.00	☐	☐	☐	☐
23000	$10.00	☐	☐	☐	☐
23001	$10.00	☐	☐	☐	☐

1943 COMMEMORATIVES

#908 1¢ FOUR FREEDOMS

		UL	UR	LL	LR
23006	$.70	☐	☐	☐	☐
23007	$.70	☐	☐	☐	☐
23008	$.70	☐	☐	☐	☐
23009	$.70	☐	☐	☐	☐
23010	$.70	☐	☐	☐	☐
23011	$.70	☐	☐	☐	☐
23015	$.70	☐	☐	☐	☐
23016	$.70	☐	☐	☐	☐
23017	$.70	☐	☐	☐	☐
23018	$1.00	☐	☐	☐	☐
23019	$6.00	☐	☐	☐	☐
23020	$5.00	☐	☐	☐	☐
23021	$1.00	☐	☐	☐	☐
23022	$1.50	☐	☐	☐	☐

1943-44 OVERRUN COUNTRIES

FLAG STAMPS FLAT PRESS

This issue was printed by the American Banknote Co.

13 Varieties Name Blocks of 4

		UR
#909 POLAND	$7.00	☐
#910 CZECHOSLOVAKIA	$3.50	☐
#911 NORWAY	$1.50	☐
#912 LUXEMBOURG	$1.50	☐
#913 NETHERLANDS	$1.50	☐
#914 BELGIUM	$1.50	☐
#915 FRANCE	$1.50	☐
#916 GREECE	$15.00	☐
#917 YUGOSLAVIA	$7.00	☐
#918 ALBANIA	$7.00	☐
#919 AUSTRIA	$5.00	☐
#920 DENMARK	$7.50	☐
#921 KOREA	$6.50	☐

1944 COMMEMORATIVES

ROTARY PRESS

#922 3¢ RAILROAD

		UL	UR	LL	LR
23142	$1.75	☐	☐	☐	☐
23143	$1.75	☐	☐	☐	☐

#923 3¢ STEAMSHIP

23145	$1.50	☐	☐	☐	☐
23146	$1.50	☐	☐	☐	☐

#924 3¢ TELEGRAPH

23151	$1.00	☐	☐	☐	☐
23152	$1.00	☐	☐	☐	☐

#925 3¢ CORREGIDOR

23162	$1.25	☐	☐	☐	☐
23163	$1.25	☐	☐	☐	☐

1944 COMMEMORATIVES

#926 3¢ MOTION PICTURES

		UL	UR	LL	LR
23180	$1	☐	☐	☐	☐
23181	$1	☐	☐	☐	☐

1945 COMMEMORATIVES

#927 3¢ FLORIDA

23237	$.75	☐	☐	☐	☐
23239	$.75	☐	☐	☐	☐

#928 5¢ UNITED NATIONS

23265	$.50	☐	☐	☐	☐
23266	$.50	☐	☐	☐	☐
23267	$.50	☐	☐	☐	☐
23276	$.50	☐	☐	☐	☐

#929 3¢ IWO JIMA

23295	$.45	☐	☐	☐	☐
23296	$.45	☐	☐	☐	☐
23297	$.45	☐	☐	☐	☐
23298	$.45	☐	☐	☐	☐
23305	$.45	☐	☐	☐	☐
23306	$.45	☐	☐	☐	☐

#930 1¢ ROOSEVELT

23307	$.20	☐	☐	☐	☐
23308	$.20	☐	☐	☐	☐
23309	$.20	☐	☐	☐	☐
23310	$.20	☐	☐	☐	☐
23311	$.20	☐	☐	☐	☐
23312	$.20	☐	☐	☐	☐

#931 2¢ ROOSEVELT

23313	$.30	☐	☐	☐	☐
23314	$.30	☐	☐	☐	☐

#932 3¢ ROOSEVELT

23285	$.35	☐	☐	☐	☐
23286	$.35	☐	☐	☐	☐
23287	$.35	☐	☐	☐	☐
23288	$.35	☐	☐	☐	☐
23293	$.35	☐	☐	☐	☐
23294	$.35	☐	☐	☐	☐

#933 5¢ ROOSEVELT (1946)

23381	$.50	☐	☐	☐	☐
23382	$.50	☐	☐	☐	☐

#934 3¢ ARMY

23324	$.35	☐	☐	☐	☐
23325	$.35	☐	☐	☐	☐
23326	$.35	☐	☐	☐	☐
23327	$.35	☐	☐	☐	☐

#935 3¢ NAVY

23338	$.35	☐	☐	☐	☐
23339	$.35	☐	☐	☐	☐
23340	$.35	☐	☐	☐	☐
23341	$.35	☐	☐	☐	☐
23342	$.35	☐	☐	☐	☐
23343	$.35	☐	☐	☐	☐

1945 COMMEMORATIVES

#936 3¢ COAST GUARD

		UL	UR	LL	LR
23334	$.35	☐	☐	☐	☐
23335	$.35	☐	☐	☐	☐
23336	$.35	☐	☐	☐	☐
23337	$.35	☐	☐	☐	☐

#937 3¢ AL SMITH

23353	$.35	☐	☐	☐	☐
23354	$.35	☐	☐	☐	☐
23355	$.35	☐	☐	☐	☐
23358	$.35	☐	☐	☐	☐

#938 3¢ TEXAS

23365	$.35	☐	☐	☐	☐
23366	$.35	☐	☐	☐	☐
23367	$.35	☐	☐	☐	☐
23368	$.35	☐	☐	☐	☐

1946 COMMEMORATIVES

#939 3¢ MERCHANT MARINE

23398	$.35	☐	☐	☐	☐
23399	$.35	☐	☐	☐	☐
23400	$.35	☐	☐	☐	☐
23405	$.35	☐	☐	☐	☐

#940 3¢ DISCHARGE EMBLEM

23428	$.35	☐	☐	☐	☐
23429	$.35	☐	☐	☐	☐
23430	$.35	☐	☐	☐	☐
23435	$.35	☐	☐	☐	☐
23438	$.35	☐	☐	☐	☐
23439	$.35	☐	☐	☐	☐

#941 3¢ TENNESSEE

23447	$.35	☐	☐	☐	☐
23448	$.35	☐	☐	☐	☐
23449	$.35	☐	☐	☐	☐
23450	$.35	☐	☐	☐	☐

#942 3¢ IOWA

23467	$.35	☐	☐	☐	☐
23468	$.35	☐	☐	☐	☐
23469	$.35	☐	☐	☐	☐
23470	$.35	☐	☐	☐	☐
23471	$.35	☐	☐	☐	☐
23472	$.35	☐	☐	☐	☐

#943 3¢ SMITHSONIAN

23463	$.35	☐	☐	☐	☐
23464	$.35	☐	☐	☐	☐
23465	$.35	☐	☐	☐	☐
23466	$.35	☐	☐	☐	☐
23473	$.35	☐	☐	☐	☐
23474	$.35	☐	☐	☐	☐

#944 3¢ KEARNY EXPEDITION

23511	$.35	☐	☐	☐	☐
23512	$.35	☐	☐	☐	☐
23513	$.35	☐	☐	☐	☐
23514	$.35	☐	☐	☐	☐
23519	$.35	☐	☐	☐	☐
23520	$.35	☐	☐	☐	☐
23521	$1.00	☐	☐	☐	☐
23522	$1.00	☐	☐	☐	☐

1947 COMMEMORATIVES

#945 3¢ EDISON

		UL	UR	LL	LR
23559	$.35	☐	☐	☐	☐
23560	$.35	☐	☐	☐	☐
23561	$.35	☐	☐	☐	☐
23562	$.35	☐	☐	☐	☐
23563	$.35	☐	☐	☐	☐
23564	$.35	☐	☐	☐	☐

#946 3¢ PULITZER

23622	$.35	☐	☐	☐	☐
23623	$.35	☐	☐	☐	☐
23624	$.35	☐	☐	☐	☐
23625	$.35	☐	☐	☐	☐
23626	$.35	☐	☐	☐	☐
23627	$.35	☐	☐	☐	☐

#947 3¢ POSTAGE CENTENARY

23596	$.35	☐	☐	☐	☐
23597	$.35	☐	☐	☐	☐
23598	$.35	☐	☐	☐	☐
23599	$.35	☐	☐	☐	☐

#948 15¢ CIPEX SHEET (IMPERF.)

The plate numbers of this souvenir sheet were trimmed off after printing so no plate numbers were regularly issued.

#949 3¢ DOCTOR

23656	$.35	☐	☐	☐	☐
23657	$.35	☐	☐	☐	☐
23658	$.35	☐	☐	☐	☐
23659	$.35	☐	☐	☐	☐
23660	$.35	☐	☐	☐	☐
23661	$.35	☐	☐	☐	☐
23665	$.35	☐	☐	☐	☐
23666	$.35	☐	☐	☐	☐

#950 3¢ UTAH

23686	$.35	☐	☐	☐	☐
23687	$.35	☐	☐	☐	☐
23688	$.35	☐	☐	☐	☐
23689	$.35	☐	☐	☐	☐
23690	$.35	☐	☐	☐	☐
23691	$.35	☐	☐	☐	☐

#951 3¢ FRIGATE CONSTITUTION

23710	$.35	☐	☐	☐	☐
23711	$.35	☐	☐	☐	☐
23712	$.35	☐	☐	☐	☐
23713	$.35	☐	☐	☐	☐
23714	$.35	☐	☐	☐	☐
23715	$.35	☐	☐	☐	☐

#952 3¢ EVERGLADES

23736	$.35	☐	☐	☐	☐
23737	$.35	☐	☐	☐	☐
23738	$.35	☐	☐	☐	☐
23739	$.35	☐	☐	☐	☐
23744	$.35	☐	☐	☐	☐
23745	$.35	☐	☐	☐	☐

1948 COMMEMORATIVES

#953 3¢ CARVER

		UL	UR	LL	LR
23653	$.35	☐	☐	☐	☐
23654	$.35	☐	☐	☐	☐
23655	$.35	☐	☐	☐	☐
23664	$.35	☐	☐	☐	☐

#954 3¢ CALIFORNIA GOLD

23772	$.35	☐	☐	☐	☐
23773	$.35	☐	☐	☐	☐
23774	$.35	☐	☐	☐	☐
23775	$.35	☐	☐	☐	☐
23776	$.35	☐	☐	☐	☐
23777	$.35	☐	☐	☐	☐

#955 3¢ MISSISSIPPI

23802	$.35	☐	☐	☐	☐
23803	$.35	☐	☐	☐	☐
23804	$.35	☐	☐	☐	☐
23805	$.35	☐	☐	☐	☐
23806	$.35	☐	☐	☐	☐
23807	$.35	☐	☐	☐	☐

#956 3¢ FOUR CHAPLAINS

23819	$.35	☐	☐	☐	☐
23820	$.35	☐	☐	☐	☐
23821	$.35	☐	☐	☐	☐
23822	$.35	☐	☐	☐	☐
23825	$.35	☐	☐	☐	☐
23826	$.35	☐	☐	☐	☐

#957 3¢ WISCONSIN

23812	$.35	☐	☐	☐	☐
23813	$.35	☐	☐	☐	☐
23814	$.35	☐	☐	☐	☐
23816	$.35	☐	☐	☐	☐

#958 5¢ SWEDISH PIONEER

23829	$.55	☐	☐	☐	☐
23830	$.55	☐	☐	☐	☐
23831	$.55	☐	☐	☐	☐
23832	$.55	☐	☐	☐	☐

#959 3¢ PROGRESS OF WOMEN

23841	$.35	☐	☐	☐	☐
23842	$.35	☐	☐	☐	☐
23843	$.35	☐	☐	☐	☐
23844	$.35	☐	☐	☐	☐

#960 3¢ WILLIAM ALLEN WHITE

23855	$.50	☐	☐	☐	☐
23856	$.50	☐	☐	☐	☐
23857	$.50	☐	☐	☐	☐
23858	$.50	☐	☐	☐	☐

#961 3¢ CANADA FRIENDSHIP

23853	$.35	☐	☐	☐	☐
23854	$.35	☐	☐	☐	☐
23859	$.35	☐	☐	☐	☐
23860	$.35	☐	☐	☐	☐

#962 3¢ FRANCIS SCOTT KEY

23835	$.35	☐	☐	☐	☐
23836	$.35	☐	☐	☐	☐

1948 COMMEMORATIVES

#963 3¢ SALUTE TO YOUTH

		UL	UR	LL	LR
23864	$.35	☐	☐	☐	☐
23865	$.35	☐	☐	☐	☐
23866	$.35	☐	☐	☐	☐
23867	$.35	☐	☐	☐	☐

#964 3¢ OREGON

23872	$.50	☐	☐	☐	☐
23873	$.50	☐	☐	☐	☐
23874	$.50	☐	☐	☐	☐
23875	$.50	☐	☐	☐	☐

#965 3¢ HARLAN FISKE STONE

23890	$.80	☐	☐	☐	☐
23891	$.80	☐	☐	☐	☐
23892	$2.25	☐	☐	☐	☐
23893	$2.25	☐	☐	☐	☐

#966 3¢ PALOMAR

23884	$1.25	☐	☐	☐	☐
23885	$1.25	☐	☐	☐	☐
23888	$2.50	☐	☐	☐	☐
23889	$2.50	☐	☐	☐	☐

#967 3¢ CLARA BARTON

23896	$.35	☐	☐	☐	☐
23897	$.35	☐	☐	☐	☐
23898	$.35	☐	☐	☐	☐
23899	$.35	☐	☐	☐	☐

#968 3¢ POULTRY INDUSTRY

23900	$.40	☐	☐	☐	☐
23901	$.40	☐	☐	☐	☐
23902	$.40	☐	☐	☐	☐
23903	$.40	☐	☐	☐	☐

#969 3¢ GOLD STAR

23833	$.40	☐	☐	☐	☐
23834	$.40	☐	☐	☐	☐

#970 3¢ FORT KEARNY

23907	$.40	☐	☐	☐	☐
23908	$.40	☐	☐	☐	☐
23912	$.40	☐	☐	☐	☐
23913	$.40	☐	☐	☐	☐

#971 3¢ VOLUNTEER FIREMAN

23918	$.40	☐	☐	☐	☐
23919	$.40	☐	☐	☐	☐
23924	$.40	☐	☐	☐	☐
23925	$.40	☐	☐	☐	☐

#972 3¢ INDIAN CENTENNIAL

23920	$.40	☐	☐	☐	☐
23921	$.40	☐	☐	☐	☐
23922	$.40	☐	☐	☐	☐
23923	$.40	☐	☐	☐	☐

#973 3¢ ROUGH RIDERS

23947	$.50	☐	☐	☐	☐
23948	$.50	☐	☐	☐	☐
23949	$.50	☐	☐	☐	☐
23950	$.50	☐	☐	☐	☐

1948 COMMEMORATIVES

#974 3¢ JULIETTE LOW

		UL	UR	LL	LR
23953	$.40	☐	☐	☐	☐
23954	$.40	☐	☐	☐	☐
23955	$.40	☐	☐	☐	☐
23956	$.40	☐	☐	☐	☐

#975 3¢ WILL ROGERS

23943	$.50	☐	☐	☐	☐
23944	$.50	☐	☐	☐	☐
23945	$.50	☐	☐	☐	☐
23946	$.50	☐	☐	☐	☐

#976 3¢ FORT BLISS

23935	$1.50	☐	☐	☐	☐
23936	$1.50	☐	☐	☐	☐
23937	$1.50	☐	☐	☐	☐
23938	$1.50	☐	☐	☐	☐

#977 3¢ MOINA MICHAEL

23965	$.40	☐	☐	☐	☐
23966	$.40	☐	☐	☐	☐
23967	$.40	☐	☐	☐	☐
23968	$.40	☐	☐	☐	☐

#978 3¢ GETTYSBURG

23961	$.40	☐	☐	☐	☐
23962	$.40	☐	☐	☐	☐
23963	$.40	☐	☐	☐	☐
23964	$.40	☐	☐	☐	☐

#979 3¢ TURNERS SOCIETY

23939	$.40	☐	☐	☐	☐
23940	$.40	☐	☐	☐	☐
23941	$.40	☐	☐	☐	☐
23942	$.40	☐	☐	☐	☐

#980 3¢ JOEL CHANDLER HARRIS

23882	$.60	☐	☐	☐	☐
23883	$.60	☐	☐	☐	☐

1949 COMMEMORATIVES

#981 3¢ MINNESOTA

24029	$.35	☐	☐	☐	☐
24030	$.35	☐	☐	☐	☐
24032	$.35	☐	☐	☐	☐
24033	$.35	☐	☐	☐	☐
24034	$.35	☐	☐	☐	☐
24035	$.35	☐	☐	☐	☐

#982 3¢ WASHINGTON & LEE

24036	$.35	☐	☐	☐	☐
24037	$.35	☐	☐	☐	☐
24038	$.35	☐	☐	☐	☐
24039	$.35	☐	☐	☐	☐
24040	$.35	☐	☐	☐	☐
24041	$.35	☐	☐	☐	☐

#983 3¢ PUERTO RICO

24062	$.35	☐	☐	☐	☐
24063	$.35	☐	☐	☐	☐
24064	$.35	☐	☐	☐	☐
24065	$.35	☐	☐	☐	☐

1949 COMMEMORATIVES

#984 3¢ ANNAPOLIS

		UL	UR	LL	LR
24093	$.35	☐	☐	☐	☐
24094	$.35	☐	☐	☐	☐
24095	$.35	☐	☐	☐	☐
24096	$.35	☐	☐	☐	☐
24097	$.35	☐	☐	☐	☐
24098	$.35	☐	☐	☐	☐

#985 3¢ G. A. R. VETERANS

24135	$.35	☐	☐	☐	☐
24136	$.35	☐	☐	☐	☐
24137	$.35	☐	☐	☐	☐
24138	$.35	☐	☐	☐	☐
24139	$.35	☐	☐	☐	☐
24140	$.35	☐	☐	☐	☐

#986 3¢ EDGAR ALLAN POE

24143	$.50	☐	☐	☐	☐
24144	$.50	☐	☐	☐	☐
24145	$.50	☐	☐	☐	☐
24146	$.50	☐	☐	☐	☐

1950 COMMEMORATIVES

#987 3¢ BANKERS ASSOCIATION

24160	$.35	☐	☐	☐	☐
24161	$.35	☐	☐	☐	☐
24162	$.35	☐	☐	☐	☐
24163	$.35	☐	☐	☐	☐
24164	$.35	☐	☐	☐	☐
24165	$.35	☐	☐	☐	☐

#988 3¢ SAMUEL GOMPERS

24166	$.35	☐	☐	☐	☐
24167	$.35	☐	☐	☐	☐
24168	$.35	☐	☐	☐	☐
24169	$.35	☐	☐	☐	☐

#989 3¢ STATUE OF FREEDOM

24183	$.35	☐	☐	☐	☐
24184	$.35	☐	☐	☐	☐
24185	$.35	☐	☐	☐	☐
24186	$.35	☐	☐	☐	☐
24187	$.35	☐	☐	☐	☐
24188	$.35	☐	☐	☐	☐

#990 3¢ EXECUTIVE MANSION

24209	$.40	☐	☐	☐	☐
24210	$.40	☐	☐	☐	☐
24211	$.40	☐	☐	☐	☐
24212	$.40	☐	☐	☐	☐
24218	$.40	☐	☐	☐	☐
24219	$.40	☐	☐	☐	☐

#991 3¢ SUPREME COURT BLDG.

24243	$.35	☐	☐	☐	☐
24244	$.35	☐	☐	☐	☐
24245	$.35	☐	☐	☐	☐
24246	$.35	☐	☐	☐	☐

#992 3¢ U.S. CAPITOL

24284	$.40	☐	☐	☐	☐
24285	$.40	☐	☐	☐	☐

1950 COMMEMORATIVES

#993 3¢ CASEY JONES

		UL	UR	LL	LR
24191	$.35	☐	☐	☐	☐
24192	$.35	☐	☐	☐	☐
24193	$.35	☐	☐	☐	☐
24194	$.35	☐	☐	☐	☐
24195	$.35	☐	☐	☐	☐
24196	$.35	☐	☐	☐	☐

#994 3¢ KANSAS CITY

24203	$.35	☐	☐	☐	☐
24204	$.35	☐	☐	☐	☐
24205	$.35	☐	☐	☐	☐
24206	$.35	☐	☐	☐	☐
24208	$.35	☐	☐	☐	☐
24217	$.35	☐	☐	☐	☐

#995 3¢ BOY SCOUTS

24224	$.40	☐	☐	☐	☐
24225	$.40	☐	☐	☐	☐
24227	$.40	☐	☐	☐	☐
24228	$.40	☐	☐	☐	☐
24229	$.40	☐	☐	☐	☐
24230	$.40	☐	☐	☐	☐

#996 3¢ INDIANA TERRITORY

24233	$.35	☐	☐	☐	☐
24234	$.35	☐	☐	☐	☐
24235	$.35	☐	☐	☐	☐
24236	$.35	☐	☐	☐	☐
24237	$.35	☐	☐	☐	☐
24238	$.35	☐	☐	☐	☐

#997 3¢ CALIFORNIA STATEHOOD

24259	$.35	☐	☐	☐	☐
24260	$.35	☐	☐	☐	☐
23261	$.35	☐	☐	☐	☐
24262	$.35	☐	☐	☐	☐

1951 COMMEMORATIVES

#998 3¢ CONFEDERATE VETERANS

24366	$.35	☐	☐	☐	☐
24367	$.35	☐	☐	☐	☐
24368	$.35	☐	☐	☐	☐
24369	$.35	☐	☐	☐	☐

#999 3¢ NEVADA

24414	$.35	☐	☐	☐	☐
24415	$.35	☐	☐	☐	☐
24416	$.35	☐	☐	☐	☐
24417	$.35	☐	☐	☐	☐
24430	$.35	☐	☐	☐	☐
24431	$.35	☐	☐	☐	☐

#1000 3¢ LANDING OF CADILLAC

24436	$.35	☐	☐	☐	☐
24437	$.35	☐	☐	☐	☐
24438	$.35	☐	☐	☐	☐
24439	$.35	☐	☐	☐	☐
24440	$.35	☐	☐	☐	☐
24441	$.35	☐	☐	☐	☐

1951 COMMEMORATIVES

#1001 3¢ COLORADO

		UL	UR	LL	LR
24446	$.35	□	□	□	□
24447	$.35	□	□	□	□
24448	$.35	□	□	□	□
24449	$.35	□	□	□	□
24450	$.35	□	□	□	□
24451	$.35	□	□	□	□

#1002 3¢ AMERICAN CHEMICAL SOCIETY

24463	$.35	□	□	□	□
24464	$.35	□	□	□	□
24465	$.35	□	□	□	□
24466	$.35	□	□	□	□
24473	$.35	□	□	□	□
24474	$.35	□	□	□	□

#1003 3¢ BATTLE OF BROOKLYN

24556	$.35	□	□	□	□
24557	$.35	□	□	□	□
24558	$.35	□	□	□	□
24559	$.35	□	□	□	□
24560	$.35	□	□	□	□
24561	$.35	□	□	□	□

1952 COMMEMORATIVES

#1004 3¢ BETSY ROSS

24574	$.50	□	□	□	□
24575	$.50	□	□	□	□
24576	$.50	□	□	□	□
24577	$.50	□	□	□	□
24578	$.50	□	□	□	□
24579	$.50	□	□	□	□

#1005 3¢ 4-H CLUB

24580	$.35	□	□	□	□
24581	$.35	□	□	□	□
24582	$.35	□	□	□	□
24583	$.35	□	□	□	□

#1006 3¢ B. & O. RAILROAD

24603	$.50	□	□	□	□
24604	$.50	□	□	□	□
24605	$.50	□	□	□	□
24606	$.50	□	□	□	□
24607	$.50	□	□	□	□
24608	$.50	□	□	□	□

#1007 3¢ A. A. A. ANNIVERSARY

24611	$.35	□	□	□	□
24612	$.35	□	□	□	□
24613	$.35	□	□	□	□
24614	$.35	□	□	□	□
24615	$.35	□	□	□	□
24616	$.35	□	□	□	□

#1008 3¢ NATO

24629	$.35	□	□	□	□
24630	$.35	□	□	□	□
24631	$.35	□	□	□	□
24632	$.35	□	□	□	□

1952 COMMEMORATIVES

#1008 3¢ NATO Cont.

		UL	UR	LL	LR
24633	$.35	□	□	□	□
24634	$.35	□	□	□	□
24635	$.35	□	□	□	□
24636	$.35	□	□	□	□
24637	$.35	□	□	□	□
24638	$.35	□	□	□	□
24639	$.35	□	□	□	□
24640	$.35	□	□	□	□
24641	$.35	□	□	□	□
24642	$.35	□	□	□	□
24643	$.35	□	□	□	□
24644	$.35	□	□	□	□
24645	$.35	□	□	□	□
24646	$.35	□	□	□	□

#1009 3¢ GRAND COULEE DAM

24647	$.35	□	□	□	□
24648	$.35	□	□	□	□
24649	$.35	□	□	□	□
24650	$.35	□	□	□	□
24651	$.35	□	□	□	□
24652	$.35	□	□	□	□

#1010 3¢ LaFAYETTE

24661	$.35	□	□	□	□
24662	$.35	□	□	□	□
24663	$.35	□	□	□	□
24664	$.35	□	□	□	□
24665	$.35	□	□	□	□
24666	$.35	□	□	□	□

#1011 3¢ MT. RUSHMORE

24669	$.40	□	□	□	□
24670	$.40	□	□	□	□
24671	$.40	□	□	□	□
24672	$.40	□	□	□	□
24673	$.40	□	□	□	□
24674	$.40	□	□	□	□

#1012 3¢ CIVIL ENGINEERS

24675	$.35	□	□	□	□
24676	$.35	□	□	□	□
24677	$.35	□	□	□	□
24678	$.35	□	□	□	□
24679	$.35	□	□	□	□
24680	$.35	□	□	□	□

#1013 3¢ SERVICE WOMEN

24681	$.35	□	□	□	□
24682	$.35	□	□	□	□
24683	$.35	□	□	□	□
24684	$.35	□	□	□	□
24685	$.35	□	□	□	□
24686	$.35	□	□	□	□

#1014 3¢ GUTENBURG BIBLE

24687	$.35	□	□	□	□
24688	$.35	□	□	□	□
24689	$.35	□	□	□	□

1952 COMMEMORATIVES

#1014 3¢ GUTENBURG BIBLE Cont.

		UL	UR	LL	LR
24690	$.35	☐	☐	☐	☐
24691	$.35	☐	☐	☐	☐
24692	$.35	☐	☐	☐	☐

#1015 3¢ NEWS BOYS

24693	$.35	☐	☐	☐	☐
24694	$.35	☐	☐	☐	☐
24695	$.35	☐	☐	☐	☐
24696	$.35	☐	☐	☐	☐
24697	$.35	☐	☐	☐	☐
24698	$.35	☐	☐	☐	☐

#1016 3¢ RED CROSS

24701	$.35	☐	☐	☐	☐
24702	$.35	☐	☐	☐	☐
24719	$.35	☐	☐	☐	☐
24720	$.35	☐	☐	☐	☐
24725	$.35	☐	☐	☐	☐
24726	$.35	☐	☐	☐	☐

1953 COMMEMORATIVES

#1017 3¢ NATIONAL GUARD

24745	$.40	☐	☐	☐	☐
24746	$.40	☐	☐	☐	☐
24747	$.40	☐	☐	☐	☐
24748	$.40	☐	☐	☐	☐
24749	$.40	☐	☐	☐	☐
24750	$.40	☐	☐	☐	☐

#1018 3¢ OHIO

24751	$.50	☐	☐	☐	☐
24752	$.50	☐	☐	☐	☐
24753	$.50	☐	☐	☐	☐
24754	$.50	☐	☐	☐	☐

#1019 3¢ WASHINGTON TERRITORY

24759	$.35	☐	☐	☐	☐
24760	$.35	☐	☐	☐	☐
24761	$.35	☐	☐	☐	☐
24762	$.35	☐	☐	☐	☐
24763	$.35	☐	☐	☐	☐
24764	$.35	☐	☐	☐	☐

#1020 3¢ LOUISIANA

24767	$.35	☐	☐	☐	☐
24768	$.35	☐	☐	☐	☐
24769	$.35	☐	☐	☐	☐
24770	$.35	☐	☐	☐	☐
24771	$.35	☐	☐	☐	☐
24772	$.35	☐	☐	☐	☐

#1021 5¢ PERRY

24803	$1	☐	☐	☐	☐
24804	$1	☐	☐	☐	☐
24805	$1	☐	☐	☐	☐
24806	$1	☐	☐	☐	☐

#1022 3¢ BAR ASSOCIATION

24829	$.35	☐	☐	☐	☐
24830	$.35	☐	☐	☐	☐
24831	$.35	☐	☐	☐	☐

1953 COMMEMORATIVES

#1022 3¢ BAR ASSOCIATION Cont.

		UL	UR	LL	LR
24832	$.35	☐	☐	☐	☐
24833	$.35	☐	☐	☐	☐
24834	$.35	☐	☐	☐	☐

#1023 3¢ SAGAMORE HILL

24849	$.35	☐	☐	☐	☐
24850	$.35	☐	☐	☐	☐
24851	$.35	☐	☐	☐	☐
24852	$.35	☐	☐	☐	☐
24853	$.35	☐	☐	☐	☐
24854	$.35	☐	☐	☐	☐

#1024 3¢ FUTURE FARMERS

24825	$.35	☐	☐	☐	☐
24826	$.35	☐	☐	☐	☐
24827	$.35	☐	☐	☐	☐
24828	$.35	☐	☐	☐	☐

#1025 3¢TRUCKING INDUSTRY

24867	$.35	☐	☐	☐	☐
24868	$.35	☐	☐	☐	☐
24869	$.35	☐	☐	☐	☐
24870	$.35	☐	☐	☐	☐
24871	$.35	☐	☐	☐	☐
24872	$.35	☐	☐	☐	☐

#1026 3¢ PATTON

24875	$.50	☐	☐	☐	☐
24876	$.50	☐	☐	☐	☐
24877	$.50	☐	☐	☐	☐
24878	$.50	☐	☐	☐	☐
24879	$.50	☐	☐	☐	☐
24880	$.50	☐	☐	☐	☐

#1027 3¢ NEW YORK CITY

24881	$.40	☐	☐	☐	☐
24882	$.40	☐	☐	☐	☐
24883	$.40	☐	☐	☐	☐
24884	$.40	☐	☐	☐	☐
24885	$.40	☐	☐	☐	☐
24886	$.40	☐	☐	☐	☐

#1028 3¢ GADSDEN PURCHASE

24888	$.35	☐	☐	☐	☐
24889	$.35	☐	☐	☐	☐
24890	$.35	☐	☐	☐	☐
24891	$.35	☐	☐	☐	☐
24892	$.35	☐	☐	☐	☐
24893	$.35	☐	☐	☐	☐

1954 COMMEMORATIVES

#1029 3¢ COLUMBIA UNIVERSITY

24894	$.35	☐	☐	☐	☐
24895	$.35	☐	☐	☐	☐
24896	$.35	☐	☐	☐	☐
24897	$.35	☐	☐	☐	☐

#1030-59A

See page 151

1954 COMMEMORATIVES

			UL	UR	LL	LR
#1060	**3¢**	**NEBRASKA**				
24967	$.35		□	□	□	□
24968	$.35		□	□	□	□
24969	$.35		□	□	□	□
24970	$.35		□	□	□	□
#1061	**3¢**	**KANSAS**				
24986	$.35		□	□	□	□
24987	$.35		□	□	□	□
24988	$.35		□	□	□	□
24989	$.35		□	□	□	□
#1062	**3¢**	**EASTMAN**				
25008	$.40		□	□	□	□
25009	$.40		□	□	□	□
25010	$.40		□	□	□	□
#1063	**3¢**	**LEWIS AND CLARK**				
Dry Printed						
25021	$.40		□	□	□	□
25022	$.40		□	□	□	□
25023	$.40		□	□	□	□
25024	$.40		□	□	□	□

1954 REGULAR ISSUE

The 1954 regular issue is also known as the Liberty Series.

The advent of this series brought a sharp increase in the collecting of plate number blocks. Collectors took advantage of the opportunity to start at the beginning of a new and interesting group of plates.

The Bureau of Engraving and Printing did considerable experimenting during this period. By the end of this series, stamps were printed by a dry process on pre-gummed paper instead of the wet method initially used. New equipment made startling changes in printing methods. The 3-color web intaglio press manufactured by Giori which used one plate with separate inking-in rollers for multicolored stamp production was used for #1042 and #1044a.

The monthly publishing of reports on cancelled plates with the number of impressions gave collectors ample advance warning of short runs in time to search the Post Offices. This prevented many of these plates from being considered rare.

ROTARY PRESS

#1030 .5¢ FRANKLIN 2 Plates

		UL	UR	LL	LR
Wet Printed					
25263	$.25	☐	☐	☐	☐
25264	$.25	☐	☐	☐	☐

#1030a .5¢ FRANKLIN 10 Plates

Dry Printed					
25980	$.25	☐	☐	☐	☐
25981	$.25	☐	☐	☐	☐
26002	$.25	☐	☐	☐	☐
26003	$.25	☐	☐	☐	☐
26708	$.90	☐	☐	☐	☐
26709	$.90	☐	☐	☐	☐
26906	$.25	☐	☐	☐	☐
26907	$.25	☐	☐	☐	☐
26911	$.60	☐	☐	☐	☐
26912	$.60	☐	☐	☐	☐

#1031b 1¢ WASHINGTON 6 Plates

Wet Printed					
25030	$.20	☐	☐	☐	☐
25031	$.20	☐	☐	☐	☐
25032	$.20	☐	☐	☐	☐
25033	$.20	☐	☐	☐	☐
25281	$.20	☐	☐	☐	☐
25282	$.20	☐	☐	☐	☐

#1031 1¢ WASHINGTON 58 Plates

Dry Printed					
25326	$.20	☐	☐	☐	☐
25327	$.20	☐	☐	☐	☐

#1031 1¢ WASHINGTON Cont.

		UL	UR	LL	LR
25361	$.20	☐	☐	☐	☐
25362	$.20	☐	☐	☐	☐
25677	$.20	☐	☐	☐	☐
25678	$.20	☐	☐	☐	☐
25679	$.20	☐	☐	☐	☐
25680	$.20	☐	☐	☐	☐
25681	$.20	☐	☐	☐	☐
25682	$.20	☐	☐	☐	☐
25687	$.20	☐	☐	☐	☐
25688	$.20	☐	☐	☐	☐
25691	$.20	☐	☐	☐	☐
25692	$.20	☐	☐	☐	☐
25695	$.20	☐	☐	☐	☐
25696	$.20	☐	☐	☐	☐
25703	$.60	☐	☐	☐	☐
25704	$.60	☐	☐	☐	☐
25707	$.20	☐	☐	☐	☐
25708	$.20	☐	☐	☐	☐
25714	$.20	☐	☐	☐	☐
25715	$.20	☐	☐	☐	☐
25727	$.60	☐	☐	☐	☐
25728	$.60	☐	☐	☐	☐
25991	$.20	☐	☐	☐	☐
25992	$.20	☐	☐	☐	☐
26063	$.20	☐	☐	☐	☐
26064	$.20	☐	☐	☐	☐
26163	$.20	☐	☐	☐	☐
26164	$.20	☐	☐	☐	☐
26189	$.20	☐	☐	☐	☐
26190	$.20	☐	☐	☐	☐
26408	$.20	☐	☐	☐	☐
26409	$.20	☐	☐	☐	☐
26429	$.20	☐	☐	☐	☐
26430	$.20	☐	☐	☐	☐
26460	$.20	☐	☐	☐	☐
26461	$.20	☐	☐	☐	☐
26606	$.20	☐	☐	☐	☐
26607	$.20	☐	☐	☐	☐
26612	$.20	☐	☐	☐	☐
26613	$.20	☐	☐	☐	☐
26927	$.60	☐	☐	☐	☐
26928	$.60	☐	☐	☐	☐
26929	$.20	☐	☐	☐	☐
26930	$.20	☐	☐	☐	☐
26971	$.20	☐	☐	☐	☐
26972	$.20	☐	☐	☐	☐
26987	$.20	☐	☐	☐	☐
26988	$.20	☐	☐	☐	☐
26994	$.20	☐	☐	☐	☐
26995	$.20	☐	☐	☐	☐
27151	$.20	☐	☐	☐	☐
27152	$.20	☐	☐	☐	☐
27221	$.20	☐	☐	☐	☐
27222	$.20	☐	☐	☐	☐
27228	$.20	☐	☐	☐	☐
27229	$.20	☐	☐	☐	☐

1954 REGULAR ISSUE

#1031A 1.25¢ SANTA FE 6 Plates

Dry Printed		UL	UR	LL	LR
26619	$.60	□	□	□	□
26620	$.60	□	□	□	□
26641	$.60	□	□	□	□
26642	$.60	□	□	□	□
26724	$.60	□	□	□	□
26725	$.60	□	□	□	□

#1032 1.5¢ MOUNT VERNON 5 Plates

Dry Printed

25365	$3.00	□	□	□	□
25366	$3.00	□	□	□	□
25368	$3.00	□	□	□	□
25369	$3.00	□	□	□	□
25410	$3.00	□	□	□	□

#1033 2¢ JEFFERSON 78 Plates

Dry Printed

25046	$.25	□	□	□	□
25047	$.25	□	□	□	□
25050	$.25	□	□	□	□
25051	$10.00	□	□	□	□
25056	$.25	□	□	□	□
25057	$.25	□	□	□	□
25061	$.25	□	□	□	□
25062	$.25	□	□	□	□
25079	$.25	□	□	□	□
25080	$.25	□	□	□	□
25129	$.25	□	□	□	□
25130	$.25	□	□	□	□
25131	$.25	□	□	□	□
25132	$.25	□	□	□	□
25137	$.25	□	□	□	□
25138	$.25	□	□	□	□
25143	$.50	□	□	□	□
25144	$.50	□	□	□	□
25149	$.25	□	□	□	□
25150	$.25	□	□	□	□
25189	$.25	□	□	□	□
25190	$.25	□	□	□	□
25203	$.25	□	□	□	□
25204	$.25	□	□	□	□
25213	$.60	□	□	□	□
25214	$.60	□	□	□	□
25215	$.90	□	□	□	□
25216	$.90	□	□	□	□
25241	$.60	□	□	□	□
25242	$.60	□	□	□	□
25277	$.25	□	□	□	□
25278	$.60	□	□	□	□
25283	$.60	□	□	□	□
25284	$.25	□	□	□	□
25290	$.25	□	□	□	□
25291	$.25	□	□	□	□
25457	$.25	□	□	□	□
25458	$.25	□	□	□	□
25459	$.25	□	□	□	□
25460	$.60	□	□	□	□
25461	$.25	□	□	□	□
25462	$.25	□	□	□	□
25463	$.25	□	□	□	□
25464	$.60	□	□	□	□

#1033 2¢ JEFFERSON Cont.

		UL	UR	LL	LR
25465	$.25	□	□	□	□
25466	$.25	□	□	□	□
25467	$.25	□	□	□	□
25468	$.25	□	□	□	□
25471	$.60	□	□	□	□
25472	$.60	□	□	□	□
25565	$.25	□	□	□	□
25566	$.90	□	□	□	□
25573	$.25	□	□	□	□
25574	$.25	□	□	□	□
25579	$.25	□	□	□	□
25580	$.25	□	□	□	□
25585	$.25	□	□	□	□
25586	$.25	□	□	□	□
25589	$.25	□	□	□	□
25590	$.25	□	□	□	□
25591	$.50	□	□	□	□
25592	$.50	□	□	□	□
25594	$.25	□	□	□	□
25595	$.25	□	□	□	□
25596	$.25	□	□	□	□
25817	$.25	□	□	□	□
25818	$.25	□	□	□	□
25823	$.25	□	□	□	□
25824	$.25	□	□	□	□
25872	$.25	□	□	□	□
25875	$.25	□	□	□	□
25876	$.25	□	□	□	□
25877	$.25	□	□	□	□
25878	$.25	□	□	□	□
25887	$.25	□	□	□	□
25888	$.25	□	□	□	□
25901	$.25	□	□	□	□
25902	$.25	□	□	□	□

#1033a 2¢ JEFFERSON 2 Plates

Dry Printed Silkote Paper

25061	—	□	□	□	□
25062	—	□	□	□	□

#1034 2.5¢ BUNKER HILL 6 Plates

Dry printed

26308	$.60	□	□	□	□
26309	$.60	□	□	□	□
26310	$.60	□	□	□	□
26322	$.60	□	□	□	□
27090	$50.00	□	□$_6$	†	□$_2$
27091	$50.00	□	†	†	□$_2$

1954 REGULAR ISSUE

#1035e 3¢ LIBERTY 64 Plates

Wet Printed

		UL	UR	LL	LR
24943	$.40	☐	☐	☐	☐
24944	$.40	☐	☐	☐	☐
24945	$.40	☐	☐	☐	☐
24946	$.40	☐	☐	☐	☐
24947	$.40	☐	☐	☐	☐
24948	$.40	☐	☐	☐	☐
24949	$.40	☐	☐	☐	☐
24950	$.40	☐	☐	☐	☐
24951	$.40	☐	☐	☐	☐
24952	$.40	☐	☐	☐	☐
24953	$.40	☐	☐	☐	☐
24954	$.40	☐	☐	☐	☐
24955	$.40	☐	☐	☐	☐
24957	$.40	☐	☐	☐	☐
24958	$.40	☐	☐	☐	☐
24961	$.40	☐	☐	☐	☐
24962	$.40	☐	☐	☐	☐
24963	$.40	☐	☐	☐	☐
24964	$.40	☐	☐	☐	☐
24965	$.40	☐	☐	☐	☐
24966	$.40	☐	☐	☐	☐
24979	$.40	☐	☐	☐	☐
24994	$.40	☐	☐	☐	☐
24998	$.40	☐	☐	☐	☐
24999	$.40	☐	☐	☐	☐
25000	$.40	☐	☐	☐	☐
25001	$.40	☐	☐	☐	☐
25004	$.40	☐	☐	☐	☐
25005	$.40	☐	☐	☐	☐
25011	$.40	☐	☐	☐	☐
25012	$.40	☐	☐	☐	☐
25028	$.40	☐	☐	☐	☐
25029	$.40	☐	☐	☐	☐
25073	$.40	☐	☐	☐	☐
25074	$.40	☐	☐	☐	☐
25077	$.40	☐	☐	☐	☐
25078	$.40	☐	☐	☐	☐
25083	$.40	☐	☐	☐	☐
25084	$.40	☐	☐	☐	☐
25085	$.40	☐	☐	☐	☐
25086	$.40	☐	☐	☐	☐
25092	$.40	☐	☐	☐	☐
25093	$.40	☐	☐	☐	☐
25109	$.40	☐	☐	☐	☐
25110	$.40	☐	☐	☐	☐
25111	$.40	☐	☐	☐	☐
25112	$.40	☐	☐	☐	☐
25113	$.40	☐	☐	☐	☐
25114	$.40	☐	☐	☐	☐
25115	$.40	☐	☐	☐	☐
25116	$.40	☐	☐	☐	☐
25187	$.40	☐	☐	☐	☐
25188	$.40	☐	☐	☐	☐
25199	$.40	☐	☐	☐	☐
25200	$.40	☐	☐	☐	☐
25201	$.40	☐	☐	☐	☐

#1035e 3¢ LIBERTY Cont.

		UL	UR	LL	LR
25202	$.40	☐	☐	☐	☐
25205	$.40	☐	☐	☐	☐
25206	$.40	☐	☐	☐	☐
25211	$.40	☐	☐	☐	☐
25212	$.40	☐	☐	☐	☐
25229	$1.00	☐	☐	☐	☐
25230	$1.00	☐	☐	☐	☐
25233	$.40	☐	☐	☐	☐

#1035 3¢ LIBERTY 224 Plates

Dry Printed - UNTAGGED

		UL	UR	LL	LR
25235	$1.00	☐	☐	☐	☐
25236	$25.00	☐3	☐3	☐	☐2
25239	$1.00	☐	☐	☐	☐
25240	$1.00	☐	☐	☐	☐
25253	$.40	☐	☐	☐	☐
25254	$2.00	☐	☐	☐	☐
25255	$2.00	☐	☐	☐	☐
25256	$.40	☐	☐	☐	☐
25259	$.40	☐	☐	☐	☐
25260	$1.25	☐	☐	☐	☐
25261	$.40	☐	☐	☐	☐
25262	$.40	☐	☐	☐	☐
25265	$.40	☐	☐	☐	☐
25266	$.40	☐	☐	☐	☐
25268	$1.25	☐	☐	☐	☐
25269	$.40	☐	☐	☐	☐
25270	$1.00	☐	☐	☐	☐
25271	$4.00	☐	☐	☐	☐
25272	$.40	☐	☐	☐	☐
25273	$.40	☐	☐	☐	☐
25274	$.40	☐	☐	☐	☐
25275	$.40	☐	☐	☐	☐
25276	$.40	☐	☐	☐	☐
25279	$.40	☐	☐	☐	☐
25280	$.40	☐	☐	☐	☐
25285	$1.50	☐	☐	☐	☐
25286	$1.50	☐	☐	☐	☐
25287	$1.75	☐	☐	☐	☐
25288	$.40	☐	☐	☐	☐
25292	$.40	☐	☐	☐	☐

1954 REGULAR ISSUE

#1035 3¢ LIBERTY Cont.

		UL	UR	LL	LR
25293	$1.00	☐	☐	☐	☐
25294	$.40	☐	☐	☐	☐
25295	$1.00	☐	☐	☐	☐
25296	$.40	☐	☐	☐	☐
25297	$.40	☐	☐	☐	☐
25298	$1.00	☐	☐	☐	☐
25306	$.40	☐	☐	☐	☐
25307	$.40	☐	☐	☐	☐
25308	$.40	☐	☐	☐	☐
25311	$.40	☐	☐	☐	☐
25312	$.40	☐	☐	☐	☐
25351	$.40	☐	☐	☐	☐
25352	$.40	☐	☐	☐	☐
25504	$.40	☐	☐	☐	☐
25505	$.40	☐	☐	☐	☐
25506	$1.00	☐	☐	☐	☐
25507	$1.00	☐	☐	☐	☐
25508	$.40	☐	☐	☐	☐
25509	$.40	☐	☐	☐	☐
25510	$3.50	☐	☐	☐	☐
25511	$.40	☐	☐	☐	☐
25512	$.40	☐	☐	☐	☐
25513	$.40	☐	☐	☐	☐
25514	$1.00	☐	☐	☐	☐
25515	$.40	☐	☐	☐	☐
25516	$.40	☐	☐	☐	☐
25517	$2.00	☐	☐	☐	☐
25518	$2.00	☐	☐	☐	☐
25519	$.40	☐	☐	☐	☐
25520	$3.00	☐	☐	☐	☐
25521	$3.00	☐	☐	☐	☐
25522	$.40	☐	☐	☐	☐
25523	$.40	☐	☐	☐	☐
25524	$1.50	☐	☐	☐	☐
25525	$.40	☐	☐	☐	☐
25526	$4.00	☐	☐	☐	☐
25528	$.40	☐	☐	☐	☐
25529	$.40	☐	☐	☐	☐
25530	$.40	☐	☐	☐	☐
25531	$.40	☐	☐	☐	☐
25532	$.40	☐	☐	☐	☐
25537	$.40	☐	☐	☐	☐
25538	$.40	☐	☐	☐	☐
25539	$.40	☐	☐	☐	☐
25540	$7.50	☐	☐	☐	☐
25543	$.40	☐	☐	☐	☐
25544	$.40	☐	☐	☐	☐
25545	$.40	☐	☐	☐	☐
25546	$.40	☐	☐	☐	☐
25547	$.40	☐	☐	☐	☐
25548	$.40	☐	☐	☐	☐
25549	$.40	☐	☐	☐	☐
25550	$.40	☐	☐	☐	☐
25551	$.40	☐	☐	☐	☐
25552	$.40	☐	☐	☐	☐
25553	$.40	☐	☐	☐	☐
25554	$.40	☐	☐	☐	☐
25555	$.40	☐	☐	☐	☐
25556	$.40	☐	☐	☐	☐
25557	$.40	☐	☐	☐	☐

#1035 3¢ LIBERTY Cont.

		UL	UR	LL	LR
25558	$1.00	☐	☐	☐	☐
25559	$1.00	☐	☐	☐	☐
25560	$.40	☐	☐	☐	☐
25561	$.40	☐	☐	☐	☐
25562	$.40	☐	☐	☐	☐
25563	$.40	☐	☐	☐	☐
25564	$.40	☐	☐	☐	☐
25581	$.40	☐	☐	☐	☐
25582	$.40	☐	☐	☐	☐
25583	$.40	☐	☐	☐	☐
25584	$.40	☐	☐	☐	☐
25587	$.40	☐	☐	☐	☐
25588	$.40	☐	☐	☐	☐
25607	$.40	☐	☐	☐	☐
25608	$.40	☐	☐	☐	☐
25609	$.40	☐	☐	☐	☐
25610	$.40	☐	☐	☐	☐
25661	$.40	☐	☐	☐	☐
25662	$.40	☐	☐	☐	☐
25671	$.40	☐	☐	☐	☐
25672	$.40	☐	☐	☐	☐
25716	$.40	☐	☐	☐	☐
25717	$.40	☐	☐	☐	☐
25731	$.40	☐	☐	☐	☐
25732	$.40	☐	☐	☐	☐
25733	$.40	☐	☐	☐	☐
25734	$.40	☐	☐	☐	☐
25792	$.40	☐	☐	☐	☐
25793	$.40	☐	☐	☐	☐
25794	$.40	☐	☐	☐	☐
25795	$.40	☐	☐	☐	☐
25810	$.40	☐	☐	☐	☐
25811	$.40	☐	☐	☐	☐
25813	$.40	☐	☐	☐	☐
25814	$.40	☐	☐	☐	☐
25815	$.40	☐	☐	☐	☐
25816	$.40	☐	☐	☐	☐
25819	$.40	☐	☐	☐	☐
25820	$.40	☐	☐	☐	☐
25821	$.40	☐	☐	☐	☐
25822	$.40	☐	☐	☐	☐
25827	$.40	☐	☐	☐	☐
25828	$.40	☐	☐	☐	☐
25829	$.40	☐	☐	☐	☐
25830	$.40	☐	☐	☐	☐
25831	$.40	☐	☐	☐	☐
25832	$.40	☐	☐	☐	☐
25833	$.40	☐	☐	☐	☐
25835	$.40	☐	☐	☐	☐
25836	$.40	☐	☐	☐	☐
25837	$.40	☐	☐	☐	☐
25838	$.40	☐	☐	☐	☐
25839	$.40	☐	☐	☐	☐
25840	$.40	☐	☐	☐	☐
25841	$.40	☐	☐	☐	☐
25842	$.40	☐	☐	☐	☐
25849	$.40	☐	☐	☐	☐
25850	$.40	☐	☐	☐	☐
25851	$.40	☐	☐	☐	☐
25852	$.40	☐	☐	☐	☐

1954 REGULAR ISSUE

#1035 3¢ LIBERTY Cont.

		UL	UR	LL	LR
25873	$1.00	□	□	□	□
25874	$1.00	□	□	□	□
25880	$.40	□	□	□	□
25881	$.40	□	□	□	□
25885	$.40	□	□	□	□
25886	$.40	□	□	□	□
25895	$.40	□	□	□	□
25896	$.40	□	□	□	□
25906	$.40	□	□	□	□
25907	$.40	□	□	□	□
25914	$2.00	□	□	□	□
25915	$.40	□	□	□	□
25916	$1.00	□	□	□	□
25917	$1.00	□	□	□	□
25918	$.40	□	□	□	□
25919	$.40	□	□	□	□
25920	$.40	□	□	□	□
25921	$.40	□	□	□	□
25922	$.40	□	□	□	□
25926	$.40	□	□	□	□
25927	$.40	□	□	□	□
25928	$.40	□	□	□	□
25929	$.40	□	□	□	□
25933	$.40	□	□	□	□
25934	$.40	□	□	□	□
25935	$.40	□	□	□	□
25936	$.40	□	□	□	□
26362	$.40	□	□	□	□
26363	$.40	□	□	□	□
26378	$.40	□	□	□	□
26426	$.40	□	□	□	□
26427	$.40	□	□	□	□
26480	$.40	□	□	□	□
26509	$.40	□	□	□	□
26510	$.40	□	□	□	□
26545	$.40	□	□	□	□
26546	$.40	□	□	□	□
26571	$.40	□	□	□	□
26572	$.40	□	□	□	□
26583	$.40	□	□	□	□
26584	$.40	□	□	□	□
26595	$.40	□	□	□	□
26824	$.40	□	□	□	□
26825	$.40	□	□	□	□
26850	$.40	□	□	□	□
26851	$.40	□	□	□	□
27004	$.40	□	□	□	□
27005	$.40	□	□	□	□
27010	$.40	□	□	□	□
27011	$.40	□	□	□	□
27020	$.40	□	□	□	□
27021	$.40	□	□	□	□
27049	$.40	□	□	□	□
27050	$.40	□	□	□	□
27051	$.40	□	□	□	□
27052	$.40	□	□	□	□
27054	$.40	□	□	□	□
27055	$ 40	□	□	□	□
27056	$.40	□	□	□	□
27057	$.40	□	□	□	□

#1035 3¢ LIBERTY Cont.

		UL	UR	LL	LR
27058	$.40	□	□	□	□
27059	$.40	□	□	□	□
27163	$.40	□	□	□	□
27164	$.40	□	□	□	□
27165	$.40	□	□	□	□
27166	$.40	□	□	□	□
27271	$.40	□	□	□	□
27272	$.40	□	□	□	□
27273**o**	$.40	□	□	□	□
27274**o**	$.40	□	□	□	□
27280**o**	$.40	□	□	□	□
27281**o**	$.40	□	□	□	□
27323	$.40	□	□	□	□
27324	$.40	□	□	□	□

#1035b 3¢ LIBERTY 4 Plates

Dry Printed - TAGGED

27273**o**	$5.00	□	□	□	□
27274**o**	$5.00	□	□	□	□
27280**o**	$7.00	□	□	□	□
27281**o**	$7.00	□	□	□	□

o Issued both TAGGED and UNTAGGED

#1036c 4¢ LINCOLN 4 Plates

Wet Printed

25075	$.50	□	□	□	□
25076	$.50	□	□	□	□
25081	$.50	□	□	□	□
25082	$.50	□	□	□	□

#1036 4¢ LINCOLN 199 Plates

Dry Printed - UNTAGGED

25445	$.50	□	□	□	□
25446	$12.00	□	□	□	□2
25447	$.50	□	□	□	□
25448	$.50	□	□	□	□
25449	$.50	□	□	□	□
25450	$3.00	□	□	□	□
25451	$1.00	□	□	□	□
25452	$.50	□	□	□	□
25453	$.50	□	□	□	□
25454	$.50	□	□	□	□

1954 REGULAR ISSUE

#1036 4¢ LINCOLN Cont.

		UL	UR	LL	LR
25455	$.50	☐	☐	☐	☐
25456	$.50	☐	☐	☐	☐
25689	$.50	☐	☐	☐	☐
25690	$.50	☐	☐	☐	☐
25697	$.50	☐	☐	☐	☐
25698	$.50	☐	☐	☐	☐
25747	$.50	☐	☐	☐	☐
25748	$.50	☐	☐	☐	☐
25780	$.50	☐	☐	☐	☐
25781	$.50	☐	☐	☐	☐
25782	$.50	☐	☐	☐	☐
25783	$.50	☐	☐	☐	☐
25787	$.50	☐	☐	☐	☐
25788	$.50	☐	☐	☐	☐
25956	$.50	☐	☐	☐	☐
25957	$.50	☐	☐	☐	☐
26065	$.50	☐	☐	☐	☐
26066	$.50	☐	☐	☐	☐
26067	$.50	☐	☐	☐	☐
26068	$.50	☐	☐	☐	☐
26074	$.50	☐	☐	☐	☐
26075	$.50	☐	☐	☐	☐
26082	$.50	☐	☐	☐	☐
26083	$.50	☐	☐	☐	☐
26099	$.50	☐	☐	☐	☐
26100	$.50	☐	☐	☐	☐
26101	$.50	☐	☐	☐	☐
26102	$.50	☐	☐	☐	☐
26122	$.50	☐	☐	☐	☐
26123	$.50	☐	☐	☐	☐
26130	$.50	☐	☐	☐	☐
26131	$.50	☐	☐	☐	☐
26132	$.50	☐	☐	☐	☐
26133	$.50	☐	☐	☐	☐
26134	$.50	☐	☐	☐	☐
26135	$.50	☐	☐	☐	☐
26136	$.50	☐	☐	☐	☐
26137	$.50	☐	☐	☐	☐
26140	$.50	☐	☐	☐	☐
26141	$.50	☐	☐	☐	☐
26142	$.50	☐	☐	☐	☐
26143	$.50	☐	☐	☐	☐
26168	$.50	☐	☐	☐	☐
26169	$.50	☐	☐	☐	☐
26171	$.50	☐	☐	☐	☐
26172	$.50	☐	☐	☐	☐
26173	$.50	☐	☐	☐	☐
26174	$.50	☐	☐	☐	☐
26179	$.50	☐	☐	☐	☐
26180	$.50	☐	☐	☐	☐
26181	$.50	☐	☐	☐	☐
26183	$.50	☐	☐	☐	☐
26184	$.50	☐	☐	☐	☐
26185	$.50	☐	☐	☐	☐
26186	$.50	☐	☐	☐	☐
26187	$.50	☐	☐	☐	☐
26188	$.50	☐	☐	☐	☐
26266	$.50	☐	☐	☐	☐
26267	$.50	☐	☐	☐	☐
26268	$.50	☐	☐	☐	☐

#1036 4¢ LINCOLN Cont.

		UL	UR	LL	LR
26293	$.50	☐	☐	☐	☐
26294	$.50	☐	☐	☐	☐
26295	$.50	☐	☐	☐	☐
26296	$.50	☐	☐	☐	☐
26311	$.50	☐	☐	☐	☐
26312	$.50	☐	☐	☐	☐
26313	$.50	☐	☐	☐	☐
26314	$.50	☐	☐	☐	☐
26330	$.50	☐	☐	☐	☐
26331	$.50	☐	☐	☐	☐
26332	$.50	☐	☐	☐	☐
26338	$.50	☐	☐	☐	☐
26339	$.50	☐	☐	☐	☐
26340	$.50	☐	☐	☐	☐
26341	$.50	☐	☐	☐	☐
26346	$.50	☐	☐	☐	☐
26347	$.50	☐	☐	☐	☐
26348	$.50	☐	☐	☐	☐
26349	$.50	☐	☐	☐	☐
26364	$.50	☐	☐	☐	☐
26365	$.50	☐	☐	☐	☐
26369	$.50	☐	☐	☐	☐
26370	$.50	☐	☐	☐	☐
26372	$.50	☐	☐	☐	☐
26373	$.50	☐	☐	☐	☐
26379	$.50	☐	☐	☐	☐
26380	$.50	☐	☐	☐	☐
26388	$.50	☐	☐	☐	☐
26389	$.50	☐	☐	☐	☐
26393	$.50	☐	☐	☐	☐
26394	$.50	☐	☐	☐	☐
26401	$.50	☐	☐	☐	☐
26402	$.50	☐	☐	☐	☐
26403	$.50	☐	☐	☐	☐
26421	$.50	☐	☐	☐	☐
26422	$.50	☐	☐	☐	☐
26473	$.50	☐	☐	☐	☐
26474	$.50	☐	☐	☐	☐
26490	$.50	☐	☐	☐	☐
26491	$.50	☐	☐	☐	☐
26496	$.50	☐	☐	☐	☐
26497	$.50	☐	☐	☐	☐
26503	$.50	☐	☐	☐	☐
26504	$.50	☐	☐	☐	☐
26526	$.50	☐	☐	☐	☐
26527	$.50	☐	☐	☐	☐
26559	$.50	☐	☐	☐	☐
26560	$.50	☐	☐	☐	☐
26573	$.50	☐	☐	☐	☐
26574	$.50	☐	☐	☐	☐
26580	$.50	☐	☐	☐	☐
26581	$.50	☐	☐	☐	☐
26604	$.50	☐	☐	☐	☐
26605	$.50	☐	☐	☐	☐
26614	$.50	☐	☐	☐	☐
26615	$.50	☐	☐	☐	☐
26658	$.50	☐	☐	☐	☐
26659	$.50	☐	☐	☐	☐
26672	$.50	☐	☐	☐	☐
26673	$.50	☐	☐	☐	☐

1954 REGULAR ISSUE

#1036 4¢ LINCOLN Cont.

		UL	UR	LL	LR
26691	$.50	☐	☐	☐	☐
26701	$.50	☐	☐	☐	☐
26702	$.50	☐	☐	☐	☐
26727	$.50	☐	☐	☐	☐
26728	$.50	☐	☐	☐	☐
26765	$.50	☐	☐	☐	☐
26766	$.50	☐	☐	☐	☐
26808	$.50	☐	☐	☐	☐
26809	$.50	☐	☐	☐	☐
26810	$.50	☐	☐	☐	☐
26811	$.50	☐	☐	☐	☐
26837	$.50	☐	☐	☐	☐
26838	$.50	☐	☐	☐	☐
26854	$.50	☐	☐	☐	☐
26855	$.50	☐	☐	☐	☐
26868	$.50	☐	☐	☐	☐
26869	$.50	☐	☐	☐	☐
26883	$.50	☐	☐	☐	☐
26884	$.50	☐	☐	☐	☐
26887	$.50	☐	☐	☐	☐
26888	$.50	☐	☐	☐	☐
26889	$.50	☐	☐	☐	☐
26890	$.50	☐	☐	☐	☐
26920	$.50	☐	☐	☐	☐
26921	$.50	☐	☐	☐	☐
26931	$.50	☐	☐	☐	☐
26932	$.50	☐	☐	☐	☐
26939	$.50	☐	☐	☐	☐
26940	$.50	☐	☐	☐	☐
26945	$.50	☐	☐	☐	☐
26946	$.50	☐	☐	☐	☐
26960	$.50	☐	☐	☐	☐
26961	$.50	☐	☐	☐	☐
26966	$.50	☐	☐	☐	☐
26967	$.50	☐	☐	☐	☐
26980	$.50	☐	☐	☐	☐
26981	$.50	☐	☐	☐	☐
26982	$.50	☐	☐	☐	☐
26983	$.50	☐	☐	☐	☐
26996	$.50	☐	☐	☐	☐
26997	$.50	☐	☐	☐	☐
26998	$.50	☐	☐	☐	☐
28999	$.50	☐	☐	☐	☐
27008**o**	$.50	☐	☐	☐	☐
27009**o**	$.50	☐	☐	☐	☐
27037	$.50	☐	☐	☐	☐
27038	$.50	☐	☐	☐	☐
27102	$.50	☐	☐	☐	☐
27103	$.50	☐	☐	☐	☐
27104	$.50	☐	☐	☐	☐
27105	$.50	☐	☐	☐	☐
27108**o**	$.50	☐	☐	☐	☐
27109**o**	$.50	☐	☐	☐	☐
27110	$.50	☐	☐	☐	☐
27111	$.50	☐	☐	☐	☐
27117	$.50	☐	☐	☐	☐
27118	$.50	☐	☐	☐	☐
27119**o**	$.50	☐	☐	☐	☐
27120**o**	$.50	☐	☐	☐	☐
27146**o**	$.50	☐	☐	☐	☐

#1036 4¢ LINCOLN Cont.

		UL	UR	LL	LR
27168**o**	$.50	☐	☐	☐	☐
27169	$.50	☐	☐	☐	☐
27980	$.50	☐	☐	☐	☐
27981	$.50	☐	☐	☐	☐
28004	$.50	☐	☐	☐	☐
28005	$.50	☐	☐	☐	☐
28006**P**	$20.00	☐	☐	☐	☐
28007**P**	$20.00	☐	☐	☐	☐
28221	$.50	☐	☐	☐	☐

P These plate numbers have been reported only on precancelled stamps.

#1036b 4¢ LINCOLN

Dry Printed - TAGGED **8 Plates**

27008**o**	$12.50	☐	☐	☐	☐
27009**o**	$12.50	☐	☐	☐	☐
27108**o**	$6.50	☐	☐	☐	☐
27109**o**	$6.50	☐	☐	☐	☐
27119**o**	$15.00	☐	☐	☐	☐
27120**o**	$15.00	☐	☐	☐	☐
27146**o**	$15.00	☐	☐	☐	☐
27168**o**	$15.00	☐	☐	☐	☐

#1037 4.5¢ HERMITAGE 4 Plates

Dry Printed

26264	$.75	☐	☐	☐	☐
26265	$.75	☐	☐	☐	☐
26269	$3.00	☐	☐	☐	☐
26270	$3.00	☐	☐	☐	☐

#1038 5¢ MONROE 16 Plates

Dry Printed

25087	$.65	☐	☐	☐	☐
25088	$.65	☐	☐	☐	☐
25090	$.65	☐	☐	☐	☐
25091	$.65	☐	☐	☐	☐
25858	$.65	☐	☐	☐	☐
25859	$.65	☐	☐	☐	☐
25865	$.65	☐	☐	☐	☐
25866	$.65	☐	☐	☐	☐

o Issued both TAGGED and UNTAGGED

1954 REGULAR ISSUE

#1038 5¢ MONROE Cont.

		UL	UR	LL	LR
25924	$.65	☐	☐	☐	☐
25925	$.65	☐	☐	☐	☐
25930	$.65	☐	☐	☐	☐
25931	$.65	☐	☐	☐	☐
26710	$1.00	☐	☐	☐	☐
26711	$1.00	☐	☐	☐	☐
26720	$.65	☐	☐	☐	☐
26721	$.65	☐	☐	☐	☐

#1039a 6¢ THEODORE ROOSEVELT

Wet Printed **2 Plates**

25191	$1.75	☐	☐	☐	☐
25192	$1.75	☐	☐	☐	☐

#1039 6¢ THEODORE ROOSEVELT

Dry Printed **8 Plates**

25427	$1.25	☐	☐	☐	☐
25428	$1.25	☐	☐	☐	☐
25843	$1.25	☐	☐	☐	☐
25844	$1.25	☐	☐	☐	☐
25853	$1.25	☐	☐	☐	☐
25854	$1.25	☐	☐	☐	☐
26004	$1.25	☐	☐	☐	☐
26005	$1.25	☐	☐	☐	☐

#1040 7¢ WILSON

Dry Printed **8 Plates**

25299	$1.25	☐	☐	☐	☐
25300	$1.25	☐	☐	☐	☐
25304	$1.25	☐	☐	☐	☐
25305	$1.25	☐	☐	☐	☐
25309	$1.25	☐	☐	☐	☐
25310	$1.25	☐	☐	☐	☐
25313	$3.00	☐	☐	☐	☐
25314	$3.00	☐	☐	☐	☐

8¢ LIBERTY BICOLORED

Plate blocks from either a rotary press or a flat press printing are both corner blocks of 4 with 2 plate numbers and can only be distinguished by the specific plate numbers that appear.

The centering of the issue, especially that of the earlier printings, is so far below standard that completion of all combinations in well centered condition is nearly impossible.

#1041B 8¢ LIBERTY

ROTARY PRESS

5 Frame Plates 2 Vignette Plates

Frame-Vignette

24923-24927	$3.00	☐	☐	☐	☐
24923-24938	$5.00	☐	☐	☐	☐
24924-24927	$8.00	☐	☐3	☐	☐
24924-24938	$8.00	☐	☐3	☐3	☐

#1041B 8¢ LIBERTY Cont.

		UL	UR	LL	LR
24928-24927	$3.00	☐	☐	☐	☐
24928-24938	$5.00	☐	☐	☐	☐
24940-24927	$3.00	☐	☐	☐	☐
24940-24938	$3.00	☐	☐	☐	☐
24942-24927	$6.00	☐	☐	☐	☐
24942-24938	$6.00	☐	☐	☐	☐

#1041 8¢ LIBERTY

FLAT PRESS

9 Frame Plates 9 Vignette Plates

Frame-Vignette

24912-24916	$5.00	☐	☐	☐	☐
24912-24917	$5.00	☐	☐	☐	☐
24912-24918	$5.00	☐	☐	☐	☐
24912-24919	$5.00	☐2	☐	☐	☐
24912-24935	$3.00	☐	☐	☐	☐
24912-24936	$3.00	☐	☐	☐	☐
24912-24937	$3.00	☐	☐	☐	☐
24912-24939	$3.00	☐	☐	☐	☐
24913-24916	$7.00	☐	☐	☐	☐
24913-24917	$7.00	☐	☐	☐	☐
24913-24918	$7.00	☐	☐	☐	☐
24913-24919	$7.00	☐	☐	☐	☐

24913-24920	$100	☐	☐	☐	☐
N24913-24920	$40	☐	☐	☐	☐
24913-24935	$3.00	☐	☐	☐	☐
24913-24936	$3.00	☐	☐	☐	☐
24913-24937	$3.00	☐	☐	☐	☐
24913-24939	$3.00	☐	☐	☐	☐
24914-24916	$5.00	☐	☐	☐	☐
24914-24917	$6.00	☐	☐	☐	☐
24914-24918	$6.00	☐	☐	☐	☐
24914-24919	$6.00	☐2	☐	☐	☐
24914-24935	$3.00	☐	☐	☐	☐
24914-24936	$3.00	☐	☐	☐	☐
24914-24937	$3.00	☐	☐	☐	☐
24914-24939	$3.00	☐	☐	☐	☐

N This Bureau precancel was applied to finished sheet stock using a flat bed press. Normal Bureau precancels are printed on a rotary press.

1954 REGULAR ISSUE

#1041 8¢ LIBERTY Cont.

		UL	UR	LL	LR
24915-24916	$7.00	☐2	☐	☐	☐
24915-24917	$10.00	☐2	☐	☐	☐
24915-24918	$8.00	☐4	☐	☐	☐
24915-24919	$25.00	☐	☐	☐	☐
24915-24920	$3500.00	†	☐	☐	☐
24915-24935	$3.00	☐	☐	☐	☐
24915-24936	$3.00	☐	☐	☐	☐
24915-24937	$3.00	☐	☐	☐	☐
24915-24939	$3.00	☐	☐	☐	☐
24926-24916	$100.00	☐	☐	☐	☐
24926-24917	$45.00	☐	☐	☐	☐
24926-24918	$30.00	☐	☐	☐	☐
24926-24919	$30.00	☐	☐	☐	☐
24929-24935	$6.00	☐	☐	☐	☐
24929-24936	$6.00	☐	☐	☐	☐
24929-24937	$6.00	☐	☐	☐	☐
24929-24939	$6.00	☐	☐	☐	☐
24930-24935	$6.00	☐	☐	☐	☐
24930-24936	$6.00	☐	☐	☐	☐
24930-24937	$6.00	☐	☐	☐	☐
24930-24939	$7.00	☐	☐	☐	☐
24932-24935	$6.00	☐	☐	☐	☐
24932-24936	$6.00	☐	☐	☐	☐
24932-24937	$6.00	☐	☐	☐	☐
24932-24939	$6.00	☐	☐	☐	☐
24933-24935	$6.00	☐	☐	☐	☐
24933-24936	$6.00	☐	☐	☐	☐
24933-24937	$7.00	☐	☐	☐	☐
24933-24939	$6.00	☐	☐	☐	☐

#1042 8¢ LIBERTY 12 Plates

ROTARY PRESS

25932	$1.25	☐	☐	☐	☐
25937	$1.25	☐	☐	☐	☐
25950	$1.25	☐	☐	☐	☐
25955	$1.25	☐	☐	☐	☐
26221	$1.25	☐	☐	☐	☐
26224	$1.25	☐	☐	☐	☐
26230	$1.25	☐	☐	☐	☐
26231	$1.25	☐	☐	☐	☐
26242	$1.25	☐	☐	☐	☐
26524	$1.25	☐	☐	☐	☐
26525	$1.25	☐	☐	☐	☐
26821	$15.00	☐	☐	☐	☐

#1042A 8¢ PERSHING 4 Plates

Dry Printed

		UL	UR	LL	LR
27075	$1.25	☐	☐	☐	☐
27076	$1.25	☐	☐	☐	☐
27705	$1.25	☐	☐	☐	☐
27706	$1.25	☐	☐	☐	☐

#1043 9¢ ALAMO 6 Plates

Dry Printed

25393	$1.40	☐	☐	☐	☐
25394	$1.40	☐	☐	☐	☐
25415	$1.40	☐	☐	☐	☐
25416	$1.40	☐	☐	☐	☐
26260	$1.40	☐	☐	☐	☐
26261	$1.40	☐	☐	☐	☐

#1044 10¢ INDEPENDENCE HALL

Dry Printed UNTAGGED **15 Plates**

25423	$1.25	☐	☐	☐	☐
25424	$1.25	☐	☐	☐	☐
25426	$3.50	☐	☐	☐	☐
25601	$1.25	☐	☐	☐	☐
25602	$1.25	☐	☐	☐	☐
25860	$1.25	☐	☐	☐	☐
25861	$1.25	☐	☐	☐	☐
25938	$1.25	☐	☐	☐	☐
25939	$1.25	☐	☐	☐	☐
26951	$1.25	☐	☐	☐	☐
26952	$1.25	☐	☐	☐	☐
27684**o**	$1.65	☐	☐	☐	☐
27685**o**	$1.65	☐	☐	☐	☐
27773**o**	$1.65	☐	☐	☐	☐
27774**o**	$1.65	☐	☐	☐	☐

#1044b 10¢ INDEPENDENCE HALL

Dry Printed TAGGED **4 Plates**

27684**o**	$25.00	☐	☐	☐	☐
27685**o**	$25.00	☐	☐	☐	☐
27773**o**	$20.00	☐	☐	☐	☐
27774**o**	$20.00	☐	☐	☐	☐

#1044A 11¢ LIBERTY 4 Plates

Dry Printed UNTAGGED

26976**o**	$1.50	☐	☐	☐	☐
26978**o**	$1.50	☐	☐	☐	☐
26979**o**	$1.50	☐	☐	☐	☐
26986	$1.50	☐	☐	☐	☐

#1044c 11¢ LIBERTY 3 Plates

Dry Printed TAGGED

26976**o**	$35.00	☐	☐	☐	☐
26978**o**	$35.00	☐	☐	☐	☐
26979**o**	$50.00	☐	☐	☐	☐

o Issued both TAGGED and UNTAGGED

1954 REGULAR ISSUE

#1045 12¢ HARRISON 4 Plates

Dry Printed UNTAGGED

		UL	UR	LL	LR
26281o	$2.00	☐	☐	☐	☐
26282o	$2.00	☐	☐	☐	☐
26283o	$2.00	☐	☐	☐	☐
26284o	$2.00	☐	☐	☐	☐

#1045a 12¢ HARRISON 4 Plates

Dry Printed TAGGED

26281o	$4.00	☐	☐	☐	☐
26282o	$4.00	☐	☐	☐	☐
26283o	$4.00	☐	☐	☐	☐
26284o	$4.00	☐	☐	☐	☐

#1046 15¢ JAY 4 Plates

Dry Printed UNTAGGED

26138	$4.00	☐	☐	☐	☐
26139o	$4.00	☐	☐	☐	☐
26165o	$4.00	☐	☐	☐	☐
26166o	$4.00	☐	☐	☐	☐

#1046a 15¢ JAY 5 Plates

Dry Printed TAGGED

26139o	$8.50	☐	☐	☐	☐
26165o	$8.50	☐	☐	☐	☐
26166o	$12.50	☐	☐	☐	☐
27968	$7.50	☐	☐	☐	☐
27969	$7.50	☐	☐	☐	☐

#1047 20¢ MONTICELLO 20 Plates

Dry Printed

25391	$2.50	☐	☐	☐	☐
25392	$2.50	☐	☐	☐	☐
25653	$2.50	☐	☐	☐	☐
25654	$2.50	☐	☐	☐	☐
25655	$2.50	☐	☐	☐	☐
25656	$2.50	☐	☐	☐	☐
25988	$2.50	☐	☐	☐	☐
25989	$2.50	☐	☐	☐	☐
26256	$2.50	☐	☐	☐	☐
26257	$2.50	☐	☐	☐	☐
26315	$2.50	☐	☐	☐	☐
26316	$2.50	☐	☐	☐	☐
26528	$2.50	☐	☐	☐	☐
26529	$2.50	☐	☐	☐	☐
27002	$2.50	☐	☐	☐	☐
27003	$2.50	☐	☐	☐	☐
28021	$2.50	☐	☐	☐	☐
28022	$2.50	☐	☐	☐	☐
28034	$7.00	☐	☐	☐	☐
28035	$7.00	☐	☐	☐	☐

#1048 25¢ REVERE 4 Plates

Dry Printed

25962	$6.00	☐	☐	☐	☐
25963	$6.00	☐	☐	☐	☐
25964	$6.00	☐	☐	☐	☐
25965	$6.00	☐	☐	☐	☐

o Issued both TAGGED and UNTAGGED

#1049a 30¢ LEE 2 Plates

Wet Printed

		UL	UR	LL	LR
25251	$5.00	☐	☐	☐	☐
25252	$5.00	☐	☐	☐	☐

#1049 30¢ LEE 10 Plates

Dry Printed

25487	$5.00	☐	☐	☐	☐
25488	$5.00	☐	☐	☐	☐
25948	$5.00	☐	☐	☐	☐
25949	$5.00	☐	☐	☐	☐
26324	$5.00	☐	☐	☐	☐
26325	$5.00	☐	☐	☐	☐
26602	$5.00	☐	☐	☐	☐
26603	$5.00	☐	☐	☐	☐
29207	$5.00	☐	☐	☐	☐
29208	$5.00	☐	☐	☐	☐

#1050a 40¢ MARSHALL 2 Plates

Wet Printed

25249	$13.00	☐	☐	☐	☐
25250	$13.00	☐	☐	☐	☐

#1050 40¢ MARSHALL 6 Plates

Dry Printed

25571	$9.00	☐	☐	☐	☐
25572	$9.00	☐	☐	☐	☐
26203	$9.00	☐	☐	☐	☐
26204	$9.00	☐	☐	☐	☐
27814	$9.00	☐	☐	☐	☐
27815	$9.00	☐	☐	☐	☐

#1051a 50¢ SUSAN ANTHONY 4 Plates

Wet Printed

25231	$10.00	☐	☐	☐	☐
25232	$10.00	☐	☐	☐	☐
25237	$10.00	☐	☐	☐	☐
25238	$10.00	☐	☐	☐	☐

#1051 50¢ SUSAN ANTHONY 6 Plates

Dry Printed

25897	$7.00	☐	☐	☐	☐
25898	$7.00	☐	☐	☐	☐
26205	$7.00	☐	☐	☐	☐
26206	$7.00	☐	☐	☐	☐
27957	$7.00	☐	☐	☐	☐
27958	$7.00	☐	☐	☐	☐

#1052a $1 PATRICK HENRY 2 Plates

Wet Printed

25257	$25.00	☐	☐	☐	☐
25258	$25.00	☐	☐	☐	☐

#1052 $1 PATRICK HENRY 6 Plates

Dry Printed

25541	$25.00	☐	☐	☐	☐
25542	$25.00	☐	☐	☐	☐
26207	$25.00	☐	☐	☐	☐
26208	$25.00	☐	☐	☐	☐
27990	$25.00	☐	☐	☐	☐
27991	$25.00	☐	☐	☐	☐

#1053 $5 HAMILTON Dry Printed

FLAT PRESS **Block of 4**

25367	$375.00	☐	☐	☐	☐

1954 REGULAR ISSUE

BOOKLET PANES

ROTARY PRESS — **PANES OF 6**

#1035a 3¢ LIBERTY

Wet Printed — **14 Plates**

24975	24976	24980	24981	25002
25003	25006	25007	25013	25014
25334	25335	25353	25354	

#1035f 3¢ LIBERTY

Dry Printed — **22 Plates**

25355	25356	25357	25358	25363
25364	25372	25373	25417	25418
25567	25568	25569	25570	25743
25744	25757	25758	25774	25775
25789	25790			

#1036a 4¢ LINCOLN 43 Plates

Dry Printed

26013	26014	26032	26033	26038
26039	26111	26112	26154	26155
26191	26192	26287	26288	26468
26469	26515	26516	26518	26519
26520	26521	26593	26594	26652
26653	*26689	26690	26699	26700
26817	26818	26819	26822	26823
26829	26830	26955	26956	27188
27189	27215	27216		

See Appendix G for largest reported plate number percentage by position.

SIDE COILS

On the early 384 Subject coil plates the numbers were located further from the stamps than usual and consequently very few have been found. These wide-spaced plates are marked w in the following lists, after the plate number. The plate numbers on the 432 subject plates are located under the first and last stamps in the bottom row only. Therefore these are collected in bottom strips of six stamps with a plate number from the companion plates on each side of the join line.

SIDE COILS

#1054c 1¢ WASHINGTON

Wet Printed — **6 Plates**

170 Subject Plates — **STRIPS OF 5**

25036 25037 25048 25049 25161
25162

#1054 1¢ WASHINGTON

Dry Printed — **8 Plates**

384 Subject Plates — **STRIPS OF 5**

†25479w †25480w 25721 25722 25868
25869 26006 26007

432 Subject Plates — **6 Plates**
STRIPS OF 6

26411 26412 26462 26463 †27043
†27044

#1054A 1.25¢ SANTA FE

Dry Printed — **2 Plates**

384 Subject Plates — **STRIPS OF 5**

26670 26671

432 Subject Plates — **6 Plates**
STRIPS OF 6

26621 26622 †26656 †26657 †28120
†28121

#1055d 2¢ JEFFERSON

Wet Printed — **14 Plates**

170 Subject Plates — **STRIPS OF 5**

25044 25045 25067 25068 25094
25095 25096 25097 25151 25152
25153 25157 25411 25412

#1055 2¢ JEFFERSON

Dry Printed — **14 Plates**

384 Subject Plates — **STRIPS OF 5**

†25443w †25444w †25629w †25630w 25673
25674 25759 25760 25951 25952
25968 25969 26008 26009

432 Subject Plates — **6 Plates**

UNTAGGED — **STRIPS OF 6**

†26360 †26361 26399**o** 26400**o** 27977
†27978

#1055a 2¢ JEFFERSON

432 Subject Plates — **20 Plates**

TAGGED — **STRIPS OF 6**

SHINY and DULL GUM

26399**o** 26400**o** 32119 32120 †32129
†32130 33487 33647 †34353 †34354
35232 †35575 35773 *36208 †37602
†37603 †37612 †37613 37992 37993

o Issued both TAGGED and UNTAGGED

#1056 2.5¢ BUNKER HILL

Dry Printed — **2 Plates**

384 Subject Plates — **STRIPS OF 5**

26279 26280

432 Subject Plates — **4 Plates**
STRIPS OF 6

†26436 †26437 †26449 †26450

1954 REGULAR ISSUE

SIDE COILS

#1057c 3¢ LIBERTY 64 Plates

Wet Printed
170 Subject Plates **STRIPS OF 5**

24971 24972 24973 24974 24977
24978 24982 24983 24984 24985
24990 24991 24992 24993 24995
24996 25052 25053 25063 25064
25102 25103 25121 25122 25123
25124 25133 25134 25135 25136
25139 25140 25141 25142 25145
25146 25147 25148 25154 25155
25156 25159 25217 25218 25219
25220 25221 25222 25223 25224
25225 25226 25227 25228 25336
25337 25338 25339 25399 25400
25401 25402 25403 25404

#1057 3¢ LIBERTY

Dry Printed **48 Plates**
384 Subject Plates **STRIPS OF 5**

†25433w †25434w †25435w †25436w 25481w
25482w †25575w †25576w †25577w †25578w
†25617w †25618w 25639 25640 25649
25650 †25663 25664 25665 †25666
25667 25668 25669 25670 25675
25676 25693 25694 25718 25719
25753 25754 25767 25768 25769
25770 25845 25846 25847 25848
25856 25857 26209 26210 26442
26443

432 Subject Plates **16 Plates**
UNTAGGED **STRIPS OF 6**

25825 25826 †25899 †25900 25953
25954 †25975 †25976 27028 27029
†27030 †27031 27236**o** 27237**o** 27238
27239

#1057b 3¢ LIBERTY

432 Subject Plates **2 Plates**
TAGGED **STRIPS OF 6**

27236**o** 27237**o**

#1058b 4¢ LINCOLN

Wet Printed **2 Plates**
170 Subject Plates **STRIPS OF 5**

25098**P** 25099**P**

P These Plate numbers have been reported only on precancelled coils.

#1058 4¢ LINCOLN

Dry Printed **42 Plates**
384 Subject Plates **STRIPS OF 5**

25705 25706 25709 25710 25755
25756 26040 26041 26072 26073
26084 26085 26086 26087 26089
26090 26093 26094 26109 26110
26144 26145 26146 26147 26150
26151 26152 26153 26232 26233
26258 26259 26383 26384 26395
26396 26404 26405 26650 26651
26663 26664

SIDE COILS

#1058 4¢ LINCOLN 167 Plates

432 Subject Plates **STRIPS OF 6**

26015 26016 †26034 †26035 26113
26114 †26193 †26194 †26211 †26212
†26213 †26214 26285 26286 26297
26298 26326 26327 26352 26353
†26478 †26479 †26484 †26485 26492
26493 †26505 †26506 †26513 †26514
†26538 †26539 †26547 †26548 †26585
†26586 26616 26617 26654 26655
†26703 †26704 26718 26719 †26732
†26733 †26748 †26749 26801 26802
†26812 †26813 †26835 †26836 †26839
†26840 26842 26843 26856 †26857
†26861 †26862 †26872 26873 †26876
†26877 †26879 †26880 †26881 †26882
†26891 †26892 †26893 †26894 †26902
†26903 26908 26909 †26918 †26919
†26922 †26923 †26924 †26925 †26933
†26934 †26941 †26942 †26947 †26948
†26949 †26950 †26953 †26954 †26957
†26958 †26962 †26963 †26968 †26969
†26973 †26974 †26984 †26985 27000
27001 27006 27007 †27012 †27013
†27018 †27019 †27022 †27023 27047
27048 †27069 †27070 †27077 †27078
†27084 †27085 †27094 †27095 †27097
†27098 †27100 †27101 †27123 †27124
27130 27131 27132 †27133 †27135
†27136 27137 27138 †27139 †27140
†27141 †27143 †27144 †27158 27159
27182 †27183 †27234 †27235 †27240
†27241 †27244 †27245 †27256 †27257
†27258 †27259 27267 27268 †27269
†27270 †27284 †27285 †27287 †27288
†27291 †27292

#1059 4.5¢ HERMITAGE

Dry Printed **2 Plates**
384 Subject Plates **STRIPS OF 5**

26262 26263

432 Subject Plates **4 Plates**
STRIPS OF 6

†26374 †26375 †26381 †26382

#1059A 25¢ REVERE

Dry Printed
432 Subject Plates **4 Plates**
UNTAGGED **STRIPS OF 6**

28011 28012 30767**o** 30768**o**

#1059b 25¢ REVERE

432 Subject Plates **4 Plates**
TAGGED **STRIPS OF 6**
SHINY and DULL GUM

30767**o** 30768**o** *37606 *37607

o Issued both TAGGED and UNTAGGED

#1060-#1063

See page 150

1955 COMMEMORATIVES

#1064 3¢ PENNSYLVANIA ACADEMY OF FINE ARTS

		UL	UR	LL	LR
25104	$.35	□	□	□	□
25105	$.35	□	□	□	□
25106	$.35	□	□	□	□
25107	$.35	□	□	□	□

#1065 3¢ LAND GRANT COLLEGES

25117	$.35	□	□	□	□
25118	$.35	□	□	□	□
25119	$.35	□	□	□	□
25120	$.35	□	□	□	□

#1066 8¢ ROTARY CLUB

25125	$1	□	□	□	□
25126	$1	□	□	□	□
25127	$1	□	□	□	□
25128	$1	□	□	□	□

#1067 3¢ ARMED FORCES RESERVE

25175	$.35	□	□	□	□
25176	$.35	□	□	□	□
25177	$.35	□	□	□	□
25178	$.35	□	□	□	□

#1068 3¢ NEW HAMPSHIRE

25183	$.35	□	□	□	□
25184	$.35	□	□	□	□
25185	$.35	□	□	□	□
25186	$.35	□	□	□	□

#1069 3¢ SOO LOCKS

25193	$.35	□	□	□	□
25194	$.35	□	□	□	□
25195	$.35	□	□	□	□
25196	$.35	□	□	□	□
25197	$.35	□	□	□	□
25198	$.35	□	□	□	□

#1070 3¢ ATOMS FOR PEACE

25207	$.45	□	□	□	□
25208	$.45	□	□	□	□
25209	$.45	□	□	□	□
25210	$.45	□	□	□	□

#1071 3¢ TICONDEROGA

25245	$.35	□	□	□	□
25246	$.35	□	□	□	□
25247	$.35	□	□	□	□
25248	$.35	□	□	□	□

#1072 3¢ ANDREW MELLON

Dry Printed

25301	$.35	□	□	□	□
25302	$.35	□	□	□	□

1956 COMMEMORATIVES

#1073 3¢ FRANKLIN

		UL	UR	LL	LR
25328	$.35	□	□	□	□
25329	$.35	□	□	□	□
25330	$.35	□	□	□	□
25331	$.35	□	□	□	□

#1074 3¢ BOOKER T. WASHINGTON

25380	$.35	□	□	□	□
25381	$.35	□	□	□	□
25382	$.35	□	□	□	□
25383	$.35	□	□	□	□

#1075 3¢ FIPEX SHEET (Imperf.)

The plate numbers of this souvenir sheet were trimmed off after printing so no plate numbers were regularly issued.

#1076 3¢ FIPEX

25374	$.35	□	□	□	□
25375	$.35	□	□	□	□
25386	$.35	□	□	□	□
25387	$.35	□	□	□	□

#1077 3¢ WILD TURKEY

25395	$.40	□	□	□	□
25397	$.40	□	□	□	□
25398	$.40	□	□	□	□
25409	$.40	□	□	□	□

#1078 3¢ PRONGHORN ANTELOPE

25429	$.40	□	□	□	□
25430	$.40	□	□	□	□
25431	$.40	□	□	□	□
25432	$.40	□	□	□	□

#1079 3¢ KING SALMON

Dry Printed

25496	$.40	□	□	□	□
25497	$.40	□	□	□	□
25498	$.40	□	□	□	□
25499	$.40	□	□	□	□

#1080 3¢ PURE FOOD & DRUG LAWS

25437	$.35	□	□	□	□
25438	$.35	□	□	□	□
25439	$.35	□	□	□	□
25440	$.35	□	□	□	□

From #1081 to date
all issues are Dry Printed

#1081 3¢ WHEATLAND

25475	$.35	□	□	□	□
25476	$.35	□	□	□	□
25477	$.35	□	□	□	□
25478	$.35	□	□	□	□

1956 COMMEMORATIVES

#1082 3¢ LABOR DAY

		UL	UR	LL	LR
25484	$.35	☐	☐	☐	☐
25485	$.35	☐	☐	☐	☐
25486	$.35	☐	☐	☐	☐
25489	$.35	☐	☐	☐	☐

#1083 3¢ NASSAU HALL

25469	$.35	☐	☐	☐	☐
25470	$.35	☐	☐	☐	☐
25473	$.35	☐	☐	☐	☐
25474	$.35	☐	☐	☐	☐

#1084 3¢ DEVIL'S TOWER

25500	$.35	☐	☐	☐	☐
25501	$.35	☐	☐	☐	☐
25502	$.35	☐	☐	☐	☐
25503	$.35	☐	☐	☐	☐

#1085 3¢ CHILDREN

25533	$.35	☐	☐	☐	☐
25534	$.35	☐	☐	☐	☐
25535	$.35	☐	☐	☐	☐
25536	$.35	☐	☐	☐	☐

1957 COMMEMORATIVES

#1086 3¢ ALEXANDER HAMILTON

25597	$.35	☐	☐	☐	☐
25598	$.35	☐	☐	☐	☐
25599	$.35	☐	☐	☐	☐
25600	$.35	☐	☐	☐	☐

#1087 3¢ POLIO

25603	$.35	☐	☐	☐	☐
25604	$.35	☐	☐	☐	☐
25605	$.35	☐	☐	☐	☐
25606	$.35	☐	☐	☐	☐
25647	$.35	☐	☐	☐	☐
25648	$.35	☐	☐	☐	☐
25651	$.35	☐	☐	☐	☐
25652	$.35	☐	☐	☐	☐

#1088 3¢ GEODETIC SURVEY

25621	$.35	☐	☐	☐	☐
25622	$.35	☐	☐	☐	☐
25623	$.35	☐	☐	☐	☐
25624	$.35	☐	☐	☐	☐

#1089 3¢ ARCHITECTS

25625	$.35	☐	☐	☐	☐
25626	$.35	☐	☐	☐	☐
25627	$.35	☐	☐	☐	☐
25628	$.35	☐	☐	☐	☐

#1090 3¢ STEEL INDUSTRY

25699	$.35	☐	☐	☐	☐
25700	$.35	☐	☐	☐	☐
25701	$.35	☐	☐	☐	☐
25702	$.35	☐	☐	☐	☐

1957 COMMEMORATIVES

#1091 3¢ NAVAL REVIEW

		UL	UR	LL	LR
25724	$.35	☐	☐	☐	☐
25725	$.35	☐	☐	☐	☐
25726	$.35	☐	☐	☐	☐
25730	$.35	☐	☐	☐	☐

#1092 3¢ OKLAHOMA

25683	$.35	☐	☐	☐	☐
25684	$.35	☐	☐	☐	☐
25685	$.35	☐	☐	☐	☐
25686	$.35	☐	☐	☐	☐

#1093 3¢ TEACHERS

25735	$.35	☐	☐	☐	☐
25736	$.35	☐	☐	☐	☐
25737	$.35	☐	☐	☐	☐
25738	$.35	☐	☐	☐	☐

#1094 4¢ U. S. FLAG

25711	$.50	☐	☐	☐	☐
25712	$.50	☐	☐	☐	☐

#1095 3¢ SHIPBUILDING

25776	$.35	☐	☐	☐	☐
25777	$.35	☐	☐	☐	☐
25778	$.35	☐	☐	☐	☐
25779	$.35	☐	☐	☐	☐

#1096 8¢ MAGSAYSAY

Frame Plate-Vignette Plate

25771-25805	$1	☐	☐	☐	☐
25771-25808	$1	☐	☐	☐	☐
25772-25805	$1	☐	☐	☐	☐
25772-25808	$1	☐	☐	☐	☐

#1097 3¢ LAFAYETTE BICENTENNIAL

25798	$.35	☐	☐	☐	☐
25799	$.35	☐	☐	☐	☐
25800	$.35	☐	☐	☐	☐
25801	$.35	☐	☐	☐	☐

#1098 3¢ WHOOPING CRANE

25862	$.35	☐	☐	☐	☐
25863	$.35	☐	☐	☐	☐
25864	$.35	☐	☐	☐	☐
25867	$.35	☐	☐	☐	☐
25879	$.35	☐	☐	☐	☐
25884	$.35	☐	☐	☐	☐

#1099 3¢ RELIGIOUS FREEDOM

25891	$.35	☐	☐	☐	☐
25892	$.35	☐	☐	☐	☐
25893	$.35	☐	☐	☐	☐
25905	$.35	☐	☐	☐	☐

1958 COMMEMORATIVES

#1100 3¢ GARDENING

25942	$.35	☐	☐	☐	☐
25943	$.35	☐	☐	☐	☐
25944	$.35	☐	☐	☐	☐
25945	$.35	☐	☐	☐	☐

1958 COMMEMORATIVES

#1104 3¢ BRUSSELS EXHIBITION

		UL	UR	LL	LR
25958	$.35	☐	☐	☐	☐
25959	$.35	☐	☐	☐	☐
25960	$.35	☐	☐	☐	☐
25961	$.35	☐	☐	☐	☐

#1105 3¢ MONROE BICENTENNIAL

25971	$.35	☐	☐	☐	☐
25972	$.35	☐	☐	☐	☐
25973	$.35	☐	☐	☐	☐
25974	$.35	☐	☐	☐	☐

#1106 3¢ MINNESOTA STATEHOOD

25994	$.35	☐	☐	☐	☐
25995	$.35	☐	☐	☐	☐
25996	$.35	☐	☐	☐	☐
25997	$.35	☐	☐	☐	☐

#1107 3¢ GEOPHYSICAL YEAR

25978	$.50	☐	☐	☐	☐
25985	$.50	☐	☐	☐	☐
25990	$.50	☐	☐	☐	☐
25993	$.50	☐	☐	☐	☐
26010	$.50	☐	☐	☐	☐

#1108 3¢ GUNSTON HALL

26017	$.35	☐	☐	☐	☐
26018	$.35	☐	☐	☐	☐
26019	$.35	☐	☐	☐	☐
26020	$.35	☐	☐	☐	☐

#1109 3¢ MACKINAC BRIDGE

26028	$.35	☐	☐	☐	☐
26029	$.35	☐	☐	☐	☐
26030	$.35	☐	☐	☐	☐
26031	$.35	☐	☐	☐	☐

#1110 4¢ BOLIVAR

26057	$.45	☐	☐	☐	☐
26058	$.45	☐	☐	☐	☐
26059	$.45	☐	☐	☐	☐
26060	$.45	☐	☐	☐	☐

#1111 8¢ BOLIVAR

Frame Plate-Vignette Plate

26056-26021	$2	☐	☐	☐	☐
26056-26026	$2	☐	☐	☐	☐
26061-26021	$2	☐	☐	☐	☐
26061-26026	$2	☐	☐	☐	☐
26062-26021	$2	☐	☐	☐	☐
26062-26026	$2	☐	☐	☐	☐

#1112 4¢ ATLANTIC CABLE

26076	$.45	☐	☐	☐	☐
26077	$.45	☐	☐	☐	☐
26078	$.45	☐	☐	☐	☐
26079	$.45	☐	☐	☐	☐

#1113 1¢ LINCOLN

		UL	UR	LL	LR
26245	$.25	☐	☐	☐	☐
26246	$.25	☐	☐	☐	☐
26247	$.25	☐	☐	☐	☐
26248	$.25	☐	☐	☐	☐

#1114 3¢ LINCOLN

26251	$.45	☐	☐	☐	☐
26252	$.45	☐	☐	☐	☐
26253	$.45	☐	☐	☐	☐
26254	$.45	☐	☐	☐	☐

#1115 4¢ LINCOLN DOUGLAS

26105	$.50	☐	☐	☐	☐
26106	$.50	☐	☐	☐	☐
26107	$.50	☐	☐	☐	☐
26108	$.50	☐	☐	☐	☐

#1116 4¢ LINCOLN

26271	$.50	☐	☐	☐	☐
26272	$.50	☐	☐	☐	☐
26273	$.50	☐	☐	☐	☐
26274	$.50	☐	☐	☐	☐

#1117 4¢ KOSSUTH

26124	$.45	☐	☐	☐	☐
26125	$.45	☐	☐	☐	☐
26126	$.45	☐	☐	☐	☐
26127	$.45	☐	☐	☐	☐

#1118 8¢ KOSSUTH

Frame Plate-Vignette Plate

26056-26098	$15.00	☐	☐	☐	☐
26056-26119	$1.50	☐	☐	☐	☐
26062-26098	$1.50	☐	☐	☐	☐
26062-26119	$15.00	☐	☐	☐	☐
26088-26092	$1.50	☐	☐	☐	☐
26088-26095	$1.50	☐	☐	☐	☐
26088-26098	$1.50	☐	☐	☐	☐
26088-26119	$1.50	☐	☐	☐	☐
26091-26092	$1.50	☐	☐	☐	☐
26091-26095	$1.50	☐	☐	☐	☐
26091-26098	$1.50	☐	☐	☐	☐
26091-26119	$1.50	☐	☐	☐	☐

1958 COMMEMORATIVES

#1119 4¢ FREEDOM OF PRESS

Plate	Price	UL	UR	LL	LR
26115	$.45	□	□	□	□
26116	$.45	□	□	□	□
26117	$.45	□	□	□	□
26118	$.45	□	□	□	□

#1120 4¢ OVERLAND MAIL

Plate	Price	UL	UR	LL	LR
26158	$.45	□	□	□	□
26159	$.45	□	□	□	□
26160	$.45	□	□	□	□
26161	$.45	□	□	□	□

#1121 4¢ NOAH WEBSTER

Plate	Price	UL	UR	LL	LR
26103	$.45	□	□	□	□
26104	$.45	□	□	□	□
26120	$.45	□	□	□	□
26121	$.45	□	□	□	□

#1122 4¢ FOREST CONSERVATION

Plate	Price	UL	UR	LL	LR
26149	$.45	□	□	□	□
26156	$.45	□	□	□	□
26157	$.45	□	□	□	□
26162	$.45	□	□	□	□
26167	$.45	□	□	□	□
26170	$.45	□	□	□	□

#1123 4¢ FORT DUQUESNE

Plate	Price	UL	UR	LL	LR
26197	$.45	□	□	□	□
26198	$.45	□	□	□	□
26199	$.45	□	□	□	□
26200	$.45	□	□	□	□

1959 COMMEMORATIVES

#1124 4¢ OREGON STATEHOOD

Plate	Price	UL	UR	LL	LR
26235	$.45	□	□	□	□
26236	$.45	□	□	□	□
26237	$.45	□	□	□	□
26243	$.45	□	□	□	□

#1125 4¢ SAN MARTIN

Plate	Price	UL	UR	LL	LR
26238	$.45	□	□	□	□
26239	$.45	□	□	□	□
26240	$.45	□	□	□	□
26241	$.45	□	□	□	□

#1126 8¢ SAN MARTIN

Plate	Price	UL	UR	LL	LR
26244	$1	□	□	□	□
26249	$1	□	□	□	□

#1127 4¢ NATO

Plate	Price	UL	UR	LL	LR
26299	$.45	□	□	□	□
26300	$.45	□	□	□	□
26301	$.45	□	□	□	□
26302	$.45	□	□	□	□

#1128 4¢ ARCTIC EXPLORATION

Plate	Price	UL	UR	LL	LR
26303	$.45	□	□	□	□
26304	$.45	□	□	□	□
26305	$.45	□	□	□	□
26306	$.45	□	□	□	□

1959 COMMEMORATIVES

#1129 8¢ WORLD PEACE

Plate	Price	UL	UR	LL	LR
26317	$1	□	□	□	□
26318	$1	□	□	□	□
26319	$1	□	□	□	□
26320	$1	□	□	□	□

#1130 4¢ SILVER CENTENNIAL

Plate	Price	UL	UR	LL	LR
26356	$.45	□	□	□	□
26357	$.45	□	□	□	□
26358	$.45	□	□	□	□
26359	$.45	□	□	□	□

#1131 4¢ ST. LAWRENCE SEAWAY

Plate	Price	UL	UR	LL	LR
26328	$.45	□	□	□	□
26333	$.45	□	□	□	□
26334	$.45	□	□	□	□
26335	$.45	□	□	□	□
26336	$.45	□	□	□	□
26343	$4500	□	†	†	†

photo of 26343 on next page

#1132 4¢ FLAG (49 STARS)

Plate	Price	UL	UR	LL	LR
26344	$.45	□	□	□	□
26354	$.45	□	□	□	□
26366	$.45	□	□	□	□
26368	$.45	□	□	□	□

#1133 4¢ SOIL CONSERVATION

Plate	Price	UL	UR	LL	LR
26406	$.45	□	□	□	□
26407	$.45	□	□	□	□
26410	$.45	□	□	□	□
26415	$.45	□	□	□	□
26423	$.45	□	□	□	□
26425	$.45	□	□	□	□

#1134 4¢ PETROLEUM

Plate	Price	UL	UR	LL	LR
26416	$.45	□	□	□	□
26417	$.45	□	□	□	□
26419	$.45	□	□	□	□
26431	$.45	□	□	□	□

#1135 4¢ DENTAL HEALTH

Plate	Price	UL	UR	LL	LR
26438	$.45	□	□	□	□
26439	$.45	□	□	□	□
26440	$.45	□	□	□	□
26441	$.45	□	□	□	□

#1136 4¢ REUTER

Plate	Price	UL	UR	LL	LR
26451	$.45	□	□	□	□
26452	$.45	□	□	□	□
26453	$.45	□	□	□	□
26454	$.45	□	□	□	□

#1137 8¢ REUTER

Plate	Price	UL	UR	LL	LR
26464	$1	□	□	□	□
26466	$1	□	□	□	□

#1138 4¢ MACDOWELL

Plate	Price	UL	UR	LL	LR
26498	$.45	□	□	□	□
26499	$.45	□	□	□	□
26500	$.45	□	□	□	□
26501	$.45	□	□	□	□

1960 COMMEMORATIVES

#1139 4¢ WASHINGTON CREDO

Plate	Price	UL	UR	LL	LR
26488	$.45	☐	☐	☐	☐
26489	$1.00	☐	☐	☐	☐
26494	$.45	☐	☐	☐	☐
26495	$.45	☐	☐	☐	☐
26508	$.45	☐	☐	☐	☐

#1140 4¢ FRANKLIN CREDO

Plate	Price	UL	UR	LL	LR
26582	$.45	☐	☐	☐	☐
26587	$.45	☐	☐	☐	☐
26589	$.45	☐	☐	☐	☐
26591	$.45	☐	☐	☐	☐

#1141 4¢ JEFFERSON CREDO

Plate	Price	UL	UR	LL	LR
26608	$.50	☐	☐	☐	☐
26611	$.50	☐	☐	☐	☐
26618	$.50	☐	☐	☐	☐
26623	$.50	☐	☐	☐	☐
26628	$.50	☐	☐	☐	☐
26629	$.50	☐	☐	☐	☐

#1142 4¢ FRANCIS SCOTT KEY CREDO

Plate	Price	UL	UR	LL	LR
26683	$.50	☐	☐	☐	☐
26693	$.50	☐	☐	☐	☐
26695	$.50	☐	☐	☐	☐
26696	$.50	☐	☐	☐	☐

#1143 4¢ LINCOLN CREDO

Plate	Price	UL	UR	LL	LR
26797	$.60	☐	☐	☐	☐
26803	$.60	☐	☐	☐	☐
26805	$.60	☐	☐	☐	☐
26806	$.60	☐	☐	☐	☐

#1144 4¢ PATRICK HENRY CREDO('61)

Plate	Price	UL	UR	LL	LR
26738	$.60	☐	☐	☐	☐
26741	$.60	☐	☐	☐	☐
26747	$.60	☐	☐	☐	☐
26752	$.60	☐	☐	☐	☐

#1145 4¢ BOY SCOUTS

Plate	Price	UL	UR	LL	LR
26530	$.45	☐	☐	☐	☐
26531	$.45	☐	☐	☐	☐
26535	$.45	☐	☐	☐	☐
26536	$.45	☐	☐	☐	☐

#1146 4¢ WINTER GAMES

Plate	Price	UL	UR	LL	LR
26540	$.50	☐	☐	☐	☐
26541	$.50	☐	☐	☐	☐
26542	$.50	☐	☐	☐	☐
26550	$.50	☐	☐	☐	☐

#1147 4¢ MASARYK

Plate	Price	UL	UR	LL	LR
26552	$.45	☐	☐	☐	☐
26553	$.45	☐	☐	☐	☐
26554	$.45	☐	☐	☐	☐
26555	$.45	☐	☐	☐	☐

#1148 8¢ MASARYK

Plate	Price	UL	UR	LL	LR
26557	$1.25	☐	☐	☐	☐
26562	$1.25	☐	☐	☐	☐

#1149 4¢ REFUGEE YEAR

Plate	Price	UL	UR	LL	LR
26596	$.45	☐	☐	☐	☐
26597	$.45	☐	☐	☐	☐
26598	$.45	☐	☐	☐	☐
26599	$.45	☐	☐	☐	☐

#1150 4¢ WATER CONSERVATION

Plate	Price	UL	UR	LL	LR
26588	$.45	☐	☐	☐	☐
26590	$.45	☐	☐	☐	☐
26592	$.45	☐	☐	☐	☐
26600	$.45	☐	☐	☐	☐

#1151 4¢ SEATO

Plate	Price	UL	UR	LL	LR
26632	$.45	☐	☐	☐	☐
26633	$.45	☐	☐	☐	☐
26634	$.45	☐	☐	☐	☐
26638	$.45	☐	☐	☐	☐

#1152 4¢ AMERICAN WOMAN

Plate	Price	UL	UR	LL	LR
26643	$.45	☐	☐	☐	☐
26644	$.45	☐	☐	☐	☐
26645	$.45	☐	☐	☐	☐
26646	$.45	☐	☐	☐	☐

#1153 4¢ AMERICAN FLAG (50 STARS)

Plate	Price	UL	UR	LL	LR
26639	$.45	☐	☐	☐	☐
26640	$.45	☐	☐	☐	☐
26647	$.45	☐	☐	☐	☐
26648	$.45	☐	☐	☐	☐

1960 COMMEMORATIVES

#1154 4¢ PONY EXPRESS

		UL	UR	LL	LR
26624	$.45	☐	☐	☐	☐
26625	$.45	☐	☐	☐	☐
26626	$.45	☐	☐	☐	☐
26627	$.45	☐	☐	☐	☐

#1155 4¢ EMPLOY THE HANDICAPPED

26679	$.45	☐	☐	☐	☐
26680	$.45	☐	☐	☐	☐
26681	$.45	☐	☐	☐	☐
26682	$.45	☐	☐	☐	☐

#1156 4¢ FORESTRY CONGRESS

26685	$.45	☐	☐	☐	☐
26686	$.45	☐	☐	☐	☐
26687	$.45	☐	☐	☐	☐
26688	$.45	☐	☐	☐	☐

#1157 4¢ MEXICAN INDEPENDENCE

26707	$.45	☐	☐	☐	☐
26713	$.45	☐	☐	☐	☐
26717	$.45	☐	☐	☐	☐
26722	$.45	☐	☐	☐	☐

#1158 4¢ U.S. - JAPAN AMITY

26726	$.45	☐	☐	☐	☐
26729	$.45	☐	☐	☐	☐
26730	$.45	☐	☐	☐	☐
26731	$.45	☐	☐	☐	☐

#1159 4¢ PADEREWSKI

26742	$.45	☐	☐	☐	☐
26743	$.45	☐	☐	☐	☐
26744	$.45	☐	☐	☐	☐
26745	$.45	☐	☐	☐	☐

#1160 8¢ PADEREWSKI

26753	$1.25	☐	☐	☐	☐
26763	$1.25	☐	☐	☐	☐

#1161 4¢ ROBERT TAFT

26759	$.45	☐	☐	☐	☐
26760	$.45	☐	☐	☐	☐
26761	$.45	☐	☐	☐	☐
26762	$.45	☐	☐	☐	☐

#1162 4¢ WHEELS OF FREEDOM

26774	$.45	☐	☐	☐	☐
26775	$.45	☐	☐	☐	☐
26776	$.45	☐	☐	☐	☐
26777	$.45	☐	☐	☐	☐

#1163 4¢ BOYS' CLUBS

26662	$.45	☐	☐	☐	☐
26665	$.45	☐	☐	☐	☐
26666	$.45	☐	☐	☐	☐
26669	$.45	☐	☐	☐	☐

#1164 4¢ AUTOMATED P.O.

		UL	UR	LL	LR
26785	$.45	☐	☐	☐	☐
26787	$.45	☐	☐	☐	☐
26798	$.45	☐	☐	☐	☐
26799	$.45	☐	☐	☐	☐
26804	$.45	☐	☐	☐	☐
26807	$.45	☐	☐	☐	☐

#1165 4¢ MANNERHEIM

26755	$.45	☐	☐	☐	☐
26756	$.45	☐	☐	☐	☐
26757	$.45	☐	☐	☐	☐
26758	$.45	☐	☐	☐	☐

#1166 8¢ MANNERHEIM

26764	$1	☐	☐	☐	☐
26769	$1	☐	☐	☐	☐

#1167 4¢ CAMPFIRE GIRLS

26740	$.45	☐	☐	☐	☐
26746	$.45	☐	☐	☐	☐
26751	$.45	☐	☐	☐	☐
26754	$.45	☐	☐	☐	☐
26816	$.45	☐	☐	☐	☐
26826	$.45	☐	☐	☐	☐

#1168 4¢ GARIBALDI

26792	$.45	☐	☐	☐	☐
26793	$.45	☐	☐	☐	☐
26794	$.45	☐	☐	☐	☐
26795	$.45	☐	☐	☐	☐

#1169 8¢ GARIBALDI

26779	$1	☐	☐	☐	☐
26788	$1	☐	☐	☐	☐
26790	$1	☐	☐	☐	☐

#1170 4¢ GEORGE

26780	$.45	☐	☐	☐	☐
26781	$.45	☐	☐	☐	☐
26782	$.45	☐	☐	☐	☐
26783	$.45	☐	☐	☐	☐

#1171 4¢ CARNEGIE

26674	$.45	☐	☐	☐	☐
26675	$.45	☐	☐	☐	☐
26676	$.45	☐	☐	☐	☐
26677	$.45	☐	☐	☐	☐

#1172 4¢ DULLES

26770	$.45	☐	☐	☐	☐
26771	$.45	☐	☐	☐	☐
26772	$.45	☐	☐	☐	☐
26773	$.45	☐	☐	☐	☐

#1173 4¢ ECHO I

26845	$1.00	☐	☐	☐	☐
26846	$1.00	☐	☐	☐	☐
26847	$1.00	☐	☐	☐	☐
26848	$1.00	☐	☐	☐	☐

1961 COMMEMORATIVES

#1174 4¢ GHANDI

		UL	UR	LL	LR
26864	$.45	□	□	□	□
26865	$.45	□	□	□	□
26866	$.45	□	□	□	□
26867	$.45	□	□	□	□

#1175 8¢ GHANDI

26841	$1.25	□	□	□	□
26844	$1.25	□	□	□	□

#1176 4¢ RANGE CONSERVATION

26849	$.45	□	□	□	□
26860	$.45	□	□	□	□
26870	$.45	□	□	□	□
26874	$.45	□	□	□	□
26901	$.45	□	□	□	□
26904	$.45	□	□	□	□

#1177 4¢ GREELEY

26895	$.45	□	□	□	□
26896	$.45	□	□	□	□
26897	$.45	□	□	□	□
26898	$.45	□	□	□	□

1961-65 CIVIL WAR ISSUE

#1178 4¢ FORT SUMTER

26913	$.75	□	□	□	□
26914	$.75	□	□	□	□
26915	$.75	□	□	□	□
26916	$.75	□	□	□	□

#1179 4¢ SHILOH

27178	$.55	□	□	□	□
27179	$.55	□	□	□	□
27180	$.55	□	□	□	□
27181	$.55	□	□	□	□

#1180 5¢ GETTYSBURG

27477	$.65	□	□	□	□
27508	$.65	□	□	□	□
27510	$.65	□	□	□	□
27513	$.65	□	□	□	□
27519	$.65	□	□	□	□
27520	$.65	□	□	□	□

#1181 5¢ BATTLE OF THE WILDERNESS

27763	$.65	□	□	□	□
27764	$.65	□	□	□	□
27765	$.65	□	□	□	□
27766	$.65	□	□	□	□
27771	$.65	□	□	□	□
27772	$.65	□	□	□	□

#1182 5¢ APPOMATTOX

28064	$1.10	□	□	□	□
28067	$1.10	□	□	□	□
28068	$1.10	□	□	□	□
28073	$1.10	□	□	□	□
28074	$1.10	□	□	□	□
28075	$1.10	□	□	□	□

1961 COMMEMORATIVES

#1183 4¢ KANSAS

		UL	UR	LL	LR
26935	$.45	□	□	□	□
26936	$.45	□	□	□	□
26937	$.45	□	□	□	□
26938	$.45	□	□	□	□

#1184 4¢ NORRIS

26990	$.45	□	□	□	□
26991	$ 45	□	□	□	□
26992	$.45	□	□	□	□
26993	$.45	□	□	□	□

#1185 4¢ NAVAL AVIATION

27014	$.45	□	□	□	□
27015	$.45	□	□	□	□
27016	$.45	□	□	□	□
27017	$.45	□	□	□	□

#1186 4¢ COMPENSATION LAW

27024	$.45	□	□	□	□
27025	$.45	□	□	□	□
27026	$.45	□	□	□	□
27027	$.45	□	□	□	□

All of the LL & LR plate numbers of this commemorative are inverted. Value: $.60

#1187 4¢ REMINGTON

27033	$.70	□	□	□	□
27034	$.70	□	□	□	□
27035	$.70	□	□	□	□
27036	$.70	□	□	□	□

#1188 4¢ SUN YAT-SEN

27039	$.45	□	□	□	□
27040	$.45	□	□	□	□
27041	$.45	□	□	□	□
27042	$.45	□	□	□	□

#1189 4¢ BASKETBALL

27060	$.50	□	□	□	□
27061	$.50	□	□	□	□
27062	$.50	□	□	□	□
27063	$.50	□	□	□	□

#1190 4¢ NURSING

27081-27080	$.45	□	□	□	□
27081-27082	$.45	□	□	□	□
27081-27089	$.45	□	□	□	□
27081-27092	$.45	□	□	□	□
27083-27080	$.45	□	□	□	□
27083-27082	$.45	□	□	□	□
27083-27089	$.45	□	□	□	□
27096-27082	$.45	□	□	□	□
27096-27089	$.45	□	□	□	□
27096-27092	$.45	□	□	□	□
27099-27089	$7.00	□	□	□	□
27099-27092	$7.00	□	□	□	□

1962 COMMEMORATIVES

#1191 4¢ NEW MEXICO

		UL	UR	LL	LR
27107	$.45	☐	☐	☐	☐
27112	$.45	☐	☐	☐	☐
27113	$.45	☐	☐	☐	☐
27114	$.45	☐	☐	☐	☐

#1192 4¢ ARIZONA

27125	$.45	☐	☐	☐	☐
27126	$.45	☐	☐	☐	☐
27127	$.45	☐	☐	☐	☐
27128	$.45	☐	☐	☐	☐

#1193 4¢ PROJECT MERCURY

27064	$.45	☐	☐	☐	☐
27065	$.45	☐	☐	☐	☐
27066	$.45	☐	☐	☐	☐
27067	$.45	☐	☐	☐	☐
27068	$.45	☐	☐	☐	☐
27071	$.45	☐	☐	☐	☐

#1194 4¢ MALARIA

27153	$.45	☐	☐	☐	☐
27154	$.45	☐	☐	☐	☐
27155	$.45	☐	☐	☐	☐
27157	$.45	☐	☐	☐	☐

#1195 4¢ HUGHES

27171	$.45	☐	☐	☐	☐
27172	$.45	☐	☐	☐	☐
27173	$.45	☐	☐	☐	☐
27174	$.45	☐	☐	☐	☐

#1196 4¢ SEATTLE FAIR

27167	$.45	☐	☐	☐	☐
27175	$.45	☐	☐	☐	☐
27176	$.45	☐	☐	☐	☐
27177	$.45	☐	☐	☐	☐
27198	$.45	☐	☐	☐	☐
27203	$.45	☐	☐	☐	☐
27204	$.45	☐	☐	☐	☐

#1197 4¢ LOUISIANA

27184	$.45	☐	☐	☐	☐
27185	$.45	☐	☐	☐	☐
27186	$.45	☐	☐	☐	☐
27187	$.45	☐	☐	☐	☐
27205	$.45	☐	☐	☐	☐
27210	$.45	☐	☐	☐	☐

#1198 4¢ HOMESTEAD

27147	$.45	☐	☐	☐	☐
27148	$.45	☐	☐	☐	☐
27149	$.45	☐	☐	☐	☐
27150	$.45	☐	☐	☐	☐

#1199 4¢ GIRL SCOUTS

		UL	UR	LL	LR
27217	$.45	☐	☐	☐	☐
27218	$.45	☐	☐	☐	☐
27219	$.45	☐	☐	☐	☐
27220	$.45	☐	☐	☐	☐

#1200 4¢ McMAHON

27224	$.45	☐	☐	☐	☐
27225	$.45	☐	☐	☐	☐
27226	$.45	☐	☐	☐	☐
27227	$.45	☐	☐	☐	☐

#1201 4¢ APPRENTICE

27247	$.45	☐	☐	☐	☐
27248	$.45	☐	☐	☐	☐
27249	$.45	☐	☐	☐	☐
27250	$.45	☐	☐	☐	☐

#1202 4¢ RAYBURN

27255	$.45	☐	☐	☐	☐
27260	$.45	☐	☐	☐	☐
27262	$.45	☐	☐	☐	☐
27263	$.45	☐	☐	☐	☐
27264	$.45	☐	☐	☐	☐
27265	$.45	☐	☐	☐	☐

#1203 4¢ HAMMARSKJOLD

27266-27275	$.45	☐	☐	☐	☐
27266-27277	$.45	☐	☐	☐	☐
27276-27275	$.45	☐	☐	☐	☐
27276-27277	$.45	☐	☐	☐	☐
27279-27278	$.45	☐	☐	☐	☐
27279 27282	$.45	☐	☐	☐	☐
27283-27278	$.45	☐	☐	☐	☐
27283-27282	$.45	☐	☐	☐	☐

#1204 4¢ HAMMARSKJOLD INVERT

27266-27275	$1.25	☐	☐	☐	☐
27266-27277	$1.25	☐	☐	☐	☐
27276-27275	$1.25	☐	☐	☐	☐
27276-27277	$1.25	☐	☐	☐	☐
27279-27278	$1.25	☐	☐	☐	☐
27279-27282	$1.25	☐	☐	☐	☐
27283-27278	$1.25	☐	☐	☐	☐
27283-27282	$1.25	☐	☐	☐	☐

#1205 4¢ CHRISTMAS

27301	$.45	☐	☐	☐	☐
27306	$.45	☐	☐	☐	☐
27311	$.45	☐	☐	☐	☐
27314	$.45	☐	☐	☐	☐
27325	$.45	☐	☐	☐	☐
27330	$.45	☐	☐	☐	☐

1962 COMMEMORATIVES

#1206 4¢ HIGHER EDUCATION

		UL	UR	LL	LR
27286-27289	$.45	□	□	□	□
27286-27295	$.45	□	□	□	□
27290-27289	$.45	□	□	□	□
27290-27295	$.45	□	□	□	□
27293-27299	$.45	□	□	□	□
27293-27300	$.45	□	□	□	□
27296-27299	$.45	□	□	□	□
27296-27300	$.45	□	□	□	□

#1207 4¢ WINSLOW HOMER

27362	$.45	□	□	□	□
27374	$.45	□	□	□	□
27379	$.45	□	□	□	□
27380	$.45	□	□	□	□
27381	$.45	□	□	□	□
27386	$.45	□	□	□	□

1963 REGULAR ISSUE

#1208 5¢ U.S. FLAG 26 Plates

UNTAGGED

27392	$.45	□	□	□	□
27393	$.45	□	□	□	□
27398	$.45	□	□	□	□
27403	$.45	□	□	□	□
27408	$.45	□	□	□	□
27411	$.45	□	□	□	□
27558	$.45	□	□	□	□
27559	$.45	□	□	□	□
27561	$.45	□	□	□	□
27568	$.45	□	□	□	□
27569	$.45	□	□	□	□
27572	$.45	□	□	□	□
27716	$.45	□	□	□	□
27718	$.45	□	□	□	□
27725	$.45	□	□	□	□
27732	$1.75	□	□	□	□
27965	$.45	□	□	□	□
27970	$.45	□	□	□	□
28430	$1.75	□	□	□	□
28431	$2.50	□	□	□	□
28432	$1.75	□	□	□	□
28433o	$.75	□	□	□	□
28442o	$.75	□	□	□	□
28445o	$ 75	□	□	□	□
28449o	$2.25	□	□	□	□
28453o	$2.25	□	□	□	□

#1208a 5¢ U.S. FLAG

TAGGED **16 Plates**

28433o	$2.00	□	□	□	□
28442o	$2.00	□	□	□	□
28445o	$2.00	□	□	□	□
28449o	$15.00	□	□	□	□
28453o	$2.00	□	□	□	□

1963 REGULAR ISSUE

#1208a 5¢ U.S. FLAG Cont.

		UL	UR	LL	LR
28631	$2.00	□	□	□	□
28664	$2.00	□	□	□	□
28681	$6.00	□	□	□	□
28684	$4.00	□	□	□	□
28685	$3.50	□	□	□	□
28911	$2.00	□	□	□	□
28914	$4.00	□	□	□	□
28915	$2.00	□	□	□	□
28918	$7.00	□	□	□	□
28919	$7.00	□	□	□	□
28921	$10.00	□	□	□	□

#1209 1¢ JACKSON 18 Plates

UNTAGGED

27382	$.25	□	□	□	□
27383	$.25	□	□	□	□
27387	$.25	□	□	□	□
27388	$.25	□	□	□	□
27459	$.25	□	□	□	□
27460	$.25	□	□	□	□
27464	$.25	□	□	□	□
27465 o	$.25	□	□	□	□
27473	$.25	□	□	□	□
27474	$.25	□	□	□	□
27695 o	$.25	□	□	□	□
27696 o	$.25	□	□	□	□
27779 o	$.25	□	□	□	□
27780 o	$.25	□	□	□	□
29184 o	$.25	□	□	□	□
29185 o	$.25	□	□	□	□
29389 o	$.25	□	□	□	□
29390 o	$.25	□	□	□	□

#1209a 1¢ JACKSON 13 Plates

TAGGED

27465 o	$1.00	□	□	□	□
27695 o	$.50	□	□	□	□
27696 o	$.50	□	□	□	□
27779 o	$.50	□	□	□	□
27780 o	$.50	□	□	□	□
28062	$.25	□	□	□	□
28063	$.25	□	□	□	□
29182	$.25	□	□	□	□
29183	$.25	□	□	□	□
29184 o	$.50	□	□	□	□
29185 o	$.50	□	□	□	□
29389 o	$.50	□	□	□	□
29390 o	$.50	□	□	□	□

#1213 5¢ WASHINGTON 64 Plates

UNTAGGED

27194	$.50	□	□	□	□
27195	$.50	□	□	□	□
27196	$.50	□	□	□	□
27197	$.50	□	□	□	□
27230	$.50	□	□	□	□

o Issued both TAGGED and UNTAGGED

1963 REGULAR ISSUE

#1213 5¢ WASHINGTON Cont.

UNTAGGED		UL	UR	LL	LR
27231	$.55	☐	☐	☐	☐
27232	$.55	☐	☐	☐	☐
27233	$.55	☐	☐	☐	☐
27297	$.55	☐	☐	☐	☐
27298	$.55	☐	☐	☐	☐
27307	$.55	☐	☐	☐	☐
27308	$.55	☐	☐	☐	☐
27315	$.55	☐	☐	☐	☐
27316	$.55	☐	☐	☐	☐
27317	$.55	☐	☐	☐	☐
27318	$.55	☐	☐	☐	☐
27326	$.55	☐	☐	☐	☐
27327	$.55	☐	☐	☐	☐
27328	$.55	☐	☐	☐	☐
27329	$.55	☐	☐	☐	☐
27337	$.55	☐	☐	☐	☐
27338	$.55	☐	☐	☐	☐
27339	$.55	☐	☐	☐	☐
27340	$.55	☐	☐	☐	☐
27341	$.55	☐	☐	☐	☐
27342	$.55	☐	☐	☐	☐
27343	$.55	☐	☐	☐	☐
27344	$.55	☐	☐	☐	☐
27425	$.55	☐	☐	☐	☐
27426	$.55	☐	☐	☐	☐
27478	$.55	☐	☐	☐	☐
27479	$.55	☐	☐	☐	☐
27486**o**	$.55	☐	☐	☐	☐
27487	$.55	☐	☐	☐	☐
27493	$.55	☐	☐	☐	☐
27494	$.55	☐	☐	☐	☐
27501	$.55	☐	☐	☐	☐
27502	$.55	☐	☐	☐	☐
27517**o**	$.55	☐	☐	☐	☐
27518**o**	$.55	☐	☐	☐	☐
27553	$.55	☐	☐	☐	☐
27554	$.55	☐	☐	☐	☐
27555	$.55	☐	☐	☐	☐
27556	$.55	☐	☐	☐	☐
27597	$7.50	☐	☐	☐	☐
27598	$7.50	☐	☐	☐	☐
27701	$.55	☐	☐	☐	☐
27702	$.55	☐	☐	☐	☐
27703**o**	$.55	☐	☐	☐	☐
27704**o**	$.55	☐	☐	☐	☐
27727	$.55	☐	☐	☐	☐
27728	$.55	☐	☐	☐	☐
27748**o**	$.55	☐	☐	☐	☐
27749**o**	$.55	☐	☐	☐	☐
27864	$.55	☐	☐	☐	☐
27865	$.55	☐	☐	☐	☐
27866	$50.00	☐	☐	☐	☐
27867	$50.00	☐	☐	☐	☐
27873	$.55	☐	☐	☐	☐
27874	$.55	☐	☐	☐	☐
27961	$7.50	☐	☐	☐	☐
27962	$7.50	☐	☐	☐	☐
27993	$7.50	☐	☐	☐	☐
27994	$7.50	☐	☐	☐	☐

o Issued both TAGGED and UNTAGGED

#1213b 5¢ WASHINGTON 7 Plates

TAGGED		UL	UR	LL	LR
27486 **o**	$12.50	☐	☐	☐	☐
27517 **o**	$5.00	☐	☐	☐	☐
27518 **o**	$5.00	☐	☐	☐	☐
27703 **o**	$12.50	☐	☐	☐	☐
27704 **o**	$12.50	☐	☐	☐	☐
27748 **o**	$12.50	☐	☐	☐	☐
27749 **o**	$12.50	☐	☐	☐	☐

BOOKLET PANES **PANES OF 5**

#1213a 5¢ WASHINGTON

UNTAGGED

Slogan 1 "Your Mailman" **14 Plates**

27347 27348 27349 27350 27351
27352 27357 27358 27412 27413
27435 27436 27438 27439

Slogan 2 "Use Zone Nos." **18 Plates**

27498 27499 27503 27504 27505
27506 27523 27524 27525 27526
27546 27547 27563**o** 27564**o** 27565
27566 27650 27651

Slogan 3 "Always Use ZIP" **44 Plates**

27669 27670 27671**o** 27672 27675
27676 27678**o** 27679**o** 27723 27724
27734**o** 27735**o** 27736 27737 27738
27739 27827**o** 27828 27829**o** 27830
27833 27834 28013 28014 28039
28040 28080 28081**o** 28084 28085
28090 28091**o** 28214**o** 28215**o** 28216**o**
28217**o** 28338 28339**o** 28345**o** 28346
28440**o** 28441**o** 28471**o** 28472**o**

#1213c 5¢ WASHINGTON

TAGGED

Slogan 2 "Use Zone Nos." **2 Plates**

27563**o** 27564**o**

Slogan 3 "Always Use ZIP" **47 plates**

27671**o** 27678**o** 27679**o** 27734**o** 27735**o**
27827**o** 27829**o** 28081**o** 28091**o** 28214**o**
28215**o** 28216**o** 28217**o** 28339**o** 28345**o**
28440**o** 28441**o** 28471**o** 28472**o** 28491
28492 28513 28514 28518 28538
28539 28567 28568 28569 28570
28619 28849 28850 28854 28904
28905 29053 29054 29058 29130
29131 29213 29214 29283 29284
29336 29337

See Appendix G for largest reported plate number percentage by position.

SIDE COILS

432 Subject Plates **STRIPS OF 6**

#1225 1¢ JACKSON 12 Plates

UNTAGGED

27384 †27385 †27419 †27420 27775**o**
27776**o** 28009**o** 28010**o** 29117 29118
29134 29135

#1225a 1¢ JACKSON 4 Plates

TAGGED

27775**o** 27776**o** 28009**o** 28010**o**

1963 REGULAR ISSUE

SIDE COILS

#1229 5¢ WASHINGTON 223 Plates

UNTAGGED

27190 27191 27192 27193 27206
27207 †27208 †27209 27211 27212
†27302 †27303 27304 27305 †27309
†27310 †27319 †27320 †27321 †27322
27333 †27334 27335 †27336 †27394
†27395 †27396 †27397 †27399 †27400
†27404 †27405 †27406 †27407 †27421
†27422 †27423 †27424 †27429 †27430
†27440 †27441 †27442 †27443 †27444
†27445 †27448 †27449 †27451 †27452
†27470 †27471 †27480 †27481 †27495
†27496 †27531 †27532 †27533 †27534
†27536 †27537 †27538 †27539 †27542
†27543 †27544 †27545 †27549**o** 27550**o**
†27551 †27552 †27580**o**†27581**o**†27582
†27583**o**†27617**o**†27618**o**†27619 †27620
†27628 †27629 27630**o** †27631**o**†27632**o**
†27633**o**†27634**o**†27635**o**†27648**o** 27649**o**
27652**o** 27653**o**†27665 †27666 †27667
†27668 †27690 †27691 †27708 †27709
†27710 †27711 †27712 †27713 †27729
†27730 †27752 †27753 †27755 †27756
†27757 †27758 †27759 †27760 †27761
†27762 †27767 †27768 †27769 †27770
†27781 †27782 †27783 27784 †27810
27811**o** 27816**o** †27817 †27835 27836
†27837 27838 27855 27856 27858
27890 27894 27903**o** 27904**o** 27905**o**
27906**o**†27907 †27908 27913 27914
27923 27924 †27938**o**†27939**o** 27943
27944 27949 27950 27951**o** 27952**o**
27959 27960 †27963 †27964 †28052
†28053 28058 28059 28071 28072
28078 28079 †28125**o**†28126**o** 28136
28137 28197 28198 †28199**o**†28200**o**
28202 28203 28206 28207 28208
28209 †28288 †28289 28290 28291
28318 28319 28320 28321 28322
28323 28324 28325 28386 28387
†28388**o**†28389**o** 28390**o** 28391**o** 28392
28393 28415**o** 28416**o** 28443**o** 28444**o**
†28446 †28447 †28454**o**†28455**o** 28456**o**
28457**o**†28464**o** †28465**o**†28477 †28489**o**
†28490**o**†28502 †28503 †28504 28534**o**
†28535**o** 28549**o** 28550**o**

#1229a 5¢ WASHINGTON 57 Plates

TAGGED

†27549**o** 27550**o**†27580**o**†27581**o**†27583**o**
†27617**o**†27618**o** 27630**o**†27631**o**†27632**o**
†27633**o**†27634**o** †27635**o**†27648**o** 27649**o**
27652**o** 27653**o** 27811**o** 27816**o** 27903**o**

1963 REGULAR ISSUE

SIDE COILS

#1229a 5¢ WASHINGTON Cont.

27904**o** 27905**o** 27906**o** 27938**o** 27939**o**
27951**o** 27952**o** 28125**o** 28126**o**†28199**o**
†28200**o** 28388**o** 28389**o** 28390**o** 28391**o**
28415**o** 28416**o** 28443**o** 28444**o**†28451
†28452 †28454**o** †28455**o** 28456**o** 28457**o**
†28464**o**†28465**o**†28489**o**†28490**o**†28534**o**
†28535**o**†28549**o**†28550**o** †28551 †28552
†28555 †28556

o Issued both TAGGED and UNTAGGED

1963 COMMEMORATIVES

#1230 5¢ NORTH CAROLINA

		UL	UR	LL	LR
27428	$.50	☐	☐	☐	☐
27431	$.50	☐	☐	☐	☐
27432	$.50	☐	☐	☐	☐
27433	$.50	☐	☐	☐	☐
27434	$.50	☐	☐	☐	☐
27437	$.50	☐	☐	☐	☐

#1231 5¢ FOOD FOR PEACE

27482	$.50	☐	☐	☐	☐
27484	$.50	☐	☐	☐	☐
27485	$.50	☐	☐	☐	☐
27488	$.50	☐	☐	☐	☐
27489	$.50	☐	☐	☐	☐
27492	$.50	☐	☐	☐	☐

#1232 5¢ WEST VIRGINIA

27500	$.50	☐	☐	☐	☐
27507	$.50	☐	☐	☐	☐
27509	$.50	☐	☐	☐	☐
27511	$.50	☐	☐	☐	☐
27512	$.50	☐	☐	☐	☐
27514	$.50	☐	☐	☐	☐

#1233 5¢ EMANCIPATION

27453-27456	$.50	☐	☐	☐	☐
27453-27458	$.50	☐	☐	☐	☐
27455-27456	$.50	☐	☐	☐	☐
27455-27458	$.50	☐	☐	☐	☐
27457-27462	$.50	☐	☐	☐	☐
27457-27468	$.50	☐	☐	☐	☐
27461-27462	$.50	☐	☐	☐	☐
27461-27468	$.50	☐	☐	☐	☐

#1234 5¢ ALLIANCE FOR PROGRESS

27562	$.50	☐	☐	☐	☐
27567	$.50	☐	☐	☐	☐
27570	$.50	☐	☐	☐	☐
27571	$.50	☐	☐	☐	☐
27574	$.50	☐	☐	☐	☐
27576	$.50	☐	☐	☐	☐

#1235 5¢ CORDELL HULL

27613	$.50	☐	☐	☐	☐
27614	$.50	☐	☐	☐	☐
27615	$.50	☐	☐	☐	☐
27616	$.50	☐	☐	☐	☐

1963 COMMEMORATIVES

#1236 5¢ ELEANOR ROOSEVELT

		UL	UR	LL	LR
27604	$.50	☐	☐	☐	☐
27605	$.50	☐	☐	☐	☐
27606	$.50	☐	☐	☐	☐
27607	$.50	☐	☐	☐	☐

#1237 5¢ SCIENCE

		UL	UR	LL	LR
27623	$.50	☐	☐	☐	☐
27624	$.50	☐	☐	☐	☐
27626	$.50	☐	☐	☐	☐
27627	$.50	☐	☐	☐	☐
27636	$.50	☐	☐	☐	☐
27639	$.50	☐	☐	☐	☐

#1238 5¢ CITY DELIVERY
TAGGED

		UL	UR	LL	LR
27596	$.50	☐	☐	☐	☐
27600	$.50	☐	☐	☐	☐
27611	$.50	☐	☐	☐	☐
27612	$.50	☐	☐	☐	☐
27621	$.50	☐	☐	☐	☐
27622	$.50	☐	☐	☐	☐

#1239 5¢ RED CROSS

		UL	UR	LL	LR
27641	$.50	☐	☐	☐	☐
27642	$.50	☐	☐	☐	☐
27654	$2.00	☐	☐	☐	☐
27656	$.50	☐	☐	☐	☐
27657	$.50	☐	☐	☐	☐
27658	$.50	☐	☐	☐	☐
27659	$.50	☐	☐	☐	☐
27660	$.50	☐	☐	☐	☐

#1240 5¢ CHRISTMAS
UNTAGGED

		UL	UR	LL	LR
27560	$.50	☐	☐	☐	☐
27573	$.50	☐	☐	☐	☐
27575	$1.25	☐	☐	☐	☐
27577	$.50	☐	☐	☐	☐
27578	$.50	☐	☐	☐	☐
27579	$.50	☐	☐	☐	☐
27587	$.50	☐	☐	☐	☐
27589**o**	$.50	☐	☐	☐	☐
27591	$.50	☐	☐	☐	☐
27595	$.50	☐	☐	☐	☐
27599	$.50	☐	☐	☐	☐
27601**o**	$.50	☐	☐	☐	☐
27602	$2.75	☐	☐	☐	☐
27608	$.50	☐	☐	☐	☐
27638	$.50	☐	☐	☐	☐
27640	$.50	☐	☐	☐	☐
27655	$.50	☐	☐	☐	☐

#1240a 5¢ CHRISTMAS
TAGGED

		UL	UR	LL	LR
27589**o**	$5.00	☐	☐	☐	☐
27601**o**	$5.00	☐	☐	☐	☐

o Issued both TAGGED and UNTAGGED

#1241 5¢ AUDUBON

		UL	UR	LL	LR
27586	$.50	☐	☐	☐	☐
27588	$.50	☐	☐	☐	☐
27590	$.50	☐	☐	☐	☐
27594	$.50	☐	☐	☐	☐
27603	$.50	☐	☐	☐	☐
27609	$.50	☐	☐	☐	☐

#1242 5¢ SAM HOUSTON

		UL	UR	LL	LR
27661	$.50	☐	☐	☐	☐
27662	$.50	☐	☐	☐	☐
27663	$.50	☐	☐	☐	☐
27664	$.50	☐	☐	☐	☐

#1243 5¢ C.M. RUSSELL

		UL	UR	LL	LR
27740	$.50	☐	☐	☐	☐
27741	$.50	☐	☐	☐	☐
27742	$.50	☐	☐	☐	☐
27747	$.50	☐	☐	☐	☐
27750	$.50	☐	☐	☐	☐
27751	$.50	☐	☐	☐	☐

#1244 5¢ N.Y. FAIR

		UL	UR	LL	LR
27743	$.50	☐	☐	☐	☐
27744	$.50	☐	☐	☐	☐
27745	$.50	☐	☐	☐	☐
27746	$.50	☐	☐	☐	☐

#1245 5¢ MUIR

		UL	UR	LL	LR
27687	$.50	☐	☐	☐	☐
27688	$.50	☐	☐	☐	☐
27692	$.50	☐	☐	☐	☐
27693	$.50	☐	☐	☐	☐

#1246 5¢ KENNEDY

		UL	UR	LL	LR
27800	$.50	☐	☐	☐	☐
27801	$.50	☐	☐	☐	☐
27802	$.50	☐	☐	☐	☐
27803	$.50	☐	☐	☐	☐
27804	$.50	☐	☐	☐	☐
27805	$.50	☐	☐	☐	☐
27806	$.50	☐	☐	☐	☐
27807	$.50	☐	☐	☐	☐
27808	$.50	☐	☐	☐	☐
27809	$.50	☐	☐	☐	☐
27818	$.50	☐	☐	☐	☐
27819	$.50	☐	☐	☐	☐

#1247 5¢ NEW JERSEY

		UL	UR	LL	LR
27786	$.50	☐	☐	☐	☐
27787	$.50	☐	☐	☐	☐
27788	$.50	☐	☐	☐	☐
27789	$.50	☐	☐	☐	☐

#1248 5¢ NEVADA

		UL	UR	LL	LR
27785	$.50	☐	☐	☐	☐
27790	$.50	☐	☐	☐	☐
27797	$.50	☐	☐	☐	☐
27798	$.50	☐	☐	☐	☐

1964 COMMEMORATIVES

#1249 5¢ REGISTER & VOTE

		UL	UR	LL	LR
27831	$ 50	☐	☐	☐	☐
27832	$.50	☐	☐	☐	☐
27839	$.50	☐	☐	☐	☐
27840	$.50	☐	☐	☐	☐
27841	$.50	☐	☐	☐	☐
27847	$.50	☐	☐	☐	☐
28548	$.50	☐	☐	☐	☐
28554	$.50	☐	☐	☐	☐
28557	$.50	☐	☐	☐	☐
28560	$1.00	☐	☐	☐	☐
28561	$.50	☐	☐	☐	☐
28562	$.50	☐	☐	☐	☐
28571	$.50	☐	☐	☐	☐
28587	$.50	☐	☐	☐	☐
28591	$.50	☐	☐	☐	☐
28592	$.50	☐	☐	☐	☐
28598	$.50	☐	☐	☐	☐
28599	$.50	☐	☐	☐	☐
28602	$.50	☐	☐	☐	☐
28603	$.50	☐	☐	☐	☐
28604	$.50	☐	☐	☐	☐
28606	$.50	☐	☐	☐	☐
28609	$.50	☐	☐	☐	☐
28615	$.50	☐	☐	☐	☐
28616	$.50	☐	☐	☐	☐
28622	$.50	☐	☐	☐	☐
28623	$.50	☐	☐	☐	☐
28628	$.50	☐	☐	☐	☐
28680	$.50	☐	☐	☐	☐
28682	$1.75	☐	☐	☐	☐

#1250 5¢ SHAKESPEARE

27842	$.50	☐	☐	☐	☐
27843	$.50	☐	☐	☐	☐
27844	$.50	☐	☐	☐	☐
27845	$.50	☐	☐	☐	☐

#1251 5¢ DOCTORS MAYO

27869	$.50	☐	☐	☐	☐
27870	$.50	☐	☐	☐	☐
27871	$.50	☐	☐	☐	☐
27872	$.50	☐	☐	☐	☐

#1252 5¢ AMERICAN MUSIC

27846	$.50	☐	☐	☐	☐
27848	$.50	☐	☐	☐	☐
27849	$.50	☐	☐	☐	☐
27852	$.50	☐	☐	☐	☐
27853	$.50	☐	☐	☐	☐
27854	$.50	☐	☐	☐	☐

#1253 5¢ HOMEMAKERS

27917	$.50	☐	☐	☐	☐
27918	$.50	☐	☐	☐	☐
27919	$.50	☐	☐	☐	☐
27920	$.50	☐	☐	☐	☐
27921	$.50	☐	☐	☐	☐
27922	$.50	☐	☐	☐	☐

#1254-57 5¢ CHRISTMAS 29 Plates

UNTAGGED		UL	UR	LL	LR
27875	$1.25	☐	☐	☐	☐
27876	$1.25	☐	☐	☐	☐
27878	$1.25	☐	☐	☐	☐
27879	$1.25	☐	☐	☐	☐
27880	$1.25	☐	☐	☐	☐
27883	$1.25	☐	☐	☐	☐
27884	$1.25	☐	☐	☐	☐
27885o	$1.25	☐	☐	☐	☐
27888	$1.25	☐	☐	☐	☐
27889	$1.25	☐	☐	☐	☐
27892	$1.25	☐	☐	☐	☐
27893o	$1.25	☐	☐	☐	☐
27896	$1.25	☐	☐	☐	☐
27897	$1.25	☐	☐	☐	☐
27902	$1.25	☐	☐	☐	☐
27909	$1.25	☐	☐	☐	☐
27910	$1.25	☐	☐	☐	☐
27911	$1.25	☐	☐	☐	☐
27915	$1.25	☐	☐	☐	☐
27925	$1.25	☐	☐	☐	☐
27926	$1.25	☐	☐	☐	☐
27929	$1.25	☐	☐	☐	☐
27930	$1.25	☐	☐	☐	☐
27931	$1.25	☐	☐	☐	☐
27932	$1.25	☐	☐	☐	☐
27953	$1.25	☐	☐	☐	☐
27954	$1.25	☐	☐	☐	☐
27955	$1.25	☐	☐	☐	☐
27956	$1.25	☐	☐	☐	☐

#1254a-57a 5¢ CHRISTMAS

TAGGED **2 Plates**

27885o	$5.00	☐	☐	☐	☐
27893o	$5.00	☐	☐	☐	☐

#1258 5¢ VERRAZANO BRIDGE

27945	$.50	☐	☐	☐	☐
27946	$.50	☐	☐	☐	☐
27947	$.50	☐	☐	☐	☐
27948	$.50	☐	☐	☐	☐

#1259 5¢ FINE ARTS

27933-27936	$.50	☐	☐	☐	☐
27933-27941	$.50	☐	☐	☐	☐
27934-27936	$.50	☐	☐	☐	☐
27934-27941	$.50	☐	☐	☐	☐
27935-27937	$.50	☐	☐	☐	☐
27935-27942	$.50	☐	☐	☐	☐
27940-27937	$.50	☐	☐	☐	☐
27940-27942	$.50	☐	☐	☐	☐

#1260 5¢ AMATEUR RADIO

27898	$.50	☐	☐	☐	☐
27899	$.50	☐	☐	☐	☐
27900	$.50	☐	☐	☐	☐
27901	$.50	☐	☐	☐	☐

o Issued both TAGGED and UNTAGGED

1965 COMMEMORATIVES

#1261 5¢ NEW ORLEANS

		UL	UR	LL	LR
27982	$.50	☐	☐	☐	☐
27983	$.50	☐	☐	☐	☐
27984	$.50	☐	☐	☐	☐
27985	$.50	☐	☐	☐	☐
27987	$.50	☐	☐	☐	☐
27992	$.50	☐	☐	☐	☐

#1262 5¢ SOKOL

27995	$.50	☐	☐	☐	☐
27996	$.50	☐	☐	☐	☐
27998	$.50	☐	☐	☐	☐
28002	$.50	☐	☐	☐	☐
28003	$.50	☐	☐	☐	☐
28008	$.50	☐	☐	☐	☐

#1263 5¢ CANCER CRUSADE

28036-28038	$.50	☐	☐	☐	☐
28036-28044	$.50	☐	☐	☐	☐
28037-28038	$.50	☐	☐	☐	☐
28037-28044	$.50	☐	☐	☐	☐
28043-28048	$.50	☐	☐	☐	☐
28043-28049	$.50	☐	☐	☐	☐
28047-28048	$.50	☐	☐	☐	☐
28047-28049	$.50	☐	☐	☐	☐
28054-28057	$.50	☐	☐	☐	☐
28054-28060	$.50	☐	☐	☐	☐
28055-28057	$.50	☐	☐	☐	☐
28055-28060	$.50	☐	☐	☐	☐

#1264 5¢ CHURCHILL

28104	$.50	☐	☐	☐	☐
28105	$.50	☐	☐	☐	☐
28106	$.50	☐	☐	☐	☐
28107	$.50	☐	☐	☐	☐

#1265 5¢ MAGNA CARTA

28082-28088	$.50	☐	☐	☐	☐
28082-28089	$.50	☐	☐	☐	☐
28083-28088	$.50	☐	☐	☐	☐
28083-28089	$.50	☐	☐	☐	☐
28086-28092	$.50	☐	☐	☐	☐
28086-28093	$.50	☐	☐	☐	☐
28087-28092	$.50	☐	☐	☐	☐
28087-28093	$.50	☐	☐	☐	☐

#1266 5¢ U.N. COOPERATION

28124	$.50	☐	☐	☐	☐
28127	$.50	☐	☐	☐	☐
28130	$.50	☐	☐	☐	☐
28131	$.50	☐	☐	☐	☐
28132	$.50	☐	☐	☐	☐
28133	$.50	☐	☐	☐	☐

#1267 5¢ SALVATION ARMY

		UL	UR	LL	LR
28113	$.50	☐	☐	☐	☐
28114	$.50	☐	☐	☐	☐
28117	$.50	☐	☐	☐	☐
28118	$.50	☐	☐	☐	☐
28122	$.50	☐	☐	☐	☐
28123	$.50	☐	☐	☐	☐

#1268 5¢ DANTE

28108	$.50	☐	☐	☐	☐
28109	$.50	☐	☐	☐	☐
28110	$.50	☐	☐	☐	☐
28111	$.50	☐	☐	☐	☐

#1269 5¢ HOOVER

28161	$.50	☐	☐	☐	☐
28162	$.50	☐	☐	☐	☐
28163	$.50	☐	☐	☐	☐
28164	$.50	☐	☐	☐	☐

#1270 5¢ FULTON

28145	$.50	☐	☐	☐	☐
28148	$.50	☐	☐	☐	☐
28149	$.50	☐	☐	☐	☐
28151	$.50	☐	☐	☐	☐
28160	$.50	☐	☐	☐	☐
28168	$.50	☐	☐	☐	☐

#1271 5¢ FLORIDA 32 Plates

28150-28155-28179	$.50	☐	☐	☐	☐
28150-28155-28183	$.50	☐	☐	☐	☐
28150-28159-28179	$.50	☐	☐	☐	☐
28150-28159-28183	$.50	☐	☐	☐	☐
28150-28166-28184	$.50	☐	☐	☐	☐
28150-28166-28185	$.50	☐	☐	☐	☐
28150-28169-28184	$.50	☐	☐	☐	☐
28150-28169-28185	$.50	☐	☐	☐	☐
28152-28155-28179	$.50	☐	☐	☐	☐
28152-28155-28183	$.50	☐	☐	☐	☐
28152-28159 28179	$.50	☐	☐	☐	☐
28152-28159-28183	$.50	☐	☐	☐	☐
28152-28166-28184	$.50	☐	☐	☐	☐
28152-28166-28185	$.50	☐	☐	☐	☐
28152-28169-28184	$.50	☐	☐	☐	☐
28152-28169-28185	$.50	☐	☐	☐	☐
28153-28155-28179	$.50	☐	☐	☐	☐
28153-28155-28183	$.50	☐	☐	☐	☐
28153-28159-28179	$.50	☐	☐	☐	☐
28153-28159-28183	$.50	☐	☐	☐	☐
28153-28166-28184	$.50	☐	☐	☐	☐
28153-28166-28185	$.50	☐	☐	☐	☐
28153-28169-28184	$.50	☐	☐	☐	☐
28153-28169-28185	$.50	☐	☐	☐	☐

1965 COMMEMORATIVES

#1271 5¢ FLORIDA Cont.

		UL	UR	LL	LR
28158-28155-28179	$.50	☐	☐	☐	☐
28158-28155-28183	$.50	☐	☐	☐	☐
28158-28159-28179	$.50	☐	☐	☐	☐
28158-28159-28183	$.50	☐	☐	☐	☐
28158-28166-28184	$.50	☐	☐	☐	☐
28158-28166-28185	$.50	☐	☐	☐	☐
28158-28169-28184	$.50	☐	☐	☐	☐
28158-28169-28185	$.50	☐	☐	☐	☐

#1272 5¢ TRAFFIC 24 Plates

28187-28189	$.50	☐	☐	☐	☐
28187-28192	$.50	☐	☐	☐	☐
28187-28195	$.50	☐	☐	☐	☐
28187-28201	$.50	☐	☐	☐	☐
28188-28189	$1.25	☐	☐	☐	☐
28188-28192	$1.25	☐	☐	☐	☐
28188-28195	$1.25	☐	☐	☐	☐
28188-28201	$1.25	☐	☐	☐	☐
28190-28189	$.50	☐	☐	☐	☐
28190-28192	$.50	☐	☐	☐	☐
28190-28195	$.50	☐	☐2	☐	☐
28190-28201	$.50	☐	☐2	☐	☐
28191 28189	$.50	☐	☐	☐	☐
28191-28192	$.50	☐	☐	☐	☐
28191-28195	$.50	☐	☐	☐	☐
28191-28201	$.50	☐	☐	☐	☐
28193-28189	$2.25	☐	☐	☐	☐
28193-28192	$2.25	☐	☐	☐	☐
28193-28195	$2.00	☐	☐	☐	☐
28193-28201	$2.25	☐	☐	☐	☐
28194-28189	$4.00	☐	☐	☐	☐
28194-28192	$4.00	☐	☐	☐	☐
28194-28195	$2.00	☐	☐	☐	☐
28194-28201	$2.25	☐	☐	☐	☐

#1273 5¢ J. S. COPLEY

28210	$.50	☐	☐	☐	☐
28211	$.50	☐	☐	☐	☐
28212	$.50	☐	☐	☐	☐
28213	$.50	☐	☐	☐	☐
28218	$.50	☐	☐	☐	☐
28219	$.50	☐	☐	☐	☐

#1274 11¢ I. T. U.

28143-28139	$6.00	☐	☐	☐	☐
28143-28147	$6.00	☐	☐	☐	☐
28144-28139	$6.00	☐	☐	☐	☐
28144-28147	$6.00	☐	☐	☐	☐

#1275 5¢ STEVENSON

28232	$.50	☐	☐	☐	☐
28233	$.50	☐	☐	☐	☐
28234	$2.00	☐	☐	☐	☐
28239	$.50	☐	☐	☐	☐
28240	$.50	☐	☐	☐	☐

1965 COMMEMORATIVES

#1275 5¢ STEVENSON Cont.

		UL	UR	LL	LR
28246	$.50	☐	☐	☐	☐
28258	$.50	☐	☐	☐	☐
28259	$.50	☐	☐	☐	☐
28281	$.50	☐	☐	☐	☐

#1276 5¢ CHRISTMAS

UNTAGGED

28172	$.50	☐	☐	☐	☐
28173	$.50	☐	☐	☐	☐
28174	$.50	☐	☐	☐	☐
28175	$.50	☐	☐	☐	☐
28176	$.50	☐	☐	☐	☐
28177	$.50	☐	☐	☐	☐
28178	$.50	☐	☐	☐	☐
28182	$.50	☐	☐	☐	☐
28224	$1.50	☐	☐	☐	☐
28230	$.50	☐	☐	☐	☐
28231	$.50	☐	☐	☐	☐
28235**o**	$.50	☐	☐	☐	☐
28241**o**	$.50	☐	☐	☐	☐
28251**o**	$.50	☐	☐	☐	☐
28256**o**	$.50	☐	☐	☐	☐
28275	$.50	☐	☐	☐	☐
28294	$.50	☐	☐	☐	☐

#1276a 5¢ CHRISTMAS

TAGGED

28235**o**	$7.50	☐	☐	☐	☐
28241**o**	$7.50	☐	☐	☐	☐
28251**o**	$7.50	☐	☐	☐	☐
28256**o**	$7.50	☐	☐	☐	☐

o Issued both TAGGED and UNTAGGED

1965 REGULAR ISSUE

The 1965 regular issue is also known as the Prominent American Series.

Plates before 29600 had no ZIP or MAIL EARLY markings. Plates following 29600 have these markings.

#1278 1¢ JEFFERSON 32 Plates

TAGGED Only

29450	$.20	☐	☐	☐	☐
29451	$.20	☐	☐	☐	☐
29458	$.20	☐	☐	☐	☐
29459	$.20	☐	☐	☐	☐
29479	$.20	☐	☐	☐	☐
29480	$.20	☐	☐	☐	☐
29491	$.20	☐	☐	☐	☐
29492	$.20	☐	☐	☐	☐
29997	$.20	☐	☐	☐	☐
29998	$.20	☐	☐	☐	☐
30086	$.20	☐	☐	☐	☐
30087	$.20	☐	☐	☐	☐
30946	$.20	☐	☐	☐	☐
30947	$.20	☐	☐	☐	☐
30956	$.20	☐	☐	☐	☐
30987	$.20	☐	☐	☐	☐

1965 REGULAR ISSUE

#1278 1¢ JEFFERSON Cont.

		UL	UR	LL	LR
30988	$.20	☐	☐	☐	☐
30989	$.20	☐	☐	☐	☐
30990	$.20	☐	☐	☐	☐
31006	$.20	☐	☐	☐	☐
31007	$.20	☐	☐	☐	☐
31008	$.20	☐	☐	☐	☐
31009	$.20	☐	☐	☐	☐
31301	$.20	☐	☐	☐	☐
31302	$.20	☐	☐	☐	☐
31303	$.20	☐	☐	☐	☐
31639	$.20	☐	☐	☐	☐
31640	$.20	☐	☐	☐	☐
31644	$.20	☐	☐	☐	☐
31645	$.20	☐	☐	☐	☐
37615	$.20	☐	☐	☐	☐
37616	$.20	☐	☐	☐	☐

#1279 1.25¢ GALLATIN 2 Plates

UNTAGGED Only

28930	$8.00	☐	☐	☐	☐
28931	$8.00	☐	☐	☐	☐

#1280 2¢ WRIGHT 22 Plates

TAGGED Only

28506	$.25	☐	☐	☐	☐
28507	$.25	☐	☐	☐	☐
28511	$.25	☐	☐	☐	☐
28512	$.25	☐	☐	☐	☐
29874	$.25	☐	☐	☐	☐
29875	$.25	☐	☐	☐	☐
32061	$.25	☐	☐	☐	☐
32062	$.25	☐	☐	☐	☐
32127	$.25	☐	☐	☐	☐
32128	$.25	☐	☐	☐	☐
32290	$.25	☐	☐	☐	☐
32291	$.25	☐	☐	☐	☐
32329	$.25	☐	☐	☐	☐
32330	$.25	☐	☐	☐	☐
32529	$.25	☐	☐	☐	☐
32574	$.25	☐	☐	☐	☐
32575	$.25	☐	☐	☐	☐
32576	$.25	☐	☐	☐	☐
33136	$.25	☐	☐	☐	☐
33137	$.25	☐	☐	☐	☐
37696	$.25	☐	☐	☐	☐
37697	$.25	☐	☐	☐	☐

#1281 3¢ PARKMAN 8 Plates

TAGGED

29258	$.40	☐	☐	☐	☐
29259	$.40	☐	☐	☐	☐
34243	$.40	☐	☐	☐	☐
34244	$.40	☐	☐	☐	☐
35775	$.40	☐	☐	☐	☐
35776	$.40	☐	☐	☐	☐
37623	$.40	☐	☐	☐	☐
37624	$.40	☐	☐	☐	☐

#1281a 3¢ PARKMAN 4 Plates

UNTAGGED

		UL	UR	LL	LR
36123**P**	$5	☐	☐	☐	☐
36124**P**	$5	☐	☐	☐	☐
37622**N**	$25	☐	☐	☐	☐
37625**N**	$25	☐	☐	☐	☐

P These plate numbers have been reported only on precancelled stamps.

N The UL and LR positions are precancelled Dallas, TX. The UR and LL are precancelled Seattle, WA.

#1282 4¢ LINCOLN 20 Plates

UNTAGGED

28242	$.50	☐	☐	☐	☐
28243	$.50	☐	☐	☐	☐
28244	$.50	☐	☐	☐	☐
28245	$.50	☐	☐	☐	☐
28247**o**	$.50	☐	☐	☐	☐
28248**o**	$.50	☐	☐	☐	☐
28303**o**	$.50	☐	☐	☐	☐
28304**o**	$.50	☐	☐	☐	☐
28305**o**	$.50	☐	☐	☐	☐
28306**o**	$.50	☐	☐	☐	☐
28312**o**	$15.00	☐	☐	☐	☐
28313**o**	$15.00	☐	☐	☐	☐
28314**o**	$.50	☐	☐	☐	☐
28315**o**	$.50	☐	☐	☐	☐
28329**o**	$3.00	☐	☐	☐	☐
28330**o**	$3.00	☐	☐	☐	☐
28331**o**	$3.00	☐	☐	☐	☐
28332**o**	$3.00	☐	☐	☐	☐
28600**o**	$.50	☐	☐	☐	☐
28601**o**	$.50	☐	☐	☐	☐

#1282a 4¢ LINCOLN 27 Plates

TAGGED

28247**o**	$1.50	☐	☐	☐	☐
28248**o**	$1.50	☐	☐	☐	☐
28303**o**	$.45	☐	☐	☐	☐
28304**o**	$.45	☐	☐	☐	☐
28305**o**	$.45	☐	☐	☐	☐
28306**o**	$2.00	☐	☐	☐	☐
28307	$.45	☐	☐	☐	☐
28308	$.45	☐	☐	☐	☐
28312**o**	$.45	☐	☐	☐	☐
28313**o**	$.45	☐	☐	☐	☐
28314**o**	$.45	☐	☐	☐	☐
28315**o**	$.45	☐	☐	☐	☐
28329**o**	$.45	☐	☐	☐	☐
28330**o**	$.45	☐	☐	☐	☐
28331**o**	$.45	☐	☐	☐	☐
28332**o**	$.45	☐	☐	☐	☐
28600**o**	$.45	☐	☐	☐	☐
28601**o**	$.45	☐	☐	☐	☐
28831	$.45	☐	☐	☐	☐
28832	$.45	☐	☐	☐	☐

o Issued both TAGGED and UNTAGGED

1965 REGULAR ISSUE

#1282a 4¢ LINCOLN Cont.

		UL	UR	LL	LR
28833	$.45	☐	☐	☐	☐
28834	$.45	☐	☐	☐	☐
28863	$.45	☐	☐	☐	☐
28868	$.45	☐	☐	☐	☐
28869	$.45	☐	☐	☐	☐
29407	$.45	☐	☐	☐	☐
29408	$.45	☐	☐	☐	☐

#1283 5¢ WASHINGTON 16 Plates

UNTAGGED

28349**o**	$.60	☐	☐	☐	☐
28350**o**	$.60	☐	☐	☐	☐
28351**o**	$.60	☐	☐	☐	☐
28352**o**	$.60	☐	☐	☐	☐
28353**o**	$.60	☐	☐	☐	☐
28354**o**	$.60	☐	☐	☐	☐
28355**o**	$.60	☐	☐	☐	☐
28356**o**	$.60	☐	☐	☐	☐
28357**o**	$.60	☐	☐	☐	☐
28358**o**	$.60	☐	☐	☐	☐
28360**o**	$.60	☐	☐	☐	☐
28361**o**	$.60	☐	☐	☐	☐
28363**o**	$4.00	☐	☐	☐	☐
28364**o**	$.60	☐	☐	☐	☐
28366**o**	$4.00	☐	☐	☐	☐
28367**o**	$4.00	☐	☐	☐	☐

#1283a 5¢ WASHINGTON 38 Plates

TAGGED

28349**o**	$.60	☐	☐	☐	☐
28350**o**	$.60	☐	☐	☐	☐
28351**o**	$.60	☐	☐	☐	☐
28352**o**	$.60	☐	☐	☐	☐
28353**o**	$.60	☐	☐	☐	☐
28354**o**	$.60	☐	☐	☐	☐
28355**o**	$.60	☐	☐	☐	☐
28356**o**	$.60	☐	☐	☐	☐
28357**o**	$.60	☐	☐	☐	☐
28358**o**	$5.00	☐	☐	☐	☐
28359	$.60	☐	☐	☐	☐
28360**o**	$10.00	☐	☐	☐	☐
28361**o**	$.60	☐	☐	☐	☐
28362	$.60	☐	☐	☐	☐
28363**o**	$.60	☐	☐	☐	☐
28364**o**	$.60	☐	☐	☐	☐
28366**o**	$.60	☐	☐	☐	☐
28367**o**	$.60	☐	☐	☐	☐
28369	$.60	☐	☐	☐	☐
28370	$.60	☐	☐	☐	☐
28371	$.60	☐	☐	☐	☐
28372	$.60	☐	☐	☐	☐
28373	$.60	☐	☐	☐	☐
28374	$.60	☐	☐	☐	☐
28378	$.60	☐	☐	☐	☐
28379	$.60	☐	☐	☐	☐
28380	$.60	☐	☐	☐	☐

o Issued both TAGGED and UNTAGGED

#1283a 5¢ WASHINGTON Cont.

		UL	UR	LL	LR
28381	$.60	☐	☐	☐	☐
28382	$.60	☐	☐	☐	☐
28383	$.60	☐	☐	☐	☐
28384	$.60	☐	☐	☐	☐
28385	$.60	☐	☐	☐	☐
28651	$.60	☐	☐	☐	☐
23652	$.60	☐	☐	☐	☐
28675	$10.00	☐	☐	☐	☐
28676	$10.00	☐	☐	☐	☐
28678	$10.00	☐	☐	☐	☐
28679	$10.00	☐	☐	☐	☐

#1283B 5¢ WASHINGTON 16 Plates

TAGGED **(redrawn)** SHINY GUM

29320	$.55	☐	☐	☐	☐
29323	$.55	☐	☐	☐	☐
29324	$.55	☐	☐	☐	☐
29356	$.55	☐	☐	☐	☐
29357	$.55	☐	☐	☐	☐
29362	$.55	☐	☐	☐	☐
29363	$.55	☐	☐	☐	☐
29371	$.55	☐	☐	☐	☐
38854	$.55	☐	☐	☐	☐
38855	$.55	☐	☐	☐	☐
39155	$1.50	☐	☐	☐	☐
39156	$1.50	☐	☐	☐	☐
39242	$.55	☐	☐	☐	☐
39312	$.55	☐	☐	☐	☐
39369	$1.00	☐	☐	☐	☐
39370	$1.00	☐	☐	☐	☐

#1283B 5¢ WASHINGTON 12 Plates

TAGGED **(redrawn)** DULL GUM

39412	$1.50	☐	☐	☐	☐
39413	$1.50	☐	☐	☐	☐
39425	$1.50	☐	☐	☐	☐
39426	$1.50	☐	☐	☐	☐
39467	$1.50	☐	☐	☐	☐
39468	$1.50	☐	☐	☐	☐
39550	$1.50	☐	☐	☐	☐
39551	$2.00	☐	☐	☐	☐
39556	$1.50	☐	☐	☐	☐
39557	$1.50	☐	☐	☐	☐
39584	$1.50	☐	☐	☐	☐
39585	$1.50	☐	☐	☐	☐

#1284 6¢ F.D. ROOSEVELT 6 Plates

UNTAGGED

28341**o**	$.75	☐	☐	☐	☐
28342**o**	$.75	☐	☐	☐	☐
28343**o**	$.75	☐	☐	☐	☐
28344**o**	$.75	☐	☐	☐	☐
30976**P**	$15.00	†	☐	☐	☐
31462**P**	$15.00	†	☐	☐	☐

P Issued precancelled only

1965 REGULAR ISSUE

#1284a 6¢ F.D. ROOSEVELT 57 Plates

TAGGED

		UL	UR	LL	LR
28341o	$1.25	☐	☐	☐	☐
28342o	$1.25	☐	☐	☐	☐
28343o	$1.25	☐	☐	☐	☐
28344o	$1.25	☐	☐	☐	☐
29202	$3.00	☐	☐	☐	☐
29211	$.75	☐	☐	☐	☐
29212	$.75	☐	☐	☐	☐
29232	$.75	☐	☐	☐	☐
29233	$.75	☐	☐	☐	☐
29244	$3.00	☐	☐	☐	☐
29254	$.75	☐	☐	☐	☐
29255	$.75	☐	☐	☐	☐
29481	$.75	☐	☐	☐	☐
29482	$.75	☐	☐	☐	☐
29487	$.75	☐	☐	☐	☐
29488	$.75	☐	☐	☐	☐
29496	$.75	☐	☐	☐	☐
29497	$.75	☐	☐	☐	☐
29526	$.75	☐	☐	☐	☐
29527	$4.00	☐	☐	☐	☐
29530	$.75	☐	☐	☐	☐
29531	$.75	☐	☐	☐	☐
29534	$.75	☐	☐	☐	☐
29535	$.75	☐	☐	☐	☐
29614	$.75	☐	☐	☐	☐
29615	$.75	☐	☐	☐	☐
29622	$.75	☐	☐	☐	☐
29623	$4.00	☐	☐	☐	☐
29631	$5.00	☐	☐	☐	☐
29632	$.75	☐	☐	☐	☐
29653	$.75	☐	☐	☐	☐
29654	$.75	☐	☐	☐	☐
29660	$.75	☐	☐	☐	☐
29694	$.75	☐	☐	☐	☐
30366	$.75	☐	☐	☐	☐
30367	$.75	☐	☐	☐	☐
30368	$.75	☐	☐	☐	☐
30369	$.70	☐	☐	☐	☐
30376	$.75	☐	☐	☐	☐
30377	$6.00	☐	☐	☐	☐
30400	$.75	☐	☐	☐	☐
30401	$.75	☐	☐	☐	☐
30455	$.75	☐	☐	☐	☐
30468	$10.00	☐5	☐	☐	☐
30469	$.75	☐	☐	☐	☐
30508	$.75	☐	☐	☐	☐
30509	$.75	☐	☐	☐	☐
30512	$.75	☐	☐	☐	☐
30513	$.75	☐	☐	☐	☐
30554	$.75	☐	☐	☐	☐
30555	$.75	☐	☐	☐	☐
31012	$.75	☐	☐	☐	☐
31013	$.75	☐	☐	☐	☐
31364	$.75	☐	☐	☐	☐
31365	$.75	☐	☐	☐	☐
31367	$.75	☐	☐	☐	☐
31368	$.75	☐	☐	☐	☐

#1393D 7¢ FRANKLIN 4 Plates

TAGGED Only SHINY GUM

		UL	UR	LL	LR
33412	$1.00	☐	☐	☐	☐
33413	$1.00	☐	☐	☐	☐
33422	$1.00	☐	☐	☐	☐
33423	$1.00	☐	☐	☐	☐

#1393D 7¢ FRANKLIN 2 Plates

TAGGED Only DULL GUM

39870	$2.00	☐	☐	☐	☐
39902	$2.00	☐	☐	☐	☐

#1285 8¢ EINSTEIN 4 Plates

UNTAGGED

28398o	$1.00	☐	☐	☐	☐
28399o	$1.00	☐	☐	☐	☐
28400o	$1.00	☐	☐	☐	☐
28406o	$1.00	☐	☐	☐	☐

#1285a 8¢ EINSTEIN 16 Plates

TAGGED

28398o	$1.50	☐	☐	☐	☐
28399o	$1.50	☐	☐	☐	☐
28400o	$2.50	☐	☐	☐	☐
28406o	$2.50	☐	☐	☐	☐
29341	$1.00	☐	☐	☐	☐
29342	$1.00	☐	☐	☐	☐
31896	$1.00	☐	☐	☐	☐
31913	$1.00	☐	☐	☐	☐
31914	$1.00	☐	☐	☐	☐
31915	$1.00	☐	☐	☐	☐
31916	$1.00	☐	☐	☐	☐
32048	$1.00	☐	☐	☐	☐
32049	$1.00	☐	☐	☐	☐
32179	$40.00	☐	☐	☐	☐
32180	$40.00	☐	☐	☐	☐
32201	$1.00	☐	☐	☐	☐

#1286 10¢ JACKSON 12 Plates

TAGGED

28968	$1.00	☐	☐	☐	☐
28969	$1.00	☐	☐	☐	☐
29009	$1.00	☐	☐	☐	☐
29010	$1.00	☐	☐	☐	☐
30650	$1.00	☐	☐	☐	☐
30651	$1.00	☐	☐	☐	☐
30994	$1.00	☐	☐	☐	☐
30995	$1.00	☐	☐	☐	☐
34348	$1.00	☐	☐	☐	☐
34349	$1.00	☐	☐	☐	☐
34369	$1.00	☐	☐	☐	☐
34370	$1.00	☐	☐	☐	☐

o Issued both TAGGED and UNTAGGED

1965 REGULAR ISSUE

#1286A 12¢ FORD 6 Plates

TAGGED		UL	UR	LL	LR
29548	$1.20	□	□	□	□
29549	$1.20	□	□	□	□
31266	$1.20	□	□	□	□
31267	$1.20	□	□	□	□
31911	$1.20	□	□	□	□
31912	$1.20	□	□	□	□

#1287 13¢ KENNEDY 4 Plates

TAGGED					
29113	$1.30	□	□	□	□
29114	$1.30	□	□	□	□
29392	$1.30	□	□	□	□
29393	$1.30	□	□	□	□

#1397 14¢ LaGUARDIA 4 Plates

TAGGED					
33457	$1.25	□	□	□	□
33458	$1.25	□	□	□	□
33469	$1.25	□	□	□	□
33470	$1.25	□	□	□	□

#1288 15¢ HOLMES (DIE I) 24 Plates

TAGGED					
29602	$1.60	□	□	□	□
29603	$1.60	□	□	□	□
38152	$1.60	□	□	□	□
38160	$1.60	□	□	□	□
38618	$1.60	□	□	□	□
38619	$1.60	□	□	□	□
38623	$1.60	□	□	□	□
38624	$1.60	□	□	□	□
38631	$1.60	□	□	□	□
38641	$1.60	□	□	□	□
38642	$1.60	□	□	□	□
38643	$1.60	□	□	□	□
38644	$1.60	□	□	□	□
38676	$10.00	□	□	□2	□
38677	$1.60	□	□	□	□
38678	$1.60	□	□	□	□
38902	$1.60	□	□	□	□
38904	$1.60	□	□	□	□
38936	$1.60	□	□	□	□
38957	$1.60	□	□	□	□
38959	$1.60	□	□	□	□
38960	$1.60	□	□	□	□
38972	$1.60	□	□	□	□
38973	$1.60	□	□	□	□

#1288d 15¢ HOLMES (DIE II) 8 Plates

TAGGED					
39023	$8.00	□	□	□	□
39024	$8.00	□	□	□	□
39025	$8.00	□	□	□	□
39026	$8.00	□	□	□	□

#1288d 15¢ HOLMES (DIE II) Cont.

		UL	UR	LL	LR
39043	$8.00	□	□	□	□
39044	$8.00	□	□	□	□
39069	$8.00	□	□	□	□
39070	$8.00	□	□	□	□

#1398 16¢ PYLE 4 Plates

TAGGED					
32886	$1.40	□	□	□	□
32887	$1.40	□	□	□	□
32888	$1.40	□	□	□	□
32889	$1.40	□	□	□	□

#1399 18¢ BLACKWELL 4 Plates

TAGGED					
34660	$1.50	□	□	□	□
34661	$1.50	□	□	□	□
34662	$1.50	□	□	□	□
34926	$1.50	□	□	□	□

#1289 20¢ MARSHALL 6 Plates

UNTAGGED				SHINY GUM	
29261	$1.80	□	□	□	□
29262	$1.80	□	□	□	□
29425	$1.80	□	□	□	□
29426**o**	$1.80	□	□	□	□
29773**o**	$1.80	□	□	□	□
30918**o**	$1.80	□	□	□	□

#1289a 20¢ MARSHALL 13 Plates

TAGGED				SHINY GUM	
29426**o**	$3.00	□	□	□	□
29773**o**	$1.80	□	□	□	□
30918**o**	$1.80	□	□	□	□
33964	$1.80	□	□	□	□
34103	$1.80	□	□	□	□
35342	$1.80	□	□	□	□
35343	$1.80	□	□	□	□
38536	$1.80	□	□	□	□
38537	$1.80	□	□	□	□
38873	$1.80	□	□	□	□
38915	$1.80	□	□	□	□
38938	$3.00	□	□	□	□
38939	$3.00	□	□	□	□

#1289a 20¢ MARSHALL 2 Plates

TAGGED				DULL GUM	
38938	$5.00	□	□	□	□
38939	$5.00	□	□	□	□

#1400 21¢ GIANNINI 4 Plates

TAGGED Only				SHINY GUM	
34180	$1.70	□	□	□	□
34184	$1.70	□	□	□	□
34185	$1.70	□	□	□	□
34201	$1.70	□	□	□	□

o Issued both TAGGED and UNTAGGED

1965 REGULAR ISSUE

#1290 25¢ DOUGLASS 4 Plates
UNTAGGED SHINY GUM

		UL	UR	LL	LR
28940o	$2.50	☐	☐	☐	☐
28946o	$2.50	☐	☐	☐	☐
31289o	$2.50	☐	☐	☐	☐
31290o	$2.50	☐	☐	☐	☐

#1290a 25¢ DOUGLASS 6 Plates
TAGGED SHINY GUM

28940o	$4.00	☐	☐	☐	☐
28946o	$4.00	☐	☐	☐	☐
31289o	$2.00	☐	☐	☐	☐
31290o	$2.00	☐	☐	☐	☐
37604	$2.00	☐	☐	☐	☐
37605	$2.00	☐	☐	☐	☐

#1290a 25¢ DOUGLASS 4 Plates
TAGGED DULL GUM

37604	$3.00	☐	☐	☐	☐
37605	$3.00	☐	☐	☐	☐
39378	$3.00	☐	☐	☐	☐
39432	$3.00	☐	☐	☐	☐

#1290b 25¢ DOUGLASS (maroon)**2Plates**
TAGGED SHINY GUM

37604	$50.00	☐	☐	☐	☐
37605	$50.00	☐	☐	☐	☐

#1291 30¢ DEWEY 4 Plates
UNTAGGED SHINY GUM

30320o	$3.00	☐	☐	☐	☐
30321o	$3.00	☐	☐	☐	☐
31292o	$3.00	☐	☐	☐	☐
31293o	$3.00	☐	☐	☐	☐

#1291a 30¢ DEWEY 4 Plates
TAGGED SHINY GUM

30320o	$2.50	☐	☐	☐	☐
30321o	$2.50	☐	☐	☐	☐
31292o	$2.50	☐	☐	☐	☐
31293o	$3.50	☐	☐	☐	☐

#1292 40¢ PAINE 4 Plates
UNTAGGED SHINY GUM

29537o	$3.25	☐	☐	☐	☐
29545o	$3.25	☐	☐	☐	☐
31337o	$3.25	☐	☐	☐	☐
31338o	$3.25	☐	☐	☐	☐

#1292a 40¢ PAINE 8 Plates
TAGGED SHINY GUM

29537o	$3.00	☐	☐	☐	☐
29545o	$3.00	☐	☐	☐	☐
31337o	$3.00	☐	☐	☐	☐
31338o	$3.00	☐	☐	☐	☐
34074	$3.00	☐	☐	☐	☐
37044	$3.00	☐	☐	☐	☐
37045	$3.00	☐	☐	☐	☐
37046	$3.00	☐	☐	☐	☐

#1292a 40¢ PAINE 4 Plates
TAGGED DULL GUM

29537o	$4.50	☐	☐	☐	☐
34074	$4.50	☐	☐	☐	☐
37044	$4.50	☐	☐	☐	☐
37045	$4.50	☐	☐	☐	☐

#1293 50¢ STONE 6 Plates
UNTAGGED SHINY GUM

		UL	UR	LL	LR
30133	$4.50	☐	☐	☐	☐
30134	$4.50	☐	☐	☐	☐
31588o	$4.50	☐	☐	☐	☐
31589o	$4.50	☐	☐	☐	☐
33077o	$4.50	☐	☐	☐	☐
33079o	$4.50	☐	☐	☐	☐

#1293a 50¢ STONE 4 Plates
TAGGED SHINY GUM

31588o	$4.00	☐	☐	☐	☐
31589o	$4.00	☐	☐	☐	☐
33077o	$4.00	☐	☐	☐	☐
33079o	$4.00	☐	☐	☐	☐

#1294 $1 O'NEILL 8 Plates
UNTAGGED SHINY GUM

29105	$10.00	☐	☐	☐	☐
29264	$10.00	☐	☐	☐	☐
31613	$10.00	☐	☐	☐	☐
31614	$10.00	☐	☐	☐	☐
32847o	$10.00	☐	☐	☐	☐
32848o	$10.00	☐	☐	☐	☐
32902o	$12.50	☐	☐	☐	☐
32903o	$12.50	☐	☐	☐	☐

#1294a $1 O'NEILL 8 Plates
TAGGED SHINY GUM

32847o	$8.00	☐	☐	☐	☐
32848o	$8.00	☐	☐	☐	☐
32902o	$12.50	☐	☐	☐	☐
32903o	$12.50	☐	☐	☐	☐
37564	$8.00	☐	☐	☐	☐
37565	$8.00	☐	☐	☐	☐
37994	$8.00	☐	☐	☐	☐
37995	$8.00	☐	☐	☐	☐

#1295 $5 MOORE 2 Plates
UNTAGGED SHINY GUM

28766o	$40.00	☐	☐	☐	☐
28767o	$40.00	☐	☐	☐	☐

#1295a $5 MOORE 2 Plates
TAGGED SHINY GUM

28766o	$30.00	☐	☐	☐	☐
28767o	$30.00	☐	☐	☐	☐

o Issued both TAGGED and UNTAGGED

Much of our plate number information stems from studies made by members of the Bureau Issues Association and published in their magazine. Serious plate number collectors should join this organization. For further information write to:

Executive Secretary
P.O. Box 2641, Reston, VA 20195

1965 REGULAR ISSUE

BOOKLET PANES

#1278a 1¢ JEFFERSON PANES OF 8

320 Subject Plates

†29440 †29441 †29444 †29445 †29477
†29478 †29596 †29597 †29644 †29645
†29646 †29647 *29674 †29675 †30309
†30310

400 Subject Plates

†30330 †30331 †30335 †30336 *30656
†30657 †30911 †30912 †31743 †31744
†31745 †31746 †31774 *31775

#1278b 1¢ JEFFERSON PANES OF 4

400 Subject Plates

32904 32905 32906 32907

#1280a 2¢ WRIGHT PANES OF 5

360 Subject Plates

Slogan 4 "Mail Early"

29558 29562

Slogan 5 "Use ZIP Code"

29559 29561

#1280c 2¢ WRIGHT PANES OF 6

360 Subject Plates SHINY GUM

32966 32967 32996 32997 33985
34102

360 Subject Plates DULL GUM

33985 34102 36882 36883 36884
†36885

#1284b 6¢ ROOSEVELT PANES OF 8

320 Subject Plates

†29397 †29398 †29455 †29456 †29463
†29464 †29498 †29499 †29521 †29522
†29528 †29529 †29538 †29539 †29540
†29541 †29550 †29551 †29676 †29677
†29680 †29681 †29698 †29699 †29703
†29704 †29710 †29711 †29713 †29714
†29732 †29733 †30109 †30110 †30113
†30114 †30115 †30307 †30308 †30324
†30325 †30409 †30410 †30641 †30642
†30666 †30667 †30682 †30683 †30699
†30700 †30776 †30777 †30784 †30785

400 Subject Plates

†30136 *30137 *30199 *30200 *30281
*30282 *30603 *30604 †30652 †30653
*30670 †30792 *30803 †30813 †30814
†30823 †30824 †30834 *30835 †30848
†30849 †31014 †31015 †31795 †31872

#1284c 6¢ ROOSEVELT PANES OF 5

360 Subject Plates

Slogan 4 "Mail Early"

*29556 *29566 †31244

Slogan 5 "Use ZIP Code"

*29557 *29565

#1288c 15¢ HOLMES PANES OF 8

288 Subject Plates DULL GUM

†38658 †38659 †38660 †38661 †38674
†38675 †38681 †38682 †38683 †38684
†38745 †38746 †38828 †38829 †38830
†38831 †38846 †38847 †38848 †38849
†38878 †38879 †38970 †38971 †39045
†39046 †39059 †39060 †39067 †39068

See Appendix G for largest reported plate number percentage by position.

END COILS

PERF. 10 HORIZONTALLY

432 Subject Plates **STRIPS OF 6**

#1297 3¢ PARKMAN 12 Plates

SHINY and DULL GUM

35708 35709 35762 35763 36090
36091 36092 36093 †38423 †38483
†38492 38493

#1298 6¢ F.D. ROOSEVELT 48 Plates

†29138 †29139 29155 29166 29167
29168 †29171 †29172 †29175 †29176
†29178 †29179 †29188 29190 29191
29194 29195 29215 †29238 29533
†29554 †29555 29572 29573 29574
29575 †29577 †29578 29582 29583
†29584 †29585 †29606 †29607 29611
29612 29625 †29626 †29628 29629
29636 29637 29638 29639 29640
29641 29651 29652

SIDE COILS

PERF. 10 VERTICALLY

432 Subject Plates **STRIPS OF 6**

#1299 1¢ JEFFERSON 30 Plates

29452 29453 29460 29461 29483
29484 29489 29490 30974 30975
†32288 †32289 33404 33696 33903
33904 †37608 †37609 †37654 †37655
38427 38428 38495 38496 38550
38551 †38914 †39021 †39073 †39074

#1303 4¢ LINCOLN 14 Plates

28271 28272 28273 28309 28699
28700 28902 28903 †28952 †28953
29024 29025 †29302 †29303

1965 REGULAR ISSUE

SIDE COILS

432 Subject Plates **STRIPS OF 6**

#1304 5¢ WASHINGTON 136 Plates

SHINY GUM

†28546 †28547 28558 28559 †28563
28564 28565 †28566 28573 28574
†28583 †28584 †28585 †28586 28589
28590 28594 28595 †28596 †28597
28701 28702 28703 28704 28748
28749 28805 28806 †28811 †28812
28825 28826 28871 28872 28879
28880 †28886 †28887 †28891 †28892
28896 28897 28900 †28901 28906
†28907 28909 28910 28912 †28913
†28916 28917 28923 †28924 †28926
28927 †28928 28929 †28932 †28933
†28934 †28935 †28936 †28937 28938
†28939 28942 28943 28947 28948
28949 †28950 †28959 28960 28961
28962 28964 †28965 28973 †28974
29039 29040 29059 29060 29062
29063 29066 29067 29068 29069
29077 29078 29079 29080 29081
†29082 29083 29084 29088 28089
29108 29109 29119 29120 †29150
†29151 †29156 †29157 †29219 †29220
†29273 †29274 29281 29282 †29285
†29286 †29290 †29291 †29338 †29339
29347 29348 †29360 †29361 †29386
†29387 29402 29403 29404 29405
†29410 †29411 29415 29416 29422
29423

#1304 5¢ WASHINGTON 9 Plates

DULL GUM

†39451 †39452 †39455 †39456 †39552
†39553 39555 39558 †39573

#1304C 5¢ WASHINGTON 2 Plates

DULL GUM **(redrawn)**

39479 39480

#1305 6¢ F.D. ROOSEVELT 220 Plates

SHINY GUM

29663 29664 29665 29666 29667
29668 29669 29670 29671 29672
29685 29686 29687 29688 29689
29690 29696 29697 29708 29709
†29724 †29725 29734 29735 †29747
†29748 †29770 †29771 †29776 †29777
†29783 †29784 †29788 †29789 †29797
†29798 †29804 29805 †29812 †29813
†29815 29816 29828 29829 29840
29841 29848 29849 †29853 29854
29855 †29856 †29866 †29867 29883
29884 29916 29917 29937 29938
†29960 †29981 †29982 30029 †30030
30037 †30038 †30053 †30054 30066
†30067 30083 30084 †30090 †30091
†30107 †30108 †30118 †30119 30148
†30149 30150 30151 †30158 †30159

SIDE COILS

#1305 6¢ F.D. ROOSEVELT Cont.

30167 30168 30171 30172 30187
30188 30196 †30197 30214 30215
30264 30265 30292 30293 30352
30353 †30361 30362 30364 30390
†30391 30402 30403 30407 30408
†30429 †30430 30443 30444 30478
30479 30496 30497 30500 †30501
†30519 30520 30529 30530 30537
†30538 †30539 30540 30545 30546
†30549 30550 30568 †30569 †30584
†30585 30600 30601 †30639 †30640
†30661 30662 †30674 30675 30676
30677 30678 30679 30688 30689
30691 30692 30721 30722 30754
30755 30787 30788 30797 30798
30826 30827 30844 30845 †30860
30861 30869 30870 †30878 30879
30881 30882 30884 30885 †30890
†30891 †30902 †30903 †30919 †30920
30935 30936 30939 30940 30943
†30959 †30960 †30971 †30972 †31243
31342 31343 31348 31349 31362
31363 31379 31380 31421 31422
†31427 †31428 31434 31435 †31438
†31439 31445 31446 †31450 †31451
31466 31467 †31471 †31477 31535
31536 †31543 †31544 †31573 †31574

#1305E 15¢ HOLMES (DIE I) 36 Plates

SHINY GUM

38625 38626 38628 38629 38645
38646 38647 38648 38679 38680
38690 38691 38760 38761 †38768
38769 38770 38775 38776 38780
38781 38782 38783 38784 †38785
38786 38814 38815 38816 38817
38818 †38819 38835 †38836 †38837
38838

#1305E 15¢ HOLMES (DIE I) 11 Plates

DULL GUM

38770 38922 †38923 †38932 †38933
†38934 †38935 38961 38962 †38963
†38964

#1305i 15¢ HOLMES (DIE II) 30 Plates

DULL GUM

38992 38993 38994 39027 †39028
†39029 †39030 39031 39041 39042
†39061 †39062 †39065 †39066 †39071
39103 39104 †39165 †39433 †39434
†39435 †39436 †39473 †39474 †39481
†39482 †39491 †39492 †39510 †39511

#1305C $1 O'NEILL 2 Plates

SHINY GUM

33983 33984

DULL GUM

33983 33984

1966 COMMEMORATIVES

#1306 5¢ MIGRATORY BIRDS

		UL	UR	LL	LR
28394-28395	$.50	☐	☐	☐	☐
28394-28401	$.50	☐	☐	☐	☐
28396-28395	$.50	☐	☐	☐	☐
28396-28401	$.50	☐	☐	☐	☐
28402-28408	$.50	☐	☐	☐	☐
28402-28409	$.50	☐	☐	☐	☐
28407-28408	$.50	☐	☐	☐	☐
28407-28409	$.50	☐	☐	☐	☐

#1307 5¢ HUMANE TREATMENT

28413	$1.25	☐	☐	☐	☐
28417	$.50	☐	☐	☐	☐
28418	$.50	☐	☐	☐	☐
28419	$.50	☐	☐	☐	☐
28420	$.50	☐	☐	☐	☐
28425	$.50	☐	☐	☐	☐
28429	$.50	☐	☐	☐	☐
28462	$.50	☐	☐	☐	☐
28466	$.50	☐	☐	☐	☐

#1308 5¢ INDIANA

28326-28365	$.50	☐	☐	☐	☐
28326-28368	$.50	☐	☐	☐	☐
28326-28375	$.50	☐	☐	☐	☐
28327-28365	$.50	☐	☐	☐	☐
28327-28368	$.50	☐	☐	☐	☐
28327-28375	$.50	☐	☐	☐	☐
28328-28334	$.50	☐	☐	☐	☐
28328-28347	$.50	☐	☐	☐	☐
28328-28348	$.50	☐	☐	☐	☐
28333-28334	$.50	☐	☐	☐	☐
28333-28347	$.50	☐	☐	☐	☐
28333-28348	$.50	☐	☐	☐	☐

#1309 5¢ CIRCUS

28450-28460	$.50	☐	☐	☐	☐
28450-28461	$.50	☐	☐	☐	☐
28458-28460	$.50	☐	☐	☐	☐
28458-28461	$.50	☐	☐	☐	☐
28459-28460	$.50	☐	☐	☐	☐
28459-28461	$.50	☐	☐	☐	☐
28463-28467	$.50	☐	☐	☐	☐
28463-28473	$.50	☐	☐	☐	☐
28486-28467	$.50	☐	☐	☐	☐
28486-28473	$.50	☐	☐	☐	☐
28488-28467	$.50	☐	☐	☐	☐
28488-28473	$.50	☐	☐	☐	☐

#1310 5¢ SIPEX

28468	$.50	☐	☐	☐	☐
28474	$.50	☐	☐	☐	☐
28479	$.50	☐	☐	☐	☐
28482	$.50	☐	☐	☐	☐
28522	$.50	☐	☐	☐	☐
28531	$.50	☐	☐	☐	☐

#1311 5¢ SIPEX SHEET (Imperf.)

The plate numbers of this souvenir sheet were trimmed off after printing so no plate numbers were regularly issued.

#1312 5¢ BILL OF RIGHTS

		UL	UR	LL	LR
28572-28580	$.50	☐	☐	☐	☐
28572-28582	$.50	☐	☐	☐	☐
28572-28588	$.50	☐	☐	☐	☐
28578-28580	$.50	☐	☐	☐	☐
28578-28582	$.50	☐	☐	☐	☐
28578-28588	$.50	☐	☐	☐	☐
28579-28580	$.50	☐	☐	☐	☐
28579-28582	$.50	☐	☐	☐	☐
28579-28588	$.50	☐	☐	☐	☐
28581-28593	$.50	☐	☐	☐	☐
28581-28618	$.50	☐	☐	☐	☐
28581-28621	$.50	☐	☐	☐	☐
28607-28593	$.50	☐	☐	☐	☐
28607-28618	$.50	☐	☐	☐	☐
28607-28621	$.50	☐	☐	☐	☐
28610-28593	$.50	☐	☐	☐	☐
28610-28618	$.50	☐	☐	☐	☐
28610-28621	$.50	☐	☐	☐	☐

#1313 5¢ POLISH MILLENNIUM

28625	$.50	☐	☐	☐	☐
28626	$.50	☐	☐	☐	☐
28629	$.50	☐	☐	☐	☐
28630	$.50	☐	☐	☐	☐

#1314 5¢ NATIONAL PARK SERVICE

UNTAGGED

28632**o**	$.50	☐	☐	☐	☐
28637**o**	$.50	☐	☐	☐	☐
28642**o**	$.50	☐	☐	☐	☐
28649**o**	$.50	☐	☐	☐	☐
28668**o**	$.50	☐	☐	☐	☐
28670**o**	$.50	☐	☐	☐	☐

#1314a 5¢ NATIONAL PARK SERVICE

TAGGED

28632**o**	$2.00	☐	☐	☐	☐
28637**o**	$10.00	☐	☐	☐	☐
28642**o**	$2.00	☐	☐	☐	☐
28649**o**	$2.00	☐	☐	☐	☐
28668**o**	$2.00	☐	☐	☐	☐
28670**o**	$4.50	☐	☐	☐	☐

#1315 5¢ MARINE CORPS RESERVE

UNTAGGED

28638**o**	$.50	☐	☐	☐	☐
28639**o**	$.50	☐	☐	☐	☐
28640**o**	$.50	☐	☐	☐	☐
28646**o**	$.50	☐	☐	☐	☐
28647**o**	$.50	☐	☐	☐	☐
28648**o**	$.50	☐	☐	☐	☐
28720**o**	$2.00	☐	☐	☐	☐
28721**o**	$4.00	☐	☐	☐	☐

o Issued both TAGGED and UNTAGGED

1966 COMMEMORATIVES

#1315a 5¢ MARINE CORPS RESERVE
TAGGED

		UL	UR	LL	LR
28638o	$2	☐	☐	☐	☐
28639o	$2	☐	☐	☐	☐
28640o	$2	☐	☐	☐	☐
28646o	$2	☐	☐	☐	☐
28647o	$2	☐	☐	☐	☐
28648o	$2	☐	☐	☐	☐
28720o	$7	☐	☐	☐	☐
28721o	$10	☐	☐	☐	☐

#1316 5¢ WOMEN'S CLUBS
UNTAGGED

28705-28707o	$.60	☐	☐	☐	☐
28705-28712o	$.60	☐	☐	☐	☐
28705-28714o	$.60	☐	☐	☐	☐
28706-28707o	$.60	☐	☐	☐	☐
28706-28712o	$.60	☐	☐	☐	☐
28706-28714o	$.60	☐	☐	☐	☐
28708-28707o	$.60	☐	☐	☐	☐
28708-28712o	$.60	☐	☐	☐	☐
28708-28714o	$.60	☐	☐	☐	☐
28711-28707o	$.60	☐	☐	☐	☐
28711-28712o	$.60	☐	☐	☐	☐
28711-28714o	$.60	☐	☐	☐	☐
28713-28724o	$.60	☐	☐	☐	☐
28713-28726o	$.60	☐	☐	☐	☐
28713-28728o	$.60	☐	☐	☐	☐
28715-28724o	$.60	☐	☐	☐	☐
28715-28726o	$.60	☐	☐	☐	☐
28715-28728o	$.60	☐	☐	☐	☐
28722-28724o	$.60	☐	☐	☐	☐
28722-28726o	$.60	☐	☐	☐	☐
28722-28728o	$.60	☐	☐	☐	☐
28723-28724o	$.60	☐	☐	☐	☐
28723-28726o	$.60	☐	☐	☐	☐
28723-28728o	$.60	☐	☐	☐	☐

#1316a 5¢ WOMEN'S CLUBS
TAGGED

28705-28707o	$7.50	☐	☐	☐	☐
28705-28712o	$10.00	☐	☐	☐	☐
28705-28714o	$2.00	☐	☐	☐	☐
28706-28707o	$7.50	☐	☐	☐	☐
28706-28712o	$10.00	☐	☐	☐	☐
28706-28714o	$2.00	☐	☐	☐	☐
28708-28707o	$7.50	☐	☐	☐	☐
28708-28712o	$10.00	☐	☐	☐	☐
28708-28714o	$2.00	☐	☐	☐	☐
28711-28707o	$7.50	☐	☐	☐	☐
28711-28712o	$10.00	☐	☐	☐	☐
28711-28714o	$2.00	☐	☐	☐	☐
28713-28724o	$2.00	☐	☐	☐	☐
28713-28726o	$2.00	☐	☐	☐	☐
28713-28728o	$2.00	☐	☐	☐	☐

#1316a 5¢ WOMEN'S CLUBS Cont.

		UL	UR	LL	LR
28715-28724o	$2	☐	☐	☐	☐
28715-28726o	$2	☐	☐	☐	☐
28715-28728o	$2	☐	☐	☐	☐
28722-28724o	$2	☐	☐	☐	☐
28722-28726o	$2	☐	☐	☐	☐
28722-28728o	$2	☐	☐	☐	☐
28723-28724o	$2	☐	☐	☐	☐
28723-28726o	$2	☐	☐	☐	☐
28723-28728o	$2	☐	☐	☐	☐

#1317 5¢ JOHNNY APPLESEED
UNTAGGED

28669-28673o	$.60	☐	☐	☐	☐
28669-28674o	$.60	☐	☐	☐	☐
28669-28677o	$.60	☐	☐	☐	☐
28671-28673o	$.60	☐	☐	☐	☐
28671-28674o	$.60	☐	☐	☐	☐
28671-28677o	$.60	☐	☐	☐	☐
28672-28686o	$.60	☐	☐	☐	☐
28672-28718o	$.60	☐	☐	☐	☐
28672-28719o	$.60	☐	☐	☐	☐
28683-28686o	$.60	☐	☐	☐	☐
28683-28718o	$.60	☐	☐	☐	☐
28683-28719o	$.60	☐	☐	☐	☐

#1317a 5¢ JOHNNY APPLESEED
TAGGED

28669-28673o	$5.00	☐	☐	☐	☐
28669-28674o	$6.00	☐	☐	☐	☐
28669-28677o	$2.00	☐	☐	☐	☐
28671-28673o	$4.00	☐	☐	☐	☐
28671-28674o	$4.50	☐	☐	☐	☐
28671-28677o	$2.00	☐	☐	☐	☐
28672-28686o	$2.00	☐	☐	☐	☐
28672-28718o	$4.50	☐	☐	☐	☐
28672-28719o	$5.00	☐	☐	☐	☐
28683-28686o	$2.00	☐	☐	☐	☐
28683-28718o	$4.50	☐	☐	☐	☐
28683-28719o	$5.00	☐	☐	☐	☐

#1318 5¢ U.S. BEAUTIFICATION
UNTAGGED **32 Plates**

28727-28733o	$.60	☐	☐	☐	☐
28727-28736o	$.60	☐	☐	☐	☐
28727-28775o	$.60	☐	☐	☐	☐
28727-28779o	$.60	☐	☐	☐	☐
28727-28780	$.60	☐	☐	☐	☐
28727-28781	$.60	☐	☐	☐	☐
28727-28786	$.60	☐	☐	☐	☐
28727-28788	$.60	☐	☐	☐	☐
28729-28733o	$.60	☐	☐	☐	☐
28729-28736o	$.60	☐	☐	☐	☐
28729-28775o	$.60	☐	☐	☐	☐

o Issued both TAGGED and UNTAGGED

1966 COMMEMORATIVES

#1318 5¢ U. S. BEAUTIFICATION Cont.

		UL	UR	LL	LR
28729-28779**o**	$.60	☐	☐	☐	☐
28729-28780	$.60	☐	☐	☐	☐
28729-28781	$.60	☐	☐	☐	☐
28729-28786	$.60	☐	☐	☐	☐
28729-28788	$.60	☐	☐	☐	☐
28732-28733	$.60	☐	☐	☐	☐
28732-28736	$.60	☐	☐	☐	☐
28732-28775	$.60	☐	☐	☐	☐
28732-28779	$.60	☐	☐	☐	☐
28732-28780	$.60	☐	☐	☐	☐
28732-28781	$.60	☐	☐	☐	☐
28732-28786	$.60	☐	☐	☐	☐
28732-28788	$.60	☐	☐	☐	☐
28735-28733	$.60	☐	☐	☐	☐
28735-28736	$.60	☐	☐	☐	☐
28735-28775	$.60	☐	☐	☐	☐
28735-28779	$.60	☐	☐	☐	☐
28735-28780	$.60	☐	☐	☐	☐
28735-28781	$.60	☐	☐	☐	☐
28735-28786	$.60	☐	☐	☐	☐
28735-28788	$.60	☐	☐	☐	☐

#1318a 5¢ U.S. BEAUTIFICATION

TAGGED

28727-28733**o**	$2	☐	☐	☐	☐
28727-28736**o**	$2	☐	☐	☐	☐
28727-28775**o**	$2	☐	☐	☐	☐
28727-28779**o**	$2	☐	☐	☐	☐
28729-28733**o**	$2	☐	☐	☐	☐
28729-28736**o**	$2	☐	☐	☐	☐
28729-28775**o**	$2	☐	☐	☐	☐
28729-28779**o**	$2	☐	☐	☐	☐

#1319 5¢ GREAT RIVER ROAD

UNTAGGED

28813	$.50	☐	☐	☐	☐
28816	$.50	☐	☐	☐	☐
28817	$.50	☐	☐	☐	☐
28820	$.50	☐	☐	☐	☐
28821**o**	$.50	☐	☐	☐	☐
28828**o**	$.50	☐	☐	☐	☐
28829**o**	$.50	☐	☐	☐	☐
28840**o**	$.50	☐	☐	☐	☐
28844	$.50	☐	☐	☐	☐
28884	$.50	☐	☐	☐	☐

#1319a 5¢ GREAT RIVER ROAD

TAGGED

28821**o**	$2	☐	☐	☐	☐
28828**o**	$2	☐	☐	☐	☐
28829**o**	$2	☐	☐	☐	☐
28840**o**	$2	☐	☐	☐	☐

#1320 5¢ SAVINGS BONDS

UNTAGGED

		UL	UR	LL	LR
28741**o**	$.50	☐	☐	☐	☐
28752**o**	$.50	☐	☐	☐	☐
28754**o**	$.50	☐	☐	☐	☐
28759	$.50	☐	☐	☐	☐
28761	$.50	☐	☐	☐	☐
28763	$.50	☐	☐	☐	☐
28769**o**	$.50	☐	☐	☐	☐
28772	$.50	☐	☐	☐	☐

#1320a 5¢ SAVINGS BONDS

TAGGED

28741**o**	$2	☐	☐	☐	☐
28752**o**	$2	☐	☐	☐	☐
28754**o**	$2	☐	☐	☐	☐
28769**o**	$2	☐	☐	☐	☐

#1321 5¢ CHRISTMAS 29 Plates

UNTAGGED

28739**o**	$1.00	☐	☐	☐	☐
28740	$.50	☐	☐	☐	☐
28743**o**	$.50	☐	☐	☐	☐
28745**o**	$.50	☐	☐	☐	☐
28747	$2.00	☐	☐	☐	☐
28751**o**	$1.00	☐	☐	☐	☐
28753**o**	$.50	☐	☐	☐	☐
28756	$.50	☐	☐	☐	☐
28758**o**	$ 50	☐	☐	☐	☐
28760**o**	$.50	☐	☐	☐	☐
28762	$.50	☐	☐	☐	☐
28768	$.50	☐	☐	☐	☐
28771	$.50	☐	☐	☐	☐
28808	$.50	☐	☐	☐	☐
28810	$.50	☐	☐	☐	☐
28815	$.50	☐	☐	☐	☐
28818	$.50	☐	☐	☐	☐
28822	$.50	☐	☐	☐	☐
28827	$.50	☐	☐	☐	☐
28830	$.50	☐	☐	☐	☐
28836	$.50	☐	☐	☐	☐
28839	$.50	☐	☐	☐	☐
28870	$.50	☐	☐	☐	☐
28875	$.50	☐	☐	☐	☐
28877	$.50	☐	☐	☐	☐
28883**o**	$6.00	☐	☐	☐	☐
28889**o**	$6.00	☐	☐	☐	☐
28890**o**	$6.00	☐	☐	☐	☐
28893**o**	$6.00	☐	☐	☐	☐

o Issued both TAGGED and UNTAGGED

1966 COMMEMORATIVES

#1321a 5¢ CHRISTMAS

TAGGED		UL	UR	LL	LR
28739**o**	$4.00	☐	☐	☐	☐
28743**o**	$2.00	☐	☐	☐	☐
28745**o**	$7.50	☐	☐	☐	☐
28751**o**	$4.00	☐	☐	☐	☐
28753**o**	$2.00	☐	☐	☐	☐
28758**o**	$4.00	☐	☐	☐	☐
28760**o**	$4.00	☐	☐	☐	☐
28883**o**	$2.00	☐	☐	☐	☐
28889**o**	$2.00	☐	☐	☐	☐
28890**o**	$5.00	☐	☐	☐	☐
28893**o**	$5.00	☐	☐	☐	☐

#1322 5¢ MARY CASSATT

UNTAGGED					
28776 28793	$1	☐	☐	☐	☐
28776-28802	$1	☐	☐	☐	☐
28782 28793	$1	☐	☐	☐	☐
28782-28802	$1	☐	☐	☐	☐
28785-28793	$1	☐	☐	☐	☐
28785-28802	$1	☐	☐	☐	☐
28792-28807**o**	$1	☐	☐	☐	☐
28792-28809**o**	$1	☐	☐	☐	☐
28876 28807**o**	$1	☐	☐	☐	☐
28876-28809**o**	$1	☐	☐	☐	☐
28878-28807	$1	☐	☐	☐	☐
28878-28809	$1	☐	☐	☐	☐

#1322a 5¢ MARY CASSATT

TAGGED					
28792-28807**o**	$2.00	☐	☐	☐	☐
28792-28809**o**	$2.00	☐	☐	☐	☐
28876-28807**o**	$2.00	☐	☐	☐	☐
28876-28809**o**	$2.00	☐	☐	☐	☐

o Issued both TAGGED and UNTAGGED

From #1323 to date all issues are TAGGED unless otherwise designated

1967 COMMEMORATIVES

#1323 5¢ NATIONAL GRANGE

28951-28954	$.50	☐	☐	☐	☐
28951-28956	$.50	☐	☐	☐	☐
28955-28954	$.50	☐	☐	☐	☐
28955-28956	$.50	☐	☐	☐	☐
28957-28958	$.50	☐	☐	☐	☐
28957-28972	$.50	☐	☐	☐	☐
28963-28958	$.50	☐	☐	☐	☐
28963-28972	$.50	☐	☐	☐	☐

#1324 5¢ CANADA 42 Plates

28979 29090	$.50	☐	☐	☐	☐
28979-29091	$.50	☐	☐	☐	☐
28979-29094	$.50	☐	☐	☐	☐
28979-29097	$.50	☐	☐	☐	☐

1967 COMMEMORATIVES

#1324 5¢ CANADA Cont.

		UL	UR	LL	LR
28980-29090	$.50	☐	☐	☐	☐
28980-29091	$.50	☐	☐	☐	☐
28980-29094	$.50	☐	☐	☐	☐
28980-29097	$.50	☐	☐	☐	☐
28982-29090	$.50	☐	☐	☐	☐
28982-29091	$.50	☐	☐	☐	☐
28982-29094	$.50	☐	☐	☐	☐
28982-29097	$.50	☐	☐	☐	☐
28985-29090	$.50	☐	☐	☐	☐
28985-29091	$.50	☐	☐	☐	☐
28985-29094	$.50	☐	☐	☐	☐
28985-29097	$.50	☐	☐	☐	☐
28987-29074	$.50	☐	☐	☐	☐
28987-29075	$.50	☐	☐	☐	☐
28987-29076	$.50	☐	☐	☐	☐
28987-29086	$.50	☐	☐	☐	☐
28988-29074	$.50	☐	☐	☐	☐
28988-29075	$.50	☐	☐	☐	☐
28988-29076	$.50	☐	☐	☐	☐
28988-29086	$.50	☐	☐	☐	☐
28991-29074	$.50	☐	☐	☐	☐
28991-29075	$.50	☐	☐	☐	☐
28991-29076	$.50	☐	☐	☐	☐
28991-29086	$.50	☐	☐	☐	☐
28994-29074	$.50	☐	☐	☐	☐
28994-29075	$.50	☐	☐	☐	☐
28994-29076	$.50	☐	☐	☐	☐
28994-29086	$.50	☐	☐	☐	☐
29110-29137	$.50	☐	☐	☐	☐
29110-29146	$.50	☐	☐	☐	☐
29121-29147	$.50	☐	☐	☐	☐
29121-29153	$.50	☐	☐	☐	☐
29125-29137	$.50	☐	☐	☐	☐
29125-29146	$.50	☐	☐	☐	☐
29133-29147	$.50	☐	☐	☐	☐
29133-29153	$.50	☐	☐	☐	☐
29173-29137	$.50	☐	☐	☐	☐
29173-29146	$.50	☐	☐	☐	☐

#1325 5¢ ERIE CANAL

28990	$.50	☐	☐	☐	☐
28995	$.50	☐	☐	☐	☐
28998	$.50	☐	☐	☐	☐
28999	$.50	☐	☐	☐	☐
29003	$.50	☐	☐	☐	☐
29008	$.50	☐	☐	☐	☐

#1326 5¢ SEARCH FOR PEACE

29227	$.50	☐	☐	☐	☐
29239	$.50	☐	☐	☐	☐
29243	$.50	☐	☐	☐	☐
29246	$.50	☐	☐	☐	☐
29247	$.50	☐	☐	☐	☐

1967 COMMEMORATIVES

#1326 5¢ SEARCH FOR PEACE Cont.

Plate	Price	UL	UR	LL	LR
29248	$.50	☐	☐	☐	☐
29250	$.50	☐	☐	☐	☐
29256	$.50	☐	☐	☐	☐
29265	$.50	☐	☐	☐	☐
29266	$.50	☐	☐	☐	☐

#1327 5¢ THOREAU

Plate	Price	UL	UR	LL	LR
29106	$.50	☐	☐	☐	☐
29129	$.50	☐	☐	☐	☐
29136	$.50	☐	☐	☐	☐
29140	$.50	☐	☐	☐	☐
29143	$.50	☐	☐	☐	☐
29144	$.50	☐	☐	☐	☐
29145	$.50	☐	☐	☐	☐
29148	$.50	☐	☐	☐	☐

#1328 5¢ NEBRASKA

Plate	Price	UL	UR	LL	LR
29198	$.50	☐	☐	☐	☐
29199	$.50	☐	☐	☐	☐
29203	$.50	☐	☐	☐	☐
29206	$.50	☐	☐	☐	☐
29210	$.50	☐	☐	☐	☐
29216	$.50	☐	☐	☐	☐
29221	$.50	☐	☐	☐	☐
29223	$.50	☐	☐	☐	☐

#1329 5¢ VOICE OF AMERICA

Plate	Price	UL	UR	LL	LR
29038	$.50	☐	☐	☐	☐
29043	$.50	☐	☐	☐	☐
29048	$.50	☐	☐	☐	☐
29052	$.50	☐	☐	☐	☐

#1330 5¢ DAVY CROCKETT

Plate	Price	UL	UR	LL	LR
29222	$.50	☐	☐	☐	☐
29224	$.50	☐	☐	☐	☐
29235	$.50	☐	☐	☐	☐
29242	$.50	☐	☐	☐	☐

#1331-32 5¢ SPACE

Plate	Price	UL	UR	LL	LR
29307	$4	☐	☐	☐	☐
29312	$4	☐	☐	☐	☐
29315	$4	☐	☐	☐	☐
29322	$4	☐	☐	☐	☐
29325	$4	☐	☐	☐	☐

#1333 5¢ URBAN RENEWAL

Plate	Price	UL	UR	LL	LR
29349	$.50	☐	☐	☐	☐
29350	$.50	☐	☐	☐	☐
29359	$.50	☐	☐	☐	☐
29364	$.50	☐	☐	☐	☐
29367	$.50	☐	☐	☐	☐
29369	$.50	☐	☐	☐	☐

#1334 5¢ FINLAND

Plate	Price	UL	UR	LL	LR
29305	$.50	☐	☐	☐	☐
29306	$.50	☐	☐	☐	☐
29308	$.50	☐	☐	☐	☐
29311	$.50	☐	☐	☐	☐
29313	$.50	☐	☐	☐	☐
29314	$.50	☐	☐	☐	☐
29316	$.50	☐	☐	☐	☐
29321	$.50	☐	☐	☐	☐
29365	$.50	☐	☐	☐	☐
29366	$.50	☐	☐	☐	☐

#1335 5¢ EAKINS

This issue was printed at the Photogravure and Color Co. by the gravure method.

Plate	Price	UL	UR	LL	LR
29275-29276-29277-29278-29279-29280	$5.00	☐	☐	☐	☐
29275-29276-29277-29278-29333-29280	$1.00	☐	☐	☐	☐

#1336 5¢ CHRISTMAS 42 Plates

Plate	Price	UL	UR	LL	LR
29093	$.50	☐	☐	☐	☐
29095	$.50	☐	☐	☐	☐
29098	$.50	☐	☐	☐	☐
29099	$.50	☐	☐	☐	☐
29102	$.50	☐	☐	☐	☐
29107	$.50	☐	☐	☐	☐
29111	$.50	☐	☐	☐	☐
29149	$.50	☐	☐	☐	☐
29152	$.50	☐	☐	☐	☐
29158	$.50	☐	☐	☐	☐
29159	$.50	☐	☐	☐	☐
29162	$.50	☐	☐	☐	☐
29163	$.50	☐	☐	☐	☐
29164	$.50	☐	☐	☐	☐
29170	$.50	☐	☐	☐	☐
29174	$.50	☐	☐	☐	☐
29177	$.50	☐	☐	☐	☐
29193	$.50	☐	☐	☐	☐
29197	$.50	☐	☐	☐	☐
29200	$.50	☐	☐	☐	☐
29288	$.50	☐	☐	☐	☐
29289	$.50	☐	☐	☐	☐
29293	$.50	☐	☐	☐	☐
29296	$.50	☐	☐	☐	☐
29304	$2.00	☐	☐	☐	☐
29358	$.50	☐	☐	☐	☐
29396	$.50	☐	☐	☐	☐
29399	$.50	☐	☐	☐	☐
29400	$.50	☐	☐	☐	☐
29401	$.50	☐	☐	☐	☐
29412	$2.25	☐	☐	☐	☐
29413	$2.25	☐	☐	☐	☐
29414	$5.50	☐	☐	☐	☐

1967 COMMEMORATIVES

#1336 5¢ CHRISTMAS Cont.

		UL	UR	LL	LR
29417	$2.25	□	□	□	□
29418	$.50	□	□	□	□
29419	$.50	□	□	□	□
29430	$2.00	□	□	□	□
29431	$.50	□	□	□	□
29432	$.50	□	□	□	□
29433	$.50	□	□	□	□
29434	$.50	□	□	□	□
29435	$3.00	□	□	□	□

#1337 5¢ MISSISSIPPI

29375-29376	$.50	□	□	□	□
29375-29383	$.50	□	□	□	□
29377-29376	$.50	□	□	□	□
29377-29383	$.50	□	□	□	□
29384-29388	$.50	□	□	□	□
29384-29394	$.50	□	□	□	□
29391-29388	$.50	□	□	□	□
29391-29394	$.50	□	□	□	□
29420-29424	$.50	□	□	□	□
29420-29427	$.50	□	□	□	□
29421-29424	$.50	□	□	□	□
29421-29427	$.50	□	□	□	□

1968-71 REGULAR ISSUE

#1338 6¢ U. S. FLAG 118 Plates

GIORI PRESS

29604	$.60	□	□	□	□
29605	$2.00	□	□	□	□
29610	$.60	□	□	□	□
29613	$2.00	□	□	□	□
29616	$.60	□	□	□	□
29617	$3.00	□	□	□	□
29618	$.60	□	□	□	□
29619	$.60	□	□	□	□
29620	$.60	□	□	□	□
29621	$3.00	□	□	□	□
29624	$.60	□	□	□	□
29630	$.60	□	□	□	□
29633	$.60	□	□	□	□
29634	$3.00	□	□	□	□
29635	$.60	□	□	□	□
29643	$2.50	□	□	□	□
29649	$.60	□	□	□	□
29655	$2.50	□	□	□	□
29656	$.60	□	□	□	□
29657	$.60	□	□	□	□
29658	$2.50	□	□	□	□
29659	$.60	□	□	□	□
29662	$.60	□	□	□	□

1968-71 REGULAR ISSUE

#1338 6¢ U. S. FLAG Cont.

		UL	UR	LL	LR
29702	$.60	□	□	□	□
29707	$.60	□	□	□	□
29715	$.60	□	□	□	□
29717	$.60	□	□	□	□
29718	$.60	□	□	□	□
29722	$2.50	□	□	□	□
29728	$.60	□	□	□	□
29737	$.60	□	□	□	□
29749	$3.00	□	□	□	□
29757	$.60	□	□	□	□
29794	$.60	□	□	□	□
29795	$.60	□	□	□	□
29801	$.60	□	□	□	□
29807	$3.00	□	□	□	□
29811	$.60	□	□	□	□
29845	$.60	□	□	□	□
29857	$.60	□	□	□	□
30088	$.60	□	□	□	□
30089	$.60	□	□	□	□
30104	$.60	□	□	□	□
30111	$.60	□	□	□	□
30116	$.60	□	□	□	□
30146	$.60	□	□	□	□
30166	$.60	□	□	□	□
30179	$.60	□	□	□	□
30180	$3.00	□	□	□	□
30195	$.60	□	□	□	□
30213	$.60	□	□	□	□
30223	$3.00	□	□	□	□
30236	$.60	□	□	□	□
30243	$.60	□	□	□	□
30256	$.60	□	□	□	□
30279	$.60	□	□	□	□
30289	$.60	□	□	□	□
30291	$3.00	□	□	□	□
30302	$.60	□	□	□	□
30312	$2.50	□	□	□	□
30317	$3.50	□	□	□	□
30322	$3.50	□	□	□	□
30503	$.60	□	□	□	□
30543	$.60	□	□	□	□
30547	$4.00	□	□	□	□
30548	$.60	□	□	□	□
30551	$6.00	□	□	□	□
30654	$3.00	□	□	□	□
30681	$.60	□	□	□	□
30685	$.60	□	□	□	□
30687	$5.00	□	□	□	□
30690	$.60	□	□	□	□
30703	$.60	□	□	□	□
30704	$.60	□	□	□	□
30756	$3.00	□	□	□	□
30793	$.60	□	□	□	□
30799	$.60	□	□	□	□
30804	$.60	□	□	□	□
30806	$3.00	□	□	□	□

1968-71 REGULAR ISSUE

#1338 6¢ U.S. FLAG Cont.

		UL	UR	LL	LR
30815	$.60	☐	☐	☐	☐
30816	$.60	☐	☐	☐	☐
30836	$.60	☐	☐	☐	☐
30843	$7.50	☐	☐	☐	☐
30850	$.60	☐	☐	☐	☐
30859	$6.00	☐	☐	☐	☐
30862	$.60	☐	☐	☐	☐
30871	$.60	☐	☐	☐	☐
30954	$.60	☐	☐	☐	☐
30957	$.60	☐	☐	☐	☐
30958	$5.00	☐	☐	☐	☐
30964	$.60	☐	☐	☐	☐
30967	$5.00	☐	☐	☐	☐
30970	$.60	☐	☐	☐	☐
31138	$.60	☐	☐	☐	☐
31151	$.60	☐	☐	☐	☐
31245	$.60	☐	☐	☐	☐
31313	$.60	☐	☐	☐	☐
31315	$.60	☐	☐	☐	☐
31317	$.60	☐	☐	☐	☐
31339	$2.00	☐	☐	☐	☐
31340	$2.50	☐	☐	☐	☐
31341	$1.50	☐	☐	☐	☐
31468	$.60	☐	☐	☐	☐
31469	$.60	☐	☐	☐	☐
31470	$.60	☐	☐	☐	☐
31473	$.60	☐	☐	☐	☐
31476	$.60	☐	☐	☐	☐
31479	$.60	☐	☐	☐	☐
31637	$.60	☐	☐	☐	☐
31657	$.60	☐	☐	☐	☐
31660	$.60	☐	☐	☐	☐
31661	$3.00	☐	☐	☐	☐
31662	$5.00	☐	☐	☐	☐
31677	$.60	☐	☐	☐	☐
31755	$6.00	☐	☐	☐	☐
31762	$6.00	☐	☐	☐	☐
31871	$6.00	☐	☐	☐	☐
31880	$.60	☐	☐	☐	☐

#1338A 6¢ U. S. FLAG COIL

72 Subject Plates 9 Color Huck

Of the 471 plates used to print this issue, only the following have been reported.

30713	30719	30738	30745	30747
30772	30807	30810	30811	30817
30818	30819	30829	30840	30841
30854	30855	30856	30864	30895
30896	30910	30927	31514	31517

#1338D 6¢ U.S. FLAG 135 Plates

80 Subject Plates 9 Color Huck

Positions T, B only

Basic Price $3.25

Block of 20 (10 x 2)

#1338D 6¢ U.S. FLAG Cont.

It is possible to collect both the top and the bottom plate strips in four different combinations. Using Z to represent the Zip Code, M to represent Mail Early, N to represent the plate number and B to represent a blank tab, the following are the margin positions reading from left to right in a plate block of 20.

1) Z N B M Z N B M Z N

2) N B M Z N B M Z N B

3) B M Z N B M Z N B M

4) M Z N B M Z N B M Z

31816	31817	31818	31819	31820
31821	31828	31829	31830	*31831
31832	31833	31842	31843	31844
31845	31846	31847	31856	31857
31858	31859	31860	31861	31864
31866	31867	31868	31869	31874
31875	31876	31877	31878	31879
31882	31883	31884	31885	31886
31887	32065	32066	32067	32068
32069	32072	32073	32074	32075
32076	32077	32078	32079	32080
32081	32082	32083	32084	32085
32086	32087	32088	32089	32092
32093	32094	32095	32096	32098
32099	32100	32101	32102	32103
32110	32111	32112	32113	32114
32115	32121	32122	32123	32124
32125	32126	32132	32133	32134
32135	32136	32137	32139	*32140
32141	*32142	*32143	32144	*32156
32157	32158	32159	32160	*32161
32164	32165	32166	32167	*32168
†32169	32173	32174	*32175	32176
32177	*32178	32181	32182	32183
32184	32185	32186	32188	*32189
*32190	32191	32192	32193	*32195
32196	32197	*32198	*32199	32200

#1338F 8¢ U. S. FLAG 166 Plates

80 Subject Plates 9 Color Huck

Positions T, B only

Basic Price $3.75

Block of 20 (10 x 2)

It is possible to collect both the top and the bottom plate strips in four different combinations. Using Z to represent the Zip Code, M to represent Mail Early, N to represent the plate number and B to represent a blank tab, the following are the margin positions reading from left to right in a plate block of 20.

1) Z N B M Z N B M Z N

2) N B M Z N B M Z N B

3) B M Z N B M Z N B M

4) M Z N B M Z N B M Z

1968-71 REGULAR ISSUE

#1338F 8¢ U.S. FLAG Cont.

32547	32548	32549	32550	32551
32552	32554	32555	32556	32557
32558	32559	32568	32569	32570
32571	32572	32573	32584	32585
32586	32587	32588	32589	32597
32598	32599	32600	32601	32602
32611	32612	32613	32614	32615
32616	32626	32627	32628	32629
32630	32631	32639	32640	32641
32642	32643	32644	32655	32656
32657	32658	32659	32660	32668
32669	32670	32671	32672	32673
32681	32682	32683	32684	32685
32686	32695	32696	32697	32698
32699	32700	32730	32731	32732
32733	32734	32735	32745	32746
32747	32748	32749	32750	32762
32763	32764	32765	32766	32767
32794	32795	32796	32797	32798
32799	32811	32812	32813	32814
32815	32816	32824	32825	32826
32827	32828	32829	†32839	32840
32841	32842	32843	32844	32861
32862	32863	32864	32865	32866
32878	32879	32880	32881	32882
32883	32896	32897	32898	32899
†32900	32901	33659	33660	33661
33662	†33663	†33664	33668	33669
†33670	33671	33672	33673	33676
†33677	*33678	33679	†33680	†33681
†33720	†33721	†33722	†33723	†33724
†33725	†33867	†33868	†33870	†33871
†33872	†33875	†33876	†33877	†33878
†33879				

#1338G 8¢ U.S. FLAG COIL

72 Subject Plates 9 Color Huck

Of the 373 plates used to print this issue, only the following have been reported.

32818 32834 32934

1968 COMMEMORATIVES

#1339 6¢ ILLINOIS

		UL	UR	LL	LR
29560	$.60	☐	☐	☐	☐
29570	$.60	☐	☐	☐	☐
29571	$.60	☐	☐	☐	☐
29576	$.60	☐	☐	☐	☐
29586	$.60	☐	☐	☐	☐
29590	$.60	☐	☐	☐	☐

1968 COMMEMORATIVES

#1340 6¢ HEMISFAIR

		UL	UR	LL	LR
29712	$.60	☐	☐	☐	☐
29716	$.60	☐	☐	☐	☐
29723	$.60	☐	☐	☐	☐
29731	$.60	☐	☐	☐	☐
29738	$.60	☐	☐	☐	☐
29742	$.60	☐	☐	☐	☐
29751	$.60	☐	☐	☐	☐
29753	$.60	☐	☐	☐	☐
29768	$.60	☐	☐	☐	☐

#1341 $1 AIRLIFT

UNTAGGED

29761	$13.50	☐	☐	☐	☐
29762	$13.50	☐	☐	☐	☐
29763	$13.50	☐	☐	☐	☐
29766	$13.50	☐	☐	☐	☐
29769	$13.50	☐	☐	☐	☐
29774	$13.50	☐	☐	☐	☐
29779	$13.50	☐	☐	☐	☐
29781	$13.50	☐	☐	☐	☐

#1342 5¢ SUPPORT OUR YOUTH

29814	$.60	☐	☐	☐	☐
29817	$.60	☐	☐	☐	☐
29824	$.60	☐	☐	☐	☐
29830	$.60	☐	☐	☐	☐
29834	$.60	☐	☐	☐	☐
29837	$.60	☐	☐	☐	☐

#1343 6¢ LAW AND ORDER

29833	$.60	☐	☐	☐	☐
29835	$.60	☐	☐	☐	☐
29836	$.60	☐	☐	☐	☐
29839	$.60	☐	☐	☐	☐
29843	$.60	☐	☐	☐	☐
29846	$.60	☐	☐	☐	☐
29847	$.60	☐	☐	☐	☐
29851	$.60	☐	☐	☐	☐
29946	$.60	☐	☐	☐	☐

#1344 6¢ REGISTER & VOTE

29760	$.60	☐	☐	☐	☐
29764	$.60	☐	☐	☐	☐
29782	$.60	☐	☐	☐	☐
29786	$.60	☐	☐	☐	☐
29823	$.60	☐	☐	☐	☐
29996	$.60	☐	☐	☐	☐
30055	$.60	☐	☐	☐	☐

#1345-54 6¢ HISTORIC FLAGS

Block of 20 (2 x 10)

29995	$7.50	☐	☐	☐	☐
30028	$7.50	☐	☐	☐	☐

1968 COMMEMORATIVES

#1345-54 6¢ HISTORIC FLAGS Cont.

		UL	UR	LL	LR
30045	$7.50	☐	☐	☐	☐
30052	$7.50	☐	☐	☐	☐
30074	$7.50	☐	☐	☐	☐
30085	$7.50	☐	☐	☐	☐
30306	$7.50	☐	☐	☐	☐
30311	$7.50	☐	☐	☐	☐
30705	$7.50	☐	☐	☐	☐
30706	$7.50	☐	☐	☐	☐

#1355 6¢ WALT DISNEY

This issue was printed by the Achrovure Division of the Union-Camp Corp.

30006-30008-30009-30010-30012	$1.00	☐	☐	☐	☐
N30006-30008-30009-30010-30012-	$1.00	☐	☐	☐	☐

N with hyphen after plate numbers

#1356 6¢ FR. MARQUETTE

30120	$.60	☐	☐	☐	☐
30121	$.60	☐	☐	☐	☐
30123	$.60	☐	☐	☐	☐
30124	$.60	☐	☐	☐	☐
30135	$.60	☐	☐	☐	☐
30147	$.60	☐	☐	☐	☐

#1357 6¢ DANIEL BOONE

30257	$.60	☐	☐	☐	☐
30266	$.60	☐	☐	☐	☐
30280	$.60	☐	☐	☐	☐
30294	$.60	☐	☐	☐	☐
30301	$.60	☐	☐	☐	☐
30303	$.60	☐	☐	☐	☐
30341	$.60	☐	☐	☐	☐

#1358 6¢ ARKANSAS RIVER

30326	$.60	☐	☐	☐	☐
30327	$.60	☐	☐	☐	☐
30328	$.60	☐	☐	☐	☐
30329	$.60	☐	☐	☐	☐
30334	$.60	☐	☐	☐	☐
30337	$.60	☐	☐	☐	☐
30338	$.60	☐	☐	☐	☐
30339	$.60	☐	☐	☐	☐

#1359 6¢ ERIKSON

30435	$.60	☐	☐	☐	☐
30436	$.60	☐	☐	☐	☐
30445	$.60	☐	☐	☐	☐
30446	$.60	☐	☐	☐	☐
30447	$.60	☐	☐	☐	☐
30458	$.60	☐	☐	☐	☐
30471	$.60	☐	☐	☐	☐
30480	$.60	☐	☐	☐	☐

#1360 6¢ CHEROKEE STRIP

		UL	UR	LL	LR
30371	$.60	☐	☐	☐	☐
30372	$.60	☐	☐	☐	☐
30388	$.60	☐	☐	☐	☐
30389	$.60	☐	☐	☐	☐

#1361 6¢ TRUMBULL

30383	$.75	☐	☐	☐	☐
30385	$.75	☐	☐	☐	☐
30386	$.75	☐	☐	☐	☐
30387	$.75	☐	☐	☐	☐
30392	$.75	☐	☐	☐	☐
30393	$.75	☐	☐	☐	☐
30406	$.75	☐	☐	☐	☐
30415	$.75	☐	☐	☐	☐

#1362 6¢ WATERFOWL

30347	$.80	☐	☐	☐	☐
30350	$.80	☐	☐	☐	☐
30351	$.80	☐	☐	☐	☐
30358	$.80	☐	☐	☐	☐
30360	$.80	☐	☐	☐	☐
30370	$.80	☐	☐	☐	☐

#1363/1363a 6¢ CHRISTMAS

40 Subject Plates 9 Color Huck

Issued TAGGED and UNTAGGED

Position L, R only

Basic Price $2.25

Block of 10 (2 x 5)

YELLOW PLATES **30 plates**

29868	29869	29870	29871	29872
29873	29893	29894	29895	29896
29910	29912	29913	29914	29915
29926	29950	29951	29952	29983
29984	29985	29986	29987	30022
30023	30024	30025	30026	30027

BLUE PLATES **116 Plates**

29897	29898	29899	†29923	29939
29940	29941	29942	29944	29962
29965	29966	29967	29975	29977
29979	29999	30000	30001	30002
30004	30031	30032	30033	30034
30035	30036	30056	30057	30058
30059	30060	30061	30077	30078
30079	30080	30081	30082	30098
30099	30100	30101	30102	30103
30127	30128	30129	30130	30131
30132	30152	30153	30154	30155
30156	30157	30173	30174	30175
30176	30177	30178	30189	30190
30191	30192	30193	30194	30207
30208	30209	30210	30211	30212

1968 COMMEMORATIVES

#1363/1363a 6¢ CHRISTMAS

BLUE PLATES **Cont.**

30217	30218	30219	30220	30221
30222	30230	30231	30232	30233
30234	30235	30244	*30245	30246
30247	30248	30249	30423	30424
30425	*30426	*30427	†30428	30437
30438	30439	30440	30441	30442
30472	30473	30475	30476	30477
30487	30488	30489	30490	†30491
30492				

BROWN PLATES **160 Plates**

29885	29886	29887	29888	29889
29890	29904	29905	29906	29907
29908	29909	29931	29932	29933
29934	29935	29936	29953	29954
29955	29956	29957	29958	29969
29970	29971	29972	29973	29974
29990	29991	30016	30017	30018
30019	30020	30021	30039	30040
30041	30042	30043	30044	30068
30069	30070	30071	30072	30073
30092	30093	30094	30095	30096
30097	30160	30161	30162	30181
30182	30183	30184	30185	30186
30224	30225	30226	30227	30228
30229	30237	30238	30239	30240
30241	30250	30251	30252	30253
30254	30255	30258	30259	30260
30261	30262	30263	30267	30268
30269	30270	30271	30272	30273
30274	30275	30276	30277	30278
30283	30284	30285	30286	30287
30288	30295	30296	30297	30298
30299	30300	30394	*30395	*30396
30397	30398	30399	*30416	30417
30418	30419	30420	*30421	30449
30450	30451	*30452	30453	30454
30460	30461	30462	30463	30464
30465	30523	30524	30525	30526
30527	30528	*30531	30532	30533
30534	30535	30536	30560	30561
30562	30563	*30564	30565	30577
*30578	*30579	30580	*30581	*30582

#1364 6¢ AMERICAN INDIAN

		UL	UR	LL	LR
30448	$.75	☐	☐	☐	☐
30459	$.75	☐	☐	☐	☐
30481	$.75	☐	☐	☐	☐
30493	$.75	☐	☐	☐	☐
30495	$.75	☐	☐	☐	☐
30499	$.75	☐	☐	☐	☐

1969 COMMEMORATIVES

#1365-68 6¢ CIVIC BEAUTY

		UL	UR	LL	LR
30583	$3	☐	☐	☐	☐
30586	$3	☐	☐	☐	☐
30587	$3	☐	☐	☐	☐
30588	$3	☐	☐	☐	☐
30593	$3	☐	☐	☐	☐
30607	$3	☐	☐	☐	☐
30626	$3	☐	☐	☐	☐
30627	$3	☐	☐	☐	☐
30660	$3	☐	☐	☐	☐
30663	$3	☐	☐	☐	☐
30664	$3	☐	☐	☐	☐
30665	$3	☐	☐	☐	☐
30668	$3	☐	☐	☐	☐
30671	$3	☐	☐	☐	☐

#1369 6¢ AMERICAN LEGION

30759	$.60	☐	☐	☐	☐
30769	$.60	☐	☐	☐	☐
30782	$.60	☐	☐	☐	☐
30783	$.60	☐	☐	☐	☐
30786	$.60	☐	☐	☐	☐
30789	$.60	☐	☐	☐	☐
30790	$.60	☐	☐	☐	☐
30825	$.60	☐	☐	☐	☐

#1370 6¢ GRANDMA MOSES

30886	$.60	☐	☐	☐	☐
30889	$.60	☐	☐	☐	☐
30900	$.60	☐	☐	☐	☐
30901	$.60	☐	☐	☐	☐
30904	$.60	☐	☐	☐	☐
30921	$.60	☐	☐	☐	☐
30930	$.60	☐	☐	☐	☐
30933	$.60	☐	☐	☐	☐
30985	$.60	☐	☐	☐	☐
30986	$.60	☐	☐	☐	☐

#1371 6¢ APOLLO 8

30923	$.60	☐	☐	☐	☐
30931	$.60	☐	☐	☐	☐
30932	$.60	☐	☐	☐	☐
30934	$.60	☐	☐	☐	☐
30937	$.60	☐	☐	☐	☐
30938	$.60	☐	☐	☐	☐
30941	$.60	☐	☐	☐	☐
30945	$.60	☐	☐	☐	☐

#1372 6¢ W.C. HANDY

30707	$.60	☐	☐	☐	☐
30714	$.60	☐	☐	☐	☐
30725	$.60	☐	☐	☐	☐
30732	$.60	☐	☐	☐	☐
30735	$.60	☐	☐	☐	☐
30744	$.60	☐	☐	☐	☐
30751	$.60	☐	☐	☐	☐
30760	$.60	☐	☐	☐	☐

1969 COMMEMORATIVES

#1373 5¢ CALIFORNIA

		UL	UR	LL	LR
31016	$.60	☐	☐	☐	☐
31030	$.60	☐	☐	☐	☐
31043	$.60	☐	☐	☐	☐
31064	$.60	☐	☐	☐	☐
31078	$.60	☐	☐	☐	☐
31095	$.60	☐	☐	☐	☐
31105	$.60	☐	☐	☐	☐
31124	$.60	☐	☐	☐	☐
31262	$.60	☐	☐	☐	☐
31268	$.60	☐	☐	☐	☐

#1374 6¢ J.W. POWELL

31160	$.60	☐	☐	☐	☐
31173	$.60	☐	☐	☐	☐
31174	$.60	☐	☐	☐	☐
31175	$.60	☐	☐	☐	☐
31182	$.60	☐	☐	☐	☐
31189	$.60	☐	☐	☐	☐
31202	$.60	☐	☐	☐	☐
31211	$.60	☐	☐	☐	☐

#1375 6¢ ALABAMA

31275	$.60	☐	☐	☐	☐
31276	$.60	☐	☐	☐	☐
31277	$.60	☐	☐	☐	☐
31288	$.60	☐	☐	☐	☐
31291	$.60	☐	☐	☐	☐
31300	$.60	☐	☐	☐	☐
31304	$.60	☐	☐	☐	☐
31312	$.60	☐	☐	☐	☐

#1376-79 6¢ BOTANICAL CONGRESS

30973	$4.00	☐	☐	☐	☐
30977	$4.00	☐	☐	☐	☐
30983	$4.00	☐	☐	☐	☐
30984	$4.00	☐	☐	☐	☐
30993	$4.00	☐	☐	☐	☐
30996	$4.00	☐	☐	☐	☐
30997	$4.00	☐	☐	☐	☐
31004	$4.00	☐	☐	☐	☐

#1380 6¢ DANIEL WEBSTER

31056	$.60	☐	☐	☐	☐
31057	$.60	☐	☐	☐	☐
31079	$.60	☐	☐	☐	☐
31080	$.60	☐	☐	☐	☐

#1381 6¢ BASEBALL

31399	$3	☐	☐	☐	☐
31402	$3	☐	☐	☐	☐
31404	$3	☐	☐	☐	☐
31407	$3	☐	☐	☐	☐
31409	$3	☐	☐	☐	☐

#1381 6¢ BASEBALL Cont.

		UL	UR	LL	LR
31410	$3	☐	☐	☐	☐
31413	$3	☐	☐	☐	☐
31414	$3	☐	☐	☐	☐
31436	$3	☐	☐	☐	☐

#1382 6¢ FOOTBALL

31383	$1	☐	☐	☐	☐
31386	$1	☐	☐	☐	☐
31389	$1	☐	☐	☐	☐
31391	$1	☐	☐	☐	☐
31398	$1	☐	☐	☐	☐
31403	$1	☐	☐	☐	☐
31406	$1	☐	☐	☐	☐
31408	$1	☐	☐	☐	☐

#1383 6¢ EISENHOWER

31423	$.60	☐	☐	☐	☐
31424	$.60	☐	☐	☐	☐
31426	$.60	☐	☐	☐	☐
31429	$.60	☐	☐	☐	☐
31430	$.60	☐	☐	☐	☐
31431	$.60	☐	☐	☐	☐
31432	$.60	☐	☐	☐	☐
31433	$.60	☐	☐	☐	☐

#1384 6¢ CHRISTMAS

40 Subject Plates — 9 Color Huck
Basic Price — $1.50
Block of 10 (5 x 2) — Positions **T, B**

RED PLATES — **65 Plates**

31024	31025	31026	31027	31028
31029	31044	31045	31047	31048
31049	31050	31051	31052	31053
31054	31055	31066	31067	31068
31069	31070	31071	31083	31084
31085	31086	31087	31088	31096
31097	31098	31099	31100	31101
31145	31146	31147	31148	31149
31150	31161	31162	31163	31164
31165	31166	31176	31177	31178
31179	31180	31181	31190	31191
31192	31193	31194	31195	31205
31206	31207	31208	31209	31210

GREEN PLATES — **119 Plates**

31031	31032	31033	31034	31035
31036	31037	31038	31039	31040
31041	31042	31058	31059	31060
31061	31062	31063	31072	31073
31074	31075	31076	31077	31089
31090	31091	31092	31093	31094
31106	31107	31108	31109	31110
31111	31112	31113	31114	31115
31117	31118	31119	31120	31121
31122	31123	31125	31126	31127
31128	31129	31130	31132	31133
31134	31135	31136	31137	31139
31140	31141	31142	31144	31152

1969 COMMEMORATIVES

#1384 6¢ CHRISTMAS
GREEN PLATES Cont.

31153	31154	31155	31156	31157
31167	31168	31169	31170	31171
31172	31183	31184	31185	31186
31187	31188	31196	31212	31213
31214	31215	31216	31217	31224
31225	31226	31227	31228	31229
31236	31237	31238	31239	31240
31241	31256	31257	31258	31259
31260	31261	31269	31270	31271
31272	31273	31274	31294	31295
31296	31297	31298	31299	

#1385 6¢ CRIPPLED CHILDREN

		UL	UR	LL	LR
31447	$.60	☐	☐	☐	☐
31448	$.60	☐	☐	☐	☐
31449	$.60	☐	☐	☐	☐
31452	$.60	☐	☐	☐	☐
31455	$.60	☐	☐	☐	☐
31456	$.60	☐	☐	☐	☐
31461	$.60	☐	☐	☐	☐
31464	$.60	☐	☐	☐	☐

#1386 6¢ WILLIAM M. HARNETT

31486	$.60	☐	☐	☐	☐
31488	$.60	☐	☐	☐	☐
31489	$.60	☐	☐	☐	☐
31493	$.60	☐	☐	☐	☐
31494	$.60	☐	☐	☐	☐
31496	$.60	☐	☐	☐	☐
31502	$.60	☐	☐	☐	☐
31503	$.60	☐	☐	☐	☐
31505	$.60	☐	☐	☐	☐
31508	$.60	☐	☐	☐	☐
31509	$.60	☐	☐	☐	☐
31511	$.60	☐	☐	☐	☐
31512	$.60	☐	☐	☐	☐
31513	$.60	☐	☐	☐	☐

1970 COMMEMORATIVES

#1387-90 6¢ NATURAL HISTORY

31678	$.75	☐	☐	☐	☐
31686	$.75	☐	☐	☐	☐
31702	$.75	☐	☐	☐	☐
31711	$.75	☐	☐	☐	☐
31720	$.75	☐	☐	☐	☐
31728	$.75	☐	☐	☐	☐
31729	$.75	☐	☐	☐	☐
31736	$.75	☐	☐	☐	☐
31834	$.75	☐	☐	☐	☐
31848	$.75	☐	☐	☐	☐
31862	$.75	☐	☐	☐	☐

1970 COMMEMORATIVES

#1387-90 6¢ NATURAL HISTORY Cont.

		UL	UR	LL	LR
31870	$.75	☐	☐	☐	☐
31888	$.75	☐	☐	☐	☐
31889	$.75	☐	☐	☐	☐
31929	$1.75	☐	☐	☐	☐
31930	$1.75	☐	☐	☐	☐

#1391 6¢ MAINE

31951	$.60	☐	☐	☐	☐
31957	$.60	☐	☐	☐	☐
31958	$.60	☐	☐	☐	☐
31963	$.60	☐	☐	☐	☐
31968	$.60	☐	☐	☐	☐
31969	$.60	☐	☐	☐	☐
31983	$.60	☐	☐	☐	☐
31992	$.60	☐	☐	☐	☐

#1392 6¢ BUFFALO

31959	$.60	☐	☐	☐	☐
31960	$.60	☐	☐	☐	☐
31977	$.60	☐	☐	☐	☐
31978	$.60	☐	☐	☐	☐

1970-71 REGULAR ISSUE

#1393 6¢ EISENHOWER

SHINY GUM					
31919	$.60	☐	☐	☐	☐
31920	$.60	☐	☐	☐	☐
31927	$.60	☐	☐	☐	☐
31928	$.60	☐	☐	☐	☐
31934	$.60	☐	☐	☐	☐
31935	$.60	☐	☐	☐	☐
31947	$.60	☐	☐	☐	☐
31948	$.60	☐	☐	☐	☐
32007	$.60	☐	☐	☐	☐
32008	$.60	☐	☐	☐	☐
32050	$.60	☐	☐	☐	☐
32051	$.60	☐	☐	☐	☐
DULL GUM					
31947	$1.30	☐	☐	☐	☐
31948	$1.30	☐	☐	☐	☐
32007	$1.30	☐	☐	☐	☐
32008	$1.30	☐	☐	☐	☐

#1393D 7¢ FRANKLIN
See Page 180

#1394 8¢ EISENHOWER 68 Plates

32694	$.65	☐	☐	☐	☐
32701	$.65	☐	☐	☐	☐
32724	$.65	☐	☐	☐	☐
32725	$.65	☐	☐	☐	☐
32736	$.65	☐	☐	☐	☐
32743	$.65	☐	☐	☐	☐
32744	$.65	☐	☐	☐	☐
32751	$.65	☐	☐	☐	☐
32768	$.65	☐	☐	☐	☐
32769	$.65	☐	☐	☐	☐

1970-71 REGULAR ISSUE

#1394 8¢ EISENHOWER Cont.

		UL	UR	LL	LR
32778	$.65	☐	☐	☐	☐
32779	$.65	☐	☐	☐	☐
32780	$.65	☐	☐	☐	☐
32781	$.65	☐	☐	☐	☐
32784	$.65	☐	☐	☐	☐
32785	$.65	☐	☐	☐	☐
32800	$.65	☐	☐	☐	☐
32817	$.65	☐	☐	☐	☐
32830	$.65	☐	☐	☐	☐
32845	$.65	☐	☐	☐	☐
32846	$.65	☐	☐	☐	☐
32867	$.65	☐	☐	☐	☐
32930	$.65	☐	☐	☐	☐
32933	$.65	☐	☐	☐	☐
33011	$2.00	☐	☐	☐	☐
33026	$.65	☐	☐	☐	☐
33061	$.65	☐	☐	☐	☐
33063	$17.50	☐	☐	☐	☐
33071	$.65	☐	☐	☐	☐
33078	$.65	☐	☐	☐	☐
33135	$.65	☐	☐	☐	☐
33163	$.65	☐	☐	☐	☐
33230	$.65	☐	☐	☐	☐
33232	$.65	☐	☐	☐	☐
33373	$12.00	☐	☐	☐	☐
33377	$.65	☐	☐	☐	☐
33381	$.65	☐	☐	☐	☐
33382	$.65	☐	☐	☐	☐
33385	$.65	☐	☐	☐	☐
33394	$.65	☐	☐	☐	☐
33400	$12.00	☐	☐	☐	☐
33445	$13.50	☐	☐	☐	☐
33446	$22.00	☐	☐	☐	☐
33490	$.65	☐	☐	☐	☐
33506	$.65	☐	☐	☐	☐
33507	$.65	☐	☐	☐	☐
33514	$.65	☐	☐	☐	☐
33515	$.65	☐	☐	☐	☐
33531	$.65	☐	☐	☐	☐
33543	$.65	☐	☐	☐	☐
33553	$.65	☐	☐	☐	☐
33572	$.65	☐	☐	☐	☐
33582	$.65	☐	☐	☐	☐
33598	$.65	☐	☐	☐	☐
33667	$.65	☐	☐	☐	☐
33674	$.65	☐	☐	☐	☐
33682	$.65	☐	☐	☐	☐
33685	$.65	☐	☐	☐	☐
33686	$.65	☐	☐	☐	☐
33687	$.65	☐	☐	☐	☐
33838	$2.00	☐	☐	☐	☐
34037	$.65	☐	☐	☐	☐
34073	$.65	☐	☐	☐	☐
34152	$17.50	☐	☐	☐	☐
38120	$5.00	☐	☐	☐	☐
38126	$5.00	☐	☐	☐	☐

#1396 8¢ U.S. POSTAL SERVICE

Block of 12 (2 x 6)		UL	UR	LL	LR
32918-32919-32920-32921-32922-32923	$3.00	☐	☐	☐	☐
32924-32925-32926-32927-32928-32929	$3.00	☐	☐	☐	☐

#1397-#1400

See page 181

BOOKLET PANES

#1393a 6¢ EISENHOWER PANES OF 8

400 Subject Plates

†31917 †31918 †31925 †31926 *31932
†31933 †31961 †31962 †32010 *32011
†32170 †32171

#1393b 6¢ EISENHOWER PANES OF 5

360 Subject Plates

Slogan 4 "Mail Early"
*31956

Slogan 5 "Use ZIP Code"
*31955

#1395a 8¢ EISENHOWER PANES OF 8

400 Subject Plates

*32716 *32717 *32728 *32729 *32758
*32759 *32760 †32761 †32770 †32771
†32772 †32773

#1395b 8¢ EISENHOWER PANES OF 6

360 Subject Plates

*32908 *32909 *32910 *32911

#1395c 8¢ EISENHOWER PANES OF 4

400 Subject Plates

†33297 †33298 *33338 †33339 †33425
†33426 †34100 †34234

#1395d 8¢ EISENHOWER PANES OF 7

400 Subject Plates

Slogan 4 "Mail Early"
†33294 †33296 †33301 †33302 †33419
†33420 *33767 *33768 †33821 †33822

Slogan 5 "Use ZIP Code"
†33293 †33295 †33299 †33300 †33401
†33402 †33414 †33763 †33764 †33765
†33766 †33796 †33797 †34402 †34403

See Appendix G for largest reported plate number percentage by position.

SIDE COILS

PERF. 10 VERTICALLY

#1401 6¢ EISENHOWER

432 Subject Plates **STRIPS OF 6**

†31936 †31937 31949 31950 †31953
†31954 †31966 †31967 32036 †32037
†32339 †32372 †32373 †32395 †32396
†32470 †32471

1970-71 REGULAR ISSUE

SIDE COILS

#1402 8¢ EISENHOWER

432 Subject Plates **STRIPS OF 6**

32714	32726	32727	32752	32753
32754	32755	32756	32757	32774
32775	32776	32777	32782	32783
32793	32801	32802	32803	32804
32831	32832	32849	32850	32857
32858	32859	†32860	32870	32871
†32884	†32885	33410	33435	33436
33437	†33455	33456	33516	33517
†33539	33540	33791	33792	†33873
†33889	33890	†33962	†33963	†34038
†34039	34052	34093	†34150	

1970 COMMEMORATIVES

#1405 6¢ E.L. MASTERS

		UL	UR	LL	LR
31685	$.60	☐	☐	☐	☐
31687	$.60	☐	☐	☐	☐
31694	$.60	☐	☐	☐	☐
31701	$.60	☐	☐	☐	☐
31703	$.60	☐	☐	☐	☐
31712	$.60	☐	☐	☐	☐
31719	$.60	☐	☐	☐	☐

#1406 6¢ WOMAN SUFFRAGE

32131	$.60	☐	☐	☐	☐
32138	$.60	☐	☐	☐	☐
32155	$.60	☐	☐	☐	☐
32162	$.60	☐	☐	☐	☐
32163	$.60	☐	☐	☐	☐
32172	$.60	☐	☐	☐	☐
32187	$.60	☐	☐	☐	☐
32194	$.60	☐	☐	☐	☐

#1407 6¢ SOUTH CAROLINA

32012	$.60	☐	☐	☐	☐
32020	$.60	☐	☐	☐	☐
32027	$.60	☐	☐	☐	☐
32028	$.60	☐	☐	☐	☐
32029	$.60	☐	☐	☐	☐
32038	$.60	☐	☐	☐	☐
32047	$.60	☐	☐	☐	☐
32052	$.60	☐	☐	☐	☐

#1408 6¢ STONE MOUNTAIN

32246	$.60	☐	☐	☐	☐
32247	$.60	☐	☐	☐	☐
32248	$.60	☐	☐	☐	☐
32256	$.60	☐	☐	☐	☐
32259	$.60	☐	☐	☐	☐
32261	$.60	☐	☐	☐	☐
32262	$.60	☐	☐	☐	☐
32263	$.60	☐	☐	☐	☐

1970 COMMEMORATIVES

#1409 6¢ FORT SNELLING

		UL	UR	LL	LR
32298	$.60	☐	☐	☐	☐
32302	$.60	☐	☐	☐	☐
32305	$.60	☐	☐	☐	☐
32311	$.60	☐	☐	☐	☐
32318	$.60	☐	☐	☐	☐
32320	$.60	☐	☐	☐	☐
32327	$.60	☐	☐	☐	☐
32331	$.60	☐	☐	☐	☐

#1410-13 6¢ ANTI-POLLUTION

Block of 10 (2 x 5)

32251-32252-32253-32254-32255	$3	☐	☐	☐	☐
32281-32282-32283-32284-32285	$3	☐	☐	☐	☐

#1414 6¢ CHRISTMAS NATIVITY

Block of 8 (4 x 2)

31942-31939-31940-31941	$1.25	☐	☐	☐	☐
31942-32150-32151-32152	$1.25	☐	☐	☐	☐
31946-31939-31940-31941	$1.25	☐	☐	☐	☐
31946-31943-31944-31945	$1.25	☐	☐	☐	☐
31946-32150-32151-32152	$1.25	☐	☐	☐	☐
32332-31939-31940-31941	$1.25	☐	☐	☐	☐
32332-31943-31944-31945	$1.25	☐	☐	☐	☐

#1414a 6¢ CHRISTMAS NATIVITY

PRECANCELLED

Block of 8 (4 x 2)

32153-31939-31940-31941	$2.25	☐	☐	☐	☐
32153-31943-31944-31945	$2.25	☐	☐	☐	☐
32154-31939-31940-31941	$2.25	☐	☐	☐	☐
32154-31943-31944-31945	$2.25	☐	☐	☐	☐
32154-32150-32151-32152	$2.25	☐	☐	☐	☐

#1415-18 6¢ CHRISTMAS TOYS

Block of 8 (2 x 4)

31903-31900-31901-31902	$4	☐	☐	☐	☐
31903-31904-31905-31906	$4	☐	☐	☐	☐
31903-32145-32146-32147	$4	☐	☐	☐	☐

1970 COMMEMORATIVES

#1415-18 6¢ CHRISTMAS TOYS Cont.

		UL	UR	LL	LR
31907-31900-31901-31902	$4	☐	☐	☐	☐
31907-31904-31905-31906	$4	☐	☐	☐	☐
31907-32145-32146-32147	$4	☐	☐	☐	☐

#1415a-18a 6¢ CHRISTMAS TOYS

PRECANCELLED

Block of 8 (2 x 4)

		UL	UR	LL	LR
32148-31900-31901-31902	$8	☐	☐	☐	☐
32148-31904-31905-31906	$8	☐	☐	☐	☐
32148-32145-32146-32147	$8	☐	☐	☐	☐
32149-31900-31901-31902	$8	☐	☐	☐	☐
32149-31904-31905-31906	$8	☐	☐	☐	☐
32149-32145-32146-32147	$16	☐	☐	☐	☐

#1419 6¢ UNITED NATIONS

		UL	UR	LL	LR
32299	$.60	☐	☐	☐	☐
32300	$.60	☐	☐	☐	☐
32303	$.60	☐	☐	☐	☐
32306	$.60	☐	☐	☐	☐
32308	$.60	☐	☐	☐	☐
32310	$.60	☐	☐	☐	☐
32316	$.60	☐	☐	☐	☐
32317	$.60	☐	☐	☐	☐

#1420 6¢ PILGRIM LANDING

		UL	UR	LL	LR
32264	$.60	☐	☐	☐	☐
32269	$.60	☐	☐	☐	☐
32271	$.60	☐	☐	☐	☐
32272	$.60	☐	☐	☐	☐
32273	$.60	☐	☐	☐	☐
32279	$.60	☐	☐	☐	☐
32286	$.60	☐	☐	☐	☐
32287	$.60	☐	☐	☐	☐

#1421-22 6¢ DAV-POW

		UL	UR	LL	LR
32409	$1.20	☐	☐	☐	☐
32410	$1.20	☐	☐	☐	☐
32427	$1.20	☐	☐	☐	☐
32434	$1.20	☐	☐	☐	☐
32435	$1.20	☐	☐	☐	☐
32436	$1.20	☐	☐	☐	☐
32441	$1.20	☐	☐	☐	☐
32442	$1.20	☐	☐	☐	☐

1971 COMMEMORATIVES

#1423 6¢ AMERICAN WOOL

		UL	UR	LL	LR
32478	$.60	☐	☐	☐	☐
32485	$.60	☐	☐	☐	☐
32492	$.60	☐	☐	☐	☐
32501	$.60	☐	☐	☐	☐
32516	$.60	☐	☐	☐	☐
32523	$.60	☐	☐	☐	☐
32539	$.60	☐	☐	☐	☐
32541	$.60	☐	☐	☐	☐

#1424 6¢ GEN. MacARTHUR

		UL	UR	LL	LR
32301	$.60	☐	☐	☐	☐
32304	$.60	☐	☐	☐	☐
32307	$.60	☐	☐	☐	☐
32309	$.60	☐	☐	☐	☐
32319	$.60	☐	☐	☐	☐
32328	$.60	☐	☐	☐	☐
32340	$.60	☐	☐	☐	☐
32347	$.60	☐	☐	☐	☐

#1425 6¢ BLOOD DONORS

		UL	UR	LL	LR
32590	$.60	☐	☐	☐	☐
32603	$.60	☐	☐	☐	☐
32617	$.60	☐	☐	☐	☐
32632	$.60	☐	☐	☐	☐
32645	$.60	☐	☐	☐	☐
32661	$.60	☐	☐	☐	☐
32674	$.60	☐	☐	☐	☐
32687	$.60	☐	☐	☐	☐

#1426 8¢ MISSOURI

Block of 12 (2 x 6)

		UL	UR	LL	LR
32702-32703-32704-32705-32706-32707	$2.00	☐	☐	☐	☐
32708-32709-32710-32711-32712-32713	$2.00	☐	☐	☐	☐

#1427-30 8¢ WILDLIFE

		UL	UR	LL	LR
33032	$.80	☐	☐	☐	☐
33039	$.80	☐	☐	☐	☐
33045	$.80	☐	☐	☐	☐
33048	$.80	☐	☐	☐	☐
33050	$.80	☐	☐	☐	☐
33056	$.80	☐	☐	☐	☐
33060	$.80	☐	☐	☐	☐
33062	$.80	☐	☐	☐	☐
33080	$.80	☐	☐	☐	☐
33083	$.80	☐	☐	☐	☐

#1431 8¢ ANTARCTIC TREATY

		UL	UR	LL	LR
32940	$.80	☐	☐	☐	☐
32947	$.80	☐	☐	☐	☐
32954	$.80	☐	☐	☐	☐

1971 COMMEMORATIVES

#1431 8¢ ANTARCTIC TREATY Cont.

		UL	UR	LL	LR
32955	$.80	☐	☐	☐	☐
32963	$.80	☐	☐	☐	☐
32969	$.80	☐	☐	☐	☐
32976	$.80	☐	☐	☐	☐
32978	$.80	☐	☐	☐	☐
33014	$.80	☐	☐	☐	☐

#1432 8¢ AMER. REVOLUTION

33031	$1.00	☐	☐	☐	☐
33033	$1.00	☐	☐	☐	☐
33040	$1.00	☐	☐	☐	☐
33043	$1.00	☐	☐	☐	☐
33044	$1.00	☐	☐	☐	☐
33046	$1.00	☐	☐	☐	☐
33049	$1.00	☐	☐	☐	☐
33059	$1.00	☐	☐	☐	☐

#1433 8¢ JOHN SLOAN

33102	$.80	☐	☐	☐	☐
33124	$.80	☐	☐	☐	☐
33125	$.80	☐	☐	☐	☐
33130	$.80	☐	☐	☐	☐
33131	$.80	☐	☐	☐	☐
33132	$.80	☐	☐	☐	☐
33133	$1.50	☐	☐	☐	☐
33134	$1.50	☐	☐	☐	☐
33168	$1.50	☐	☐	☐	☐
33169	$1.50	☐	☐	☐	☐

#1434-35 8¢ MOON ROVER

33138	$.80	☐	☐	☐	☐
33147	$.80	☐	☐	☐	☐
33148	$.80	☐	☐	☐	☐
33153	$.80	☐	☐	☐	☐
33154	$.80	☐	☐	☐	☐
33155	$.80	☐	☐	☐	☐
33156	$.80	☐	☐	☐	☐
33162	$.80	☐	☐	☐	☐

#1436 8¢ EMILY DICKINSON

33171	$.80	☐	☐	☐	☐
33173	$.80	☐	☐	☐	☐
33174	$.80	☐	☐	☐	☐
33175	$.80	☐	☐	☐	☐
33176	$.80	☐	☐	☐	☐
33196	$.80	☐	☐	☐	☐
33199	$.80	☐	☐	☐	☐
33200	$.80	☐	☐	☐	☐

#1437 8¢ SAN JUAN

33201	$.80	☐	☐	☐	☐
33202	$.80	☐	☐	☐	☐
33203	$.80	☐	☐	☐	☐

#1437 8¢ SAN JUAN Cont.

		UL	UR	LL	LR
33212	$.80	☐	☐	☐	☐
33213	$.80	☐	☐	☐	☐
33218	$.80	☐	☐	☐	☐
33219	$.80	☐	☐	☐	☐
33222	$.80	☐	☐	☐	☐

#1438 8¢ DRUG ABUSE

Block of 6 (3 x 2)

33064-33065-33066	$1.00	☐	☐	☐	☐
33067-33068-33069	$1.00	☐	☐	☐	☐

#1439 8¢ CARE

Block of 8 (4 x 2)

33139-33140-33141-33142	$1.50	☐	☐	☐	☐
33143-33144-33145-33146	$1.50	☐	☐	☐	☐

#1440-43 8¢ HISTORIC PRESERVATION

33233	$.80	☐	☐	☐	☐
33234	$.80	☐	☐	☐	☐
33235	$.80	☐	☐	☐	☐
33236	$.80	☐	☐	☐	☐
33237	$.80	☐	☐	☐	☐
33238	$.80	☐	☐	☐	☐
33239	$.80	☐	☐	☐	☐
33247	$.80	☐	☐	☐	☐

#1444 8¢ NATIVITY

Block of 12 (6 x 2)

33178-33179-33180-33181-33182-33183	$2.00	☐	☐	☐	☐
33184-33185-33186-33187-33188-33189	$2.00	☐	☐	☐	☐
33190-33191-33192-33193-33194-33195	$2.00	☐	☐	☐	☐

#1445 8¢ PARTRIDGE

Block of 12 (6 x 2)

33106-33107-33108-33109-33110-33111	$2.00	☐	☐	☐	☐
33106-33107-33108-33109-33211-33111	$2.00	☐	☐	☐	☐
33112-33113-33114-33115-33116-33117	$2.00	☐	☐	☐	☐
33118-33119-33120-33121-33122-33123	$2.00	☐	☐	☐	☐

1972 COMMEMORATIVES

#1446 8¢ LANIER

		UL	UR	LL	LR
33360	$.80	☐	☐	☐	☐
33361	$.80	☐	☐	☐	☐
33362	$.80	☐	☐	☐	☐
33364	$.80	☐	☐	☐	☐
33367	$.80	☐	☐	☐	☐
33374	$.80	☐	☐	☐	☐
33375	$.80	☐	☐	☐	☐
33376	$.80	☐	☐	☐	☐

#1447 8¢ PEACE CORPS

Block of 6 (3 x 2)

33223-33224-33225	$1.00	☐	☐	☐	☐
33226-33227-33228	$1.00	☐	☐	☐	☐

#1448-51 2¢ NATIONAL PARK

33460	$.50	☐	☐	☐	☐
33462	$.50	☐	☐	☐	☐
33467	$.50	☐	☐	☐	☐
33482	$.50	☐	☐	☐	☐
33483	$.50	☐	☐	☐	☐
33488	$.50	☐	☐	☐	☐
33489	$.50	☐	☐	☐	☐
33499	$.50	☐	☐	☐	☐

#1452 6¢ NATIONAL PARK

33603	$.60	☐	☐	☐	☐
33604	$.60	☐	☐	☐	☐
33618	$.60	☐	☐	☐	☐
33625	$.60	☐	☐	☐	☐
33632	$.60	☐	☐	☐	☐
33639	$.60	☐	☐	☐	☐
33646	$.60	☐	☐	☐	☐
33658	$.60	☐	☐	☐	☐

#1453 8¢ NATIONAL PARK

33411	$.80	☐	☐	☐	☐
33415	$.80	☐	☐	☐	☐
33416	$.80	☐	☐	☐	☐
33417	$.80	☐	☐	☐	☐
33418	$.80	☐	☐	☐	☐
33421	$.80	☐	☐	☐	☐
33424	$.80	☐	☐	☐	☐
33427	$.80	☐	☐	☐	☐

#1454 15¢ NATIONAL PARK

33717	$1.25	☐	☐	☐	☐
33719	$1.25	☐	☐	☐	☐
33726	$1.25	☐	☐	☐	☐
33727	$1.25	☐	☐	☐	☐
33728	$1.25	☐	☐	☐	☐

#1455 8¢ FAMILY PLANNING

		UL	UR	LL	LR
33383	$.80	☐	☐	☐	☐
33384	$.80	☐	☐	☐	☐
33386	$.80	☐	☐	☐	☐
33392	$.80	☐	☐	☐	☐
33395	$.80	☐	☐	☐	☐
33396	$.80	☐	☐	☐	☐
33397	$.80	☐	☐	☐	☐
33399	$.80	☐	☐	☐	☐

#1456-59 8¢ COLONIAL CRAFTSMEN

33580	$.80	☐	☐	☐	☐
33589	$.80	☐	☐	☐	☐
33590	$.80	☐	☐	☐	☐
33611	$.80	☐	☐	☐	☐
33665	$.80	☐	☐	☐	☐
33666	$.80	☐	☐	☐	☐

#1460 6¢ OLYMPICS

Block of 10 (2 x 5)

33312-33313-33314-33315-33316	$1.50	☐	☐	☐	☐

#1461 8¢ OLYMPICS

Block of 10 (2 x 5)

33327-33328-33329-33336-33331	$2.00	☐	☐	☐	☐
33333-33334-33335-33330-33337	$2.00	☐	☐	☐	☐

#1462 15¢ OLYMPICS

Block of 10 (2 x 5)

33317-33318-33319-33320-33321	$3.00	☐	☐	☐	☐

#1463 8¢ PARENT TEACHER

33654-33655	$.80	☐	☐	☐	☐
33656-33657	$.80	☐	☐	☐	☐

The lower right position of yellow plate number 33656 is printed in reverse.

#1464-67 8¢ WILDLIFE CONSERVATION

33729	$.80	☐	☐	☐	☐
33731	$.80	☐	☐	☐	☐
33738	$.80	☐	☐	☐	☐
33739	$.80	☐	☐	☐	☐
33757	$.80	☐	☐	☐	☐
33758	$.80	☐	☐	☐	☐
33759	$.80	☐	☐	☐	☐
33762	$.80	☐	☐	☐	☐
33805	$.80	☐	☐	☐	☐

1972 COMMEMORATIVES

#1468 8¢ MAIL ORDER

Block of 12 (2 x 6)		UL	UR	LL	LR
33745-33746-33747-33748-33749-33750	$2.00	☐	☐	☐	☐
33751-33752-33753-33754-33755-33756	$2.00	☐	☐	☐	☐

#1469 8¢ OSTEOPATHIC MEDICINE

Block of 6 (3 x 2)					
33784-33785-33786	$1.00	☐	☐	☐	☐
33787-33788-33789	$1.00	☐	☐	☐	☐

#1470 8¢ TOM SAWYER

33809	$.80	☐	☐	☐	☐
33811	$.80	☐	☐	☐	☐
33815	$.80	☐	☐	☐	☐
33819	$.80	☐	☐	☐	☐
33820	$.80	☐	☐	☐	☐
33828	$.80	☐	☐	☐	☐
33833	$.80	☐	☐	☐	☐
33834	$.80	☐	☐	☐	☐
33911	$.80	☐	☐	☐	☐
33924	$.80	☐	☐	☐	☐

#1471 8¢ ST. LUCY LEGEND

Block of 12 (6 x 2)					
33554-33555-33556-33557-33558-33559	$2.00	☐	☐	☐	☐
33560-33561-33562-33563-33564-33565	$2.00	☐	☐	☐	☐
33566-33567-33568-33569-33570-33571	$2.00	☐	☐	☐	☐

#1472 8¢ SANTA CLAUS

Block of 12 (6 x 2)					
33698-33699-33700-33701-33702-33703	$2.00	☐	☐	☐	☐
33704-33705-33700-33707-33708-33709	$2.00	☐	☐	☐	☐
33704-33705-33706-33707-33708-33709	$2.00	☐	☐	☐	☐
33710-33711-33712-33713-33714-33715	$2.00	☐	☐	☐	☐

#1473 8¢ PHARMACY

33808	$.80	☐	☐	☐	☐
33810	$.80	☐	☐	☐	☐
33812	$.80	☐	☐	☐	☐
33813	$.80	☐	☐	☐	☐
33814	$.80	☐	☐	☐	☐
33816	$.80	☐	☐	☐	☐
33818	$.80	☐	☐	☐	☐
33856	$.80	☐	☐	☐	☐

1972 COMMEMORATIVES

#1474 8¢ STAMP COLLECTING

		UL	UR	LL	LR
33847	$.80	☐	☐	☐	☐
33850	$.80	☐	☐	☐	☐
33851	$.80	☐	☐	☐	☐
33852	$.80	☐	☐	☐	☐
33857	$.80	☐	☐	☐	☐
33858	$.80	☐	☐	☐	☐
33861	$.80	☐	☐	☐	☐
33866	$.80	☐	☐	☐	☐

1973 COMMEMORATIVES

#1475 8¢ LOVE

Block of 6 (2 x 3)					
33931-33932-33933	$1.00	☐	☐	☐	☐
33934-33935-33937	$1.00	☐	☐	☐	☐

#1476 8¢ PAMPHLETEER

34046	$.80	☐	☐	☐	☐
34047	$.80	☐	☐	☐	☐
34048	$.80	☐	☐	☐	☐
34049	$.80	☐	☐	☐	☐
34050	$.80	☐	☐	☐	☐
34051	$.80	☐	☐	☐	☐
34053	$.80	☐	☐	☐	☐
34054	$.80	☐	☐	☐	☐

#1477 8¢ BROADSIDE

34116	$.80	☐	☐	☐	☐
34117	$.80	☐	☐	☐	☐
34119	$.80	☐	☐	☐	☐
34120	$.80	☐	☐	☐	☐
34121	$.80	☐	☐	☐	☐
34122	$.80	☐	☐	☐	☐
34123	$.80	☐	☐	☐	☐
34124	$.80	☐	☐	☐	☐

#1478 8¢ POST RIDER

34193	$.80	☐	☐	☐	☐
34196	$.80	☐	☐	☐	☐
34199	$.80	☐	☐	☐	☐
34200	$.80	☐	☐	☐	☐
34210	$.80	☐	☐	☐	☐
34211	$.80	☐	☐	☐	☐
34212	$.80	☐	☐	☐	☐
34226	$.80	☐	☐	☐	☐
34227	$.80	☐	☐	☐	☐
34229	$.80	☐	☐	☐	☐

1973 COMMEMORATIVES

#1479 8¢ DRUMMER

		UL	UR	LL	LR
34288	$.80	☐	☐	☐	☐
34313	$.80	☐	☐	☐	☐
34345	$.80	☐	☐	☐	☐
34346	$.80	☐	☐	☐	☐
34347	$.80	☐	☐	☐	☐
34350	$.80	☐	☐	☐	☐
34351	$.80	☐	☐	☐	☐
34352	$.80	☐	☐	☐	☐

#1480-83 8¢ BOSTON TEA PARTY

34225	$.80	☐	☐	☐	☐
34230	$.80	☐	☐	☐	☐
34236	$.80	☐	☐	☐	☐
34247	$.80	☐	☐	☐	☐
34250	$.80	☐	☐	☐	☐
34252	$.80	☐	☐	☐	☐
34261	$.80	☐	☐	☐	☐
34272	$.80	☐	☐	☐	☐

#1484 8¢ GEORGE GERSHWIN

Block of 12 (2 x 6)

33950-33951-33952-33953-33960-33955	$2.00	☐	☐	☐	☐
33956-33957-33958-33959-33954-33961	$2.00	☐	☐	☐	☐

#1485 8¢ ROBINSON JEFFERS

Block of 12 (2 x 6)

34301-34302-34303-34304-34305-34306	$2.00	☐	☐	☐	☐
34307-34308-34309-34310-34311-34312	$2.00	☐	☐	☐	☐

#1486 8¢ HENRY O. TANNER

Block of 12 (2 x 6)

34315-34316-34317-34318-34319-34320	$2.00	☐	☐	☐	☐
34321-34322-34323-34324-34325-34326	$2.00	☐	☐	☐	☐

#1487 8¢ WILLA CATHER

Block of 12 (2 x 6)

34355-34356-34357-34358-34359-34366	$2.00	☐	☐	☐	☐
34361-34362-34363-34364-34365-34366	$2.00	☐	☐	☐	☐

#1488 8¢ COPERNICUS

34105	$.80	☐	☐	☐	☐
34106	$.80	☐	☐	☐	☐
34107	$2.00	☐	☐	☐	☐
34110	$.80	☐	☐	☐	☐
34111	$.80	☐	☐	☐	☐
34112	$.80	☐	☐	☐	☐
34114	$.80	☐	☐	☐	☐
34115	$.80	☐	☐	☐	☐
34118	$.80	☐	☐	☐	☐

#1489-98 8¢ POSTAL PEOPLE

Block of 20 (10 x 2)

		UL	UR	LL	LR
34075-34076-34077-34078-34079	$3.25	☐	☐	☐	☐
34081-34082-34089-34084-34085	$3.25	☐	☐	☐	☐
34087-34088-34083-34090-34091	$3.25	☐	☐	☐	☐

Back Plate Numbers
†34080 †34086 *34092

#1499 8¢ HARRY S. TRUMAN

34153	$.80	☐	☐	☐	☐
34154	$.80	☐	☐	☐	☐
34155	$.80	☐	☐	☐	☐
34156	$.80	☐	☐	☐	☐
34159	$.80	☐	☐	☐	☐
34160	$.80	☐	☐	☐	☐
34161	$.80	☐	☐	☐	☐
34163	$.80	☐	☐	☐	☐
34164	$.80	☐	☐	☐	☐
34165	$.80	☐	☐	☐	☐
34167	$.80	☐	☐	☐	☐
34168	$.80	☐	☐	☐	☐
34169	$1.50	☐	☐	☐	☐
34177	$1.50	☐	☐	☐	☐

#1500 6¢ ELECTRONICS

34269	$.60	☐	☐	☐	☐
34270	$.60	☐	☐	☐	☐
34274	$.60	☐	☐	☐	☐
34275	$.60	☐	☐	☐	☐
34277	$.60	☐	☐	☐	☐
34278	$.60	☐	☐	☐	☐

#1501 8¢ ELECTRONICS

34233	$.80	☐	☐	☐	☐
34242	$.80	☐	☐	☐	☐
34249	$.80	☐	☐	☐	☐
34251	$.80	☐	☐	☐	☐
34260	$.80	☐	☐	☐	☐
34268	$.80	☐	☐	☐	☐
34273	$.80	☐	☐	☐	☐
34276	$.80	☐	☐	☐	☐

#1502 15¢ ELECTRONICS

34279	$1.50	☐	☐	☐	☐
34285	$1.50	☐	☐	☐	☐
34287	$1.50	☐	☐	☐	☐
34293	$1.50	☐	☐	☐	☐
34300	$1.50	☐	☐	☐	☐

#1503 8¢ LYNDON JOHNSON

Block of 12 (6 x 2)		UL	UR	LL	LR
34213-34214-34215-34216-34217-34218	$2.00	☐	☐	☐	☐
34219-34220-34221-34222-34223-34224	$2.00	☐	☐	☐	☐

1973-74 COMMEMORATIVES

#1504 8¢ ANGUS CATTLE

34379	$.80	☐	☐	☐	☐
34380	$.80	☐	☐	☐	☐
34382	$.80	☐	☐	☐	☐
34383	$.80	☐	☐	☐	☐
34384	$.80	☐	☐	☐	☐
34385	$.80	☐	☐	☐	☐
34386	$.80	☐	☐	☐	☐
34387	$.80	☐	☐	☐	☐
34390	$.80	☐	☐	☐	☐
34391	$.80	☐	☐	☐	☐
34394	$.80	☐	☐	☐	☐
34395	$.80	☐	☐	☐	☐
34401	$.80	☐	☐	☐	☐
34404	$.80	☐	☐	☐	☐

#1505 10¢ CHAUTAUQUA

35495	$.90	☐	☐	☐	☐
35498	$.90	☐	☐	☐	☐
35499	$.90	☐	☐	☐	☐
35500	$.90	☐	☐	☐	☐
35502	$.90	☐	☐	☐	☐
35503	$.90	☐	☐	☐	☐
35508	$.90	☐	☐	☐	☐
35509	$.90	☐	☐	☐	☐
35510	$.90	☐	☐	☐	☐
35511	$.90	☐	☐	☐	☐
35515	$.90	☐	☐	☐	☐
35526	$.90	☐	☐	☐	☐

#1506 10¢ KANSAS WHEAT

35543	$.90	☐	☐	☐	☐
35544	$.90	☐	☐	☐	☐
35545	$.90	☐	☐	☐	☐
35550	$.90	☐	☐	☐	☐
35551	$.90	☐	☐	☐	☐
35552	$.90	☐	☐	☐	☐
35553	$.90	☐	☐	☐	☐
35554	$.90	☐	☐	☐	☐
35555	$.90	☐	☐	☐	☐
35558	$.90	☐	☐	☐	☐
35561	$.90	☐	☐	☐	☐
35563	$.90	☐	☐	☐	☐

1973-74 COMMEMORATIVES

#1507 6¢ MADONNA

Block of 12 (6 x 2)		UL	UR	LL	LR
34125-34126-34127-34128-34129-34130	$2.00	☐	☐	☐	☐
34131-34132-34133-34134-34135-34136	$2.00	☐	☐	☐	☐
34137-34138-34139-34140-34141-34142	$2.00	☐	☐	☐	☐

#1508 8¢ CHRISTMAS TREE

Block of 12 (6 x 2)

34327-34328-34329-34330-34331-34332	$2.00	☐	☐	☐	☐
34333-34334-34335-34336-34337-34338	$2.00	☐	☐	☐	☐
34339-34340-34341-34342-34343-34344	$2.00	☐	☐	☐	☐

1973-74 REGULAR ISSUE

#1509 10¢ CROSSED FLAGS

80 Subject Plates 9 Color Huck

Positions T, B only

Block of 20 (10 x 2)

It is possible to collect both the top and the bottom plate strips in four different combinations. Using Z to represent the Zip Code, M to represent Mail Early, N to represent the plate number and B to represent a blank tab, the following are the margin positions reading from left to right in a plate block of 20.

1) B R M Z B R M Z B R
2) R M Z B R M Z B R M
3) M Z B R M Z B R M Z
4) Z B R M Z B R M Z B

Basic Price $4.00

ALTERNATE PRINTING

1) R B Z M R B Z M R B
2) B Z M R B Z M R B Z
3) Z M R B Z M R B Z M
4) M R B Z M R B Z M R

Basic Price $8.00

BLUE PLATES **95 Plates**

34641	34642	34643	34644	34645
34646	34663	34664	34665	34666
34667	34668	34669	34670	34671
34672	34673	34674	34687	34688
34689	34690	34691	34692	34699

1973-74 REGULAR ISSUE

#1509 10¢ CROSSED FLAGS

BLUE PLATES **Cont.**

34700	34701	34702	34703	34704
34705	34706	34707	34708	34709
34710	34723	34724	34725	34726
34727	34728	34744	34745	34746
34747	34748	34749	34876	34877
34878	34879	34880	34881	34892
34893	34894	34895	34896	34897
34908	34909	34910	34911	34912
34913	34943	34944	34945	34946
34947	34948	34960	34961	34962
34963	34964	34965	34972	34973
34974	34975	34976	34977	34986
34987	34988	34989	34990	34991
35179	35180	†35181	35183	35184

RED PLATES **197 Plates**

34647	34648	34649	34650	34651
34652	34675	34676	34677	34678
34679	34680	34681	34682	34683
34684	34685	34686	34693	34694
34695	34696	34697	34711	34712
34713	34714	34715	34717	34718
34719	34720	34721	34722	34733
34734	34735	34736	34737	34738
34750	34751	34752	34753	34754
34755	34768	34769	34770	34771
34772	34773	34885	34886	34887
34888	34889	34890	34899	34900
34901	34902	34903	34904	34914
34915	34916	34917	34918	34919
34935	34936	34937	34938	34939
34940	34949	34950	†34951	34953
34954	34966	34967	34968	34969
34970	34971	34979	34980	34981
34982	34983	34984	34993	34994
34995	34996	34997	34998	35000
35001	*35002	35003	35004	35005
35006	35007	35008	35009	†35010
35011	35012	35013	35014	35015
35016	35017	35018	35019	†35020
35021	35022	35023	35030	35031
35032	35033	35034	35035	35173
35174	35175	35176	35177	35178
35185	35186	35187	*35188	35189
35190	35200	*35345	†35451	35452
†35464	†35469	†35478	†35479	†35480
†35481	35881	*35882	*35883	*35884
*35885	*35886	35899	35900	35901
35902	35903	35910	35911	35912
35913	35914	35915	35923	35924
35925	35926	35927	35928	35935
35936	35937	35938	35939	35940
35954	35955	35956	35957	35958
35959	35969	†35970	35971	35972
35973	35978	35979	35980	†35981
35982	35983			

#1510 10¢ JEFFERSON MEMORIAL

20 Plates		UL	UR	LL	LR
34591	$.90	□	□	□	□
34592	$.90	□	□	□	□
34593	$.90	□	□	□	□
34594	$.90	□	□	□	□
34595	$.90	□	□	□	□
34596	$.90	□	□	□	□
35042	$.90	□	□	□	□
35043	$.90	□	□	□	□
35191	$.90	□	□	□	□
35192	$.90	□	□	□	□
35680	$.90	□	□	□	□
35681	$.90	□	□	□	□
35766	$.90	□	□	□	□
35767	$.90	□	□	□	□
35781	$.90	□	□	□	□
35782	$.90	□	□	□	□
35783	$.90	□	□	□	□
35784	$.90	□	□	□	□
36003	$.90	□	□	□	□
36004	$.90	□	□	□	□

#1511 10¢ ZIP CODE

Block of 8 (2 x 4)

34415-34416-34417-34418	$1.90	□	□	□	□
34420-34421-34422-34423	$1.90	□	□	□	□

BOOKLET PANES

#1510b 10¢ JEFFERSON MEMORIAL

360 Subject Plates **PANES OF 5**

*34729 †34730 *34731 *34732 †34957 *34958

#1510c 10¢ JEFFERSON MEMORIAL

400 Subject Plates **PANES OF 8**

†34482 †34483 †34499 †34500 †34526 †34527 †34534 †34535 †34536 †34537 †35293 †35294 †35674 †35675 †35682 †35764 †35765 †35785 †35786 †35787 †35788 †36005 †36006 †36068 †36121 †36122

#1510d 10¢ JEFFERSON MEMORIAL

360 Subject Plates **PANES OF 6**

*35211 †35212

See Appendix G for largest reported plate number percentage by position.

1974 REGULAR ISSUE

SIDE COILS

PERF. 10 VERTICALLY

#1518 6.3¢ LIBERTY BELL

432 Subject Plates **STRIPS OF 6**

35612 35613 35614 35615

#1519 10¢ CROSSED FLAGS

72 Subject Plates 9 Color Huck

Of the 191 plates used to print the red portion of this stamp, only the following plates have been reported.

34528	34562	34604	34605	34607
34608	34813	34825	34830	35038
35040	35156	35158	35194	35286
35290	35370	35383	35397	35398
35427	35429	35439	35442	35459
35471	35473	35483	35487	35488

Of the 155 plates used to print the blue portion of this stamp, only the following plates have been reported.

34476	34508	34551	34556	34598
34618	34786	34797	34799	34802
34823	34849	34850	35029	35061
35845	35871	35872	35873	35891
35892	35894	35907	35932	

#1520 10¢ JEFFERSON MEMORIAL

432 Subject Plates **STRIPS OF 6**

34388	34389	34413	34414	34497
34498	34654	34655	34656	†34657
†34658	†34659	34924	35280	35281
35323	†35504	†35505	†35506	†35507
†35547	†35548	†35549	†35560	†35570
†35624	†35625	†35626	†35627	†35695
†35696	†35697	†35698	†35699	†35700
†35701	†35702	†35705	†35706	†35758
35759	35760	35761	36008	†36012
36013	†36014	36087	†36088	†36119
36120	36205	†36206	†36207	†36359
†36360	36827	36828	†36849	36850
37122	37148	†37149	†37595	

1974 COMMEMORATIVES

#1525 10¢ VETERANS OF FOREIGN WARS

		UL	UR	LL	LR
34868	$.90	☐	☐	☐	☐
34884	$.90	☐	☐	☐	☐
34891	$.90	☐	☐	☐	☐
34898	$.90	☐	☐	☐	☐
34905	$.90	☐	☐	☐	☐
34920	$.90	☐	☐	☐	☐
34929	$2.50	☐	☐	☐	☐
34933	$.90	☐	☐	☐	☐
34934	$.90	☐	☐	☐	☐
34985	$.90	☐	☐	☐	☐
34999	$.90	☐	☐	☐	☐

#1526 10¢ ROBERT FROST

34882	$.90	☐	☐	☐	☐
34883	$.90	☐	☐	☐	☐
34922	$.90	☐	☐	☐	☐
34923	$.90	☐	☐	☐	☐

1974 COMMEMORATIVES

#1527 10¢ EXPO '74

Block of 12 (2 x 6)

		UL	UR	LL	LR
34442-34443-34444-34445-34446-34447	$2.50	☐	☐	☐	☐
34448-34449-34450-34451-34452-34453	$2.50	☐	☐	☐	☐

#1528 10¢ HORSE RACING

Block of 12 (2 x 6)

35108-35109-35110-35111-35112-35113	$2.50	☐	☐	☐	☐
35114-35115-35116-35117-35118-35119	$2.50	☐	☐	☐	☐

#1529 10¢ SKYLAB

35213	$.90	☐	☐	☐	☐
35214	$.90	☐	☐	☐	☐
35215	$.90	☐	☐	☐	☐
35216	$.90	☐	☐	☐	☐
35217	$.90	☐	☐	☐	☐
35218	$.90	☐	☐	☐	☐
35219	$.90	☐	☐	☐	☐
35220	$.90	☐	☐	☐	☐
35221	$.90	☐	☐	☐	☐
35222	$.90	☐	☐	☐	☐
35227	$.90	☐	☐	☐	☐
35256	$.90	☐	☐	☐	☐

#1530-37 10¢ UNIVERSAL POSTAL UNION

Block of 10 (5 x 2)

35263-35264-36265-35266-35267	$2.50	☐	☐	☐	☐
35268-35269-35270-35271-35272	$2.50	☐	☐	☐	☐

#1538-41 10¢ MINERAL HERITAGE

35062	$.90	☐	☐	☐	☐
35063	$.90	☐	☐	☐	☐
35064	$.90	☐	☐	☐	☐
35067	$.90	☐	☐	☐	☐
35068	$.90	☐	☐	☐	☐
35069	$.90	☐	☐	☐	☐
35077	$.90	☐	☐	☐	☐
35078	$.90	☐	☐	☐	☐
35079	$.90	☐	☐	☐	☐
35080	$.90	☐	☐	☐	☐

#1542 10¢ FORT HARROD

35245	$.90	☐	☐	☐	☐
35246	$.90	☐	☐	☐	☐
35248	$.90	☐	☐	☐	☐
35255	$.90	☐	☐	☐	☐
35258	$.90	☐	☐	☐	☐
35259	$.90	☐	☐	☐	☐
35260	$.90	☐	☐	☐	☐
35261	$.90	☐	☐	☐	☐
35262	$.90	☐	☐	☐	☐
35273	$.90	☐	☐	☐	☐
35279	$.90	☐	☐	☐	☐
35284	$.90	☐	☐	☐	☐

1974 COMMEMORATIVES

#1543-46 10¢CONTINENTAL CONGRESS

		UL	UR	LL	LR
35308	$.90	☐	☐	☐	☐
35309	$.90	☐	☐	☐	☐
35310	$.90	☐	☐	☐	☐
35311	$.90	☐	☐	☐	☐
35312	$.90	☐	☐	☐	☐
35313	$.90	☐	☐	☐	☐
35314	$.90	☐	☐	☐	☐
35315	$.90	☐	☐	☐	☐
35325	$.90	☐	☐	☐	☐
35326	$.90	☐	☐	☐	☐
35335	$.90	☐	☐	☐	☐
35336	$.90	☐	☐	☐	☐
35350	$.90	☐	☐	☐	☐
35358	$.90	☐	☐	☐	☐
35394	$.90	☐	☐	☐	☐
35401	$.90	☐	☐	☐	☐

#1547 10¢ ENERGY

35100	$.90	☐	☐	☐	☐
35101	$.90	☐	☐	☐	☐
35102	$.90	☐	☐	☐	☐
35103	$.90	☐	☐	☐	☐
35104	$.90	☐	☐	☐	☐
35105	$.90	☐	☐	☐	☐
35106	$.90	☐	☐	☐	☐
35107	$.90	☐	☐	☐	☐
35120	$.90	☐	☐	☐	☐
35121	$.90	☐	☐	☐	☐
35122	$.90	☐	☐	☐	☐
35123	$.90	☐	☐	☐	☐
35124	$.90	☐	☐	☐	☐
35125	$.90	☐	☐	☐	☐

#1548 10¢ SLEEPY HOLLOW

35617	$.90	☐	☐	☐	☐
35618	$.90	☐	☐	☐	☐
35619	$.90	☐	☐	☐	☐
35622	$.90	☐	☐	☐	☐
35623	$.90	☐	☐	☐	☐
35650	$.90	☐	☐	☐	☐
35651	$.90	☐	☐	☐	☐
35652	$.90	☐	☐	☐	☐

#1549 10¢ RETARDED CHILDREN

35496	$.90	☐	☐	☐	☐
35497	$.90	☐	☐	☐	☐
35501	$.90	☐	☐	☐	☐
35514	$.90	☐	☐	☐	☐
35525	$.90	☐	☐	☐	☐
35528	$.90	☐	☐	☐	☐
35529	$.90	☐	☐	☐	☐
35535	$.90	☐	☐	☐	☐

1974 COMMEMORATIVES

#1550 10¢ CHRISTMAS ANGEL

Block of 10 (5 x 2)

		UL	UR	LL	LR
35591-35592-35593-35594-35595	$2	☐	☐	☐	☐
35596-35597 35598-35599-35600	$2	☐	☐	☐	☐
35596-35597-35598-35599-35673	$2	☐	☐	☐	☐
35596-35597-35598-35599-35688	$2	☐	☐	☐	☐
35601-35602-35603-35604-35605	$2	☐	☐	☐	☐
35601-35602-35603-35604-35690	$2	☐	☐	☐	☐

#1551 10¢ CURRIER & IVES

Block of 12 (2 x 6)

35408-35409-35410-35411-35412-35413	$2.50	☐	☐	☐	☐
35414-35415-35416-35417-35418-35419	$2.50	☐	☐	☐	☐
35420-35421-35422-35423-35424-35425	$2.50	☐	☐	☐	☐

#1552 10¢ CHRISTMAS PEACE

UNTAGGED

Block of 12 (2 x 6)

35634-35635-35636-35637-35638-35639	$3	☐	☐	☐	☐
35640-35641-35642-35643-35644-35645	$3	☐	☐	☐	☐

1975 COMMEMORATIVES

#1553 10¢ BENJAMIN WEST

Block of 10 (5 x 2)

35384-35385-35386-35387-35388	$2	☐	☐	☐	☐
35389-35390-35391-35392-35393	$2	☐	☐	☐	☐

#1554 10¢ P.L. DUNBAR

Block of 10 (5 x 2)

36027-36028-36029-36030-36031	$2	☐	☐	☐	☐

#1555 10¢ D.W. GRIFFITH

36037	$1.00	☐	☐	☐	☐
36039	$1.00	☐	☐	☐	☐
36040	$1.00	☐	☐	☐	☐
36045	$1.50	☐	☐	☐	☐
36046	$1.50	☐	☐	☐	☐
36047	$1.00	☐	☐	☐	☐
36048	$1.50	☐	☐	☐	☐
36050	$1.00	☐	☐	☐	☐

1975 COMMEMORATIVES

#1555 10¢ D.W. GRIFFITH Cont.

		UL	UR	LL	LR
36065	$.90	☐	☐	☐	☐
36072	$.90	☐	☐	☐	☐
36073	$.90	☐	☐	☐	☐
36079	$.90	☐	☐	☐	☐

#1556 10¢ JUPITER

35813	$.90	☐	☐	☐	☐
35820	$.90	☐	☐	☐	☐
35821	$.90	☐	☐	☐	☐
35822	$.90	☐	☐	☐	☐
35823	$.90	☐	☐	☐	☐
35824	$.90	☐	☐	☐	☐
35831	$.90	☐	☐	☐	☐
35832	$.90	☐	☐	☐	☐
35838	$.90	☐	☐	☐	☐
35841	$.90	☐	☐	☐	☐
35848	$.90	☐	☐	☐	☐
35849	$.90	☐	☐	☐	☐
35850	$.90	☐	☐	☐	☐
35863	$.90	☐	☐	☐	☐

#1557 10¢ MARINER

35947	$.90	☐	☐	☐	☐
35966	$.90	☐	☐	☐	☐
35967	$.90	☐	☐	☐	☐
35968	$.90	☐	☐	☐	☐
35975	$.90	☐	☐	☐	☐
35976	$.90	☐	☐	☐	☐
35977	$.90	☐	☐	☐	☐
35984	$.90	☐	☐	☐	☐
35985	$.90	☐	☐	☐	☐
35989	$.90	☐	☐	☐	☐
35990	$.90	☐	☐	☐	☐
35991	$.90	☐	☐	☐	☐
35992	$.90	☐	☐	☐	☐
35993	$.90	☐	☐	☐	☐
35997	$.90	☐	☐	☐	☐
36002	$.90	☐	☐	☐	☐

#1558 10¢ COLLECTIVE BARGAINING

Block of 8 (2 x 4)

35583-35584-35585-35586
$1.75 ☐ ☐ ☐ ☐

35587-35588-35589-35590
$1.75 ☐ ☐ ☐ ☐

#1559 8¢ SYBIL LUDINGTON

Block of 10 (2 x 5)

35722-35723-35730-35725-35726
$1.60 ☐ ☐ ☐ ☐

Back Plate Number

†35727

#1560 10¢ SALEM POOR

Block of 10 (2 x 5)

35734-35735-35736-35737-35738
$2.00 ☐ ☐ ☐ ☐

Back Plate Number

*35739

#1561 10¢ HAYM SALOMON

Block of 10 (2 x 5) UL UR LL LR

35716-35711-35712-35719-35720
$2.00 ☐ ☐ ☐ ☐

35716-35717-35718-35719-35720
$2.00 ☐ ☐ ☐ ☐

Back Plate Number

†35715 †35721

#1562 18¢ PETER FRANCISCO

Block of 10 (2 x 5)

35746-35747-34748-34749-34750
$3.75 ☐ ☐ ☐ ☐

Back Plate Number

†35751

#1563 10¢ LEXINGTON-CONCORD

Block of 12 (2 x 6)

35789-35790-35791-35792-35793-35794
$2.50 ☐ ☐ ☐ ☐

35795-35796-35797-35798-35799-35800
$2.50 ☐ ☐ ☐ ☐

#1564 10¢ BUNKER HILL

Block of 12 (6 x 2)

36015-36016-36017-36018-36019-36020
$2.50 ☐ ☐ ☐ ☐

36015-36016-36017-36024-36019-36026
$2.50 ☐ ☐ ☐ ☐

#1565-68 10¢ MILITARY UNIFORMS

Block of 12 (6 x 2)

36053-36054-36055-36056-36057-36058
$2.50 ☐ ☐ ☐ ☐

36059-36060-36061-36062-36063-36064
$2.50 ☐ ☐ ☐ ☐

#1569-70 10¢ APOLLO-SOYUZ

Block of 12 (2 x 6)

36297-36298-36299-36306-36301-36302
$2.50 ☐ ☐ ☐ ☐

36297-36577-36299-36306-36301-36302
$2.50 ☐ ☐ ☐ ☐

36303-36304-36305-36300-36307-36308
$2.50 ☐ ☐ ☐ ☐

#1571 10¢ WOMEN'S YEAR

Block of 6 (2 x 3)

36431-36432-36433
$1.25 ☐ ☐ ☐ ☐

36434-36435-36436
$1.25 ☐ ☐ ☐ ☐

#1572-75 10¢ U.S.P.S. BICENTENNIAL

Block of 12 (2 x 6)

36331-36332-36333-36334-36335-36336
$2.50 ☐ ☐ ☐ ☐

36337-36338-36339-36340-36341-36342
$5.00 ☐ ☐ ☐ ☐

1975 COMMEMORATIVES

#1580 (10¢) CHRISTMAS CARD

Block of 12 (6 x 2)

"L" Perforator 10.9 x 10.9

Plate Numbers	Price	UL	UR	LL	LR
36630-36631-36632-36633-36634-36635	$5.00	□	□	□	□
36636-36637-36638-36639-36640-36641	$2.60	□	□	□	□
36642-36643-36644-36645-36646-36647	$2.60	□	□	□	□

EXAMPLE OF IN-LINE PERFORATION

#1580 (10¢) CHRISTMAS CARD

Block of 12 (6 x 2)

In-Line Perforator 11.2 x 11.2

Plate Numbers	Price	UL	UR	LL	LR
36630-36631-36632-36633-36634-36635	$5.00	□	□	□	□
36636-36637-36638-36639-36640 -36641	$2.60	□	□	□	□
36642-36643-36644-36645-36646-36647	$2.60	□	□	□	□
36886-36637-36638-36639-36640-36641	$2.60	□	□	□	□

EXAMPLE OF EE PERFOPATION

#1580b (10¢) CHRISTMAS CARD

Block of 12 (6 x 2)

EE Perforator 10.5 x 11.3

Plate Numbers	Price	UL	UR	LL	LR
36642-36643-36644-36645-36646-36647	$50.00	□	□	□	□
36886-36637-36638-36639-36640-36641	$15.00	□	□	□	□

EXAMPLE OF "L" PERFORATION

NOTE:

"L" PERFORATION 10.9 x 10.9
HORIZONTAL & VERTICAL perfs through margins

EE PERFORATION 10.5 x 11.3
HORIZONTAL perfs through side margin
VERTICAL perfs NOT through side margin

IN-LINE PERFORATION 11.2 x 11.2
NO perforations through margins

1975 COMMEMORATIVES

#1576 10¢ WORLD PEACE

		UL	UR	LL	LR
36467	$.90	☐	☐	☐	☐
36487	$.90	☐	☐	☐	☐
36488	$.90	☐	☐	☐	☐
36489	$.90	☐	☐	☐	☐
36496	$.90	☐	☐	☐	☐
36497	$.90	☐	☐	☐	☐
36506	$.90	☐	☐	☐	☐
36513	$.90	☐	☐	☐	☐
36514	$.90	☐	☐	☐	☐
36515	$.90	☐	☐	☐	☐
36526	$.90	☐	☐	☐	☐
36527	$.90	☐	☐	☐	☐
36528	$.90	☐	☐	☐	☐
36535	$.90	☐	☐	☐	☐
36538	$.90	☐	☐	☐	☐
36552	$.90	☐	☐	☐	☐

#1577-78 10¢ BANKING

36835	$1.25	☐	☐	☐	☐
36843	$.90	☐	☐	☐	☐
36844	$.90	☐	☐	☐	☐
36845	$1.25	☐	☐	☐	☐
36846	$.90	☐	☐	☐	☐
36847	$1.25	☐	☐	☐	☐
36848	$.90	☐	☐	☐	☐
36852	$.90	☐	☐	☐	☐
36864	$1.25	☐	☐	☐	☐
36865	$.90	☐	☐	☐	☐
36866	$.90	☐	☐	☐	☐
36867	$.90	☐	☐	☐	☐
36868	$.90	☐	☐	☐	☐
36879	$.90	☐	☐	☐	☐

#1579 (10¢) MADONNA

Block of 12 (6 x 2)

36741-36742-36743-36744-36745-36746	$2.60	☐	☐	☐	☐
36747-36748-36749-36750-36751-36752	$2.60	☐	☐	☐	☐
36753-36754-36755-36756-36757-36758	$5.00	☐	☐	☐	☐

#1580 (10¢) CHRISTMAS CARD

See page 209

1975 REGULAR ISSUE

The 1975 regular issue is also known as the Americana Series.

#1581 1¢ ABILITY TO WRITE 6 Plates

SHINY GUM GREENISH PAPER

38251	$.25	☐	☐	☐	☐
38252	$.25	☐	☐	☐	☐
38255	$.25	☐	☐	☐	☐
38256	$.25	☐	☐	☐	☐
38257	$.25	☐	☐	☐	☐
38258	$.25	☐	☐	☐	☐

1975 REGULAR ISSUE

#1581 1¢ ABILITY TO WRITE 8 Plates

DULL GUM GREENISH PAPER

		UL	UR	LL	LR
38252	$.25	☐	☐	☐	☐
38256	$.25	☐	☐	☐	☐
38257	$.25	☐	☐	☐	☐
38258	$.25	☐	☐	☐	☐
39423	$.25	☐	☐	☐	☐
39424	$.25	☐	☐	☐	☐
39682	$.25	☐	☐	☐	☐
39683	$.25	☐	☐	☐	☐

#1581c 1¢ ABILITY TO WRITE 2 Plates

DULL GUM WHITE PAPER

38257	$25.00	☐	☐	☐	☐
38258	$25.00	☐	☐	☐	☐

#1582 2¢ FREEDOM TO SPEAK OUT 10 Plates

SHINY GUM TINTED PAPER

38281	$.30	☐	☐	☐	☐
38282	$.30	☐	☐	☐	☐
38287	$.30	☐	☐	☐	☐
38288	$.30	☐	☐	☐	☐
38601	$.30	☐	☐	☐	☐
38602	$.30	☐	☐	☐	☐
38603	$.30	☐	☐	☐	☐
38604	$.30	☐	☐	☐	☐
38605	$.30	☐	☐	☐	☐
38606	$.30	☐	☐	☐	☐

#1582 2¢ FREEDOM TO SPEAK OUT 7 Plates

DULL GUM TINTED PAPER

38281	$2.50	☐	☐	☐	☐
38287	$2.50	☐	☐	☐	☐
38601	$2.50	☐	☐	☐	☐
38602	$2.50	☐	☐	☐	☐
38603	$2.50	☐	☐	☐	☐
38604	$2.50	☐	☐	☐	☐
38606	$2.50	☐	☐	☐	☐

#1582 2¢ FREEDOM TO SPEAK OUT 9 Plates

DULL GUM WHITE PAPER

38287	$.30	☐	☐	☐	☐
38602	$.30	☐	☐	☐	☐
38603	$.30	☐	☐	☐	☐
38604	$.30	☐	☐	☐	☐
38606	$.30	☐	☐	☐	☐
39773	$.30	☐	☐	☐	☐
39774	$.30	☐	☐	☐	☐
39817	$.30	☐	☐	☐	☐
39818	$.30	☐	☐	☐	☐

1975 REGULAR ISSUE

#1584 3¢ TO CAST A FREE BALLOT

SHINY GUM — GREENISH PAPER

4 Plates

Plate	Price	UL	UR	LL	LR
38277	$.35	☐	☐	☐	☐
38278	$.35	☐	☐	☐	☐
38279	$.35	☐	☐	☐	☐
38280	$.35	☐	☐	☐	☐

#1584 3¢ TO CAST A FREE BALLOT

16 Plates

DULL GUM — GREENISH PAPER

Plate	Price	UL	UR	LL	LR
38277	$.50	☐	☐	☐	☐
38278	$.50	☐	☐	☐	☐
38279	$.50	☐	☐	☐	☐
38290	$.50	☐	☐	☐	☐
39535	$.50	☐	☐	☐	☐
39536	$.50	☐	☐	☐	☐
39548	$.50	☐	☐	☐	☐
39549	$.50	☐	☐	☐	☐
39562	$.50	☐	☐	☐	☐
39563	$.50	☐	☐	☐	☐
39601	$.50	☐	☐	☐	☐
39602	$.50	☐	☐	☐	☐
39603	$.50	☐	☐	☐	☐
39604	$.50	☐	☐	☐	☐
39616	$.50	☐	☐	☐	☐
39617	$.50	☐	☐	☐	☐

#1585 4¢ A PUBLIC THAT READS

4 Plates

SHINY GUM — CREAM PAPER

Plate	Price	UL	UR	LL	LR
38283	$.45	☐	☐	☐	☐
38284	$.45	☐	☐	☐	☐
38291	$.45	☐	☐	☐	☐
38398	$.45	☐	☐	☐	☐

#1585 4¢ A PUBLIC THAT READS

9 Plates

DULL GUM — CREAM PAPER

Plate	Price	UL	UR	LL	LR
38284	$1.25	☐	☐	☐	☐
39457	$1.25	☐	☐	☐	☐
39458	$1.25	☐	☐	☐	☐
39524	$1.25	☐	☐	☐	☐
39525	$1.25	☐	☐	☐	☐
39586	$1.25	☐	☐	☐	☐
39587	$1.25	☐	☐	☐	☐
39591	$1.25	☐	☐	☐	☐
39592	$1.25	☐	☐	☐	☐

#1591 9¢ FREEDOM TO ASSEMBLE

10 Plates

SHINY GUM — GREY PAPER

Plate	Price	UL	UR	LL	LR
36922	$.90	☐	☐	☐	☐
36923	$.90	☐	☐	☐	☐
36939	$.90	☐	☐	☐	☐
36940	$.90	☐	☐	☐	☐
36941	$.90	☐	☐	☐	☐
36942	$.90	☐	☐	☐	☐
37443	$.90	☐	☐	☐	☐
37444	$.90	☐	☐	☐	☐
38348	$.90	☐	☐	☐	☐
38349	$.90	☐	☐	☐	☐

#1591 9¢ FREEDOM TO ASSEMBLE

DULL GUM — GREY PAPER

4 Plates

Plate	Price	UL	UR	LL	LR
38348	$5.00	☐	☐	☐	☐
38349	$5.00	☐	☐	☐	☐
38895	$5.00	☐	☐	☐	☐
38896	$5.00	☐	☐	☐	☐

#1592 10¢ RIGHT TO PETITION 8 Plates

SHINY GUM — GREY PAPER

Plate	Price	UL	UR	LL	LR
37245	$1.00	☐	☐	☐	☐
37246	$1.00	☐	☐	☐	☐
37247	$1.00	☐	☐	☐	☐
37248	$1.00	☐	☐	☐	☐
37249	$1.00	☐	☐	☐	☐
37250	$1.00	☐	☐	☐	☐
37251	$1.00	☐	☐	☐	☐
37641	$1.00	☐	☐	☐	☐

#1592 10¢ RIGHT TO PETITION 8 Plates

DULL GUM — GREY PAPER

Plate	Price	UL	UR	LL	LR
37248	$1.00	☐	☐	☐	☐
37250	$1.00	☐	☐	☐	☐
37251	$1.00	☐	☐	☐	☐
37641	$1.00	☐	☐	☐	☐
39453	$1.00	☐	☐	☐	☐
39454	$1.00	☐	☐	☐	☐
39459	$1.00	☐	☐	☐	☐
39460	$1.00	☐	☐	☐	☐

#1593 11¢ FREEDOM OF PRESS 8 Plates

SHINY GUM — GREY PAPER

Plate	Price	UL	UR	LL	LR
36915	$1.10	☐	☐	☐	☐
36916	$1.10	☐	☐	☐	☐
36924	$1.10	☐	☐	☐	☐
36925	$1.10	☐	☐	☐	☐
36929	$1.10	☐	☐	☐	☐
36935	$1.10	☐	☐	☐	☐
36936	$1.10	☐	☐	☐	☐
36943	$1.10	☐	☐	☐	☐

#1594 12¢ FREEDOM OF CONSCIENCE

6 Plates

DULL GUM — BEIGE PAPER

Plate	Price	UL	UR	LL	LR
37808	$1.50	☐	☐	☐	☐
37842	$1.50	☐	☐	☐	☐
37843	$1.50	☐	☐	☐	☐
37929	$1.50	☐	☐	☐	☐
37930	$1.50	☐	☐	☐	☐
37931	$1.50	☐	☐	☐	☐

#1595 13¢ LIBERTY BELL

See page 213

#1596 13¢ EAGLE and SHIELD

Block of 12 (2 x 6) — 29 Combinations

In-Line Perforator 11.2 x 11.2

Plates	Price				
36309-36310-36311-36312-36313-36314	$3.50	☐	☐	☐	☐
36315-36316-36317-36318-36319-36320	$3.50	☐	☐	☐	☐
36315-37917-36317-37663-37664-37921	$3.50	☐	☐	☐	☐

1975 REGULAR ISSUE

#1596 13¢ EAGLE and SHIELD Cont.

Plate Numbers	Price	UL	UR	LL	LR
36315-37918-38204-37920-37664-37921	$3.50	☐	☐	☐	☐
37231-37232-37233-37234-37235-37236	$3.50	☐	☐	☐	☐
37231-37232-37237-37234-37235-37236	$3.50	☐	☐	☐	☐
37347-37348-37349-37350-37351-37352	$3.50	☐	☐	☐	☐
37347-37460-37233-37919-36319-37921	$3.50	☐	☐	☐	☐
37347-37460-37349-37462-37351-37464	$3.50	☐	☐	☐	☐
37347-37666-37233-37920-37463-37921	$3.50	☐	☐	☐	☐
37347-37918-37233-37920-37463-37921	$3.50	☐	☐	☐	☐
37459-37460-37461-37462-37463-37464	$3.50	☐	☐	☐	☐
37459-37666-37461-37350-37463-37352	$3.50	☐	☐	☐	☐
37459-37666-37461-37350-37463-37464	$3.50	☐	☐	☐	☐
37459-37666-37461-37462-37463-37464	$20.00	☐	☐	☐	☐
37660-37661-37233-37663-37351-37464	$3.50	☐	☐	☐	☐
37660-37661-37233-37663-37664-37464	$3.50	☐	☐	☐	☐
37660-37661-37461-37350-36319-37464	$3.50	☐	☐	☐	☐
37660-37661-37461-37350-37351-37464	$3.50	☐	☐	☐	☐
37660-37661-36461-37663-37351-37464	$3.50	☐	☐	☐	☐
37660-37661-37662-37663-37664-37464	$3.50	☐	☐	☐	☐
37660-37661-37662-37663-37664-37665	$3.50	☐	☐	☐	☐
38195-37918-37349-38198-38199-38200	$15.00	☐	☐	☐	☐
38195-38203-37349-38198-38199-38200	$15.00	☐	☐	☐	☐
38202-38196-38197-38205-38206-38207	$3.50	☐	☐	☐	☐
38202-38203-38204-38205-38206-38207	$15.00	☐	☐	☐	☐
38271-38272-38273-38205-38206-38276	$3.50	☐	☐	☐	☐
38271-38272-38273-38205-38275-38276	$3.50	☐	☐	☐	☐
38271-38272-38273-38274-38275-38276	$3.50	☐	☐	☐	☐

#1596d 13¢ EAGLE and SHIELD

L - Perf. 10.9 x 10.9

Plate Numbers	Price				
37231-37232-37233-37234-37235-37236	$400.00	☐	☐	☐	☐

#1597 15¢ FT. McHENRY FLAG

A Press (floating) **5 Plates**

Block of 6 (2 x 3)

Plate	Price	L	R
38650	$2.00	☐	☐
38797	$2.00	☐	☐
39365	$2.00	☐	☐
39380	$2.00	☐	☐

#1598a 15¢ FT. McHENRY FLAG

see page 213

#1599 16¢ LIBERTY HEAD 6 Plates

SHINY GUM		UL	UR	LL	LR
38467	$2.00	☐	☐	☐	☐
38468	$2.00	☐	☐	☐	☐
38481	$2.00	☐	☐	☐	☐
38482	$2.00	☐	☐	☐	☐
38506	$2.00	☐	☐	☐	☐
38507	$2.00	☐	☐	☐	☐

#1603 24¢ OLD NORTH CHURCH 6 Plates

SHINY GUM BLUE PAPER

36759	$2.50	☐	☐	☐	☐
36760	$2.50	☐	☐	☐	☐
36766	$2.50	☐	☐	☐	☐
36767	$2.50	☐	☐	☐	☐
36933	$2.50	☐	☐	☐	☐
36934	$2.50	☐	☐	☐	☐

#1604 28¢ FORT NISQUALLY 4 Plates

SHINY GUM BLUE PAPER

38772	$2.75	☐	☐	☐	☐
38773	$2.75	☐	☐	☐	☐
38778	$2.75	☐	☐	☐	☐
38779	$2.75	☐	☐	☐	☐

#1604 28¢ FORT NISQUALLY 2 Plates

DULL GUM BLUE PAPER

38772	$10.00	☐	☐	☐	☐
38778	$10.00	☐	☐	☐	☐

#1605 29¢ LIGHTHOUSE 4 Plates

SHINY GUM LIGHT BLUE PAPER

38485	$3.00	☐	☐	☐	☐
38486	$3.00	☐	☐	☐	☐
38499	$3.00	☐	☐	☐	☐
38500	$3.00	☐	☐	☐	☐

#1605 29¢ LIGHTHOUSE 4 Plates

DULL GUM LIGHT BLUE PAPER

38485	$15.00	☐	☐	☐	☐
38486	$15.00	☐	☐	☐	☐

#1606 30¢ SCHOOLHOUSE 5 Plates

DULL GUM BLUE PAPER

39131	$3.00	☐	☐	☐	☐
39133	$3.00	☐	☐	☐	☐
39134	$3.00	☐	☐	☐	☐
39195	$3.00	☐	☐	☐	☐
39196	$3.00	☐	☐	☐	☐

1975 REGULAR ISSUE

#1608 50¢ IRON LAMP 6 Plates

SHINY GUM		UL	UR	LL	LR
39146	$4	☐	☐	☐	☐
39149	$4	☐	☐	☐	☐
39157	$4	☐	☐	☐	☐
39159	$4	☐	☐	☐	☐
39588	$4	☐	☐	☐	☐
39589	$4	☐	☐	☐	☐

#1610 $1 CANDLE HOLDER 14 Plates

SHINY GUM					
39076	$8	☐	☐	☐	☐
39086	$8	☐	☐	☐	☐
39087	$8	☐	☐	☐	☐
39088	$8	☐	☐	☐	☐
40310	$8	☐	☐	☐	☐
40311	$8	☐	☐	☐	☐
40312	$8	☐	☐	☐	☐
40313	$8	☐	☐	☐	☐
40314	$8	☐	☐	☐	☐
40709	$8	☐	☐	☐	☐
40710	$8	☐	☐	☐	☐
40970	$8	☐	☐	☐	☐
40971	$8	☐	☐	☐	☐
41125	$8	☐	☐	☐	☐

#1611 $2 KEROSENE LAMP 5 Plates

SHINY GUM					
38900	$16	☐	☐	☐	☐
38905	$16	☐	☐	☐	☐
38906	$16	☐	☐	☐	☐
38907	$16	☐	☐	☐	☐
39075	$16	☐	☐	☐	☐

#1612 $5 RAILROAD LANTERN9 Plates

SHINY GUM					
39135	$50	☐	☐	☐	☐
39141	$50	☐	☐	☐	☐
39142	$50	☐	☐	☐	☐
39143	$50	☐	☐	☐	☐
39164	$50	☐	☐	☐	☐
39169	$50	☐	☐	☐	☐
39173	$32	☐	☐	☐	☐
39174	$32	☐	☐	☐	☐

BOOKLET PANES

#1595a 13¢ LIBERTY BELL

360 Subject Plates **PANES OF 6**

*36516 †36517 *36722 *36723 *36770 *36771

#1595b 13¢ LIBERTY BELL

400 Subject Plates **PANES OF 7**

†36502 †36503 †36724 *36725 †36774 †36775 †36902 †36903 †36917 †36918 †36944 †36945 †37699 †37850 †37851 †37852 †37970 †37971 †37972 †37973 †38045 †38046 †38049 †38050

288 Subject Plates

‡38487 ‡38488 ‡38490 ‡38534

ALL PRODUCT WAS DESTROYED.

#1595c 13¢ LIBERTY BELL

400 Subject Plates **PANES OF 8**

†36504 †36505 †36650 *36651 †36772 †36773 †36904 †36905 †36910 †36911 *37031 *37032 *37033 †37151 †37574 †37575 †37824 †37825 †37826 †37827 †37853 †37854 †37855 †37856 †37975 †37986 †37987 †38042 †38043 †38047 †38048 †38055 †38056 †38233

288 Subject Plates

‡38487 ‡38488 ‡38490 ‡38534

ALL PRODUCT WAS DESTROYED.

#1595d 13¢ LIBERTY BELL

360 Subject Plates **PANES OF 5**

†37253 37254 37255 37256 †37258 †37321 *37327 *37328 37345 37346 37374 37375 37376 †37377 †37572 †37573

#1598a 15¢ FT. McHENRY FLAG

832 Subject Plates **PANES OF 8**

†38657 †38908

See Appendix G for largest reported plate number percentage by position.

SIDE COILS

PERF. 10 VERTICALLY **STRIPS OF 6**

#1811 1¢ ABILITY TO WRITE

432 Subject Plates SHINY and DULL GUM

38253 38254 38259 38851 39342 39343

#1613 3.1¢ GUITAR

432 Subject Plates DULL GUM

39181 39182 †39183 †39184

#1813 3.5¢ VIOLINS

432 Subject Plates DULL GUM

39360 39361 †39366 †39367 †39943 †39955

1975 REGULAR ISSUE

SIDE COILS

PERF. 10 VERTICALLY **STRIPS OF 6**

#1614 7.7¢ SAX HORNS

432 Subject Plates SHINY GUM

37670 37671 37672 37673 †38351
†38352 †38396 †38397

#1615 7.9¢ DRUM

432 Subject Plates SHINY and DULL GUM

37275 37276 37278 37279 †37304
37305 †40011 40012 †40167 †40168

#1615C 8.4¢ GRAND PIANO

432 Subject Plates SHINY and DULL GUM

38715 38725 38726 †38747 38748
38751 38752 38832 *38893 †38894
†39344 †39345 †39414 †39415 †39449
†39450

#1616 9¢ FREEDOM TO ASSEMBLE

432 Subject Plates SHINY and DULL GUM

36984 36985 37152 37153 37166
37167 37168 †37169 †37536 †37537

#1617 10¢ RIGHT TO PETITION

432 Subject Plates SHINY and DULL GUM

38244 38245 38246 38247 38248
38249 †40222 †40223

#1816 12¢ FREEDOM OF CONSCIENCE

432 Subject Plates DULL GUM

37810 37811 37844 37845 †37948
†37949

#1618 13¢ LIBERTY BELL

432 Subject Plates SHINY and DULL GUM

36193 36194 36195 36196 36273
36274 36800 36813 36814 36815
36816 †36817 †36853 †36854 36855
36856 36857 36858 36859 36860
37548 †37549 †37550 †37551 37559
37560 †37576 †37577 †37715 †37716
†37717 †37718 †37976 †37977 †37988
†37989 †38116 †38117 †38118 †38119
†38148 38149 †38182 †38183 †38184
†38185 38214 †38215 †38216 38217
*38228 *38229 †38230 †38231 †38261
†38262 †38263 †38264 †38342 †38343
†38345 †38420 †38456 †38457 †38458

#1618C 15¢ FT. McHENRY FLAG

936 Subject Plates SHINY GUM

†38692 *38759 †38850 †38877 †38996
†39048 †39199 †39283 †39399

#1619 16¢ LIBERTY HEAD

432 Subject Plates SHINY GUM

38429 38430 38460 38461 †38529
†38532

#1619a 16¢ LIBERTY HEAD

936 Subject Plate SHINY GUM

†38563

SHEET STAMP

#1622 13¢ FLAG OVER INDEPENDENCE HALL

80 Subject Plates 9 Color Huck

297 Plates **Positions T, B only**

Block of 20 (10 x 2) $5.50

It is possible to collect both the top and the bottom plate strips in four different combinations. Using Z to represent the Zip Code, M to represent Mail Early, N to represent the plate number and B to represent a blank tab, the following are the margin positions reading from left to right in a plate block of 20.

1) Z N B M Z N B M Z N
2) N B M Z N B M Z N B
3) B M Z N B M Z N B M
4) M Z N B M Z N B M Z

36106	36107	36109	36117	36118
36125	36126	36127	36128	36129
36130	36136	36137	36138	36141
36144	36145	36146	36147	36148
36149	36150	36151	36152	36153
36154	36155	36168	36169	36170
36171	36172	36173	36174	36175
36176	36177	36178	36179	36180
36181	36182	36183	36184	36185
36215	36216	36217	36218	36219
36220	36227	36228	36229	36230
36231	36232	36239	36240	36241
36242	36243	36244	36251	†36252
36253	36254	*36255	36256	36776
36777	36778	36779	36780	36781
36794	36795	36796	36797	36798
36799	36801	36802	36803	36804
36805	36806	36807	36808	36809
36810	36811	36812	36821	36822
36823	36825	36829	36830	36831
36832	36833	36834	36837	36838
36839	36840	36841	36842	37005
37006	37007	37008	37009	37024
37025	37026	37027	37028	37029
37035	37036	37037	37038	37039
37040	37048	37050	37051	37052
37056	37057	37058	37059	37060
37061	37067	37068	37069	37070
37072	37074	37075	37076	37077
37078	37090	*37091	37092	37093
37095	37096	37097	37098	37099
37100	37101	37102	37103	37104
37105	37106	37107	37116	37117
37118	37119	37120	37123	37125
37126	37127	37128	37130	37131
37132	37133	37137	37138	37139
37143	37144	37145	37146	37147
37154	37155	37156	37157	37158
37159	37160	37161	37162	37163
*37164	37165	37170	37171	37172

1975 REGULAR ISSUE

#1622 13¢ FLAG OVER INDEPENDENCE HALL Cont.

37173	37175	37176	37177	37178
37179	37180	37181	37182	37183
*37184	*37185	*37186	37187	37188
37189	37190	37191	37192	37193
37194	37195	37196	37197	37198
*37199	37200	37201	37202	37203
37204	37205	37206	37207	37208
37209	37210	37211	*37212	37213
37218	37219	*37220	37221	37222
37223	37225	37226	37227	37228
37229	37238	37239	37240	37241
37243	37700	37701	37702	*37703
*37704	37705	37746	37747	37748
37749	37750	37751	*37752	37753
*37754	37755	*37756	37757	37758
37759	37760	37761	37762	37763
37764	37765	37766	37767	37768
37769	†37786	37787	37788	*37789
37790	37791	*37798	37799	37800
37801	*37802	†37803		

#1622c 13¢ FLAG OVER INDEPENDENCE HALL

A Press (floating)

Block of 20 (10 x 2)		L	R
39913	$75.00	☐	☐

BOOKLET PANE

#1623a 13¢ FLAG OVER CAPITOL

Perf. 11 **PANES OF 8**

Consisting of 7-1623 & 1-1590

†37706 †37829

#1623c 13¢ FLAG OVER CAPITOL

Perf. 10 **PANES OF 8**

Consisting of 7-1623b & 1-1590a

†37706 †37829

SIDE COIL

#1625 13¢ FLAG OVER INDEPENDENCE HALL

72 Subject Plates 9 Color Huck

Of the 55 plates used to print this stamp, no plate numbers have been reported.

936 Subject Plates B Press

Of the 22 plates used to print this stamp, no plate numbers have been reported.

1976 COMMEMORATIVES

#1629-31 13¢ SPIRIT OF '76

Block of 12 (6 x 2)		UL	UR	LL	LR
36946-36947-36948-36949-36950	$3.50	☐	☐	☐	☐
36951-36952-36953-36954-36955	$3.50	☐	☐	☐	☐

#1632 13¢ INTERPHIL

36958	$1.15	☐	☐	☐	☐
36960	$1.15	☐	☐	☐	☐

1976 COMMEMORATIVES

#1632 13¢ INTERPHIL Cont.

		UL	UR	LL	LR
36975	$1.15	☐	☐	☐	☐
36978	$1.15	☐	☐	☐	☐
36980	$1.15	☐	☐	☐	☐
36982	$1.15	☐	☐	☐	☐
36987	$40.00	☐	☐	☐	☐
36990	$40.00	☐	☐	☐	☐
37003	$40.00	☐	☐	☐	☐
37011	$40.00	☐	☐	☐	☐
37141	$1.15	☐	☐	☐	☐
37150	$1.15	☐	☐	☐	☐

#1633-82 13¢ STATE FLAGS

Pane of 50

36782-36783-36784-36785-36786-36787	$25.00	☐	☐	☐	☐
36782-36783-36784-36791-36786-36787	$15.00	☐	☐	☐	☐
36782-36783-36784-37244-36786-36787	$15.00	☐	☐	☐	☐
36782-36789-36784-36791-36786-36787	$25.00	☐	☐	☐	☐
36788-36789-36790-37244-36786-36787	$15.00	☐	☐	☐	☐
36788-36789-36790-37244-36792-36793	$15.00	☐	☐	☐	☐

#1683 13¢ TELEPHONE

37280	$1.15	☐	☐	☐	☐
37281	$1.15	☐	☐	☐	☐
37282	$1.15	☐	☐	☐	☐
37283	$1.15	☐	☐	☐	☐
37284	$1.15	☐	☐	☐	☐
37285	$1.15	☐	☐	☐	☐
37289	$1.15	☐	☐	☐	☐
37290	$1.15	☐	☐	☐	☐
37291	$1.15	☐	☐	☐	☐
37292	$1.15	☐	☐	☐	☐
37293	$1.15	☐	☐	☐	☐
37294	$1.15	☐	☐	☐	☐
37295	$1.15	☐	☐	☐	☐
37296	$1.15	☐	☐	☐	☐
37297	$1.15	☐	☐	☐	☐
37306	$1.15	☐	☐	☐	☐

#1684 13¢ COMMERCIAL AVIATION

Block of 10 (2 x 5)

36991-36992-36993-36994-36995	$3.00	☐	☐	☐	☐
36996-36997-36998-36999-37000	$3.00	☐	☐	☐	☐

#1685 13¢ CHEMISTRY

Block of 12 (2 x 6)

36963-36964-36965-36966-36967-36968	$3.50	☐	☐	☐	☐
36969-36970-36971-36972-36973-36974	$3.50	☐	☐	☐	☐

1976 COMMEMORATIVES

BICENTENNIAL ISSUE

SOUVENIR SHEETS

#1686 13¢ SURRENDER OF CORNWALLS

#1687 18¢ DECLARATION OF INDEPENDENCE

#1688 24¢ CROSSING THE DELAWARE

#1689 31¢ ARMY AT VALLEY FORGE

The plate numbers of these souvenir sheets were trimmed off after printing so no plate numbers were regularly issued.

#1690 13¢ BENJAMIN FRANKLIN

		UL	UR	LL	LR
37338	$1.15	☐	☐	☐	☐
37339	$1.15	☐	☐	☐	☐
37343	$1.15	☐	☐	☐	☐
37353	$1.15	☐	☐	☐	☐
37354	$1.15	☐	☐	☐	☐
37355	$1.15	☐	☐	☐	☐
37356	$1.15	☐	☐	☐	☐
37357	$1.15	☐	☐	☐	☐
37364	$1.15	☐	☐	☐	☐
37365	$1.15	☐	☐	☐	☐
37366	$1.15	☐	☐	☐	☐
37395	$1.15	☐	☐	☐	☐

#1691-94 13¢ SIGNING THE DECLARATION

Block of 16 (8 x 2)

37480-37481-37482-37483-37484	$4.50	☐	☐	☐	☐
37486-37487-37488-37563-37490	$4.50	☐	☐	☐	☐

#1695-98 13¢ OLYMPIC GAMES

Block of 12 (6 x 2)

37429-37430-37431-37432-37433-37434	$7.50	☐	☐	☐	☐
37435-37430-37431-37438-37439-37440	$4.00	☐	☐	☐	☐

#1699 13¢ CLARA MAASS

Block of 12 (6 x 2)

37261-37262-37263-37264-37265-37266	$3.50	☐	☐	☐	☐
37267-37268-37269-37270-37271-37272	$3.50	☐	☐	☐	☐

#1700 13¢ ADOLPH OCHS

		UL	UR	LL	LR
37592	$1.15	☐	☐	☐	☐
37593	$1.15	☐	☐	☐	☐
37594	$1.15	☐	☐	☐	☐
37596	$1.15	☐	☐	☐	☐
37597	$1.15	☐	☐	☐	☐
37598	$1.15	☐	☐	☐	☐
37599	$1.15	☐	☐	☐	☐
37610	$1.15	☐	☐	☐	☐
37626	$1.15	☐	☐	☐	☐
37627	$1.15	☐	☐	☐	☐
37628	$1.15	☐	☐	☐	☐
37629	$1.15	☐	☐	☐	☐
37632	$1.15	☐	☐	☐	☐

#1701 13¢ NATIVITY

Block of 12 (2 x 6)

37492-37493-37494-37495-37496-37497	$3.50	☐	☐	☐	☐
37498-37499-37500-37501-37502-37503	$3.50	☐	☐	☐	☐
37498-37499-37500-37501-37502-37640	$3.50	☐	☐	☐	☐
37504-37505-37506-37507-37508-37509	$3.50	☐	☐	☐	☐

#1702 13¢ CURRIER & IVES

Andreotti Press

Block of 10 (2 x 5)

37465-37466-37467-37468-37479	$3.00	☐	☐	☐	☐
37470-37471-37472-37473-37474	$3.00	☐	☐	☐	☐
37475-37476-37477-37478-37469	$3.00	☐	☐	☐	☐

#1703 13¢ CURRIER & IVES

A Press (floating)

Block of 20 (2 x 10)

These are the "Floating Plate Numbers" which move up and down in the right and left vertical margins. There are 23 different positions of the plate numbers on each side.

		L	R
37617-37618-37619-37620-37621	$6.00	☐	☐
37634-37635-37636-37637-37638	$6.00	☐	☐

#1704 13¢ WASHINGTON AT PRINCETON

Block of 10 (5 x 2)		UL	UR	LL	LR
37642-37643-37644-37645-37646	$3.00	☐	☐	☐	☐
37647-37648-37649-37650-37651	$3.00	☐	☐	☐	☐

1977 COMMEMORATIVES

#1705 13¢ SOUND RECORDING

		UL	UR	LL	LR
37858	$1.15	☐	☐	☐	☐
37859	$1.15	☐	☐	☐	☐
37860	$1.15	☐	☐	☐	☐
37862	$1.15	☐	☐	☐	☐
37865	$1.15	☐	☐	☐	☐
37867	$1.15	☐	☐	☐	☐
37868	$1.15	☐	☐	☐	☐
37869	$1.15	☐	☐	☐	☐

#1706-09 13¢ PUEBLO ART

Block of 10 (5 x 2)

37770-37771-37772-37773-37774	$3.00	☐	☐	☐	☐
37775-37776-37777-37778-37779	$3.00	☐	☐	☐	☐

#1710 13¢ LINDBERGH FLIGHT

Block of 12 (2 x 6)

37933-37934-37935-37936-37937-37938	$3.50	☐	☐	☐	☐
37939-37940-37941-37942-37943-37944	$3.50	☐	☐	☐	☐

#1711 13¢ COLORADO

Block of 12 (6 x 2)
"L" Perforator 10.9 x 10.9

37956-37957-37958-37959-37960-37961	$3	☐	☐	☐	☐
37962-37963-37964-37965-37966-37967	$3	☐	☐	☐	☐

#1711c 13¢ COLORADO

Block of 12 (6 x 2)
In-Line Perforator 11.2 x 11.2

37956-37957-37958-37959-37960-37961	$15	☐	☐	☐	☐
37956-37963-37964-37965-37966-37967	$15	☐	☐	☐	☐
37962-37963-37964-37965-37966-37967	$15	☐	☐	☐	☐

#1712-15 13¢ BUTTERFLIES

Block of 12 (2 x 6)

37830-37831-37832-37833-37834-37835	$3.50	☐	☐	☐	☐
37836-37837-37838-37839-37840-37841	$3.50	☐	☐	☐	☐

#1716 13¢ LAFAYETTE

37916	$1.15	☐	☐	☐	☐
37923	$1.15	☐	☐	☐	☐
37925	$1.15	☐	☐	☐	☐
37928	$1.15	☐	☐	☐	☐
37945	$1.15	☐	☐	☐	☐
37952	$2.50	☐	☐	☐	☐
37954	$1.15	☐	☐	☐	☐
37968	$1.15	☐	☐	☐	☐
37978	$1.15	☐	☐	☐	☐
38269	$150.00	☐	☐	☐	☐

#1717-20 13¢ SKILLED HANDS

Block of 12 (2 x 6)		UL	UR	LL	LR
37812-37813-37814-37815-37816-37817	$3.50	☐	☐	☐	☐
37818-37919-37820-37821-37822-37823	$3.50	☐	☐	☐	☐

#1721 13¢ PEACE BRIDGE

38051	$1.15	☐	☐	☐	☐
38052	$1.15	☐	☐	☐	☐
38053	$1.15	☐	☐	☐	☐
38054	$1.15	☐	☐	☐	☐

#1722 13¢ ORISKANY

Block of 10 (2 x 5)

37682-37683-37684-37685-37686	$3.00	☐	☐	☐	☐
37687-37688-37689-37690-37691	$3.00	☐	☐	☐	☐

#1723-24 13¢ ENERGY

Block of 12 (2 x 6)

38088-38089-38090-38091-38092-38093	$3.50	☐	☐	☐	☐
38094-38095-38096-38097-38098-38099	$3.50	☐	☐	☐	☐

#1725 13¢ ALTA CALIFORNIA

38191	$1.15	☐	☐	☐	☐
38192	$1.15	☐	☐	☐	☐
38209	$1.15	☐	☐	☐	☐
38210	$1.15	☐	☐	☐	☐
38211	$1.15	☐	☐	☐	☐
38212	$1.15	☐	☐	☐	☐
38213	$1.15	☐	☐	☐	☐
38218	$1.15	☐	☐	☐	☐

#1726 13¢ CONFEDERATION

37875	$1.15	☐	☐	☐	☐
37890	$1.15	☐	☐	☐	☐
37914	$1.15	☐	☐	☐	☐
37915	$1.15	☐	☐	☐	☐
37922	$1.15	☐	☐	☐	☐
37924	$1.15	☐	☐	☐	☐
37926	$1.15	☐	☐	☐	☐
37932	$1.15	☐	☐	☐	☐
37951	$1.15	☐	☐	☐	☐

#1727 13¢ TALKING PICTURES

37991	$1.15	☐	☐	☐	☐
37996	$1.15	☐	☐	☐	☐
37997	$1.15	☐	☐	☐	☐
38000	$1.15	☐	☐	☐	☐
38001	$1.15	☐	☐	☐	☐
38014	$1.15	☐	☐	☐	☐
38021	$1.15	☐	☐	☐	☐
38034	$1.15	☐	☐	☐	☐

1977 COMMEMORATIVES

#1728 13¢ SARATOGA

Block of 10 (2 x 5)		UL	UR	LL	LR
38133-38134-38135-38136-38137	$3.00	□	□	□	□
38138-38139-38140-38141-38142	$3.00	□	□	□	□

#1729 13¢ VALLEY FORGE

A Press (floating)
Block of 20 (2 x 10)

These are the "Floating Plate Numbers" which move up and down in the right and left vertical margins. There are 23 different positions of the plate numbers on each side.

		L	R
37892-37893-37894-37895-37896	$6.00	□	□
37898-37899-37900-37901-37902	$6.00	□	□
38121-38122-38123-38124-38125	$6.00	□	□

#1730 13¢ RURAL MAILBOX

Block of 10 (2 x 5)		UL	UR	LL	LR
37904-37905-37906-37907-37908	$3.00	□	□	□	□
37909-37910-37911-37912-37913	$6.00	□	□	□	□
38155-38156-38157-38158-38159	$3.00	□	□	□	□

1978 COMMEMORATIVES

#1731 13¢ CARL SANDBURG

38317	$1.15	□	□	□	□
38330	$1.15	□	□	□	□
38332	$1.15	□	□	□	□
38334	$1.15	□	□	□	□
38336	$1.15	□	□	□	□
38338	$1.15	□	□	□	□
38341	$1.15	□	□	□	□
38346	$1.15	□	□	□	□

#1732 13¢ CAPTAIN COOK
Portraits

38362	$1.15	□	‡	□	‡
38372	$1.15	□	‡	□	‡
38374	$1.15	□	‡	□	‡
38379	$1.15	□	‡	□	‡
38381	$2.50	□	‡	□	‡
38382	$1.15	□	‡	□	‡
38384	$1.15	□	‡	□	‡
38385	$1.15	□	‡	□	‡
38388	$1.15	□	‡	□	‡
38389	$1.15	□	‡	□	‡
38390	$1.15	□	‡	□	‡
38391	$1.15	□	‡	□	‡
38392	$1.15	□	‡	□	‡

1978 COMMEMORATIVES

#1733 13¢ CAPTAIN COOK
Ships

		UL	UR	LL	LR
38362	$1.15	‡	‡	□	□
38372	$1.15	‡	‡	□	□
38374	$1.15	‡	‡	□	□
38379	$1.15	‡	‡	□	□
38381	$2.50	‡	‡	□	□
38382	$1.15	‡	‡	□	□
38384	$1.15	‡	‡	□	□
38385	$1.15	‡	‡	□	□
38388	$1.15	‡	‡	□	□
38389	$1.15	‡	‡	□	□
38390	$1.15	‡	‡	□	□
38391	$1.15	‡	‡	□	□
38392	$1.15	‡	‡	□	□

#1734 13¢ INDIAN HEAD PENNY

38353	$1.50	□	□	□	□
38356	$1.50	□	□	□	□
38357	$1.50	□	□	□	□
38358	$1.50	□	□	□	□
38360	$1.50	□	□	□	□
38363	$1.50	□	□	□	□
38373	$1.50	□	□	□	□
38376	$1.50	□	□	□	□

1978-80 REGULAR ISSUE

#1735 (15¢)A EAGLE

"L" Perforator 10.9 x 10.9

35768	$3	□	□	□	□
35769	$3	□	□	□	□

#1735c (15¢)A EAGLE

In-Line Perforator 11.2 x 11.2

35768	$1.50	□	□	□	□
35769	$1.50	□	□	□	□
35770	$1.50	□	□	□	□
35771	$1.50	□	□	□	□

BOOKLET PANES

#1736a (15¢)A EAGLE

400 Subject Plates **PANES OF 8**

†36074 †36097 †36098 †36142 †36281 †36282

#1737a 15¢ ROSES

832 Subject Plates **PANES OF 8**

†38724 †38827 †38983

#1742a 15¢ WINDMILLS

480 Subject Plates **PANES OF 10**

†39212 †39214 †39215 †39216 †39217 †39218 †39225 †39227 †39228 †39230 †39240 †39251 †39252 †39253 †39254 †39255 †39256 †39257 †39469 †39471 †39472 †39476 †39477 †39483 †39484 †39493 †39494 †39496 †39497

1978-80 REGULAR ISSUE

SIDE COILS

PERF. 10 VERTICALLY

#1743 (15¢)A EAGLE

432 Subject Plates **STRIPS OF 6**

35840	35858	35859	35860	35861
35862	35875	35876	†35877	35878

1978 COMMEMORATIVES

#1744 13¢ HARRIET TUBMAN

Block of 12 (6 x 2) **UL UR LL LR**

38294-38295-38296-38297-38298-38299 $3.25 ☐ ☐ ☐ ☐

38300-38301-38302-38303-38304-38305 $3.25 ☐ ☐ ☐ ☐

#1745-48 13¢ QUILTS

Block of 12 (2 x 6)

38318-38319-38320-38321-38322-38323 $3.25 ☐ ☐ ☐ ☐

38324-38325-38326-38327-38328-38329 $3.25 ☐ ☐ ☐ ☐

#1749-52 13¢ AMERICAN DANCE

Block of 12 (2 x 6)

38443-38444-38445-38446-38447-38448 $3.25 ☐ ☐ ☐ ☐

38449-38450-38451-38452-38453-38454 $3.25 ☐ ☐ ☐ ☐

#1753 13¢ FRENCH ALLIANCE

38497	$1.15	☐	☐	☐	☐
38509	$1.15	☐	☐	☐	☐
38510	$1.15	☐	☐	☐	☐
38511	$1.15	☐	☐	☐	☐
38512	$1.15	☐	☐	☐	☐
38513	$1.15	☐	☐	☐	☐
38514	$1.15	☐	☐	☐	☐
38535	$1.15	☐	☐	☐	☐
38538	$1.15	☐	☐	☐	☐
38539	$1.15	☐	☐	☐	☐
38543	$1.15	☐	☐	☐	☐

#1754 13¢ CANCER DETECTION

38238	$1.15	☐	☐	☐	☐
38239	$1.15	☐	☐	☐	☐
38240	$1.15	☐	☐	☐	☐
38241	$1.15	☐	☐	☐	☐

#1755 13¢ JIMMIE RODGERS

Block of 12 (6 x 2)

38475-38476-38477-38478-38479-38480 $3.25 ☐ ☐ ☐ ☐

#1756 15¢ GEORGE M. COHAN

Block of 12 (6 x 2)

38406-38407-38408-38709-38410-38584 $3.75 ☐ ☐ ☐ ☐

38412-38413-38414-38710-38416-38585 $3.75 ☐ ☐ ☐ ☐

1978 COMMEMORATIVES

#1757 13¢ CAPEX ISSUE

Individual souvenir pane with 1 plate number

		UL	UR	LL	LR
38615	$2.25	☐	☐	☐	☐
38617	$2.25	☐	☐	☐	☐
38620	$2.25	☐	☐	☐	☐
38621	$2.25	☐	☐	☐	☐
38622	$2.25	☐	☐	☐	☐
38627	$2.25	☐	☐	☐	☐
38638	$2.25	☐	☐	☐	☐
38649	$2.25	☐	☐	☐	☐

#1758 15¢ PHOTOGRAPHY

Block of 12 (6 x 2)

38515-38516-38517-38518-38519-38583 $4.00 ☐ ☐ ☐ ☐

38522-38523-38524-38525-38526-38582 $4.00 ☐ ☐ ☐ ☐

#1759 15¢ VIKING

38712	$1.40	☐	☐	☐	☐
38713	$1.40	☐	☐	☐	☐
38714	$1.40	☐	☐	☐	☐
38717	$1.40	☐	☐	☐	☐
38727	$1.40	☐	☐	☐	☐
38728	$1.40	☐	☐	☐	☐
38729	$1.40	☐	☐	☐	☐
38730	$1.40	☐	☐	☐	☐
38743	$1.40	☐	☐	☐	☐

#1760-63 15¢ AMERICAN OWLS

38792	$1.50	☐	☐	☐	☐
38793	$1.50	☐	☐	☐	☐
38794	$1.50	☐	☐	☐	☐
38796	$1.50	☐	☐	☐	☐
38798	$1.50	☐	☐	☐	☐
38799	$1.50	☐	☐	☐	☐
38800	$1.50	☐	☐	☐	☐
38806	$1.50	☐	☐	☐	☐

#1764-67 15¢ AMERICAN TREES

Block of 12 (2 x 6)

38808-38809-38810-38811-38812-38813 $4.00 ☐ ☐ ☐ ☐

#1768 15¢ MADONNA

Block of 12 (2 x 6)

38731-38732-38733-38734-38735-38736 $3.75 ☐ ☐ ☐ ☐

38737-33738-38739-38740-38741-38742 $3.75 ☐ ☐ ☐ ☐

#1769 15¢ HOBBY HORSE

Block of 12 (2 x 6)

38662-38663-38664-38665-38666-38667 $3.75 ☐ ☐ ☐ ☐

38668-38669-38670-38671-38672-38673 $3.75 ☐ ☐ ☐ ☐

1979 COMMEMORATIVES

#1770 15¢ ROBERT KENNEDY

		UL	UR	LL	LR
38916	$1.50	☐	☐	☐	☐
38917	$1.50	☐	☐	☐	☐
38918	$1.50	☐	☐	☐	☐
38919	$1.50	☐	☐	☐	☐
38920	$1.50	☐	☐	☐	☐
38921	$1.50	☐	☐	☐	☐
38926	$1.50	☐	☐	☐	☐
38927	$1.50	☐	☐	☐	☐

#1771 15¢ MARTIN LUTHER KING

Block of 12 (6 x 2)

38820-38821-38822-38823-38824-38825

$3.75 ☐ ☐ ☐ ☐

#1772 15¢ YEAR OF THE CHILD

38976	$1.50	☐	☐	☐	☐
38977	$1.50	☐	☐	☐	☐
38978	$1.50	☐	☐	☐	☐
38979	$1.50	☐	☐	☐	☐
38980	$1.50	☐	☐	☐	☐
38981	$1.50	☐	☐	☐	☐
38984	$1.50	☐	☐	☐	☐
38985	$1.50	☐	☐	☐	☐

#1773 15¢ JOHN STEINBECK

38940	$1.50	☐	☐	☐	☐
38941	$1.50	☐	☐	☐	☐
38942	$1.50	☐	☐	☐	☐
38943	$1.50	☐	☐	☐	☐

#1774 15¢ ALBERT EINSTEIN

38966	$1.50	☐	☐	☐	☐
38967	$1.50	☐	☐	☐	☐
38968	$1.50	☐	☐	☐	☐
38969	$1.50	☐	☐	☐	☐

#1775-78 15¢ AMERICAN FOLK ART

Block of 10 (5 x 2)

38997-38998-38999-39000-39001

$3.50 ☐ ☐ ☐ ☐

#1779-82 15¢ ARCHITECTURE

39035	$1.50	☐	☐	☐	☐
39036	$1.50	☐	☐	☐	☐
39038	$1.50	☐	☐	☐	☐
39039	$1.50	☐	☐	☐	☐
39040	$1.50	☐	☐	☐	☐
39055	$1.50	☐	☐	☐	☐
39056	$1.50	☐	☐	☐	☐
39058	$1.50	☐	☐	☐	☐

#1783-86 15¢ ENDANGERED FLORA

Block of 12 (6 x 2)

39049-39050-39051-39052-39053-39054

$3.75 ☐ ☐ ☐ ☐

#1787 15¢ SEEING EYE DOGS

A Press (floating)

Block of 20 (10 x 2) **T B**

These are the "Floating Plate Numbers" which move in the top and bottom horizontal margins. There are 23 different positions of the plate numbers on each position.

38986-38987-38988-38989-39037

$6.00 ☐ ☐

#1788 15¢ SPECIAL OLYMPICS

Block of 10 (5 x 2) **UL UR LL LR**

39096-39097-39098-39099-39100

$3.50 ☐ ☐ ☐ ☐

#1789 15¢ JOHN PAUL JONES

Block of 10 (2 x 5) Perf. 11 x 12

A0001-A0002-A0003-A0004-A0005

$3.50 ☐ ☐ ☐ ☐

A0006-A0007-A0008-A0009-A0010

$3.50 ☐ ☐ ☐ ☐

#1789a 15¢ JOHN PAUL JONES

Block of 10 (2 x 5) Perf. 11 x 11

A0006-A0007-A0008-A0009-A0010

$4.00 ☐ ☐ ☐ ☐

#1789b 15¢ JOHN PAUL JONES

Block of 10 (2 x 5) Perf. 12 x 12

A0001-A0002-A0003-A0004-A0005

$20,000 ☐ † ☐ †

see pg. 213 for photograph

#1790 10¢ OLYMPICS

Block of 12 (6 x 2) **UL UR LL LR**

39111-39112-39113-39114-39115-39116

$3.50 ☐ ☐ ☐ ☐

#1791-94 15¢ SUMMER OLYMPICS

Block of 12 (2 x 6)

39089-39090-39091-39092-39093-39094

$4.00 ☐ ☐ ☐ ☐

#1795-98 15¢ WINTER OLYMPICS(1980)

Block of 12 (2 x 6)

EE Perforator 11.3 x 10.5

39204-39205-39206-39207-39208-39209

$5.00 ☐ ☐ ☐ ☐

#1795a-98a 15¢ WINTER OLYMPICS('80)

Block of 12 (2 x 6)

In-Line Perforator 11.2 x 11.2

39204-39205-39206-39207-39208-39209

$15.00 ☐ ☐ ☐ ☐

#1799 15¢ MADONNA

Block of 12 (2 x 6)

38944-38945-38946-38947-38948-38949

$3.75 ☐ ☐ ☐ ☐

38950-38951-38952-38953-38954-38955

$3.75 ☐ ☐ ☐ ☐

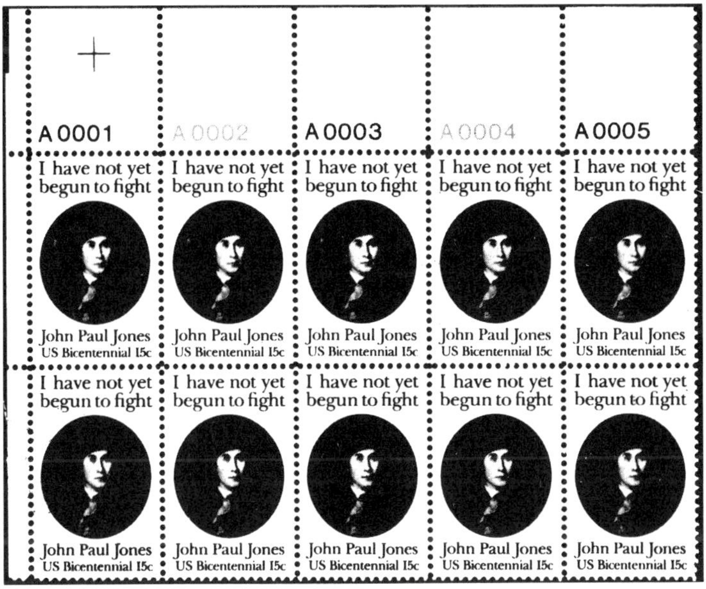

PERF. 12 x 12

1979 COMMEMORATIVES

#1800 15¢ SANTA CLAUS

Block of 12 (2 x 6) UL UR LL LR

38880-38881-38882-38883-38884-38885
$3.75 ☐ ☐ ☐ ☐

38886-38887-38888-38889-38890-38891
$3.75 ☐ ☐ ☐ ☐

#1801 15¢ WILL ROGERS

Block of 12 (6 x 2)

39080-39081-39082-39083-39084-39085
$3.75 ☐ ☐ ☐ ☐

#1802 15¢ VIETNAM VETERANS

Block of 10 (2 x 5)

39150-39151-39152-39153-39154
$3.25 ☐ ☐ ☐ ☐

1980 COMMEMORATIVES

#1803 15¢ W.C. FIELDS

Block of 12 (6 x 2)

39219-39220-39221-39222-39223-39224
$3.75 ☐ ☐ ☐ ☐

#1804 15¢ BENJAMIN BANNEKER

Block of 12 (6 x 2)

A0011-A0012-A0013-A0014-A0015-A0016
$3.75 ☐ ☐ ☐ ☐

A0017-A0018-A0019-A0020-A0021-A0022
$3.75 ☐ ☐ ☐ ☐

#1805-10 15¢ LETTER WRITING

Block of 36 (6 x 6)

39231-39232-39233-39234-39235-39236
$12.00 ☐ ☐ ☐ ☐

1975 REGULAR ISSUE

#1811 1¢ ABILITY TO WRITE

See page 213

#1813 3.5¢ VIOLINS

See page 213

#1816 12¢ FREEDOM OF CONSCIENCE

See Page 214

1980 REGULAR ISSUE

#1818 (18¢)B EAGLE

		UL	UR	LL	LR
36470	$1.80	☐	☐	☐	☐
36471	$1.80	☐	☐	☐	☐
36472	$1.80	☐	☐	☐	☐

BOOKLET PANE

#1819a (18¢)B EAGLE

288 Subject Plates **PANES OF 8**

†39002 †39003 †39004 †39005 †39200
†39201 †39202 †39203 †39581 †39582

SIDE COILS

#1820 (18¢)B EAGLE

432 Subject Plates **STRIPS OF 6**

*36569 *36761 *36762 *39033 *39247
*39248 *39249 *39250 *39276 *39277
†39288 †39289 †39291 †39292 †39300
†39315 †39346 †39347 †39373 †39374

1980 COMMEMORATIVES

#1821 15¢ FRANCES PERKINS

		UL	UR	LL	LR
39270	$1.25	☐	☐	☐	☐
39271	$1.25	☐	☐	☐	☐
39272	$1.25	☐	☐	☐	☐
39273	$1.25	☐	☐	☐	☐

#1822 15¢ DOLLEY MADISON

39293	$1.50	☐	☐	☐	☐
39294	$1.50	☐	☐	☐	☐
39295	$1.50	☐	☐	☐	☐
39296	$1.50	☐	☐	☐	☐
39297	$1.50	☐	☐	☐	☐

#1823 15¢ EMILY BISSELL

39278	$1.25	☐	☐	☐	☐
39279	$1.25	☐	☐	☐	☐
39280	$1.25	☐	☐	☐	☐
39281	$1.25	☐	☐	☐	☐
39284	$1.25	☐	☐	☐	☐
39285	$1.25	☐	☐	☐	☐
39286	$1.25	☐	☐	☐	☐
39287	$1.25	☐	☐	☐	☐

#1824 15¢ HELEN KELLER

39313	$1.25	☐	☐	☐	☐
39314	$1.25	☐	☐	☐	☐
39316	$1.25	☐	☐	☐	☐
39340	$1.25	☐	☐	☐	☐
39341	$1.25	☐	☐	☐	☐
39348	$1.25	☐	☐	☐	☐
39349	$1.25	☐	☐	☐	☐
39350	$1.25	☐	☐	☐	☐
39352	$1.25	☐	☐	☐	☐
39383	$1.25	☐	☐	☐	☐

#1825 15¢ VETERANS ADMIN.

A0023-A0024	$1.25	☐	☐	☐	☐
A0025-A0026	$1.25	☐	☐	☐	☐

#1826 15¢ GENERAL GALVEZ

39359	$1.25	☐	☐	☐	☐
39364	$1.25	☐	☐	☐	☐
39368	$1.25	☐	☐	☐	☐
39381	$1.25	☐	☐	☐	☐
39382	$1.25	☐	☐	☐	☐
39391	$1.25	☐	☐	☐	☐
39397	$1.25	☐	☐	☐	☐

#1827-30 15¢ CORAL REEFS

Block of 12 (6 x 2)

39385-39386-39387-39388-39389-39390

$4.00 ☐ ☐ ☐ ☐

#1831 15¢ ORGANIZED LABOR

Block of 12 (6 x 2)

39405-39406-39407-39408-39409-39410

$4.00 ☐ ☐ ☐ ☐

#1832 15¢ EDITH WHARTON

		UL	UR	LL	LR
39393	$1.25	☐	☐	☐	☐
39394	$1.25	☐	☐	☐	☐
39395	$1.25	☐	☐	☐	☐
39396	$1.25	☐	☐	☐	☐

#1833 15¢ EDUCATION

Block of 6 (3 x 2)

A0027-A0028-A0029

$2.00 ☐ ☐ ☐ ☐

A0030-A0031-A0032

$2.00 ☐ ☐ ☐ ☐

#1834-37 15¢ INDIAN MASKS

Block of 10 (5 x 2)

39265-39266-39267-39268-39269

$3.50 ☐ ☐ ☐ ☐

#1838-41 15¢ ARCHITECTURE

39417	$1.50	☐	☐	☐	☐
39421	$1.50	☐	☐	☐	☐
39422	$1.50	☐	☐	☐	☐
39427	$1.50	☐	☐	☐	☐
39428	$2.00	☐	☐	☐	☐
39429	$1.50	☐	☐	☐	☐
39430	$1.50	☐	☐	☐	☐
39431	$1.50	☐	☐	☐	☐

#1842 15¢ MADONNA

Block of 12 (6 x 2)

39327-39328-39329-39330-39331-39332

$4.00 ☐ ☐ ☐ ☐

39333-39334-39335-39336-39337-39338

$4.00 ☐ ☐ ☐ ☐

#1843 15¢ CHRISTMAS WREATH

A Press (floating)

Block of 20 (10 x 2)

These are the “Floating Plate Numbers” which move in the margins. There are 23 different positions of the plate numbers for each position.

		T	B
39317-39318-39319-39320-39321	$6.00	☐	☐
39322-39323-39324-39325-39326	$6.00	☐	☐

THE NEW PLATE IDENTIFICATION NUMBERING SYSTEM

The printing plates used by the BEP for printing postage stamps have been sequentially numbered starting from plate 1 in 1894. The **actual number** of the printing plate usually appeared on the finished product. Starting in 1981 with the Everett Dirksen commemorative, the actual plate number no longer appears on the finished product, but in the place where the actual plate number normally appeared, a **representative number** is now used. The traditional numbering of the printing plates has not changed and has continued for accounting purposes, but the actual number is placed in an area where it cannot appear on the finished product. The representative number is chosen according to the following selection scheme. The first plate of each type prepared for an issue is given the number 1, and subsequent plates of the same type are given consecutive numbers. A type of plate includes an intaglio plate, and an offset or gravure plate for a given color. For example, the first intaglio plate for an issue is given the number 1, and the first offset or gravure plate of a given color for the same issue would also be given the number 1. A replacement plate for any of these plates would be given the number 2.

A question that must be addressed is "What is a PLATE BLOCK?" We will define a plate block to be the minimum quantity of stamps which maintains the intended design and at the same time shows all of the plate numbers involved, in an aesthetically pleasing block format.

In most cases for stamps produced on a rotary press, a plate block will consist of four stamps with selvage on two adjacent sides. In most cases for stamps produced on a flat press, a plate block consists of 6 stamps with selvage on one side.

The size of a plate block for an issue produced on the A Press depends on the plate layout and the number of printing sections employed. Early issues were printed from plates where the number of subjects was some multiple of 23 (230, 460, 920), creating the so-called "floating" plate numbers. If only one section (either intaglio or gravure) of the press was used, these issues are collected as blocks of SIX with selvage on one side where there is one stamp with blank selvage at either side of the plate number. If both printing sections were used, a plate block consists of a block of FOUR stamps with selvage on one side with the intaglio number adjacent to one stamp and the gravure numbers adjacent to the other stamp. Some collectors prefer to collect plate strips of 20 stamps for all early issues of the A Press. Later issues were printed from plates where the number of subjects is a multiple of 200 (200, 400, 800), creating normal corner plate blocks of FOUR stamps with selvage on two sides.

When a plate block consists of more than four stamps, we will list the size of the plate block in the heading of the issue.

The changeover in the identifying numbering system also resulted in a change in the collectability of plate numbers on coil and booklet pane stamps. Since the introduction of the rotary press, plate numbers were placed in a position where they would normally be trimmed off in the manufacturing process. Where formerly a partial plate number might be found by accident, now the representative number is an INTEGRAL part of the finished product. The representative number is placed under the design of one stamp in each row of the printing plate used for coil stamps. The representative number is placed on the tab of booklet panes for printing plates used for booklet stamps.

We will define a plate number strip of coil stamps as having five stamps with the plate number on the middle stamp.

We will define a plate number pane of booklet stamps as the full pane as issued with the plate number in the tab.

KEY TO PRIVATE CONTRACTORS

After this point contractors other than the Bureau of Engraving and Printing were employed to supply stamps to the USPS. The stamps printed by the private contractors have plate numbers which are preceeded by a single letter identifying the contractor. A key to these symbols is given below.

Letter	Contractor
"no letter"	Bureau of Engraving and Printing
A	American Bank Note Company
B	Banknote Corp. of America
D	Dittler Brothers Incorporated
K	KCS Industries
P	Ashton-Potter America
S	Stamp Venturers
U	United States Bank Note
V	Avery

1980 REGULAR ISSUE

This series is also known as the Great Americans series.

#1844 1¢ DOROTHEA DIX
A Press(floating) Block tagged
Bull's Eye Perf. 11.2 x 11.1
Block of 6

		L	R
1	$1.00	☐	☐

#1844c 1¢ DOROTHEA DIX
A Press(floating) Block tagged
L - Perf. 10.8 x 10.9
Block of 6

1	$2.00	☐	☐
2	$2.00	☐	☐

#2168 1¢ MARGARET MITCHELL
A Press(4 position) Block tagged
Bull's Eye Perf. 11.2 x 11.1

		UL	UR	LL	LR
1	$0.20	☐	☐	☐	☐

#1845 2¢ IGOR STRAVINSKY
Cottrell Press Overall tagged
EE Perf. 11.2 x 10.5

1	$0.25	☐	☐	☐	☐
2	$0.25	☐	☐	☐	☐
3	$0.25	☐	☐	☐	☐
4	$0.25	☐	☐	☐	☐
5	$4.00	☐	☐	☐	☐
6	$4.00	☐	☐	☐	☐

#2169 2¢ MARY LYON
A Press(4 position) Block tagged
Bull's Eye Perf. 11.2 x 11.1

1	$0.25	☐	☐	☐	☐
2	$0.25	☐	☐	☐	☐

#2169a 2¢ MARY LYON
C Press Untagged
Bull's Eye Perf. 11.2 x 11.1

3	$0.25	☐	☐	☐	☐

#1846 3¢ HENRY CLAY
Cottrell Press Overall tagged
EE Perf. 11.2 x 10.5

1	$0.35	☐	☐	☐	☐
2	$0.35	☐	☐	☐	☐

#2170 3¢ PAUL DUDLEY WHITE
Bull's Eye Perf. 11.2 x 11.1
A Press(4 position) Block tagged

1	$0.35	☐	☐	☐	☐
2	$0.35	☐	☐	☐	☐
3	$0.35	☐	☐	☐	☐

C Press shiny gum Untagged

4	$0.35	☐	☐	☐	☐

C Press dull gum Untagged

4	$0.35	☐	☐	☐	☐

#1847 4¢ CARL SCHURZ
Cottrell Press Overall tagged
EE Perf. 11.2 x 10.5

		UL	UR	LL	LR
1	$0.40	☐	☐	☐	☐
2	$0.40	☐	☐	☐	☐
3	$0.40	☐	☐	☐	☐
4	$0.40	☐	☐	☐	☐

#2171 4¢ FATHER FLANAGAN
A Press(4 position) Block tagged
Bull's Eye Perf. 11.2 x 11.1

1	$0.40	☐	☐	☐	☐

#2171a 4¢ FATHER FLANAGAN
Bull's Eye Perf. 11.2 x 11.1
A Press(4 position) Untagged

1	$0.40	☐	☐	☐	☐

C Press Untagged

2	$0.40	☐	☐	☐	☐

#1848 5¢ PEARL BUCK
Cottrell Press Overall tagged
EE Perf. 11.2 x 10.5

1	$0.50	☐	☐	☐	☐
2	$0.50	☐	☐	☐	☐
3	$0.50	☐	☐	☐	☐
4	$0.50	☐	☐	☐	☐

#2172 5¢ HUGO BLACK
A Press(4 position) Block tagged
Bull's Eye Perf. 11.2 x 11.1

1	$0.40	☐	☐	☐	☐
2	$0.40	☐	☐	☐	☐

#2173 5¢ LUIS MUNOZ MARIN
C Press Overall tagged
Bull's Eye Perf. 11.2 x 11.1

1	$0.50	☐	☐	☐	☐

#2173a 5¢ LUIS MUNOZ MARIN
C Press Untagged
Bull's Eye Perf. 11.2 x 11.1

2	$0.50	☐	☐	☐	☐

#1849 6¢ WALTER LIPPMAN
A Press(floating) Block tagged
L - Perf. 10.8 x 10.9
Block of 6

		L	R
1	$0.75	☐	☐

#1850 7¢ ABRAHAM BALDWIN
A Press(floating) Block tagged
L - Perf. 10.8 x 10.9
Block of 6

1	$0.75	☐	☐

1980 REGULAR ISSUE

#1851 8¢ HENRY KNOX

I-8 Press Overall tagged

L - Perf. 10.8 x 10.9

		UL	UR	LL	LR
3	$0.75	☐	☐	☐	☐
4	$0.75	☐	☐	☐	☐
5	$0.75	☐	☐	☐	☐
6	$0.75	☐	☐	☐	☐

#1852 9¢ SYLVANUS THAYER

A Press(floating) Block tagged

L - Perf. 10.8 x 10.9

Block of 6		L	R
1	$1.25	☐	☐

#1853 10¢ RICHARD RUSSELL

A Press(floating) Block tagged

L - Perf. 10.8 x 10.9

Block of 6			
1	$1.50	☐	☐

#2175 10¢ RED CLOUD (lake)

A Press(4 position) Block tagged

Bull's Eye Perf. 11.2 x 11.1

		UL	UR	LL	LR
1	$0.75	☐	☐	☐	☐

#2175a 10¢ RED CLOUD (lake)

Bull's Eye Perf. 11.2 x 11.1

A Press(4 position)		Overall tagged			
1	$5.00	☐	☐	☐	☐
C Press		Overall tagged			
2	$1.25	☐	☐	☐	☐

#2175c 10¢ RED CLOUD (lake)

Bull's Eye Perf. 11.2 x 11.1

C Press		Mottled prephosphored			
2	$1.00	☐	☐	☐	☐
C Press		Uniform prephosphored			
2	$1.00	☐	☐	☐	☐

#2175d 10¢ RED CLOUD (carmine)

C Press Mottled prephosphored

Bull's Eye Perf. 11.2 x 11.1

2	$0.75	☐	☐	☐	☐

#1854 11¢ ALLEN PARTRIDGE

I-8 Press Overall tagged

L - Perf. 10.8 x 10.9

2	$1.00	☐	☐	☐	☐
3	$1.00	☐	☐	☐	☐
4	$1.00	☐	☐	☐	☐
5	$1.00	☐	☐	☐	☐

#1855 13¢ CRAZY HORSE

Cottrell Press Overall tagged

EE Perf. 11.2 x 10.5

		UL	UR	LL	LR
1	$1.50	☐	☐	☐	☐
2	$1.50	☐	☐	☐	☐
3	$1.50	☐	☐	☐	☐
4	$1.50	☐	☐	☐	☐

#1856 14¢ SINCLAIR LEWIS

A Press(floating) Block tagged

L - Perf. 10.8 x 10.9

Block of 6		L	R
1	$2.00	☐	☐

#2176 14¢ JULIA WARD HOWE

A Press(4 position) Block tagged

Bull's Eye Perf. 11.2 x 11.1

		UL	UR	LL	LR
1	$1.00	☐	☐	☐	☐
2	$1.50	☐	☐	☐	☐

#2177 15¢ BUFFALO BILL CODY

A Press(4 position) Block tagged

Bull's Eye Perf. 11.2 x 11.1

1	$3.00	☐	☐	☐	☐
3	$3.00	☐	☐	☐	☐

#2177a 15¢ BUFFALO BILL CODY

Bull's Eye Perf. 11.2 x 11.1

D Press		Overall tagged			
2	$1.50	☐	☐	☐	☐
A Press(4 position)		Overall tagged			
3	$1.50	☐	☐	☐	☐

#2177b 15¢ BUFFALO BILL CODY

A Press(4 position) Uniform prephosphored

Bull's Eye Perf. 11.2 x 11.1

1	$1.50	☐	☐	☐	☐

#1857 17¢ RACHEL CARSON

Cottrell Press Overall tagged

EE Perf. 11.2 x 10.5

1	$1.75	☐	☐	☐	☐
2	$1.75	☐	☐	☐	☐
3	$1.75	☐	☐	☐	☐
4	$1.75	☐	☐	☐	☐
13	$1.75	☐	☐	☐	☐
14	$1.75	☐	☐	☐	☐
15	$7.50	☐	☐	☐	☐
16	$7.50	☐	☐	☐	☐

#2178 17¢ BELVA LOCKWOOD

A Press(4 position) Block tagged

Bull's Eye Perf. 11.2 x 11.1

1	$1.50	☐	☐	☐	☐
2	$1.50	☐	☐	☐	☐

1980 REGULAR ISSUE

#1858 18¢ GEORGE MASON
Cottrell Press Overall tagged
EE Perf. 11.2 x 10.5

		UL	UR	LL	LR
1	$2.00	☐	☐	☐	☐
2	$2.00	☐	☐	☐	☐
3	$3.00	☐	☐	☐	☐
4	$3.00	☐	☐	☐	☐
5	$2.00	☐	☐	☐	☐
6	$2.00	☐	☐	☐	☐

#1859 19¢ SEQUOYAH
Cottrell Press Overall tagged
EE Perf. 11.2 x 10.5

39529	$2.00	☐	☐	☐	☐
39530	$2.00	☐	☐	☐	☐

#1860 20¢ RALPH BUNCHE
Cottrell Press Overall tagged
EE Perf. 11.2 x 10.5

1	$3.00	☐	☐	☐	☐
2	$3.00	☐	☐	☐	☐
3	$6.00	☐	☐	☐	☐
4	$6.00	☐	☐	☐	☐
5	$3.00	☐	☐	☐	☐
6	$3.00	☐	☐	☐	☐
7	$3.00	☐	☐	☐	☐
8	$6.00	☐	☐	☐	☐
10	$3.00	☐	☐	☐	☐
11	$6.00	☐	☐	☐	☐
13	$12.00	☐	☐	☐	☐

#1861 20¢ THOMAS GALLAUDET
Cottrell Press Overall tagged
EE Perf. 11.2 x 10.5

1	$3.00	☐	☐	☐	☐
2	$3.00	☐	☐	☐	☐
5	$6.00	☐	☐	☐	☐
6	$6.00	☐	☐	☐	☐
8	$40.00	☐	☐	☐	☐
9	$40.00	☐	☐	☐	☐

#1862 20¢ HARRY TRUMAN
A Press(floating) Block tagged
L - Perf. 10.8 x 10.9

Block of 6		L	R
1	$5.00	☐	☐

#1862a 20¢ HARRY TRUMAN
A Press(4 position) Block tagged
Bull's Eye Perf. 11.2 x 11.1

		UL	UR	LL	LR
2	$2.00	☐	☐	☐	☐

#1862b 20¢ HARRY TRUMAN
A Press(4 position) Overall tagged
Bull's Eye Perf. 11.2 x 11.1

3	$2.00	☐	☐	☐	☐

#1862d 20¢ HARRY TRUMAN
C Press Mottled prephosphored
Bull's Eye Perf. 11.2 x 11.1

		UL	UR	LL	LR
4	$2.00	☐	☐	☐	☐

#2179 20¢ VIRGINIA APGAR
T/A Press Mottled prephosphored
Bull's Eye Perf. 11.2 x 11.1

B1	$2.00	☐	☐	☐	☐
B2	$2.00	☐	☐	☐	☐

#2180 21¢ CHESTER CARLSON
A Press(4 position) Block tagged
Bull's Eye Perf. 11.2 x 11.1

1	$1.75	☐	☐	☐	☐

#1863 22¢ JOHN AUDUBON
A Press(floating) Block tagged
L - Perf. 10.8 x 10.9

Block of 6		L	R
1	$15.00	☐	☐

#1863d 22¢ JOHN AUDUBON
A Press(4 position) Block tagged
Bull's Eye Perf. 11.2 x 11.1

		UL	UR	LL	LR
3	$3.00	☐	☐	☐	☐

#2181 23¢ MARY CASSATT
A Press(4 position) Block tagged
Bull's Eye Perf. 11.2 x 11.1

1	$2.00	☐	☐	☐	☐

#2181a 23¢ MARY CASSATT
Bull's Eye Perf. 11.2 x 11.1

A Press(4 position)		Overall tagged			
1	$3.00	☐	☐	☐	☐
C Press		Overall tagged			
2	$2.50	☐	☐	☐	☐

#2181b 23¢ MARY CASSATT
Bull's Eye Perf. 11.2 x 11.1

C Press		Uniform prephosphored			
2	$2.00	☐	☐	☐	☐
C Press		Mottled prephosphored			
3	$2.00	☐	☐	☐	☐

#2182 25¢ JACK LONDON
A Press(4 position) Block tagged
Bull's Eye Perf. 11.2 x 11.1

1	$2.00	☐	☐	☐	☐
2	$4.00	☐	☐	☐	☐

#2183 28¢ SITTING BULL
A Press(4 position) Block tagged
Bull's Eye Perf. 11.2 x 11.1

1	$2.25	☐	☐	☐	☐

1980 REGULAR ISSUE

#2184 29¢ EARL WARREN

T/A Press Mottled prephosphored

Bull's Eye Perf. 10.9

	UL	UR	LL	LR	CUR	CLR
S1 $2.25	□	□	□	□	□	□
S2 $2.25	□	□	□	□	□	□

#2185 29¢ THOMAS JEFFERSON

T/A Press Mottled prephosphored

Bull's Eye Perf. 10.9

		UL	UR	LL	LR
S1	$2.25	□	□	□	□
S2	$2.25	□	□	□	□

#1864 30¢ FRANK LAUBACH

A Press(floating) Block tagged

L - Perf. 10.8 x 10.9

Block of 6		L	R
1	$10.00	□	□

#1864a 30¢ FRANK LAUBACH

Bull's Eye Perf. 11.2 x 11.1

A Press(4 position) Block tagged

		UL	UR	LL	LR
2	$3.00	□	□	□	□

#1864b 30¢ FRANK LAUBACH

Bull's Eye Perf. 11.2 x 11.1

A Press(4 position) Overall tagged

2	$25.00	□	□	□	□

#2933 32¢ MILTON S. HERSHEY

T/A Press Uniform prephosphored

Bull's Eye Perf. 11.2 x 11.1

B1	$2.50	□	□	□	□
B2	$2.50	□	□	□	□

#2934 32¢ CAL FARLEY

Bull's Eye Perf. 11.2 x 11.1

T/A Press Uniform prephosphored

B1	$2.50	□	□	□	□

Lightly coated examples appear mottled.

#1865 35¢ CHARLES DREW

Cottrell Press Overall tagged

EE Perf. 11.2 x 10.5

1	$3.00	□	□	□	□
2	$3.00	□	□	□	□
3	$12.00	□	□	□	□
4	$12.00	□	□	□	□

#2186 35¢ DENNIS CHAVEZ

T/A Press Mottled prephosphored

L - Perf. 10.9

	UL	UR	LL	LR	CUR	CLR
S1 $3.00	□	□	□	□	□	□
S2 $3.00	□	□	□	□	□	□

#1866 37¢ ROBERT MILLIKAN

Cottrell Press Overall tagged

EE Perf. 11.2 x 10.5		UL	UR	LL	LR
1	$3.00	□	□	□	□
2	$3.00	□	□	□	□
3	$3.00	□	□	□	□
4	$3.00	□	□	□	□

#1867 39¢ GRENVILLE CLARK

A Press(floating) Block tagged

L - Perf. 10.8 x 10.9

Block of 6		L	R
1	$15.00	□	□

#1867c 39¢ GRENVILLE CLARK

A Press(4 position) Block tagged

Bull's Eye Perf. 11.2 x 11.1

		UL	UR	LL	LR
2	$3.50	□	□	□	□

#1868 40¢ LILLIAN GILBRETH

A Press(floating) Block tagged

L - Perf. 10.8 x 10.9

Block of 6		L	R
1	$15.00	□	□

#1868a 40¢ LILLIAN GILBRETH

A Press(4 position) Block tagged

Bull's Eye Perf. 11.2 x 11.1

		UL	UR	LL	LR
2	$3.25	□	□	□	□

#2187 40¢ CLAIRE LEE CHENNAULT

A Press(4 position) Overall tagged

Bull's Eye Perf. 11.2 x 11.1

1	$3.25	□	□	□	□

#2187a 40¢ CLAIRE LEE CHENNAULT

Bull's Eye Perf. 11.2 x 11.1

C Press dull gum Uniform prephosphored

2	$3.25	□	□	□	□

C Press shiny gum Mottled prephosphored

2	$3.25	□	□	□	□

#2188 45¢ HARVEY CUSHING

A Press(4 position) Block tagged

Bull's Eye Perf. 11.2 x 11.1

1	$3.50	□	□	□	□

#2188a 45¢ HARVEY CUSHING

A Press(4 position) Overall tagged

Bull's Eye Perf. 11.2 x 11.1

1	$7.00	□	□	□	□

#2938 46¢ RUTH BENEDICT

D Press Mottled prephosphored

Bull's Eye Perf. 11.2 x 11.1

1	$3.75	□	□	□	□

1980 REGULAR ISSUE

#1869 50¢ CHESTER NIMITZ

I-8 Press — Overall tagged

L - Perf. 10.8 x 10.9

		UL	UR	LL	LR
1	$4.00	☐	☐	☐	☐
2	$4.00	☐	☐	☐	☐
3	$4.00	☐	☐	☐	☐
4	$4.00	☐	☐	☐	☐

#1869a 50¢ CHESTER NIMITZ

Bull's Eye Perf. 11.2 x 11.1

A Press(4 position) — Block tagged

1	$4.00	☐	☐	☐	☐
2	$4.00	☐	☐	☐	☐

#1869d 50¢ CHESTER NIMITZ

Bull's Eye Perf. 11.2 x 11.1

A Press(4 position)		Overall tagged			
2	$7.50	☐	☐	☐	☐
C Press		Overall tagged			
3	$7.50	☐	☐	☐	☐
C Press		Mottled prephosphored			
3	$7.50	☐	☐	☐	☐

#2189 52¢ HUBERT HUMPHREY

Bull's Eye Perf. 11.2 x 11.1

C Press		Uniform prephosphored			
1	$4.00	☐	☐	☐	☐
C Press		Mottled prephosphored			
1	$4.00	☐	☐	☐	☐
2	$4.00	☐	☐	☐	☐

#2940 55¢ ALICE HAMILTON

T/A Press — Mottled prephosphored

Bull's Eye Perf. 11.2 x 11.1

B1	$4.25	☐	☐	☐	☐
B2	$4.25	☐	☐	☐	☐

#2190 56¢ JOHN HARVARD

A Press(4 position) — Block tagged

Bull's Eye Perf. 11.2 x 11.1

1	$4.25	☐	☐	☐	☐

#2191 65¢ "HAP" ARNOLD

A Press(4 position) — Block tagged

Bull's Eye Perf. 11.2 x 11.1

1	$4.50	☐	☐	☐	☐

#2192 75¢ WENDELL WILKIE

Bull's Eye Perf. 11.2 x 11.1

C Press		Mottled prephosphored			
1	$5.00	☐	☐	☐	☐
C Press		Uniform prephosphored			
1	$5.00	☐	☐	☐	☐

#2943 78¢ ALICE PAUL

Bull's Eye Perf. 11.2 x 11.1

		UL	UR	LL	LR
T/A Press		Uniform prephosphored			
B1	$5.50	☐	☐	☐	☐
B2	$5.50	☐	☐	☐	☐
T/A Press		Mottled prephosphored			
B1	$5.50	☐	☐	☐	☐

#2193 $1.00 BERNARD REVEL

A Press(4 position) — Block tagged

Bull's Eye Perf. 11.2 x 11.1

1	$9.00	☐	☐	☐	☐

#2194 $1.00 JOHNS HOPKINS

A Press(4 position) — Block tagged

Bull's Eye Perf. 11.2 x 11.1

1	$7.00	☐	☐	☐	☐

#2194b $1.00 JOHNS HOPKINS

A Press(4 position) — Overall tagged

Bull's Eye Perf. 11.2 x 11.1

1	$7.00	☐	☐	☐	☐

#2194d $1.00 JOHNS HOPKINS

Bull's Eye Perf. 11.2 x 11.1

C Press		Mottled prephosphored			
2	$7.00	☐	☐	☐	☐
C Press		Uniform prephosphored			
2	$7.00	☐	☐	☐	☐

#2195 $2.00 WILLIAM JENNINGS BRYAN

A Press(4 position) — Block tagged

Bull's Eye Perf. 11.2 x 11.1

2	$14.00	☐	☐	☐	☐

#2196 $5.00 BRET HARTE

A Press(4 position) — Block tagged

Bull's Eye Perf. 11.2 x 11.1

1	$30.00	☐	☐	☐	☐

#2196b $5.00 BRET HARTE

A Press(4 position) Uniform prephosphored

Bull's Eye Perf. 11.2 x 11.1

2	$30.00	☐	☐	☐	☐

BOOKLET PANES

#2182a 25¢ JACK LONDON

$5.00 - **BK150** - 2 panes of 10 stamps

		T
1	$9.50	☐
2	$9.50	☐

#2197a 25¢ JACK LONDON

$1.50 - **BK151** - 1 pane of 6 stamps

1	$2.50	☐

$3.00 - **BK152** - 2 panes of 6 stamps

1	$5.00	☐

1981 COMMEMORATIVES

#1874 15¢ EVERETT DIRKSEN

		UL	UR	LL	LR
1	$1.35	☐	☐	☐	☐
2	$1.35	☐	☐	☐	☐
3	$1.35	☐	☐	☐	☐
4	$1.35	☐	☐	☐	☐
5	$1.35	☐	☐	☐	☐
6	$1.35	☐	☐	☐	☐
7	$1.35	☐	☐	☐	☐
8	$1.35	☐	☐	☐	☐

#1875 15¢ WHITNEY YOUNG

111111	$1.60	☐	☐	☐	☐

#1876-79 18¢ FLOWERS

111111	$1.80	☐	☐	☐	☐

#1889a 18¢ WILDLIFE BOOKLET

$3.60 - **BK137** - 2 panes of 10 stamps

		T
1	$15	☐
2	$15	☐
3	$15	☐
4	$15	☐
5	$15	☐
6	$15	☐
7	$15	☐
8	$15	☐
9	$15	☐
10	$15	☐
11	$40	☐
12	$40	☐
13	$40	☐
14	$40	☐
15	$30	☐
16	$30	☐

1981 REGULAR ISSUES

#1890 18¢ FLAG

Block of 6 (2 x 3)

		L	R
1	$2.00	☐	☐
2	$2.00	☐	☐

#1891 18¢ FLAG COIL

Strips of 5

		B
1	$400	☐
2	$40	☐
3	$900	☐
4	$9	☐
5	$5	☐
6	$4,000	☐
7	$35	☐

#1893a 18¢/6¢ FLAG BOOKLET

$1.20 - **BK138** - 1 pane of 6-18¢ and 2-6¢ stamps

		T
1	$3.00	☐

The above price is for booklets with the plate number over the left stamp. This booklet also occurs with the plate number over the right stamp and commands a premium.

1981 REGULAR ISSUES

#1894 20¢ FLAG OVER SUPREME COURT

Block of 6 (2 x 3)

L-Perf. 10.9 x 10.9

		L	R
2	$5.00	☐	☐
3	$5.00	☐	☐
4	$5.00	☐	☐

#1894e 20¢ FLAG OVER SUPREME COURT

Block of 6 (2 x 3)

Bull's Eye Perf. 11.2 x 11.2

2	$2.50	☐	☐
3	$2.50	☐	☐
4	$2.50	☐	☐

#1895 20¢ FLAG OVER SUPREME COURT COIL

Strips of 5

		B
B Press		
1	$75	☐
2	$8	☐
3	$5	☐
5	$5	☐
11	$8	☐
13	$5	☐
14	$5	☐
C Press		
4	$750	☐
6	$150	☐
8	$14	☐
9	$5	☐
10	$5	☐
12	$8	☐

#1895e 20¢ FLAG OVER SUPREME COURT COIL

PRECANCEL Style 2

Strips of 5

B Press

14	$60.00	☐

#1896a 20¢ FLAG OVER SUPREME COURT BOOKLET

$1.20 - **BK139** - 1 pane of 6 stamps

		T
1	$2.50	☐

#1896b 20¢ FLAG OVER SUPREME COURT BOOKLET

$2.00 - **BK140** - 1 pane of 10 stamps		
1	$4.50	☐
4	$25.00	☐
$4.00 - **BK140A** - 2 panes of 10 stamps		
2	$9.00	☐
3	$9.00	☐
4	$500.00	☐

PRECANCEL STYLES

STYLE 2

STYLE 3

STYLE 13-A

STYLE 13-B

STYLE 4

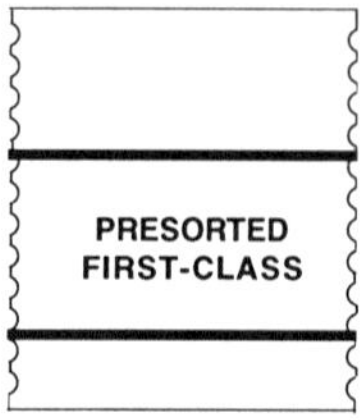

STYLE 5-A

STYLE 14

STYLE 15

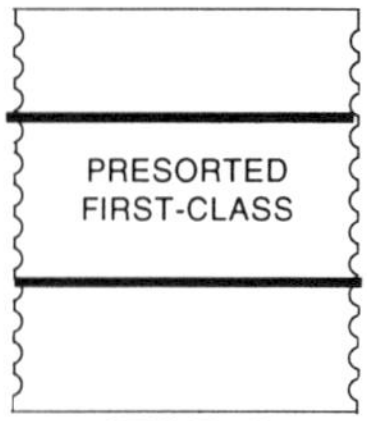

STYLE 5-B

STYLE 5-C

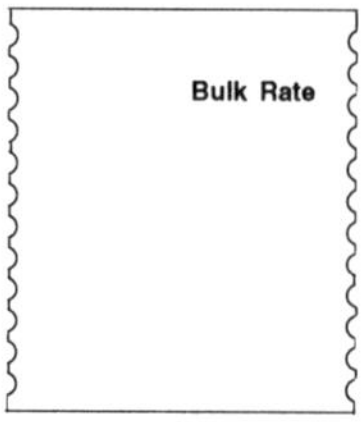

STYLE 16

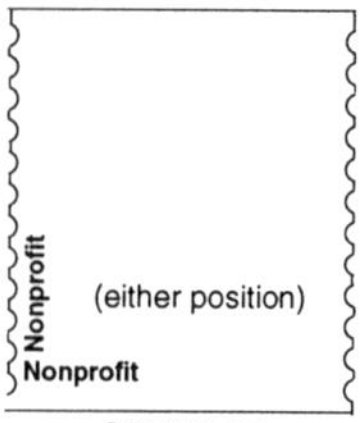

STYLE 17

STYLE 7

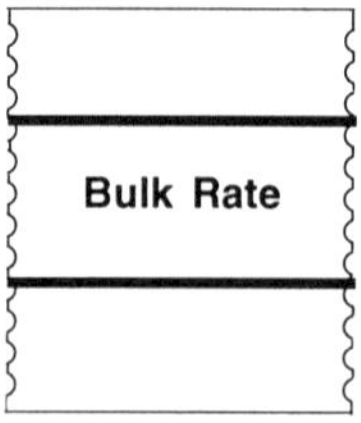

STYLE 8

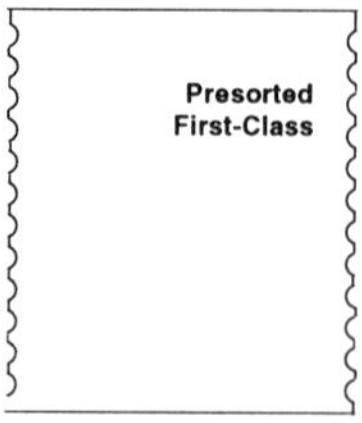

STYLE 18

STYLE 19

STYLE 9

STYLE 10

STYLE 20

STYLE 21

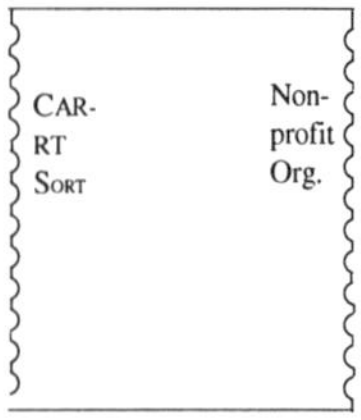

STYLE 11

STYLE 12

STYLE 22

STYLE 23

1981 TRANSPORTATION COILS

Cottrell Press stamps shows join line;
stamps from other presses do not.
Strips of 5

#1897 1¢ OMNIBUS

Cottrell Press Overall tagged

		B
1	$0.50	☐
2	$0.50	☐
3	$0.50	☐
4	$0.50	☐
5	$0.50	☐
6	$0.50	☐

#2225 1¢ OMNIBUS (revised)

B Press Block tagged

1	$0.50	☐
2	$0.50	☐

C Press Mottled prephosphored

3	$6.00	☐

#2225a 1¢ OMNIBUS (revised)

B Press Untagged

2	$0.50	☐

C Press dull gum Untagged

3	$0.50	☐

C Press shiny gum Untagged

3	$0.50	☐

#1897A 2¢ LOCOMOTIVE

Cottrell Press Overall tagged

2	$0.50	☐
3	$0.50	☐
4	$0.50	☐
6	$0.50	☐
8	$0.50	☐
10	$0.50	☐

#2226 2¢ LOCOMOTIVE (revised)

B Press Block tagged

1	$0.50	☐

#2226a 2¢ LOCOMOTIVE (revised)

C Press Untagged

2	$0.50	☐

#1898 3¢ HANDCAR

Cottrell Press Overall tagged

1	$0.75	☐
2	$0.75	☐
3	$0.75	☐
4	$0.75	☐

#2252 3¢ CONESTOGA WAGON

B Press Block tagged

1	$0.90	☐

#2252a 3¢ CONESTOGA WAGON

B Press **B** Untagged

2	$0.90	☐

C Press dull gum Untagged

3	$0.90	☐

C Press shiny gum Untagged

3	$0.90	☐
5	$0.90	☐
6	$1.50	☐

#2123 3.4¢ SCHOOL BUS

Cottrell Press Overall tagged

1	$1.10	☐
2	$1.10	☐

#2123a 3.4¢ SCHOOL BUS

Cottrell Press Untagged

PRECANCEL Style 3

1	$7.00	☐
2	$7.00	☐

#1898A 4¢ STAGECOACH

Cottrell Press Overall tagged

1	$1.25	☐
2	$1.25	☐
3	$1.25	☐
4	$1.25	☐
5	$2.00	☐
6	$2.00	☐

#1898b 4¢ STAGECOACH

Cottrell Press Untagged

PRECANCEL Style 4

3	$7.00	☐
4	$7.00	☐
5	$7.00	☐
6	$7.00	☐

#2228 4¢ STAGECOACH (revised)

B Press Block tagged

1	$1.00	☐

#2228a 4¢ STAGECOACH (revised)

B Press Overall tagged

1	$15.00	☐

#2451 4¢ STEAM CARRIAGE

B Press Overall tagged

1	$1.00	☐

#2451b 4¢ STEAM CARRIAGE

B Press Untagged

1	$1.00	☐

1981 TRANSPORTATION COILS

#2124 4.9¢ BUCKBOARD
Cottrell Press — Overall tagged

		B
3	$1.00	☐
4	$1.00	☐

#2124a 4.9¢ BUCKBOARD
Cottrell Press — Untagged
PRECANCEL Style 4

1	$1.75	☐
2	$1.75	☐
3	$1.75	☐
4	$1.75	☐
5	$1.75	☐
6	$1.75	☐

#1899 5¢ POPE MOTORCYCLE
Cottrell Press — Overall tagged

1	$1.00	☐
2	$1.00	☐
3	$1.00	☐
4	$1.00	☐

#2253 5¢ MILK WAGON
B Press — Block tagged

1	$1.00	☐

#2452 5¢ CIRCUS WAGON (intaglio)
B Press — Overall tagged

1	$1.25	☐

#2452a 5¢ CIRCUS WAGON (intaglio)
B Press — Untagged

1	$1.25	☐

#2452B 5¢ CIRCUS WAGON (gravure)
Andreotti Press — Untagged

A1	$1.50	☐
A2	$1.50	☐
A3	$1.50	☐

#2452D 5¢ CIRCUS WAGON (gravure)
Champlain Press — Untagged

S1	$1.50	☐
S2	$1.50	☐

#2453 5¢ CANOE (intaglio)
C Press — Untagged
PRECANCEL Style 22

1	$1.50	☐
2	$1.50	☐
3	$1.50	☐

#2454 5¢ CANOE (gravure)
PRECANCEL Style 22
Champlain Press shiny gum Untagged

S11	$1.50	☐

Champlain Press semi-gloss gum Untagged

S11	$1.50	☐

#1900 5.2¢ SLEIGH
Cottrell Press — Overall tagged

		B
1	$9.00	☐
2	$9.00	☐
3	$250.00	☐
5	$180.00	☐

#1900a 5.2¢ SLEIGH
Cottrell Press — Untagged
PRECANCEL Style 2

1	$12.00	☐
2	$12.00	☐
3	$12.00	☐
4	$16.00	☐
5	$12.00	☐
6	$16.00	☐

#2254 5.3¢ ELEVATOR
B Press — Untagged
PRECANCEL Style 19

1	$1.00	☐

#2125 5.5¢ STAR ROUTE TRUCK
B Press — Block tagged

1	$2.00	☐

#2125a 5.5¢ STAR ROUTE TRUCK
B Press — Untagged
PRECANCEL STYLE 11

1	$1.50	☐
2	$3.00	☐

#1901 5.9¢ BICYCLE
Cottrell Press — Overall tagged

3	$15.00	☐
4	$15.00	☐

#1901a 5.9¢ BICYCLE
Cottrell Press — Untagged
PRECANCEL Style 2

3	$30.00	☐
4	$30.00	☐
5	$80.00	☐
6	$80.00	☐

#2126 6¢ TRICYCLE
B Press — Block tagged

1	$1.30	☐

#2126a 6¢ TRICYCLE
B Press — Untagged
PRECANCEL Style 4

1	$1.50	☐
2	$7.50	☐

1981 TRANSPORTATION COILS

#2127 7.1¢ TRACTOR
B Press Block tagged

		B
1	$2.50	☐

#2127a 7.1¢ TRACTOR
B Press Untagged
PRECANCEL Style 12

1	$3.00	☐

PRECANCEL Style 21

1	$2.50	☐

#1902 7.4¢ BABY BUGGY
B Press Block tagged

2	$8.50	☐

#1902a 7.4¢ BABY BUGGY
B Press Untagged
PRECANCEL Style 7

2	$4.25	☐

#2255 7.6¢ CARRETA
B Press Untagged
PRECANCEL Style 17 Horizontal

1	$2.25	☐
2	$2.25	☐
3	$6.00	☐

#2128 8.3¢ AMBULANCE
Cottrell Press Overall tagged

1	$1.50	☐
2	$1.50	☐

#2128a 8.3¢ AMBULANCE
Cottrell Press Untagged
PRECANCEL Style 7

1	$1.80	☐
2	$1.80	☐
3	$5.25	☐
4	$5.25	☐

#2231 8.3¢ AMBULANCE
B Press Untagged
PRECANCEL Style 7

1	$4.50	☐
2	$6.00	☐

#2256 8.4¢ WHEEL CHAIR
PRECANCEL Style 17 Vertical
B Press Untagged

1	$2.25	☐

C Press Untagged

2	$2.25	☐
3	$14.00	☐

#2129 8.5¢ TOW TRUCK
B Press Block tagged

		B
1	$2.50	☐

#2129a 8.5¢ TOW TRUCK
B Press Untagged
PRECANCEL Style 14

1	$2.50	☐
2	$12.00	☐

#1903 9.3¢ MAIL WAGON
Cottrell Press Overall tagged

1	$12.00	☐
2	$12.00	☐
3	$33.00	☐
4	$33.00	☐
5	$275.00	☐
6	$275.00	☐

#1903a 9.3¢ MAIL WAGON
Cottrell Press Untagged
PRECANCEL Style 2

1	$16.00	☐
2	$12.00	☐
3	$30.00	☐
4	$20.00	☐
5	$2.75	☐
6	$2.75	☐
8	$200.00	☐

#2257 10¢ CANAL BOAT
B Press Block tagged

1	$1.50	☐

#2257a 10¢ CANAL BOAT
B Press Overall tagged

1	$4.00	☐

B Press Mottled prephosphored

1	$3.00	☐
2	$3.00	☐

C Press Mottled prephosphored

3	$4.00	☐

#2457 10¢ TRACTOR TRAILER
C Press Untagged
PRECANCEL Style 23

1	$2.00	☐

#2458 10¢ TRACTOR TRAILER
(gravure)
Andreotti Press Untagged
PRECANCEL Style 23

11	$2.00	☐
22	$2.00	☐

1981 TRANSPORTATION COILS

#2130 10.1¢ OIL WAGON
B Press Block tagged

		B
1	$2.50	☐

#2130a 10.1¢ OIL WAGON
B Press Untagged
PRECANCEL Style 8

1	$2.50	☐
2	$2.50	☐

PRECANCEL Style 15

2	$2.50	☐
3	$2.50	☐

#1904 10.9¢ HANSOM CAB
Cottrell Press Overall tagged

1	$30.00	☐
2	$30.00	☐

#1904a 10.9¢ HANSOM CAB
Cottrell Press Untagged
PRECANCEL Style 2

1	$30.00	☐
2	$30.00	☐
3	$350.00	☐
4	$350.00	☐

#1905 11¢ RAILROAD CABOOSE
B Press Block tagged

1	$4.00	☐

#1905a 11¢ RAILROAD CABOOSE
B Press Untagged

2	$2.00	☐

PRECANCEL Style 2

1	$3.50	☐

#2131 11¢ STUTZ BEARCAT
Cottrell Press Overall tagged

1	$1.50	☐
2	$1.50	☐
3	$1.50	☐
4	$1.50	☐

#2132 12¢ STANLEY STEAMER
Cottrell Press Overall tagged

1	$2.00	☐
2	$2.00	☐

#2132a 12¢ STANLEY STEAMER
Cottrell Press Untagged
PRECANCEL Style 5-A

1	$2.40	☐
2	$2.40	☐

#2132b 12¢ STANLEY STEAMER
B Press Untagged
PRECANCEL Style 5-A

		B
1	$20.00	☐

#2133 12.5¢ PUSHCART
B Press Block tagged

1	$2.75	☐
2	$5.00	☐

#2133a 12.5¢ PUSHCART
B Press Untagged
PRECANCEL Style 8

1	$3.00	☐
2	$4.50	☐

#2258 13¢ POLICE PATROL
B Press Untagged
PRECANCEL Style 18

1	$3.00	☐

#2259 13.2¢ RAILROAD COAL CAR
B Press Untagged
PRECANCEL Style 16

1	$3.00	☐
2	$3.00	☐

#2134 14¢ ICEBOAT (Type I)
Cottrell Press Overall tagged

1	$2.25	☐
2	$2.25	☐
3	$2.25	☐
4	$2.25	☐

#2134b 14¢ ICEBOAT (Type II)
B Press Block tagged

2	$3.50	☐

#2260 15¢ TUGBOAT
B Press Block tagged

1	$2.50	☐
2	$3.00	☐

#2260a 15¢ TUGBOAT
B Press Overall tagged

2	$3.00	☐

#2261 16.7¢ POPCORN WAGON
B Press Untagged
PRECANCEL Style 16

1	$3.50	☐
2	$5.00	☐

1981 TRANSPORTATION COILS

#1906 17¢ ELECTRIC AUTO
Cottrell Press — Overall tagged

		B
1	$2.25	☐
2	$2.25	☐
3	$2.25	☐
4	$2.25	☐
5	$2.25	☐
6	$13.00	☐
7	$5.00	☐

#1906a 17¢ ELECTRIC AUTO
Cottrell Press — Untagged
PRECANCEL Style 5-A
"PRESORTED" is 11 mm long

3	$3.50	☐
4	$3.50	☐
5	$3.50	☐
6	$12.00	☐
7	$12.00	☐

#1906a 17¢ ELECTRIC AUTO
Cottrell Press — Untagged
PRECANCEL Style 5-B
"PRESORTED" is 12.5 mm long

3	$25.00	☐
4	$25.00	☐
5	$20.00	☐
6	$20.00	☐

#1906a 17¢ ELECTRIC AUTO
Cottrell Press — Untagged
PRECANCEL Style 5-C
"PRESORTED" is 13.5 mm long

1	$10.00	☐
2	$10.00	☐
3	$10.00	☐
4	$10.00	☐
5	$30.00	☐
7	$30.00	☐

#2135 17¢ DOG SLED
B Press — Block tagged

2	$3.00	☐

#2262 17.5¢ RACING CAR
B Press — Block tagged

1	$3.00	☐

#2262a 17.5¢ RACING CAR
B Press — Untagged
PRECANCEL Style 13-A

1	$3.25	☐

#1907 18¢ SURREY
Cottrell Press — Overall tagged

		B
1	$90.00	☐
2	$3.25	☐
3	$70.00	☐
4	$70.00	☐
5	$3.25	☐
6	$3.25	☐
7	$35.00	☐
8	$3.25	☐
9	$14.00	☐
10	$14.00	☐
11	$14.00	☐
12	$14.00	☐
13	$3.25	☐
14	$3.25	☐
15	$14.00	☐
16	$14.00	☐
17	$3.25	☐
18	$3.25	☐

#1908 20¢ FIRE PUMPER
Cottrell Press — Overall tagged

1	$140.00	☐
2	$750.00	☐
3	$5.00	☐
4	$5.00	☐
5	$3.00	☐
6	$35.00	☐
7	$175.00	☐
8	$175.00	☐
9	$3.00	☐
10	$3.00	☐
11	$80.00	☐
12	$8.00	☐
13	$5.00	☐
14	$8.00	☐
15	$5.00	☐
16	$5.00	☐

#2263 20¢ CABLE CAR
C Press — Block tagged

1	$3.00	☐
2	$3.00	☐

#2263b 20¢ CABLE CAR
C Press — Overall tagged

2	$6.00	☐

#2463 20¢ COG RAILWAY
C Press — Mottled prephosphored

1	$4.00	☐
2	$4.00	☐

#2264 20.5¢ FIRE ENGINE
B Press — Untagged
PRECANCEL Style 13-B

1	$3.00	☐

1981 TRANSPORTATION COILS

#2265 21¢ RAILROAD MAIL CAR

PRECANCEL Style 18

B Press		Untagged
		B
1	$3.00	□
C Press		Untagged
2	$3.00	□

#2464 23¢ LUNCH WAGON

B Press		Uniform prephosphored
2	$4.00	□
3	$4.00	□
B Press shiny gum		Mottled prephosphored
3	$4.00	□
B Press dull gum		Mottled prephosphored
3	$4.00	□
C Press shiny gum		Mottled prephosphored
4	$4.00	□

#2266 24.1¢ TANDEM BICYCLE

B Press Untagged

PRECANCEL Style 20

1	$3.75	□

#2136 25¢ BREADWAGON

B Press		Block tagged
1	$4.00	□
5	$4.00	□
C or D Press		Block tagged
2	$4.00	□
3	$4.00	□
4	$4.00	□

#2466 32¢ FERRYBOAT

C Press shiny gum		Mottled prephosphored
2	$6.00	□
3	$6.00	□
4	$6.00	□
5	$6.00	□
C Press semi-gloss gum		Mottled prephos.
3	$6.00	□
4	$15.00	□
5	$6.00	□

#2468 $1.00 SEAPLANE

B Press		Overall tagged
1	$9.00	□
C Press		Mottled prephosphored
3	$9.00	□

1981 REGULAR ISSUE

#1909a $9.35 EAGLE BOOKLET

$28.05 - **BK140B** - 1 pane of 3 stamps

		L
1111	$60.00	□

1981 COMMEMORATIVES

#1910 18¢ AMERICAN RED CROSS

		UL	UR	LL	LR
111111	$1.60	□	□	□	□

#1911 18¢ SAVINGS & LOAN

111111	$1.60	□	□	□	□

#1912-19 18¢ SPACE ACHIEVEMENTS

Block of 8 (4 x 2)

111111	$3.50	□	□	□	□
222222	$3.50	□	□	□	□

#1920 18¢ PROFESSIONAL MANAGEMENT

11	$1.60	□	□	□	□

#1921-24 18¢ WILDLIFE HABITAT

11111	$2.00	□	□	□	□

#1925 18¢ DISABLED PERSONS

111111	$1.60	□	□	□	□

#1926 18¢ EDNA ST. VINCENT MILLAY

111111-4	$1.60	□	□	□	□
111111-6	$1.60	□	□	□	□
111111-7	$1.60	□	□	□	□
111111-8	$1.60	□	□	□	□

#1927 18¢ ALCOHOLISM

Block of 6 (2 x 3)

		L	R
1	$15.00	□	□

#1928-31 18¢ ARCHITECTURE

		UL	UR	LL	LR
1	$2.00	□	□	□	□
2	$2.00	□	□	□	□
3	$2.00	□	□	□	□
4	$2.00	□	□	□	□
5	$2.00	□	□	□	□
6	$2.00	□	□	□	□
7	$2.00	□	□	□	□
8	$2.00	□	□	□	□

#1932 18¢ BABE ZAHARIAS

1	$3.00	□	□	□	□
2	$3.00	□	□	□	□
3	$3.00	□	□	□	□
4	$3.00	□	□	□	□

#1933 18¢ BOBBY JONES

1	$3.00	□	□	□	□
2	$3.00	□	□	□	□
3	$3.00	□	□	□	□
4	$3.00	□	□	□	□

1981 COMMEMORATIVES

#1934 18¢ REMINGTON

		UL	UR	LL	LR
11-1	$1.60	□	□	□	□
11-2	$1.60	□	□	□	□
11-3	$1.60	□	□	□	□
11-4	$1.60	□	□	□	□
11-5	$1.60	□	□	□	□
11-6	$1.60	□	□	□	□
11-7	$1.60	□	□	□	□
11-8	$1.60	□	□	□	□
12-3	$1.60	□	□	□	□
12-6	$1.60	□	□	□	□
12-7	$1.60	□	□	□	□
12-8	$1.60	□	□	□	□

#1935 18¢ HOBAN

111111	$2.00	□	□	□	□

#1936 20¢ HOBAN

111112	$1.75	□	□	□	□

#1937-38 18¢ YORKTOWN CAPES

111111-1	$4.00	□	□	□	□
111111-2	$4.00	□	□	□	□
111111-3	$4.00	□	□	□	□
111111-4	$4.00	□	□	□	□
111111-5	$2.00	□	□	□	□
111111-6	$2.00	□	□	□	□
111111-7	$2.00	□	□	□	□
111111-8	$2.00	□	□	□	□
211111-1	$2.00	□	□	□	□
211111-5	$20.00	†	□	†	†
211111-6	$2.00	□	□	□	□
211111-7	$2.00	□	□	□	□
211111-8	$2.00	□	□	□	□
211112-1	$20.00	†	†	□	□
211112-6	$20.00	†	†	□	□
211112-7	$20.00	†	†	□	□
211112-8	$20.00	□	†	□	□
212112-1	$2.00	□	□	□	□
212112-2	$2.00	□	□	□	□
212112-3	$5.00	□	□	□	□
212112-4	$5.00	□	□	□	□
212112-5	$5.00	□	□	□	□
212112-6	$2.00	□	□	□	□
212112-7	$2.00	□	□	□	□
212112-8	$2.00	□	□	□	□
212122-2	$2.00	□	□	□	□
212122-3	$2.00	□	□	□	□
212122-4	$2.00	□	□	□	□
212122-5	$2.00	□	□	□	□
212222-2	$2.00	□	□	□	□
212222-3	$2.00	□	□	□	□
212222-4	$2.00	□	□	□	□
212222-5	$2.00	□	□	□	□

#1937-38 18¢ YORKTOWN CAPES Cont.

		UL	UR	LL	LR
222222-2	$2.00	□	□	□	□
222222-3	$2.00	□	□	□	□
222222-4	$2.00	□	□	□	□
222222-5	$2.00	□	□	□	□
223222-2	$5.00	□	□	□	□
223222-3	$5.00	□	□	□	□
223222-4	$5.00	□	□	□	□
223222-5	$5.00	□	□	□	□
223223-2	$2.25	□	□	□	□
223223-3	$2.25	□	□	□	□
223223-4	$2.25	□	□	□	□
223223-5	$2.25	□	□	□	□
323223-2	$2.25	□	□	□	□
323223-3	$2.25	□	□	□	□
323223-4	$2.25	□	□	□	□
323223-5	$2.25	□	□	□	□

#1939 (20¢) MADONNA

111111	$1.75	□	□	□	□
222222	$1.75	□	□	□	□

#1940 (20¢) TEDDY BEAR

11111	$1.75	□	□	□	□
12222	$5.00	□	□	□	□
22222	$1.75	□	□	□	□

#1941 20¢ JOHN HANSON

11111	$1.75	□	□	□	□

#1942-45 20¢ DESERT PLANTS

111111-1	$4.00	□	□	□	□
111111-2	$2.00	□	□	□	□
111111-3	$4.00	□	□	□	□
111111-4	$2.00	□	□	□	□
111111-5	$4.00	□	□	□	□
111111-6	$2.00	□	□	□	□
111111-7	$4.00	□	□	□	□
111111-8	$2.00	□	□	□	□
111112-1	$4.00	□	□	□	□
111112-3	$4.00	□	□	□	□
111112-5	$4.00	□	□	□	□
111112-7	$4.00	□	□	□	□
121112-1	$2.00	□	□	□	□
121112-3	$2.00	□	□	□	□
121112-5	$2.00	□	□	□	□
121112-7	$2.00	□	□	□	□
121113-1	$4.00	□	□	□	□
121113-3	$4.00	□	□	□	□
121113-5	$4.00	□	□	□	□
121113-7	$4.00	□	□	□	□

1981 COMMEMORATIVES

#1942-45 20¢ DESERT PLANTS Cont.

		UL	UR	LL	LR
221113-1	$2.00	☐	☐	☐	☐
221113-3	$2.00	☐	☐	☐	☐
221113-5	$2.00	☐	☐	☐	☐
221113-7	$2.00	☐	☐	☐	☐
221123-1	$2.00	☐	☐	☐	☐
221123-3	$2.00	☐	☐	☐	☐
221123-5	$2.00	☐	☐	☐	☐
221123-7	$2.00	☐	☐	☐	☐

1981 REGULAR ISSUE

#1946 (20¢)C EAGLE

39566	$1.80	☐	☐	☐	☐
39567	$1.80	☐	☐	☐	☐
39568	$1.80	☐	☐	☐	☐

#1947 (20¢)C EAGLE COIL

432 Subject Plates Strips of 6

†39437 †39438 †39439 †39440 †39441
†39442 †39443 †39444 †39445 †39446
†39447 †39448 †39564 *39569 †39570
†39571 †39572 †39575 †39576 *39577
†39578 †39583 †39614 †39615

#1948a (20¢)C EAGLE BOOKLET

$4.00 - **BK141** - 2 panes of 10 stamps

†39528 †39543

1982 REGULAR ISSUE

#1949a 20¢ BIGHORN SHEEP BOOKLET (Type I)

$4.00 - **BK142** - 2 panes of 10 stamps

		T
1	$15.00	☐
2	$15.00	☐
3	$15.00	☐
4	$15.00	☐
5	$15.00	☐
6	$15.00	☐
9**N**	$15.00	☐
10**N**	$15.00	☐
11	$35.00	☐
12	$35.00	☐
14**N**	$35.00	☐
15**N**	$35.00	☐
16**N**	$70.00	☐
17**N**	$70.00	☐
18**N**	$70.00	☐
19**N**	$70.00	☐
20**N**	$100.00	☐
21	$500.00	☐

1982 REGULAR ISSUE

#1949a 20¢ BIGHORN SHEEP BOOKLET (Type I) Cont.

		T
22**N**	$100.00	☐
23**N**	$100.00	☐
24**N**	$100.00	☐
25**N**	$150.00	☐
26**N**	$150.00	☐
28	$500.00	☐
29	$500.00	☐

N The above prices are for booklets with the plate number on only the top pane. These booklets also occur with the plate number on only the bottom pane and command a premium.

#1949d 20¢ BIGHORN SHEEP BOOKLET (Type II)

$4.00 - **BK142a** - 2 panes of 10 stamps

34**N**	$15.00	☐

N The above price is for booklets with the plate number on only the top pane. This booklet also occurs with the plate number on only the bottom pane and commands a premium.

1982 COMMEMORATIVES

#1950 20¢ ROOSEVELT

		UL	UR	LL	LR
1	$1.75	☐	☐	☐	☐
2	$1.75	☐	☐	☐	☐
3	$1.75	☐	☐	☐	☐
4	$1.75	☐	☐	☐	☐

#1951 20¢ LOVE

EE Perf. 11.3 x 10.5

11111	$2.50	☐	☐	☐	☐

#1951a 20¢ LOVE

Bull's Eye Perf. 11.2 x 11.2

11111	$1.75	☐	☐	☐	☐
22222	$1.75	☐	☐	☐	☐

#1952 20¢ WASHINGTON

111111	$1.75	☐	☐	☐	☐

#2002b 20¢ STATE BIRDS & FLOWERS

Pane of 50

EE Perf. 10.5 x 11.3

11111	$25.00	☐	☐	☐	☐
22222	$25.00	☐	☐	☐	☐

#2002c 20¢ STATE BIRDS & FLOWERS

Pane of 50

Bull's Eye Perf. 11.2 x 11.2

11111	$30.00	☐	☐	☐	☐
22222	$30.00	☐	☐	☐	☐

1982 COMMEMORATIVES

#2003 20¢ NETHERLANDS

Block of 6 (2 x 3)		L	R
111	$3.00	☐	☐

#2004 20¢ LIBRARY OF CONGRESS

		UL	UR	LL	LR
1	$1.75	☐	☐	☐	☐
2	$1.75	☐	☐	☐	☐
3	$1.75	☐	☐	☐	☐
4	$1.75	☐	☐	☐	☐

1982 REGULAR ISSUE

#2005 20¢ CONSUMER EDUCATION COIL

Strips of 5		B
1	$150.00	☐
2	$150.00	☐
3	$100.00	☐
4	$100.00	☐

1982 COMMEMORATIVES

#2006-09 20¢ KNOXVILLE FAIR

		UL	UR	LL	LR
111111	$2.00	☐	☐	☐	☐

#2010 20¢ HORATIO ALGER

1	$1.75	☐	☐	☐	☐
2	$1.75	☐	☐	☐	☐
3	$1.75	☐	☐	☐	☐
4	$1.75	☐	☐	☐	☐

#2011 20¢ AGING

1	$1.75	☐	☐	☐	☐
2	$1.75	☐	☐	☐	☐
3	$1.75	☐	☐	☐	☐
4	$1.75	☐	☐	☐	☐

#2012 20¢ THE BARRYMORES

111111	$1.75	☐	☐	☐	☐

#2013 20¢ DR. MARY WALKER

111111	$1.75	☐	☐	☐	☐

#2014 20¢ PEACE GARDEN

1111-1	$2.00	☐	☐	☐	☐
1111-2	$2.00	☐	☐	☐	☐
1111-3	$2.00	☐	☐	☐	☐
1111-4	$2.00	☐	☐	☐	☐
1211-1	$10.00	☐	☐	☐	☐
1211-2	$10.00	☐	☐	☐	☐
1211-3	$10.00	☐	☐	☐	☐
1211-4	$10.00	☐	☐	☐	☐
1221-1	$2.00	☐	☐	☐	☐
1221-2	$2.00	☐	☐	☐	☐
1221-3	$2.00	☐	☐	☐	☐
1221-4	$2.00	☐	☐	☐	☐

1982 COMMEMORATIVES

#2014 20¢ PEACE GARDEN Cont.

		UL	UR	LL	LR
1321-1	$2.00	☐	☐	☐	☐
1321-2	$2.00	☐	☐	☐	☐
1321-3	$2.00	☐	☐	☐	☐
1321-4	$2.00	☐	☐	☐	☐
1322-1	$10.00	☐	☐	☐	☐
1322-2	$10.00	☐	☐	☐	☐
1322-3	$10.00	☐	☐	☐	☐
1322-4	$10.00	☐	☐	☐	☐
2322-1	$2.00	☐	☐	☐	☐
2322-2	$2.00	☐	☐	☐	☐
2322-3	$2.00	☐	☐	☐	☐
2322-4	$2.00	☐	☐	☐	☐
2422-1	$2.00	☐	☐	☐	☐
2422-2	$2.00	☐	☐	☐	☐
2422-3	$2.00	☐	☐	☐	☐
2422-4	$2.00	☐	☐	☐	☐
2432-1	$2.00	☐	☐	☐	☐
2432-2	$2.00	☐	☐	☐	☐
2432-3	$2.00	☐	☐	☐	☐
2432-4	$2.00	☐	☐	☐	☐
2532-1	$2.00	☐	☐	☐	☐
2532-2	$2.00	☐	☐	☐	☐
2532-3	$2.00	☐	☐	☐	☐
2532-4	$2.00	☐	☐	☐	☐
3532-1	$2.00	☐	☐	☐	☐
3532-2	$2.00	☐	☐	☐	☐
3532-3	$2.00	☐	☐	☐	☐
3532-4	$2.00	☐	☐	☐	☐
3632-1	$50.00	☐	☐	☐	☐
3632-2	$50.00	☐	☐	☐	☐
3632-3	$50.00	☐	☐	☐	☐
3632-4	$50.00	☐	☐	☐	☐
3633-1	$10.00	☐	☐	☐	☐
3633-2	$10.00	☐	☐	☐	☐
3633-3	$10.00	☐	☐	☐	☐
3633-4	$10.00	☐	☐	☐	☐
3733-1	$2.00	☐	☐	☐	☐
3733-2	$2.00	☐	☐	☐	☐
3733-3	$2.00	☐	☐	☐	☐
3733-4	$2.00	☐	☐	☐	☐
3734-1	$2.00	☐	☐	☐	☐
3734-2	$2.00	☐	☐	☐	☐
3734-3	$2.00	☐	☐	☐	☐
3734-4	$2.00	☐	☐	☐	☐

1982 COMMEMORATIVES

#2014 20¢ PEACE GARDEN Cont.

		UL	UR	LL	LR
3744-1	$2.00	☐	☐	☐	☐
3744-2	$2.00	☐	☐	☐	☐
3744-3	$2.00	☐	☐	☐	☐
3744-4	$2.00	☐	☐	☐	☐
3844-1	$10.00	☐	☐	☐	☐
3844-2	$10.00	☐	☐	☐	☐
3844-3	$10.00	☐	☐	☐	☐
3844-4	$10.00	☐	☐	☐	☐

#2015 20¢ LIBRARIES OF AMERICA

1	$1.75	☐	☐	☐	☐
2	$1.75	☐	☐	☐	☐
3	$1.75	☐	☐	☐	☐
4	$1.75	☐	☐	☐	☐
5	$3.00	☐	☐	☐	☐

#2016 20¢ JACKIE ROBINSON

11111	$5.00	☐	☐	☐	☐

#2017 20¢ TOURO SYNAGOGUE

Block of 4 (2 x 2)

		L	R
11111-1	$1.75	☐	☐

#2018 20¢ WOLF TRAP FARM PARK

		UL	UR	LL	LR
11111	$1.75	☐	☐	☐	☐

#2019-22 20¢ ARCHITECTURE

1	$2.00	☐	☐	☐	☐
2	$2.00	☐	☐	☐	☐
3	$2.00	☐	☐	☐	☐
4	$2.00	☐	☐	☐	☐
5	$2.00	☐	☐	☐	☐
6	$2.00	☐	☐	☐	☐

#2023 20¢ ST. FRANCIS OF ASSISI

A111111	$1.75	☐	☐	☐	☐

#2024 20¢ PONCE DE LEON

Block of 6 (2 x 3)

		L	R
11111	$3.00	☐	☐
22222	$3.00	☐	☐

#2025 13¢ KITTEN & PUPPY

		UL	UR	LL	LR
1111	$1.10	☐	☐	☐	☐
1121	$1.10	☐	☐	☐	☐
2222	$1.10	☐	☐	☐	☐

1982 COMMEMORATIVES

#2026 20¢ MADONNA

Block of 6 (2 x 3)

		T	B
11111	$3.00	☐	☐
12122	$10.00	☐	†
13131	$3.00	☐	☐
13133	$5.00	☐	☐
13233	$5.00	☐	☐
13243	$5.00	☐	☐
22222	$3.00	☐	☐
24243	$3.00	☐	☐
35354	$3.00	☐	☐
44265	$3.00	☐	☐
44465	$3.00	☐	☐
45266	$5.00	☐	☐
45364	$3.00	☐	☐
45365	$5.00	☐	☐
45366	$3.00	☐	☐
46365	$5.00	☐	☐
46465	$5.00	☐	☐

#2027-30 20¢ SNOW SCENES

		UL	UR	LL	LR
1111	$2.25	☐	☐	☐	☐
1311	$2.25	☐	☐	☐	☐
2111	$2.25	☐	☐	☐	☐
2122	$2.25	☐	☐	☐	☐
2222	$2.25	☐	☐	☐	☐

1983 COMMEMORATIVES

#2031 20¢ SCIENCE & INDUSTRY

658-5	$1.75	☐	☐	☐	☐
658-6	$1.75	☐	☐	☐	☐
658-7	$1.75	☐	☐	☐	☐
658-8	$1.75	☐	☐	☐	☐
777-1	$50.00	†	†	☐	†
777-3	$50.00	☐	†	☐	†
777-5	$1.75	☐	☐	☐	☐
777-6	$1.75	☐	☐	☐	☐
777-7	$1.75	☐	☐	☐	☐
777-8	$1.75	☐	☐	☐	☐
779-5	$5.00	☐	☐	☐	☐
779-6	$5.00	☐	☐	☐	☐
779-7	$5.00	☐	☐	☐	☐
779-8	$5.00	☐	☐	☐	☐
788-5	$1.75	☐	☐	☐	☐
788-6	$1.75	☐	☐	☐	☐
788-7	$1.75	☐	☐	☐	☐
788-8	$1.75	☐	☐	☐	☐
798-5	$3.00	☐	☐	☐	☐
798-6	$3.00	☐	☐	☐	☐
798-7	$3.00	☐	☐	☐	☐
798-8	$3.00	☐	☐	☐	☐

1983 COMMEMORATIVES

#2031 20¢ SCIENCE & INDUSTRY Cont.

		UL	UR	LL	LR
799-5	$1.75	☐	☐	☐	☐
799-6	$1.75	☐	☐	☐	☐
799-7	$1.75	☐	☐	☐	☐
799-8	$1.75	☐	☐	☐	☐
855-5	$1.75	☐	☐	☐	☐
855-6	$1.75	☐	☐	☐	☐
855-7	$1.75	☐	☐	☐	☐
855-8	$1.75	☐	☐	☐	☐
858-5	$1.75	☐	☐	☐	☐
858-6	$1.75	☐	☐	☐	☐
858-7	$1.75	☐	☐	☐	☐
858-8	$1.75	☐	☐	☐	☐
884-5	$5.00	☐	☐	☐	☐
884-6	$5.00	☐	☐	☐	☐
884-7	$5.00	☐	☐	☐	☐
884-8	$5.00	☐	☐	☐	☐
885-5	$1.75	☐	☐	☐	☐
885-6	$1.75	☐	☐	☐	☐
885-7	$1.75	☐	☐	☐	☐
885-8	$1.75	☐	☐	☐	☐
886-5	$1.75	☐	☐	☐	☐
886-6	$1.75	☐	☐	☐	☐
886-7	$1.75	☐	☐	☐	☐
886-8	$1.75	☐	☐	☐	☐
888-5	$1.75	☐	☐	☐	☐
888-6	$1.75	☐	☐	☐	☐
888-7	$1.75	☐	☐	☐	☐
888-8	$1.75	☐	☐	☐	☐

#2032-35 20¢ BALLOONS

11112	$1.75	☐	☐	☐	☐
11132	$3.25	☐	☐	☐	☐
11142	$1.75	☐	☐	☐	☐
22141	$1.75	☐	☐	☐	☐
22221	$1.75	☐	☐	☐	☐
22222	$1.75	☐	☐	☐	☐
22241	$1.75	☐	☐	☐	☐
22242	$3.25	☐	☐	☐	☐

#2036 20¢ AMITY AND COMMERCE

1	$1.75	☐	☐	☐	☐
2	$1.75	☐	☐	☐	☐
3	$1.75	☐	☐	☐	☐
4	$1.75	☐	☐	☐	☐
9	$1.75	☐	☐	☐	☐
10	$1.75	☐	☐	☐	☐

#2037 20¢ CCC

111111	$1.75	☐	☐	☐	☐

#2038 20¢ JOSEPH PRIESTLEY

A111111	$1.75	☐	☐	☐	☐

#2039 20¢ VOLUNTARISM

Block of 6 (2 x 3)

		L	R
3	$3.00	☐	☐

#2040 20¢ CONCORD

		UL	UR	LL	LR
1	$1.75	☐	☐	☐	☐
2	$1.75	☐	☐	☐	☐
3	$1.75	☐	☐	☐	☐
4	$1.75	☐	☐	☐	☐

#2041 20¢ BROOKLYN BRIDGE

1	$1.75	☐	☐	☐	☐
4	$1.75	☐	☐	☐	☐
5	$1.75	☐	☐	☐	☐
6	$1.75	☐	☐	☐	☐

#2042 20¢ TVA

Block of 4 (2 x 2)

		L	R
1111-1	$1.75	☐	☐
1121-1	$1.75	☐	☐

#2043 20¢ PHYSICAL FITNESS

Block of 6 (2 x 3)

1111	$3.00	☐	☐

#2044 20¢ SCOTT JOPLIN

		UL	UR	LL	LR
111111	$1.75	☐	☐	☐	☐

#2045 20¢ MEDAL OF HONOR

1111-1	$1.75	☐	☐	☐	☐
1111-2	$1.75	☐	☐	☐	☐
1111-3	$1.75	☐	☐	☐	☐
1111-5	$1.75	☐	☐	☐	☐
2121-1	$10.00	☐	☐	☐	☐
2121-2	$10.00	☐	☐	☐	☐
2121-3	$10.00	☐	☐	☐	☐
2121-5	$10.00	☐	☐	☐	☐
2122-1	$1.75	☐	☐	☐	☐
2122-2	$1.75	☐	☐	☐	☐
2122-3	$1.75	☐	☐	☐	☐
2122-5	$1.75	☐	☐	☐	☐
2222-1	$1.75	☐	☐	☐	☐
2222-2	$1.75	☐	☐	☐	☐
2222-3	$1.75	☐	☐	☐	☐
2222-5	$1.75	☐	☐	☐	☐
2223-1	$3.00	☐	☐	☐	☐
2223-2	$3.00	☐	☐	☐	☐
2223-3	$3.00	☐	☐	☐	☐
2223-5	$3.00	☐	☐	☐	☐
3223-1	$3.00	☐	☐	☐	☐
3223-2	$3.00	☐	☐	☐	☐
3223-3	$3.00	☐	☐	☐	☐
3223-5	$3.00	☐	☐	☐	☐

1983 COMMEMORATIVES

#2046 20¢ BABE RUTH

		UL	UR	LL	LR
2	$6.00	☐	☐	☐	☐
3	$6.00	☐	☐	☐	☐
4	$6.00	☐	☐	☐	☐
5	$6.00	☐	☐	☐	☐

#2047 20¢ NATHANIEL HAWTHORNE

1111	$1.75	☐	☐	☐	☐

#2048-51 13¢ OLYMPIC GAMES

1111	$1.75	☐	☐	☐	☐

#2052 20¢ TREATY OF PARIS

1111	$1.75	☐	☐	☐	☐

#2053 20¢ CIVIL SERVICE

Block of 4 (2 x 2)		T	B
1-1	$1.75	☐	☐

#2054 20¢ METROPOLITAN OPERA

		UL	UR	LL	LR
1-1	$1.75	☐	☐	☐	☐
1-2	$1.75	☐	☐	☐	☐
1-3	$1.75	☐	☐	☐	☐
1-4	$1.75	☐	☐	☐	☐
2-1	$1.75	☐	☐	☐	☐
2-2	$1.75	☐	☐	☐	☐
2-3	$1.75	☐	☐	☐	☐
2-4	$1.75	☐	☐	☐	☐

#2055-58 20¢ INVENTORS

3-1	$2.00	☐	☐	☐	☐
3-2	$2.00	☐	☐	☐	☐
3-4	$2.00	☐	☐	☐	☐
3-5	$2.00	☐	☐	☐	☐
3-6	$5.00	☐	☐	☐	☐
4-1	$2.00	☐	☐	☐	☐
4-2	$2.00	☐	☐	☐	☐
4-4	$2.00	☐	☐	☐	☐
4-5	$2.00	☐	☐	☐	☐
5-1	$2.00	☐	☐	☐	☐
5-2	$2.00	☐	☐	☐	☐
5-4	$2.00	☐	☐	☐	☐
5-5	$2.00	☐	☐	☐	☐
6-1	$2.00	☐	☐	☐	☐
6-2	$2.00	☐	☐	☐	☐
6-4	$2.00	☐	☐	☐	☐
6-5	$2.00	☐	☐	☐	☐
6-6	$2.00	☐	☐	☐	☐
7-2	$2.00	☐	☐	☐	☐
7-4	$2.00	☐	☐	☐	☐
7-5	$2.00	☐	☐	☐	☐
7-6	$2.00	☐	☐	☐	☐
8-2	$2.00	☐	☐	☐	☐
8-4	$2.00	☐	☐	☐	☐
8-5	$2.00	☐	☐	☐	☐
8-6	$2.00	☐	☐	☐	☐

1983 COMMEMORATIVES

#2055-58 20¢ INVENTORS Cont.

		UL	UR	LL	LR
9-2	$2.00	☐	☐	☐	☐
9-4	$2.00	☐	☐	☐	☐
9-5	$2.00	☐	☐	☐	☐
9-6	$2.00	☐	☐	☐	☐
10-2	$2.00	☐	☐	☐	☐
10-4	$2.00	☐	☐	☐	☐
10-5	$2.00	☐	☐	☐	☐
10-6	$2.00	☐	☐	☐	☐
11-2	$20.00	☐	☐	☐	☐
11-4	$20.00	☐	☐	☐	☐
11-5	$20.00	☐	☐	☐	☐
12-2	$2.00	☐	☐	☐	☐
12-4	$2.00	☐	☐	☐	☐
12-5	$2.00	☐	☐	☐	☐
12-6	$2.00	☐	☐	☐	☐

#2059-62 20¢ STREETCARS

1111-1	$1.75	☐	☐	☐	☐
1111-2	$1.75	☐	☐	☐	☐
1111-3	$1.75	☐	☐	☐	☐
1111-4	$1.75	☐	☐	☐	☐
2222-1	$1.75	☐	☐	☐	☐
2222-2	$1.75	☐	☐	☐	☐
2222-3	$1.75	☐	☐	☐	☐
2222-4	$1.75	☐	☐	☐	☐
3333-1	$10.00	☐	☐	☐	☐
3333-2	$10.00	☐	☐	☐	☐
3333-3	$10.00	☐	☐	☐	☐
3333-4	$10.00	☐	☐	☐	☐

#2063 20¢ MADONNA

11111	$1.75	☐	☐	☐	☐
11112	$4.00	☐	☐	☐	☐
12111	$1.75	☐	☐	☐	☐
12112	$1.75	☐	☐	☐	☐
21222	$1.75	☐	☐	☐	☐
22112	$1.75	☐	☐	☐	☐
32111	$1.75	☐	☐	☐	☐

#2064 20¢ SANTA CLAUS

Block of 6 (2 x 3)		L	R
11211	$3.00	☐	☐
22322	$3.00	☐	☐

#2065 20¢ MARTIN LUTHER

		UL	UR	LL	LR
A11111	$1.75	☐	☐	☐	☐

1984 COMMEMORATIVES

#2066 20¢ ALASKA STATEHOOD

A11111	$1.75	☐	☐	☐	☐

#2067-70 20¢ WINTER OLYMPICS

1111	$2.00	☐	☐	☐	☐

1984 COMMEMORATIVES

#2071 20¢ FEDERAL DEPOSIT INSURANCE

This issue was part of a quadrant printing. See also #2074, #2075 and #2081 for the other stamps. Only one position of the plate number exists for this issue.

		UL	UR	LL	LR
122221	$1.75	☐	‡	‡	‡
122222	$1.75	☐	‡	‡	‡
222221	$1.75	☐	‡	‡	‡
222222	$1.75	☐	‡	‡	‡

#2072 20¢ LOVE

Block of 4 (2 x 2)

		T	B
11111-1	$1.75	☐	☐
11111-2	$1.75	☐	☐
11112-2	$5.00	☐	☐
12222-2	$5.00	☐	☐
22221-2	$1.75	☐	☐
22222-2	$1.75	☐	☐
22223-2	$1.75	☐	☐

#2073 20¢ CARTER G. WOODSON

		UL	UR	LL	LR
A111111	$1.75	☐	☐	☐	☐

#2074 20¢ SOIL AND WATER CONSERVATION

This issue was part of a quadrant printing. See also #2071, #2075 and #2081 for the other stamps. Only one position of the plate number exists for this issue.

122221	$1.75	‡	☐	‡	‡
122222	$1.75	‡	☐	‡	‡
222221	$1.75	‡	☐	‡	‡
222222	$1.75	‡	☐	‡	‡

#2075 20¢ CREDIT UNION

This issue was part of a quadrant printing. See also #2071, #2074 and #2081 for the other stamps. Only one position of the plate number exists for this issue.

122221	$1.75	‡	‡	‡	☐
122222	$1.75	‡	‡	‡	☐
222221	$1.75	‡	‡	‡	☐
222222	$1.75	‡	‡	‡	☐

#2076-79 20¢ ORCHIDS

11111	$1.75	☐	☐	☐	☐
11121	$1.75	☐	☐	☐	☐
11122	$1.75	☐	☐	☐	☐

#2080 20¢ HAWAII STATEHOOD

		UL	UR	LL	LR
A11111	$1.75	☐	☐	☐	☐

#2081 20¢ NATIONAL ARCHIVES

This issue was part of a quadrant printing. See also #2071, #2074 and #2075 for the other stamps. Only one position of the plate number exists for this issue.

122221	$1.75	‡	‡	☐	‡
122222	$1.75	‡	‡	☐	‡
222221	$1.75	‡	‡	☐	‡
222222	$1.75	‡	‡	☐	‡

#2082-85 20¢ SUMMER OLYMPICS

1111	$3.00	☐	☐	☐	☐
1121	$3.00	☐	☐	☐	☐
1131	$3.00	☐	☐	☐	☐
1141	$3.00	☐	☐	☐	☐

#2086 20¢ LOUISIANA WORLD EXPO

11111	$1.75	☐	☐	☐	☐

#2087 20¢ HEALTH RESEARCH

A11111	$1.75	☐	☐	☐	☐

#2088 20¢ DOUGLAS FAIRBANKS

Block of 4 (2 x 2)

		T	B
1111-1	$1.75	☐	☐
1111-2	$1.75	☐	☐

#2089 20¢ JIM THORPE

		UL	UR	LL	LR
3	$1.75	☐	☐	☐	☐
4	$1.75	☐	☐	☐	☐
7	$1.75	☐	☐	☐	☐
9	$50.00	☐	☐	☐	☐
10	$1.75	☐	☐	☐	☐
11	$1.75	☐	☐	☐	☐
12	$1.75	☐	☐	☐	☐
13	$1.75	☐	☐	☐	☐
14	$1.75	☐	☐	☐	☐
17	$1.75	☐	☐	☐	☐
18	$1.75	☐	☐	☐	☐
19	$1.75	☐	☐	☐	☐
20	$1.75	☐	☐	☐	☐
22	$1.75	☐	☐	☐	☐
25	$1.75	☐	☐	☐	☐
26	$1.75	☐	☐	☐	☐
27	$1.75	☐	☐	☐	☐

#2090 20¢ JOHN McCORMACK

11111	$1.75	☐	☐	☐	☐

#2091 20¢ ST. LAWRENCE SEAWAY

A1111	$1.75	☐	☐	☐	☐

1984 COMMEMORATIVES

#2092 20¢ MIGRATORY BIRD HUNTING

		UL	UR	LL	LR
18	$2.00	☐	☐	☐	☐
19	$2.00	☐	☐	☐	☐
20	$2.00	☐	☐	☐	☐
21	$2.00	☐	☐	☐	☐
22	$2.00	☐	☐	☐	☐
23	$2.00	☐	☐	☐	☐
24	$2.00	☐	☐	☐	☐
25	$2.00	☐	☐	☐	☐

#2093 20¢ ROANOKE VOYAGERS

A11111	$1.75	☐	☐	☐	☐

#2094 20¢ HERMAN MELVILLE

14	$1.75	☐	☐	☐	☐
15	$1.75	☐	☐	☐	☐
16	$1.75	☐	☐	☐	☐
17	$1.75	☐	☐	☐	☐

#2095 20¢ HORACE A. MOSES

Block of 6 (3 x 2)		T	B
1	$3.00	☐	☐

#2096 20¢ SMOKEY BEAR

		UL	UR	LL	LR
1121-3	$2.00	☐	☐	☐	☐
1221-3	$50.00	†	†	☐	†
1313-3	$2.00	☐	☐	☐	☐
1321-3	$2.00	☐	☐	☐	☐
1323-3	$20.00	☐	☐	☐	☐
2232-3	$2.00	☐	☐	☐	☐
3232-3	$2.00	☐	☐	☐	☐
5656-3	$2.00	☐	☐	☐	☐
6667-3	$2.00	☐	☐	☐	☐
6868-3	$2.00	☐	☐	☐	☐
6888-3	$2.00	☐	☐	☐	☐
8888-3	$2.00	☐	☐	☐	☐
8989-3	$2.00	☐	☐	☐	☐
8999-3	$2.00	☐	☐	☐	☐
9212-3	$2.00	☐	☐	☐	☐
9213-3	$4.25	☐	☐	☐	☐
9991-3	$2.00	☐	☐	☐	☐
10101010-3	$20.00	☐	☐	†	☐
10111010-3	$2.00	☐	☐	☐	☐
10111110-3	$2.00	☐	☐	☐	☐
10111111-3	$100.00	☐	†	†	☐
10141411-3	$2.00	☐	☐	☐	☐
11141414-3	$2.00	☐	☐	☐	☐
13131212-3	$2.00	☐	☐	☐	☐
13131213-3	$2.00	☐	☐	☐	☐
14151515-3	$4.00	☐	☐	☐	☐
14151516-3	$2.00	☐	☐	☐	☐
14161616-3	$4.00	☐	☐	☐	☐
17171717-3	$2.00	☐	☐	☐	☐

#2097 20¢ ROBERTO CLEMENTE

111111	$6.00	☐	☐	☐	☐

1984 COMMEMORATIVES

#2098-2101 20¢ DOGS

		UL	UR	LL	LR
1111	$2.50	☐	☐	☐	☐
1112	$3.50	☐	☐	☐	☐

#2102 20¢ CRIME PREVENTION

A1111	$1.75	☐	☐	☐	☐

#2103 20¢ HISPANIC AMERICANS

111111	$1.75	☐	☐	☐	☐
122211	$1.75	☐	☐	☐	☐

#2104 20¢ FAMILY UNITY

Block of 4 (2 x 2)

		T	B
12-2	$1.75	☐	☐
21-2	$1.75	☐	☐
22-2	$1.75	☐	☐

#2105 20¢ ELEANOR ROOSEVELT

		UL	UR	LL	LR
2	$1.75	☐	☐	☐	☐
3	$1.75	☐	☐	☐	☐
4	$1.75	☐	☐	☐	☐
6	$1.75	☐	☐	☐	☐
8	$1.75	☐	☐	☐	☐
9	$1.75	☐	☐	☐	☐
11	$1.75	☐	☐	☐	☐
12	$1.75	☐	☐	☐	☐

#2106 20¢ A NATION OF READERS

1	$1.75	☐	☐	☐	☐
2	$1.75	☐	☐	☐	☐
3	$1.75	☐	☐	☐	☐
4	$1.75	☐	☐	☐	☐
5	$1.75	☐	☐	☐	☐
6	$1.75	☐	☐	☐	☐
7	$1.75	☐	☐	☐	☐
8	$1.75	☐	☐	☐	☐

#2107 20¢ MADONNA

11111	$1.75	☐	☐	☐	☐
22222	$1.75	☐	☐	☐	☐

#2108 20¢ SANTA CLAUS

11111	$1.75	☐	☐	☐	☐
22222	$1.75	☐	☐	☐	☐

#2109 20¢ VIETNAM VETERANS

2	$1.75	☐	☐	☐	☐
3	$1.75	☐	☐	☐	☐
4	$1.75	☐	☐	☐	☐
6	$1.75	☐	☐	☐	☐
7	$1.75	☐	☐	☐	☐
8	$1.75	☐	☐	☐	☐
9	$1.75	☐	☐	☐	☐
10	$1.75	☐	☐	☐	☐

1985 COMMEMORATIVE

#2110 22¢ JEROME KERN

A11111	$1.75	☐	☐	☐	☐

1985 REGULAR ISSUES

#2111 (22¢)D EAGLE

Block of 6 (2 x 3)

		L	R
1	$4.50	□	□
2	$4.50	□	□
3	$4.50	□	□
4	$4.50	□	□

#2112 (22¢)D EAGLE COIL

Strips of 5

		B
1	$6.50	□
2	$6.50	□

#2113a (22¢)D EAGLE BOOKLET

$4.40 - **BK143** - 2 panes of 10 stamps

		L
1N	$15.00	□
2	$500.00	□
3N	$15.00	□
4N	$15.00	□

N The above prices are for booklets with the plate number on only the top pane. These booklets also occur with the plate number on only the bottom pane and command a premium.

#2114 22¢ FLAG OVER CAPITOL

		UL	UR	LL	LR
1	$1.75	□	□	□	□
3	$1.75	□	□	□	□
4	$1.75	□	□	□	□
5	$1.75	□	□	□	□
6	$1.75	□	□	□	□

#2115 22¢ FLAG OVER CAPITOL COIL

Strips of 5

		B
B Press		
2	$3.50	□
4	$6.00	□
6	$6.00	□
10	$6.00	□
13	$12.00	□
14	$30.00	□
15	$3.50	□
16	$6.00	□
C or D Press		
1	$12.00	□
3	$55.00	□
5	$6.00	□
7	$12.00	□
8	$3.50	□
11	$6.00	□
12	$3.50	□
17	$6.00	□
18	$6.00	□
19	$3.50	□
20	$6.00	□
21	$6.00	□
22	$3.50	□

1985 REGULAR ISSUES

#2115b 22¢ FLAG OVER CAPITOL COIL (TEST)

Strip of 5

C Press

		B
T1	$3.50	□

#2116a 22¢ FLAG OVER CAPITOL BOOKLET

$1.10 - **BK144** - 1 pane of 5 stamps

		T
1	$2.25	□
3	$2.25	□

$2.20 - **BK145** - 2 panes of 5 stamps

1	$4.50	□
3	$4.50	□

#2121a 22¢ SEASHELLS BOOKLET

$4.40 - **BK146** - 2 panes of 10 stamps

floating cover

1	$8.50	□
2	$8.50	□
3	$8.50	□

$4.40 - **BK147** - 2 panes of 10 stamps

non-floating cover

1	$8.50	□
3	$8.50	□
5	$8.50	□
6	$8.50	□
7	$8.50	□
8N	$8.50	□
10	$8.50	□

N The above price is for booklets with the plate number over the left stamp. This booklet also occurs with the plate number over the right stamp and commands a premium.

#2122a $10.75 EAGLE BOOKLET (TYPE I)

$32.25 - **BK148** - 1 pane of 3 stamps

		L
11111	$55.00	□

#2122c $10.75 EAGLE BOOKLET (TYPE II)

$32.25 - **BK149** - 1 pane of 3 stamps

22222	$55.00	□

1981 TRANSPORTATION COILS

#2123 THROUGH #2136

See pages 228-235

1985 COMMEMORATIVES

#2137 22¢ MARY McLEOD BETHUNE

		UL	UR	LL	LR
A111111	$2.00	□	□	□	□

#2138-41 22¢ DUCK DECOYS

A11111	$5.00	□	□	□	□

1985 COMMEMORATIVES

#2142 22¢ WINTER SPECIAL OLYMPICS

		UL	UR	LL	LR
111111	$1.75	☐	☐	☐	☐
112121	$1.75	☐	☐	☐	☐

#2143 22¢ LOVE

		UL	UR	LL	LR
111312	$1.75	☐	☐	☐	☐
112111	$1.75	☐	☐	☐	☐
112211	$1.75	☐	☐	☐	☐
112212	$1.75	☐	☐	☐	☐
221221	$1.75	☐	☐	☐	☐
222221	$1.75	☐	☐	☐	☐

#2144 22¢ R. E. A.

Block of 4 (2 x 2)

		L	R
1111-1	$1.75	☐	☐
1131-1	$3.50	☐	☐

#2145 22¢ AMERIPEX

		UL	UR	LL	LR
11-1	$1.75	☐	☐	☐	☐
11-2	$7.50	☐	☐	☐	☐
11-3	$1.75	☐	☐	☐	☐
11-4	$1.75	☐	☐	☐	☐
11-5	$1.75	☐	☐	☐	☐
13-1	$1.75	☐	☐	☐	☐
13-3	$1.75	☐	☐	☐	☐
13-4	$1.75	☐	☐	☐	☐
13-5	$1.75	☐	☐	☐	☐
22-1	$1.75	☐	☐	☐	☐
22-3	$1.75	☐	☐	☐	☐
22-4	$1.75	☐	☐	☐	☐
22-5	$1.75	☐	☐	☐	☐
24-1	$1.75	☐	☐	☐	☐
24-3	$1.75	☐	☐	☐	☐
24-4	$1.75	☐	☐	☐	☐
24-5	$1.75	☐	☐	☐	☐
33-1	$1.75	☐	☐	☐	☐
33-3	$1.75	☐	☐	☐	☐
33-4	$1.75	☐	☐	☐	☐
33-5	$1.75	☐	☐	☐	☐
35-1	$5.00	☐	☐	☐	☐
35-3	$5.00	☐	☐	☐	☐
35-4	$5.00	☐	☐	☐	☐
35-5	$5.00	☐	☐	☐	☐
44-1	$1.75	☐	☐	☐	☐
44-3	$1.75	☐	☐	☐	☐
44-4	$1.75	☐	☐	☐	☐
44-5	$1.75	☐	☐	☐	☐
46-1	$1.75	☐	☐	☐	☐
46-3	$1.75	☐	☐	☐	☐
46-4	$1.75	☐	☐	☐	☐
46-5	$1.75	☐	☐	☐	☐

#2145 22¢ AMERIPEX Cont.

		UL	UR	LL	LR
55-1	$1.75	☐	☐	☐	☐
55-3	$1.75	☐	☐	☐	☐
55-4	$1.75	☐	☐	☐	☐
55-5	$1.75	☐	☐	☐	☐
65-1	$1.75	☐	☐	☐	☐
65-3	$1.75	☐	☐	☐	☐
65-4	$1.75	☐	☐	☐	☐
65-5	$1.75	☐	☐	☐	☐
99-1	$1.75	☐	☐	☐	☐
99-3	$1.75	☐	☐	☐	☐
99-4	$1.75	☐	☐	☐	☐
99-5	$1.75	☐	☐	☐	☐
1010-1	$1.75	☐	☐	☐	☐
1010-3	$1.75	☐	☐	☐	☐
1010-4	$1.75	☐	☐	☐	☐
1010-5	$1.75	☐	☐	☐	☐
11 9-1	$1.75	☐	☐	☐	☐
11 9-3	$1.75	☐	☐	☐	☐
11 9-4	$1.75	☐	☐	☐	☐
11 9-5	$1.75	☐	☐	☐	☐
1210-1	$1.75	☐	☐	☐	☐
1210-3	$1.75	☐	☐	☐	☐
1210-4	$1.75	☐	☐	☐	☐
1210-5	$1.75	☐	☐	☐	☐
13 9-1	$3.50	☐	☐	☐	☐
13 9-3	$3.50	☐	☐	☐	☐
13 9-4	$3.50	☐	☐	☐	☐
13 9-5	$3.50	☐	☐	☐	☐
1311-1	$1.75	☐	☐	☐	☐
1311-3	$1.75	☐	☐	☐	☐
1311-4	$1.75	☐	☐	☐	☐
1311-5	$1.75	☐	☐	☐	☐
1410-1	$3.50	☐	☐	☐	☐
1410-3	$3.50	☐	☐	☐	☐
1410-4	$3.50	☐	☐	☐	☐
1410-5	$3.50	☐	☐	☐	☐
1412-1	$1.75	☐	☐	☐	☐
1412-3	$1.75	☐	☐	☐	☐
1412-4	$1.75	☐	☐	☐	☐
1412-5	$1.75	☐	☐	☐	☐
1511-1	$1.75	☐	☐	☐	☐
1511-3	$1.75	☐	☐	☐	☐
1511-4	$1.75	☐	☐	☐	☐
1511-5	$1.75	☐	☐	☐	☐
1612-1	$1.75	☐	☐	☐	☐
1612-3	$1.75	☐	☐	☐	☐
1612-4	$1.75	☐	☐	☐	☐
1612-5	$1.75	☐	☐	☐	☐
1711-1	$1.75	☐	☐	☐	☐
1711-3	$1.75	☐	☐	☐	☐
1711-4	$1.75	☐	☐	☐	☐
1711-5	$1.75	☐	☐	☐	☐

1985 COMMEMORATIVES

#2146 22¢ ABIGAIL ADAMS

		UL	UR	LL	LR
1111	$1.75	□	□	□	□

#2147 22¢ BARTHOLDI

1111-1	$1.75	□	□	□	□
2222-1	$1.75	□	□	□	□
2242-1	$1.75	□	□	□	□
2252-1	$1.75	□	□	□	□
3535-1	$1.75	□	□	□	□
3555-1	$1.75	□	□	□	□

1985 REGULAR ISSUES

Strips of 5

#2149 18¢ WASHINGTON AND MONUMENT COIL

		B
1112	$3.00	□
3333	$3.50	□

#2149a 18¢ WASHINGTON AND MONUMENT COIL

PRECANCEL Style 9

dull gum

11121	$7.00	□
33333	$3.00	□
43444	$7.00	□

semi-gloss gum

11121	$4.00	□

#2150 21.1¢ LETTERS COIL

111111	$3.50	□
111121	$4.50	□

#2150a 21.1¢ LETTERS COIL

PRECANCEL Style 10

111111	$3.50	□
111121	$4.50	□

1985 COMMEMORATIVES

#2152 22¢ KOREAN WAR VETERANS

		UL	UR	LL	LR
1	$1.75	□	□	□	□
2	$1.75	□	□	□	□
3	$1.75	□	□	□	□
4	$1.75	□	□	□	□
5	$1.75	□	□	□	□

#2153 22¢ SOCIAL SECURITY ACT

A11	$1.75	□	□	□	□

#2154 22¢ WORLD WAR I VETERANS

1	$2.00	□	□	□	□
2	$2.00	□	□	□	□
3	$2.00	□	□	□	□
4	$2.00	□	□	□	□

#2155-58 22¢ HORSES

11111	$6.00	□	□	□	□

1985 COMMEMORATIVES

#2159 22¢ PUBLIC EDUCATION

		UL	UR	LL	LR
A11111	$2.25	□	□	□	□

#2160-63 22¢ INTERNATIONAL YOUTH YEAR

A11111	$3.00	□		□	□

#2164 22¢ HELP END HUNGER

A11111	$1.75	□	□	□	□

#2165 22¢ MADONNA

1111	$1.75	□	□	□	□
1112	$1.75	□	□	□	□
2222	$1.75	□	□	□	□

#2166 22¢ POINSETTIA

11111	$1.75	□	□	□	□
12111	$1.75	□	□	□	□
21222	$1.75	□	□	□	□
22222	$1.75	□	□	□	□

1986 COMMEMORATIVE

#2167 22¢ ARKANSAS STATEHOOD

A111111	$1.75	□	□	□	□

1986 REGULAR ISSUES

#2168 THROUGH #2197a

See pages 224-228

1986 COMMEMORATIVES

#2201a 22¢ STAMP COLLECTING BOOKLET

$1.76 - **BK153** - 2 panes of 4 stamps

		L
1	$4.00	□

#2202 22¢ LOVE

		UL	UR	LL	LR
11112	$1.75	□	□	□	□
12221	$1.75	□	□	□	□
21112	$1.75	□	□	□	□

#2203 22¢ SOJOURNER TRUTH

A111111	$1.75	□	□	□	□

#2204 22¢ REPUBLIC OF TEXAS

A111	$1.75	□	□	□	□

#2209a 22¢ FISH BOOKLET

$2.20 - **BK154** - 2 panes of 5 stamps

		T
11111	$6.00	□
22222	$6.00	□

#2210 22¢ PUBLIC HOSPITALS

		UL	UR	LL	LR
A11111	$1.75	□	□	□	□

#2211 22¢ "DUKE" ELLINGTON

A111111	$1.75	□	□	□	□
A222222	$1.75	□	□	□	□

1986 COMMEMORATIVES

AMERIPEX SOUVENIR SHEETS

#2216 PRESIDENTS: I
#2217 PRESIDENTS: II
#2218 PRESIDENTS: III
#2219 PRESIDENTS: IV

The plate numbers of these souvenir sheets were trimmed off after printing, so no plate numbers were regularly issued.

#2220-23 22¢ POLAR EXPLORERS

		UL	UR	LL	LR
A11111	$3.00	☐	☐	☐	☐

#2224 22¢ STATUE OF LIBERTY

1	$2.00	☐	☐	☐	☐

1981 TRANSPORTATION COILS

#2225 THROUGH #2231

See pages 221-24

1986 COMMEMORATIVES

#2235-38 22¢ NAVAJO ART

1111-1	$2.50	☐	☐	☐	☐
1211-1	$2.50	☐	☐	☐	☐
2211-1	$2.50	☐	☐	☐	☐
2222-1	$20.00	☐	☐	☐	☐
2322-1	$2.50	☐	☐	☐	☐

#2239 22¢ T.S. ELIOT

2	$1.75	☐	☐	☐	☐

#2240-43 22¢ WOODCARVED FIGURINES

A11111	$2.50	☐	☐	☐	☐

#2244 22¢ MADONNA

22222	$1.75	☐	☐	☐	☐

#2245 22¢ VILLAGE SCENE

111121	$1.75	☐	☐	☐	☐
111122	$20.00	☐	☐	☐	☐

1987 COMMEMORATIVES

#2246 22¢ MICHIGAN STATEHOOD

11111	$1.75	☐	☐	☐	☐

#2247 22¢ PAN AMERICAN GAMES

11111	$1.75	☐	☐	☐	☐

#2248 22¢ LOVE

11111	$1.75	☐	☐	☐	☐
11121	$1.75	☐	☐	☐	☐
11131	$1.75	☐	☐	☐	☐
11231	$1.75	☐	☐	☐	☐
12222	$3.50	☐	☐	☐	☐
12232	$1.75	☐	☐	☐	☐

#2249 22¢ JEAN BAPTISTE

11111	$1.75	☐	☐	☐	☐

#2250 22¢ CARUSO

A1111	$1.75	☐	☐	☐	☐

1987 COMMEMORATIVES

#2251 22¢ GIRL SCOUTS

		UL	UR	LL	LR
11111-1	$1.75	☐	☐	☐	☐
11112-1	$1.75	☐	☐	☐	☐
22223-1	$1.75	☐	☐	☐	☐

1981 TRANSPORTATION COILS

#2252 THROUGH #2266

See pages 228-235

1987 COMMEMORATIVES

#2274a 22¢ SPECIAL OCCASIONS BOOKLET

$2.20 - **BK155** - 1 panes of 10 stamps

		T
11111	$7.00	☐
22222	$7.00	☐

#2275 22¢ UNITED WAY

		UL	UR	LL	LR
21211-1	$1.75	☐	☐	☐	☐
21221-1	$1.75	☐	☐	☐	☐
21222-1	$3.50	☐	☐	☐	☐
21322-1	$1.75	☐	☐	☐	☐
32332-1	$1.75	☐	☐	☐	☐
32432-1	$1.75	☐	☐	☐	☐
32442-1	$1.75	☐	☐	☐	☐

1987-88 REGULAR ISSUES

#2276 22¢ FLAG WITH FIREWORKS

1111	$1.75	☐	☐	☐	☐
2222	$1.75	☐	☐	☐	☐

#2276a 22¢ FLAG WITH FIREWORKS BOOKLET

prepared from sheet stamps
$4.40 - **BK156** - 1 pane of 20 stamps

1111	$10.00	☐	‡	☐	‡
2122	$16.00	☐	‡	☐	‡
2222	$10.00	☐	‡	☐	‡

#2277 (25¢)E EARTH

1111	$2.00	☐	☐	☐	☐

#2278 25¢ FLAG WITH CLOUDS

1111	$2.00	☐	☐	☐	☐
1222	$2.00	☐	☐	☐	☐
2131	$2.00	☐	☐	☐	☐
2222	$2.00	☐	☐	☐	☐
2231	$2.00	☐	☐	☐	☐
2232	$2.00	☐	☐	☐	☐

#2279 (25¢)E EARTH COIL

Strips of 5		B
1111	$2.75	☐
1211	$4.50	☐
1222	$2.75	☐
2222	$4.50	☐

1987-88 REGULAR ISSUES

#2280 25¢ FLAG OVER YOSEMITE COIL

Strips of 5

Block tagged		B
1	$6.50	☐
2	$3.50	☐
3	$3.50	☐
4	$3.50	☐
5	$3.50	☐
7	$6.50	☐
8	$3.50	☐
9	$10.00	☐

Mottled prephosphored		
1	$45.00	☐
2	$3.50	☐
3	$3.50	☐
5	$6.50	☐
6	$14.00	☐
7	$3.50	☐
8	$3.50	☐
9	$3.50	☐
10	$3.50	☐
11	$3.50	☐
13	$3.50	☐
14	$3.50	☐
15	$6.50	☐

#2281 25¢ HONEYBEE COIL

Strips of 5

1	$3.50	☐
2	$3.50	☐

#2282a (25¢)E EARTH BOOKLET

$5.00 - **BK157** - 2 panes of 10 stamps

		T
1111	$12.00	☐
2122	$12.00	☐
2222	$12.00	☐

#2283a 25¢ PHEASANT BOOKLET

$5.00 - **BK158** - 2 panes of 10 stamps

		L
A1111	$10.00	☐

#2283c 25¢ PHEASANT BOOKLET

(red color removed from sky)

$5.00 - **BK159** - 2 panes of 10 stamps

A3111	$100.00	☐
A3222	$100.00	☐

#2285b 25¢ OWL AND GROSBEAK BOOKLET

$5.00 - **BK160** - 2 panes of 10 stamps

		T
1111	$10.00	☐
1112	$10.00	☐
1133	$15.00	☐
1211	$10.00	☐
1414	$15.00	☐
1433	$10.00	☐
1434	$10.00	☐
1634	$50.00	☐

1987-88 REGULAR ISSUES

#2285b 25¢ OWL AND GROSBEAK BOOKLET Cont.

		T
1734	$10.00	☐
2111	$10.00	☐
2121	$10.00	☐
2122	$15.00	☐
2221	$10.00	☐
2222	$10.00	☐
2321	$10.00	☐
3133	$10.00	☐
3233	$15.00	☐
3333	$10.00	☐
3412	$15.00	☐
3413	$15.00	☐
3422	$15.00	☐
3512	$15.00	☐
3521	$15.00	☐
3822	$20.00	☐
4642	$15.00	☐
4644	$15.00	☐
4911	$15.00	☐
4941	$15.00	☐
5453	$150.00	☐
5955	$15.00	☐

The above plates appear in covers with one bud. Plates 1111, 1211, 2122 and 2222 also appear in covers with two buds and plate 2122 commands a premium.

#2285c 25¢ FLAG WITH CLOUDS BOOKLET

$3.00 - **BK161** - 2 panes of 6 stamps

		L
1111	$5.00	☐

1987 COMMEMORATIVES

#2335a 22¢ WILDLIFE

Pane of 50		UL	UR	LL	LR
11111	$40.00	☐	☐	☐	☐

1987-90 RATIFICATION OF THE CONSTITUTION BICENTENNIAL

#2336 22¢ DELAWARE

1111-1	$1.75	☐	☐	☐	☐
2122-1	$1.75	☐	☐	☐	☐
2132-1	$1.75	☐	☐	☐	☐
3243-1	$1.75	☐	☐	☐	☐
3253-1	$1.75	☐	☐	☐	☐
4254-1	$1.75	☐	☐	☐	☐
6666-1	$1.75	☐	☐	☐	☐
7666-1	$3.00	☐	†	☐	☐
8666-1	$1.75	☐	☐	☐	☐
8676-1	$1.75	☐	☐	☐	☐

1987-90 RATIFICATION OF THE CONSTITUTION BICENTENNIAL

#2337 22¢ PENNSYLVANIA

		UL	UR	LL	LR
A11111	$1.75	□	□	□	□

#2338 22¢ NEW JERSEY

A11111	$1.75	□	□	□	□

#2339 22¢ GEORGIA

A1111	$1.75	□	□	□	□

#2340 22¢ CONNECTICUT

1111-1	$1.75	□	□	□	□
1112-1	$1.75	□	□	□	□
1113-1	$1.75	□	□	□	□
1213-1	$3.50	□	□	□	□
2223-1	$1.75	□	□	□	□
2224-1	$1.75	□	□	□	□
2225-1	$1.75	□	□	□	□
2325-1	$1.75	□	□	□	□
2335-1	$1.75	□	□	□	□
2336-1	$3.50	□	□	□	□
2337-1	$1.75	□	□	□	□
2438-1	$1.75	□	□	□	□

#2341 22¢ MASSACHUSETTS

1	$1.75	□	□	□	□

#2342 22¢ MARYLAND

11111-1	$1.75	□	□	□	□
11211-1	$1.75	□	□	□	□

#2343 25¢ SOUTH CAROLINA

A11111	$2.00	□	□	□	□

#2344 25¢ NEW HAMPSHIRE

A1111	$2.00	□	□	□	□

#2345 25¢ VIRGINIA

1111-1	$2.00	□	□	□	□
2222-1	$2.00	□	□	□	□
2223-1	$2.00	□	□	□	□
3223-1	$2.00	□	□	□	□
3323-1	$2.00	□	□	□	□
3333-1	$2.00	□	□	□	□

#2346 25¢ NEW YORK

1111-1	$2.00	□	□	□	□
2111-1	$2.00	□	□	□	□
2131-1	$2.00	□	□	□	□
2232-1	$4.00	□	□	□	□
2242-1	$2.00	□	□	□	□

#2347 25¢ NORTH CAROLINA

A11111	$2.00	□	□	□	□

#2348 25¢ RHODE ISLAND

111111-1	$2.00	□	□	□	□
222222-1	$2.00	□	□	□	□
222223-1	$2.00	□	□	□	□
343334-1	$2.00	□	□	□	□

1987 COMMEMORATIVES

#2349 22¢ MOROCCO TREATY

		UL	UR	LL	LR
1-1	$1.75	□	□	□	□
2-1	$5.00	□	□2	□	□
3-1	$1.75	□	□	□	□
4-1	$1.75	□	□	□	□
5-1	$1.75	□	□	□	□

#2350 22¢ WILLIAM FAULKNER

1	$1.75	□	□	□	□

#2351-54 22¢ LACEMAKING

111-1	$2.50	□	□	□	□
112-1	$2.50	□	□	□	□
122-1	$2.50	□	□	□	□
123-1	$2.50	□	□	□	□
123-2	$2.50	□	□	□	□
124-1	$2.50	□	□	□	□
124-2	$2.50	□	□	□	□
224-2	$2.50	□	□	□	□
225-2	$2.50	□	□	□	□
235-1	$2.50	□	□	□	□
235-2	$2.50	□	□	□	□
236-2	$2.50	□	□	□	□

#2359a 22¢ CONSTITUTION BOOKLET

$4.40 - **BK162** - 4 panes of 5 stamps

		T
1111	$9.00	□
1112	$9.00	□

#2360 22¢ CONSTITUTION

		UL	UR	LL	LR
12111-1	$1.75	□	□	□	□
12311-1	$1.75	□	□	□	□
12312-1	$1.75	□	□	□	□
22322-1	$1.75	□	□	□	□
23322-1	$1.75	□	□	□	□
33322-1	$1.75	□	□	□	□

#2361 22¢ C. P. A.

1111-1	$6.00	□	□	□	□
1112-1	$6.00	□	□	□	□
1113-1	$6.00	□	□	□	□
1124-1	$6.00	□	□	□	□

#2366a 22¢ LOCOMOTIVE BOOKLET

$4.40 - **BK163** - 4 panes of 5 stamps

		T
1	$9.00	□
2	$9.00	□

#2367 22¢ MADONNA

		UL	UR	LL	LR
111111	$1.75	□	□	□	□
121112	$1.75	□	□	□	□

#2368 22¢ CHRISTMAS TREE

111111	$1.75	□	□	□	□

1988 COMMEMORATIVES

#2369 22¢ WINTER OLYMPICS

		UL	UR	LL	LR
A1111	$1.75	☐	☐	☐	☐

#2370 22¢ AUSTRALIA

11111	$1.75	☐	☐	☐	☐
12111	$1.75	☐	☐	☐	☐

#2371 22¢ JAMES JOHNSON

A11111	$1.75	☐	☐	☐	☐

#2372-75 22¢ CATS

A11111	$2.50	☐	☐	☐	☐

#2376 22¢ KNUTE ROCKNE

111111-1	$2.25	☐	☐	☐	☐

#2377 25¢ FRANCIS OUIMET

A11111	$2.00	☐	☐	☐	☐

#2378 25¢ LOVE

11111	$2.00	☐	☐	☐	☐

#2379 45¢ LOVE

1111	$2.75	☐	☐	☐	☐

#2380 25¢ SUMMER OLYMPICS

12111	$2.00	☐	☐	☐	☐

#2385a 25¢ CLASSIC AUTO BOOKLET

$5.00 - **BK164** - 4 panes of 5 stamps

		T
1	$15.00	☐

#2386-89 25¢ EXPLORERS

		UL	UR	LL	LR
A111111	$3.50	☐	☐	☐	☐

#2390-93 25¢ CAROUSEL ANIMALS

111111-1	$3.00	☐	☐	☐	☐
111121-1	$3.00	☐	☐	☐	☐
222232-1	$3.00	☐	☐	☐	☐
323232-1	$3.00	☐	☐	☐	☐
323243-1	$3.00	☐	☐	☐	☐

1988 REGULAR ISSUE

#2394 $8.75 EAGLE

11111-1	$50.00	☐	☐	☐	☐
22232-1	$50.00	☐	☐	☐	☐
33333-1	$50.00	☐	☐	☐	☐
55555-1	$50.00	☐	☐	☐	☐

Each position occurs with and without color bars.

1988 COMMEMORATIVES

#2396a,98a 25¢ SPECIAL OCCASIONS BOOKLET

$3.00 - **BK165** - 2 panes of 6 stamps

		C
A1111	$7.00	☐

1988 COMMEMORATIVES

#2399 25¢ MADONNA

		UL	UR	LL	LR	CUL	CUR
11111-1	$2.00	☐	☐	☐	☐	☐	☐
22222-2	$2.00	☐	☐	☐	☐	☐	☐
22323-2	$2.00	☐	☐	☐	☐	☐	☐
22333-2	$2.00	☐	☐	☐	☐	☐	☐
32333-2	$2.00	☐	☐	☐	☐	☐	☐
32433-2	$2.00	☐	☐	☐	☐	☐	☐
42433-2	$2.00	☐	☐	☐	☐	☐	☐
42443-2	$2.00	☐	☐	☐	☐	☐	☐
42444-2	$5.00	☐	☐	☐	☐	☐	☐
43444-2	$2.00	☐	☐	☐	☐	☐	☐
43454-1	$5.00	☐	☐	☐	☐	☐	☐
53454-1	$2.00	☐	☐	☐	☐	☐	☐
53554-1	$5.00	☐	☐	☐	☐	☐	☐
63554-1	$2.00	☐	☐	☐	☐	☐	☐
63554-2	$2.00	☐	☐	☐	☐	☐	☐
63565-2	$5.00	☐	☐	☐	☐	☐	☐
63665-2	$2.00	☐	☐	☐	☐	☐	☐

#2400 25¢ SLEIGH AND VILLAGE

		UL	UR	LL	LR	CUL	CLL
111111	$2.00	☐	☐	☐	☐	☐	☐

1989 COMMEMORATIVES

#2401 25¢ MONTANA STATEHOOD

		UL	UR	LL	LR
1111-1	$2.00	☐	☐	☐	☐
1211-1	$5.00	☐	☐	☐	☐
2211-1	$20.00	†	☐	†	☐
2222-1	$2.00	☐	☐	☐	☐
2232-1	$2.00	☐	☐	☐	☐
3332-1	$2.00	☐	☐	☐	☐
4332-1	$2.00	☐	☐	☐	☐
4352-1	$4.00	☐	☐	☐	☐
5352-1	$2.00	☐	☐	☐	☐
5362-1	$2.00	☐	☐	☐	☐
6362-1	$5.00	☐	☐	☐	☐
6363-1	$2.00	☐	☐	☐	☐
6463-1	$2.00	☐	☐	☐	☐
6473-1	$2.00	☐	☐	☐	☐
6483-1	$2.00	☐	☐	☐	☐
6494-1	$2.00	☐	☐	☐	☐

#2402 25¢ RANDOLPH

11111	$2.00	☐	☐	☐	☐
12111	$2.00	☐	☐	☐	☐

#2403 25¢ NORTH DAKOTA STATEHOOD

A1111	$2.00	☐	☐	☐	☐

#2404 25¢ WASHINGTON STATEHOOD

A1111	$2.00	☐	☐	☐	☐

1989 COMMEMORATIVES

#2409a 25¢ STEAMBOAT BOOKLET
UNFOLDED & UNBOUND pane of 5

		T
1	$7.50	☐
2	$15.00	☐

$5.00 - **BK166** - 4 panes of 5 stamps

1	$9.50	☐
2	$9.50	☐

#2410 25¢ WORLD STAMP EXPO

		UL	UR	LL	LR
111-1	$2.00	☐	☐	☐	☐
212-1	$2.00	☐	☐	☐	☐

#2411 25¢ ARTURO TOSCANINI

A11111	$2.00	☐	☐	☐	☐

1989-90 CONSTITUTION BICENTENIAL ISSUE

#2412 25¢ HOUSE OF REPRESENTATIVES

111-1	$2.00	☐	☐	☐	☐
211-1	$2.00	☐	☐	☐	☐
221-1	$5.00	☐	☐	☐	☐
321-1	$2.00	☐	☐	☐	☐
422-1	$2.00	☐	☐	☐	☐
522-1	$2.00	☐	☐	☐	☐
622-1	$2.00	☐	☐	☐	☐
722-1	$2.00	☐	☐	☐	☐
723-1	$5.00	☐	☐	☐	☐
724-1	$2.00	☐	☐	☐	☐
823-1	$2.00	☐	☐	☐	☐

#2413 25¢ U. S. SENATE

111-1	$2.00	☐	☐	☐	☐
211-1	$2.00	☐	☐	☐	☐
212-1	$2.00	☐	☐	☐	☐
213-1	$2.00	☐	☐	☐	☐
314-1	$2.00	☐	☐	☐	☐
315-1	$2.00	☐	☐	☐	☐
414-1	$2.00	☐	☐	☐	☐
514-1	$2.00	☐	☐	☐	☐
615-1	$2.00	☐	☐	☐	☐
715-1	$2.00	☐	☐	☐	☐

#2414 25¢ EXECUTIVE BRANCH

111-1	$2.00	☐	☐	☐	☐
211-1	$2.00	☐	☐	☐	☐
311-1	$10.00	☐	☐	†	†
312-1	$2.00	☐	☐	☐	☐

#2415 25¢ U.S. SUPREME COURT

211-1	$2.00	☐	☐	☐	☐
212-1	$2.00	☐	☐	☐	☐
214-1	$2.00	☐	☐	☐	☐

1989 COMMEMORATIVES

#2416 25¢ SOUTH DAKOTA

		UL	UR	LL	LR
A1111	$2.00	☐	☐	☐	☐

#2417 25¢ LOU GEHRIG

A111111	$2.25	☐	☐	☐	☐

#2418 25¢ ERNEST HEMINGWAY

A11111	$2.00	☐	☐	☐	☐

1989 REGULAR ISSUE

#2419 $2.40 MOON LANDING

11111-1	$16.00	☐	☐	☐	☐
11112-1	$16.00	☐	☐	☐	☐
11113-1	$16.00	☐	☐	☐	☐
11114-1	$16.00	☐	☐	☐	☐
11124-1	$16.00	☐	☐	☐	☐
11211-1	$16.00	☐	☐	☐	☐
33437-1	$16.00	☐	☐	☐	☐
43437-1	$16.00	☐	☐	☐	☐

1989 COMMEMORATIVES

#2420 25¢ LETTER CARRIERS

A11111	$2.00	☐	☐	☐	☐

#2421 25¢ BILL OF RIGHTS

111-1	$2.50	☐	☐	☐	☐
112-1	$2.50	☐	☐	☐	☐
122-1	$2.50	☐	☐	☐	☐
123-1	$5.00	☐	☐	☐	☐
223-1	$2.50	☐	☐	☐	☐
234-1	$2.50	☐	☐	☐	☐
235-1	$2.50	☐	☐	☐	☐
376-1	$2.50	☐	☐	☐	☐
377-1	$2.50	☐	☐	☐	☐
446-1	$2.50	☐	☐	☐	☐
456-1	$2.50	☐	☐	☐	☐
466-1	$10.00	†	☐	†	☐
467-1	$2.50	☐	☐	☐	☐
477-1	$2.50	☐	☐	☐	☐
676-1	$2.50	☐	☐	☐	☐

#2422-25 25¢ DINOSAURS

11111-1	$2.50	☐	☐	☐	☐
12111-1	$2.50	☐	☐	☐	☐
12121-1	$2.50	☐	☐	☐	☐
12122-1	$2.50	☐	☐	☐	☐
12232-1	$2.50	☐	☐	☐	☐
27367-1	$2.50	☐	☐	☐	☐
28367-1	$3.50	☐	☐	☐	☐
29367-1	$2.50	☐	☐	☐	☐
29368-1	$2.50	☐	☐	☐	☐
29668-1	$2.50	☐	☐	☐	☐
29669-1	$2.50	☐	☐	☐	☐
44443-1	$2.50	☐	☐	☐	☐
44444-1	$2.50	☐	☐	☐	☐
44445-1	$3.50	☐	☐	☐	☐
44455-1	$2.50	☐	☐	☐	☐
45555-1	$2.50	☐	☐	☐	☐
45556-1	$2.50	☐	☐	☐	☐
46556-1	$2.50	☐	☐	☐	☐

1989 COMMEMORATIVES

#2426 25¢ AMERICAS ISSUE

		UL	UR	LL	LR
A111111	$2.00	□	□	□	□

#2427 25¢ MADONNA

		UL	UR	LL	LR	CUL	CUR
1111-1	$2.00	□	□	□	□	□	□
2211-1	$15.00	†	□	□	□	□	□
2221-1	$2.00	□	□	□	□	□	□
3342-1	$2.00	□	□	□	□	□	□
4453-1	$2.00	□	□	□	□	□	□
5564-1	$2.00	□	□	□	□	□	□
6675-1	$2.00	□	□	□	□	□	□

#2427a 25¢ MADONNA BOOKLET
UNFOLDED & UNBOUND pane of 10

		T
1	$10.00	□

$5.00 - **BK167** - 2 panes of 10 stamps

1	$9.50	□

#2428 25¢ SLEIGH

		UL	UR	LL	LR	CUR	CLR
A11111	$2.00	□	□	□	□	□	□

#2429a 25¢ SLEIGH BOOKLET
UNFOLDED & UNBOUND pane of 10

		L
1111	$10.00	□

$5.00 - **BK168** - 2 panes of 10 stamps

1111	$9.50	□
2111	$9.50	□

#2431a 25¢ EAGLE AND SHIELD SELF ADHESIVE BOOKLET

$5.00 - 1 pane of 18 stamps

		UL	UR	LL	LR
A1111	$9.50	□	‡	‡	□

Also issued in coil strips of 18 without plate numbers.

#2433 $3.60 WORLD STAMP EXPO SOUVENIR SHEET

Issued without plate numbers

#2434-37 25¢ 20th UPU CONGRESS

1112-1	$10.00	†	□	□	□
2112-1	$3.00	□	□	□	□
2122-1	$3.00	□	□	□	□
3223-1	$3.00	□	□	□	□
3232-1	$3.00	□	□	□	□
3234-1	$3.00	□	□	□	□
4345-1	$3.00	□	□	□	□
4356-1	$3.00	□	□	□	□

#2438 $1.00 20th UPU CONGRESS SOUVENIR SHEET

Issued without plate numbers

1990 COMMEMORATIVES

#2439 25¢ IDAHO STATEHOOD

		UL	UR	LL	LR
A11111	$2.00	□	□	□	□

#2440 25¢ LOVE

		UL	UR	LL	LR	CUL	CLL
U1111	$2.00	□	□	□	□	□	□
U1211	$2.00	□	□	□	□	□	□
U1212	$5.00	□	†	□	□	□	□
U2222	$2.00	□	□	□	□	□	□
U3223	$2.00	□	□	□	□	□	□
U3224	$5.00	□	□	□	□	□	□
U3323	$2.00	□	□	□	□	□	□
U3333	$2.00	□	□	□	□	□	□
U3353	$2.00	□	□	□	□	□	□
U3354	$10.00	†	□	□	†	†	†
U3443	$2.00	□	□	□	□	□	□

#2441a 25¢ LOVE BOOKLET
UNFOLDED & UNBOUND pane of 10

		L
1211	$30.00	□

$5.00 - **BK169** - 2 panes of 10 stamps

1211	$9.50	□
2111	$20.00	□
2211	$20.00	□
2222	$9.50	□

#2442 25¢ IDA B. WELLS

		UL	UR	LL	LR
A11111	$2.00	□	□	□	□

#2443a 15¢ BEACH UMBRELLA BOOKLET
UNFOLDED & UNBOUND pane of 10

		T
111111	$8.00	□

$3.00 - **BK170** - 2 panes of 10 stamps

111111	$6.00	□
221111	$12.00	□

#2444 25¢ WYOMING STATEHOOD

		UL	UR	LL	LR
1112-1	$2.00	□	□	□	□
1122-1	$2.00	□	□	□	□
1132-1	$2.00	□	□	□	□
1142-1	$2.00	□	□	□	□
1152-1	$2.00	□	□	□	□
2251-1	$2.00	□	□	□	□
2261-1	$2.00	□	□	□	□
2363-1	$2.00	□	□	□	□

#2445-48 25¢ CLASSIC FILMS

A11111	$4.50	□	□	□	□

#2449 25¢ MARIANNE MOORE

A111	$2.00	□	□	□	□

1981 TRANSPORTATION COILS

#2451 THROUGH #2468

See pages 231-235

1990 COMMEMORATIVES

#2474a 25¢ LIGHTHOUSES BOOKLET

UNFOLDED & UNBOUND pane of 5

		L
1	$5.00	☐
2	$5.00	☐
3	$5.00	☐
4	$250.00	☐
5	$5.00	☐

$5.00 - **BK171** - 4 panes of 5 stamps

1	$9.50	☐
2	$9.50	☐
3	$9.50	☐
4	$9.50	☐
5	$9.50	☐

1990-96 REGULAR ISSUES

#2475 25¢ FLAG ATM SHEETLET

$3.00 - 1 pane of 12 stamps

Issued without plate numbers

#2476 1¢ KESTREL

UNTAGGED ONLY

		UL	UR	LL	LR
A1111	$0.15	☐	☐	☐	☐
A1112	$0.15	☐	☐	☐	☐
A1113	$0.15	☐	☐	☐	☐
A1213	$0.30	☐	☐	☐	☐
A1313	$0.30	☐	☐	☐	☐
A2313	$0.15	☐	☐	☐	☐
A2314	$0.50	☐	☐	☐	☐
A2324	$0.15	☐	☐	☐	☐
A2334	$0.15	☐	☐	☐	☐
A3334	$0.15	☐	☐	☐	☐
A4334	$0.15	☐	☐	☐	☐
A4335	$0.30	☐	☐	☐	☐
A4345	—	†	†	†	†
A6456	$0.15	☐	☐	☐	☐
A6457	$0.15	☐	☐	☐	☐
A7568	$0.30	☐	☐	☐	☐
A7569	$0.15	☐	☐	☐	☐
A8568	$0.15	☐	☐	☐	☐
A10101010	$0.15	☐	☐	☐	☐
A11101010	$0.30	☐	☐	☐	☐

The 15 plate combinations, A1111-A6457, were printed with 800 subject plates (400 #2476 and 400 #2478).

#2477 1¢ KESTREL (revised)

UNTAGGED ONLY

1111	$0.15	☐	☐	☐	☐
1112	$0.50	☐	☐	☐	☐
2222	$0.15	☐	☐	☐	☐
3333	$0.15	†	☐	†	☐

1990-96 REGULAR ISSUES

#2478 3¢ BLUEBIRD

UNTAGGED ONLY		UL	UR	LL	LR
A1111	$0.25	☐	☐	☐	☐
A1112	$0.25	☐	☐	☐	☐
A1113	$0.25	☐	☐	☐	☐
A1213	$0.50	☐	☐	☐	☐
A1313	$0.50	☐	☐	☐	☐
A2313	$0.25	☐	☐	☐	☐
A2314	$0.50	☐	☐	☐	☐
A2324	$0.25	☐	☐	☐	☐
A2334	$0.25	☐	☐	☐	☐
A3334	$0.25	☐	☐	☐	☐
A4334	$0.25	☐	☐	☐	☐
A4335	$0.50	☐	☐	☐	☐
A4345	$0.25	☐	☐	☐	☐
A6456	$0.25	☐	☐	☐	☐
A6457	$0.25	☐	☐	☐	☐
A7568	$0.50	☐	☐	☐	☐
A7578	$0.50	†	☐	☐	☐
A8588	$0.25	☐	☐	☐	☐
A9588	$0.25	☐	☐	☐	☐

The 15 plate combinations, A1111-A6457, were printed with 800 subject plates (400 #2476 and 400 #2478).

#2479 19¢ FAWN

11111	$1.50	☐	☐	☐	☐
21111	$2.00	☐	☐	☐	☐
22222	$1.50	☐	☐	☐	☐

#2480 30¢ CARDINAL

S1111	$2.40	☐	☐	☐	☐

#2481 45¢ PUMPKINSEED SUNFISH

1111-S1	$3.60	☐	☐	☐	☐
2222-S1	$3.60	☐	☐	☐	☐
3333-S1	$3.60	☐	☐	☐	☐
4444-S1	$3.60	☐	☐	☐	☐

#2482 $2.00 BOBCAT

1111-1	$14	☐	☐	☐	☐
1211-1	$14	☐	☐	☐	☐
2222-1	$14	☐	☐	☐	☐
2322-1	$14	☐	☐	☐	☐
4644-1	$20	☐	☐	☐	☐
4654-1	$14	☐	☐	☐	☐
5654-1	$14	☐	☐	☐	☐
6876-1	$14	☐	☐	☐	☐
6886-1	$14	☐	☐	☐	☐
9999-1	$14	☐	☐	☐	☐

#2483a 20¢ BLUE JAY BOOKLET

UNFOLDED & UNBOUND pane of 10

		T
S1111	$4.00	☐

$2.00 - **BK172** - 1 pane of 10 stamps

S1111	$4.00	☐

1990-96 REGULAR ISSUES

#2484a 29¢ WOOD DUCK BOOKLET
UNFOLDED & UNBOUND pane of 10

		L
1111	$8.00	☐

$2.90 - **BK173** - 1 pane of 10 stamps

4444	$5.25	☐

$5.80 - **BK174** - 2 panes of 10 stamps

1111	$10.50	☐
1211	$100.00	☐
2122	$15.00	☐
2222	$10.50	☐
3221	$100.00	☐
3222	$15.00	☐
3331	$100.00	☐
3333	$15.00	☐
4444	$10.50	☐

#2485a 29¢ WOOD DUCK BOOKLET
UNFOLDED & UNBOUND pane of 10

K11111	$10.00	☐

$5.80 - **BK175** - 2 panes of 10 stamps

K11111	$10.50	☐

#2486a 29¢ AFRICAN VIOLET BOOKLET
UNFOLDED & UNBOUND pane of 10

K1111	$5.25	☐

$2.90 - **BK176** - 1 pane of 10 stamps

K1111	$5.25	☐

$5.80 - **BK177** - 2 panes of 10 stamps

K1111	$10.50	☐

#2488a 32¢ PEACHES & PEAR BOOKLET
UNFOLDED & UNBOUND pane of 10

		T
11111	$6.00	☐

$6.40 - **BK178** - 2 panes of 10 stamps

11111	$11.50	☐

#2489a 29¢ RED SQUIRREL SELF ADHESIVE BOOKLET

$5.22 - 1 pane of 18 stamps

		C
D11111	$10.00	☐
D22211	$10.00	☐
D22221	$12.50	☐
D22222	$12.50	☐
D23133	$12.50	☐

Also issued in coil strips of 18 without plate numbers

#2490a 29¢ RED ROSE SELF ADHESIVE BOOKLET

$5.22 - 1 pane of 18 stamps

		C
S111	$10.00	☐

Also issued in coil strips of 18 without plate numbers

#2491a 29¢ PINE CONE SELF-ADHESIVE BOOKLET

$5.22 - 1 pane of 18 stamps

		C
B1	$20.00	☐
B2	$10.00	☐
B3	$10.00	☐
B4	$10.00	☐
B5	$15.00	☐
B6	$10.00	☐
B7	$10.00	☐
B8	$10.00	☐
B9	$10.00	☐
B10	$10.00	☐
B11	$10.00	☐
B12	$15.00	☐
B13	$10.00	☐
B14	$10.00	☐
B15	$15.00	☐
B16	$10.00	☐

Also issued in coil strips of 18 with plate numbers.

Strip of 5		B
B1	$6.00	☐

#2492a 32¢ PINK ROSE SELF-ADHESIVE BOOKLET

$6.40 - 1 pane of 20 stamps

		C
S111	$11.50	☐
S112	$11.50	☐
S333	$11.50	☐
S444	$11.50	☐
S555	$11.50	☐

Also issued in coil strips of 18 with plate numbers.

Strip of 5		B
S111	$5.00	☐

#2492b 32¢ PINK ROSE SELF-ADHESIVE BOOKLET

See Appendix K for "MDI" booklets.

#2494a 32¢ PEACHES & PEAR SELF-ADHESIVE BOOKLET

$6.40 - 1 pane of 20 stamps

		C
V11111	$11.50	☐
V11122	$11.50	☐
V11131	$11.50	☐
V11132	$11.50	☐
V11232	$11.50	☐
V12131	$11.50	☐
V12132	$11.50	☐
V12211	$11.50	☐
V12221	$11.50	☐
V12232	$11.50	☐
V22212	$11.50	☐
V22221	$11.50	☐
V22222	$11.50	☐
V33142	$11.50	☐

1990-96 REGULAR ISSUES

#2494a 32¢ PEACHES & PEAR SELF-ADHESIVE BOOKLET Cont.

		C
V33143	$11.50	□
V33243	$11.50	□
V33323	$11.50	□
V33333	$11.50	□
V33343	$11.50	□
V33353	$11.50	□
V33363	$11.50	□
V33453	$11.50	□
V44424	$11.50	□
V44434	$11.50	□
V44454	$11.50	□
V45434	$11.50	□
V45464	$11.50	□
V54365	$11.50	□
V54565	$11.50	□
V55365	$11.50	□
V55565	$11.50	□

#2495-95A 32¢ PEACHES & PEAR SELF-ADHESIVE COIL

		B
V11111	$5.00	□

1990 COMMEMORATIVES

#2496-2500 25¢ OLYMPIANS

Block of 10 (5 x 2)		UL	UR	LL	LR
A1111	$6.00	□	□	□	□

#2505a 25¢ INDIAN HEADRESSES BOOKLET

UNFOLDED & UNBOUND pane of 10

		L
1	$15.00	□
2	$15.00	□

$5.00 - **BK179** - 2 panes of 10 stamps

1	$9.50	□
2	$9.50	□

#2506-07 25¢ MICRONESIA & MARSHALL ISLANDS

		UL	UR	LL	LR
22121-1	$2.00	□	□	□	□
22122-1	$2.00	□	□	□	□
22321-1	$2.00	□	□	□	□
22423-1	$10.00	†	□	†	□
22523-1	$2.00	□	□	□	□

#2508-11 25¢ SEA CREATURES

1111-1	$2.00	□	□	□	□
2122-1	$2.00	□	□	□	□
2132-1	$2.00	□	□	□	□
4233-1	$2.00	□	□	□	□
5233-1	$2.00	□	□	□	□
5243-1	$2.00	□	□	□	□
5244-1	$5.00	□	□	†	□
5254-1	$2.00	□	□	□	□
6254-1	$5.00	□	□	□	□
6354-1	$2.00	□	□	□	□
6364-1	$2.00	□	□	□	□

1990 COMMEMORATIVES

#2512 25¢ AMERICA

		UL	UR	LL	LR
A1111	$2.00	‡	□	□	□

See #C127 for upper left position.

#2513 25¢ EISENHOWER

A11111	$2.00	□	□	□	□

#2514 25¢ MADONNA

		UL	UR	LL	LR	CUL	CUR
1112-1	$2.00	□	□	□	□	□	□
1113-1	$2.00	□	□	□	□	□	□
1213-1	$2.00	□	□	□	□	□	□
1223-1	$2.00	□	□	□	□	□	□
2221-1	$2.00	□	□	□	□	□	□
2223-1	$2.00	□	□	□	□	□	□
2224-1	$2.00	□	□	□	□	□	□
2234-1	$2.00	□	□	□	□	□	□
2335-1	$2.00	□	□	□	□	□	□
3446-1	$2.00	□	□	□	□	□	□
5556-1	$2.00	□	□	□	□	□	□
6556-1	$2.00	□	□	□	□	□	□
6557-1	$2.00	□	□	□	□	□	□

#2514a 25¢ MADONNA BOOKLET

UNFOLDED & UNBOUND pane of 10

		T
1	$10.00	□

$5.00 - **BK180** - 2 panes of 10 stamps

1	$9.50	□

#2515 25¢ CHRISTMAS TREE

		UL	UR	LL	LR	CUL	CUR
A1111	$2.00	□	□	□	□	□	□

#2516a 25¢ CHRISTMAS TREE BOOKLET

UNFOLDED & UNBOUND pane of 10

		T
1211	$10.00	□

$5.00 - **BK181** - 2 panes of 10 stamps

1211	$9.50	□

1991 REGULAR ISSUES

#2517 (29¢)F FLOWER

		UL	UR	LL	LR
U1111	$2.25	□	□	□	□
U1112	$2.25	□	□	□	□
U1211	$2.25	□	□	□	□
U1212	$2.25	□	□	□	□
U1213	$5.00	□	□	□	□
U1221	$2.25	□	□	□	□

#2518 (29¢)F FLOWER COIL

Strips of 5		B
1111	$3.50	□
1211	$25.00	□
1222	$3.50	□
2211	$5.00	□
2222	$3.50	□

1991 REGULAR ISSUES

#2519a (29¢)F FLOWER BOOKLET

$2.90 - **BK182** - 1 pane of 10 stamps

		T
2222	$5.25	☐

$5.80 - **BK183** - 2 panes of 10 stamps

1111	$10.50	☐
1222	$25.00	☐
2111	$20.00	☐
2121	$10.50	☐
2212	$20.00	☐
2222	$10.50	☐

#2520a (29¢)F FLOWER BOOKLET

$2.90 - **BK184** - 1 pane of 10 stamps

K1111	$7.50	☐

#2521 (4¢) MAKE-UP

UNTAGGED ONLY

		UL	UR	LL	LR	CUL	CLL
A11	$0.35	☐	☐	☐	☐	☐	☐
A22	$0.35	☐	☐	☐	☐	☐	☐
A33	$0.35	☐	☐	☐	☐	☐	☐
A44	$0.35	☐	☐	☐	☐	☐	☐
A55	$0.35	☐	☐	☐	☐	☐	☐
A66	$0.35	☐	☐	☐	☐	☐	☐
A77	$0.35	☐	☐	☐	☐	☐	☐
A88	$0.35	☐	☐	☐	☐	☐	☐
A99	$0.35	☐	☐	☐	☐	☐	☐

#2522 (29¢)F FLAG ATM SHEETLET

$3.48 - 1 pane of 12 stamps

Issued without plate numbers

#2523 29¢ FLAG OVER MT. RUSHMORE COIL

Strips of 5		B
1	$4.50	☐
2	$4.50	☐
3	$4.50	☐
4	$4.50	☐
5	$4.50	☐
6	$4.50	☐
7	$4.50	☐
8	$8.00	☐
9	$8.00	☐

#2523c 29¢ FLAG OVER MT. RUSHMORE COIL

Strips of 5		(Toledo brown)
7	$130.00	☐

#2523A 29¢ FLAG OVER MT. RUSHMORE COIL

Strips of 5		
A11111	$4.50	☐
A22211	$4.50	☐

#2524 29¢ FLOWER

L - Perf. 10.8 x 10.9		UL	UR	LL	LR
U1111	$2.25	☐	☐	☐	☐
U1121	$2.25	☐	☐	☐	☐
U1122	$2.25	☐	☐	☐	☐
U1132	$10.00	☐	☐	☐	☐
U2132	$2.25	☐	☐	☐	☐
U2232	$2.25	☐	☐	☐	☐
U2342	$2.25	☐	☐	☐	☐

#2524a 29¢ FLOWER

Bull's Eye Perf. 12.5 x 13

U3342	$2.75	☐	☐	☐	☐
U3343	$2.75	☐	☐	☐	☐

#2525 29¢ FLOWER COIL

Strips of 5		B	(Rouletted)
S1111	$4	☐	
S2222	$4	☐	

#2526 29¢ FLOWER COIL

Strips of 5		(Perforated)
S2222	$4	☐

#2527a 29¢ FLOWER BOOKLET

UNFOLDED & UNBOUND pane of 10

		T
K1111	$6.00	☐

$5.80 - **BK185** - 2 panes of 10 stamps

K1111	$10.50	☐
K2222	$10.50	☐
K3333	$10.50	☐

#2528a 29¢ FLAG WITH OLYMPIC RINGS BOOKLET

UNFOLDED & UNBOUND pane of 10

		L
K11111	$5.25	☐

$2.90 - **BK186** - 1 pane of 10 stamps

K11111	$5.25	☐

$2.90 - **BK186A** - 1 pane of 10 stamps

K11111	$5.25	☐

#2529 19¢ FISHING BOAT COIL

Strips of 5		B
A1111	$3.50	☐
A1112	$6.00	☐
A1212	$3.50	☐
A2424	$3.50	☐

#2529a 19¢ FISHING BOAT COIL

Strips of 5		
A5555	$3.50	☐
A5556	$3.50	☐
A6667	$3.50	☐
A7667	$3.50	☐
A7679	$3.50	☐
A7766	$3.50	☐
A7779	$3.50	☐

#2529b 19¢ FISHING BOAT COIL

Strips of 5		UNTAGGED
A5555	$10.00	☐

1991 REGULAR ISSUES

#2529C 19¢ FISHING BOAT COIL

Strips of 5		B
S111	$4.50	☐

#2530a 19¢ BALLOON BOOKLET

UNFOLDED & UNBOUND pane of 10

		T
1111	$4.00	☐

$3.80 - **BK187** - 2 panes of 10 stamps

1111	$8.00	☐
1222	$15.00	☐
2222	$8.00	☐

#2531 29¢ FLAGS ON PARADE

		UL	UR	LL	LR
1111	$2.25	☐	☐	☐	☐
1112**N**	$2.25	☐	☐	☐	☐
1121	$2.25	☐	☐	☐	☐
2211	$2.25	☐	☐	☐	☐
2221	$4.00	☐	☐	☐	☐
2222	$2.25	☐	☐	☐	☐

N Also exists of prephosphored paper

#2531A 29¢ TORCH ATM BOOKLET

$5.22 - 1 pane of 18 stamps

Issued without plate numbers

1991 COMMEMORATIVES

#2532 50¢ SWITZERLAND

A11111	$4.00	☐	☐	☐	☐

#2533 29¢ VERMONT

A1111	$2.25	☐	☐	☐	☐

#2534 29¢ SAVINGS BONDS

111111	$2.25	☐	☐	☐	☐

#2535 29¢ LOVE

Bull's Eye Perf. 12.5 x 13

		UL	UR	LL	LR	CUL	CLL
U11111	$2.25	☐	☐	☐	☐	☐	☐
U21112	$2.25	☐	☐	☐	☐	☐	☐
U21121	$2.25	☐	☐	☐	☐	☐	☐
U21122	$2.25	☐	☐	☐	☐	☐	☐
U21123	$10.00	†	☐	†	☐	☐	†
U21124	$2.25	☐	☐	☐	☐	☐	☐
U32213	$2.25	☐	☐	☐	☐	☐	☐
U42213	$2.25	☐	☐	☐	☐	☐	☐
U52213	$2.25	☐	☐	☐	☐	☐	☐

#2535a 29¢ LOVE

L - Perf. 10.8 x 10.9

U21122	$10.00	†	†	†	☐	†	†
U21124	$2.75	☐	☐	☐	☐	☐	☐
U31113	$5.00	☐	☐	☐	☐	☐	☐
U31123	$2.75	☐	☐	☐	☐	☐	☐
U31124	$2.75	☐	☐	☐	☐	☐	☐
U32213	$2.75	☐	☐	☐	☐	☐	☐
U53234	$2.75	☐	☐	☐	☐	☐	☐

1991 COMMEMORATIVES

#2536a 29¢ LOVE BOOKLET

UNFOLDED & UNBOUND pane of 10

		L
1111	$6.50	☐
1112	$6.50	☐

$5.80 - **BK188** - 2 panes of 10 stamps

1111	$10.50	☐
1112	$10.50	☐
1113	$15.00	☐
1123	$15.00	☐
1212	$20.00	☐
2223	$15.00	☐

#2537 52¢ LOVE

		UL	UR	LL	LR
A111	$4.00	☐	☐	☐	☐

#2538 29¢ WILLIAM SAROYAN

A11111	$2.25	☐	☐	☐	☐

1991-93 REGULAR ISSUES

#2539 $1.00 OLYMPICS

S111111	$8.00	☐	☐	☐	☐

#2540 $2.90 EAGLE

A1111-1	$20	☐	☐	☐	☐
A2111-1	$20	☐	☐	☐	☐
A2111-2	$20	☐	☐	☐	☐
A3111-1	$35	☐	☐	☐	☐
A3111-2	$20	☐	☐	☐	☐
A4121-2	$20	☐	☐	☐	☐
A4122-2	$20	☐	☐	☐	☐
A4222-1	$20	☐	☐	☐	☐
A4232-1	$20	☐	☐	☐	☐
A4232-2	$20	☐	☐	☐	☐
A5233-2	$20	☐	☐	☐	☐
A5233-3	$20	☐	☐	☐	☐
A5244-3	$20	☐	☐	☐	☐
A5344-3	$20	☐	☐	☐	☐
A5345-3	$20	☐	☐	☐	☐
A5346-3	$20	☐	☐	☐	☐
A6356-3	$20	☐	☐	☐	☐
A8467-4	$20	☐	☐	☐	☐
A8467-5	$20	☐	☐	☐	☐
A8468-5	$20	☐	☐	☐	☐
A8468-6	$20	☐	☐	☐	☐

#2541 $9.95 EAGLE

A1111-1	$70	☐	☐	☐	☐
A1111-2	$70	☐	☐	☐	☐
A2111-2	$70	☐	☐	☐	☐
A3222-2	$70	☐	☐	☐	☐
A3222-3	$70	☐	☐	☐	☐
A3232-2	$70	☐	☐	☐	☐
A3232-3	$70	☐	☐	☐	☐

1991-93 REGULAR ISSUES

#2542 $14.00 EAGLE

		UL	UR	LL	LR
A1111-1	$100	□	□	□	□

#2543 $2.90 SPACE VEHICLE

11111-1	$20	□	□	□	□
22222-1	$20	□	□	□	□
22322-1	$20	□	□	□	□
32322-1	$20	□	□	□	□
32332-1	$20	□	□	□	□
32333-1	$20	□	□	□	□
43333-1	$20	□	□	□	□
86666-1	$20	□	□	□	□
99999-1	$30	□	□	□	□

#2544 $3.00 CHALLENGER SHUTTLE

1995 year date					
P1111-1	$20	□	□	□	□
P2222-1	$20	□	□	□	□
P3333-1	$20	□	□	□	□
1996 year date					
P4444-2	$20	□	□	□	□
P5555-2	$20	□	□	□	□

#2544A $10.75 ENDEAVOR SHUTTLE

P1111-1	$100	□	□	□	□
P2222-1	$100	□	□	□	□

1991 COMMEMORATIVES

#2549a 29¢ FISHING FLIES BOOKLET UNFOLDED & UNBOUND pane of 5

		T
A11111	$1000.00	□
A22122	$250.00	□
A23124	$20.00	□
A23133	$20.00	□
A23213	$5.00	□
A33213	$250.00	□
A32225	$20.00	□
A33233	$20.00	□

$5.80 - **BK189** - 4 panes of 5 stamps

A11111	$40.00	□
A22122	$10.50	□
A22132	$10.50	□
A22133	$20.00	□
A23123	$10.50	□
A23124	$10.50	□
A23133	$40.00	□
A23213	$20.00	□
A31224	$20.00	□
A32224	$10.50	□
A32225	$20.00	□
A33233	$20.00	□
A33235	$10.50	□
A44446	$10.50	□
A45546	$10.50	□
A45547	$10.50	□

Each booklet may contain more than one plate number.

1991 COMMEMORATIVES

#2550 29¢ COLE PORTER

		UL	UR	LL	LR
A11111	$2.25	□	□	□	□

#2551 29¢ DESERT STORM

S1111111	$2.25	□	□	□	□
S1111121	$2.25	□	□	□	□

#2552a 29¢ DESERT STORM BOOKLET UNFOLDED & UNBOUND pane of 5

		R
A11121111	$3.50	□

$5.80 - **BK190** - 4 panes of 5 stamps

A11111111	$20.00	□
A11121111	$10.50	□

Each booklet may contain more than one plate number.

#2553-57 29¢ SUMMER OLYMPICS

Block of 10 (5 x 2)

		UL	UR	LL	LR
A11111	$6.50	□	□	□	□

#2558 29¢ NUMISMATICS

111111-1	$2.25	□	□	□	□
111211-1	$2.25	□	□	□	□
112221-1	$2.25	□	□	□	□
112222-1	$2.25	□	□	□	□
112322-1	$2.25	□	□	□	□
122322-1	$2.25	□	□	□	□
123422-1	$2.25	□	□	□	□
123432-1	$2.25	□	□	□	□
124432-1	$2.25	□	□	□	□
125432-1	$2.25	□	□	□	□

#2559 29¢ WORLD WAR II (1991)

Block of 10 (5x2) and central label

1111-1	$5.25	□	□	□	□
1112-1	$5.25	□	□	□	□
2112-1	$5.25	□	□	□	□
2113-1	$7.50	□	□	□	□
2213-1	$10.00	□	□	□	□
2223-1	$5.25	□	□	□	□
2224-1	$5.25	□	□	□	□
2234-1	$5.25	□	□	□	□
3244-1	$5.25	□	□	□	□
3344-1	$5.25	□	□	□	□
3354-1	$5.25	□	□	□	□
3364-1	$5.25	□	□	□	□
4354-1	$7.50	□	□	□	□
5354-1	$5.25	□	□	□	□
5455-1	$5.25	□	□	□	□
5475-1	$5.25	□	□	□	□
5476-2	$5.25	□	□	□	□
6476-2	$7.50	□	□	□	□
6486-2	$5.25	□	□	□	□
6586-2	$10.50	□	□	□	□

1991 COMMEMORATIVES

#2560 29¢ BASKETBALL

		UL	UR	LL	LR
1111	$2.25	☐	☐	☐	☐

#2561 29¢ DISTRICT OF COLUMBIA

1111-1	$2.25	☐	☐	☐	☐
1212-1	$2.25	☐	☐	☐	☐
2212-1	$3.50	☐	☐	☐	☐
2312-1	$2.25	☐	☐	☐	☐
2423-1	$2.25	☐	☐	☐	☐

#2566a 29¢ COMEDIANS BOOKLET
UNFOLDED & UNBOUND pane of 10

		L
1	$6.50	☐

$5.80 - **BK191** - 2 panes of 10 stamps

1	$10.50	☐
2	$10.50	☐

#2567 29¢ JAN MATZELIGER

		UL	UR	LL	LR
A111111	$2.25	☐	☐	☐	☐

#2577a 29¢ SPACE EXPLORATION BOOKLET
UNFOLDED & UNBOUND pane of 10

		L
111111	$6.50	☐

$5.80 - **BK192** - 2 panes of 10 stamps

111111	$10.50	☐
111112	$10.50	☐

#2578 (29¢) MADONNA

		UL	UR	LL	LR	CUL	CUR
1111-1	$2.25	☐	☐	☐	☐	☐	☐
1121-1	$2.25	☐	☐	☐	☐	☐	☐
2121-1	$2.25	☐	☐	☐	☐	☐	☐
2232-1	$2.25	☐	☐	☐	☐	☐	☐
2232-2	$5.00	☐	☐	☐	☐	☐	☐
3342-2	$2.25	☐	☐	☐	☐	☐	☐
4453-1	$2.25	☐	☐	☐	☐	☐	☐
5564-1	$5.00	☐	☐	☐	☐	☐	☐
5564-2	$2.25	☐	☐	☐	☐	☐	☐
5575-2	$2.25	☐	☐	☐	☐	☐	☐
5585-2	$2.25	☐	☐	☐	☐	☐	☐
6696-1	$2.25	☐	☐	☐	☐	☐	☐
7696-1	$2.25	☐	☐	☐	☐	☐	☐

#2578a (29¢) MADONNA BOOKLET
UNFOLDED & UNBOUND pane of 10

		T
1	$6.50	☐

$5.80 - **BK193** - 2 panes of 10 stamps

1	$10.50	☐

#2579 (29¢) SANTA CLAUS

		UL	UR	LL	LR	CUL	CLL
A111	$2.25	☐	☐	☐	☐	☐	☐

1991 COMMEMORATIVES

#2581b,2a-5a (29¢) SANTA CLAUS BOOKLET
UNFOLDED & UNBOUND - set of 5 panes of 4 stamps

		L
A11111	$20.00	☐

$5.80 - **BK194** - 5 panes of 4 stamps

A11111	$10.50	☐
A12111	$10.50	☐

1991-95 REGULAR ISSUES

#2587 32¢ JAMES K. POLK

		UL	UR	LL	LR
B1	$2.50	☐	☐	☐	☐

#2590 $1.00 SARATOGA

S1	$7.00	☐	☐	☐	☐
S2	$7.00	☐	☐	☐	☐

#2592 $5.00 WASHINGTON AND JACKSON

S1	$35.00	☐	☐	☐	☐

BOOKLET STAMPS

#2593a 29¢ FLAG WITH PLEDGE
Perf. 10.0 x 9.8
UNFOLDED & UNBOUND pane of 10

		T
1111	$6.50	☐

$2.90 - **BK195** - 1 pane of 10 stamps

1111	$6.50	☐
2222	$6.50	☐

$5.80 - **BK196** - 2 panes of 10 stamps

1111	$10.50	☐
1211	$15.00	☐
2122	$15.00	☐
2222N	$10.50	☐

N This number also appears in books with the plate number over the right stamp.

#2593c 29¢ FLAG WITH PLEDGE
Perf. 10.9 x 9.8
$5.80 - **BK197** - 2 panes of 10 stamps

1111	$10.50	☐
1211	$10.50	☐
2122	$10.50	☐
2222	$10.50	☐
2232	$10.50	☐
2333	$150.00	☐
3333	$10.50	☐
4444	$10.50	☐

#2594a 29¢ FLAG WITH PLEDGE
UNFOLDED & UNBOUND pane of 10

K1111	$6.50	☐

$2.90 - **BK198** - 1 pane of 10 stamps

K1111	$6.50	☐

$5.80 - **BK199** - 2 panes of 10 stamps

K1111	$10.50	☐

1991-95 REGULAR ISSUES

#2595a 29¢ EAGLE AND SHIELD SELF ADHESIVE (brown)

$4.93 - 1 pane of 17 stamps and 1 label

		C
B1111-1	$10	☐
B1111-2	$10	☐
B2222-1	$10	☐
B2222-2	$10	☐
B3333-1	$10	☐
B3333-3	$10	☐
B3434-1	$10	☐
B3434-3	$10	☐
B4344-1	$10	☐
B4344-3	$175	☐
B4444-1	$10	☐
B4444-3	$10	☐

Also issued in coil strips of 17 stamps without plate numbers

#2596a 29¢ EAGLE AND SHIELD SELF-ADHESIVE (green)

$4.93 - 1 pane of 17 stamps and 1 label

D11111	$10	☐
D21221	$10	☐
D22322	$10	☐
D32322	$10	☐
D32332	$10	☐
D32342	$25	☐
D42342	$10	☐
D43342	$25	☐
D43352	$10	☐
D43452	$10	☐
D43453	$10	☐
D54561	$10	☐
D54563	$10	☐
D54571	$10	☐
D54573	$10	☐
D54673	$20	☐
D61384	$20	☐
D65784	$10	☐

Also issued in coil strips of 17 stamps without plate numbers

#2597a 29¢ EAGLE AND SHIELD SELF-ADHESIVE (red)

$4.93 - 1 pane of 17 stamps and 1 label

S1111	$10	☐

Also issued in coil strips of 17 stamps without plate numbers

#2598a 29¢ EAGLE SELF-ADHESIVE

$5.22 - 1 pane of 18 stamps

M111	$10	☐
M112	$10	☐

Also issued in coil strips of 18 with plate numbers.

Strip of 5		B
111	$6	☐

#2599a 29¢ STATUE OF LIBERTY SELF-ADHESIVE

$5.22 - 1 pane of 18 stamps

		C
D1111	$10	☐
D1212	$10	☐

Also issued in coil strips of 18 with plate numbers.

Strip of 5		B
D1111	$6	☐

COIL STAMPS

Strips of 5

#2602 (10¢) EAGLE AND SHIELD

UNTAGGED

A11111	$3	☐
A11112	$3	☐
A12213	$20	☐
A21112	$3	☐
A21113	$3	☐
A22112	$3	☐
A22113	$3	☐
A32333	$225	☐
A33333	$3	☐
A33334	$85	☐
A33335	$4	☐
A34424	$4	☐
A34426	$4	☐
A43324	$4	☐
A43325	$4	☐
A43326	$4	☐
A43334	$3	☐
A43335	$3	☐
A43426	$3	☐
A53335	$3	☐
A54444	$3	☐
A54445	$3	☐
A77777	$3	☐
A88888	$3	☐
A88889	$3	☐
A89999	$3	☐
A99998	$3	☐
A99999	$3	☐
A1010101010	$3	☐
A1011101010	$4	☐
A1011101011	$3	☐
A1011101012	$3	☐
A1110101010	$3	☐
A1110101011	$12	☐
A1110111010	$3	☐
A1111101010	$3	☐
A1111111010	$3	☐
A1211101010	$4	☐
A1411101010	$3	☐
A1411101011	$3	☐
A1412111110	$3	☐
A1412111111	$3	☐

1991-95 REGULAR ISSUES

#2603 (10¢) EAGLE AND SHIELD

UNTAGGED shiny gum

		B
11111	$3	☐
22221	$3	☐
22222	$3	☐
33333	$3	☐

UNTAGGED dull gum

22222	$3	☐

#2603b (10¢) EAGLE AND SHIELD

TAGGED

11111	$10	☐
22221	$10	☐
22222	$200	☐

#2604 (10¢) EAGLE AND SHIELD

UNTAGGED

S11111	$3	☐
S22222	$3	☐

#2605 23¢ FLAG

UNTAGGED

A111	$3.50	☐
A112	$3.50	☐
A122	$3.50	☐
A212	$3.50	☐
A222	$3.50	☐
A333	$3.50	☐

#2606 23¢ FLAG AND USA

UNTAGGED

A1111	$3.50	☐
A2222	$3.50	☐
A2232	$3.50	☐
A2233	$3.50	☐
A3333	$3.50	☐
A4364	$3.50	☐
A4443	$3.50	☐
A4444	$3.50	☐
A4453	$3.50	☐

#2607 23¢ FLAG AND USA

UNTAGGED shiny gum

1111	$3.50	☐

UNTAGGED dull gum

1111	$3.50	☐

#2608 23¢ FLAG AND USA

UNTAGGED

S111	$3.50	☐

#2609 29¢ FLAG OVER WHITE HOUSE

1	$4.50	☐
2	$4.50	☐
3	$4.50	☐
4	$4.50	☐
5	$4.50	☐
6	$4.50	☐
7	$4.50	☐
8	$4.50	☐
9	$4.50	☐

1991-95 REGULAR ISSUES

#2609 29¢ FLAG OVER WHITE HOUSE Cont.

		B
10	$4.50	☐
11	$4.50	☐
12	$4.50	☐
13	$4.50	☐
14	$4.50	☐
15	$4.50	☐
16	$4.50	☐
18	$4.50	☐

1992 COMMEMORATIVES

#2611-15 29¢ WINTER OLYMPICS

Block of 10 (5 x 2)		UL	UR	LL	LR
S1111	$5.25	☐	☐	☐	☐

#2616 29¢ WORLD COLUMBIAN STAMP EXPO

111-1	$2.25	☐	☐	☐	☐
211-1	$2.25	☐	☐	☐	☐
212-1	$2.25	☐	☐	☐	☐
322-1	$2.25	☐	☐	☐	☐
423-1	$2.25	☐	☐	☐	☐

#2617 29¢ W.E.B. DUBOIS

111122-1	$2.25	☐	☐	☐	☐
112322-1	$2.25	☐	☐	☐	☐
113222-1	$2.25	☐	☐	☐	☐
113422-1	$3.50	☐	☐	☐	☐
233433-1	$3.50	☐	☐	☐	☐
234433-1	$2.25	☐	☐	☐	☐

#2618 29¢ LOVE

		UL	UR	LL	LR	CLL	CLR
U11111	$2.25	☐	☐	☐	☐	☐	☐
U21111	$2.25	☐	☐	☐	☐	☐	☐
U21112	$2.25	☐	☐	☐	☐	☐	☐
U21212	$2.25	☐	☐	☐	☐	☐	☐
U21222	$2.25	☐	☐	☐	☐	☐	☐
U22222	$2.25	☐	☐	☐	☐	☐	☐
U22223	$2.25	☐	☐	☐	☐	☐	☐
U32223	$2.25	☐	☐	☐	☐	☐	☐
U33223	$2.25	☐	☐	☐	☐	☐	☐
U43224	$4.00	☐	☐	†	†	☐	☐
U43234	$4.00	☐	☐	†	†	☐	☐
U43334	$4.00	☐	☐	†	†	☐	☐

#2619 29¢ OLYMPIC BASEBALL

		UL	UR	LL	LR
11111	$2.25	☐	☐	☐	☐

#2620-23 29¢ VOYAGES OF COLUMBUS

1111-1	$2.25	☐	☐	☐	☐
2111-1	$2.25	☐	☐	☐	☐
2122-1	$2.25	☐	☐	☐	☐
2222-1	$2.25	☐	☐	☐	☐
2232-1	$2.25	☐	☐	☐	☐
2242-1	$2.25	☐	☐	☐	☐
3242-1	$2.25	☐	☐	☐	☐
3252-1	$2.25	☐	☐	☐	☐
4463-1	$3.50	☐	☐	☐	☐

1992 COMMEMORATIVES

#2624-29 COLUMBIAN SOUVENIR SHEETS

Set of 6 sheets issued without plate numbers.

#2630 29¢ STOCK EXCHANGE

		UL	UR	LL	LR
A11-1	$2.25	□	□	□	□
A11-2	$2.25	□	□	□	□
A12-2	$2.25	□	□	□	□
A13-2	$2.25	□	□	□	□
A23-2	$2.25	□	□	□	□
A33-2	$2.25	□	□	□	□
A44-2	$2.25	□	□	□	□
A55-2	$2.25	□	□	□	□
A55-3	$3.50	□	□	□	□
A66-3	$2.25	□	□	□	□

#2631-34 29¢ SPACE

1111	$2.25	□	□	□	□

#2635 29¢ ALASKA HIGHWAY

11111-1	$2.25	□	□	□	□
11211-1	$2.25	□	□	□	□
22211-1	$2.25	□	□	□	□
22311-1	$2.25	□	□	□	□

#2636 29¢ KENTUCKY STATEHOOD

S11111	$2.25	□	□	□	□

#2637-41 29¢ SUMMER OLYMPICS

Block of 10 (5 x 2)

S11111	$5.25	□	□	□	□

#2646a 29¢ HUMMINGBIRDS BOOKLET UNFOLDED & UNBOUND pane of 5

		L
A1111111	$7.50	□
A2212112	$7.50	□
A2212122	$7.50	□
A2212222	$7.50	□
A2222222	$7.50	□

$5.80 - **BK201** - 4 panes of 5 stamps

A1111111	$10.50	□
A2212112	$10.50	□
A2212122	$15.00	□
A2212222	$10.50	□
A2222222	$10.50	□

#2696a 29¢ WILDFLOWERS

Pane of 50 (10 x 5)

		UL	UR	LL	LR
P1111	$25	□	□	□	□
P3333	$25	□	□	□	□

		UL	UR	LL	LR	CUL	CLL
P2222	$25	□	□	□	□	□	□
P4444	$25	□	□	□	□	□	□

#2697 29¢ WORLD WAR II (1992)

Block of 10 (5 x 2)		UL	UR	LL	LR
1111-1	$5.25	□	□	□	□
1211-1	$5.25	□	□	□	□
1212-1	$5.25	□	□	□	□
1213-1	$5.25	□	□	□	□
1223-1	$5.25	□	□	□	□
2223-1	$5.25	□	□	□	□
3223-1	$5.25	□	□	□	□
3323-1	$5.25	□	□	□	□
3423-1	$5.25	□	□	□	□
4422-1	$5.25	□	□	□	□
4432-1	$5.25	□	□	□	□
4442-1	$5.25	□	□	□	□
4532-1	$5.25	□	□	□	□
4542-1	$5.25	□	□	□	□
4632-1	$10.00	□	†	□	†
5632-1	$5.25	□	□	□	□

#2698 29¢ DOROTHY PARKER

S11111	$2.25	□	□	□	□

#2699 29¢ THEODORE VON KARMAN

S1111	$2.25	□	□	□	□

#2700-03 29¢ MINERALS

11111-1	$2.25	□	□	□	□
21111-1	$2.25	□	□	□	□
32111-1	$2.25	□	□	□	□
32121-1	$2.25	□	□	□	□
32221-1	$3.50	□	□	□	□
42232-1	$2.25	□	□	□	□
42233-1	$2.25	□	□	□	□
43233-1	$2.25	□	□	□	□
53233-1	$2.25	□	□	□	□
54233-1	$3.50	□	□	□	□
55233-1	$2.25	□	□	□	□

#2704 29¢ JUAN RODRIQUEZ CABRILLO

S111111-S1	$2.25	□	□	□	□
S222222-S1	$2.25	□	□	□	□
S333333-S1	$2.25	□	□	□	□
S444444-S1	$2.25	□	□	□	□

#2709a 29¢ WILD ANIMALS BOOKLET UNFOLDED & UNBOUND pane of 5

		T
K1111	$2.75	□

$5.80 - **BK202** - 4 panes of 5 stamps

K1111	$10.50	□

#2710 29¢ MADONNA

		UL	UR	LL	LR	CUL	CUR
1111-1	$2.25	□	□	□	□	□	□
1112-1	$2.25	□	□	□	□	□	□
2223-1	$2.25	□	□	□	□	□	□
3334-1	$2.25	□	□	□	□	□	□
4445-1	$2.25	□	□	□	□	□	□

1992 COMMEMORATIVES

#2710a 29¢ MADONNA BOOKLET

UNFOLDED & UNBOUND pane of 10

		T
1	$5.25	☐

$5.80 - **BK202A** - 2 panes of 10 stamps

1	$10.50	☐

#2711-14 29¢ CHRISTMAS TOYS

		UL	UR	LL	LR	CUL	CLL
P11111	$2.25	☐	☐	☐	☐	☐	☐
P22222	$2.25	☐	☐	☐	☐	☐	☐
P33333	$2.25	☐	☐	☐	☐	☐	☐
P44444	$2.25	☐	☐	☐	☐	☐	☐

#2718a 29¢ CHRISTMAS TOYS BOOKLET

UNFOLDED & UNBOUND pane of 4

		L
A111111	$2.75	☐
A112211	$250.00	☐
A222222	$2.75	☐

$5.80 - **BK203** - 5 panes of 4 stamps

A111111	$10.50	☐
A112211	$10.50	☐
A222222	$10.50	☐

#2719a 29¢ TOY TRAIN ATM BOOKLET

$5.22 - 1 pane of 18 stamps

		C
V11111	$10.00	☐

#2720 29¢ HAPPY NEW YEAR

		UL	UR	LL	LR
1111-A1	$2.25	☐	☐	☐	☐
1111-A4	$2.25	☐	☐	☐	☐
2222-A2	$2.25	☐	☐	☐	☐
3333-A2	$2.25	☐	☐	☐	☐
3333-A3	$2.25	☐	☐	☐	☐
3333-A4	$2.25	☐	☐	☐	☐
3333-A5	$2.25	☐	☐	☐	☐
4444-A4	$3.50	☐	☐	☐	☐
4444-A5	$2.25	☐	☐	☐	☐
6226-A4	$2.25	☐	☐	☐	☐
6266-A4	$5.00	☐	☐	☐	☐
6622-A2	$5.00	☐	☐	☐	☐
7266-A4	$2.25	☐	☐	☐	☐
7333-A5	$2.25	☐	☐	☐	☐
8333-A5	$2.25	☐	☐	☐	☐

1993 COMMEMORATIVES

#2721 29¢ ELVIS PRESLEY

11111	$2.25	☐	☐	☐	☐
22212	$2.25	☐	☐	☐	☐
22222	$2.25	☐	☐	☐	☐

#2722 29¢ OKLAHOMA

S1111	$2.25	☐	☐	☐	☐

1993 COMMEMORATIVES

#2723 29¢ HANK WILLIAMS

Perf. 10		UL	UR	LL	LR
S111111	$2.25	☐	☐	☐	☐

#2723a 29¢ HANK WILLIAMS

Perf. 11.1 x 11.45

S111111	$100.00	☐	☐	☐	☐

#2724-30 29¢ ROCK & ROLL

Block of 8 (2 x 4)

S111111	$4.50	☐	☐	☐	☐

Block of 10 (5 x 2) with banner

		T
S111111	$5.25	☐

#2737a,b 29¢ ROCK & ROLL BOOKLET

UNFOLDED & UNBOUND pane of 8 (a)

A13113	$40.00	☐
A22222	$4.50	☐

Unfolded panes of 7 from plate A11111 exist and were available only in year sets.

UNFOLDED & UNBOUND pane of 4 (b)

A13113	$40.00	☐
A22222	$2.25	☐

$5.80 - **BK204** - 1 pane of 4 stamps and 2 panes of 8 stamps

A11111	$10.50	☐
A13113	$10.50	☐
A22222	$10.50	☐
A44444	$10.50	☐

Panes in the booklet may contain different plate numbers.

#2745a 29¢ SPACE FANTASY BOOKLET

UNFOLDED & UNBOUND pane of 5

		L
1111	$2.75	☐
1211	$2.75	☐
2222	$2.75	☐

$5.80 - **BK207** - 4 panes of 5 stamps

1111	$10.50	☐
1211	$10.50	☐
2222	$10.50	☐

#2746 29¢ PERCY JULIAN

		UL	UR	LL	LR
111111-1	$2.25	☐	☐	☐	☐
112211-1	$2.25	☐	☐	☐	☐
122211-1	$2.25	☐	☐	☐	☐

#2747 29¢ OREGON TRAIL

11111-1	$2.25	☐	☐	☐	☐
11121-1	$2.25	☐	☐	☐	☐
11131-1	$2.25	☐	☐	☐	☐
21131-1	$4.00	☐	☐	☐	☐

#2748 29¢ WORLD UNIVERSITY GAMES

11111	$2.25	☐	☐	☐	☐

1993 COMMEMORATIVES

#2749 29¢ GRACE KELLY

		UL	UR	LL	LR
S1	$2.25	☐	☐	☐	☐
S2	$2.25	☐	☐	☐	☐

#2750-53 29¢ CIRCUS

P11111	$2.25	☐	☐	☐	☐
P22222	$2.25	☐	☐	☐	☐
P33333	$2.25	☐	☐	☐	☐

#2754 29¢ CHEROKEE STRIP

1111-A1	$2.25	☐	☐	☐	☐
1111-A2	$2.25	☐	☐	☐	☐
1111-A3	$2.25	☐	☐	☐	☐
2222-A2	$2.25	☐	☐	☐	☐
3333-A3	$2.25	☐	☐	☐	☐
3333-A4	$2.25	☐	☐	☐	☐
4444-A4	$2.25	☐	☐	☐	☐
4444-A5	$2.25	☐	☐	☐	☐
5555-A5	$2.25	☐	☐	☐	☐

#2755 29¢ DEAN ACHESON

S1	$2.25	☐	☐	☐	☐
S2	$2.25	☐	☐	☐	☐

#2756-59 29¢ SPORTING HORSES

1111-S1	$2.25	☐	☐	☐	☐
2222-S2	$2.25	☐	☐	☐	☐
3333-S1	$2.25	☐	☐	☐	☐
3333-S2	$2.25	☐	☐	☐	☐
3333-S3	$2.25	☐	☐	☐	☐
4444-S1	$2.25	☐	☐	☐	☐
4444-S2	$2.25	☐	☐	☐	☐
4444-S3	$2.25	☐	☐	☐	☐
5555-S3	$4.50	☐	☐	☐	☐

#2764a 29¢ SPRING GARDEN FLOWERS BOOKLET

UNFOLDED & UNBOUND pane of 5

		L
1	$3.25	☐

$5.80 - **BK208** - 4 panes of 5 stamps

1	$10.50	☐
2	$10.50	☐

#2765 29¢ WORLD WAR II (1993)

Block of 10 (5 x 2)		UL	UR	LL	LR
1111-1	$5.25	☐	☐	☐	☐
1112-1	$5.25	☐	☐	☐	☐
1122-1	$5.25	☐	☐	☐	☐
1232-1	$5.25	☐	☐	☐	☐
2232-1	$5.25	☐	☐	☐	☐
3242-1	$5.25	☐	☐	☐	☐
3243-1	$5.25	☐	☐	☐	☐
3353-1	$5.25	☐	☐	☐	☐
5355-1	$5.25	☐	☐	☐	☐
5555-1	$5.25	☐	☐	☐	☐
5566-1	$5.25	☐	☐	☐	☐
5576-1	$5.25	☐	☐	☐	☐

#2766 29¢ JOE LOUIS

		UL	UR	LL	LR
1111-1	$2.25	☐	☐	☐	☐
1112-1	$2.25	☐	☐	☐	☐
2222-1	$2.25	☐	☐	☐	☐
3222-1	$2.25	☐	☐	☐	☐
3322-1	$8.00	☐	†	☐	☐
3332-1	$2.25	☐	☐	☐	☐

#2770a 29¢ BROADWAY MUSICALS BOOKLET

UNFOLDED & UNBOUND pane of 4

		T
A11111	$2.25	☐
A11121	$2.25	☐
A22222	$2.25	☐

$5.80 - **BK209** - 5 panes of 4 stamps

A11111	$10.50	☐
A11121	$10.50	☐
A22222	$10.50	☐
A23232	$10.50	☐
A23233	$10.50	☐

#2771-74 29¢ COUNTRY MUSIC

		UL	UR	LL	LR
S111111	$2.25	☐	☐	☐	☐

Block of 8 (4 x 2) with banner

		T
S111111	$4.50	☐

#2778a 29¢ COUNTRY MUSIC BOOKLET

UNFOLDED & UNBOUND pane of 4

A222222	$2.25	☐

$5.80 - **BK210** - 5 panes of 4 stamps

A111111	$10.50	☐
A222222	$10.50	☐
A333323	$400.00	☐
A333333	$10.50	☐
A422222	$10.50	☐

#2779-82 29¢ NATIONAL POSTAL MUSEUM

		UL	UR	LL	LR
111111-A1	$2.25	☐	☐	☐	☐
115115-A1	$2.25	☐	☐	☐	☐
115155-A1	$2.25	☐	☐	☐	☐
155155-A1	$2.25	☐	☐	☐	☐
222222-A2	$2.25	☐	☐	☐	☐
232222-A1	$2.25	☐	☐	☐	☐
232222-A2	$10.00	☐	☐	☐	☐
232222-A3	$2.25	☐	☐	☐	☐
333333-A1	$2.25	☐	☐	☐	☐
433433-A1	$2.25	☐	☐	☐	☐
433444-A1	$2.25	☐	☐	☐	☐
433444-A3	$2.25	☐	☐	☐	☐
434444-A1	$2.25	☐	☐	☐	☐
434444-A3	$2.25	☐	☐	☐	☐
444444-A1	$2.25	☐	☐	☐	☐
444444-A3	$2.25	☐	☐	☐	☐

Plate numbers read from outside inwards.

1993 COMMEMORATIVES

#2783-84 29¢ SIGN LANGUAGE

		UL	UR	LL	LR
S1111	$2.25	☐	☐	☐	☐

#2785-88 29¢ YOUTH CLASSICS

1111-A1	$2.75	☐	☐	☐	☐
2222-A2	$2.75	☐	☐	☐	☐
2232-A2	$10.00	☐	†	☐	†
2332-A2	$2.75	☐	☐	☐	☐
3332-A1	$2.75	☐	☐	☐	☐
3332-A2	$2.75	☐	☐	☐	☐
3443-A1	$2.75	☐	☐	☐	☐
3443-A3	$2.75	☐	☐	☐	☐
3443-A4	$2.75	☐	☐	☐	☐
3443-A5	$5.00	☐	☐	☐	☐
4554-A5	$2.75	☐	☐	☐	☐
4655-A6	$2.75	☐	☐	☐	☐
4765-A6	$2.75	☐	☐	☐	☐
5877-A6	$2.75	☐	☐	☐	☐

#2789 29¢ MADONNA

		UL	UR	LL	LR	CUL	CUR
111-1	$2.25	☐	☐	☐	☐	☐	☐
211-1	$2.25	☐	☐	☐	☐	☐	☐
212-1	$2.25	☐	☐	☐	☐	☐	☐
222-1	$2.25	☐	☐	☐	☐	☐	☐
433-1	$2.25	☐	☐	☐	☐	☐	☐
434-1	$2.25	☐	☐	☐	☐	☐	☐
435-1	$10.00	†	☐	☐	†	☐	☐
535-1	$5.00	☐	☐	☐	☐	☐	☐
546-1	$5.00	☐	☐	☐	☐	☐	☐
547-1	$2.25	☐	☐	☐	☐	☐	☐
647-1	$4.00	☐	☐	☐	☐	☐	☐

#2790a 29¢ MADONNA BOOKLET

UNFOLDED & UNBOUND pane of 4

		T
11111-K1	$2.25	☐
33333-K1	$2.25	☐
44444-K1	$2.25	☐
55555-K2	$75.00	☐

$5.80 - **BK211** - 5 panes of 4 stamps

11111-K1	$10.50	☐
22222-K2	$10.50	☐
33333-K1	$10.50	☐
44444-K1	$10.50	☐
55555-K2	$10.50	☐
66666-K2	$10.50	☐

#2791-94 29¢ HOLIDAY DESIGNS

		UL	UR	LL	LR	CLL	CLR
111111	$2.25	☐	☐	☐	☐	☐	☐
222222	$2.25	☐	☐	☐	☐	☐	☐

#2798a,b 29¢ HOLIDAY DESIGNS BOOKLET

UNFOLDED & UNBOUND pane of 10

		T
111111	$5.25	☐

$5.80 - **BK212** - 2 panes of 10 stamps

111111	$10.50	☐
222222	$10.50	☐

These booklet panes exist in two arrangements:
#2798a with #2795 in UL corner.
#2798b with #2797 in UL corner.

#2802a 29¢ HOLIDAY DESIGNS SELF ADHESIVE BOOKLET

$3.48 - 1 pane of 12 stamps

		C
V111-1111	$6.75	☐
V222-1222	$6.75	☐
V222-2112	$6.75	☐
V222-2122	$6.75	☐
V222-2221	$6.75	☐
V222-2222	$6.75	☐
V333-3333	$6.75	☐

Also issued in coil strips of 12 with plate numbers.

Strip of 8		B
V1111111	$6.50	☐

#2803a 29¢ SNOWMAN ATM BOOKLET

$5.22 - 1 pane of 18 stamps

		C
V1111	$10.00	☐
V2222	$10.00	☐

#2804 29¢ MARIANA ISLANDS

		UL	UR	LL	LR
12111-1	$2.25	☐	☐	☐	☐
12321-1	$2.25	☐	☐	☐	☐
12331-1	$2.25	☐	☐	☐	☐
13331-1	$2.25	☐	☐	☐	☐
13332-1	$2.25	☐	☐	☐	☐
13432-1	$2.25	☐	☐	☐	☐
23432-1	$2.25	☐	☐	☐	☐
33442-1	$2.25	☐	☐	☐	☐
33443-1	$2.25	☐	☐	☐	☐
45653-1	$2.25	☐	☐	☐	☐
45753-1	$2.25	☐	☐	☐	☐

#2805 29¢ PUERTO RICO

S11111	$2.25	☐	☐	☐	☐

#2806 29¢ AIDS AWARENESS

S111	$2.25	☐	☐	☐	☐

#2806a 29¢ AIDS AWARENESS BOOKLET

UNFOLDED & UNBOUND pane of 5

		T
K111	$2.75	☐

$2.90 - **BK213** - 2 panes of 5 stamps

K111	$5.25	☐

1994 COMMEMORATIVES

#2807-11 29c WINTER OLYMPICS

Block of 10 (5 x 2)		T	B
P1111	$5.25	□	□
P2222	$5.25	□	□

#2812 29c EDWARD R. MURROW

		UL	UR	LL	LR
1	$2.25	□	□	□	□

#2813a 29c LOVE SUNRISE SELF ADHESIVE BOOKLET

$5.22 - 1 pane of 18 stamps

		C
B111-1	$10.00	□
B111-2	$10.00	□
B111-3	$10.00	□
B111-4	$10.00	□
B111-5	$125.00	□
B121-5	$10.00	□
B221-5	$10.00	□
B222-4	$10.00	□
B222-5	$10.00	□
B222-6	$10.00	□
B333-5	$25.00	□
B333-7	$10.00	□
B333-8	$10.00	□
B333-9	$10.00	□
B333-10	$10.00	□
B333-11	$10.00	□
B333-12	$10.00	□
B333-14	$100.00	□
B333-17	$10.00	□
B334-11	$500.00	□
B344-11	$50.00	□
B344-12	$10.00	□
B344-13	$10.00	□
B434-10	$125.00	□
B444-7	$10.00	□
B444-8	$10.00	□
B444-9	$10.00	□
B444-10	$10.00	□
B444-13	$10.00	□
B444-14	$10.00	□
B444-15	$10.00	□
B444-16	$10.00	□
B444-17	$10.00	□
B444-18	$10.00	□
B444-19	$10.00	□
B555-20	$10.00	□
B555-21	$10.00	□

The colors on combination 555 appear in a different order

Also issued in coil strips of 18 with plate numbers.

Strip of 5		above denomination
B1	$6.00	□

#2814a 29c VICTORIAN LOVE BOOKLET

UNFOLDED & UNBOUND pane of 10

		T
A11111	$5.25	□

$5.80 - **BK214** - 2 panes of 10 stamps

A11111	$10.50	□
A11311	$10.50	□
A12111	$15.00	□
A12112	$10.50	□
A12211	$15.00	□
A12212	$10.50	□
A21222	$10.50	□
A21311	$20.00	□
A22122	$10.50	□
A22222	$15.00	□
A22322	$10.50	□

#2814C 29c LOVE

		UL	UR	LL	LR
1111-1	$2.25	□	□	□	□

#2815 52c LOVE

1111-1	$4.50	□	□	□	□
2222-1	$12.00	□	□	□	□

#2816 29c ALLISON DAVIS

S1	$2.25	□	□	□	□
S2	$3.00	□	□	□	□

#2817 29c YEAR OF THE DOG

S1111	$2.25	□	□	□	□

#2818 29c BUFFALO SOLDIERS

S1111-1	$2.25	□	□	□	□
S2222-2	$2.25	□	□	□	□

#2819-28 29c SILENT SCREEN STARS

Block of 10 (5 x 2)

111-1	$5.25	‡	‡	□	□
211-1	$5.25	‡	‡	□	□

#2833a 29c SUMMER GARDEN FLOWERS BOOKLET

UNFOLDED & UNBOUND pane of 5

		L
2	$2.75	□

$5.80 - **BK215** - 4 panes of 5 stamps

1	$10.50	□
2	$10.50	□

#2834 29c WORLD CUP SOCCER

		UL	UR	LL	LR
S1111	$2.25	□	□	□	□

#2835 40c WORLD CUP SOCCER

S1111	$3.00	□	□	□	□

#2836 50c WORLD CUP SOCCER

S1111	$4.00	□	□	□	□

1994 COMMEMORATIVES

#2837 $1.19 WORLD CUP SOUVENIR SHEET

issued without plate numbers

#2838 29c WORLD WAR II (1994)

Block of 10 (5 x 2)		UL	UR	LL	LR
111111-1	$5.25	☐	☐	☐	☐
222121-1	$5.25	☐	☐	☐	☐
322131-1	$5.25	☐	☐	☐	☐
322232-1	$5.25	☐	☐	☐	☐
323232-1	$5.25	☐	☐	☐	☐
323242-1	$5.25	☐	☐	☐	☐
434353-1	$5.25	☐	☐	☐	☐
434363-1	$5.25	☐	☐	☐	☐
434373-1	$8.00	☐	☐	☐	☐
434383-1	$8.00	☐	☐	☐	☐
534383-1	$5.25	☐	☐	☐	☐
554383-1	$5.25	☐	☐	☐	☐
554393-1	$5.25	☐	☐	☐	☐
654393-1	$5.25	☐	☐	☐	☐
754393-1	$5.25	☐	☐	☐	☐
754494-1	$5.25	☐	☐	☐	☐
846796-1	$5.25	☐	☐	☐	☐
854494-1	$5.25	☐	☐	☐	☐

#2839 29c NORMAN ROCKWELL

1111-1	$2.25	☐	☐	☐	☐

#2840 $2.00 NORMAN ROCKWELL SOUVENIR SHEET

issued without plate numbers

#2841 29c MOON LANDING

issued without plate numbers

#2842 $9.95 MOON LANDING

B1111-1	$70.00	☐	☐	☐	☐
B2222-1	$120.00	☐	☐	☐	☐

#2847a 29c LOCOMOTIVES BOOKLET
UNFOLDED & UNBOUND pane of 5

		T
S11111	$2.75	☐

$5.80 - **BK216** - 4 panes of 5 stamps

S11111	$10.50	☐

#2848 29c GEORGE MEANY

		UL	UR	LL	LR
1	$2.25	☐	☐	☐	☐

#2849-53 29c POPULAR SINGERS

Block of 6 (2 x 3)					
S111111	$3.50	☐	☐	☐	☐

Block of 12 (4 x 3) with banner

		T
S111111	$6.75	☐

#2854-61 29c BLUES AND JAZZ SINGERS

Block of 9 (3 x 3)		UL	UR	LL	LR
P11111	$5.00	☐	☐	☐	☐
P22222	$5.00	☐	☐	☐	☐
P33333	$5.00	☐	☐	☐	☐
Block of 10 (2 x 5)					
P11111	$5.25	☐	☐	☐	☐
P22222	$5.25	☐	☐	☐	☐
P33333	$5.25	☐	☐	☐	☐

Block of 10 (5 x 2) with banner

		T
P11111	$5.25	☐
P22222	$5.25	☐
P33333	$5.25	☐

#2862 29c JAMES THURBER

		UL	UR	LL	LR
1-1	$2.25	☐	☐	☐	☐

#2863-66 29c WONDERS OF THE SEA

B1111	$2.25	☐	☐	☐	☐
B2222	$2.25	☐	☐	☐	☐
B3333	$4.00	☐	☐	☐	☐

#2867-68 29c WHOOPING CRANES

B1111-1	$2.25	☐	☐	☐	☐
B2222-1	$2.25	☐	☐	☐	☐

#2869 29c LEGENDS OF THE WEST

Pane of 20		(revised)			
S11111	$10.50	‡	‡	☐	‡

#2870 29c LEGENDS OF THE WEST

Pane of 20		(recalled)			
S11111	$150.00	‡	‡	☐	‡

#2871 29c MADONNA

shiny gum					
1111-1	$2.25	☐	☐	☐	☐
1111-2	$4.00	☐	☐	☐	☐
dull gum					
1111-1	$2.25	☐	☐	☐	☐
1111-2	$4.00	☐	☐	☐	☐

#2871b 29c MADONNA BOOKLET
UNFOLDED & UNBOUND pane of 10

		T
1	$5.25	☐
2	$5.25	☐

$5.80 - **BK217** -2 panes of 10 stamps

1	$10.50	☐
2	$10.50	☐

#2872 29c CHRISTMAS STOCKING

		UL	UR	LL	LR
P11111	$2.25	☐	☐	☐	☐
P22222	$2.25	☐	☐	☐	☐
P33333	$2.25	☐	☐	☐	☐

1994 COMMEMORATIVES

#2872a 29c CHRISTMAS STOCKING BOOKLET

UNFOLDED & UNBOUND pane of 20

		R
P11111	$10.50	□
P22222	$10.50	□
P33333	$1000.00	□
P44444	$10.50	□

$5.80 - **BK218** - 1 pane of 20 stamps

P11111	$10.50	□
P22222	$10.50	□
P33333	$10.50	□
P44444	$10.50	□

#2873a 29c SANTA SELF ADHESIVE BOOKLET

$3.48 - 1 pane of 12 stamps

		C
V1111	$6.75	□

Also issued in coil strips of 12 with plate numbers.

Strip of 5		B
V1111	$6.00	□

#2874a 29c CARDINAL ATM BOOKLET

$5.22 - 1 pane of 18 stamps

V1111	$10.00	□
V2222	$10.00	□

#2875 $8.00 BEP ANNIVERSARY SOUVENIR SHEET

issued without plate numbers

#2876 29c YEAR OF THE BOAR

		UL	UR	LL	LR
S1111	$2.25	□	□	□	□

RATE CHANGE AND 1995 REGULAR ISSUES

#2877 (3c) DOVE MAKE UP RATE

		UL	UR	LL	LR
A111	$0.35	□	†	□	□
A121	$0.35	□	†	□	□
A131	$0.70	□	†	□	□
A241	$0.35	□	□	□	□
A242	$0.35	□	□	□	□
A252	$0.50	□	□	□	□
A352	$0.70	□	□	□	□
A353	$0.50	□	□	□	□
A363	$0.50	□	□	□	□
A364	$0.35	□	□	□	□
A374	$0.50	□	□	□	□
A375	$0.50	□	□	□	□
A475	$0.50	□	□	□	□
A575	$0.35	□	□	□	□

RATE CHANGE AND 1995 REGULAR ISSUES

#2877 (3c) DOVE MAKE UP RATE

		UL	UR	LL	LR
A686	$0.50	□	□	□	□
A687	$0.50	□	□	□	□
A697	$0.50	□	□	□	□
A797	$0.50	□	□	□	□
A798	$1.00	□	□	□	□
A10 10 10	$0.50	□	□	□	□
A11 10 10	$0.50	□	□	□	□
A11 11 11	$0.35	□	□	□	□
A14 14 14	$0.35	□	□	□	□
A14 15 14	$2.00	†	□	□	□
A14 16 14	$0.70	□	□	□	□
A14 17 14	$0.35	□	□	□	□
A15 18 15	$0.50	□	□	□	□
A16 18 15	$0.70	□	□	□	□
A16 19 15	$0.35	□	□	□	□
A16 19 16	$0.35	□	□	□	□
A17 20 16	$0.35	□	□	□	□
A17 22 16	$0.35	□	□	□	□
A17 23 17	$1.00	□	□	□	□
A17 25 17	$0.35	□	□	□	□
A18 25 17	$0.70	□	□	□	□
A18 26 17	$0.50	□	□	□	□
A18 26 18	$0.50	□	□	□	□
A19 26 18	$1.00	□	□	□	□
A19 28 18	$0.35	□	□	□	□
A19 29 18	$0.35	□	□	□	□
A21 21 21	$0.50	□	□	□	□
A21 24 21	$5.00	□	†	□	†
A21 24 22	$0.50	□	□	□	□
A21 27 22	$0.35	□	□	□	□

#2878 (3c) DOVE MAKE UP RATE

S111	$0.35	□	□	□	□

#2879 (20c) G OLD GLORY
Postcard Rate (yellow)

11111	$1.75	□	□	□	□

#2880 (20c) G OLD GLORY
Postcard Rate (yellow)

S11111	$1.75	□	□	□	□

#2881 (32c) G OLD GLORY

1111	$4.00	□	□	□	□

#2881a (32c) G OLD GLORY BOOKLET

Perf. 11.2 x 11.1

$3.20 - **BK219** - 1 pane of 10 stamps

		T
1111	$6.00	□

#2882 (32c) G OLD GLORY

		UL	UR	LL	LR
S1111	$2.50	□	□	□	□

RATE CHANGE AND 1995 REGULAR ISSUES

#2883a (32c) G OLD GLORY BOOKLET

Perf. 10.0 x 9.8

$3.20 - **BK220** - 1 pane of 10 stamps

		T
1111	$6.00	☐
2222	$6.00	☐

$6.40 - **BK221** - 2 panes of 10 stamps

1111	$11.50	☐
2222	$11.50	☐

#2884a (32c) G OLD GLORY BOOKLET

$6.40 - **BK222** - 2 panes of 10 stamps

A1111	$11.50	☐
A1211	$11.50	☐
A2222	$11.50	☐
A3333	$11.50	☐
A4444	$11.50	☐

Some books exist with a combination of numbers.

#2885a (32c) G OLD GLORY BOOKLET

$6.40 - **BK223** - 2 panes of 10 stamps

K1111	$11.50	☐

#2886a (32c) G OLD GLORY SELF ADHESIVE BOOKLET

$5.76 - 1 pane of 18 stamps

		C
V11111	$11.50	☐
V22222	$11.50	☐

Also issued in coil strips of 18 with plate numbers.

Strip of 5		B
V11111	$5.00	☐

#2887a (32c) G OLD GLORY ATM BOOKLET

$5.76 - 1 pane of 18 stamps
issued without plate numbers

#2888 (25c) G OLD GLORY COIL

First Class Presort Rate (blue)

Strips of 5		B
S11111	$5.00	☐

#2889 (32c) G OLD GLORY COIL

Strips of 5

1111	$5.50	☐
2222	$5.50	☐

> Much of our plate number information stems from studies made by members of the Bureau Issues Association and published in their magazine. Serious plate number collectors should join this organization. For further information write to:
> **Executive Secretary**
> **P.O. Box 2641, Reston, VA 20195**

#2890 (32c) G OLD GLORY COIL

Strips of 5		B
A1111	$5.50	☐
A1112	$5.50	☐
A1113	$5.50	☐
A1211	$5.50	☐
A1212	$5.50	☐
A1222	$5.50	☐
A1311	$5.50	☐
A1313	$5.50	☐
A1314	$5.50	☐
A1324	$5.50	☐
A1417	$5.50	☐
A1433	$5.50	☐
A2211	$5.50	☐
A2212	$5.50	☐
A2213	$5.50	☐
A2214	$5.50	☐
A2223	$5.50	☐
A2313	$5.50	☐
A3113	$5.50	☐
A3114	$5.50	☐
A3314	$5.50	☐
A3315	$5.50	☐
A3323	$5.50	☐
A3324	$5.50	☐
A3423	$5.50	☐
A3426	$5.50	☐
A3433	$5.50	☐
A3435	$5.50	☐
A3436	$5.50	☐
A4426	$5.50	☐
A4427	$5.50	☐
A4435	$150.00	☐
A5327	$5.50	☐
A5417	$5.50	☐
A5427	$5.50	☐
A5437	$5.50	☐

#2891 (32c) G OLD GLORY COIL

Strips of 5 perforated

S1111	$5.50	☐

#2892 (32c) G OLD GLORY COIL

Strips of 5 rouletted

S1111	$5.50	☐
S2222	$5.50	☐

#2893 (5c) G OLD GLORY COIL

Strips of 5 Non-Profit Rate (green)

A11111	$2.00	☐
A21111	$2.00	☐

#2897 32c FLAG OVER PORCH

		UL	UR	LL	LR
S11111	$2.50	☐	☐	☐	☐
S22222	$2.50	☐	☐	☐	☐

1995 REGULAR ISSUES

COIL STAMPS

Strips of 5

#2902 (5c) BUTTE COIL

B

S111 $1.50 ☐
S222 $1.50 ☐
S333 $1.50 ☐

#2902B (5c) BUTTE SELF ADHESIVE COIL

S111 $1.50 ☐

#2903 (5c) MOUNTAIN COIL

11111 $1.50 ☐

#2904 (5c) MOUNTAIN COIL

S111 $1.50 ☐

#2904A (5c) MOUNTAIN SELF ADHESIVE COIL

V222222 $1.50 ☐
V333323 $1.50 ☐
V333333 $1.50 ☐
V333342 $1.50 ☐
V333343 $1.50 ☐

#2905 (10c) AUTOMOBILE COIL

S111 $2.50 ☐
S222 $2.50 ☐
S333 $2.50 ☐

#2906 (10c) AUTOMOBILE SELF ADHESIVE COIL

S111 $2.50 ☐

#2907 (10c) EAGLE AND SHIELD SELF ADHESIVE COIL

S11111 $2.50 ☐

#2908 (15c) AUTO TAIL FIN COIL

11111 $3.00 ☐

#2909 (15c) AUTO TAIL FIN COIL

S11111 $3.00 ☐

#2910 (15c) AUTO TAIL FIN SELF ADHESIVE COIL

S11111 $3.00 ☐

#2911 (25c) JUKE BOX COIL

111111 $3.50 ☐
212222 $3.50 ☐
222222 $3.50 ☐
332222 $3.50 ☐

#2912 (25c) JUKE BOX COIL

S11111 $3.50 ☐
S22222 $3.50 ☐

#2912A (25c) JUKE BOX SELF ADHESIVE COIL

B

S11111 $3.50 ☐

#2913 32c FLAG OVER PORCH COIL

shiny gum
11111 $5.50 ☐
22221 $5.50 ☐
22222 $5.50 ☐
semi-gloss gum
11111 $5.50 ☐
22222 $5.50 ☐
22322 $12.50 ☐
33333 $5.50 ☐
34333 $5.50 ☐
44444 $5.50 ☐
45444 $5.50 ☐
66646 $5.50 ☐
66666 $5.50 ☐
77767 $5.50 ☐
78767 $5.50 ☐
99969 $5.50 ☐

#2914 32c FLAG OVER PORCH COIL

S11111 $5.50 ☐

#2915 32c FLAG OVER PORCH SELF ADHESIVE COIL

V11111 $5.50 ☐

#2915A 32c FLAG OVER PORCH SELF ADHESIVE COIL

Perf. 10
66666 $5.50 ☐
78777 $5.50 ☐
87888 $5.50 ☐
87898 $5.50 ☐
88888 $5.50 ☐
88898 $5.50 ☐
89878 $5.50 ☐
89888 $5.50 ☐
89898 $5.50 ☐
89899 $5.50 ☐
97898 $5.50 ☐
98878 $5.50 ☐
99899 $5.50 ☐
99999 $5.50 ☐

#2915B 32c FLAG OVER PORCH SELF ADHESIVE COIL

S11111 $5.50 ☐

#2915C 32c FLAG OVER PORCH SELF ADHESIVE COIL

Perf. 11
55555 $5.50 ☐
66666 $5.50 ☐

1995 REGULAR ISSUES

#2916a 32c FLAG OVER PORCH BOOKLET

UNFOLDED & UNBOUND pane of 10

		T
11111	$6.00	☐
$3.20 - **BK225** - 1 pane of 10 stamps		
11111	$6.00	☐
22222	$6.00	☐
33332	$6.00	☐
$6.40 - **BK226** - 2 panes of 10 stamps		
11111	$11.50	☐
22222	$11.50	☐
23222	$11.50	☐
33332	$11.50	☐
44444	$11.50	☐

#2919a 32c FLAG OVER FIELD ATM BOOKLET

$5.76 - 1 pane of 18 stamps

		C
V1111	$11.00	☐

#2920a 32c FLAG OVER PORCH SELF ADHESIVE BOOKLET

$6.40 - 1 pane of 20 stamps and 1 label

V11111	$11.50	☐

#2920c 32c FLAG OVER PORCH SELF ADHESIVE BOOKLET

$6.40 - 1 pane of 20 stamps and 1 label

V12211	$11.50	☐
V12212	$11.50	☐
V12312	$11.50	☐
V12321	$11.50	☐
V12322	$11.50	☐
V12331	$11.50	☐
V13322	$11.50	☐
V13831	$11.50	☐
V13834	$11.50	☐
V13836	$11.50	☐
V22211	$11.50	☐
V23322	$11.50	☐
V23422	$11.50	☐
V23432	$11.50	☐
V34743	$11.50	☐
V34745	$11.50	☐
V42556	$11.50	☐
V45554	$11.50	☐
V56665	$11.50	☐
V65976	$11.50	☐

See Appendix M for a listing of those issues which show a plate position diagram in the margin. Please report any unreported positions to the editor.

1995 REGULAR ISSUES

#2920e 32c FLAG OVER PORCH SELF ADHESIVE BOOKLET

$3.20 - 1 pane of 10 stamps

		T
V11111	$6.00	☐
V12111	$6.00	☐
V23222	$6.00	☐
V31121	$6.00	☐
V32111	$6.00	☐
V32121	$6.00	☐
V44444	$6.00	☐
V55555	$6.00	☐

#2920f 32c FLAG OVER PORCH SELF ADHESIVE BOOKLET

See Appendix K for "MDI" booklets.

#2921a 32c FLAG OVER PORCH SELF ADHESIVE BOOKLET

UNFOLDED & UNBOUND pane of 10

21221	$6.00	☐
22221	$6.00	☐
22222	$6.00	☐
$6.40 - **BK228** - 2 panes of 10 stamps		
11111	$11.50	☐
13111	$11.50	☐
21221	$11.50	☐
22221	$11.50	☐
22222	$11.50	☐
44434	$11.50	☐

#2933//2943

See pages 227-228

1995 COMMEMORATIVES

#2948 (32c) LOVE

		UL	UR	LL	LR
1111-1	$2.50	☐	☐	☐	☐
1112-1	$2.50	☐	☐	☐	☐

#2949a (32c) LOVE SELF ADHESIVE BOOKLET

$6.40 - 1 pane of 20 stamps and 1 label

		C
B1111-1	$11.50	☐
B2222-1	$11.50	☐
B2222-2	$11.50	☐
B3333-2	$11.50	☐

#2950 32c FLORIDA

		UL	UR	LL	LR
P11111	$2.50	☐	☐	☐	☐
P22222	$2.50	☐	☐	☐	☐
P33333	$2.50	☐	☐	☐	☐

1995 COMMEMORATIVES

#2951-54 32c EARTH DAY

		UL	UR	LL	LR
P11111	$2.50	□	□	□	□
P22222	$2.50	□	□	□	□
P33333	$2.50	□	□	□	□
P44444	$2.50	□	□	□	□
P55555	$4.00	□	□	□	□

Block of 8 (4 x 2) with banner

		T	B
P11111	$5.00	□	□
P22222	$5.00	□	□
P33333	$5.00	□	□
P44444	$5.00	□	□
P55555	$8.00	□	□

#2955 32c RICHARD NIXON

		UL	UR	LL	LR
B1111-1	$2.50	□	□	□	□
B1111-2	$5.00	□	□	□	□

#2956 32c BESSIE COLEMAN

1	$2.50	□	□	□	□

#2957 32c LOVE

1111-1	$2.50	□	□	□	□
2111-1	$2.50	□	□	□	□
4222-1	$4.00	□	□	□	□

#2958 55c LOVE

1111-1	$5.00	□	□	□	□

#2959a 32c LOVE BOOKLET
UNFOLDED & UNBOUND pane of 10

		T
1	$6.00	□

$6.40 - **BK229** - 2 panes of 10 stamps

1	$11.50	□

#2960a 55c LOVE
SELF ADHESIVE BOOKLET
$11.00 - 1 pane of 20 stamps and 1 label

		C
B1111-1	$11.50	□
B2222-1	$11.50	□

#2961-65 32c RECREATIONAL SPORTS

Block of 6 (2 x 3)		UL	UR	LL	LR
B1111	$3.75	□	□	□	□

#2966 32c POW/MIA

P11111	$2.50	□	□	□	□
P22222	$2.50	□	□	□	□

The above plate combinations do not include a sixth plate number for the transparent lacquor "color".

#2967 32c MARILYN MONROE

		UL	UR	LL	LR
S111111	$2.50	□	□	□	□
S112211	$2.50	□	□	□	□

#2968 32c TEXAS

P111111	$2.50	□	□	□	□
P222222	$2.50	□	□	□	□
P333333	$4.00	□	□	□	□

#2973a 32c LIGHTHOUSES BOOKLET
UNFOLDED & UNBOUND pane of 5

		L
S11111	$3.00	□

$6.40 - **BK230** - 4 panes of 5 stamps

S11111	$11.50	□

#2974 32c UNITED NATIONS

		UL	UR	LL	LR
B1	$2.50	□	□	□	□

#2975 32c CIVIL WAR
Pane of 20

S1111	$11.50	‡	‡	□	‡

#2976-79 32c CAROUSEL HORSES

P11111	$2.50	□	□	□	□
P22222	$2.50	□	□	□	□
P33333	$2.50	□	□	□	□
P44444	$2.50	□	□	□	□

#2980 32c WOMEN'S SUFFRAGE

P1111-1	$2.50	□	□	□	□
P2222-1	$2.50	□	□	□	□

#2981 32c WORLD WAR II (1995)
Block of 10 (5 x 2)

111111-1	$6.00	□	□	□	□
221111-1	$7.50	□	□	□	□
321111-1	$6.00	□	□	□	□
321121-1	$6.00	□	□	□	□
421121-1	$6.00	□	□	□	□
432121-1	$6.00	□	□	□	□
532221-1	$10.00	†	□	†	□
533231-1	$6.00	□	□	□	□
534231-1	$6.00	□	□	□	□
544231-1	$6.00	□	□	□	□
644231-1	$6.00	□	□	□	□
645231-1	$6.00	□	□	□	□
645241-1	$6.00	□	□	□	□
645242-1	$6.00	□	□	□	□

#2982 32c LOUIS ARMSTRONG

P1111	$2.50	□	□	□	□
P2222	$2.50	□	□	□	□
P3333	$2.50	□	□	□	□

1995 COMMEMORATIVES

#2983-92 32c JAZZ MUSICIANS

Block of 10 (2 x 5)		L	R
P111111	$6.00	☐	☐
P222222	$6.00	☐	☐

Block of 20 (5 x 4) with banner

		T
P111111	$11.50	☐

#2997a 32c FALL GARDEN FLOWERS BOOKLET

UNFOLDED & UNBOUND pane of 5

		L
2	$3.00	☐

$6.40 - **BK231** - 4 panes of 5 stamps

2	$11.50	☐

#2998 60c EDDIE RICHENBACKER

		UL	UR	LL	LR
11111	$5.00	☐	☐	☐	☐

#2999 32c REPUBLIC OF PALAU

P11111	$2.50	☐	☐	☐	☐
P22222	$2.50	☐	☐	☐	☐

#3000 32c AMERICAN COMIC STRIPS

Pane of 20

S1111	$11.50	‡	‡	☐	‡

#3001 32c U. S. NAVAL ACADEMY

P11111	$2.50	☐	☐	☐	☐
P22222	$2.50	☐	☐	☐	☐

#3002 32c TENNESSEE WILLIAMS

P11111	$2.50	☐	☐	☐	☐
P22222	$2.50	☐	☐	☐	☐

#3003 32c MADONNA

1111-1	$5.00	☐	☐	☐	☐
1111-2	$2.50	☐	☐	☐	☐
2222-2	$5.00	☐	☐	☐	☐
3224-2	$2.50	☐	☐	☐	☐
4224-2	$2.50	☐	☐	☐	☐
5224-2	$2.50	☐	☐	☐	☐
5324-2	$5.00	☐	☐	☐	☐
5325-1	$2.50	☐	☐	☐	☐
5427-1	$2.50	☐	☐	☐	☐
6427-1	$2.50	☐	☐	☐	☐

#3003b 32c MADONNA BOOKLET

UNFOLDED & UNBOUND pane of 10

		L
1	$6.00	☐

$6.40 - **BK232** - 2 panes of 10 stamps

1	$11.50	☐

#3004-07 32c SANTA AND CHILDREN

		UL	UR	LL	LR
P1111	$2.50	☐	☐	☐	☐
P2222	$2.50	☐	☐	☐	☐
P3333	$2.50	☐	☐	☐	☐
P4444	$2.50	☐	☐	☐	☐

#3007b,c 32c SANTA AND CHILDREN BOOKLET

UNFOLDED & UNBOUND pane of 10

		T
P1111	$6.00	☐

$6.40 - **BK233** - 2 panes of 10 stamps

P1111	$11.50	☐
P2222	$11.50	☐

Some books exist with a combination of numbers.

#3011a 32c SANTA AND CHILDREN SELF ADHESIVE BOOKLET

$6.40 - 1 pane of 20 stamps and 1 label

		C
V1111	$11.50	☐
V1121	$11.50	☐
V1212	$11.50	☐
V3233	$11.50	☐
V3333	$11.50	☐
V4444	$11.50	☐

#3012a 32c MIDNIGHT ANGEL SELF ADHESIVE BOOKLET

$6.40 - 1 pane of 20 stamps and 1 label

B1111	$11.50	☐
B2222	$11.50	☐
B3333	$11.50	☐

#3012b 32c MIDNIGHT ANGEL SELF ADHESIVE BOOKLET

See Appendix K for "MDI" booklets.

#3013a 32c CHILDREN SLEDDING ATM BOOKLET

$5.76 - 1 pane of 18 stamps

V1111	$11.00	☐

#3014-17 32c SANTA AND CHILDREN SELF ADHESIVE COIL

Strip of 8		B
V1111	$6.50	☐

#3018 32c MIDNIGHT ANGEL SELF ADHESIVE COIL

Strip of 5		
B1111	$5.00	☐

1995 COMMEMORATIVES

#3019-23 32c ANTIQUE AUTOMOBILES

Block of 6		UL	UR	LL	LR
S1111	$3.75	☐	☐	☐	☐

1996 COMMEMORATIVES

#3024 32c UTAH

P11111	$2.50	☐	☐	☐	☐
P22222	$2.50	☐	☐	☐	☐

#3029a 32c WINTER GARDEN FLOWERS BOOKLET

UNFOLDED & UNBOUND pane of 5

		L
1	$3.00	☐

$6.40 - **BK234** - 4 panes of 5 stamps

1	$11.50	☐

#3030a 32c LOVE SELF ADHESIVE BOOKLET

$6.40 - 1 pane of 20 stamps and 1 label

		C
B1111-1	$11.50	☐
B1111-2	$11.50	☐
B2222-1	$11.50	☐
B2222-2	$11.50	☐

#3030b 32c LOVE SELF ADHESIVE BOOKLET

See Appendix K for "MDI" booklets.

1996 REGULAR ISSUE

#3032 2c WOODPECKER

		UL	UR	LL	LR
11111	$0.25	☐	☐	☐	☐
11121	$0.25	☐	☐	☐	☐
22222	$0.25	☐	☐	☐	☐

#3033 3c BLUEBIRD

1111	$0.35	☐	☐	☐	☐

#3044 1c KESTREL COIL

Strip of 5		B
1111	$0.50	☐

#3048a 20c BLUE JAY SELF ADHESIVE BOOKLET

$2.00 - 1 pane of 10 stamps

		C
S1111	$4.00	☐

1996 REGULAR ISSUE

#3049a 20c YELLOW ROSE SELF ADHESIVE BOOKLET

$6.40 - 1 pane of 20 stamps and 1 label

		C
S1111	$11.50	☐
S2222	$11.50	☐

$9.60 - 1 pane of 30 stamps

		B
S1111	$17.00	☐

$4.80 - 1 pane of 15 stamps and 1 label

S1111	$8.75	☐

#3053 20c BLUE JAY SELF ADHESIVE COIL

Strip of 5		
S1111	$3.00	☐

1996 COMMEMORATIVES

#3058 32c ERNEST E. JUST

		UL	UR	LL	LR
B1111	$2.50	☐	☐	☐	☐

#3059 32c SMITHSONIAN

P1111	$2.50	☐	☐	☐	☐
P2222	$2.50	☐	☐	☐	☐

#3060 32c YEAR OF THE RAT

S1111	$2.50	☐	☐	☐	☐

#3061-64 32c PIONEERS OF COMMUNICATION

P11111	$2.50	☐	☐	☐	☐
P22222	$2.50	☐	☐	☐	☐

#3065 32c FULBRIGHT SCHOLARSHIP

1111-1	$2.50	☐	☐	☐	☐

#3066 50c JACQUELINE COCHRANE

1111-1	$4.50	☐	☐	☐	☐
2111-1	$4.50	☐	☐	☐	☐
2212-1	$10.00	☐	☐	☐	☐
2222-1	$4.50	☐	☐	☐	☐
3232-1	$4.50	☐	☐	☐	☐
4242-1	$4.50	☐	☐	☐	☐
4244-1	$4.50	☐	☐	☐	☐
5345-1	$4.50	☐	☐	☐	☐
5353-1	$4.50	☐	☐	☐	☐
6353-1	$4.50	☐	☐	☐	☐
6363-1	$4.50	☐	☐	☐	☐
7777-1	$4.50	☐	☐	☐	☐

#3067 32c MARATHON

B1111	$2.50	☐	☐	☐	☐

1996 COMMEMORATIVES

#3068 32c OLYMPIC GAMES

Pane of 20		UL	UR	LL	LR
S11111	$11.50	‡	‡	☐	‡

#3069 32c GEORGIA O'KEEFFE

S1111	$2.50	☐	‡	☐	‡

#3070 32c TENNESSEE STATEHOOD

S11111	$2.50	☐	☐	☐	☐

#3071a 32c TENNESSEE STATEHOOD SELF ADHESIVE BOOKLET

$6.40 - 1 pane of 20 stamps

		C
S11111	$11.50	☐

#3072-76 32c AMERICAN INDIAN DANCES

Block of 10 (5 x 2)		T	B
P1111	$6.00	☐	☐
P2222	$6.00	☐	☐
P3333	$6.00	☐	☐

#3077-80 32c PREHISTORIC ANIMALS

		UL	UR	LL	LR
P1111	$2.50	☐	☐	☐	☐
P2222	$2.50	☐	☐	☐	☐
P3333	$2.50	☐	☐	☐	☐

#3081 32c BREAST CANCER AWARENESS

P11111	$2.50	☐	☐	☐	☐
P22222	$2.50	☐	☐	☐	☐

#3082 32c JAMES DEAN

S1111111	$2.50	☐	☐	☐	☐

#3083-86 32c FOLK HEROES

P1111	$2.50	☐	☐	☐	☐
P2222	$2.50	☐	☐	☐	☐

#3087 32c DISCUS THROWER

P1	$2.50	☐	☐	☐	☐

#3088 32c IOWA STATEHOOD

P1111	$2.50	☐	☐	☐	☐
P2222	$2.50	☐	☐	☐	☐

#3089a 32c IOWA SELF ADHESIVE BOOKLET

$6.40 - 1 pane of 20 stamps

		C
B1111	$11.50	☐

> See Appendix M for a listing of those issues which show a plate position diagram in the margin. Please report any unreported positions to the editor.

#3090 32c RURAL FREE DELIVERY

		UL	UR	LL	LR
1111-1	$2.50	☐	☐	☐	☐
1112-1	$4.00	☐	☐	☐	☐
1122-1	$2.50	☐	☐	☐	☐
1123-1	$2.50	☐	☐	☐	☐
2223-1	$4.00	☐	☐	☐	☐
2224-1	$2.50	☐	☐	☐	☐
2235-1	$4.00	☐	☐	☐	☐
3235-1	$2.50	☐	☐	☐	☐
3236-1	$4.00	☐	☐	☐	☐

#3091-95 32c RIVERBOATS SELF ADHESIVE

Block of 6 (2 x 3 or 3 x 2)

V11111	$3.75	☐	☐	☐	☐

#3096-99 32c BIG BAND LEADERS

P111111	$2.50	☐	☐	☐	☐
P222222	$2.50	☐	☐	☐	☐

Block of 8 (4 x 2) with banner

		T
P111111	$5.00	☐
P222222	$5.00	☐

#3100-03 32c SONGWRITERS

		UL	UR	LL	LR
P111111	$2.50	☐	☐	☐	☐
P222222	$2.50	☐	☐	☐	☐

Block of 8 (4 x 2) with banner

		T
P111111	$5.00	☐
P222222	$5.00	☐

#3104 23c F. SCOTT FITZGERALD

		UL	UR	LL	LR
1111	$1.75	☐	☐	☐	☐

#3105 32c ENDANGERED SPECIES

Pane of 15					
P11111	$9.00	☐	‡	☐	‡
P22222	$9.00	☐	‡	☐	‡
P33333	$9.00	☐	‡	☐	‡
P44444	$9.00	☐	‡	☐	‡

#3106 32c COMPUTER TECHNOLOGY

P1111-11	$2.50	☐	☐	☐	☐
P2222-11	$2.50	☐	☐	☐	☐

#3107 32c MADONNA

1111-1	$2.50	☐	☐	☐	☐
1112-1	$2.50	☐	☐	☐	☐
1212-1	$4.00	☐	☐	☐	☐
2222-1	$2.50	☐	☐	☐	☐

1996 COMMEMORATIVES

#3108-11 32c CHRISTMAS FAMILY SCENES

		UL	UR	LL	LR
P1111	$2.50	☐	☐	☐	☐
P2222	$2.50	☐	☐	☐	☐
P3333	$2.50	☐	☐	☐	☐
P4444	$2.50	☐	☐	☐	☐

#3112a 32c MADONNA SELF-ADHESIVE BOOKLET

$6.40 - 1 pane of 20 stamps

		C
1111-1	$11.50	☐
1211-1	$11.50	☐
2222-1	$11.50	☐
2323-1	$11.50	☐
3323-1	$11.50	☐
3333-1	$11.50	☐
3334-1	$11.50	☐
4444-1	$11.50	☐
5544-1	$11.50	☐
5555-1	$11.50	☐
5556-1	$11.50	☐
5556-2	$11.50	☐
5656-2	$11.50	☐
6656-2	$11.50	☐
6666-1	$11.50	☐
6666-2	$11.50	☐
6766-1	$11.50	☐
7887-1	$11.50	☐
7887-2	$11.50	☐
7888-2	$11.50	☐
7988-2	$11.50	☐

#3116a 32c CHRISTMAS FAMILY SCENES SELF-ADHESIVE BOOKLET

$6.40 - 1 pane of 20 stamps

B1111	$11.50	☐
B2222	$11.50	☐
B3333	$11.50	☐

#3117a 32c SKATERS ATM BOOKLET

$5.76 - 1 pane of 18 stamps

V1111	$11.00	☐
V2111	$11.00	☐

#3118 32c HANUKKAH SELF ADHESIVE

		UL	UR	LL	LR
V11111	$2.50	☐	☐	☐	☐

#3119 50c CYCLING

issued without plate numbers

See Appendix M for a listing of those issues which show a plate position diagram in the margin. Please report any unreported positions to the editor.

See Appendix K for a listing of those issues which have appeared in "Blue Cover MDI" booklets.

AIR MAIL ISSUES

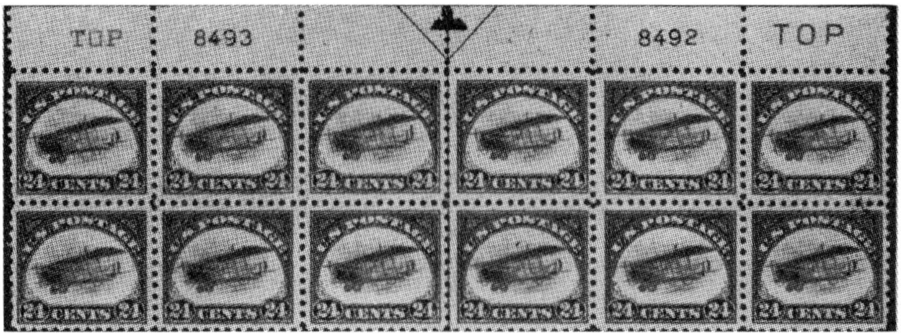

1918 ISSUE

FLAT PRESS Perf.11

#C1 6¢ CURTISS "JENNY"

Plate and Arrow Block of 6

9155 Top posltion only ☐ $750

#C2 16¢ CURTISS "JENNY"

Plate and Arrow Block of 6

8900 Top position only ☐ $1,250

#C3 24¢ CURTISS "JENNY" BICOLORED

Top Position only
Plate Combination 8493-8492
Block of 12 with plates and arrow plus blue TOP and red TOP ☐ $1,600

Block of 12 with plates and arrow plus blue TOP only ☐ $8,000

#C3a 24¢ CURTISS "JENNY" BICOLORED

Block of 4 with center inverted blue plate number only ☐ $1,000,000

1923 ISSUE

FLAT PRESS Perf.11

Block of 6

		TL	TR	L	R	B
#C4	**8¢ PROPELLER**					
14824	$300	☐	☐	☐	☐	☐
14825	$300	☐	☐	☐	☐	☐
14826	$300	☐	☐	☐	☐	☐
14827	$300	☐	☐	☐	☐	☐
#C5	**16¢ AIR SERVICE INSIGNIA**					
14828	$2,100	☐	☐	☐	☐	☐
14829	$2,100	☐	☐	☐	☐	☐
14830	$2,100	☐	☐	☐	☐	☐
14831	$2,100	☐	☐	☐	☐	☐
#C6	**24¢ DE HAVILLAND BIPLANE**					
14840	$2,500	☐	☐	☐	☐	☐
14841	$2,500	☐	☐	☐	☐	☐
14842	$2,500	☐	☐	☐	☐	☐
14843	$2,500	☐	☐	☐	☐	☐

1926-27 ISSUE

FLAT PRESS Perf.11

Block of 6

#C7	**10¢ MAP**					
18246	$50	☐	☐	☐	☐	☐
18247	$50	☐	☐	☐	☐	☐
18248	$50	☐	☐	☐	☐	☐
18249	$50	☐	☐	☐	☐	☐
18250	$60	☐	☐	☐	☐	☐
18903	$75	☐	☐	☐	☐	☐
18904	$75	☐	☐	☐	☐	☐
18905	$75	☐	☐	☐	☐	☐
#C8	**15¢ MAP**					
18745	$60	☐	☐	☐	☐	☐
18746	$60	☐	☐	☐	☐	☐
18747	$60	☐	☐	☐	☐	☐
18748	$60	☐	☐	☐	☐	☐

AIR MAIL ISSUES

1926-27 ISSUE

#C9 20¢ MAP

		TL	TR	L	R	B
18890	$120	□	□Z_1	□	□	□
18891	$120	□	□	□	□	□
18892	$120	□	□Z_2	□	□	□
18893	$120	□	□	□	□	□
18894	$120	□	□	□	□	□
18897	$120	□	□	□	□	□
18898	$120	□	□	□	□	□
18899	$120	□	□	□	□	□

Z_1 The letter F is not on the TR position. It appears on the left side bottom plate inverted with respect to the plate number.

Z_2 The letter F appears on the TR positlon and also appears on the left side bottom plate inverted with respect to the plate number.

1927 ISSUE

FLAT PRESS Perf.11

#C10 10¢ LINDBERGH

18997	$135	□	□	□	□	□
18998	$135	□	□	□	□	□
18999	$135	□	□	□	□	□
19000	$135	□	□	□	□	□
19001	$135	□	□	□	□	□
19002	$135	□	□	□	□	□
19003	$135	□	□	□	□	□
19004	$135	□	□	□	□	□
19005	$135	□	□	□	□	□
19006	$135	□	□	□	□	□
19007	$135	□	□	□	□	□
19008	$135	□	□	□	□	□

#C10a 10¢ LINDBERGH BOOKLET

PANES OF 3

*19414 *19425 19426 19427

See Appendix G for the largest reported plate number percentage by position.

1928 ISSUE

FLAT PRESS Perf.11

#C11 5¢ BEACON BICOLORED

Plate Combination Block of 6

Basic Prices: **TL, TR**

With TOP (red or blue)	$50
Without TOP	$150
With Double TOP (red and blue)	$120

40 BLUE (Vignette) Plates

19545	19546	19547	19548	19573
19574	19575	19576	19577	19578
19579	19580	19597	19598	19599
19600	19608	*19609	*19610	19611
19616	19617	19618	19619	*19639 N
19666	19667	19668	19669	19674
19675	19676	19677	19688	19689
19690	19691	19692	19693	19694

1928 ISSUE

#C11 5¢ BEACON BICOLORED

55 RED (Frame) Plates **Cont.**

19549	19550	19551	19552	19565
19566	19567	19568	19569	19570
19571	19572	19585	19586	19587
19588	*19589	19590	19591	19592
19605	19606	19607	19612	19613
19614	19615	19620	19621	19622
19623	19624	19625	19626	19627
19628	19629	19630	19631	19632
19633	19634	19635	19670	19671
19672	19673	19696	19697	19698
19699	19700	19701	19702	19703

Although between 1,000 and 1,100 number combinations have been recorded, no one plate exists in combination with all others.

The standard plate number plus TOP arrangement is:

Left Pane

RED Plate #	BLUE Plate #	RED TOP

Right Pane

BLUE TOP	BLUE F Plate #	RED F Plate #

Through error the inscription TOP was entered on the left pane of vignette plate 19597. Therefore, all combinations containing that number have the following arrangement:

Left Pane

RED Plate #	BLUE Plate #	RED&BLUE Double TOP

Right Pane

No Top	BLUE F Plate #	RED F Plate #

The F placement on frame plate 19605 is an exception to the rule. On this plate the F is on the **left** pane.

Scattered through the issue there are undoubtedly many scarce to rare plate number combinations, but no one has studied the issue seriously enough to establish their identity. A large showing of Beacon Air Mail combinations, with fine centering throughout, is unheard of.

N Four special vignette plates - 19636, 19637, 19638, 19639 - were used for an experimental printing. There were 100 impressions from each plate. It is said that most of the sheets were never distributed. The question has been raised as to whether any of the plates were placed on general sale. We know the existence of only one of them - F19639 - 19605 in a strip of 3.

AIR MAIL ISSUES

5¢ BEACON AIRMAIL of 1928

RED PLATES listed Vertically
BLUE PLATES listed Horizontally

	19545	F19545	19546	F19546	19547	F19547	19548	F19548	19573	F19573	19574	F19574	19575	F19575	19576	F19576	19577	F19577	19578	F19578	19579	F19579	19580	F19580	19597	F19597	19598	F19598	19599	F19599	19600	F19600	19608	F19608	19609	F19609	19610	F19610	19611	F19611	
19549	●	●	●	●	●	●	●	●	●	●	●	●	●	●	●	●	●	●	●	●	●	●	●	●																	19549
19550	●	●	●	●	●	●	●	●	●	●	●	●	●	●	●	●	●	●	●	●	●	●	●	●																	19550
19551	●	●	●	●	●	●	●	●	●	●	●	●	●	●	●	●	●	●	●	●	●	●	●	●																	19551
19552	●	●	●	●	●	●	●	●	●	●	●	●	●	●	●	●	●	●	●	●	●	●	●	●																	19552
19565	●	●	●	●	●	●	●	●	●	●	●	●	●	●	●	●	●	●	●	●	●	●	●	●																	19565
19566	●	●	●	●	●	●	●	●	●	●	●	●	●	●	●	●	●	●	●	●	●	●	●	●																	19566
19567	●	●	●	●	●	●	●	●	●	●	●	●	●	●	●	●	●	●	●	●	●	●	●	●																	19567
19568	●	●	●	●	●	●	●	●	●	●	●	●	●	●	●	●	●	●	●	●	●	●	●	●																	19568
19569	●	●	●	●	●	●	●	●	●	●	●	●	●	●	●	●	●	●	●	●	●	●	●	●																	19569
19570	●	●	●	●	●	●	●	●	●	●	●	●	●	●	●	●	●	●	●	●	●	●	●	●																	19570
19571	●	●	●	●	●	●	●	●	●	●	●	●	●	●	●	●	●	●	●	●	●	●	●	●	●	●	●	●													19571
19572	●	●	●	●	●	●	●	●	●	●	●	●	●	●	●	●	●	●	●	●	●	●	●	●																	19572
19585	●	●	●	●	●	●	●	●	●	●	●	●	●	●	●	●	●	●	●	●	●	●	●	●	●	●	●	●	●	●	●	●	●	●	●	●	●	●	●	●	19585
19586	●	●	●	●	●	●	●	●	●	●	●	●	●	●	●	●	●	●	●	●	●	●	●	●	●	●	●	●	●	●	●	●	●	●	●	●	●	●	●	●	19586
19587	●	●	●	●	●	●	●	●	●	●	●	●	●	●	●	●	●	●	●	●	●	●	●	●	●	●	●	●	●	●	●	●	●	●	●	●	●	●	●	●	19587
19588	●	●	●	●	●	●	●	●	●	●	●	●	●	●	●	●	●	●	●	●	●	●	●	●	●	●	●	●	●	●	●	●	●	●	●	●	●	●			19588
19589	●	●	●	●	●	●	●	●	●	●	●	●	●	●	●	●	●	●	●	●	●	●	●	●	●	●	●	●													19589
19590	●	●	●	●	●	●	●	●	●	●	●	●	●	●	●	●	●	●	●	●	●	●	●	●	●	●	●	●	●	●	●	●	●	●	●	●	●	●	●	●	19590
19591	●	●	●	●	●	●	●	●	●	●	●	●	●	●	●	●	●	●	●	●	●	●	●	●	●	●	●	●	●	●	●	●	●	●	●	●	●	●			19591
19592	●	●	●	●	●	●	●	●	●	●	●	●	●	●	●	●	●	●	●	●	●	●	●	●	●	●	●	●	●	●											19592
19605	●	●	●	●	●	●	●	●	●	●	●	●	●	●	●	●	●	●	●	●	●	●	●	●	●	●	●	●	●	●	●	●	●	●	●	●	●	●	●	●	19605
19606	●	●	●	●	●	●	●	●	●	●	●	●	●	●	●	●	●	●	●	●	●	●			●	●	●	●	●	●	●	●	●	●	●	●	●	●	●	●	19606
19607	●	●	●	●	●	●	●	●	●	●	●	●	●	●	●	●									●	●	●	●	●	●	●	●	●	●	●	●	●	●	●	●	19607
19612									●	●			●	●	●	●									●	●	●	●	●	●	●	●	●	●	●	●	●	●	●	●	19612
19613					●	●	●	●	●	●	●	●	●	●	●	●					●	●			●	●	●	●	●	●	●	●	●	●	●	●	●	●	●	●	19613
19614	●	●	●	●	●	●	●	●	●	●			●	●	●	●									●	●	●	●	●	●	●	●	●	●	●	●	●	●	●	●	19614
19615					●	●			●	●	●	●	●	●							●	●			●	●	●	●	●	●	●	●	●	●	●	●	●	●	●	●	19615
19620					●	●	●	●	●	●	●	●	●	●	●	●					●	●			●	●	●	●	●	●	●	●	●	●	●	●	●	●	●	●	19620
19621							●	●			●	●			●	●					●	●			●	●	●	●	●	●	●	●	●	●	●	●	●	●	●	●	19621
19622									●	●					●	●									●	●	●	●	●	●	●	●	●	●	●	●	●	●	●	●	19622
19623									●	●			●	●	●	●									●	●	●	●	●	●	●	●	●	●	●	●	●	●	●	●	19623
19624					●	●			●	●			●	●	●	●									●	●	●	●	●	●	●	●	●	●	●	●	●	●	●	●	19624
19625									●	●			●	●	●	●									●	●	●	●	●	●	●	●	●	●	●	●	●	●	●	●	19625
19626									●	●	●	●	●	●	●	●									●	●	●	●	●	●	●	●	●	●	●	●	●	●	●	●	19626
19627									●	●			●	●	●	●									●	●	●	●	●	●	●	●	●	●	●	●	●	●	●	●	19627
19628									●	●			●	●	●	●									●	●	●	●	●	●	●	●	●	●	●	●			●	●	19628
19629									●	●			●	●	●	●									●	●	●	●	●	●	●	●	●	●	●	●			●	●	19629
19630									●	●	●	●	●	●	●	●									●	●	●	●			●	●	●	●	●	●			●	●	19630
19631									●	●			●	●	●	●									●	●	●	●			●	●	●	●	●	●			●	●	19631
19632																									●	●	●	●					●	●	●	●			●	●	19632
19633																									●	●	●	●					●	●	●	●			●	●	19633
19634																									●	●	●	●					●	●	●	●			●	●	19634
19635																									●	●	●	●					●	●	●	●			●	●	19635
19670																									●	●	●	●					●	●					●	●	19670
19671																									●	●	●	●					●	●					●	●	19671
19672																									●	●	●	●					●	●					●	●	19672
19673																									●	●	●	●											●	●	19673
19696																																									19696
19697																																									19697
19698																																									19698
19699																									●	●	●	●											●	●	19699
19700																																									19700
19701																									●	●	●	●											●	●	19701
19702																																									19702
19703																																									19703
	19545	F19545	19546	F19546	19547	F19547	19548	F19548	19573	F19573	19574	F19574	19575	F19575	19576	F19576	19577	F19577	19578	F19578	19579	F19579	19580	F19580	19597	F19597	19598	F19598	19599	F19599	19600	F19600	19608	F19608	19609	F19609	19610	F19610	19611	F19611	

AIR MAIL ISSUES

5¢ BEACON AIRMAIL of 1928

RED PLATES listed Vertically
BLUE PLATES listed Horizontally

	19616	F19616	19617	F19617	19618	F19618	19619	F19619	19639	F19639	19666	F19666	19667	F19667	19668	F19668	19669	F19669	19674	F19674	19675	F19675	19676	F19676	19677	F19677	19688	F19688	19689	F19689	19690	F19690	19691	F19691	19692	F19692	19693	F19693	19694	F19694
19549																																								
19550																																								
19551																																								
19552																																								
19565																																								
19566																																								
19567																																								
19568																																								
19569																																								
19570																																								
19571																																								
19572																																								
19585	●	●	●	●	●	●	●	●																																
19586	●	●	●	●	●	●	●	●																																
19587	●	●	●	●	●	●	●	●																																
19588	●	●	●	●	●	●																																		
19589																																								
19590	●	●	●	●	●	●	●	●																																
19591	●	●			●	●	●	●																																
19592																																								
19605	●	●	●	●	●	●	●	●		●																														
19606	●	●	●	●	●	●	●	●			●	●	●	●			●	●																						
19607	●	●	●	●	●	●	●	●			●	●	●	●	●	●	●	●	●	●	●	●	●	●	●	●	●	●												
19612	●	●	●	●	●	●	●	●			●	●	●	●			●	●	●	●	●	●	●	●	●	●	●	●												
19613	●	●	●	●	●	●	●	●																																
19614	●	●	●	●	●	●	●	●			●	●	●	●	●	●	●	●	●	●	●	●	●	●	●	●	●	●												
19615	●	●	●	●	●	●	●	●			●	●	●	●	●	●	●	●	●	●	●	●	●	●	●	●	●	●												
19620	●	●	●	●	●	●	●	●			●	●	●	●	●	●	●	●	●	●	●	●	●	●	●	●	●	●												
19621	●	●	●	●	●	●	●	●																																
19622	●	●	●	●	●	●	●	●																																
19623	●	●	●	●	●	●	●	●			●	●	●	●	●	●	●	●	●	●	●	●	●	●	●	●	●	●												
19624	●	●	●	●	●	●	●	●			●	●	●	●			●	●	●	●	●	●					●	●												
19625	●	●	●	●	●	●	●	●			●	●	●	●	●	●	●	●	●	●	●	●	●	●	●	●	●	●												
19626	●	●	●	●	●	●	●	●			●	●	●	●	●	●	●	●	●	●	●	●	●	●	●	●	●	●												
19627	●	●	●	●	●	●	●	●			●	●	●	●	●	●	●	●	●	●	●	●	●	●	●	●	●	●												
19628	●	●	●	●	●	●	●	●			●	●	●	●			●	●	●	●	●	●	●	●	●	●	●	●												
19629	●	●	●	●	●	●	●	●			●	●	●	●	●	●	●	●	●	●	●	●	●	●	●	●	●	●												
19630	●	●	●	●	●	●	●	●			●	●	●	●	●	●	●	●	●	●	●	●	●	●	●	●	●	●												
19631	●	●	●	●	●	●	●	●			●	●	●	●	●	●	●	●	●	●	●	●	●	●	●	●	●	●												
19632	●	●	●	●	●	●	●	●			●	●	●	●	●	●	●	●	●	●	●	●	●	●	●	●	●	●	●	●	●	●	●	●	●	●	●	●	●	●
19633	●	●	●	●	●	●	●	●			●	●	●	●	●	●	●	●	●	●	●	●	●	●	●	●	●	●	●	●	●	●	●	●	●	●	●	●	●	●
19634	●	●	●	●	●	●	●	●			●	●	●	●	●	●	●	●	●	●	●	●	●	●	●	●	●	●	●	●	●	●	●	●	●	●	●	●	●	●
19635	●	●	●	●	●	●	●	●			●	●	●	●	●	●	●	●	●	●	●	●	●	●	●	●	●	●	●	●	●	●	●	●	●	●	●	●	●	●
19670	●	●	●	●	●	●	●	●			●	●	●	●	●	●	●	●	●	●	●	●	●	●	●	●	●	●	●	●	●	●	●	●	●	●	●	●	●	●
19671	●	●	●	●	●	●	●	●			●	●	●	●	●	●	●	●	●	●	●	●	●	●	●	●	●	●	●	●	●	●	●	●	●	●	●	●	●	●
19672	●	●	●	●	●	●	●	●			●	●	●	●	●	●	●	●	●	●	●	●	●	●	●	●	●	●	●	●	●	●	●	●	●	●	●	●	●	●
19673	●	●	●	●	●	●	●	●			●	●	●	●	●	●	●	●	●	●	●	●	●	●	●	●	●	●	●	●	●	●	●	●	●	●	●	●	●	●
19696											●	●			●	●			●	●	●	●	●	●	●	●	●	●	●	●	●	●	●	●	●	●	●	●	●	●
19697											●	●			●	●			●	●	●	●	●	●	●	●	●	●	●	●	●	●	●	●	●	●	●	●	●	●
19698											●	●			●	●			●	●	●	●	●	●	●	●	●	●	●	●	●	●	●	●	●	●	●	●	●	●
19699	●	●	●	●	●	●	●	●			●	●	●	●	●	●	●	●	●	●	●	●	●	●	●	●	●	●	●	●	●	●	●	●	●	●	●	●	●	●
19700											●	●			●	●			●	●	●	●	●	●	●	●	●	●	●	●	●	●	●	●	●	●	●	●	●	●
19701	●	●	●	●	●	●	●	●			●	●	●	●	●	●	●	●	●	●	●	●	●	●	●	●	●	●	●	●	●	●	●	●	●	●	●	●	●	●
19702											●	●			●	●			●	●	●	●	●	●	●	●	●	●	●	●	●	●	●	●	●	●	●	●	●	●
19703											●	●			●	●			●	●	●	●	●	●	●	●	●	●	●	●	●	●	●	●	●	●	●	●	●	●

AIR MAIL ISSUES

1930 ISSUE

FLAT PRESS Perf.11
Block of 6

#C12 5¢ WINGED GLOBE

		TL	TR	L	R	B
19941	$160	☐	☐	☐	☐	☐
19942	$160	☐	☐	☐	☐	☐
19943	$160	☐	☐	☐	☐	☐
19944	$160	☐	☐	☐	☐	☐
19945	$160	☐	☐	☐	☐	☐
19946	$160	☐	☐	☐	☐	☐
19947	$300	☐	☐	☐	☐	☐
19948	$160	☐	☐	☐	☐	☐
20187	$450	☐	☐	‡	‡	☐
20188	$450	☐	☐	‡	‡	☐
20189	$450	☐	☐	‡	‡	☐
20190	$450	☐	☐	‡	‡	☐
20323	$500	☐	☐	‡	‡	☐

#C13 65¢ ZEPPELIN

20077	$2,500	☐	☐	☐	☐	☐
20078	$2,500	☐	☐	☐	☐	☐
20079	$2,500	☐	☐	☐	☐	☐
20080	$2,500	☐	☐	☐	☐	☐

#C14 $1.30 ZEPPELIN

20085	$6,500	☐	☐	☐	☐	☐
20086	$6,500	☐	☐	☐	☐	☐
20087	$6,500	☐	☐	☐	☐	☐
20088	$6,500	☐	☐	☐	☐	☐

1930 ISSUE

#C15 $2.60 ZEPPELIN

		TL	TR	L	R	B
20090	$9,000	☐	☐	☐	☐	☐
20091	$9,000	☐	☐	☐	☐	☐
20092	$9,000	☐	☐	☐	☐	☐
20095	$9,000	☐	☐	☐	☐	☐

1931-32 ISSUE

ROTARY PRESS Perf. 10˚ x 11
Block of 4

#C16 5¢ WINGED GLOBE

		UL	UR	LL	LR
20606	$90	☐	☐	☐	☐
20607	$90	☐	☐	☐	☐

#C17 8¢ WINGED GLOBE

21028	$35	☐	☐	☐	☐
21029	$35	☐	☐	☐	☐
21030	$35	☐	☐	☐	☐
21031	$35	☐	☐	☐	☐
21032	$60	☐	☐	☐	☐
21033	$60	☐	☐	☐	☐

1933 ISSUE

FLAT PRESS Perf.11
Block of 6

#C18 50¢ GRAF ZEPPELIN

		T	B
21171	$750	☐	☐
21172	$750	☐	☐
21177	$900	☐	☐
21178	$900	☐	☐

AIR MAIL ISSUES

1934 ISSUE

ROTARY PRESS Perf.10½ x 11

Block of 4

#C19 6¢ WINGED GLOBE

		UL	UR	LL	LR
21234	$32.50	☐	☐	☐	☐
21235	$32.50	☐	☐	☐	☐
21236	$32.50	☐	☐	☐	☐
21237	$32.50	☐	☐	☐	☐
21598	$40.00	☐	☐	☐	☐
21599	$40.00	☐	☐	☐	☐

1935-37 ISSUE

FLAT PRESS Block of 6 Perf.11

#C20 25¢ CHINA CLIPPER

		TL	TR	L	R	B
21473	$30.00	☐	☐	‡	‡	☐
21474	$35.00	☐	☐	‡	‡	☐

1935-37 ISSUE

#C20 25¢ CHINA CLIPPER Cont.

		TL	TR	L	R	B
21475	$30	☐	☐	‡	‡	☐
21476	$35	☐	☐	‡	‡	☐

#C21 20¢ CHINA CLIPPER

21622	$160	☐	☐	‡	‡	☐
21623	$130	☐	☐	‡	‡	☐
21626	$130	☐	☐	‡	‡	☐
21627	$160	☐	☐	‡	‡	☐

#C22 50¢ CHINA CLIPPER

21624	$130	☐	☐	‡	‡	☐
21625	$130	☐	☐	‡	‡	☐
21628	$130	☐	☐	‡	‡	☐
21629	$130	☐	☐	‡	‡	☐

1938 ISSUE

FLAT PRESS Perf.11

Compiled and edited by Albert L. Goldman from the original Durland notes and later information.

#C23 6¢ EAGLE BICOLORED

The frame plates contained 100 subjects, divided into left and right panes of 50, with top plate numbers only. The F was not placed consistently on right panes.

Plates 22186 and 22192 had no F but the positions can be identified by differences in the registration markings. (See "The United States Specialist", pages 253-254, May 1976).

The vignette plates were single panes of 50 subjects with plate numbers at top. The first 18 numbers are preceded by an F and the remaining 20 are plain.

The plate-number combinations fall into two **major** classifications, those **with** and those **without** arrow.

All of the early printings are **with arrow.**

With arrow combinations containing vignette plates 21918, 21919, 21920 are very scarce, and we have not seen any containing 21921 or 21922.

Vignette plate 21909 occurs only in **with arrow** combinations.

All late printings are **without arrow.**

No arrows exist on any combinations containing vignette plates 22197, 22198, 22199, 22200, or frame plates 22185, 22186, 22191, 22192.

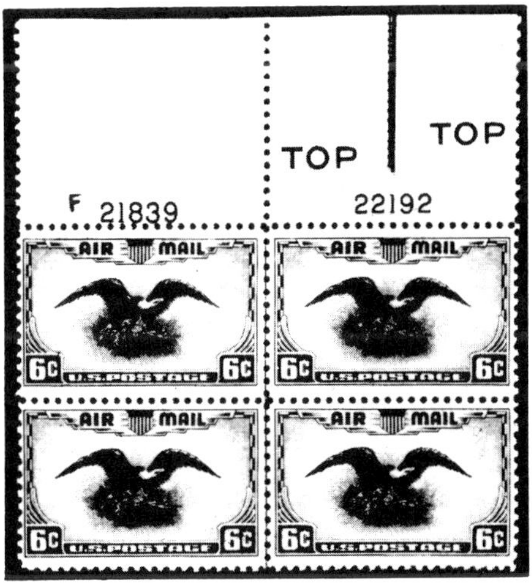

Some combinations are common with arrow and scarce without, and vice versa. There are also combinations where one pane is much scarcer than the other.

AIR MAIL ISSUES

1938 ISSUE

#C23 6¢ EAGLE BICOLORED Cont.

Of the positions for which there is no designated value, some do not exist and others are unreported.

The lack of a value designation for such positions is not necessarily an indication of relative scarcity.

16 Frame Plates

Block of 4
WITH ARROW

Vignette Plates	F21835 L	21835 R	F21836 L	21836 R	F21837 L	21837 R	F21838 L	21838 R	F21855 L	21855 R	F21856 L	21856 R	F21857 L	21857 R	F21858 L	21858 R	21948 L	F21948 R	21949 L	F21949 R	21950 L	F21950 R	21951 L	F21951 R	22185 L	F22185 R	22186 L	22186 R	22191 L	F22191 R	22192 L	22192 R
18 Vignette Plates with F																																
F21839	A	B	A	C	B	E	E	E	E	E	E	A	E	D	E	B	K	P	T	T	T	V	X	Y								
F21840	E	E	A	B	E	E	E	E	E	E	C	D	C	C	E	B	D	D	V	V	S	V	S	V								
F21841	E	B	E	E	E	C	C	B	E	D	S	B	K	E	D	E	K	T	P	X	D	X	T	T								
F21842	E	E	E	C	E	B	E	C	E	E	B	C	B	E	E	B	Y	X	Y	X	V	Y	N	X								
F21843	E	C	E	E	B	B	E	A	T	B	H	B	Y	B	X	B	T	T	X	Y	V	N	T									
F21844	N	E	K	B	B	B	E	E	E	B	Y	B	X	E	E	B	X	T	P	T	T	T	T	T								
F21845	E	E	E	B	K	B	A	B	K	B	K	B	V	B	P	B																
F21846	N	B	H	E	N	E	K	B	C	E	H	E	H	E	X	E	S															
F21847	P	E	T	E	N	E	H	B		B		B		B		B	S	Y	T	P	P	H	T	P								
F21848	B	N	B	B	E	H	K	K	B		B	Y	B		B	B	S	Y	N	S	K	P	H	N								
F21849	X	E	X	E	P	E	C	E		B		B		S	X	E	V	Y	H	H	P	Y	K	X								
F21850	X	D	X	B	X	B		C		C		E		B		B																
F21851		E		B	K	E		E		B		E		A		B																
F21852	K	P	K	P	K	T	T	T	K	K	P		S	Y	S		Y	S	P	P	X	S	X	X								
F21853	P	P	B	X	B	N	E	N	B		B	S	B	T	E	S	V	P	T	P	V	V	V	V								
F21854	E	X	B	T	E	V	E	Y	B		B	X	E	X	B	S	Y	P	S	X	X	X	T	T								
F21901	E	V	E	P	E	X	E	X	B	X	E	S	E	S	B	X	X	Y	T	P	T	X	T	X								
F21902	N	N	E	N	E	C	E	E	E	T	E	P	E	X	E	X	T	T	V	S	K	T	S	X								
20 Vignette Plates without F																																
21903	E	B	E	S	C	H	E	T	E	P	E	K	E	T	E	X	K	T	P	S	N	S	N	T								
21904	E	B	E	X	B	H	E	P	E		E		E		E	P	T	X	X	P	Z	S	N	N								
21909	K	P	H	T	K	T	H	X	K	T	H	T	H	X	H	X																
21910	E	B	E	H	E	P	E	K	C	S	E	V	E	S	E	P	X		Y		X		Z	X								
21911		E		E		E		E		E		B		B		E																
21912		E		E		E		D		E		N		B		H																
21913		E		E		E		E		E		B		E		E																
21914		E		E		E		B		E		E		E		D																
21915	C	P	E	P	E	X	E		D	P	E	P	E	X	E																	
21916	E	P	B	P	E	P	A		B	P	E		E	P	B	X																
21917	B		K	X	E		T	T	S	X	K	P	K	V	N	X																
21918								Z																								
21919				Z		Z		Z																								
21920		Z				Y																										
21921																																
21922																																
22197																																
22198																																
22199																																
22200																																
	L	R	L	R	L	R	L	R	L	R	L	R	L	R	L	R	L	R	L	R	L	R	L	R	L	R	L	R	L	R	L	R
	F21835	21835	F21836	21836	F21837	21837	F21838	21838	F21855	21855	F21856	21856	F21857	21857	F21858	21858	21948	F21948	21949	F21949	21950	F21950	21951	F21951	22185	F22185	22186	22186	22191	F22191	22192	22192

AIR MAIL ISSUES

1938 ISSUE

#C23 6¢ EAGLE BICOLORED Cont.

KEY TO VALUATIONS

E.....11.00	D.....14.00	P.....27.50	X.......52.50
A.....11.50	H.....16.00	S.....30.00	Y.......62.50
B.....12.25	K.....18.00	T.....38.50	Z.....105.00
C.....13.50	N.....22.00	V.....45.00	

Blocks of 4

WITHOUT ARROW

16 Frame Plates

		F21835	21835	F21836	21836	F21837	21837	F21838	21838	F21855	21855	F21856	21856	F21857	21857	F21858	21858	21948	F21948	21949	F21949	21950	F21950	21951	F21951	22185	F22185	22186	22186	22191	F22191	22192	22192
		L	R	L	R	L	R	L	R	L	R	L	R	L	R	L	R	L	R	L	R	L	R	L	R	L	R	L	R	L	R	L	R
18 Vignette Plates with F	F21839	E	E	E	E	E	E	E	E	E	E	E	E	E	E	E	E	E	E	E	E	E	E	E	E	H	H	K	T	K	H	Y	
	F21840	E	E	E	E	E	E	E	E	E	A	E	E	E	E	E	E	D	E	E	E	E	E	E	A	N	X						
	F21841	C	E	E	E	E	E	E	E	E	E	E	K	E	B	E	E	E	E	E	E	E	E	E	E	Y	Y						
	F21842	E	E	E	E	E	E	E	E	E	E	E	E	E	E	E	E	E	E	E	E	E	E	E	E	V	V						
	F21843	E	E	E	E	E	E	E	E	E	E	E	E	E	E	E	E	E	E	E	E	E	E	E	E	N	V	N	N	K	N	X	
	F21844	E	E	E	E	E	E	E	E	E	E	E	E	E	E	E	E	E	E	E	E	E	E	E	E	H	T	N	N	S	N	X	X
	F21845	D	C	C	T	K	N	D	C	C	C	C	D	D	C	E	E	E	E	E	E	E	E	E	E	H	N	S	N	K	K	Y	Y
	F21846	B	X	A	D	E	B	P	E	E	D	E	E	E	E	C	C	E	E	B	C	B	E	C	E	H	K	H	H	K	K	Y	Y
	F21847	E	E	E	D	E	E	D	E	E	T	E	N	E	N	E	E	E	E	E	E	E	E	E	E	H	H	K	H	H	H	T	X
	F21848	E	E	E	E	E	E	E	E	E	E	E	E	E	E	E	E	E	E	E	E	E	E	E	E	H	H	K	K	H	H	T	T
	F21849	E	E	E	E	E	E	E	E	E	Y	E	E	E	E	E	E	E	E	E	E	E	E	E	E	Y		K	K	X	X		
	F21850	E	K	E	E	E	B	E	E	E	C	E	E	C	K	E	T	E	E	C	B	C	E	D	B	S	S	K	S	X	X		
	F21851	E	E	E	E	E	E	E	E	E	D	E	H	E	B	E	E	E	E	E	E	E	E	E	E	K	K	K	K	K	K	Y	
	F21852	E	E	E	E	E	E	E	E	E	E	B	E	E	E	E	E	E	B	E	E	E	E	E	E	H	H	K	N	P	P		
	F21853	K	T	K	H	K	H	K	V	H	S	H	K	B	K	D	D	N	D	Y	Y	T	S	K	T		Y						
	F21854	C	E	E	N	E	E	E	E	C	B	K	C	C	B	E	E	E	E	E	E	E	E	E	E	H	H	K	K	H	H		
	F21901	C	C	P	C	E	P	B	N	B	H	C	H	C	C	E	A	S	E	S	K	S	E	S	D	X	X						
	F21902	E	D	C	X	E	D	B	N	B	C	N	N	E	K	K	E	E	B	E	E	C	E	B	E	K	X	K	K	P	T		
20 Vignette Plates without F	21903	E	E	B	B	D	E	B	E	K	C	S	C	D	D	B	E	E	E	E	E	E	E	E	E	K	K	K	K	K	K	X	X
	21904	T	T	K	S	S	T	T	S	D	T	H	T	K	T	K	Y	P	K	K	K	K	H	K	K	Z	Y						
	21909																																
	21910	K	B	E	E	E	E	E	E	B	B	D	C	B	C	E	E	E	E	E	E	E	E	E	E	P	P	K	K	K	K	X	T
	21911	E	D	E	E	E	E	E	E	E	E	B	K	K	T	E	E	E	E	E	E	E	E	E	E	H	H	K	K	K	H	P	V
	21912	B	E	E	A	B	B	B	D	E	E	C	D	C	X	C	K	E	E	E	B	E	E	E	H	Z	X	H	K	K	N		X
	21913	T	X	T	C	C	T	N	D	B	V	C	S	H	S	D	T	T	C	E	X	T	C	N	C		X						
	21914	C	P	C	B	D	C	D	D	E	D	D	T	B	D	E	D	E	E	B	E	B	B	K	E	Y		P	X	X	X		
	21915	K	D	T	B	P	V	T	H	P	T	D	B	N	T	T	N	B	B	C	D	B	B	B	C								
	21916	B	C	D	E	B	S	C	E	N	D	D	D	B	C	B	E	E	C	E	H	E	E	E	C	H	K	N	P	P	P		
	21917	K	E	D	E	T	E	B	B	E	E	D	C	D	D	D	C	E	B	D	K	B	C	E	E	Y	X		Z	X			
	21918	D	T	D	D	T	D	C	K	P	Y	T	V	X	K	P	X	B	B	P	C	T	T	K	T								
	21919	D	D	C	E	B	E	C	E	K	K	E	T	E	K	D	C	N	N	X	C	B	E	D	D	X	V		S	P	P		
	21920	V		V		V	Y	X	Y	Y	Y	Y	X	X	V	T	X	X	N	T	T	P	T	X	X								
	21921	T	X	V		V		K		X	X	V	X	X	X	X	S	T	T	P	P	V	V	K	T								
	21922	V	P	K	T	V	N	K	K	T	X	P	X	S	S	K	S	P	P	N	T	K	S	S	T	Y	P				Z		
	22197	X	X	T	X	Y	Y	S	Y	K	X	Z	N	N	T	X	T	P	K	T	T	K	K	P	N	P			Z		Z		
	22198	X	Y	Y		X	T	T	Z	S	S	V	X	V	P	Y	Y	T	P	S	V	X	V	V	S	T	T						
	22199	X	P		Y	X			T	S	X	S	X	Y	Y	N	X	V	S	S	S	V	V	V	Y	V							
	22200	X		X	Y	Y			T	P	Y	X	P	T	X	S	X	X	P	X	T	X	P	X	P	Z							
		L	R	L	R	L	R	L	R	L	R	L	R	L	R	L	R	L	R	L	R	L	R	L	R	L	R	L	R	L	R	L	R
		F21835	21835	F21836	21836	F21837	21837	F21838	21838	F21855	21855	F21856	21856	F21857	21857	F21858	21858	21948	F21948	21949	F21949	21950	F21950	21951	F21951	22185	F22185	22186	22186	22191	F22191	22192	22192

AIR MAIL ISSUES

1939 ISSUE

FLAT PRESS Perf.11

Block of 6

#C24 30¢ TRANS ATLANTIC WINGED GLOBE

		TL	TR	L	R	B
22381	$170	☐	☐	‡	‡	☐
22382	$170	☐	☐	‡	‡	☐
22383	$170	☐	☐	‡	‡	☐
22384	$170	☐	☐	‡	‡	☐

1941-44 ISSUES

ROTARY PRESS Perf. 11 x 10˚

Block of 4

#C25 6¢ TRANSPORT

		UL	UR	LL	LR
22752	$1.00	☐	☐	☐	☐
22753	$1.00	☐	☐	☐	☐
22754	$1.00	☐	☐	☐	☐
22755	$1.00	☐	☐	☐	☐
22888	$1.00	☐	☐	☐	☐
22889	$1.00	☐	☐	☐	☐
22890	$2.00	☐	☐2	☐	☐
22891	$2.00	☐	☐2	☐	☐
23043	$1.00	☐	☐	☐	☐
23044	$1.00	☐	☐	☐	☐
23049	$1.00	☐	☐	☐	☐
23052	$1.00	☐	☐	☐	☐
23109	$1.00	☐	☐	☐	☐
23110	$1.00	☐	☐	☐	☐
23111	$1.00	☐	☐	☐	☐
23112	$1.00	☐	☐	☐	☐
23113	$1.00	☐	☐	☐	☐
23114	$1.00	☐	☐	☐	☐
23165	$1.00	☐	☐	☐	☐
23166	$1.00	☐	☐	☐	☐
23174	$1.00	☐	☐	☐	☐
23175	$1.00	☐	☐	☐	☐
23252	$1.00	☐	☐	☐	☐
23253	$1.00	☐	☐	☐	☐
23268	$1.00	☐	☐	☐	☐
23269	$1.00	☐	☐	☐	☐
23270	$1.00	☐	☐	☐	☐
23271	$1.00	☐	☐	☐	☐

1941-44 ISSUES

#C25 6¢ TRANSPORT Cont.

		UL	UR	LL	LR
23272	$1.50	☐	☐	☐	☐
23273	$2.00	☐	☐	☐	☐
23274	$1.00	☐	☐	☐	☐
23275	$1.00	☐	☐	☐	☐
23277	$1.50	☐	☐	☐	☐
23278	$1.50	☐	☐	☐	☐
23279	$2.00	☐	☐	☐	☐
23280	$1.50	☐	☐	☐	☐
23281	$2.50	☐	☐	☐	☐
23282	$1.50	☐	☐	☐	☐
23348	$1.50	☐	☐	☐	☐
23349	$2.50	☐	☐	☐	☐

#C25a 6¢ TRANSPORT BOOKLET

PANES OF 3

22979	22980	22981	22982	*23028
*23029	*23048	*23072	*23258	*23259

See Appendix G for the largest reported plate number percentage by position.

#C26 8¢ TRANSPORT

23121	$1.50	☐	☐	☐	☐
23122	$1.50	☐	☐	☐	☐
23123	$1.50	☐	☐	☐	☐
23124	$1.50	☐	☐	☐	☐
23125	$1.50	☐	☐	☐	☐
23126	$1.50	☐	☐	☐	☐
23127	$1.50	☐	☐	☐	☐
23128	$1.50	☐	☐	☐	☐
23129	$1.50	☐	☐	☐	☐
23130	$1.50	☐	☐	☐	☐
23131	$1.50	☐	☐	☐	☐
23132	$1.50	☐	☐	☐	☐
23135	$1.50	☐	☐	☐	☐
23136	$1.50	☐	☐	☐	☐
23137	$1.50	☐	☐	☐	☐
23138	$1.50	☐	☐	☐	☐
23328	$25.00	☐	☐	☐	☐
23329	$25.00	☐	☐	☐	☐
23351	$10.00	☐	☐	☐	☐
23352	$10.00	☐	☐	☐	☐
23356	$5.00	☐	☐	☐	☐
23357	$5.00	☐	☐	☐	☐

AIR MAIL ISSUES

1941-44 ISSUES

#C27 10¢ TRANSPORT

		UL	UR	LL	LR
22756	$10.00	☐	☐	☐	☐
22757	$10.00	☐	☐	☐	☐
22758	$25.00	☐	☐	☐	☐
22759	$25.00	☐	☐	☐	☐

#C28 15¢ TRANSPORT

22764	$12.00	☐	☐	☐	☐
22765	$12.00	☐	☐	☐	☐
22766	$30.00	☐	☐	☐	☐
22767	$30.00	☐	☐	☐	☐

#C29 20¢ TRANSPORT

22760	$11.00	☐	☐	☐	☐
22761	$11.00	☐	☐	☐	☐

#C30 30¢ TRANSPORT

22774	$12.00	☐	☐	☐	☐
22775	$12.00	☐	☐	☐	☐

#C31 50¢ TRANSPORT

22778	$85.00	☐	☐	☐	☐
22779	$85.00	☐	☐	☐	☐

1946 ISSUE

#C32 5¢ SKYMASTER

23483	$.50	☐	☐	☐	☐
23484	$.50	☐	☐	☐	☐
23485	$.50	☐	☐	☐	☐
23486	$.50	☐	☐	☐	☐
23487	$.50	☐	☐	☐	☐
23488	$.50	☐	☐	☐	☐
23489	$.50	☐	☐	☐	☐
23490	$.50	☐	☐	☐	☐
23491	$.50	☐	☐	☐	☐
23492	$.50	☐	☐	☐	☐
23493	$.75	☐	☐	☐	☐
23494	$.75	☐	☐	☐	☐
23495	$.50	☐	☐	☐	☐
23496	$.50	☐	☐	☐	☐
23497	$.50	☐	☐	☐	☐
23498	$.50	☐	☐	☐	☐
23503	$.50	☐	☐	☐	☐
23504	$1.50	☐	☐	☐	☐
23505	$.50	☐	☐	☐	☐
23506	$1.50	☐	☐	☐	☐
23507	$1.00	☐	☐	☐	☐
23508	$.75	☐	☐	☐	☐
23509	$.75	☐	☐	☐	☐
23510	$1.00	☐	☐	☐	☐
23515	$1.00	☐	☐	☐	☐
23516	$1.00	☐	☐	☐	☐
23517	$.75	☐	☐	☐	☐
23518	$.75	☐	☐	☐	☐
23523	$.75	☐	☐	☐	☐

1946 ISSUE

#C32 5¢ SKYMASTER Cont.

		UL	UR	LL	LR
23524	$3.50	☐	☐	☐	☐
23525	$3.50	☐	☐	☐	☐
23526	$.75	☐	☐	☐	☐

1947 ISSUES

#C33 5¢ SKYMASTER

23580	$.60	☐	☐	☐	☐
23581	$.60	☐	☐	☐	☐
23582	$.60	☐	☐	☐	☐
23583	$.60	☐	☐	☐	☐
23586	$.60	☐	☐	☐	☐
23588	$.60	☐	☐	☐	☐
23590	$.60	☐	☐	☐	☐
23591	$.60	☐	☐	☐	☐

#C34 10¢ PAN-AM UNION BLDG.

Wet Printed

23693	$1.60	☐	☐	☐	☐
23694	$1.60	☐	☐	☐	☐
24898	$30.00	☐	☐	☐	☐
24899	$30.00	☐	☐	☐	☐

#C34a 10¢ PAN-AM UNION BLDG.

Dry printed

25613	$2.00	☐	☐	☐	☐
25614	$2.00	☐	☐	☐	☐

#C35 15¢ NEW YORK SKYLINE

Wet Printed

23683	$1.75	☐	☐	☐	☐
23684	$1.75	☐	☐	☐	☐
23685	$1.75	☐	☐	☐	☐
24505	$1.75	☐	☐	☐	☐
24584	$1.75	☐	☐	☐	☐
24585	$1.75	☐	☐	☐	☐

#C35b 15¢ NEW YORK SKYLINE

Dry Printed

25492	$6.00	☐	☐	☐	☐
25493	$6.00	☐	☐	☐	☐
25889	$6.00	☐	☐	☐	☐
25890	$6.00	☐	☐	☐	☐
25940	$3.00	☐	☐	☐	☐
25941	$3.00	☐	☐	☐	☐

#C36 25¢ OAKLAND BAY BRIDGE

Wet Printed

23667	$5.00	☐	☐	☐	☐
23668	$5.00	☐	☐	☐	☐
23669	$5.00	☐	☐	☐	☐
23670	$5.00	☐	☐	☐	☐
23671	$20.00	☐	☐	☐	☐
23672	$20.00	☐	☐	☐	☐
23681	$20.00	☐	☐	☐	☐
23682	$20.00	☐	☐	☐	☐

#C36a 25¢ OAKLAND BAY BRIDGE

Dry Printed

25615	$5.00	☐	☐	☐	☐
25616	$5.00	☐	☐	☐	☐

AIR MAIL ISSUES

1948 ISSUES

#C37 5¢ SKYMASTER COIL

170 Subject Plates STRIPS OF 5

23716 23717

#C38 5¢ NEW YORK CITY

		UL	UR	LL	LR
23846	$5.00	☐	☐	☐	☐
23851	$5.00	☐	☐	☐	☐

1949 ISSUES

#C39 6¢ SKYMASTER

Wet Printed

23973	$.60	☐	☐	☐	☐
23974	$.60	☐	☐	☐	☐
23975	$.60	☐	☐	☐	☐
23976	$.60	☐	☐	☐	☐
23977	$.60	☐	☐	☐	☐
23978	$.60	☐	☐	☐	☐
23979	$.60	☐	☐	☐	☐
23985	$.60	☐	☐	☐	☐
23986	$.60	☐	☐	☐	☐
24031	$.60	☐	☐	☐	☐
24042	$.60	☐	☐	☐	☐
24043	$.60	☐	☐	☐	☐
24550	$.60	☐	☐	☐	☐
24551	$.60	☐	☐	☐	☐
24859	$.60	☐	☐	☐	☐
24860	$.60	☐	☐	☐	☐

#C39b 6¢ SKYMASTER

Dry Printed

25340	$2.50	☐	☐	☐	☐
25341	$2.50	☐	☐	☐	☐
25413	$4.00	☐	☐	☐	☐
25414	$4.00	☐	☐	☐	☐
25421	$15.00	☐	☐	☐	☐
25422	$15.00	☐	☐	☐	☐

#C39a 6¢ SKYMASTER BOOKLET

Wet Printed PANES OF 6

24141 24142 24263 24264 24564
24565 *24908 *24909

#C39c 6¢ SKYMASTER BOOKLET

Dry Printed PANES OF 6

25359 25360 25376 *25377

See Appendix G for the largest reported plate number percentage by position.

#C40 6¢ ALEXANDRIA BICENTENNIAL

24083	$.50	☐	☐	☐	☐
24084	$.50	☐	☐	☐	☐
24085	$.50	☐	☐	☐	☐
24086	$.50	☐	☐	☐	☐
24087	$.50	☐	☐	☐	☐
24088	$.50	☐	☐	☐	☐

1949 ISSUES

#C41 6¢ SKYMASTER COIL

170 Subject Plates STRIPS OF 5

24116 24117 24122 24123 25169
25170 †25171 †25172 25173 25174

#C42 10¢ P.O.D. BUILDING

		UL	UR	LL	LR
24151	$1.50	☐	☐	☐	☐
24155	$1.50	☐	☐	☐	☐

#C43 15¢ GLOBE & DOVES

24147	$1.25	☐	☐	☐	☐
24148	$1.25	☐	☐	☐	☐
24149	$1.25	☐	☐	☐	☐
24150	$1.25	☐	☐	☐	☐

#C44 25¢ GLOBE & PLANE

24153	$6.00	☐	☐	☐	☐
24154	$6.00	☐	☐	☐	☐

#C45 6¢ WRIGHT BROTHERS

24156	$.70	☐	☐	☐	☐
24157	$.70	☐	☐	☐	☐
24158	$.70	☐	☐	☐	☐
24159	$.70	☐	☐	☐	☐

1952 ISSUE

#C46 80¢ HAWAII

24592	$25.00	☐	☐	☐	☐
24593	$25.00	☐	☐	☐	☐
24594	$37.50	☐	☐	☐	☐

1953 ISSUE

#C47 6¢ 50th ANNIVERSARY

24781	$.60	☐	☐	☐	☐
24782	$.60	☐	☐	☐	☐
24783	$.60	☐	☐	☐	☐
24784	$.60	☐	☐	☐	☐
24785	$.60	☐	☐	☐	☐
24786	$.60	☐	☐	☐	☐

1954 ISSUE

#C48 4¢ EAGLE IN FLIGHT

25034	$2.00	☐	☐	☐	☐
25035	$2.00	☐	☐	☐	☐
25040	$7.00	☐	☐	☐	☐
25041	$7.00	☐	☐	☐	☐

AIR MAIL ISSUES

1957 ISSUE

#C49 6¢ U.S. AIR FORCE

		UL	UR	LL	LR
25761	$.75	☐	☐	☐	☐
25762	$.75	☐	☐	☐	☐
25763	$.75	☐	☐	☐	☐
25764	$.75	☐	☐	☐	☐

1958 ISSUES

#C50 5¢ EAGLE IN FLIGHT

26052	$1.75	☐	☐	☐	☐
26053	$1.75	☐	☐	☐	☐
26215	$6.00	☐	☐	☐	☐
26216	$6.00	☐	☐	☐	☐

#C51 7¢ JET PLANE (blue)

26044	$.65	☐	☐	☐	☐
26045	$.65	☐	☐	☐	☐
26046	$.65	☐	☐	☐	☐
26047	$.65	☐	☐	☐	☐
26177	$.65	☐	☐	☐	☐
26178	$.65	☐	☐	☐	☐
26385**N**	$.65	☐	☐	☐	☐
26386**N**	$.65	☐	☐	☐	☐
26444**N**	$.65	☐	☐	☐	☐
26445**N**	$.65	☐	☐	☐	☐

N Also used for #C60.

#C51a 7¢ JET PLANE BOOKLET (blue)

PANES OF 6

26042 26043 26175 26176 26458**N**
26459**N**

N Also used for #C60a.

See Appendix G for the largest reported plate number percentage by position.

#C52 7¢ JET PLANE COIL (blue)

384 Subject Plates STRIPS OF 5

26048**N** 26054**N** 26055 26069

432 Subject Plates STRIPS OF 6

26446 26447

N Also used for #C61.

1959 ISSUES

#C53 7¢ ALASKA

26225	$.65	☐	☐	☐	☐
26226	$.65	☐	☐	☐	☐
26227	$.65	☐	☐	☐	☐
26228	$.65	☐	☐	☐	☐

#C54 7¢ JUPITER

26390	$.65	☐	☐	☐	☐
26391	$.65	☐	☐	☐	☐
26392	$.65	☐	☐	☐	☐
26397	$.65	☐	☐	☐	☐

#C55 7¢ HAWAII

26432	$.65	☐	☐	☐	☐
26433	$.65	☐	☐	☐	☐
26434	$.65	☐	☐	☐	☐
26435	$.65	☐	☐	☐	☐

1959 ISSUES

#C56 10¢ PAN AMERICAN GAMES

		UL	UR	LL	LR
26413	$1.75	☐	☐	☐	☐
26414	$1.75	☐	☐	☐	☐

1959-60 ISSUES

#C57 10¢ LIBERTY BELL

26630	$6.00	☐	☐	☐	☐
26635	$6.00	☐	☐	☐	☐
26636	$6.00	☐	☐	☐	☐

#C58 15¢ STATUE OF LIBERTY

26482	$1.75	☐	☐	☐	☐
26483	$1.75	☐	☐	☐	☐
26486	$1.75	☐	☐	☐	☐
26487	$7.00	☐	☐	☐	☐

#C59 25¢ ABRAHAM LINCOLN

UNTAGGED

26563**o**	$2.50	☐	☐	☐	☐
26570	$2.50	☐	☐	☐	☐
26576	$2.50	☐	☐	☐	☐

#C59a 25¢ ABRAHAM LINCOLN

TAGGED

26563**o**	$5.00	☐	☐	☐	☐
28536	$2.25	☐	☐	☐	☐
28543	$2.25	☐	☐	☐	☐
30638	$15.00	☐	☐	☐	☐
30649	$7.00	☐	☐	☐	☐
31603	$12.00	☐	☐	☐	☐
31604	$6.00	☐	☐	☐	☐
31615	$30.00	☐2	☐2	☐	☐2
31648	$30.00	☐2	☐2	☐	☐2

1960 ISSUES

#C60 7¢ JET PLANE (red)

26385**N**	$.65	☐	☐	☐	☐
26386**N**	$.65	☐	☐	☐	☐
26444**N**	$.65	☐	☐	☐	☐
26445**N**	$.65	☐	☐	☐	☐
26667	$.65	☐	☐	☐	☐
26668	$.65	☐	☐	☐	☐
26714	$.65	☐	☐	☐	☐
26715	$.65	☐	☐	☐	☐
26899	$.65	☐	☐	☐	☐
26900	$.65	☐	☐	☐	☐
27213	$.65	☐	☐	☐	☐
27214	$.65	☐	☐	☐	☐
27242	$2.00	☐	☐	☐	☐
27243	$2.00	☐	☐	☐	☐

N Also used for #C51

AIR MAIL ISSUES

1960 ISSUES

#C60a 7¢ JET PLANE BOOKLET (red)
PANES OF 6
26458**N** 26459**N** 26475 26476

N Also used for #C51a.

#C61 7¢ JET PLANE COIL (red)
432 Subject Plates STRIPS OF 6
26446**N** 26447**N**†26455 †26456
N Also used for #C52.

1961 ISSUES

#C62 13¢ LIBERTY BELL

UNTAGGED		UL	UR	LL	LR
26965**o**	$1.75	□	□	□	□
26970**o**	$1.75	□	□	□	□
26975	$1.75	□	□	□	□
26977	$1.75	□	□	□	□
28608	$1.75	□	□	□	□
28611	$1.75	□	□	□	□
28617	$1.75	□	□	□	□
28620	$1.75	□	□	□	□

#C62a 13¢ LIBERTY BELL

TAGGED					
26965**o**	$6.00	□	□	□	□
26970**o**	$6.00	□	□	□	□

#C63 15¢ STATUE OF LIBERTY REDESIGNED

UNTAGGED					
26875	$1.25	□	□	□	□
26878	$1.25	□	□	□	□
26885	$1.25	□	□	□	□
26886	$1.25	□	□	□	□
28033**o**	$1.75	□	□	□	□
28335**o**	$1.75	□	□	□	□
28336**o**	$5.00	□	□	□	□
28340**o**	$5.00	□	□	□	□
28644	$1.25	□	□	□	□
28645	$1.25	□	□	□	□
28655	$1.25	□	□	□	□
28657	$17.50	□	□	□	□
28659	$1.25	□	□	□	□

#C63a 15¢ STATUE OF LIBERTY REDESIGNED

TAGGED					
28033**o**	$2.50	□	□	□	□
28051	$1.50	□	□	□	□
28335**o**	$2.50	□	□	□	□
28336**o**	$2.50	□	□	□	□
28340**o**	$2.50	□	□	□	□
31551	$1.50	□	□	□	□
31558	$1.50	□	□	□	□
31559	$1.50	□	□	□	□
31892	$1.50	□	□	□	□
31893	$1.50	□	□	□	□

o Issued both TAGGED and UNTAGGED

1962 ISSUES

#C64 8¢ CAPITOL

UNTAGGED		UL	UR	LL	LR
27365**o**	$1.00	□	□	□	□
27366**o**	$1.00	□	□	□	□
27377	$.65	□	□	□	□
27378	$.65	□	□	□	□
27593**o**	$1.00	□	□	□	□
27625**o**	$1.00	□	□	□	□
27680**o**	$1.00	□	□	□	□
27681**o**	$1.00	□	□	□	□
27682**o**	$3.00	□	□	□	□
27683**o**	$3.00	□	□	□	□

#C64a 8¢ CAPITOL

TAGGED					
27365**o**	$4.00	□	□	□	□
27366**o**	$4.00	□	□	□	□
27593**o**	$2.00	□	□	□	□
27625**o**	$2.00	□	□	□	□
27680**o**	$2.00	□	□	□	□
27681**o**	$2.00	□	□	□	□
27682**o**	$2.00	□	□	□	□
27683**o**	$2.00	□	□	□	□
28024	$.65	□	□	□	□
28025	$.65	□	□	□	□
28041	$.65	□	□	□	□
28042	$.65	□	□	□	□
28423	$.65	□	□	□	□
28424	$.65	□	□	□	□
28475	$.65	□	□	□	□
28476	$.65	□	□	□	□
28484	$.65	□	□	□	□
28485	$.65	□	□	□	□
28612	$5.00	□	□	□	□
28613	$5.00	□	□	□	□
29029	$20.00	□	□	□	□
29030	$20.00	□	□	□	□

#C64b 8¢ CAPITOL BOOKLET
UNTAGGED PANES OF 6
Slogan 1 "Your Mailman"
27371 27372 27375 27376
Slogan 2 "Use Zone Nos."
27515 27516
Slogan 3 "Always Use ZIP"
27646**o** 27673**o** 27674**o** 27677**o** 27697**o**
27698**o**

#C64c 8¢ CAPITOL BOOKLET
TAGGED PANES OF 6
Slogan 3 "Always Use ZIP"
27646**o** 27673**o** 27674**o** 27677**o** 27697**o**
27698**o** 28030 28031 28032 28050
28115 28116 28317 28403 28404
28405 28469 28470 28480 28481
28496 28497 28575 28576

See Appendix G for the largest reported plate number percentage by position.

AIR MAIL ISSUES

1962 ISSUES

#C65 8¢ CAPITOL COIL

432 Subject Plates STRIPS OF 6

UNTAGGED

†27367 †27368 27369**o** 27370**o**

#C65a 8¢ CAPITOL COIL

432 Subject Plates STRIPS OF 6

TAGGED

27369**o** 27370**o** †27699 †27700 †28045 †28280

1963 ISSUES

#C66 15¢ MONTGOMERY BLAIR

		UL	UR	LL	LR
27463	$3.50	☐	☐	☐	☐
27466	$3.50	☐	☐	☐	☐

#C67 6¢ EAGLE

UNTAGGED

27390**o**	$2.00	☐	☐	☐	☐
27391**o**	$2.00	☐	☐	☐	☐

#C67a 6¢ EAGLE

TAGGED

27390**o**	$40.00	☐	☐	☐	☐
27391**o**	$40.00	☐	☐	☐	☐

#C68 8¢ AMELIA EARHART

27497	$1.25	☐	☐	☐	☐
27529	$1.25	☐	☐	☐	☐
27541	$1.25	☐	☐	☐	☐
27548	$1.25	☐	☐	☐	☐

1964 ISSUE

#C69 8¢ ROBERT GODDARD

27860	$2.00	☐	☐	☐	☐
27861	$2.00	☐	☐	☐	☐
27862	$2.00	☐	☐	☐	☐
27863	$2.00	☐	☐	☐	☐

1967 ISSUES

#C70 8¢ ALASKA PURCHASE

29013	$1.75	☐	☐	☐	☐
29019	$1.75	☐	☐	☐	☐
29022	$1.75	☐	☐	☐	☐
29026	$1.75	☐	☐	☐	☐

#C71 20¢ JOHN JAMES AUDUBON

29073	$4.00	☐	☐	☐	☐
29087	$4.00	☐	☐	☐	☐
29092	$4.00	☐	☐	☐	☐
29096	$4.00	☐	☐	☐	☐
29542	$4.00	☐	☐	☐	☐

o Issued both TAGGED and UNTAGGED.

1968 ISSUES

#C72 10¢ STAR RUNWAY

		UL	UR	LL	LR
29467	$1.00	☐	☐	☐	☐
29468	$1.00	☐	☐	☐	☐
29475	$1.00	☐	☐	☐	☐
29476	$1.00	☐	☐	☐	☐
29494	$1.00	☐	☐	☐	☐
29495	$1.00	☐	☐	☐	☐
29517	$1.00	☐	☐	☐	☐
29518	$1.00	☐	☐	☐	☐
30733	$1.00	☐	☐	☐	☐
30734	$1.00	☐	☐	☐	☐
30757	$1.00	☐	☐	☐	☐
30758	$1.00	☐	☐	☐	☐
31894	$1.00	☐	☐	☐	☐
31895	$1.00	☐	☐	☐	☐
31990	$3.00	☐	☐	☐	☐
32039	$3.00	☐	☐	☐	☐

BOOKLET PANES

#C72b 10¢ STAR RUNWAY

320 Subject Plates PANES OF 8

†29465 †29466 †29469 †29470 †29485
†29486 †29523 †29524 †29739 †29740

400 Subject Plates PANES OF 8

†30566 †30567 †30570 †30658

#C72c 10¢ STAR RUNWAY

360 Subject Plates PANES OF 5

Slogan 4 "Mail Early"

29564 29568

Slogan 5 "Use ZIP Code"

29563 29567

See Appendix G for the largest reported plate number percentage by position.

#C73 10¢ STAR RUNWAY COIL

432 Subject Plates STRIPS OF 6

29472 29473 29474 29500 29501
29514 29519 29520 †31908 †31909

#C74 10¢ 50th ANNIVERSARY AIR MAIL

29673	$2.75	☐	☐	☐	☐
29678	$2.75	☐	☐	☐	☐
29679	$2.75	☐	☐	☐	☐
29684	$2.75	☐	☐	☐	☐

#C75 20¢ USA and JET

30494	$2.50	☐	☐	☐	☐
30498	$2.50	☐	☐	☐	☐
30502	$2.50	☐	☐	☐	☐
30510	$2.50	☐	☐	☐	☐
30511	$7.00	☐	☐	☐	☐
30518	$8.00	☐	☐	☐	☐
30602	$2.50	☐	☐	☐	☐
30606	$2.50	☐	☐	☐	☐
31566	$2.50	☐	☐	☐	☐
31581	$2.50	☐	☐	☐	☐
31590	$2.50	☐	☐	☐	☐

AIR MAIL ISSUES

1969 ISSUES

#C76 10¢ MOON LANDING

		UL	UR	LL	LR
31371	$1.25	☐	☐	☐	☐
31374	$1.25	☐	☐	☐	☐
31375	$1.25	☐	☐	☐	☐
31376	$1.25	☐	☐	☐	☐
31378	$1.25	☐	☐	☐	☐
31381	$1.25	☐	☐	☐	☐
31382	$1.25	☐	☐	☐	☐
31384	$1.25	☐	☐	☐	☐
31387	$1.25	☐	☐	☐	☐
31388	$1.25	☐	☐	☐	☐
31390	$1.25	☐	☐	☐	☐
31392	$1.25	☐	☐	☐	☐
31400	$1.25	☐	☐	☐	☐
31401	$1.25	☐	☐	☐	☐
31405	$1.25	☐	☐	☐	☐

1971-73 ISSUES

#C77 9¢ DELTA WING

32945	$1.00	☐	☐	☐	☐
32946	$1.00	☐	☐	☐	☐

#C78 11¢ JET AIRLINER

32941	$1.00	☐	☐	☐	☐
32942	$1.00	☐	☐	☐	☐
32998	$1.00	☐	☐	☐	☐
32999	$1.00	☐	☐	☐	☐
33019	$1.00	☐	☐	☐	☐
33020	$1.00	☐	☐	☐	☐
33887	$6.50	☐	☐	☐	☐
33888	$6.50	☐	☐	☐	☐

#C78a 11¢ JET AIRLINER BOOKLET

360 Subjects PANES OF 4

32964 32965 32994 32995 33485
33486

See Appendix G for the largest reported plate number percentage by position.

#C79 13¢ WINGED ENVELOPE

34557	$1.20	☐	☐	☐	☐
34558	$1.20	☐	☐	☐	☐
34584	$1.20	☐	☐	☐	☐
34653	$1.20	☐	☐	☐	☐
35579	$1.20	☐	☐	☐	☐
35580	$1.20	☐	☐	☐	☐

#C79a 13¢ WINGED ENVELOPE BOOKLET

360 Sujects PANES OF 5

34795 34796 34843 34844 35338
35339

See Appendix G for the largest reported plate number percentage by position.

1971-73 ISSUES

#C80 17¢ STATUE OF LIBERTY

		UL	UR	LL	LR
33092	$1.70	☐	☐	☐	☐
33093	$1.70	☐	☐	☐	☐
33094	$1.70	☐	☐	☐	☐
33096	$1.70	☐	☐	☐	☐
33097	$1.70	☐	☐	☐	☐
33098	$1.70	☐	☐	☐	☐
33099	$1.70	☐	☐	☐	☐
33100	$1.70	☐	☐	☐	☐

#C81 21¢ USA and JET

33003	$1.75	☐	☐	☐	☐
33005	$1.75	☐	☐	☐	☐
33007	$1.75	☐	☐	☐	☐
33009	$1.75	☐	☐	☐	☐
33012	$4.00	☐	☐	☐	☐
33013	$4.00	☐	☐	☐	☐
33017	$1.75	☐	☐	☐	☐
33018	$4.00	☐	☐	☐	☐
33027	$4.00	☐	☐	☐	☐
33029	$4.00	☐	☐	☐	☐
33030	$4.00	☐	☐	☐	☐
33242	$1.75	☐	☐	☐	☐
33246	$1.75	☐	☐	☐	☐
33248	$1.75	☐	☐	☐	☐
33279	$1.75	☐	☐	☐	☐
33332	$1.75	☐	☐	☐	☐
33550	$1.75	☐	☐	☐	☐
35128	$1.75	☐	☐	☐	☐
35704	$1.75	☐	☐	☐	☐

#C82 11¢ JET AIRLINER COIL

432 Subject Plates STRIPS OF 6

32943 32944 33000 33001 33244
33697

#C83 13¢ WINGED ENVELOPE COIL

432 Subject Plates STRIPS OF 6

34739 34740 34741 34742 35565
35566 †35670 †35671

1972 ISSUES

#C84 11¢ NATIONAL PARKS

33454	$.90	☐	☐	☐	☐
33459	$.90	☐	☐	☐	☐
33461	$.90	☐	☐	☐	☐
33463	$.90	☐	☐	☐	☐
33465	$.90	☐	☐	☐	☐
33466	$.90	☐	☐	☐	☐
33468	$.90	☐	☐	☐	☐
33481	$.90	☐	☐	☐	☐

#C85 11¢ OLYMPICS

Block of 10 (2 x 5)

33322-33323-33324-33325-33326

	$2.25	☐	☐	☐	☐

AIR MAIL ISSUES

1973 ISSUE

#C86 11¢ ELECTRONICS

		UL	UR	LL	LR
34190	$1.00	☐	☐	☐	☐
34191	$1.00	☐	☐	☐	☐
34192	$1.00	☐	☐	☐	☐
34197	$1.00	☐	☐	☐	☐
34232	$1.00	☐	☐	☐	☐
34235	$1.00	☐	☐	☐	☐

1974 ISSUES

#C87 18¢ STATUE OF LIBERTY

34932-34928	$1.50	☐	☐	☐	☐
34932-34931	$1.50	☐	☐	☐	☐
34932-34941	$1.50	☐	☐	☐	☐
34932-34955	$1.50	☐	☐	☐	☐
34942-34928	$1.50	☐	☐	☐	☐
34942-34931	$1.50	☐	☐	☐	☐
34942-34941	$1.50	☐	☐	☐	☐
34942-34955	$1.50	☐	☐	☐	☐
34956-34928	$1.50	☐	☐	☐	☐
34956-34931	$1.50	☐	☐	☐	☐
34956-34941	$1.50	☐	☐	☐	☐
34956-34955	$1.50	☐	☐	☐	☐
34959-34928	$4.00	☐	☐	☐	☐
34959-34931	$4.00	☐	☐	☐	☐
34959-34941	$35.00	☐	☐	☐	☐
34959-34955	$4.00	☐	☐	☐	☐

#C88 26¢ MOUNT RUSHMORE

34774	$2.50	☐	☐	☐	☐
34851	$2.50	☐	☐	☐	☐
34853	$2.50	☐	☐	☐	☐
34860	$2.50	☐	☐	☐	☐
34867	$2.50	☐	☐	☐	☐
34875	$2.50	☐	☐	☐	☐
34907	$2.50	☐	☐	☐	☐
34927	$2.50	☐	☐	☐	☐

1975 ISSUES

#C89 25¢ PLANE and GLOBES

36956	$2.50	☐	☐	☐	☐
36957	$2.50	☐	☐	☐	☐
36959	$2.50	☐	☐	☐	☐
36976	$2.50	☐	☐	☐	☐
36979	$2.50	☐	☐	☐	☐
36988	$2.50	☐	☐	☐	☐
37001	$5.00	☐	☐3	☐	☐

1975 ISSUES

#C90 31¢ PLANE, GLOBE and FLAG

		UL	UR	LL	LR
36977	$2.50	☐	☐	☐	☐
36981	$2.50	☐	☐	☐	☐
36989	$2.50	☐	☐	☐	☐
37002	$2.50	☐	☐	☐	☐
37014	$2.50	☐	☐	☐	☐
37034	$2.50	☐	☐	☐	☐
37344	$2.50	☐	☐	☐	☐
37402	$2.50	☐	☐	☐	☐
37614	$2.50	☐	☐	☐	☐
37927	$2.50	☐	☐	☐	☐
37950	$2.50	☐	☐	☐	☐
38309	$2.50	☐	☐	☐	☐
38310	$2.50	☐	☐	☐	☐
38312	$2.50	☐	☐	☐	☐
38313	$2.50	☐	☐	☐	☐
38314	$2.50	☐	☐	☐	☐

1978 ISSUE

#C91-92 31¢ WRIGHT BROTHERS

38844	$3.00	☐	☐	☐	☐
38845	$3.00	☐	☐	☐	☐
38853	$3.00	☐	☐	☐	☐
38856	$3.00	☐	☐	☐	☐
38857	$3.00	☐	☐	☐	☐
38858	$3.00	☐	☐	☐	☐
38859	$3.00	☐	☐	☐	☐
38860	$3.00	☐	☐	☐	☐
38861	$3.00	☐	☐	☐	☐

1979 ISSUES

#C93-94 21¢ OCTAVE CHANUTE

39007	$4.00	☐	☐	☐	☐
39008	$4.00	☐	☐	☐	☐
39014	$4.00	☐	☐	☐	☐
39015	$4.00	☐	☐	☐	☐
39017	$15.00	☐	☐	☐	☐
39018	$15.00	☐	☐	☐	☐
39019	$15.00	☐	☐	☐	☐
39020	$15.00	☐	☐	☐	☐

#C95-96 25¢ WILEY POST

39193	$10.00	☐	☐	☐	☐
39197	$10.00	☐	☐	☐	☐
39198	$10.00	☐	☐	☐	☐
39210	$10.00	☐	☐	☐	☐

#C97 31¢ SUMMER OLYMPICS

Block of 12 (6 x 2)

39117-39118-39119-39120-39121-39122

	$10.00	☐	☐	☐	☐

AIR MAIL ISSUES

1980 ISSUES

#C98 40¢ PHILIP MAZZEI
Block of 12 (6 x 2)
Bull's Eye Perf. 11.2 x 11.2
39461-39462-39463-39464-39465-39466

		UL	UR	LL	LR
	$9.00	☐	☐	☐	☐

40518-40519-40520-40521-40522-40523

	$9.00	☐	☐	☐	☐

#C98a 40¢ PHILIP MAZZEI
Block of 12 (6 x 2)
EE Perf. 10.5 x 11.3
39461-39462-39463-39464-39465-39466

	$75.00	☐	☐	☐	☐

#C99 28¢ BLANCHE SCOTT
Block of 12 (2 x 6)
39537-39538-39539-39540-39541-39542

	$7.00	☐	☐	☐	☐

#C100 35¢ GLENN CURTISS
Block of 12 (2 x 6)
39502-39503-39504-39505-39506-39507

	$8.00	☐	☐	☐	☐

1983 ISSUES

#C101-04 28¢ OLYMPIC GAMES

2222	$4.00	☐	☐	☐	☐
3333	$7.00	☐	☐	☐	☐

#C105-08 40¢ OLYMPIC GAMES
Bull's Eye Perf. 11.2 x 11.2

2222	$4.00	☐	☐	☐	☐

#C105a,6a,7a,8c 40¢ OLYMPIC GAMES
L - Perf. 10.9 x 10.9

2222	$7.00	☐	☐	☐	☐

#C109-12 35¢ OLYMPIC GAMES

1111	$5.00	☐	☐	☐	☐

1985 ISSUES

#C113 33¢ ALFRED V. VERVILLE
(combined wlth #C114)

11111	$3.00	☐	‡	‡	☐
12111	$3.00	☐	‡	‡	☐

#C114 39¢ LAWRENCE AND ELMER SPERRY
(combined with #C113)

11111	$3.50	‡	☐	☐	‡
12111	$3.50	‡	☐	☐	‡

(new printing of four position stock of #C114 only)

1111	$3.50	☐	☐	☐	☐

#C115 44¢ TRANSPACIFIC AIRMAIL

1111	$4.00	☐	☐	☐	☐
1112	$4.00	☐	☐	☐	☐

1985 ISSUES

#C116 44¢ FR. JUNIPERO SERRA

		UL	UR	LL	LR
1111	$7.00	☐	☐	☐	☐

1988 ISSUES

#C117 44¢ NEW SWEDEN

1111-1	$7.50	☐	☐	☐	☐

#C118 45¢ SAMUEL P. LANGLEY
Block tagged

111111-1	$4.00	☐	☐	☐	☐
111121-1	$4.00	☐	☐	☐	☐
111131-1	$4.00	☐	☐	☐	☐
111231-1	$4.00	☐	☐	☐	☐
111232-1	$4.00	☐	☐	☐	☐
121232-1	$4.00	☐	☐	☐	☐
222232-1	$4.00	☐	☐	☐	☐
223232-1	$4.00	☐	☐	☐	☐
224232-1	$4.00	☐	☐	☐	☐
224233-1	$10.00	☐	☐	☐	☐
324233-1	$10.00	☐	☐	☐	☐
324343-1	$4.00	☐	☐	☐	☐
334344-1	$4.00	☐	☐	☐	☐
335344-1	$10.00	☐	☐	☐	☐
435344-1	$4.00	☐	☐	☐	☐
435364-1	$4.00	☐	☐	☐	☐
435464-1	$4.00	☐	☐	☐	☐
445564-1	$10.00	☐	☐	☐	☐
446564-1	$4.00	☐	☐	☐	☐
447564-1	$4.00	☐	☐	☐	☐
447565-1	$4.00	☐	☐	☐	☐
647565-1	$4.00	☐	☐	☐	☐
779898-1	$10.00	☐	☐	☐	☐
879898-1	$10.00	☐	☐	☐	☐
979898-1	$4.00	☐	☐	☐	☐
979899-1	$4.00	☐	☐	☐	☐

Overall tagged

999999-1	$30.00	☐	☐	☐	☐

#C119 36¢ IGOR SIKORSKY

11111-1	$3.00	☐	☐	☐	☐
12112-1	$3.00	☐	☐	☐	☐
21111-1	$3.00	☐	☐	☐	☐
21112-1	$3.00	☐	☐	☐	☐
22112-1	$3.00	☐	☐	☐	☐
32111-1	$7.50	☐	☐	☐	☐
32211-1	$3.00	☐	☐	☐	☐
42211-1	$3.00	☐	☐	☐	☐

1989 ISSUES

#C120 45¢ FRENCH REVOLUTION

111-1	$4.00	☐	☐	☐	☐
121-1	$4.00	☐	☐	☐	☐
122-1	$4.00	☐	☐	☐	☐
222-1	$4.00	☐	☐	☐	☐

AIR MAIL ISSUES

1989 ISSUES

#C121 45¢ AMERICA ISSUE

		UL	UR	LL	LR
1111	$5.00	□	□	□	□

#C122-25 45¢ 20th UPU CONGRESS

1111-1	$4.50	□	□	□	□
1112-1	$4.50	□	□	□	□
2223-1	$4.50	□	□	□	□
2233-1	$4.50	□	□	□	□
2243-1	$4.50	□	□	□	□
2263-1	$4.50	□	□	□	□

#C126 $1.80 20th UPU CONGRESS SOUVENIR SHEET

Issued without plate numbers.

1990 ISSUE

#C127 45¢ AMERICA

A1111	$5.00	□	‡	‡	‡

See #2512 for other positions.

1991-93 ISSUES

#C128 50¢ HARRIET QUIMBY

L - Perf. 10.9 Uniform prephosphored

S1111	$4.50	□	□	□	□

#C128b 50¢ HARRIET QUIMBY

Bull's Eye Perf. 11.2 Uniform prephosphored

S2222	$4.50	□	□	□	□

#C129 40¢ WILLIAM PIPER

L - Perf 10.9 Overall tagged

A1111	$3.75	□	□	□	□

#C130 50¢ ANTARCTIC TREATY

S1111	$4.50	□	□	□	□

#C131 50¢ AMERICA

111111	$4.50	□	□	□	□

#C132 40¢ WILLIAM PIPER

Bull's Eye Perf. 11.2 Uniform prephosphored

S1111	$3.75	□	□	□	□

AIR MAIL SPECIAL DELIVERY

1934 FIRST ISSUE

#CE1 16¢ BLUE

		TL	TR	L	R	B
21312	$16.00	□	□	‡	‡	□
21313	$16.00	□	□	‡	‡	□
21314	$16.00	□	□	‡	‡	□
21315	$16.00	□	□	‡	‡	□

1936 SECOND ISSUE

#CE2 16¢ BICOLORED

The prlces for the Letter Value are as shown below:

E	$8.50	P	$35.00
A	$9.00	S	$40.00
B	$9.50	T	$45.00
C	$10.00	V	$50.00
D	$12.00	X	$65.00
H	$14.00	Y	$70.00
K	$18.00	Z	$80.00
N	$20.00		

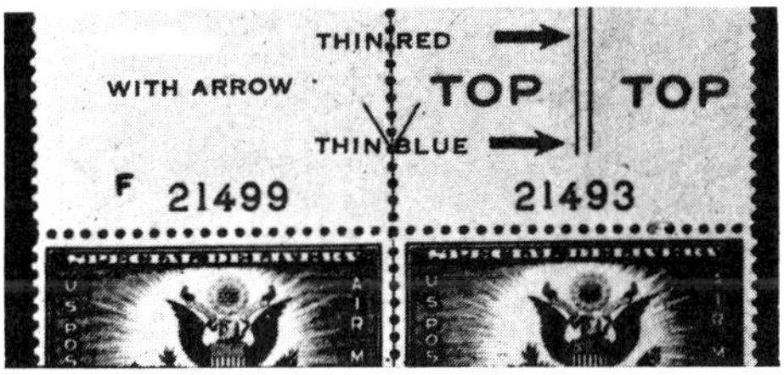

THIN RED THIN BLUE TYPE 1

Extra thin vertical red lines were added to both panes of plate 21491 and the left pane of 21493 for later printings of Type 1. See US Specialist, November 1972 for illustrations.

RELATIVE SCARCITY GRADES FOR TYPE 1

	F21495	F21496	F21497	F21498	F21499	F21500	F21501	F21502
21491	E	A	E	E	A	B	E	C
F21491	E	A	A	E	B	A	B	C
21492	E	E	E	E	E	B	A	B
F21492	E	E	E	E	E	A	B	B
21493	E	E	E	E	E	A	E	A
F21493	E	E	E	E	A	B	C	C
21494	E	E	E	E	E	B	B	A
F21494	E	E	E	E	E	E	B	B

AIR MAIL SPECIAL DELIVERY

#CE2 16¢ BICOLORED Cont.

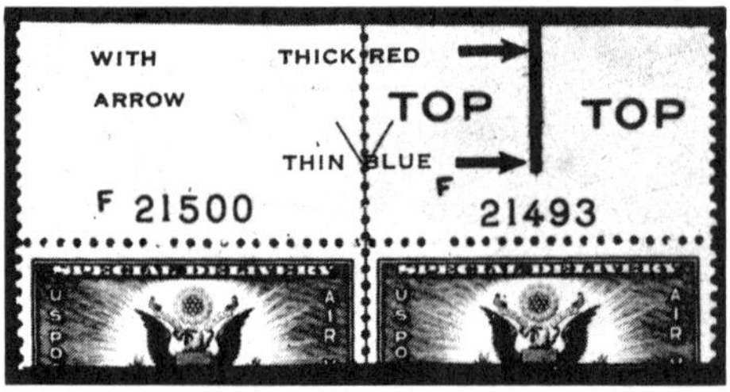

THICK RED THIN BLUE TYPE 2

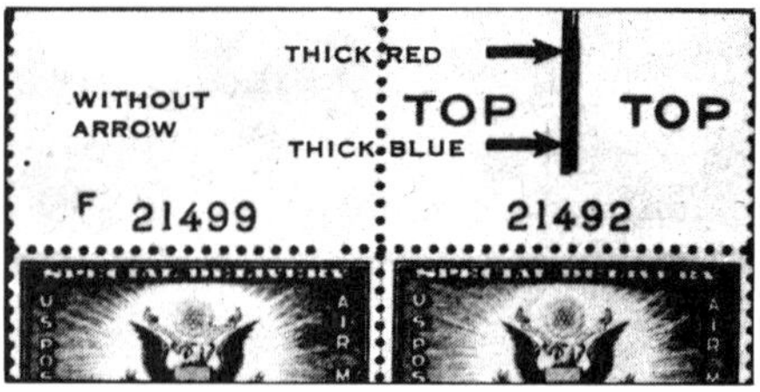

THICK RED THICK BLUE TYPE 4

RELATIVE SCARCITY GRADES FOR TYPE 2

	F21495	F21496	F21497	F21498	F21499	F21500	F21501	F21502
21491	X	X	V	T	Z	Z	†	Y
F21491	Y	Z	Z	Z	V	S	T	S
21492	V	S	T	P	Z	Z	Z	Z
F21492	Z	Y	Y	Z	T	P	T	S
21493	S	S	T	T	Z	Z	Z	Z
F21493	Z	Z	Z	Z	S	S	T	P
21494	S	T	P	X	Z	Y	Z	†
F21494	Z	Y	Z	Z	T	T	P	V

RELATIVE SCARCITY GRADES FOR TYPE 4

	F21495	F21496	F21497	F21498	F21499	F21500	F21501	F21502
21491	D	C	C	D	K	D	K	N
F21491	B	D	B	B	H	K	H	D
21492	C	C	C	C	N	K	K	H
F21492	C	C	C	C	K	K	N	K
21493	H	D	B	D	N	K	H	H
F21493	B	B	B	B	N	D	H	H
21494	D	D	D	C	H	K	D	H
F21494	C	D	C	B	D	D	H	D

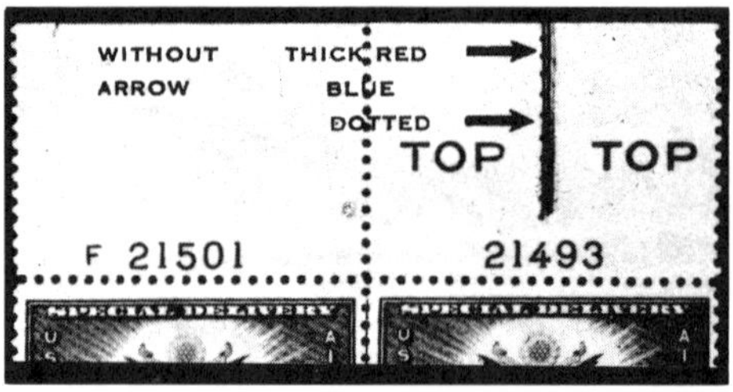

THICK RED DOTTED BLUE TYPE 3

Note for Type 3:
There are five blue dots per mm on plates ending with 96, 97, 99, 01 and 7 dots per mm on plates ending with 95, 98, 00, 02.

RELATIVE SCARCITY GRADES FOR TYPE 3

	F21495	F21496	F21497	F21498	F21499	F21500	F21501	F21502
21491	X	Y	X	Y	Y	Y	Z	Z
F21491	Z	Y	Y	Z	Z	Z	X	Z
21492	Z	X	Z	X	Z	Y	Z	X
F21492	Y	Z	Z	X	Y	X	Y	Z
21493	Y	Y	Y	Y	Y	Z	Z	Z
F21493	Z	Y	Z	Y	Z	Y	Z	Y
21494	Y	Z	X	Y	Z	Y	Y	Z
F21494	Y	Y	Y	X	Y	Y	Z	Z

SPECIAL DELIVERY ISSUES

Printed by the American Bank Note Co.

Plate numbers are in top and bottom margins only preceded by "No." The plate number follows the imprint in all positions, but in TL and BL positions the plate # stamp has a straight right edge, while in TR and BR positions it is perfed on the right side, and has or originally had the side margin attached.

Unwatermarked Perf. 12

Imprint F

1885 ISSUE

#E1 10c MESSENGER RUNNING

Imprint Strip of 4	**TL,TR,BL,BR**	$1,400
Imprint Block of 8	**TL,TR,BL,BR**	$10,000

495 496

These 2 plates have split arrows on the plate # stamp in TL and BL positions.

1888 ISSUE

#E2 10c MESSENGER RUNNING (blue)

Imprint Strip of 4	**TL,TR,BL,BR**	$1,400
Imprint Block of 8	**TL,TR,BL,BR**	$10,000

552 73

There are no top or bottom arrows on these two plates. Plate 552 was made first (it was numbered in the series of 1882, while plate 73 was numbered in the series of 1890).

1893 COLUMBUAN ISSUE

#E3 10c MESSENGER RUNNING(orange)

Imprint Strip of 4	**TL,TR,BL,BR**	$900
Imprint Block of 8	**TL,TR,BL,BR**	$5500

552 73

Printed by the
Bureau of Engraving and Printing

1894 ISSUE

The TL and TR, or BL and BR plate numbers differ slightly in position, and can be distinguished. See U.S. Specialist, May 1995, p 196.

FLAT PRESS Perf. 12

Unwatermarked

#E4 10¢ SPECIAL DELIVERY

Imprint Strip of 3	**T, B**	$3,000
Imprint Block of 6	**T, B**	$12,500

Imprint III

77

1895 ISSUE

Double Line Wmk. Perf. 12

#E5 10¢ SPECIAL DELIVERY

Basic Price:

Imprint Strip of 3	**T, B**	$700
Imprint Block of 6	**T, B**	$4,250

Imprint III

77

Imprint VI

257

Imprint VII

*381	492	*880	*881	*882
*883	*1257	*1258	*1259	*1260

SPECIAL DELIVERY ISSUES

1902 ISSUE

Double Line Wmk. Perf. 12

#E6 10¢ SPECIAL DELIVERY

Basic Price

Imprint Strip of 3	T, B	$425
Imprint Block of 6	T, B	$2,300

Imprint VII

1481 1482 1483 1484 1773
1774 1775 1776 *5240 *5243
*5244 *5245

#E6 1909 REISSUE

Basic Price

Imprint Strip of 3	T, B	$400
Imprint Block of 6	T, B	$2,100

Imprint VII

5240-09 5243-09 5244-09 5245-09

1908 ISSUE

Double Line Wmk. Perf. 12

#E7 10¢ SPECIAL DELIVERY

Basic Price

Imprint Block of 6	T	$1,000
Imprint Block of 6	L, R, B	$900

Imprint V

4916 4917 4920 4921

1911 ISSUE

Single Line Wmk. Perf. 12

#E8 10¢ SPECIAL DELIVERY

Basic Price

Imprint Block of 6	T	$2,400
Imprint Block of 6	L, R, B	$2,200

Imprint VII

5513 5514 *5520 5535 5539

Basic Price

Block of 6	T	$2,600
Block of 6	L, R, B	$2,400

Imprint IX

5854 5857 5860 5863

1914 ISSUE

Single Line Wmk. Perf. 10

#E9 10¢ SPECIAL DELIVERY

Imprint Block of 6	T	$4,800
Imprint Block of 6	L, R, B	$4,500

Imprint VII

5520

Basic Price

Block of 6	T	$4,000
Block of 6	L, R, B	$3,600

Imprint IX

5854 5857 5860 5863 6043
6046 6049

1916 ISSUE

Unwatermarked Perf. 10

#E10 10¢ SPECIAL DELIVERY

Imprint Block of 6	T	$6,000
Imprint Block of 6	L, R, B	$5,500

Imprint VII

5520

Basic Price

Block of 6	T	$5,300
Block of 6	L, R, B	$4,800

Imprint IX

6043 6046 6049

1917 ISSUE

Unwatermarked Perf. 11

#E11 10¢ SPECIAL DELIVERY

Imprint Block of 6	T	$850
Imprint Block of 6	L, R, B	$750

Imprint VII

5520

Basic Price

Block of 6	T (TL, TR)	$250
Block of 6	L, R, B	$200

Imprint IX

6043 6046 6049 7642 7643
7648 7653

Positions **TL, TR, L, R, B**

8506 8507 8508 8509 10274
10275 10276 10277 10631 10632
10634 10653 11814 11815 11816
11817 13391 13392 13393 13394
13552 13553 13554 13555 13816
13817 *13818 *13819

1922 ISSUE

Unwatermarked Perf. 11

#E12 10¢ SPECIAL DELIVERY

Basic Price	TL, TR	$350
Basic Price	L, R, B	$300

13916 13917 13918 13919 13920
13921 *13922 *13923 14262 14263
14264 14265 14328 14329 14330
14331 *14579 14614 14615 14616
14617 15101 15102 15103 15104
15231 15232 15233 15234 16091
16092 16093 16094 *16119 16120
16121 16122 17223 17224 17225
17226 17239 17240 17241 17242
17513 17514 17515 17516 17564

17565 17566 17567 17625 17626
*17627 17628 17637 17638 17639
17640 *17641 17642 17643 *17644
18683 18684 *18685 *18686

SPECIAL DELIVERY ISSUES

1925 ISSUE

Unwatermarked Perf. 11

#E13 15¢ SPECIAL DELIVERY

Basic Price **TL, TR** $250
Basic Price **L, R, B** $200

16833 16834 16835 16836 16857
*16858 16859 16860

#E14 20¢ SPECIAL DELIVERY

Basic Price **TL, TR** $45
Basic Price **L, R, B** $35

17175 17176 17177 17178 17183
17184 17185 17186 17191 17192
17193 17199 *17206 *17211 *17213
*17214

1927 ISSUE

Unwatermarked Perf. 11 x 10°
ROTARY PRESS **Block of 4**

#E15 10¢ SPECIAL DELIVERY

		UL	UR	LL	LR
18919	$10	☐	☐	☐	☐
18920	$5	☐	☐	☐	☐
19248	$15	☐	☐	☐	☐
19249	$10	☐	☐	☐	☐
19260	$20	☐	☐	☐	☐
19261	$7	☐	☐	☐	☐
19280	$5	☐	☐	☐	☐
19281	$7	☐	☐	☐	☐
19282	$10	☐	☐	☐	☐
19283	$10	☐	☐	☐	☐
22738	$5	☐	☐	☐	☐
22739	$5	☐	☐	☐	☐
22841	$15	☐	☐	☐	☐
22842	$15	☐	☐	☐	☐
23105	$20	☐	☐	☐	☐
23106	$15	☐	☐	☐	☐

1931 ISSUE

#E16 15¢ SPECIAL DELIVERY

20595	$7.50	☐	☐	☐	☐
20596	$7.50	☐	☐	☐	☐
23034	$5.00	☐	☐	☐	☐
23035	$5.00	☐	☐	☐	☐

1944 ISSUE

#E17 13¢ SPECIAL DELIVERY

23170	$3.75	☐	☐	☐	☐
23171	$3.75	☐	☐	☐	☐
23172	$3.75	☐	☐	☐	☐
23173	$3.75	☐	☐	☐	☐
23720	$5.00	☐	☐	☐	☐
23721	$5.00	☐	☐	☐	☐

#E18 17¢ SPECIAL DELIVERY

23168	$25.00	☐	☐	☐	☐
23169	$25.00	☐	☐	☐	☐

1951 ISSUE

#E19 20¢ SPECIAL DELIVERY

		UL	UR	LL	LR
24552	$7.00	☐	☐	☐	☐
24553	$7.00	☐	☐	☐	☐
24554	$10.00	☐	☐	☐	☐
24555	$10.00	☐	☐	☐	☐

1954 ISSUE

#E20 20¢ SPECIAL DELIVERY

25054	$3	☐	☐	☐	☐
25055	$3	☐	☐	☐	☐
25059	$3	☐	☐	☐	☐
25060	$3	☐	☐	☐	☐
25065	$5	☐	☐	☐	☐
25066	$5	☐	☐	☐	☐

1957 ISSUE

#E21 30¢ SPECIAL DELIVERY

25796	$3.00	☐	☐	☐	☐
25797	$3.00	☐	☐	☐	☐
25806	$3.00	☐	☐	☐	☐
25807	$3.00	☐	☐	☐	☐
27812	$3.00	☐	☐	☐	☐
27813	$3.00	☐	☐	☐	☐
28410	$3.75	☐	☐	☐	☐
28411	$3.75	☐	☐	☐	☐

1969 ISSUE

#E22 45¢ SPECIAL DELIVERY

31484	$7	☐	☐	☐	☐
31485	$7	☐	☐	☐	☐
31487	$7	☐	☐	☐	☐
31492	$15	☐	☐	☐	☐
31495	$7	☐	☐	☐	☐
31504	$7	☐	☐	☐	☐
31506	$7	☐	☐	☐	☐
31507	$7	☐	☐	☐	☐
31510	$7	☐	☐	☐	☐

1971 ISSUE

#E23 60¢ SPECIAL DELIVERY

32962	$5	☐	☐	☐	☐
32977	$5	☐	☐	☐	☐
32985	$5	☐	☐	☐	☐
32986	$5	☐	☐	☐	☐
33002	$5	☐	☐	☐	☐
33004	$5	☐	☐	☐	☐
33006	$5	☐	☐	☐	☐
33008	$5	☐	☐	☐	☐

REGISTRATION STAMP

1911 ISSUE

Single Line Wmk. Perf. 12
FLAT PRESS Block of 6

#F1 10¢ REGISTRY

Imprint XII

		T	L	R	B
5720	$1,600	☐	☐	☐	☐
5723	$1,600	☐	☐	☐	☐
5726	$1,600	☐	☐	☐	☐
5729	$1,600	☐	☐	☐	☐

CERTIFIED MAIL

1955 ISSUE

Unwatermarked Perf. 10° X 11
ROTARY PRESS Block of 4

#FA1 15¢ CERTIFIED MAIL

		UL	UR	LL	LR
25179	$5	☐	☐	☐	☐
25180	$5	☐	☐	☐	☐

POSTAGE DUE ISSUES

Printed by the American Bank Note Co. Plate numbers are in top and bottom margins only preceded by "No." In TL and BL positions the plate number follows the imprint, while in TR and BR positions it precedes it.

Unwatermarked Perf. 12

Imprint F

1879 ISSUE (brown)

#J1 1c POSTAGE DUE

Imprint strip of 5	TL,TR,BL,BR	$200
Imprint block of 10	TL,TR,BL,BR	$375

313 314

#J2 2c POSTAGE DUE

Imprint strip of 5	TL,TR,BL,BR	-
Imprint block of 10	TL,TR,BL,BR	-

315 464

In the BR position of plate 315, only the first two digits are entered.

#J3 3c POSTAGE DUE

Imprint strip of 5	TL,TR,BL,BR	$200
Imprint block of 10	TL,TR,BL,BR	$375

316 317

#J4 5c POSTAGE DUE

Imprint strip of 5	TL,TR,BL,BR	-
Imprint block of 10	TL,TR,BL,BR	-

318

#J5 10c POSTAGE DUE

Imprint strip of 5	TL,TR,BL,BR	-
Imprint block of 10	TL,TR,BL,BR	-

331

#J6 30c POSTAGE DUE

Imprint strip of 5	TL,TR,BL,BR	$1000
Imprint block of 10	TL,TR,BL,BR	$1800

332

#J7 50c POSTAGE DUE

Imprint strip of 5	TL,TR,BL,BR	-
Imprint block of 10	TL,TR,BL,BR	-

333

POSTAGE DUE ISSUES

1884 ISSUE (red brown)

#J15 1c POSTAGE DUE

Imprint strip of 5	**TL,TR,BL,BR**	$200
Imprint block of 10	**TL,TR,BL,BR**	$375

313 314

#J16 2c POSTAGE DUE

Imprint strip of 5	**TL,TR,BL,BR**	$250
Imprint block of 10	**TL,TR,BL,BR**	$450

315 464

In the BR position of plate 315, only the first two digits are entered.

#J17 3c POSTAGE DUE

Imprint strip of 5	**TL,TR,BL,BR**	-
Imprint block of 10	**TL,TR,BL,BR**	-

316 317

#J18 5c POSTAGE DUE

Imprint strip of 5	**TL,TR,BL,BR**	-
Imprint block of 10	**TL,TR,BL,BR**	-

318

#J19 10c POSTAGE DUE

Imprint strip of 5	**TL,TR,BL,BR**	-
Imprint block of 10	**TL,TR,BL,BR**	-

331

#J20 30c POSTAGE DUE

Imprint strip of 5	**TL,TR,BL,BR**	$500
Imprint block of 10	**TL,TR,BL,BR**	$900

332

#J21 50c POSTAGE DUE

Imprint strip of 5	**TL,TR,BL,BR**	-
Imprint block of 10	**TL,TR,BL,BR**	-

333

1884 ISSUE (bright claret)

#J22 1c POSTAGE DUE

Imprint strip of 5	**TL,TR,BL,BR**	$75
Imprint block of 10	**TL,TR,BL,BR**	$125

313 314

#J23 2c POSTAGE DUE

Imprint strip of 5	**TL,TR,BL,BR**	$80
Imprint block of 10	**TL,TR,BL,BR**	$150

315 464

In the BR position of plate 315, only the first two digits are entered.

#J24 3c POSTAGE DUE

Imprint strip of 5	**TL,TR,BL,BR**	$275
Imprint block of 10	**TL,TR,BL,BR**	$500

316 317

1884 ISSUE (bright claret)

#J25 5c POSTAGE DUE

Imprint strip of 5	**TL,TR,BL,BR**	$300
Imprint block of 10	**TL,TR,BL,BR**	$550

318

#J26 10c POSTAGE DUE

Imprint strip of 5	**TL,TR,BL,BR**	$400
Imprint block of 10	**TL,TR,BL,BR**	$750

331

#J27 30c POSTAGE DUE

Imprint strip of 5	**TL,TR,BL,BR**	$1500
Imprint block of 10	**TL,TR,BL,BR**	-

332

#J28 50c POSTAGE DUE

Imprint strip of 5	**TL,TR,BL,BR**	$1500
Imprint block of 10	**TL,TR,BL,BR**	-

333

Printed by the
Bureau of Engraving and Printing.

1894 ISSUE

Plate numbers follow the imprint in all positions. The TL and TR, or BL and BR plate numbers differ slightly in position, and can be distinguished. See U.S. Specialist, May 1995, p 196.

FLAT PRESS **Block of 6**
Unwatermarked Perf. 12

#J29 1¢ POSTAGE DUE

Imprint Strip of 3	**T, B**	$2,000
Imprint Block of 6	**T, B**	$7,500

Imprint I

57

#J30 2¢ POSTAGE DUE

Imprint Strip of 3	**T, B**	$850
Imprint Block of 6	**T, B**	$3,500

Imprint I

34

J29 & J30 fluoresce under long wavelength ultraviolet light, while J31 and J32 do not.

#J31 1¢ POSTAGE DUE

Basic Price

Imprint Strip of 3	**T**	$150
Imprint Strip of 3	**B**	$125
Imprint Block of 6	**T**	$475
Imprint Block of 6	**B**	$425

Imprint I

57

Imprint II

147

POSTAGE DUE ISSUES

1894 ISSUE

#J32 2¢ POSTAGE DUE

Basic Price

Imprint Strip of 3	**T**	$125
Imprint Strip of 3	**B**	$100
Imprint Block of 6	**T**	$450
Imprint Block of 6	**B**	$400

Imprint I

60 159

#J33 3¢ POSTAGE DUE

Imprint Strip of 3	**T**	$650
Imprint Strip of 3	**B**	$250
Imprint Block of 6	**T**	$1,750
Imprint Block of 6	**B**	$850

Imprint I

70

#J34 5¢ POSTAGE DUE

Imprint Strip of 3	**T**	Rare
Imprint Strip of 3	**B**	$400
Imprint Block of 6	**T**	Rare
Imprint Block of 6	**B**	$1,200

Imprint I

71

#J35 10¢ POSTAGE DUE

Imprint Strip of 3	**T, B**	$300
Imprint Block of 6	**T, B**	$1,200

Imprint I

72

#J36 30¢ POSTAGE DUE

Imprint Strip of 3	**T, B**	$700
Imprint Block of 6	**T, B**	$2,500

Imprint I

73

#J37 50¢ POSTAGE DUE

Imprint Strip of 3	**T, B**	$1,800
Imprint Block of 6	**T, B**	$6,000

Imprint II

74

1895 ISSUE

Double Line Wmk. Perf.12

#J38 1¢ POSTAGE DUE

Basic Price

Imprint Strip of 3	**T, B**	$50
Imprint Block of 6	**T, B**	$200

Imprint I

57

Imprint II

147

Imprint IV

246 267

Imprint V

1632 *1777 *1778 1779 *1780

#J39 2¢ POSTAGE DUE

Basic Price

Imprint Strip of 3	**T, B**	$50
Imprint Block of 6	**T, B**	$200

Imprint I

60 159

Imprint IV

247 268

Imprint V

*1099 1242 1243 1244 1245
*1783 *1784 *1785 *1786

#J40 3¢ POSTAGE DUE

Basic Price

Imprint Strip of 3	**T, B**	$125
Imprint Block of 6	**T, B**	$500

Imprint I

70

Imprint IV

254

Imprint V

*1631 *1787

#J41 5¢ POSTAGE DUE

Basic Price

Imprint Strip of 3	**T, B**	$150
Imprint Block of 6	**T, B**	$550

Imprint I

71

Imprint V

255 *1642 *1792

POSTAGE DUE ISSUES

1895 ISSUE

#J42 10¢ POSTAGE DUE

Basic Price		
Imprint Strip of 3	**T, B**	$160
Imprint Block of 6	**T, B**	$600

Imprint I

72

Imprint IV

256

Imprint V

1633 *1781 *1782

#J43 30¢ POSTAGE DUE

Basic Price		
Imprint Strip of 3	**T, B**	$1,200
Imprint Block of 6	**T, B**	$4,500

Imprint I

73

#J44 50¢ POSTAGE DUE

Basic Price		
Imprint Strip of 3	**T, B**	$750
Imprint Block of 6	**T, B**	$2,500

Imprint II

74

1910-12 ISSUE

Single Line Wmk. Perf.12

#J45 1¢ POSTAGE DUE

Basic Price		
Imprint Block of 6	**T**	$450
Imprint Block of 6	**L, R, B**	$400

Imprint X

5510 5522 5534 5541

#J46 2¢ POSTAGE DUE

Basic Price		
Imprint Block of 6	**T**	$425
Imprint Block of 6	**L, R, B**	$375

Imprint X

5511 5519 5530 5538

Basic Price		
Block of 6	**T**	$600
Block of 6	**L, R, B**	$550

Imprint IX

6703 6704 6705 6706

#J47 3¢ POSTAGE DUE

Basic Price		
Imprint Block of 6	**T**	$4,000
Imprint Block of 6	**L, R, B**	$3,750

Imprint X

5523 5529

#J48 5¢ POSTAGE DUE

Basic Price		
Imprint Block of 6	**T**	$700
Imprint Block of 6	**L, R, B**	$650

Imprint X

5524 5531

1910-12 ISSUE

#J49 10¢ POSTAGE DUE

Basic Price		
Imprint Block of 6	**T**	$1,200
Imprint Block of 6	**L, R, B**	$1,100

Imprint X

5525 5532 5540 6555

#J50 50¢ POSTAGE DUE

Imprint Block of 6	**T**	$7,500
Imprint Block of 6	**L, R, B**	$7,000

Imprint X

5527

1914-15 ISSUE

Single Line Wmk. Perf. 10

#J52 1¢ POSTAGE DUE

Basic Price		
Imprint Block of 6	**T**	$550
Imprint Block of 6	**L, R, B**	$525

Imprint X

5510 5522 5534 5541

#J53 2¢ POSTAGE DUE

Basic Price	**T**	$425
Basic Price	**L, R, B**	$375

Imprint IX

6703 6704 6705 6706

#J54 3¢ POSTAGE DUE

Basic Price		
Imprint Block of 6	**T**	$5,000
Imprint Block of 6	**L, R, B**	$4,500

Imprint X

5523 5529

#J55 5¢ POSTAGE DUE

Basic Price		
Imprint Block of 6	**T**	$350
Imprint Block of 6	**L, R, B**	$300

Imprint X

5524 5531

#J56 10¢ POSTAGE DUE

Basic Price		
Imprint Block of 6	**T**	$650
Imprint Block of 6	**L, R, B**	$600

Imprint X

5525 5532 5540 6555

#J57 30¢ POSTAGE DUE

Basic Price		
Imprint Block of 6	**T**	$2,250
Imprint Block of 6	**L, R, B**	$2,000

Imprint X

5526

#J58 50¢ POSTAGE DUE

Basic Price		
Imprint Block of 6	**T**	$50,000
Imprint Block of 6	**L, R, B**	$50,000

Imprint X

5527

POSTAGE DUE ISSUES

1916 ISSUE

Unwatermarked Perf.10

#J59 1¢ POSTAGE DUE

Basic Price

Imprint Block of 6 **T** $12,000

Imprint Block of 6 **L, R, B** $11,000

Imprint X

5510 5522 5534 5541

#J60 2¢ POSTAGE DUE

Basic Price **T** $1,200

Basic Price **L, R, B** $1,100

Imprint IX

6703 6704 6705 6706

1917-23 ISSUE

Unwatermarked Perf.11

#J61 1¢ POSTAGE DUE

Basic Price

Imprint Block of 6 **T** $120

Imprint Block of 6 **L, R, B** $100

Imprint X

5510 5522 5534 5541

Basic Price

Block of 6 **T (TL,TR)** $50

Block of 6 **L, R, B** $40

Imprint IX

7122 7129 7132 7141 8211
8212 8213 8214

Positions TL, TR, L, R, B

13844 13845 13846 13847**N** *14034
*14035 *14036 *14037

N Inverted F on bottom left position

#J62 2¢ POSTAGE DUE

Basic Price

Block of 6 **T (TL,TR)** $45

Block of 6 **L, R, B** $35

Imprint IX

6703 6704 6705 6706 7121
*7126 7130 7134

Positions TL, TR, L, R, B

10335 10336 10337 10338 14026
14027 14028 14029 14596 14597
14598 14599 15828 *15829 19076
19077 19078 19079 19082 *19083
*19084 *19085

1917-23 ISSUE

#J63 3¢ POSTAGE DUE

Basic Price

Imprint Block of 6 **T** $125

Imprint Block of 6 **L, R, B** $100

Imprint X

5523 5529

Basic Price

Block of 6 **TL, TR** $100

Block of 6 **L, R, B** $90

Imprint IX

8477 8478 8479 8480

Without side plate numbers

*20069 *20070 *20071 *20072

#J64 5¢ POSTAGE DUE

Basic Price

Imprint Block of 6 **T** $125

Imprint Block of 6 **L, R, B** $100

Imprint X

5524 5531

Basic Price

Block of 6 **TL, TR** $150

Block of 6 **L, R, B** $125

Imprint IX

15854 15855 15856 15857 19469
19470 *19877 *19878

#J65 10¢ POSTAGE DUE

Basic Price

Imprint Block of 6 **T** $160

Imprint Block of 6 **L, R, B** $135

Imprint X

5525 5532 5540 6555 6556

Basic Price

Block of 6 **TL, TR** $175

Block of 6 **L, R, B** $150

Imprint IX

15860 *15861 *15862 15863 18724
18725 18726 18727

#J66 30¢ POSTAGE DUE

Basic Price

Imprint Block of 6 **T** $675

Imprint Block of 6 **L, R, B** $625

Imprint X

5526 5537

Basic Price

Block of 6 **TL, TR** $700

Block of 6 **L, R, B** $650

Imprint IX

15876 15877 *19881 *19882 *19883
*19884

POSTAGE DUE ISSUES

1917-23 ISSUE

#J67 50¢ POSTAGE DUE

Basic Price

Imprint Block of 6	**T**	$850
Imprint Block of 6	**L, R, B**	$800

Imprint X

5527 5533

Basic Price

Block of 6	**TL,TR**	$900
Block of 6	**L, R, B**	$850

Imprint IX

15886 15887

Without side plate numbers

*20035 *20036

1925 ISSUE

Unwatermarked Perf.11

#J68 ° ¢ POSTAGE DUE

		TL	TR	L	R	B
17127	$12	☐	☐	☐	☐	☐
17128	$12	☐	☐	☐	☐	☐
17129	$12	☐	☐	☐	☐	☐
17130	$12	☐	☐	☐	☐	☐
17131	$12	☐	☐	☐	☐	☐

1930-31 ISSUE

#J69 ° ¢ POSTAGE DUE

20239	$40	☐	☐	‡	‡	☐
20240	$40	☐	☐	‡	‡	☐
20241	$40	☐	☐	‡	‡	☐
20242	$40	☐	☐	‡	‡	☐

#J70 1¢ POSTAGE DUE

20162	$30	☐	☐	‡	‡	☐
20163	$30	☐	☐	‡	‡	☐
20164	$30	☐	☐	‡	‡	☐
20165	$30	☐	☐	‡	‡	☐

#J71 2¢ POSTAGE DUE

20217	$45	☐	☐	‡	‡	☐
20218	$45	☐	☐	‡	‡	☐
20219	$45	☐	☐	‡	‡	☐
20220	$45	☐	☐	‡	‡	☐
20251	$50	☐	☐	‡	‡	☐
20252	$50	☐	☐	‡	‡	☐
20253	$50	☐	☐	‡	‡	☐
20254	$50	☐	☐	‡	‡	☐

#J72 3¢ POSTAGE DUE

20213	$260	☐	☐	‡	‡	☐
20214	$260	☐	☐	‡	‡	☐
20215	$260	☐	☐	‡	‡	☐
20216	$260	☐	☐	‡	‡	☐

1930-31 ISSUE

#J73 5¢ POSTAGE DUE

20209	$225	☐	☐	‡	‡	☐
20210	$225	☐	☐	‡	‡	☐
20211	$225	☐	☐	‡	‡	☐
20212	$225	☐	☐	‡	‡	☐

#J74 10¢ POSTAGE DUE

		TL	TR	L	R	B
20235	$400	☐	☐	‡	‡	☐
20236	$400	☐	☐	‡	‡	☐
20237	$400	☐	☐	‡	‡	☐
20238	$400	☐	☐	‡	‡	☐

#J75 30¢ POSTAGE DUE

20225	$1,200	☐	☐	‡	‡	☐
20226	$1,200	☐	☐	‡	‡	☐
20227	$1,200	☐	☐	‡	‡	☐
20228	$1,200	☐	☐	‡	‡	☐

#J76 50¢ POSTAGE DUE

20229	$1,300	☐	☐	‡	‡	☐
20230	$1,300	☐	☐	‡	‡	☐
20231	$1,300	☐	☐	‡	‡	☐
20232	$1,300	☐	☐	‡	‡	☐

#J77 $1 POSTAGE DUE

20130	$275	☐	☐	‡	‡	☐
20131	$275	☐	☐	‡	‡	☐
20132	$275	☐	☐	‡	‡	☐
20133	$275	☐	☐	‡	‡	☐

#J78b $5 POSTAGE DUE

Wet Printed

20158	$400	☐	☐	‡	‡	☐
20159	$400	☐	☐	‡	‡	☐
20160	$400	☐	☐	‡	‡	☐
20161	$400	☐	☐	‡	‡	☐

#J78 $5 POSTAGE DUE

Dry Printed

20158	$500	☐	☐	‡	‡	☐
20159	$500	☐	☐	‡	‡	☐
20160	$500	☐	☐	‡	‡	☐
20161	$500	☐	☐	‡	‡	☐

POSTAGE DUE ISSUES

1931-32 ISSUE

Unwatermarked Perf. 11 x 10°
ROTARY PRESS Blocks of 4

#J79 ° ¢ POSTAGE DUE

Wet Printed

		UL	UR	LL	LR
Pre-Eye Plates					
20571	$20	☐	☐	☐	☐
20572	$20	☐	☐	☐	☐
Eye Plates					
22805	$20	☐	☐	☐	☐
22806	$20	☐	☐	☐	☐

#J80b 1¢ POSTAGE DUE

Wet Printed

Pre-Eye Plates					
20579	$2	☐	☐	☐	☐
20580	$2	☐	☐	☐	☐
Eye Plates					
22807	$2	☐	☐	☐	☐
22808	$2	☐	☐	☐	☐

#J80 1¢ POSTAGE DUE

Dry Printed

25635	$2	☐	☐	☐	☐
25636	$2	☐	☐	☐	☐

#J81b 2¢ POSTAGE DUE

Wet Printed

Pre-Eye Plates					
20610	$3	☐	☐	☐	☐
20611	$3	☐	☐	☐	☐
20674	$5	☐	☐	☐	☐
20675	$5	☐	☐	☐	☐
Eye Plates					
22809	$2	☐	☐	☐	☐
22810	$2	☐	☐	☐	☐
23156	$3	☐	☐	☐	☐
23157	$3	☐	☐	☐	☐

#J81 2¢ POSTAGE DUE

Dry printed

25637	$2	☐	☐	☐	☐
25638	$2	☐	☐	☐	☐

#J82b 3¢ POSTAGE DUE

Wet Printed

Pre-Eye Plates					
20612	$3	☐	☐	☐	☐
20613	$3	☐	☐	☐	☐
20676	$5	☐	☐	☐	☐
20677	$5	☐	☐	☐	☐
Eye Plates					
22811	$3	☐	☐	☐	☐
22812	$3	☐	☐	☐	☐
22963	$3	☐	☐	☐	☐
22964	$3	☐	☐	☐	☐
23644	$3	☐	☐	☐	☐
23645	$3	☐	☐	☐	☐

#J82 3¢ POSTAGE DUE

Dry Printed

25641	$3	☐	☐	☐	☐
25642	$3	☐	☐	☐	☐

1931-32 ISSUE

#J83b 5¢ POSTAGE DUE

Wet Printed

		UL	UR	LL	LR
Pre-Eye Plates					
20615	$5	☐	☐	☐	☐
20616	$5	☐	☐	☐	☐
Eye Plates					
22813	$4	☐	☐	☐	☐
22814	$4	☐	☐	☐	☐
23148	$8	☐	☐	☐	☐
24058	$8	☐	☐	☐	☐

#J83 5¢ POSTAGE DUE

Dry Printed

25643	$4	☐	☐	☐	☐
25644	$4	☐	☐	☐	☐

#J84b 10¢ POSTAGE DUE

Wet Printed

Pre-Eye Plates					
20619	$10	☐	☐	☐	☐
20620	$10	☐	☐	☐	☐
Eye Plates					
22821	$8	☐	☐	☐	☐
22822	$8	☐	☐	☐	☐

#J84 10¢ POSTAGE DUE

Dry Printed

25645	$8	☐	☐	☐	☐
25646	$8	☐	☐	☐	☐

#J85 30¢ POSTAGE DUE

Wet Printed

Pre-Eye Plates					
20623	$50	☐	☐	☐	☐
20624	$50	☐	☐	☐	☐
Eye Plates					
22829	$40	☐	☐	☐	☐
22830	$40	☐	☐	☐	☐

#J86 50¢ POSTAGE DUE

Wet Printed

Pre-Eye Plates					
20621	$55	☐	☐	☐	☐
20622	$55	☐	☐	☐	☐
Eye Plates					
22831	$55	☐	☐	☐	☐
22832	$55	☐	☐	☐	☐

#J87 $1 POSTAGE DUE

Wet Printed

25243	$250	☐	☐	☐	☐
25244	$250	☐	☐	☐	☐

POSTAGE DUE ISSUES

1959 ISSUE

The design portion of this issue was printed on the web-fed Cottrell presses from pairs of 400 subject intaglio plates producing 800 stamps per revolution. The web then proceeded to the letterpress station were the denomination was added by four 100 subject rubber mats mounted on a cylinder overprinting 400 stamps per revolution. Shiny dextrin gum was then applied to the web. All of the plates could exist with any denomination but only those plates that have been reported on the value are shown .

In 1979 the Bureau started using pregummed paper with dull PVA gum. Six plates, all of which had been used for earlier printings, were used for these printings. Since most collectors had already acquired shiny gum examples, few dull gum plate blocks were saved. Most collections contain only a token representation of dull gum plate blocks and no collection approaches completion.

For further information on this series including overprint types please refer to the series of articles by David Stiff in the **US Specialist** (Jan 1996, Oct 1996, Nov 1996, Dec 1996, Feb 1997, and later issues).

OVERPRINT TYPES

1¢	I	squat letters
	II	tall letters
3¢	I	narrow spacing
	II	wide spacing between 3 and CENTS
5¢	I	knob of 5 over E
	II	knob of 5 between C and E
10¢	I	nadir of 0 over T ; squat letters
	II	nadir of 0 between N and T
	III	nadir of 0 over T; tall letters
30¢	I	nadir of 0 over T
	II	nadir of 0 between N and T
50¢	I	nadir of 0 over T
	II	nadir of 0 between N and T
$1	I	wide spacing between 1 and DOLLAR
	II	narrow spacing

#J88 .5¢ POSTAGE DUE

SHINY GUM		UL	UR	LL	LR
26289	$175	☐	☐	☐	☐
26290	$175	☐	☐	☐	☐
26291	$350	☐	☐	†	†
26292	$350	☐	☐	☐	†
26660	$175	☐	☐	☐	☐
26661	$175	☐	☐	☐	☐

1959 ISSUE

#J89 1¢ POSTAGE DUE

SHINY GUM Type I		UL	UR	LL	LR
26289	$.40	☐	☐	☐	☐
26290	$.40	☐	☐	☐	☐
26291	$.40	☐	☐	☐	☐
26292	$.40	☐	☐	☐	☐
26660	$.40	☐	☐	☐	☐
26661	$.40	☐	☐	☐	☐
26833	$.40	☐	☐	☐	☐
26834	$.40	☐	☐	☐	☐
27072	$.40	☐	☐	☐	☐
27694	$.40	☐	☐	☐	☐
27850	$.40	☐	☐	☐	☐
27851	$.40	☐	☐	☐	☐
29228	$.40	☐	☐	☐	☐
29229	$.40	☐	☐	☐	☐
34283	$.40	☐	☐	☐	☐
35283	$.40	☐	☐	☐	☐
35306	$.40	☐	☐	☐	☐
35307	$.40	☐	☐	☐	☐
37876	$.40	☐	☐	☐	☐
37877	$.40	☐	☐	☐	☐
DULL GUM Type II					
35306	$5.00	☐	☐	☐	☐
35307	$5.00	☐	☐	☐	☐
DULL GUM Type I					
*37876	—	†	☐	†	☐
*37877	—	†	☐	†	☐

#J90 2¢ POSTAGE DUE

SHINY GUM		UL	UR	LL	LR
26289	$.50	☐	☐	☐	☐
26290	$.50	☐	☐	☐	☐
26291	$.50	☐	☐	☐	☐
26292	$.50	☐	☐	☐	☐
26660	$.50	☐	☐	☐	☐
26661	$.50	☐	☐	☐	☐
26833	$.50	☐	☐	☐	☐
26834	$.50	☐	☐	☐	☐
27072	$.50	☐	☐	☐	☐
27694	$.50	☐	☐	☐	☐
27850	$.50	☐	☐	☐	☐
27851	$.50	☐	☐	☐	☐
29228	$.50	☐	☐	☐	☐
29229	$.50	☐	☐	☐	☐
34283	$.50	☐	☐	☐	☐
35282	$.50	☐	☐	☐	☐
35283	$.50	☐	☐	☐	☐
35306	$.50	☐	☐	☐	☐
35307	$.50	☐	☐	☐	☐
37876	$ 50	☐	☐	☐	☐
37877	$.50	☐	☐	☐	☐

POSTAGE DUE ISSUES

1959 ISSUE

#J90 2¢ POSTAGE DUE Cont.

DULL GUM		UL	UR	LL	LR
*35306	—	†	†	□	†
*35307	—	□	†	□	†
37876	$5.00	□	□	□	□
37877	$5.00	□	□	□	□

#J91 3¢ POSTAGE DUE

SHINY GUM	Type I				
26289	—	□	□	□	□
26290	—	□	□	□	□

SHINY GUM	Type II				
26289	$1.00	□	□	□	□
26290	$1.00	□	□	□	□
26660	$.60	□	□	□	□
26661	$.60	□	□	□	□
26833	$.60	□	□	□	□
26834	$.60	□	□	□	□
27072	$.60	□	□	□	□
27694	$.60	□	□	□	□
27850	$.60	□	□	□	□
27851	$.60	□	□	□	□
29228	$.60	□	□	□	□
29229	$.60	□	□	□	□
34283	$.60	□	□	□	□
35282	$3.00	□	□	□	□
35283	$.60	□	□	□	□
35306	$.60	□	□	□	□
35307	$.60	□	□	□	□

DULL GUM	Type II				
37876	$4.00	□	□	□	□
37877	$4.00	□	□	□	□

#J92 4¢ POSTAGE DUE

SHINY GUM					
26289	$.75	□	□	□	□
26290	$.75	□	□	□	□
26291	$.75	□	□	□	□
26292	$.75	□	□	□	□
26660	$.75	□	□	□	□
26661	$.75	□	□	□	□
26833	$.75	□	□	□	□
26834	$.75	□	□	□	□
27072	$.75	□	□	□	□
27694	$.75	□	□	□	□
27850	$.75	□	□	□	□
27851	$.75	□	□	□	□
29228	$.75	□	□	□	□
29229	$.75	□	□	□	□
34283	$.75	□	□	□	□
35283	$.75	□	□	□	□
35306	$.75	□	□	□	□
35307	$.75	□	□	□	□

1959 ISSUE

#J93 5¢ POSTAGE DUE

SHINY GUM	Type I	UL	UR	LL	LR
*26289	—	□	□	□	□
26290	$.70	□	□	□	□
26291	$.70	□	□	□	□
26292	$.70	□	□	□	□
26660	$.70	□	□	□	□
26661	$.70	□	□	□	□
26833	$.70	□	□	□	□
26834	$.70	□	□	□	□
27072	$.70	□	□	□	□
27694	$.70	□	□	□	□
27850	$.70	□	□	□	□
27851	$.70	□	□	□	□
29228	$.70	□	□	□	□
29229	$.70	□	□	□	□
34283	$.70	□	□	□	□
35282	$.70	□	□	□	□
35283	$.70	□	□	□	□
35306	$.70	□	□	□	□
35307	$.70	□	□	□	□
37876	$.70	□	□	□	□
37877	$.70	□	□	□	□

DULL GUM	Type I				
35306	$5.00	□	†	†	†
35307	$5.00	□	†	†	†
37876	$5.00	†	□	†	□
37877	$5.00	†	□	†	□

DULL GUM	Type II				
35306	$5.00	†	□	□	†
35307	$5.00	†	□	□	†
37876	$5.00	□	†	□	†
37877	$5.00	□	□	□	□

#J94 6¢ POSTAGE DUE

SHINY GUM					
26289	$1.25	□	□	□	□
26290	$1.25	□	□	□	□
26291	$1.25	□	□	□	□
26292	$1.25	□	□	□	□
26660	$1.25	□	□	□	□
26661	$1.25	□	□	□	□
26833	$1.25	□	□	□	□
27072	$1.25	□	□	□	□
27694	$1.25	□	□	□	□
27850	$1.25	□	□	□	□
27851	$1.25	□	□	□	□
29228	$1.25	□	□	□	□
29229	$1.25	□	□	□	□
34283	$1.25	□	□	□	□
35283	$1.25	□	□	□	□
35306	$1.25	□	□	□	□
35307	$1.25	□	□	□	□

POSTAGE DUE ISSUES

1959 ISSUE

#J94 6¢ POSTAGE DUE Cont.

DULL GUM		UL	UR	LL	LR
35306	$1500.00	†	□	□	†
35307	$1500.00	□	□	□	□

#J95 7¢ POSTAGE DUE

SHINY GUM		UL	UR	LL	LR
26289	$2.00	□	□	□	□
26290	$2.00	□	□	□	□
26291	$2.00	□	□	□	□
26292	$2.00	□	□	□	□
26660	$2.00	□	□	□	□
26661	$2.00	□	□	□	□
26833	$30.00	□	□	†	□
26834	$2.00	□	□	□	□
27072	$7.50	□	□	□	□
27694	$2.00	□	□	□	□
27850	$2.00	□	□	□	□
27851	$2.00	□	□	□	□
29228	$2.00	□	□	□	□
29229	$2.00	□	□	□	□
35306	$2.00	□	□	□	□
35307	$2.00	□	□	□	□
DULL GUM					
35306	$2000.00	†	□	†	†
35307	$2000.00	†	†	□	†

#J96 8¢ POSTAGE DUE

SHINY GUM		UL	UR	LL	LR
26291	$1.50	□	□	□	□
26292	$1.50	□	□	□	□
26834	$7.50	□	□	□	□
27072	$1.50	□	□	□	□
27694	$1.50	□	□	□	□
27850	$1.50	□	□	□	□
27851	$1.50	□	□	□	□
29228	$1.50	□	□	□	□
29229	$1.50	□	□	□	□
34283	$1.50	□	□	□	□
35282	$1.50	□	□	□	□
35283	$1.50	□	□	□	□
35306	$1.50	□	□	□	□
35307	$1.50	□	□	□	□

#J97 10¢ POSTAGE DUE

SHINY GUM					Type I
26289	$1.20	□	□	□	□
26290	$1.20	□	□	□	□
26291	$1.20	□	□	□	□
26292	$1.20	□	□	□	□
26660	$1.20	□	□	□	□
26661	$1.20	□	□	□	□
26833	$1.20	□	□	□	□
26834	$1.20	□	□	□	□
27072	$1.20	□	□	□	□
27694	$1.20	□	□	□	□

1959 ISSUE

#J97 10¢ POSTAGE DUE Cont.

		UL	UR	LL	LR
27850	$1.20	□	□	□	□
27851	$1.20	□	□	□	□
29228	$1.20	□	□	□	□
29229	$1.20	□	□	□	□
34283	$1.20	□	□	□	□
35282	$2.50	□	□	†	†
35283	$1.20	□	□	□	□
35306	$1.20	□	□	□	□
35307	$1.20	□	□	□	□
37876	$1.20	□	□	□	□
37877	$1.20	□	□	□	□
DULL GUM					Type III
35306	$7.50	□	□	□	†
35307	$7.50	□	†	□	□
DULL GUM					Type I
37876	—	†	†	†	□
37877	—	†	□	□	□
DULL GUM					Type II
37876	$5.00	□	□	□	□
37877	$5.00	□	□	□	□

#J102 11¢ POSTAGE DUE

SHINY GUM		UL	UR	LL	LR
34283	$4.50	□	□	□	□
35283	$4.50	□	□	□	□
35306	$2.00	□	□	□	□
35307	$2.00	□	□	□	□

#J103 13¢ POSTAGE DUE

SHINY GUM		UL	UR	LL	LR
34283	$2.00	□	□	□	□
35283	$2.00	□	□	□	□
35306	$2.00	□	□	□	□
35307	$2.00	□	□	□	□

#J104 17¢ POSTAGE DUE

DULL GUM		UL	UR	LL	LR
35306	$25.00	□	□	□	□
35307	$25.00	□	□	□	□

#J98 30¢ POSTAGE DUE

SHINY GUM					Type I
26289	$15.00	□	□	□	□
26290	$15.00	□	†	□	□
26291	$3.50	□	□	□	□
26292	$3.50	□	□	□	□
26660	$3.50	□	□	□	□
26661	$3.50	□	□	□	□
26833	$15.00	□	□	□	□
27072	$3.50	□	□	□	□
27694	$3.50	□	□	□	□
27850	$3.50	□	□	□	□
27851	$3.50	□	□	□	□
29228	$3.50	□	□	□	□

POSTAGE DUE ISSUES

1959 ISSUE

#J98 30¢ POSTAGE DUE Cont.

		UL	UR	LL	LR
29229	$3.50	□	□	□	□
34283	$3.50	□	□	□	□
35283	$3.50	□	□	□	□
35306	$3.50	□	□	□	□
35307	$3.50	□	□	□	□
37876	$3.50	□	□	□	□
37877	$3.50	□	□	□	□
DULL GUM					Type I
37876	$7.50	□	□	□	□
37877	$7.50	□	□	□	□
DULL GUM					Type II
37876	$25.00	□	□	□	□
37877	$25.00	□	□	□	□

#J99 50¢ POSTAGE DUE

SHINY GUM					Type I
26289	$5.00	□	□	□	□
26290	$5.00	□	□	□	□
*26291	—	□	†	†	†
26660	$5.00	□	□	□	□
26661	$5.00	□	□	□	□
26833	$20.00	□	□	□	□
*26834	—	†	□	†	†
27072	$5.00	□	□	□	□
27694	$5.00	□	□	□	□
27850	$5.00	□	□	□	□
27851	$5.00	□	□	□	□
29228	$5.00	□	□	□	□
29229	$5.00	□	□	□	□
34283	$5.00	□	□	□	□
35282	$10.00	□	□	□	□
35283	$5.00	□	□	□	□
35306	$5.00	□	□	□	□
35307	$5.00	□	□	□	□
37876	$5.00	□	□	□	□
37877	$5.00	□	□	□	□
DULL GUM					Type I
37876	$20.00	†	†	†	□
37877	$20.00	†	□	□	□
DULL GUM					Type II
37876	$10.00	□	□	□	□
37877	$10.00	□	□	□	□

#J100 $1 POSTAGE DUE

SHINY GUM					Type I
26290	$7.50	□	□	□	□
26291	$7.50	□	□	□	□
26292	$7.50	□	□	□	□
26660	$7.50	□	□	□	□
26661	$7.50	□	□	□	□
26834	$7.50	□	□	□	□
27072	$7.50	□	□	□	□
27694	$7.50	□	□	□	□

1959 ISSUE

#J100 $1 POSTAGE DUE Cont.

		UL	UR	LL	LR
27850	$7.50	□	□	□	□
27851	$7.50	□	□	□	□
29228	$7.50	□	□	□	□
29229	$7.50	□	□	□	□
34283	$7.50	□	□	□	□
35282	—	□	□	□	□
35283	$7.50	□	□	□	□
35306	$7.50	□	□	□	□
35307	$7 50	□	□	□	□
37876	$7 50	□	□	□	□
37877	$7.50	□	□	□	□
SHINY GUM					Type II
34283	—	□	□	□	□
35282	—	□	□	□	□
DULL GUM					Type I
*34283	—	□	□	□	†
*35282	—	†	†	□	†
35306	$30.00	†	□	□	†
35307	$30.00	□	□	□	†
DULL GUM					Type II
35306	$30.00	†	†	†	□
35307	$30.00	†	†	†	□
37876	$10.00	□	□	□	□
37877	$10.00	□	□	□	□

#J101 $5 POSTAGE DUE

SHINY GUM					
26291	$40.00	□	□	□	□
26292	$40.00	□	□	□	□
26660	$40.00	□	□	□	□
26661	$40.00	□	□	□	□
27072	$40.00	□	□	□	□
27694	$40.00	□	□	□	□
27850	$40.00	□	□	□	□
27851	$40.00	□	□	□	□
29228	$40.00	□	□	□	□
29229	$40.00	□	□	□	□
34283	$40.00	□	□	□	□
35282	$70.00	□	□	□	□
35283	$40.00	□	□	□	□
35306	$40.00	□	□	□	□
35307	$40.00	□	□	□	□
37876	$40.00	□	□	□	□
37877	$40.00	□	□	□	□
DULL GUM					
34283	$55.00	□	□	□	□
35282	$55.00	□	□	□	□
37876	$45.00	□	□	□	□
37877	$45.00	□	†	□	□

#J102-104

See page 309

SHANGHAI

The Shanghai China overprints have been the subject of a study by Mr. Meyer Tuchinsky for many years. Since his study enables us to differentiate the plate positions of #K1 thru #K15, we shall list those stamps in all eight possible plate block positions with the letter X and the unreported with the letter O. Should you own an unreported position, it would be appreciated if a photo or photocopy of your block be submitted to the editor.

On flat plate sheets the upper left position includes a top and a left side plate block, the upper right position includes a top and a right side plate block, the lower left position includes a bottom and a left side plate block and the lower right position includes a bottom and a right side plate block.

IDENTIFYING POSITIONS ON SHANGHAI OVERPRINTS

For each pane of 100 stamps, 4 blocks of 25 overprints (5x5) were made, clamped into a frame, and used to overprint 100 stamps at a time. Where 2 of the blocks met, there is usually more than the standard space. Thus on a plate block of 6, 4 stamps will show identical positions of the overprint, and 2 will show slightly different positions. For top and bottom plate blocks, the right 2 stamps are different on UL-T and LL-B positions, and the left 2 stamps on UR-T and LR-B. For side plates the top 2 stamps differ on LL-L and LR-R, and the bottom 2 on UL-L and UR-R. Blocks of 4 can be identified on the basis of whether the spacings are the same, or different, but plate singles can not be assigned a unique position. The 'F' marking helps identify the UR-T position in most cases, but it was placed on the UL-T position on plates 9478,9 (#K1), 9198 (#K2), 8495, 12550 (#K4); 9116 (#K5), and in both positions on 11776 (#K9) and 11729, 11787 (#K17). Plates below 8000 and 8899 (#K7), 10786 (#K8), all K18 have no F. On 9199 (#K2) the F is on the LR-R position.

#K1 2¢ on 1¢

Basic Price $300

	UL	UR	LL	LR
	T L	T R	B L	B R
8168	O O	X O	X X	X X
8431	X O	O O	X X	X X
9478	O O	X O	X X	X X
9479	X X	X X	X X	X X
13219	O O	O O	X X	X X
13220	X X	X O	X X	O O
13221	X O	X O	O X	O O
13222	X O	X O	X O	X X
13257	O O	X X	O O	O O
13301	O O	X X	O O	O O
13307	X O	X X	O O	O O
13318	O O	X X	O O	O O
*13341	O O	O O	O X	O X
*13342	X O	O O	O X	O O
*13343	X O	X O	O O	O X
*13344	O X	O O	O O	O X

#K2 4¢ on 2¢

Basic Price $300

	UL	UR	LL	LR
9190	X X	X X	O O	O O
9198	O X	O X	O O	O O
9199	X X	X X	X O	X O
9200	X O	X X	O O	X X
13438	O X	X X	O X	O X
13440	X X	OO	O X	O X
13534	O O	X X	X O	O X
13535	O O	X X	O O	O O
13540	X O	X X	O X	O O
13541	O O	X X	X O	O O
13567	O X	X O	O X	O X
13588	O O	X O	O X	O X
N13738	O O	O O	O O	O O
N13739	O O	O O	O O	O O
N13746	X O	O O	O O	O O
*13747	O O	O O	O X	O X

N Plate single left side on 13738, 739, 746

#K3 6¢ on 3¢

Basic Price $500

	UL	UR	LL	LR
	T L	T R	B L	B R
8386	O O	O O	X O	X X
8456	X O	O O	O O	O O
8462	O X	X X	O O	O X
8473	O X	O X	O X	O O
8476	X X	X X	X X	O X
8868	X X	O X	X X	O O
8869	O O	X X	X X	O X
8906	O X	X X	X X	X O

#K4 8¢ on 4¢

Basic Price $600

	UL	UR	LL	LR
8494	X O	X X	O O	O X
8495	O O	O X	X O	O X
8496	X X	X X	O X	X X
8497	O O	X X	X X	X X
12549	X X	X X	O X	O O
12550	X O	X X	X X	X X
12551	X X	O X	X O	X X
12552	X X	X X	X O	X O

#K5 10¢ on 5¢

Basic Price $575

	UL	UR	LL	LR
9115	O X	O O	X X	X O
9116	X X	O O	X X	O O
9117	O X	O O	X X	O X
9118	O X	O X	X X	X O
13272	O X	O O	X O	X X
13273	X O	O O	X X	O O
13274	X X	O O	X X	O O
13275	X O	X X	X O	O O

SHANGHAI

#K6 12¢ on 6¢

Basic Price $750

	UL T L	UR T R	LL B L	LR B R
7822	X X	O O	X X	X X
7828	X X	X O	O O	X X
7834	X X	O O	X X	O X
7837	X X	X O	X X	X X
13372	X X	O X	X O	O O
13373	X O	X X	O X	X O
13374	O O	X X	X O	O O
13375	X X	X X	O O	X O

#K7 14¢ on 7¢

Basic Price $900

8490	X O	X X	X O	O O
8898	X X	X X	X X	X X
8899	O O	X X	X O	X X
8943	X O	X X	O O	X O
12561	X O	X X	O X	O O
12562	O X	X O	X X	X X
12563	X O	X X	X X	X X
12564	O X	X O	X O	O X

#K8 16¢ on 8¢

Basic Price $700

7734	O O	O X	X O	X X
7740	O X	O X	O X	X X
7742	O O	O X	X X	X X
7748	O X	O X	X X	X X
10785	O O	X X	X O	O X
10786	O O	X O	O O	O O
10787	O O	X X	X O	X X
10788	X X	X X	X O	O O

#K9 18¢ on 9¢

Basic Price $750

6918	X X	X O	O X	O O
6922	X X	X X	O X	O X
6925	X X	X O	O O	O O
6930	X X	X O	O X	O O
11773	X O	X X	X X	X X
11774	O O	X X	O O	X O
11775	O O	X X	O O	X X
11776	O O	X X	X O	X X

#K10 20¢ on 10¢

Basic Price $650

8435	O X	X O	O O	O X
8436	X X	X X	X O	X X
8437	X X	O O	X X	X X
8438	X X	X X	O O	X X
13403	X X	X O	X X	X X
13404	X X	X O	X O	X X
13405	X O	X X	O O	X X
13406	O X	O O	O O	O X

#K11 24¢ on 12¢

Basic Price $800

6931	O X	X X	O O	X X
6934	X X	X O	X X	X X
7036	X X	X O	X O	X X
7037	X X	X X	O O	X X
10621	X O	X O	O O	O O
10622	O X	O X	O O	O X
10623	O X	O O	O O	O O
10624	O O	X O	O O	X O

#K12 30¢ on 15¢

Basic Price $1,100

	UL T L	UR T R	LL B L	LR B R
7926	O O	X O	O X	X X
7927	X O	X X	O X	X X
7928	O X	O X	O X	X X
7929	O O	O O	O O	X X
12589	X X	O O	O O	X O
12590	O X	X X	X X	X O
12591	X O	X X	X X	X X
12592	O O	O X	O O	O O

#K13 40¢ on 20¢

Basic Price $1,400

6933	X X	O X	X X	X X
6935	X O	O X	O O	O X
6938	X O	X X	O O	X X
7033	X O	X X	X O	O X
12593	O O	X O	X O	X O
12594	X X	X X	X X	O X
12595	X O	O O	O O	X X
12596	O O	X X	O O	X X

#K14 60¢ on 30¢

Basic Price $1,100

6899	X O	O O	O O	O O
6921	X O	O O	X X	X X
6924	X O	X X	X X	X O
6927	X X	X X	X X	X O
6928	O X	X X	X X	X X

#K15 $1 on 50¢

Basic Price $10,000

7040	O O	X X	X O	X X
7042	X X	X O	X X	X O
7049	X X	X O	O O	O X
7057	X X	X X	X X	O O

#K16 $2 on $1

Basic Price $7,500

	T	L	R	B
5782	X	‡	‡	X

On #K16 it is impossible to differentiate between L and R panes.

#K17 2 Cts. on 1¢

Basic Price $750

*10584	X	X	‡	‡
10592	X	X	‡	‡
10595	X	X	‡	‡
10599	X	X	‡	‡
*10600	X	X	‡	‡
11729	X	X	‡	‡
*11787	X	X	‡	‡
11790	X	X	‡	‡
*11791	X	O	‡	‡
11792	X	X	‡	‡

#K18 4 Cts. on 2¢

Basic Price $750

*13077	X	‡	X	‡
13129	X	‡	X	‡

OFFICIAL MAIL

1873 ISSUE

Most of the plates had 100 subjects and thus have only T and B positions. The 1c, 3c and 6c Post Office, the 1c, 2c and 3c Treasury, and the 2c and 3c War were printed from 200 subject plates and have **TL,TR,BL,BR** positions.

On many 100 subject plates, the imprints are centered over stamps 1 - 4, and under stamps 91 - 94, with "No." and the plate number centered in the margin over stamps 5 and 6 or under stamps 95 and 96. Thus a strip of 6 or block of 12 is needed to include the full marginal marking. For full value, these pieces should include the left margin. On a few plates the imprints were centered over stamp 3 and a strip of 5 or block of 10 will suffice to include all marginal markings. However, a full strip of 6 stamps is more pleasing, and we thus list all 100 subject plates this way. Shorter strips will sell for somewhat less than the quoted prices. We note other exceptions.

On 200 subject plates, arrows were placed in the middle of top and bottom margins so that the sheets could be cut into 100 subject panes. For TL and BL positions, the imprint is followed by "No." and the plate number, and then the next stamp shows the partial arrow and a right straight edge. For TR and BR positions, the first stamp has the partial arrow and left straight edge, and "No.", the plate number and the imprint follow. In order to show the full marginal markings, a strip of 7 or block of 14 is needed. For a few positions, 7 stamps are needed even to include the full plate number. Strips of 6 or blocks of 12 without the partial arrow are valued at 80-90% of the larger pieces.

Plates not known on stamps are marked with a dagger (†). Most plate numbers are known on card or india proofs, and on issues where more than one plate was made, we indicate those known on proofs with "p". Plate numbers reported on Special Printings made for collectors and overprinted "Specimen" are listed separately.

Printed by the Continental Bank Note Co.

Unwatermarked Perf. 12

Imprint E1

#O1 1c AGRICULTURE

†65

#O2 2c AGRICULTURE

Imprint strip of 6	**T, B**	$700
Imprint block of 12	**T, B**	-

64

1873 ISSUE

#O3 3c AGRICULTURE

Imprint strip of 6	**T, B**	$600
Imprint block of 12	**T, B**	-

57

#O4 6c AGRICULTURE

†72

#O5 10c AGRICULTURE

†114

#O6 12c AGRICULTURE

†73

#O7 15c AGRICULTURE

†105

#O8 24c AGRICULTURE

†145

The plate number precedes the imprint on this plate.

#O9 30c AGRICULTURE

†100

#O10 1c EXECUTIVE

†82

Plate number 81 was originally entered by mistake, and was crossed out and replaced by 82. Thus a strip of 7 is needed to include marginal markings.

#O11 2c EXECUTIVE

75

A plate block of 4 is known.

#O12 3c EXECUTIVE

†63

#O13 6c EXECUTIVE

†76

#O14 10c EXECUTIVE

111

A plate number pair is known.

#O15 1c INTERIOR

Imprint strip of 6	**T, B**	$200
Imprint block of 12	**T, B**	$350

52

#O16 2c INTERIOR

Imprint strip of 6	**T, B**	$150
Imprint block of 12	**T, B**	$275

45

OFFICIAL MAIL

1873 ISSUE

#O17 3c INTERIOR
Imprint strip of 6 T, B $300
Imprint block of 12 T, B $500
27

#O18 6c INTERIOR
Imprint strip of 6 T, B $250
Imprint block of 12 T, B $400
56

#O19 10c INTERIOR
Imprint strip of 6 T, B $250
Imprint block of 12 T, B $400
109

#O20 12c INTERIOR
Imprint strip of 6 T, B $350
Imprint block of 12 T, B $600
49

#O21 15c INTERIOR
Imprint strip of 6 T, B $500
Imprint block of 12 T, B -
93

#O22 24c INTERIOR
Imprint strip of 6 T, B $450
Imprint block of 12 T, B $800
104

#O23 30c INTERIOR
Imprint strip of 6 T, B $500
Imprint block of 12 T, B $1,000
95

#O24 90c INTERIOR
Imprint strip of 6 T, B $1,100
Imprint block of 12 T, B -
108

#O25 1c JUSTICE
†85

#O26 2c JUSTICE
†90

#O27 3c JUSTICE
†28

#O28 6c JUSTICE
†77

1873 ISSUE

#O29 10c JUSTICE
Imprint strip of 6 T, B -
Imprint block of 12 T, B -
97

A top strip of 4 with partial imprint was sold in 1947, a plate block of 12 sold for $2530 in 1989.

#O30 12c JUSTICE
†91

#O31 15c JUSTICE
†99

#O32 24c JUSTICE
†115

#O33 30c JUSTICE
†110

#O34 90c JUSTICE
†113

#O35 1c NAVY
Imprint strip of 6 T, B $500
Imprint block of 12 T, B $900
80

#O36 2c NAVY
Imprint strip of 6 T, B $400
Imprint block of 12 T, B $700
50

#O37 3c NAVY
Imprint strip of 6 T, B $400
Imprint block of 12 T, B $700
34

#O38 6c NAVY
Imprint strip of 6 T, B $400
Imprint block of 12 T, B $700
53

#O39 7c NAVY
†119

#O40 10c NAVY
Imprint strip of 6 T, B $500
Imprint block of 12 T, B $900
101

#O41 12c NAVY
Imprint strip of 6 T, B $600
Imprint block of 12 T, B -
92

#O42 15c NAVY
Imprint strip of 6 T, B $1,000
Imprint block of 12 T, B -
94

#O43 24c NAVY
†107

#O44 30c NAVY
†96

#O45 90c NAVY
Imprint strip of 6 T, B -
Imprint block of 12 T, B -
106

A plate block of 4 is known.

OFFICIAL MAIL

1873 ISSUE

#O47 1c POST OFFICE
Imprint strip of 7 **TL,TR,BL,BR** $175
Imprint block of 14 **TL,TR,BL,BR** $300
43 †428p

In 1882 the American Bank Note Co. made 200 subject plate 428 with its imprint. This was used only for proofs as far as is known.

#O48 2c POST OFFICE
Imprint strip of 6 **T, B** $175
Imprint block of 12 **T, B** $300
37 38 285p

#O49 3c POST OFFICE
†36 †40
Imprint strip of 7 **TL,TR,BL,BR** $75
Imprint block of 14 **TL,TR,BL,BR** $125
30 41 140 141p

#O50 6c POST OFFICE
Imprint strip of 7 **TL,TR,BL,BR** $150
Imprint block of 14 **TL,TR,BL,BR** $250
†39 47 249p

#O51 10c POST OFFICE
Imprint strip of 6 **T, B** $450
Imprint block of 12 **T, B** $800
62

#O52 12c POST OFFICE
Imprint strip of 6 **T, B** $300
Imprint block of 12 **T, B** $500
71

#O53 15c POST OFFICE
Imprint strip of 6 **T, B** $400
Imprint block of 12 **T, B** $700
66

#O54 24c POST OFFICE
Imprint strip of 6 **T, B** $400
Imprint block of 12 **T, B** -
74

#O55 30c POST OFFICE
Imprint strip of 6 **T, B** $400
Imprint block of 12 **T, B** $700
68

#O56 90c POST OFFICE
Imprint strip of 6 **T, B** $500
Imprint block of 12 **T, B** $900
88

1873 ISSUE

#O57 1c STATE DEPT.
†55

#O58 2c STATE DEPT.
†59

#O59 3c STATE DEPT.
†70

#O60 6c STATE DEPT.
Imprint strip of 6 **T, B** -
Imprint block of 12 **T, B** -
83

A rejoined plate block is known, but no intact strips.

#O61 7c STATE DEPT.
†112

#O62 10c STATE DEPT.
Imprint strip of 6 **T, B** $850
Imprint block of 12 **T, B** $1,800
98

#O63 12c STATE DEPT.
†78

#O64 15c STATE DEPT.
†118

#O65 24c STATE DEPT.
†117

#O66 30c STATE DEPT.
†116

#O67 90c STATE DEPT.
†67

The following four stamps were printed from plates of 10 subjects (2 high by 5 wide). The top margin had an imprint in black over stamp 1 and spreading to the left in the margin and to the right over stamp 2. "No." in black was over the right side of stamp 4, with the black vignette plate number 123 over the left side of stamp 5. Green "No." was over stamp 3, with the green frame plate number between stamps 3 and 4. The green imprint was in the bottom margin under stamps 7-9. Proofs exist of full panes.

#O68 $2 STATE DEPT.
frame 121
vignette 123

Plate singles are known of 121 and 123.

#O69 $5 STATE DEPT.
frame 120
vignette 123

An irregular block of 6 showing the frame plate number and both imprints was sold for $29,700 in 1989. A plate single of 123 is also known.

#O70 $10 STATE DEPT.
frame 122
vignette 123

Full sheet, $30,000

#O71 $20 STATE DEPT.
frame 124
vignette 123

Full sheet, $30,000

OFFICIAL MAIL

1873 ISSUE

#O72 1c TREASURY

Imprint strip of 7 **TL,TR,BL,BR** $275
Imprint block of 14 **TL,TR,BL,BR** $500
44

#O73 2c TREASURY

Imprint strip of 7 **TL,TR,BL,BR** $350
Imprint block of 14 **TL,TR,BL,BR** $600
42

#O74 3c TREASURY

Imprint strip of 7 **TL,TR,BL,BR** $200
Imprint block of 14 **TL,TR,BL,BR** $350
29 33p

#O75 6c TREASURY

Imprint strip of 6 **T, B** $250
Imprint block of 12 **T, B** $450
51

#O76 7c TREASURY

Imprint strip of 6 **T, B** $500
Imprint block of 12 **T, B** -
103

#O77 10c TREASURY

Imprint strip of 6 **T, B** $500
Imprint block of 12 **T, B** -
58

#O78 12c TREASURY

†46

#O79 15c TREASURY

Imprint strip of 6 **T, B** $475
Imprint block of 12 **T, B** $800
84

#O80 24c TREASURY

†134

The plate number precedes the imprint on this plate.

#O81 30c TREASURY

†69

#O82 90c TREASURY

Imprint strip of 6 **T, B** $800
Imprint block of 12 **T, B** -
61

#O83 1c WAR

Imprint strip of 6 **T, B** $600
Imprint block of 12 **T, B** $1,100
48

#O84 2c WAR

Imprint strip of 7 **TL,TR,BL,BR** $700
Imprint block of 14 **TL,TR,BL,BR** $1,200
35

#O85 3c WAR

Imprint strip of 7 **TL,TR,BL,BR** $700
Imprint block of 14 **TL,TR,BL,BR** $1,200
32

1873 ISSUE

#O86 6c WAR

Imprint strip of 6 **T, B** $2,500
Imprint block of 12 **T, B** -
60

#O87 7c WAR

Imprint strip of 6 **T, B** $700
Imprint block of 12 **T, B** $1,200
102

#O88 10c WAR

Imprint strip of 6 **T, B** $250
Imprint block of 12 **T, B** $450
79

#O89 12c WAR

Imprint strip of 6 **T, B** $800
Imprint block of 12 **T, B** $1,300
54

#O90 15c WAR

Imprint strip of 6 **T, B** $250
Imprint block of 12 **T, B** $400
87

#O91 24c WAR

Imprint strip of 6 **T, B** $275
Imprint block of 12 **T, B** $450
86

#O92 30c WAR

Imprint strip of 6 **T, B** $300
Imprint block of 12 **T, B** $475
81

#O93 90c WAR

Imprint strip of 6 **T, B** $500
Imprint block of 12 **T, B** $900
89

1879 ISSUE

Stamps on soft porous paper were mostly printed by the American Bank Note Co., but a few were printed by the Continental Bank Note Co. near the end of their contract.

#O94 1c AGRICULTURE

Imprint strip of 6 **T, B**
Imprint block of 12 **T, B**
65

Top and bottom plate singles are known.

#O95 3c AGRICULTURE

Imprint strip of 6 **T, B** $1,600
Imprint block of 12 **T, B** -
57

#O96 1c INTERIOR

Imprint strip of 6 **T, B** $1,000
Imprint block of 12 **T, B** $1,800
52

OFFICIAL MAIL

1879 ISSUE

#O97 2c INTERIOR

Imprint strip of 6	**T, B**	$75
Imprint block of 12	**T, B**	$125

45

#O98 3c INTERIOR

Imprint strip of 6	**T, B**	$75
Imprint block of 12	**T, B**	$125

27

#O99 6c INTERIOR

Imprint strip of 6	**T, B**	$125
Imprint block of 12	**T, B**	$200

56

#O100 10c INTERIOR

Imprint strip of 6	**T, B**	$400
Imprint block of 12	**T, B**	$700

109

#O101 12c INTERIOR

Imprint strip of 6	**T, B**	$750
Imprint block of 12	**T, B**	$1,200

49

#O102 15c INTERIOR

Imprint strip of 6	**T, B**	$1,600
Imprint block of 12	**T, B**	-

93

#O103 24c INTERIOR

Imprint strip of 6	**T, B**	$15,000
Imprint block of 12	**T, B**	-

104

#O106 3c JUSTICE

†28

#O107 6c JUSTICE

†77

#O108 3c POST OFFICE

Imprint strip of 7	**TL,TR,BL,BR**	$100
Imprint block of 14	**TL,TR,BL,BR**	$175

†30 †41 140 141

#O109 3c TREASURY

Imprint strip of 7	**TL,TR,BL,BR**	$300
Imprint block of 14	**TL,TR,BL,BR**	$500

†29 33

#O110 6c TREASURY

Imprint strip of 6	**T, B**	$500
Imprint block of 12	**T, B**	$900

51

1879 ISSUE

#O111 10c TREASURY

Imprint strip of 6	**T, B**	$700
Imprint block of 12	**T, B**	$1,200

58

#O112 30c TREASURY

†69

#O113 90c TREASURY

†61

#O114 1c WAR

Imprint strip of 6	**T, B**	$75
Imprint block of 12	**T, B**	$125

48

#O115 2c WAR

Imprint strip of 7	**TL,TR,BL,BR**	$100
Imprint block of 14	**TL,TR,BL,BR**	$180

35

#O116 3c WAR

Imprint strip of 7	**TL,TR,BL,BR**	$125
Imprint block of 14	**TL,TR,BL,BR**	$200

32

#O117 6c WAR

Imprint strip of 6	**T, B**	$90
Imprint block of 12	**T, B**	$150

60

#O118 10c WAR

Imprint strip of 6	**T, B**	$250
Imprint block of 12	**T, B**	$400

79

#O119 12c WAR

Imprint strip of 6	**T, B**	$200
Imprint block of 12	**T, B**	$350

54

#O120 30c WAR

Imprint strip of 6	**T, B**	$500
Imprint block of 12	**T, B**	$900

81

OFFICIAL MAIL

SPECIAL PRINTINGS

Special printings of Official stamps made for sale to collectors were overprinted "Specimen". We list the plate numbers of those known to us as plate singles, strips, blocks or larger pieces.

Hard paper

#O1S	1c	AGRICULTURE	65
#O2S	2c	AGRICULTURE	64
#O5S	10c	AGRICULTURE	114
#O10S	1c	EXECUTIVE	82
#O11S	2c	EXECUTIVE	75
#O15S	1c	INTERIOR	52
#O16S	2c	INTERIOR	45
#O25S	1c	JUSTICE	85
#O26S	2c	JUSTICE	90
#O27S	3c	JUSTICE	28
#O28S	6c	JUSTICE	77
#O29S	10c	JUSTICE	97
#O30S	12c	JUSTICE	91
#O31S	15c	JUSTICE	99
#O32S	24c	JUSTICE	115
#O33S	30c	JUSTICE	110
#O34S	90c	JUSTICE	113
#O35S	1c	NAVY	80
#O36S	2c	NAVY	50
#O39S	7c	NAVY	119
#O47S	1c	POST OFFICE	43
#O48S	2c	POST OFFICE	37
#O57S	1c	STATE DEPT.	55
#O58S	2c	STATE DEPT.	59
#O59S	3c	STATE DEPT.	70
#O61S	7c	STATE DEPT.	112
#O76S	7c	TREASURY	103
#O83S	1c	WAR	48
#O84S	2c	WAR	35

Soft porous paper

#O10xS	1c	EXECUTIVE	82
#O35xS	1c	NAVY	80
#O57xS	1c	STATE DEPT.	55

Printed by the
Bureau of Engraving and Printing

1913 ISSUES

Double Line Wmk. Perf. 12

#O121 2¢ BLACK

Imprint X

		T	L	R	B
5500	$250	□	□	□	□
5501	$300	□	□	□	□
5502	$250	□	□	□	□
5503	$250	□	□	□	□

#O122 50¢ DARK GREEN

Imprint X

5614	$2,000	□	‡	‡	□

#O123 $1 ULTRAMARINE

Imprint X

5615	$1,750	□	‡	‡	□

Single Line Watermark Perf. 12

#O124 1¢ DARK VIOLET

Imprint X

5646	$125	□	□	□	□

#O125 2¢ BLACK

Imprint X

5500	$575	□	□	□	□
5501	$700	□	□	□	□
5502	$575	□	□	□	□
5503	$575	□	□	□	□

#O126 10¢ CARMINE

Imprint X

5613	$275	□	□	□	□

OFFICIAL MAIL

1983 ISSUES

The make-up of the printing plates of this issue is the forerunner of what is now called "quadrant printing". The result is that the entire plate is no longer either the same denomination or the same design in each of the four quarters that are normally issued as post office panes. One set of plates was made with a 1¢ in UL; a 1¢ in UR; a 17¢ in LL and a 4¢ in LR. The second set of plates was made with a $1 in UL; a 13¢ in UR; a $5 in LL and a "D" in LR.

#O127 1¢ OFFICIAL MAIL

		UL	UR	LL	LR
2	$.20	□	□	‡	‡
3	$.20	□	□	‡	‡
4	$.20	□	□	‡	‡
5	$.20	□	□	‡	‡
6	$.20	□	□	‡	‡

#O128 4¢ OFFICIAL MAIL

2	$.40	‡	‡	‡	□
3	$.40	‡	‡	‡	□
4	$.40	‡	‡	‡	□
5	$.40	‡	‡	‡	□
6	$.40	‡	‡	‡	□

#O129 13¢ OFFICIAL MAIL

		UL	UR	LL	LR
1	$1.50	‡	□	‡	‡
2	$1.50	‡	□	‡	‡
3	$1.50	‡	□	‡	‡
4	$1.50	‡	□	‡	‡

#O130 17¢ OFFICIAL MAIL

2	$1.80	‡	‡	□	‡
3	$1.80	‡	‡	□	‡
4	$1.80	‡	‡	□	‡
5	$1.80	‡	‡	□	‡
6	$1.80	‡	‡	□	‡

#O132 $1.00 OFFICIAL MAIL

1	$10	□	‡	‡	‡
2	$10	□	‡	‡	‡
3	$10	□	‡	‡	‡
4	$10	□	‡	‡	‡

#O133 $5.00 OFFICIAL MAIL

1	$50	‡	‡	□	‡
2	$50	‡	‡	□	‡
3	$50	‡	‡	□	‡
4	$50	‡	‡	□	‡

#O135 20¢ OFFICIAL MAIL COIL

Strip of 5		B
1	$60	□

1983 ISSUES

#O138 (14¢)D OFFICIAL MAIL

		UL	UR	LL	LR
1	$35	‡	‡	‡	□
2	$35	‡	‡	‡	□
3	$35	‡	‡	‡	□
4	$35	‡	‡	‡	□

#O139 (22¢)D OFFICIAL MAIL COIL

Strip of 5		B
1	$65	□

The following issues occur without plate numbers.

#O129A	**14¢**	
#O136	**22¢**	**COIL**
#O138A	**15¢**	**COIL**
#O138B	**20¢**	**COIL**
#O140	**(25¢)E**	**COIL**
#O141	**25¢**	**COIL**
#O143	**1¢**	**(offset)**
#O144	**(29¢)F**	**COIL**
#O145	**29¢**	**COIL**
#O146	**4¢**	**(offset)**
#O146A	**10¢**	**(offset)**
#O147	**19¢**	
#O148	**23¢**	
#O151	**$1**	**(offset)**
#O152	**(32¢)G**	**COIL**
#O153	**32¢**	**COIL**
#O154	**1¢**	**(offset)**
#O155	**20¢**	**(offset)**
#O156	**23¢**	**(offset)**

NEWSPAPER & PERIODICAL STAMPS

1865 ISSUE

Printed by the National Bank Note Co.

Panes of 10 with top or bottom imprints and plate numbers. On the stamps with colored background, two stamps are needed to show the imprint and plate number, while on the white background stamps, only a single is needed.

#PR1 5c colored background
Imprint Pair $750
38

#PR2 10c colored background
Imprint Pair $325
39

#PR3 25c colored background
Imprint Pair $425
40

#PR4 5c white background
Imprint Single $125
38

1875 ISSUE

#PR5 5c white background
Imprint Single $150
38

#PR6 10c colored background
Imprint Pair $250
39

#PR7 25c colored background
Imprint Pair $300
40

1880 ISSUE

Printed by the American Bank Note Co.

#PR8 5c white background
Imprint Single $325
38

#PR9 - #PR101 were printed from plates made by the Continental Bank Note Co. These plates did not have the plate number entered on the plate, but only the imprint of the CBNCo. The sole exception is plate 482 of the 1c value made by the American Bank Note Co. which was used for #PR81 and #PR90.

1885 ISSUE

Printed by the American Bank Note Co.

Imprint F4

#PR81 1c black, soft porous paper
Imprint Pair T $50
Imprint Block of 4 T $90
482

1894 ISSUE

Printed by the Bureau of Engraving and Printing

The first issue printed by the Bureau of Engraving and Printing used plates that were supplied by the American Bank Note Company. Plate numbers in the regular postage stamp series were assigned to these plates, but were never entered on the plates. Since the plate numbers appear only on the proof sheets with the assigned number written in pencil in the bottom margin, Scott Catalog numbers# PR90-#PR101 will not be listed. The 1¢ stamp does have plate number 482 in the top margin.

#PR90 1c Intense black,soft wove paper
Imprint Pair T $275
Imprint Block of 4 T $500

482

1895 ISSUE

The regulations in effect at the time the unwatermarked issue (#PR102-#PR113) made its appearance in February 1895 stated that neither mint nor used stamps were to be given or sold to collectors. Since some clerks and postmasters ignored these regulations, some examples of #PR102-#PR113 exist, but plate pieces are very rare. The plates used for the unwatermarked series had arrows bisected by lines in the top, bottom, and side margins, but did not have guidelines between the stamps. Such guidelines were added to these plates between November 8 and 15, 1895. This was after the use of watermarked paper began for the lower denominations in September 1895, so that the early watermarked issues of the 1¢-50¢ values

NEWSPAPER & PERIODICAL STAMPS

1895 ISSUE

are also without guidelines. (The $2-$100 values were probably not printed on watermarked paper before the guidelines were added; please report any examples.) The regulations pertaining to the sale and distribution of these stamps were still in effect, so watermarked stamps without guidelines between the stamps are also scarce.

In 1899 the government sold 26,989 complete sets of #PR114-#PR125 to the public, and it is from this act that the majority of the plate strips and blocks were obtained by collectors. These stamps were from printings on watermarked paper, and with guidelines between the stamps. The plates in the 200 series were also included. The $5-$100 stamps had to be reprinted in February 1899 in order to have enough of the higher denominations to make up complete sets, but these printings cannot be distinguished from earlier ones.

Side plate strips or blocks of the 1¢ thru 50¢ are either upper left or lower right with half imprint and split arrow. On the $2 thru $100, the side plates are with full imprint and exist as upper left, lower left, upper right and lower right positions. The upper and lower side positions can be distinguished by the spacing of the plate numbers as follows:

$2 Plate number 136
UL 3 tilted to right, numbers level
LL 3 straight, 3 below 1 and 6
UR 1 straight
LR 1 tilted to right

$5 Plate number 137
UL 1 straight, over S. 3 over P, 7 between AP
LL 1 tilted to left, between SP 3 over A, 7 over P
UR 7 below 1 and 3, 3 evenly spaced
LR 7 level, 3 closer to 1 than 7

$10 Plate number 138
UL 8 straight, 1 over P
LL 8 tilted to left, 1 over S
UR 1 over I, 1 and 8 tilted slightly to left. 8 slightly below 13
LR 1 between IO, closer to O. Numbers level. 1 and 8 vertical

$20 Plate number 139
UL 3 level, heavier impression of 9, partly filled
LL 3 slightly below 1 and 9. lighter impression of 9
UR 9 between OD, 1 between PE, 3 evenly spaced
LR 9 over D, 1 between ER, 3 closer to 1 than to 9

1895 ISSUE

$50 Plate number 135
UL 5 over P, 3 below 1 and 5 1 over S, 3 tilted to R
LL 5 between AP, 3 straight, 1 between WS
UR 5 over I, 3 straight
LR 5 between IC, 3 tilts slightly to right

$100 Plate number 140
UL numbers close together, 4 between PA, 0 over P
LL numbers farther apart 4 over A, 0 between PE
UR numbers spaced wider, 4 level with others, 1 over I, 4 between OD, 0 between IC
LR numbers close together, 4 below 1 and 0 1 between RI, 4 over O, 0 between DI

See U.S. Specialist, November 1991, p 611, for pictures of these positions.

The top and bottom plate blocks of all denominations will have plate number, full imprint, full arrow, and on the later issues of #PR114-#PR125, vertical guideline between the stamps.

Without Vertical or Horizontal Guidelines Between Stamps

The following is a listing of potential plate positions on both the unwatermarked and the early watermarked series of stamps. Neither series has vertical or horizontal guidelines between the stamps. We will list reported positions as □ and unreported as †. All strips or plate blocks will be imprint III and there is only one plate number for each value. On the watermarked series side plates can be distinguished from the later issues with horizontal guidelines only when the panes were cut in such a manner that the absence of a horizontal guideline can be established.

Unwatermarked

Imprint III

Imprint Strips of 3

#PR102	**1¢**	**FREEDOM**				
			T	**L**	**R**	**B**
90	$200		□	□	□	□
#PR103	**2¢**	**FREEDOM**				
100	$200		□	†	†	□
#PR104	**5¢**	**FREEDOM**				
93	$250		□	†	□	□
#PR105	**10¢**	**FREEDOM**				
105	$400		□	†	†	□

NEWSPAPER & PERIODICAL STAMPS

1895 ISSUE

#PR106 25¢ JUSTICE

123	-	□	□	†	†

#PR107 50¢ JUSTICE

109	-	†	□	†	□

#PR108 $2 VICTORY

		T	UL	LL	UR	LR	B
136	-	□	†	†	†	†	□

#PR109 $5 CLIO

137	-	□	†	†	†	†	†

#PR110 $10 VESTA

138	-	†	†	†	†	†	†

#PR111 $20 PEACE

139	-	†	†	†	†	†	†

#PR112 $50 COMMERCE

135	-	†	†	†	†	†	□

#PR113 $100 INDIAN

140	-	†	†	†	†	†	†

Watermarked Double Line USPS

Imprint III

#PR114 1¢ FREEDOM

		T	L	R	B
90	$150	□	†	†	□

#PR115 2¢ FREEDOM

100	$150	□	†	†	□

#PR116 5¢ FREEDOM

93	$200	□	†	†	□

#PR117 10¢ FREEDOM

105	$200	†	†	†	□

#PR118 25¢ JUSTICE

123	$250	□	†	†	□

#PR119 50¢ JUSTICE

109	$300	□	†	†	†

1895 ISSUE

With Vertical and Horizontal Guidelines Between Stamps

Prices are for imprint strips of 3. Top or bottom imprint strips of 4 are valued at 1˚ times these prices, and plate blocks of 6 or 8 are valued at 3˚ to 4 times the value for the corresponding strip.

Watermarked Double Line USPS

#PR114 1¢ FREEDOM

		T	L	R	B
			Imprint III		
90	$35	□	□	□	□
			Imprint VI		
262	$35	□	□	□	□

#PR115 2¢ FREEDOM

			Imprint III		
100	$35	□	□	□	□
			Imprint VI		
265	$250	□	□	□	□

#PR116 5¢ FREEDOM

			Imprint III		
93	$40	□	□	□	□
			Imprint VI		
266	$40	□	□	□	□

#PR117 10¢ FREEDOM

			Imprint III		
105	$40	□	□	□	□
			Imprint VI		
269	$400	□	□	□	□

#PR118 25¢ JUSTICE

			Imprint III		
123	$50	□	□	□	□

#PR119 50¢ JUSTICE

			Imprint III		
109	$250	□	□	□	□
			Imprint VI		
259	$60	□	□	□	□

#PR120 $2 VICTORY

		T	UL	LL	UR	LR	B
			Imprint III				
136	$65	□	□	□	□	□	□

#PR121 $5 CLIO

			Imprint III				
137	$90	□	□	□	□	□	□

NEWSPAPER & PERIODICAL STAMPS

1895 ISSUE

#PR122 $10 VESTA

Imprint III

		T	UL	LL	UR	LR	B
138	$85	☐	☐	☐	☐	☐	☐

#PR123 $20 PEACE

Imprint III

139	$90	☐	☐	☐	☐	☐	☐

#PR124 $50 COMMERCE

Imprint III

135	$110	☐	☐	☐	☐	☐	☐

#PR125 $100 INDIAN

Imprint III

140	$135	☐	☐	☐	☐	☐	☐

NEWSPAPER STAMPS OVERPRINTED FOR REVENUE USE

In 1898 the $5 Newspaper stamp (#PR121) was overprinted "INT. REV. $5. DOCUMENTARY." Top panes had the overprint reading up, while bottom panes had it reading down. Thus only three positions occur on each type.

#R159 OVERPRINT READING DOWN
$5 NEWSPAPER (#PR121)

Basic price *Imprint III*

Plate single $250

Imprint strip of 3 $1500

	T	UL	LL	UR	LR	B
137	‡	‡	☐	‡	☐	☐

#R160 OVERPRINT READING UP
$5 NEWSPAPER (#PR121)

Basic price *Imprint III*

Plate single $150

Imprint strip of 3 $850

	T	UL	LL	UR	LR	B
137	☐	☐	‡	☐	‡	‡

POSTAL SAVINGS STAMPS

Double Line Wmk. Perf. 12
FLAT PRESS

#PS1 10¢ ORANGE

Imprint X

		T	L	R	B
5504	$500	☐	☐	☐	☐
5505	$500	☐	☐	☐	☐
5506	$500	☐	☐	☐	☐
5507	$500	☐	☐	☐	☐

Single Line Wmk. Perf. 12
FLAT PRESS

#PS4 10¢ DEEP BLUE

5504	$175	☐	☐	☐	☐
5505	$175	☐	☐	☐	☐
5506	$175	☐	☐	☐	☐
5507	$175	☐	☐	☐	☐

Imprint XII

Although plates 5698, 5700, 5703 and 5704 were sent to press from October 18 to 27, 1911, no stamps from these plates were issued.

IMPRINT XV

Unwatermarked Perf. 11
FLAT PRESS

#PS6 10¢ DEEP BLUE

Imprint XV

		TL	TR	L	R	B
21485	$125	☐	☐	☐	☐	☐
21486	$125	☐	☐	☐	☐	☐

#PS7 10¢ DEEP ULTRAMARINE

Imprint IX

22540	$225	☐	☐	☐	☐	☐
22541	$225	☐	☐	☐	☐	☐

#PS8 25¢ DARK CARMINE ROSE

		TL	TR	L	R	B
22542	$300	☐	☐	☐	☐	☐
22543	$300	☐	☐	☐	☐	☐

#PS9 50¢ DARK BLUE GREEN

22544	$900	☐	☐	☐	☐	☐

#PS10 $1 GRAY BLACK

22545	$1,900	☐	☐	☐	☐	☐

Unwatermarked Perf. 11 x 10°
ROTARY PRESS

#PS11 10¢ ROSE RED

		UL	UR	LL	LR
22714	$9.00	☐	☐	☐	☐
22715	$9.00	☐	☐	☐	☐
22722	$9.00	☐	☐	☐	☐
22723	$9.00	☐	☐	☐	☐
148245	$9.00	☐	☐	☐	☐
148246	$9.00	☐	☐	☐	☐

#PS12 25¢ BLUE GREEN

22716	$22.50	☐	☐	☐	☐
22717	$22.50	☐	☐	☐	☐
22724	$22.50	☐	☐	☐	☐
22725	$22.50	☐	☐	☐	☐
148247	$22.50	☐	☐	☐	☐
148248	$22.50	☐	☐	☐	☐

#PS13 50¢ ULTRAMARINE

22718	$50.00	☐	☐	☐	☐
22719	$50.00	☐	☐	☐	☐
22726	$60.00	☐	☐	☐	☐
22727	$60.00	☐	☐	☐	☐

#PS14 $1 GRAY BLACK

22720	$80.00	☐	☐	☐	☐
22728	$80.00	☐	☐	☐	☐

Unwatermarked Perf. 11
FLAT PRESS

#PS15 $5 SEPIA

		TL	TR	L	R	B
22730	$500	☐	☐	☐	☐	☐
22731	$500	☐	☐	☐	☐	☐
22732	$500	☐	☐	☐	☐	☐
22733	$500	☐	☐	☐	☐	☐
22734	$500	☐	☐	☐	☐	☐
22735	$500	☐	☐	☐	☐	☐
22736	$500	☐	☐	☐	☐	☐
22737	$500	☐	☐	☐	☐	☐
22740	$500	☐	☐	☐	☐	☐

1912-13 PARCEL POST ISSUE

On plate blocks with imprint, the imprint follows the plate number in TL,BL, LL and UR positions and precedes it in TR, BR, UL and LR positions. We have deleted a number of previously listed plates to which imprints were added, but which were not put to press thereafter.

Single Line Wmk. Perf. 12
FLAT PRESS BLOCK SIZE SHOWN ( )

#Q1 1¢ POST OFFICE CLERK

Imprint IX

Basic Price **T** (6) $105
Basic Price **L, R, B** (6) $100

6199 6200 6201 6202 6203
6204 6205 6206 6207 6208
6209 6210 6330 6331 6332
6333 6334 6335 6336 6337

Imprint XIV ONE

Basic Price **TL, TR, BL, BR** (4) $40
Basic Price **TL, TR, BL, BR** (6) $95
Basic Price **UL, LL, UR, LR** (6) $95

6330 6331 6332 6333 6335
6337 *6377 *6378 *6388 *6393
*6399

#Q2 2¢ CITY CARRIER

Imprint IX

Basic Price **T** (6) $125
Basic Price **L, R, B** (6) $115

6177 6178 6179 6180 6181
6182 6183 6184 6195 6196
6197 6198 6338 6339 6340
6341

Imprint XIV TWO

Basic Price **TL, TR, BL, BR** (4) $40
Basic Price **TL, TR, BL, BR** (6) $115
Basic Price **UL, LL, UR, LR** (6) $115

6338 6339 6340 6341 6367
6370 6371 6374 *6379 6384
*6390 6395

#Q3 3¢ RAILWAY POSTAL CLERK

Imprint XIV THREE

Basic Price **TL, TR, BL, BR** (4) $80
Basic Price **TL, TR, BL, BR** (6) $200
Basic Price **UL, LL, UR, LR** (8) $250

6254 6255 6256 6257

#Q4 4¢ RURAL CARRIER

Imprint IX

Basic Price **T** (6) $825
Basic Price **L, R, B** (6) $775

6169 6170 6171 6172 6345
6346 6347 6350

Imprint XIV FOUR

Basic Price **TL, TR, BL, BR** (4) $325
Basic Price **TL, TR, BL, BR** (6) $900
Basic Price **UL, LL, UR, LR** (6) $900

6345 6346 6347 *6359 6360
*6361 *6365 *6392

#Q5 5¢ MAIL TRAIN

Imprint IX

Basic Price **T** (6) $825
Basic Price **L, R, B** (6) $775

6211 6212 6213 6214 6215
6216 6217 6218 6219 6220
6221 6222 6245

Imprint XIV FIVE

Basic Price **TL, TR, BL, BR** (4) $300
Basic Price **TL, TR, BL, BR** (6) $900
Basic Price **UL, LL, UR, LR** (6) $900

6217 6220 6221 6222 6245
6405 6407 6411 *6417 6420
*6433 *6441

#Q6 10¢ STEAMSHIP

Imprint IX

Basic Price **T** (6) $1,100
Basic Price **L, R, B** (6) $1,000

6161 6162 6163 6164 6165
6167 6168 6266

Imprint XIV TEN

Basic Price **TL, TR, BL, BR** (4) $400
Basic Price **TL, TR, BL, BR** (6) $1,250
Basic Price **UL, LL, UR, LR** (6) $1,250

6161 6162 6163 6164 6165

#Q7 15¢ AUTOMOBILE

Imprint IX

Basic Price **T** (6) $2,300
Basic Price **L, R, B** (6) $2,100

6258 6259 6260 6261

Imprint XV FIFTEEN

Basic Price **TL, TR, BL, BR** (4) $700
Basic Price **TL, TR, BL, BR** (6) $3,000
Basic Price **UL, LL, UR, LR** (8) $3,500

6258 6259 6260 6261

1912-13 PARCEL POST ISSUE

#Q8 20¢ AEROPLANE

Imprint IX

Basic Price **T** (6) $5,500
Basic Price **L, R** (6) $5,000

6191 6192 6193 6194

Imprint XIV TWENTY

Basic Price **TL, TR, BL, BR** (4) $1,250
Basic Price **TL, TR, BL, BR** (6) $6,500
Basic Price **UL, LL, UR, LR** (8) $7,000

6191 6192 6193 6194

#Q9 25¢ MANUFACTURING

Imprint IX

Basic Price **T** (6) $2,500
Basic Price **L, R, B** (6) $2,200

6173 6174 6175 6176

Imprint XIV TWENTY FIVE

Basic Price **TL, TR, BL, BR** (6) $3,500
Basic Price **UL, LL, UR, LR** (8) $4,000

6173 6174 6175 6176

#Q10 50¢ DAIRYING

Imprint XIV FIFTY

Basic Price **TL, TR, BL, BR** (4) $2,000
Basic Price **TL, TR, BL, BR** (6) $20,000
Basic Price **UL, LL, UR, LR** (6) $20,000

6423 6424 6427 6428

#Q11 75¢ HARVESTING

Imprint IX

Basic Price **T** (6) $3,000
Basic Price **L, R, B** (6) $2,700

6287 6288 6296 6299

Imprint XIV SEVENTY-FIVE

Basic Price **TL, TR, BL, BR** (6) $4,000
Basic Price **UL, LL, UR, LR** (8) $4,500

6287 6288 6296 6299

#Q12 $1 FRUIT GROWING

Imprint IX

Basic Price **T** (6) $20,000
Basic Price **L, R, B** (6) $18,000

6262

Imprint XIV ONE DOLLAR

Basic Price **TL, TR, BL, BR** (6) $20,000
Basic Price **UL, LL, UR, LR** (8) $20,000

6262 *6263 *6264 *6265

1912 PARCEL POST POSTAGE DUE ISSUE

Single Line Wmk. Perf. 12
FLAT PRESS Block of 6

#JQ1 1¢ PARCEL POST DUE

Basic Price **T** $600
Basic Price **L, R, B** $575

Imprint IX

6225 6226 6227 6228

#JQ2 2¢ PARCEL POST DUE

Basic Price **T** $4,250
Basic Price **L, R, B** $4,000

Imprint IX

6241 6242 6243 6244

#JQ3 5¢ PARCEL POST DUE

Basic Price **T** $700
Basic Price **L, R, B** $650

Imprint IX

6229 6230 6231 6232 *6239
*6240

#JQ4 10¢ PARCEL POST DUE

Basic Price **T** $10,000
Basic Price **L, R, B** $9,500

Imprint IX

6250 6251 6252 6253

#JQ5 25¢ PARCEL POST DUE

Basic Price **T** $4,750
Basic Price **L, R, B** $4,500

Imprint IX

6246 6247 6248 6249

1925-29 SPECIAL HANDLING ISSUE

FLAT PRESS Perf. 11
Block of 6

#QE1a 10¢ SPECIAL HANDLING

Wet Printed

		TL	TR	L	R	B
19553	$20.00	☐	☐	☐	☐	☐
19554	$20.00	☐	☐	☐	☐	☐
19555	$20.00	☐	☐	☐	☐	☐
19556	$20.00	☐	☐	☐	☐	☐

#QE1 10¢ SPECIAL HANDLING

Dry Printed

19553	$32.50	☐	☐	☐	☐	☐
19554	$32.50	☐	☐	☐	☐	☐

#QE2a 15¢ SPECIAL HANDLING

Wet Printed

19557	$30.00	☐	☐	☐	☐	☐
19558	$30.00	☐	☐	☐	☐	☐
19559	$30.00	☐	☐	☐	☐	☐
19560	$30.00	☐	☐	☐	☐	☐

1925-29 SPECIAL HANDLING ISSUE

#QE2 15¢ SPECIAL HANDLING

Dry Printed

		TL	TR	L	R	B
19557	$42.50	□	□	□	□	□
19558	$42.50	□	□	□	□	□
19559	$42.50	□	□	□	□	□
19560	$42.50	□	□	□	□	□

#QE3a 20¢ SPECIAL HANDLING

Wet Printed

19541	$40.00	□	□	□	□	□
19542	$40.00	□	□	□	□	□
19543	$40.00	□	□	□	□	□
19544	$40.00	□	□	□	□	□

#QE3 20¢ SPECIAL HANDLING

Dry Printed

19541	$50.00	□	□	□	□	□
19542	$50.00	□	□	□	□	□
19543	$50.00	□	□	□	□	□
19544	$50.00	□	□	□	□	□

#QE4a 25¢ SPECIAL HANDLING

Wet Printed (deep green)

17095	$300	□	□	□	□	□
17096	$325	□	□	□	□	□
17097	$300	□	□	□	□	□
17098	$300	□	□	□	□	□
17099	$300	□	□	□	□	□
17101	$350	□	□	□	□	□
17102	$375	□	□	□	□	□
17103	$300	□	□	□	□	□

#QE4 25¢ SPECIAL HANDLING

Wet Printed (yellow green)

17095	$250	□	□	□	□	□
17096	$250	□	□	□	□	□
17097	$250	□	□	□	□	□
17098	$250	□	□	□	□	□

PROVISIONAL REVENUES

#R153 SMALL I.R. OVERPRINT 1¢ FRANKLIN (#279)

Basic Price	T	L	R	B
Imprint strip of 3				$25
Imprint block of 6				$75
440	□	†	†	‡
494	†	†	†	‡
495	□	□	□	‡
534	□	□	□	‡
535	□	□	□	‡
536	□	□	□	‡
538	†	‡	†	‡
539	□	‡	†	‡
540	□	‡	†	‡
541	□	‡	†	‡

PROVISIONAL REVENUES

#R153 SMALL I.R. OVERPRINT 1¢ FRANKLIN (#279) Cont.

	T	L	R	B
542	□	□	□	‡
543	□	□	□	‡
544	□	□	□	‡
545	□	□	□	‡
546	□	□	□	‡
547	□	□	□	‡
548	□	□	□	‡
549	□	□	□	‡

#R154 LARGE I.R. OVERPRINT 1¢ FRANKLIN (#279)

Basic Price				
Imprint strip of 3				$10
Imprint block of 6				$60
439	□	□	□	□
440	□	□	□	□
493	□	□	□	□
494	□	□	□	□
495	□	□	□	□
496	□	□	□	□
526	‡	□	‡	□
527	‡	□	□	□
528	‡	□	□	□
534	□	□	□	□
535	□	□	□	□
536	□	□	□	□
537	□	□	□	□
538	□	□	□	□
539	□	□	□	□
540	□	□	□	□
541	□	□	□	□
542	□	□	□	□
543	□	□	□	□
544	□	□	□	□
545	□	□	□	□
546	□	□	□	□
547	□	□	□	□
548	□	□	□	□
549	□	□	□	□

#R155 LARGE I.R. OVERPRINT 2¢ WASHINGTON (#267)

Basic Price				
Imprint strip of 3				$9
Imprint block of 6				$50
475	□	□	□	□
480	□	□	□	□
481	□	□	□	□
482	□	□	□	□
483	□	□	□	□
484	□	□	□	□
485	□	□	□	□
486	□	□	□	□
487	□	□	□	□
501	□	□	□	□
502	□	□	□	□
503	□	□	□	□

PROVISIONAL REVENUES

#R155 LARGE I.R. OVERPRINT
2¢ WASHINGTON (#279B)

Basic Price	T	L	R	B
Imprint strip of 3				$9
Imprint block of 6				$50
505	□	□	□	□
506	□	□	□	□
507	□	□	□	□
508	□	□	□	□
509	□	□	□	□
510	□	□	□	□
511	□	□	□	□
512	□	□	□	□
513	□	□	□	□
514	□	□	□	□
515	□	□	□	□
516	□	□	□	□
517	□	□	□	□
522	□	□	□	□
523	□	□	□	□
524	□	□	□	□
525	□	†	□	‡
550	□	□	□	□
551	□	□	□	□
552	□	□	□	□
553	□	□	□	□
556	□	□	□	□
557	□	□	□	□
558	□	□	□	□
559	□	□	□	□
560	□	□	□	□
561	□	□	□	□
562	□	□	□	□
563	□	□	□	□

The overprints on #R154a -#R160 are INVERTED.

#R154a LARGE I.R. OVERPRINT
1¢ FRANKLIN (#279)

Basic Price				
Imprint strip of 3				$750
Imprint block of 6				$5,000
495	‡	□	‡	□
534	‡	□	‡	□
535	‡	□	‡	□
536	‡	□	‡	□
542	□	□	□	□
543	‡	□	‡	□
544	‡	□	‡	□
545	‡	□	‡	□

#R155a LARGE I.R. OVERPRINT
2¢ WASHINGTON (#267)

Basic Price	T	L	R	B
Imprint strip of 3				$90
Imprint block of 6				$250
475	□	□	□	□
480	‡	□	‡	□
481	‡	□	‡	□
482	‡	□	‡	□
483	‡	□	‡	□
501	‡	□	‡	□
502	‡	□	‡	□
503	‡	□	‡	□

#R155a LARGE I.R. OVERPRINT
2¢ WASHINGTON (#279B)

Basic Price				
Imprint strip of 3				$90
Imprint block of 6				$250
505	‡	□	‡	□
508	‡	†	‡	□
509	‡	□	‡	□
510	□	□	□	□
511	□	□	□	□
512	□	□	□	□
513	□	□	□	□
515	‡	□	‡	□
516	‡	□	‡	□
517	‡	□	‡	□
522	‡	□	‡	□
523	□	□	□	□
524	□	□	□	□
551	□	□	□	□
552	‡	□	‡	□
553	‡	□	‡	□
556	‡	□	‡	□
557	‡	□	‡	□
558	‡	□	‡	□
559	‡	□	‡	□

#R159

See page 323

#R160

See page 323

HUNTING PERMIT STAMPS

FLAT PRESS — Perf. 11 — Plate Blocks of 6

Although plates of #RW1 thru #RW 25 and #RW 31 are printed on flat plate presses, we will designate the positions in the same manner as is customary for the rotary press products. The prices are for plate blocks of six with the SIDE margin intact.

BLOCKS OF SIX WITHOUT SIDE MARGIN ARE VALUED AT 80% OF PRICE SHOWN.

The placement of the letter F is not necessarily in the UR plate block. The exceptions are #RW3, #RW5 & #RW11. Starting with #RW13 the use of the letter F was discontinued.

UL (upper left)

UR (upper right)

LL (lower left)

LR (lower right)

1934 ISSUE

#RW1 $1 MALLARDS

		UL	UR	LL	LR
129199	$8,500	☐	☐	☐	☐
129200	$8,500	☐	☐	☐	☐
129201	$8,500	☐	☐	☐	☐
129202	$8,500	☐	☐	☐	☐

1935 ISSUE

#RW2 $1 CANVASBACKS

131980	$7,500	☐	☐	☐	☐
131981	$7,500	☐	☐	☐	☐
131982	$7,500	☐	☐	☐	☐
131983	$7,500	☐	☐	☐	☐

1936 ISSUE

#RW3 $1 CANADA GEESE

134317	$3,000	☐	☐	☐	☐
134318	$3,000	☐	☐	☐	☐

The "F" appears on the upper left pane of these plates.

1937 ISSUE

#RW4 $1 SCAUP DUCKS

136267	$2,000	☐	☐	☐	☐

1938 ISSUE

#RW5 $1 PINTAILS

		UL	UR	LL	LR
138602	$2,400	☐	☐	☐	☐

The “F', appears on the upper left pane of this plate.

1939 ISSUE

#RW6 $1 GREEN-WINGED TEALS

141428	$1,300	☐	☐	☐	☐

1940 ISSUE

#RW7 $1 BLACK MALLARDS

143743	$1,300	☐	☐	☐	☐
143776	$1,300	☐	☐	☐	☐

1941 ISSUE

#RW8 $1 RUDDY DUCKS

146271	$1,300	☐	☐	☐	☐
146282	$1,300	☐	☐	☐	☐

1942 ISSUE

#RW9 $1 BALDPATES

149599	$1,300	☐	☐	☐	☐
149600	$1,300	☐	☐	☐	☐

HUNTING PERMIT STAMPS

1943 ISSUE

#RW10 $1 WOOD DUCKS

		UL	UR	LL	LR
152826	$500	☐	☐	☐	☐
152827	$500	☐	☐	☐	☐

1944 ISSUE

#RW11 $1 WHITE-FRONTED GEESE

155590	$600	☐	☐	☐	☐
155603	$600	☐	☐	☐	☐

The letter F is separated from the plate number and appears in the selvage of the stamp to the left of the plate number in the UR position.

1945 ISSUE

#RW12 $1 SHOVELLER DUCKS

157248	$400	☐	☐	☐	☐
157249	$400	☐	☐	☐	☐

1946 ISSUE

#RW13 $1 REDHEAD DUCKS

158448	$300	☐	☐	☐	☐
158449	$300	☐	☐	☐	☐
158456	$300	☐	☐	☐	☐
158457	$300	☐	☐	☐	☐

Inscription printed on back by Offset. The plate number of this offset plate appears in only one place. This is in the sheet margin of stamp #24 in the upper right pane. The Offset plate number is 47510.

1947 ISSUE

#RW14 $1 SNOW GEESE

159461	$300	☐	☐	☐	☐
159462	$300	☐	☐	☐	☐
159464	$300	☐	☐	☐	☐

The back plate number is 47510.

1948 ISSUE

#RW15 $1 BUFFLEHEADS

160099	$300	☐	☐	☐	☐
160100	$300	☐	☐	☐	☐
160101	$300	☐	☐	☐	☐
160102	$300	☐	☐	☐	☐

The back plate number is 47510.

1949 ISSUE

#RW16 $1 GOLDEN EYE DUCKS

160790	$300	☐	☐	☐	☐
160791	$300	☐	☐	☐	☐
160792	$300	☐	☐	☐	☐
160793	$300	☐	☐	☐	☐

The back plate number is 47510.

1950 ISSUE

#RW17 $2 TRUMPETER SWANS

		UL	UR	LL	LR
161533	$400	☐	☐	☐	☐
161534	$400	☐	☐	☐	☐
161535	$400	☐	☐	☐	☐
161536	$400	☐	☐	☐	☐

The back plate number is 47510.

1951 ISSUE

#RW18 $2 GADWALL DUCKS

162125	$450	☐	☐	☐	☐
162126	$450	☐	☐	☐	☐
162127	$450	☐	☐	☐	☐
162128	$450	☐	☐	☐	☐

Starting with this issue the Offset plate number of the inscription on the back has been trimmed off and does NOT appear on subsequent issues.

1952 ISSUE

#RW19 $2 HARLEQUIN DUCKS

162602	$450	☐	☐	☐	☐
162603	$450	☐	☐	☐	☐
162604	$450	☐	☐	☐	☐
162605	$450	☐	☐	☐	☐

1953 ISSUE

#RW20 $2 BLUE WINGED TEALS

163622	$450	☐	☐	☐	☐
163623	$450	☐	☐	☐	☐
163624	$450	☐	☐	☐	☐
163625	$450	☐	☐	☐	☐

1954 ISSUE

#RW21 $2 RING-NECKED DUCKS

164744	$450	☐	☐	☐	☐
164745	$450	☐	☐	☐	☐
164746	$450	☐	☐	☐	☐
164747	$450	☐	☐	☐	☐

1955 ISSUE

#RW22 $2 BLUE GEESE

165282	$450	☐	☐	☐	☐
165283	$450	☐	☐	☐	☐
165284	$450	☐	☐	☐	☐
165285	$450	☐	☐	☐	☐

1956 ISSUE

#RW23 $2 MERGANSERS

165826	$450	☐	☐	☐	☐
165827	$450	☐	☐	☐	☐
165829	$450	☐	☐	☐	☐
165860	$450	☐	☐	☐	☐

HUNTING PERMIT STAMPS

1957 ISSUE

#RW24 $2 EIDERS

		UL	UR	LL	LR
166256	$450	☐	☐	☐	☐
166257	$450	☐	☐	☐	☐
166258	$450	☐	☐	☐	☐
166259	$450	☐	☐	☐	☐

1958 ISSUE

#RW25 $2 CANADA GEESE

166753	$450	☐	☐	☐	☐
166754	$450	☐	☐	☐	☐
166755	$450	☐	☐	☐	☐
166756	$450	☐	☐	☐	☐

1959 ISSUE

ROTARY PRESS Perf.11

Block of 4

#RW26 $3 LABRADOR RETRIEVER

167109	$400	☐	☐	☐	☐
167120	$400	☐	☐	☐	☐

1960 ISSUE

#RW27 $3 REDHEAD DUCKS

167498	$350	☐	☐	☐	☐
167503	$350	☐	☐	☐	☐

1961 ISSUE

#RW28 $3 MALLARDS

167768	$350	☐	☐	☐	☐
167772	$350	☐	☐	☐	☐

1962 ISSUE

#RW29 $3 PINTAILS

168073	$400	☐	☐	☐	☐

1963 ISSUE

#RW30 $3 BRANTS

168269	$400	☐	☐	☐	☐
168273	$400	☐	☐	☐	☐

1964 ISSUE

FLAT PRESS Perf. 11

Block of 6

#RW31 $3 NENE GEESE

168629	$2,000	☐	☐	☐	☐
168630	$2,000	☐	☐	☐	☐

1965 ISSUE

ROTARY PRESS Perf. 11

Block of 4

#RW32 $3 CANVASBACKS

168790	$400	☐	☐	☐	☐
168791	$400	☐	☐	☐	☐

1966 ISSUE

#RW33 $3 WHISTLING SWANS

		UL	UR	LL	LR
169058	$400	☐	☐	☐	☐
169063	$400	☐	☐	☐	☐

1967 ISSUE

#RW34 $3 OLD SQUAW DUCKS

169457	$400	☐	☐	☐	☐
169487	$400	☐	☐	☐	☐

1968 ISSUE

#RW35 $3 HOODED MERGANSERS

170436	$250	☐	☐	☐	☐
170443	$250	☐	☐	☐	☐

1969 ISSUE

#RW36 $3 WHITE WINGED SCOTERS

170765	$250	☐	☐	☐	☐
170767	$250	☐	☐	☐	☐

1970 ISSUE

#RW37 $3 ROSS GEESE

171165	$250	☐	☐	☐	☐
171169	$250	☐	☐	☐	☐

1971 ISSUE

#RW38 $3 CINNAMON TEALS

171586	$150	☐	☐	☐	☐
171587	$150	☐	☐	☐	☐

1972 ISSUE

#RW39 $5 EMPEROR GEESE

171862	$135	☐	☐	☐	☐
171864	$135	☐	☐	☐	☐

1973 ISSUE

#RW40 $5 STELLER'S EIDERS

172101	$100	☐	☐	☐	☐
172102	$100	☐	☐	☐	☐

1974 ISSUE

#RW41 $5 WOOD DUCKS

172500	$75	☐	☐	☐	☐
172505	$75	☐	☐	☐	☐

1975 ISSUE

#RW42 $5 CANVASBACK DECOY

172775	$60	☐	☐	☐	☐
172777	$60	☐	☐	☐	☐

HUNTING PERMIT STAMPS

1976 ISSUE

#RW43 $5 CANADA GEESE

		UL	UR	LL	LR
173029	$55	☐	☐	☐	☐
173030	$55	☐	☐	☐	☐

1977 ISSUE

#RW44 $5 ROSS GEESE

173205	$60	☐	☐	☐	☐
173206	$60	☐	☐	☐	☐

1978 ISSUE

#RW45 $5 HOODED MERGANSER

173331	$60	☐	☐	☐	☐
173333	$60	☐	☐	☐	☐

1979 ISSUE

#RW46 $7.50 GREEN-WINGED TEAL

173422	$60	☐	☐	☐	☐
173423	$60	☐	☐	☐	☐

1980 ISSUE

#RW47 $7.50 MALLARDS

173492	$60	☐	☐	☐	☐
173493	$60	☐	☐	☐	☐

1981 ISSUE

#RW48 $7.50 RUDDY DUCKS

173572	$60	☐	☐	☐	☐
173573	$60	☐	☐	☐	☐

1982 ISSUE

#RW49 $7.50 CANVAS BACKS

173669	$60	☐	☐	☐	☐
173672	$60	☐	☐	☐	☐

1983 ISSUE

#RW50 $7.50 PINTAILS

173765	$60	☐	☐	☐	☐
173767	$60	☐	☐	☐	☐

1984 ISSUE

#RW51 $7.50 WIGEONS

173871	$60	☐	☐	☐	☐
173872	$60	☐	☐	☐	☐

1985 ISSUE

#RW52 $7.50 CINNAMON TEAL

174343	$60	☐	☐	☐	☐
174350	$60	☐	☐	☐	☐

1986 ISSUE

#RW53 $7.50 FULVOUS WHISTLING

		UL	UR	LL	LR
176844	$60	☐	☐	☐	☐
176845	$60	☐	☐	☐	☐

1987 ISSUE

#RW54 $10.00 RED HEAD

178171	$60	☐	☐	☐	☐

1988 ISSUE

#RW55 $10.00 SNOW GOOSE

180059	$60	☐	☐	☐	☐

1989 ISSUE

#RW56 $12.50 LESSER SCAUPS

182531	$75	☐	☐	☐	☐

1990 ISSUE

#RW57 $12.50 BLACK BELLIED WHISTLING DUCK

186307	$75	☐	☐	☐	☐

1991 ISSUE

#RW58 $15.00 KING EIDERS

188404	$85	☐	☐	☐	☐

1992 ISSUE

#RW59 $15.00 SPECTACLED EIDER

190493	$85	☐	☐	☐	☐

1993 ISSUE

#RW60 $15.00 CANVASBACK

191659	$85	☐	☐	☐	☐

1994 ISSUE

#RW61 $15.00 RED BREASTED MERGANSER

193700	$85	☐	☐	☐	☐

1995 ISSUE

#RW62 $15.00 MALLARDS IN FLIGHT

195213	$85	☐	☐	☐	☐

1996 ISSUE

#RW63 $15.00 SURF SCOTERS

195744	$95	☐	☐	☐	☐

U.S. POSSESSIONS OVERPRINTS

At various times U.S. stamps were overprinted for use in U.S. possessions. For more detailed information, see "Napp's Numbers" Vol I, available from Grounds for Divorce Publications, 5 Knollwood Dr., West Orange, N.J. 07052. This book lists all reported positions on the possessions overprints.

CANAL ZONE OVERPRINTS

Some of the basic stamps of the United States were overprinted for use in the Canal Zone. We have listed these using the Scott Canal Zone Catalog numbers. We have also shown the basic Scott United States Catalog number in parentheses following the description. Other issues of Canal Zone were printed by the Bureau of Engraving and Printing but these were assigned from the miscellaneous series of numbers and we do not list them. For further information on Canal Zone Stamps, see "Canal Zone Stamps" by Plass, Brewster & Salz, Canal Zone Study Group, 1986, and "Napp's Numbers" Vol I.

1904 Overprinted "CANAL ZONE PANAMA" on two lines. Only LL panes were overprinted, except that a single right side strip of the 5¢ value (plate number 1888) is known.

Imprint V

#4 CANAL ZONE PANAMA
on 1¢ FRANKLIN (#300)

Basic Price **B, L only**
Imprint Strip of 3 $150
Imprint Block of 6 $900

2061 2062 2063 2064 2087
2088 2092 2141 2142 2143
2144

#5 CANAL ZONE PANAMA
on 2¢ SHIELD (#319)

Basic Price **B, L only**
Imprint Strip of 3 $150
Imprint Block of 6 $900

2076 2133 2134 2135 2136
2169 2170 2171 2172 2192
2201 2202 *2203 2204 2205
2206 2208 2209 2210 *2212
*2214 *2217

#6 CANAL ZONE PANAMA
on 5¢ LINCOLN (#304)

Basic Price **B, L, (R) only**
Imprint Strip of 3 $450
Imprint Block of 6 $1,350

1885 1886 1887 1888

#7 CANAL ZONE PANAMA
on 8¢ MARTHA WASHINGTON (#306)

Basic Price **B, L only**
Imprint Strip of 3 $600
Imprint Block of 6 $1,800

1497 1498 1499 1500

#8 CANAL ZONE PANAMA
on 10¢ WEBSTER (#307)

Basic Price **B, L only**
Imprint Strip of 3 $700
Imprint Block of 6 $2,200

1590 1591 1592 1593

Overprinted CANAL ZONE, with flat topped A's in the word CANAL.

These overprints are on stamps of the series of 1922 which were printed from plates with narrow or slightly wider horizontal spacing for vertically arranged stamps, or vertical spacing for horizontally arranged stamps. We will specify narrow or wide gauge (see pg. 68 for more detail). Some of the wide gauge plates were marked with a star to the left of the TR plate number or below the UR-R plate number, but star plate blocks are known with Canal Zone overprints only on #84 and #90. Stamps from some other star plates were overprinted, but the UR panes were not used. Several printings were made of some of the denominations, but we will list them separately only when the spacing of the words in the overprint differs, or the type of plate was different.

#70 CANAL ZONE
on .5¢ HALE (#551) wide gauge

Basic Price **TL, TR, L, R, B** $18

17017 17018 17020 17029 17078
17079 17080 17081

#71 CANAL ZONE
on 1¢ FRANKLIN (#552) narrow gauge

Basic Price **TL, TR, L, R, B** $35

15334 15358 15359 15374 15375
15384 15385 15437 15456 16556
16560 16561

#72 CANAL ZONE
on 1.5¢ HARDING (#553) wide gauge

Basic Price **TL, TR, L, R, B** $35

16829 16838 16848 16863

#73 CANAL ZONE
on 2¢ WASHINGTON(#554)narrow gauge

Basic Price **TL, TR, L, R, B** $200

15378 15402 15405 15496 15603
15623 15629 15630 15631 15632
16721 16722 16723 16724

wide gauge

Basic Price **TL, L, R, B** $250

17110 17115

These were star plates, but UR panes were not overprinted

U.S. POSSESSIONS OVERPRINTS

#74 CANAL ZONE
on 5¢ ROOSEVELT (#557) narrow gauge
Basic Price **TL, TR, L, R, B** $350
15148 15204 15205 15206

#75 CANAL ZONE
on 10¢ MONROE (#562) narrow gauge
Basic Price **TL, TR, L, R, B** $850
15510 15511 15512 15513

#76 CANAL ZONE
on 12¢ CLEVELAND (#564) narrow gauge
Basic Price **TL, TR, L, R, B** $500
14404 14405 14406 14407
TL,L only
15350 15351 15352 15692
Only UL panes were used for the second printing.

#77 CANAL ZONE
on 14¢ INDIAN (#565) narrow gauge
Basic Price **TL, TR, L, R, B** $500
14512 14513 14514 14515

#78 CANAL ZONE
on 15¢ STATUE OF LIBERTY (#566)
narrow gauge
Basic Price **TL, TR, L, R, B** $800
14910 14911 14912 14913

#79 CANAL ZONE
on 30¢ BISON (#569) narrow gauge
Basic Price **TL, TR, L, R, B** $500
14436 14437 14438 14439

#80 CANAL ZONE
on 50¢ AMPHITHEATER (#570)
narrow gauge
Basic Price **TL, TR, L, R, B** $1700
14042 14043 14044 14045
The first printing is red lilac with 9˘ mm spacing, and the second printing is lilac with 7˚ - 8∫ mm spacing.

#81 CANAL ZONE
on $1 LINCOLN MEMORIAL (#571)
narrow gauge
Basic Price **TL, TR, B** $4000
14268

Overprinted CANAL ZONE, with sharp topped A's in the word CANAL.
The normal spacing between the words CANAL and ZONE is 9 mm; we note exceptions.

#84 CANAL ZONE
on 2¢ WASHINGTON (#554)
wide gauge (star), 11 mm spacing
Basic Price **TL, TR, L, R, B** $400
17814 17842 17890 17892
Large five point star below side plate number of UR pane:
Plate block of 6, $1500 **Plate block 4,** $400

#85 CANAL ZONE
on 3¢ LINCOLN (#555) narrow gauge
Basic Price **TL, TR, L, R, B** $170
16400 16401 16402 16474

#86 CANAL ZONE
on 5¢ ROOSEVELT (#557) narrow gauge
Basic Price **TL, TR, L, R, B** $170
15571 15952 16331 16332
L, R, B only
16333 16363 16365 16366 16391
*16392 16393 16394
Only LL and LR panes were used for the second printing.

#87 CANAL ZONE
on 10¢ MONROE (#562) narrow gauge
Basic Price **TL, TR, L, R, B** $550
16376 16377 16378 16379

#88 CANAL ZONE
on 12¢ CLEVELAND (#564) narrow gauge
Basic Price **TL, TR, L, R, B** $400
15350 15351 15352 15693

#89 CANAL ZONE
on 14¢ INDIAN (#565) narrow gauge
Basic Price **TL, TR, L,R** $375
14526 15795 15796 15797
Only UL and UR panes were used.

#90 CANAL ZONE
on 15¢ STATUE OF LIBERTY (#566)
Basic Price $200
narrow gauge **TL, TR, L, R, B**
14910 14911 14912 14913
wide gauge (star) **TL, L, R, B**
17430 17431 17432 17433
A plate block of 4 with star and plate number 17433 in right margin is known, but the other 3 star plate blocks are unreported. Apparently few UR panes were overprinted.
wide gauge (no star) **TL, TR, L, R, B**
18928 18929 18930 19139

U.S. POSSESSIONS OVERPRINTS

#91 CANAL ZONE
on 17¢ WILSON (#623) intermediate gauge
Basic Price **TL, L, B**
9 mm spacing
18021 18022 18023 18024 18025
18026 18027 18028
7 mm spacing
18021 18022 18023 18024
Only UL and LL panes were overprinted.

#92 CANAL ZONE
on 20¢ GOLDEN GATE (#567)
Basic Price $250
narrow gauge,9mm spacing **TL, TR, L, R, B**
16646 16648 17530 17531
wide gauge(star),7mm spacing **L, R, B only**
†17227 17228 17229 17230 17426
17427 17428 17429
Only LL and LR panes were used, so no top or star plate blocks exist.
wide gauge(no star),9mm spacing,**TL,L,R,B**
19134 19468 19648 19872
Only UL and LR panes were overprinted.
wide gauge(no star), 9 mm spacing, no side plate #'s
*20033 †20034 *20037 *20038

#93 CANAL ZONE
on 30¢ BISON (#569)
Basic Price **TL, TR, L, R, B** $300
narrow gauge
14436 14437 14438 14439
wide gauge, no star
17446 17447 17448 17449

#94 CANAL ZONE
on 50¢ AMPHITHEATER (#570)
narrow gauge
Basic Price **TL, L, B** $3000
14042 14043 14044 14045
Only UL and LL panes were used.

#95 CANAL ZONE
on $1 LINCOLN MEMORIAL (#571) narrow gauge
Basic Price **TL, TR, B** $1500
14268

#96 CANAL ZONE
on 2¢ SESQUICENTENNIAL (#627)
Basic Price **L, R, B** $100
18570 18577 18582 18583
Top positions have very narrow selvage. Top plate blocks showing any part of the plate number command a premium.

#97 CANAL ZONE
on 2¢ WASHINGTON (#583)
Basic Price $300
9 mm spacing, LL, UR only
18632 18633
10 mm spacing, LR only
18809 18827 †18834 *18835 18933
18934

#98 CANAL ZONE
on 3¢ LINCOLN (#584)
Basic Price **LL, UR only** $125
18445 18446

#99 CANAL ZONE
on 10¢ MONROE (#591)
Basic Price **LR only** $200
18532 18538

#100 CANAL ZONE
on 1¢ FRANKLIN (#632)
Basic Price **LR only** $20
7 mm spacing
18730 18731

#101 CANAL ZONE
on 2¢ WASHINGTON (#634)
Basic Price $50
10mm spacing **LR only**
18809 18827 18933 18934
9 mm spacing **UL, UR, LL, LR**
18985 18986

#102 CANAL ZONE
on 3¢ LINCOLN (#635)
Basic Price $110
UL, UR, LR
18126 18803
UL, LR
18831 18833

#103 CANAL ZONE
on 5¢ ROOSEVELT (#637)
Basic Price **UL, UR, LL, LR** $200
18851 18855

#104 CANAL ZONE
on 10¢ MONROE (#642)
Basic Price **UL only** $190
10 mm spacing
19234 19235 19256 19257

#115 CANAL ZONE
on 3¢ WASHINGTON (#720)
Basic Price **UL, UR, LL, LR** $30
20932 20933 20934 20950 20954
20959 20960 21000 21001

#116 CANAL ZONE
on 14¢ INDIAN (#695)
Basic Price **LL, LR only** $55
20549 20550

#118 CANAL ZONE
on 1/2¢ FRANKLIN (#803)
Basic Price $3
Pre-eye Plates
UL, UR, LL, LR
21885 21887 21888 21889
LL only
*21899 *21900
Electric Eye Plates
UL, UR, LL, LR
22470 22471
UL, UR, LR only
22898 22899

U.S. POSSESSIONS OVERPRINTS

#119 CANAL ZONE
on 1.5¢ MARTHA WASHINGTON (#805)
Basic Price $3

Pre-eye Plates
UL, UR, LL, LR
21878 21879 21881 21882
UL, LL, LR only
*21877 *21884
POSITION UNKNOWN (UNIQUE PANE)
*21883
UL, UR, LL only
21934 *21937 *22079 *22080
UR only
*22077 †22078
UL only
*22173 *22174

Electric Eye Plates
UL, UR, LL, LR
22464 22466 22645 22646
LL only
*22876 *22877

BOOKLET PANES

#71e CANAL ZONE
on 1¢ FRANKLIN (#552a)
Basic Price **T** $500
14269 14270 14271 14272 15961
15964

#73a CANAL ZONE
on 2¢ WASHINGTON (#554c)
Basic Price **T** $600
15790 15792 16602 16603

#84d CANAL ZONE
on 2¢ WASHINGTON (#554c)
Plate number panes not reported

#97b CANAL ZONE
on 2¢ WASHINGTON (#583a)
Plate number panes not reported

#101a CANAL ZONE
on 2¢ WASHINGTON (#634d)
Basic Price **T** unique
†18719 *18721

#102a CANAL ZONE
on 3¢ LINCOLN (#635)
Basic Price $6,000
This booklet was handmade from sheet stamps. Three of the four known panes have plate numbers.
18803 18831 18833

#115c CANAL ZONE
on 3¢ WASHINGTON (#720)
Basic Price **L, R** $500
Handmade from sheet stamps
20932 20933 20934 20950 20954
20959 20960 21000 21001

POSTAGE DUES

Diagonal overprint CANAL ZONE

#J1 CANAL ZONE
on 1¢ POSTAGE DUE (#J45)
Basic Price **B, R only** $600
Imprint X
5510 5522 5534 5541
Only LR panes were overprinted

#J2 CANAL ZONE
on 2¢ POSTAGE DUE (#J46)
Basic Price **B, L, R** only $1,600
6703 6704 6705 6706
Only LL and LR panes were overprinted

#J3 CANAL ZONE
on 10¢ POSTAGE DUE (#J49)
Basic Price **B, R only** $7,000
Imprint X
5525 5532 5540 6555
Only LR panes were overprinted. Only one mint plate block (R 6555) is known. A cancelled pane of 100 of 5540 exists. Used plate singles and blocks of 4 are known, as well as some mint strips.

Overprinted CANAL ZONE, with flat topped A's in the word CANAL.

#J12 CANAL ZONE
on 1¢ POSTAGE DUE (#J61)
Basic Price **L, R, B only** $1,200
13844 13845
Only LL and LR panes were overprinted

#J13 CANAL ZONE
on 2¢ POSTAGE DUE (#J62)
Basic Price **TL, TR, L, R,B** $700
14026 14027 14028 14029

#J14 CANAL ZONE
on 10¢ POSTAGE DUE (#J65)
Basic Price **T, L, R, B** $3,200
Imprint X
5532 5540 6555 6556

POSTAGE DUE overprint in addition to CANAL ZONE overprint on regular issues.

#J15 CANAL ZONE POSTAGE DUE
on 1¢ FRANKLIN (#552)
Basic Price **R, B** $800
15334 15358 15359 15437
Only LR panes were overprinted

#J16 CANAL ZONE POSTAGE DUE
on 2¢ WASHINGTON (#554)
Basic Price **TR, R, B** $200
15629 15630 15631 15632
Only UR and LR panes were overprinted

U.S. POSSESSIONS OVERPRINTS

#J17 CANAL ZONE POSTAGE DUE
on 10¢ MONROE (#562)

Basic Price **TL, L** $500

15510 15511 15512 15513

Only UL panes were overprinted

Overprinted CANAL ZONE, with sharp topped A's in the word CANAL.

#J18 CANAL ZONE
on 1¢ POSTAGE DUE (#J61)

Basic Price **TL, TR, L, R, B** $80

9 mm spacing

8214 13844 13846 13847

11 mm spacing

13844 13845 13846 13847

F on 13847 inverted next to LL-B plate number. No F on 8214.

#J19 CANAL ZONE
on 2¢ POSTAGE DUE (#J62)

Basic Price **TL, TR, L, R, B** $140

14026 14027 14028 14029 14596
14597 14598 14599

#J20 CANAL ZONE
on 10¢ POSTAGE DUE (#J65)

Basic Price **T, L, R, B** $2000

Imprint X

6555 6556

#J20a Top plate block with top row of stamps lacking overprint (unique)

Price $17,500

6555

#J20b Overprinted on rose red shade (#J65a) No plate number copies known, but probably printed from plates 18724-7

#J20c Double overprint on rose red shade (#J65a) (unique)

18725

CUBA OVERPRINTS

The overprinted stamps of Cuba are listed in the Scott Cuba Catalog number order with the basic United States stamp shown on the next line with number in parentheses.

1899

Imprint V

#221 CUBA 1¢ de PESO
on 1¢ FRANKLIN (#279)

Basic Price **B, L only**

Imprint strip of 3 $55

Imprint block of 6 $250

564	565	566	567	572
573	574	575	766	767
768	769	770	771	772
773	*794	*795	†796	*797
*810	*811	*812	*813	

#222 CUBA 2¢ de PESO
on 2¢ WASHINGTON (#267)

Basic Price **B, L only**

Imprint strip of 3 $75

Imprint block of 6 $500

475 503

on 2¢ WASHINGTON (#279B)

Basic Price **B, L only**

Imprint strip of 3 $60

Imprint block of 6 $400

*556	*559	*560	*561	*562
*563	568	569	570	571
593	594	595	596	745
746	747	748	753	754
755	756	758	759	760
761	*762	*763	*764	*765
*774	*775	*776	*777	

#223 CUBA 2.5¢ de PESO
on 2¢ WASHINGTON (#267)

Basic Price **B, L only**

Imprint strip of 3 $75

Imprint block of 6 $400

469 475 503

on 2¢ WASHINGTON (#279B)

Basic Price **B, L only**

Imprint strip of 3 $60

Imprint block of 6 $275

*516	*552	*556	*559	560
561	562	563	568	569
570	571	593	594	595
596	745	746	747	748
753	754	755	756	758
759	760	761		

U.S. POSSESSIONS OVERPRINTS

#224 CUBA 3¢ de PESO
on 3¢ JACKSON (#268)
Basic Price **T,B only**
Imprint strip of 3 $95
Imprint block of 6 $550
447 448 449 450

#225 CUBA 5¢ de PESO
on 5¢ GRANT (#281)
Basic Price **T,B only**
Imprint strip of 3 $150
Imprint block of 6 $700
389 390 391 392 407
408 409 410
See Special Printings for plate 950

#226 CUBA 10¢ de PESO
on 10¢ WEBSTER (#282C)
Basic Price **B,L only**
Imprint strip of 3 $225
Imprint block of 6 $1,000
302 303 305 306

1899 Watermarked US-C

Imprints VII

#227 1¢ STATUE COLUMBUS
Basic Price **T, B only**
Imprint strip 5 $50
Imprint block 10 $200
879 884 889 890

#228 2¢ ROYAL PALMS
Basic Price **T, B only**
Imprint strip 5 $45
Imprint block 10 $175
871 872 873 874

#228b 2¢ BOOKLET PANE
No plate number panes known
†1323

#229 3¢ ALLEGORY "CUBA"
Basic Price **T, B only**
Imprint strip 5 $65
Imprint block 10 $250
891 892 893 894

#230 5¢ OCEAN LINER
Basic Price **T, B only**
Imprint strip 5 $125
Imprint block 10 $450
899 901 902 903

#231 10¢ CANE FIELD
Basic Price **T, B only**
Imprint strip 5 $250
Imprint block 10 $1,000
900

#232 1¢ UN CENTAVO
surcharged on #229
Basic Price **B only**
Imprint strip 5 $50
Imprint block 10 $200
891 892 893 894

SPECIAL DELIVERY

#E1 CUBA 10¢ de PESO
on 10¢ SPECIAL DELIVERY (#E5)
Price **T, B only**
Imprint strip of 3 $900
Imprint block of 6 $5,500
492

Watermarked US-C
#E2 10¢ "IMMEDIATA"
Price **T, B only**
Imprint strip of 3 $250
Imprint block of 6 $800
908

#E3 10¢ "INMEDIATA"
Price **T, B only**
Imprint strip of 3 $90
Imprint block of 6 $300
1432

POSTAGE DUE

#J1 CUBA 1¢ de PESO
on 1¢ POSTAGE DUE (#J38)
Basic Price **T, B only**
Imprint IV strip of 3 $200
Imprint IV block of 6 $750
246 267

#J2 CUBA 2¢ de PESO
on 2¢ POSTAGE DUE (#J39)
Basic Price **T, B only**
Imprint IV strip of 3 $200
Imprint IV block of 6 $750
247 268

#J3 CUBA 5¢ de PESO
on 5¢ POSTAGE DUE (#J41)
Basic Price **T, B only**
Imprint I strip of 3 $200
Imprint I block of 6 $800
71
Imprint V strip of 3 $150
Imprint V block of 6 $600
255

#J4 CUBA 10¢ de PESO
on 10¢ POSTAGE DUE (#J42)
Basic Price **T, B only**
Imprint I strip of 3 $200
Imprint I block of 6 $800
72
Imprint IV strip of 3 $150
Imprint IV block of 6 $600
256

U.S. POSSESSIONS OVERPRINTS

CUBA SPECIAL PRINTINGS

The following is a list of the plate numbers that were used for the special printing made for the exhibit in Paris in 1900. Two plate singles with positions indicated are the only known examples.

#221 **CUBA 1¢ de PESO**
†975

#222 **CUBA 2¢ de PESO**
†886

#223 **CUBA 2.5¢ de PESO**
†885

#225 **CUBA 5¢ de PESO**
950 Top

#226A **CUBA 10¢ de PESO**
935 Bottom

#E1 **CUBA 10¢ de PESO**
†882

#J1 **CUBA 1¢ de PESO**
†267

#J2 **CUBA 2¢ de PESO**
†268

#J3 **CUBA 5¢ de PESO**
†255

#J4 **CUBA 10¢ de PESO**
†256

GUAM OVERPRINTS

The overprinted stamps of Guam are listed in the Scott Guam Catalog number order with the basic United States stamp with number in parentheses. The overprint reads "GUAM". On the 1¢, 2¢ and 5¢ stamps the overprint is vertically aligned on bottom plate blocks of the first printing, while on the second printing the bottom row is shifted to the left by 0.5, 0.9 and 1.5 mm. Only bottom and left positions are known on 1¢, 2¢ and 10¢ values, and bottom positions for the other denominations of the regular issue, because top selvages were removed during overprinting. The known top positions are from the 1900 Paris Special Overprinting and are each unique. The special delivery stamp exists in both top and bottom positions, but only right panes were overprinted.

Imprint V unless noted otherwise.

#1 **GUAM**
on 1¢ FRANKLIN (#279)

First Printing **B, L only**
Basic Price
Imprint strip of 3 $90
Imprint block of 6 $500

794	795	796	797

Second Printing **B, L only**
Basic Price
Imprint strip of 3 $70
Imprint block of 6 $400

810	811	812	813	830
831	832	833		

#2 **GUAM**
on 2¢ WASHINGTON (#279B)

First Printing **B, L only**
Basic Price
Imprint strip of 3 $70
Imprint block of 6 $400

758	759	760	761	762
763	764	765	777	778
779	780	781	782	783
784	785	786	787	788
789	798	799	800	801
802	803	804	805	

Second Printing **B, L only**
Basic Price
Imprint strip of 3 $65
Imprint block of 6 $350

814	815	816	817	838
840	841	842	843	845
850	851	852	853	858
859	860	861	866	867
869	870	875	876	877
878	895	896	897	898**N**
904	905	906	907	

N A left plate single with "Specimen" overprint is the only example reported. See Napps Numbers, Vol I, p 46.

U.S. POSSESSIONS OVERPRINTS

#3 GUAM
on 3¢ JACKSON (#268)

Basic Price	**B only**	
Imprint strip of 3		$500
Imprint block of 6		$1,500

447 448 449 450

#4 GUAM
on 4¢ LINCOLN (#280a)

Basic Price	**B only**	
Imprint strip of 3		$500
Imprint block of 6		$2,200

790 791 792 793

#5 GUAM
on 5¢ GRANT (#281)

First Printing	**B only**	
Basic Price		
Imprint strip of 3		$150
Imprint block of 6		$900

389 390 391 392

Second Printing	**B only**	
Basic Price		
Imprint strip of 3		$125
Imprint block of 6		$700

834 835 836 837

#6 GUAM
on 6¢ GARFIELD (#282)

Basic Price	**B only**	
Imprint strip of 3		$500
Imprint block of 6		$1,750

922 923 924 925

#7 GUAM
on 8¢ SHERMAN (#272)

Basic Price	**B only**	
Imprint strip of 3		$500
Imprint block of 6		$1,750

928 929 930 931

#8 GUAM
on 10¢ WEBSTER (#282C)

Basic Price	**B, L only**	
Imprint strip of 3		$225
Imprint block of 6		$1,000

518 519 520 521

#10 GUAM
on 15¢ CLAY (#284)

Price	**B only**	
Imprint IV strip of 3		$600
Imprint IV block of 6		$2,500

264

#11 GUAM
on 50¢ JEFFERSON (#275)

Price	**B only**	
Imprint I strip of 3		$1,200
Imprint I block of 6		$4,000

75

#12 GUAM
on $1 PERRY (#276)

Price	**B only**	
Imprint II strip of 3		$1,600
Imprint II block of 6		$9,000

76

#E1 GUAM
on 10¢ SPECIAL DELIVERY (#E5)

Basic Price	**T, B only**	
Imprint VII strip of 3		$850
Imprint VII block of 6		$3,600

880 881 882 883

Only right panes were overprinted.

U.S. POSSESSIONS OVERPRINTS

GUAM SPECIAL PRINTINGS

The following is a list of the plate numbers that were used for the special printing made for the exhibit in Paris in 1900. These are unique items that exist as strips of 3 in most cases. The positions known to exist are listed.

#1 GUAM on 1¢ FRANKLIN (#279)
975 **B,L**

#2 GUAM on 2¢ WASHINGTON (#279B)
888 **B,L**

#3 GUAM on 3¢ JACKSON (#268)
447 **T,B**

#5 GUAM on 5¢ GRANT (#281)
949 **T**

#6 GUAM on 6¢ GARFIELD (#282)
†923

#7 GUAM on 8¢ SHERMAN (#272)
929 **B**

#8 GUAM on 10¢ WEBSTER (#282C)
932 **B,L**

#9 GUAM on 10¢ WEBSTER (#283)
No plate number examples are known. Napp believes the known copies come from surplus of a printing for the U.P.U.

#10 GUAM on 15¢ CLAY (#284)
264 **T,B**

#11 GUAM on 50¢ JEFFERSON (#275)
†75

#12 GUAM on $1 PERRY (#276)
†76 (a T imprint strip 2 is known)

#13 GUAM on $1 PERRY (#276A)
No plate number examples are known. The known copies are thought to come from a printing for the U.P.U.

#E1 GUAM
on 10¢ SPECIAL DELIVERY (#E5)
881 **TL** (strip 4)

PHILIPPINES OVERPRINTS

The overprinted U.S. stamps used in the Philippines are listed under their Scott Phillipines Catalog numbers with the basic United States stamp shown in parentheses. Other issues were printed by the Bureau of Engraving and Printing, but these were assigned from the miscellaneous series of plate numbers and we do not list them. They are listed in detail in "Napps Numbers" Vol 2 (see address on p333).

1899-1901

We list these by denomination, rather than in order of Scott numbers.

#213 PHILIPPINES
on 1¢ Franklin (#279)

Basic Price	
Imprint V strip of 3	$30
Imprint V block of 6	$200

B, L only

770	771	772	773	794
795	796	797	810	811
812	813	818	819	820
821	822	823	824	825
†969	979	984	985	986
987	992	993	995	1000
1001	1002	1003	1004	†1005
1006	1007			

B, R only

1050	1051	1052	1053	1062
1063	1064	1065	1130	1131
1132	1133	1146	1147	1148
1149	1157	1158	1159	1160
†1204	1205	†1206	1207	

B, L only

1396	1397	1398	1399	1400
1401	†1402	1403	†1407	1408
1409	1410	1411		

B, R only

1420	1421	1422	1423	1424
1427	1453	1454	1455	†1456

U.S. POSSESSIONS OVERPRINTS

#214 PHILIPPINES
on 2¢ WASHINGTON (#279B)

Basic Price
Imprint V strip of 3 $20
Imprint V block of 6 $160

B, L only

556	758	759	760	761
762	763	764	765	774
775	776	777	778	779
780	781	782	783	784
785	786	787	788	789
798	799	800	801	802
803	804	805	807	808
809	814	815	816	817
838	839	840	841	850
851	852	853	854	855
856	857	858	859	860
861	866	867	869	870
875	876	877	878	885
886	887	888	895	896
897	898	904	905	906
907				

B, R only

915	917	918	919	†1025
1026	1027	1032	1034	1039
1054	1056	1067	1068	1069
1070	1071	*1072	†1080	1081
†1082	1359	*1373	1381	1382
1383	1384	1385	1386	1387
1412	*1413	1414	1415	†1416
1417	1418	1419	1434	1435
1436	1437	1438	1439	1440

#214b 2¢ BOOKLET PANE
No plate number panes have been reported.

#215 PHILIPPINES
on 3¢ JACKSON (#268)

Basic Price **T, B only**
Imprint V strip of 3 $60
Imprint V block of 6 $500

447 448 449 450

#220 PHILIPPINES
on 4¢ LINCOLN (#280)

Basic Price **T, B only**
Imprint V strip of 3 $100
Imprint V block of 6 $600

*790 1100 1101 1102 1103

#216 PHILIPPINES
on 5¢ GRANT (#281)

Basic Price **T, B only**
Imprint V strip of 3 $55
Imprint V block of 6 $450

389	390	391	392	407
408	409	410	980	981
982	983	*1199	*1200	*1201
*1202	*1218	*1220		

#221 PHILIPPINES
on 6¢ GARFIELD (#282)

Basic Price **T, B only**
Imprint V strip of 3 $125
Imprint V block of 6 $800

922 923 924 925

#222 PHILIPPINES
on 8¢ SHERMAN (#272)

Basic Price **T, B only**
Imprint V strip of 3 $150
Imprint V block of 6 $900

928 929 930 931

#217 PHILIPPINES
on 10¢ WEBSTER (#282C)

Basic Price **B, L only**
Imprint V strip of 3 $100
Imprint V block of 6 $700

302	303	305	306	518
519	520	521		

#217A PHILIPPINES
on 10¢ WEBSTER (#283)

Basic Price **T, B only**
Imprint V strip of 3 $350
Imprint V block of 6 $2,500

1336 1337 1338 1339

#218 PHILLIPINES
on 15¢ CLAY (#284)

Price **T, B only**
Imprint IV strip of 3 $200
Imprint IV block of 6 $1000

264

#212 PHILIPPINES
on 50¢ JEFFERSON (#260)

Price **T, B only**
Imprint I strip of 3 $1,200
Imprint I block of 6 $5,000

75

#219 PHILIPPINES
on 50¢ JEFFERSON (#275)

Price **T, B only**
Imprint I strip of 3 $600
Imprint I block of 6 $2,500

75

U.S. POSSESSIONS OVERPRINTS

#223 PHILIPPINES
on $1 PERRY (#276)

Price **T, B only**
Imprint II strip of 3 $2,000
76

#223A PHILIPPINES
on $1 PERRY (#276A)

Price **T, B only**
Imprint II strip of 3 $10,000
76

#224 PHILIPPINES
on $2 MADISON (#277)

Price **T, B only**
Imprint II strip of 3 $3,000
84

#225 PHILIPPINES
on $5 MARSHALL (#278)

Price **T, B only**
Imprint II strip of 3 $6,500
85

1903-4

Imprint V

#226 PHILIPPINES
on 1¢ FRANKLIN (#300)

Basic Price
Imprint strip of 3 $20
Imprint block of 6 $175

B, L only

*1651	†1652	*1653	†1654	1655
†1656	†1657	1658	1680	1682
†1983				

T, L only

†1721	†1722	†1723	1734	1735
†1738	1739	†1740	1793	1794
1796	1801	1804		

B, L only

†2061	*2062	†2063	†2064	*2088
*2141	*2142	†2143	*2144	2173
2174	2175	2176	2193	2194
*2196	2257	2258	2259	*2260
2310	*2391	2392	2393	*2394
2407	2408	2409	2410	2415
2416	2417	2418	2451	2452
*2453	2454	2468	2469	*2470
2471	2484	2485	2486	2487
†2492	2493	2494	2495	2500
2501	2502	2503		

T, B only known

2745	2761	2762	2763	2764
†2792				

B, L only

2820	2821	2823	2907	2911
2915	2919			

#227 PHILIPPINES
on 2¢ WASHINGTON (FLAG) (#301)

Basic Price **B, L only**
Imprint strip of 3 $30
Imprint block of 6 $250

1644	1645	1646	1668	1669
1670	1671	1672	†1673	1674
1675	1676	1677	1678	1679
1696	†1697	1698	1699	1704
1705	1706	1707	1708	1709
1710	1711	1716		

#228 PHILIPPINES
on 3¢ JACKSON (#302)

Basic Price **B, L only**
Imprint strip of 3 $250
Imprint block of 6 $1,000

1586	1587	1588	1589	2516
2517	2518	2519		

#229 PHILIPPINES
on 4¢ GRANT (#303)

Basic Price **B, L only**
Imprint strip of 3 $250
Imprint block of 6 $1,000

1797	1798	1799	1800

#230 PHILIPPINES
on 5¢ LINCOLN (#304)

Basic Price
Imprint strip of 3 $40
Imprint block of 6 $325

T only known

*1537	*1538	*1540	*1663

B, L only

1885	1886	1887	†1888	2225
*2226	2227	2297		

#231 PHILIPPINES
on 6¢ GARFIELD (#305)

Basic Price **B, L only**
Imprint strip of 3 $300
Imprint block of 6 $1100

1598	1599	1600	1601

#232 PHILIPPINES
on 8¢ MARTHA WASHINGTON (#306)

Basic Price **B, L only**
Imprint strip of 3 $225
Imprint block of 6 $950

1497	1498	1499	1500

#233 PHILIPPINES
on 10¢ WEBSTER (#307)

Basic Price **B, L, R only**
Imprint strip of 3 $90
Imprint block of 6 $750

1590	1591	1592	1593

U.S. POSSESSIONS OVERPRINTS

#234 PHILIPPINES
on 13¢ HARRISON (#308)

Basic Price **T only known**

Imprint strip of 3	$140
Imprint block of 6	$1,000

1473 1474 1475 1476

#235 PHILIPPINES
on 15¢ CLAY (#309)

Basic Price **T, B only**

Imprint strip of 3	$250
Imprint block of 6	$1,500

1607 2330

#236 PHILIPPINES
on 50¢ JEFFERSON (#310)

Price **T, B only**

Imprint strip of 3	$600
Imprint block of 6	$3,800

1602

#237 PHILIPPINES
on $1 FARRAGUT (#311)

Price **T, B only**

Imprint strip of 3	$2,000
Imprint block of 6	$8,000

1629

#238 PHILIPPINES
on $2 MADISON (#312)

Price **T, B only**

Imprint strip of 3	$4,000
Imprint block of 6	$12,500

1630

#239 PHILIPPINES
on $5 MARSHALL (#313)

Price **T, B only**

Imprint strip of 3	$6,000
Imprint block of 6	$30,000

1620

#240 PHILIPPINES
on 2¢ WASHINGTON (SHIELD) (#319)

Basic Price **B, L only**

Imprint strip of 3	$35
Imprint block of 6	$250

*2211	*2212	*2214	*2217	2439
2441	2442	2459	2460	2461
2462	2712	2794	2795	2796
2810	2831**N**	2835	2839	2840
*2863	*2864	*2865	*2866	

N Top position known

#240a 2¢ BOOKLET PANE

The only plate number panes reported are 2109 and 2124. Others certainly were used.

#E1 PHILIPPINES
on 10¢ SPECIAL DELIVERY (#E5)

Basic Price **T, B only**

Imprint VII strip of 3	$500
Imprint VII block of 6	$4,000

880 881 882 883

#J1 PHILIPPINES
on 1¢ POSTAGE DUE (#J38)

Basic Price **T, B only**

Imprint IV strip of 3	$100
Imprint IV block of 6	$500

246 267

#J2 PHILIPPINES
on 2¢ POSTAGE DUE (#J39)

Basic Price **T, B only**

Imprint IV strip of 3	$100
Imprint IV block of 6	$500

247 268

Price **T, B only**

Imprint V strip of 3	$180
Imprint V block of 6	$950

1099

#J6 PHILIPPINES
on 3¢ POSTAGE DUE (#J40)

Price **T, B only**

Imprint IV strip of 3	$150
Imprint IV block of 6	$900

254

#J3 PHILIPPINES
on 5¢ POSTAGE DUE (#J41)

Price **T, B only**

Imprint I strip of 3	$150
Imprint I block of 6	$1,000

71

Price **T, B only**

Imprint V strip of 3	$175
Imprint V block of 6	$1,200

255

#J4 PHILIPPINES
on 10¢ POSTAGE DUE (#J42)

Price **T, B only**

Imprint I strip of 3	$150
Imprint I block of 6	$1,000

72

#J7 PHILIPPINES
on 30¢ POSTAGE DUE (#J43)

Price **T, B only**

Imprint I strip of 3	$850
Imprint I block of 6	$3,500

73

#J5 PHILIPPINES
on 50¢ POSTAGE DUE (#J44)

Price **T, B only**

Imprint II strip of 3	$850
Imprint II block of 6	$3,500

74

U.S. POSSESSIONS OVERPRINTS

PHILIPPINES
SPECIAL PRINTINGS

Special printings were made for the Paris Exposition in 1900, the St. Louis World's Fair in 1904, and for the Bureau of Insular Affairs in 1907. We list only those known or reported to exist as plate number pieces (strips of 3 except where noted). These are unique, and the positions known are indicated. These special printings resulted in the only use of plate 288 of the $5 Marshall (U.S. #278), and in the creation of Scott #E2A. See Napp's Numbers, Vol I, for more detail.

SCOTT #	PLATE NUMBER	
	1900 Paris Exhibition	
#213	†969	
#216	951	T
	1904 St. Louis	
#221	924	B
#223	76	B (single)
#225	288	TR (single)
#226	1946	B, L
#227	1553	B (pl 6), R
#230	1887	B
#234	1474	B
#235	1607	T
#236	1602	B
#237	1629	B
#240	1913	B, R
#J6	254	B (pl 6)
#J7	†73	

1907 Special Printing (all are plate blocks)

#226	3393	L
#228	2808	L
#230	3158	B
#231	1600	B
#232	2803	B, R
#233	2289	B, R
#234	1473	B, R
#235	3209	B
#240	3372	R
#E2A	1774	BL, BR
#JI	1632	B
#J2	1244	B
#J3	1642	B
#J4	1633	B
#J5	†74	
#J6	1631	B
#J7	†73	

UR-top position based on examination of proof sheet by J. Bruns

U.S. POSSESSIONS OVERPRINTS

PUERTO RICO OVERPRINTS

U.S. stamps were overprinted for use in Puerto Rico. The diagonal overprint at first read "PORTO RICO" but this was later changed to "PUERTO RICO." Some of the PORTO RICO overprints exist with two angles of overprint, 25 and 36 degrees, and plate strips of the 1¢, 2¢, 8¢ and postage dues can contain both angles. We list these by Scott Puerto Rico Catalog order with the basic U.S. stamp in parentheses.

#210 PORTO RICO
on 1¢ FRANKLIN (#279)

Basic Price **B, L only**

Imprint V strip of 3 $40
Imprint V block of 6 $180

564	565	566	567	574
575	768	769	770	771
772	773			

#211 PORTO RICO
on 2¢ WASHINGTON (#279B)

Basic Price **B, L only**

Imprint V strip of 3 $35
Imprint V block of 6 $180

556	561	562	563	593
594	595	596	745	746
747	748	753	754	755
756	758	759	760	761
762	763	764	765	774
775	776	777	778	779
780	781	782	783	784
785				

#212 PORTO RICO
on 5¢ GRANT (#281)

Basic Price **T, B only**

Imprint V strip of 3 $60
Imprint V block of 6 $500

389	390	391	392	*408
†410				

#213 PORTO RICO
on 8¢ SHERMAN (#272)

Basic Price **T, B only**

Imprint strip of 3 $240
Imprint block of 6 $1,500

Imprint IV

249

Imprint V

555

#214 PORTO RICO
on 10¢ WEBSTER (#282C)

Basic Price **B, L only**

Imprint strip of 3 $100
Imprint block of 6 $800

Imprint IV

302	303	305	306

Imprint V

518	519	520	521

#215 PUERTO RICO
on 1¢ FRANKLIN (#279)

Basic Price **B, L only**

Imprint V strip of 3 $28
Imprint V block of 6 $140

846	847	848	849	862
863	864	865	937	938
939	940	941	*942	*943
944	*946	*947	*953	*954
*955	*957	*958	*959	

#216 PUERTO RICO
on 2¢ WASHINGTON (#279B)

Basic Price **B,L,R only**

Imprint V strip of 3 $30
Imprint V block of 6 $140

838	839	840	841	850
851	852	853	854	855
856	857	858	859	860
861	866	867	869	870
875	876	877	878	885
886	887	888	895	896
897	898	904	905	906
907				

Left positions are very scarce

#J1 PORTO RICO
on 1¢ POSTAGE DUE (#J38)

Basic Price **T, B only**

Imprint IV strip of 3 $100
Imprint IV block of 6 $600

246 267

#J2 PORTO RICO
on 2¢ POSTAGE DUE (#J39)

Basic Price **T, B only**

Imprint IV strip of 3 $100
Imprint IV block of 6 $700

247 268

#J3 PORTO RICO
on 10¢ POSTAGE DUE (#J42)

Price **T, B only**

Imprint I strip of 3 $750
Imprint I block of 6 $3,000

72

U.S. POSSESSIONS OVERPRINTS

PUERTO RICO SPECIAL PRINTINGS

A special printing was made for exhibiting at the Paris Exhibition in 1900. These have the "PUERTO RICO" overprint, and thus some values do not currently have Scott Catalog numbers. The 1¢ and 2¢ values exist as bottom and left strips of 3, while the other denominations exist as plate singles in positions shown. Each item is unique.

#215 PUERTO RICO on 1¢ FRANKLIN (#279)
975 B, L

#216 PUERTO RICO on 2¢ WASHINGTON (#279B)
878 B, L

#"?" PUERTO RICO on 5¢ GRANT (#281)
948 B

#"?" PUERTO RICO on 8¢ SHERMAN (#272)
929 B

#"?" PUERTO RICO on 10¢ WEBSTER (#282C)
932 B, L

Lower left panes from plate 932 contained three type II stamps (Scott #283), but apparently none were saved.

#"?" PUERTO RICO on 1¢ POSTAGE DUE (#J38)
267 T, B

#"?" PUERTO RICO on 2¢ POSTAGE DUE (#J39)
268 T, B

#"?" PUERTO RICO on 10¢ POSTAGE DUE (#J42)
256 T, B

CONFEDERATE STATES

Only Scott #11 and #12 had plate numbers. Plates 1 and 2 were type I or die A (#11) and plates 3 and 4 were type II or die B (#12). The plates had 200 subjects in 2 panes of 100; full panes of 200 exist. For the first printings the plates had plate numbers preceded by "No." in the bottom margin of each pane, but no imprints. The plate numbers on plates 1 and 2 were under stamp 96 on the left pane and 95 on the right pane. On plate 3 they were under 95 on both panes, and on plate 4 they were between 95 and 96. These early printings are rare; we have seen only plate 4. Please report any other plate numbers without imprints.

For the next printings, an imprint in script letters that originally read "Archer & Daly, Bank Note Engravers, Richmond, Va." was added to the left of the plate number on 1L, 2L, 4L and 4R. It follows the plate number on 1R, 2R, 3L and 3R. This imprint is reported by Dietz to exist in five forms. In addition to the full imprint, which we have not seen, it appears with "& Daly" crossed out with horizontal lines (seen by us on 2L and 2R), with "& Daly" removed (seen on 1L, 1R, 3L and 3R), with both "& Daly" and "Richmond, Va." removed (not seen by us), and with "Archer & Daly" and the "s" of "Engravers" removed, but "Richmond, Va." still present (seen on 4L). Please report the imprints on plate numbers and positions other than those mentioned above and supply a xerox, if possible.

The left and right panes can be distinguished by the position of the imprint on plates 1 and 2; by the position of the "k" of "Bank" on plate 3 (near right of gutter on left pane; left of gutter on right pane); and on plate 4 by the fact that stamp 91 is entered lower than 92 and 100 higher than 99 on the right pane, while the stamps are entered evenly on the left pane.

In 1864, with Union armies approaching Richmond, the plates were sent to South Carolina and printings were made by Keatinge & Ball. They removed all remaining portions of the imprints except for "Bank Note Engravers" and added in block letters "Keatinge & Ball" before and "Columbia, S.C." after "Bank Note Engravers." We have seen all positions except 4L.

#11	**10¢**	**Blue Die A**	
Basic Price		**BL,BR**	
Block of 12, no imprint			$300
Archer & Daly			
Imprint block of 12			$200
Keatinge & Ball			
Imprint block of 12			$200
	1	2	

#12	**10¢**	**Blue Die B**	
Basic Price		**BL,BR**	
Block of 12, no imprint			$300
Archer & Daly			
Imprint block of 12			$200
Keatinge & Ball			
Imprint block of 12			$200
	3	4	

COMPUTER VENDED POSTAGE

#CVP31 Shield Coil (Type I)
surface tagging, dull gum

		L
1	$0.00	☐

#CVP31a Shield Coil (Type I)
embedded tagging, shiny gum

1	$0.00	☐

#CVP31b Shield Coil (Type II)
surface tagging, dull gum

1	$0.00	☐

#CVP31c Shield Coil (Type II)
embedded tagging, shiny gum

1	$0.00	☐

#CVP32 Shield Coil
dull and shiny gum

		B
A11	$0.00	☐

#CVP33 Shield Coil

11	$0.00	☐

APPENDIX A

PRIVATELY PRODUCED VENDING AND AFFIXING MACHINE COILS

The listing is arranged in alphabetical order for the various companies that produced these items. Normally the location of the plate number on the privately produced coils is at the left side or bottom whereas the government produced coils show the numbers at the right side or the top as a result of the manner in which the coils were pasted up.

THE BRINKERHOFF COMPANY

Sedalia, MO

Brinkerhoff Type I

ENDWISE COILS

#314 1¢ WASHINGTON
3228

#320 2¢ WASHINGTON & SHIELD
3451

#371 2¢ ALASKA-YUKON
5249 5250

#408 1¢ WASHINGTON
5849 5882 5884 7283

#409 2¢ WASHINGTON
5861 5995 6496 6498

Brinkerhoff Type II

#345 3¢ WASHINGTON
4926

#346 4¢ WASHINGTON
4934

#347 5¢ WASHINGTON
4931

#371 2¢ ALASKA-YUKON
5249 5250

#384 2¢ WASHINGTON
5323

Brinkerhoff Type IIb

#408 1¢ WASHINGTON
5837

THE FARWELL COMPANY

Chicago, IL

SIDEWISE COILS

Farwell Group 2 Type 2 A 3

#384 2¢ WASHINGTON
5608

Farwell Group 2 Type 2 B 3

#383 1¢ FRANKLIN
5598

#384 2¢ WASHINGTON
5608 5624

Farwell Group 4 Type A

#383 1¢ FRANKLIN
5679 5709

#408 1¢ WASHINGTON
5867 6041 7294

#409 2¢ WASHINGTON
6151 7708

Farwell Group 4 Type B

#383 1¢ FRANKLIN
5679 5715

#384 2¢ WASHINGTON
5624

#409 2¢ WASHINGTON
5740 5785

Farwell Group 4 Type A & B

#408 1¢ WASHINGTON
5831 6041

#409 2¢ WASHINGTON
5785

Farwell Group 4 Type ?

#409 2¢ WASHINGTON
6151

Farwell Group 5

#408 1¢ WASHINGTON
6615

INTERNATIONAL VENDING MACHINE CO.

Baltimore, MD

SIDEWISE COILS

PERF. 12°

#344 2¢ WASHINGTON
4868

#345 3¢ WASHINGTON
4927

THE MAILOMETER COMPANY

Detroit, MI

SIDEWISE COILS

MAIL-O-METER Type I

#320 2¢ WASH. & SHIELD
3451

MAIL-O-METER Type II

#343 1¢ FRANKLIN
4980

#344 2¢ WASHINGTON
5015

MAIL-O-METER Type III

#343 1¢ FRANKLIN
4980

#368 2¢ LINCOLN
4976

MAIL-O-METER Type IV

#343 1¢ FRANKLIN
4980

#344 2¢ WASHINGTON
4887

#345 3¢ WASHINGTON
4918

APPENDIX A

PRIVATELY PRODUCED VENDING AND AFFIXING MACHINE COILS

MAIL-O-METER Type IV Cont.

#346 4¢ WASHINGTON
5212

#347 5¢ WASHINGTON
4931

#368 2¢ LINCOLN
4981

#371 2¢ ALASKA-YUKON
5257

#383 1¢ FRANKLIN
5491 5494 5495

#384 2¢ WASHINGTON
5309 5516 5554

#408 1¢ WASHINGTON
5828 5886 5900 5901 5903
5905

#409 2¢ WASHINGTON
5872 5928 5929 5992 6281
6286 6289

#483 3¢ WASHINGTON
8130

THE SCHERMACK COMPANY

Detroit, MI

SIDEWISE COILS

SCHERMACK Type I 8 holes

#314 1¢ FRANKLIN
3119

#343 1¢ FRANKLIN
4971

#368 2¢ LINCOLN
4979

SCHERMACK Type II 6 holes

#314 1¢ FRANKLIN
3121

SCHERMACK Type III

#314 1¢ FRANKLIN
4605 4712 4713 4734

#314A 4¢ GRANT
4255

#315 5¢ LINCOLN
4073

#320 2¢ WASH. & SHIELD (DIE I)
3136 3452 4245

#320a 2¢ WASH. & SHIELD (DIE II)
4617

#343 1¢ FRANKLIN
5084

#344 2¢ WASHINGTON
4876 4879 5072

#345 3¢ WASHINGTON
4927 5131

#346 4¢ WASHINGTON
4932 4934 4935 5212

#373 2¢ HUDSON-FULTON
5389 5394

SCHERMACK Type III Cont.

#383 1¢ FRANKLIN
5484 5489 5631 5639

#384 2¢ WASHINGTON
5366 5512 5515 5589 5608
5616 5635 5686

#408 1¢ WASHINGTON
5867 5878 6007 6154 6282
6283 6301 6475 6777 6793
7301 7307 7326 7363 7364

#409 2¢ WASHINGTON
5792 5802 5815 5861 5979
6024 6051 6293 6760 6979
7084 7192 7195 7225 7229
7245 7257 7311 7318 7328
7352 7356 7396 7424 7448
7450 7478 7481 7486 7574
7594 7638

#481 1¢ WASHINGTON
7896 8040 8259 10075 10121
10264 10265 10279 10282 10290
10292 10360 10759 12494 12501
13308

#482 2¢ WASHINGTON
7698 7699 7703 7780 7809
7930 7936 7944 7995 9206
9221 9434 9437 10199 13671
13726 13946

#483 3¢ WASHINGTON (Type I)
8209

#484 3¢ WASHINGTON (Type II)
8355 8358

#534 2¢ WASHINGTON (Type Va)
11414

#534A 2¢ WASHINGTON (Type VI)
11641 11686

#535 3¢ WASHINGTON (Type IV)
8837

#575 1¢ FRANKLIN
14217 14218 15145 15410

#576 1.5¢ HARDING
16862 16870 16872

#577 2¢ WASHINGTON
14197 15699 15700 15739 16190
16208 16235 16238 16580 16651
16714 16722 16724 16739 16743
16755 17708 17876 18197 18220
18221 18228

APPENDIX A

PRIVATELY PRODUCED VENDING AND AFFIXING MACHINE COILS

U.S. AUTOMATIC VENDING COMPANY

New York, NY

ENDWISE COILS Type I

#320a 2¢ **WASH. & SHIELD (DIE II)**
4671

#343 1¢ **FRANKLIN**
4972 5336

#344 2¢ **WASHINGTON**
4876 5306

#345 3¢ **WASHINGTON**
4927

#346 4¢ **WASHINGTON**
4932

#368 2¢ **LINCOLN**
4977

#384 2¢ **WASHINGTON**
5528

#409 2¢ **WASHINGTON**
5998

SIDEWISE COILS Type II

#320 2¢ **WASH. & SHIELD (DIE I)**
4146

#344 2¢ **WASHINGTON**
4905

#345 3¢ **WASHINGTON**
4925

#346 4¢ **WASHINGTON**
4932

#371 2¢ **ALASKA-YUKON**
5208

#383 1¢ **FRANKLIN**
5634

#384 2¢ **WASHINGTON**
5528

#408 1¢ **WASHINGTON**
5878

#409 2¢ **WASHINGTON**
5819 5830

SIDEWISE COILS Type III

#320 2¢ **WASH. & SHIELD (DIE I)**
4146

#345 3¢ **WASHINGTON**
4927

#371 2¢ **ALASKA-YUKON**
5236 5257

#373 2¢ **HUDSON-FULTON**
5392 5394 5395

#408 1¢ **WASHINGTON**
5828 5878

#409 2¢ **WASHINGTON**
5819 5830

APPENDIX B

PANES OF 60 AND 160

During the period when the private vending machine operators were purchasing imperforate sheets of stamps from the Post Office Department for use in their perforating and coiling machines, the use of the "Star plates" gave birth to two collectible varieties of panes of stamps. The configuration of the star plate created a problem for the vending machine operators. The star plate was created in an attempt to solve the problem of uneven shrinkage of wetted stamp paper. The 400 subject star plate consisted of twenty horizontal rows of stamps each of twenty vertical columns. The vertical spacing was constant but the horizontal spacing consisted of six outside columns spaced at 3mm; eight internal columns spaced at 2mm and six outside columns spaced at 3mm. Since the non-uniform spacing caused problems in the perforating and coiling operation, the vending machine operators persuaded the Post Office Department to sell them imperforate sheets consisting of the 8 columns that were spaced 2mm apart as a pane of 160 stamps. Since this left a remainder on hand of two panes of 120 stamps each, the decision was made to perforate these remainders 12 x 12 and to sell panes of sixty subjects at the post office instead of the normal 100 subjects. This action created the panes of sixty of Scott #374.

The collectible positions of Scott #374 are:

a) UL pane consisting of sixty subjects with a full imprint and plate number in the left margin and imprint only over the two top right stamps.

b) UR pane consisting of sixty subjects with a full imprint and plate number in the right hand margin and a full imprint and plate number in the top margin with a straight edge at left side of imprint.

c) LL pane consisting of sixty subjects with a full imprint and plate number in the left margin and imprint only under the two bottom right stamps.

d) LR pane consisting of sixty subjects with a fuil imprint and plate number in the right margin and a full imprint and plate number in the bottom margin with a straight edge at left side of imprint.

e) A plate block of six subjects with full imprint and plate number in top margin with a full margin straight edge at left side. This is a UR plate block.

f) A full plate block of six subjects with full imprint and plate number in bottom margin with a full margin straight edge at left side. This is a LR plate block.

There are no UL top or LL bottom plate blocks. The majority of reported panes are LR. The side position plate blocks cannot be distinguished from the plate blocks from the one hundred subject sheets.

Before the vending machine operators had purchased all of the stock of the 160 subject imperforates, another change in plate configuration was made which were the "A", plates that had a constant horizontal spacing of 2 3/4mm. Since this spacing was satisfactory, the operators ceased purchasing the imperforate 160 subject panes. As a direct result, the Post Office Department sold the remainders of the 160 subject panes at the Philatelic Agency in Washington, DC. This action created the panes of 160 subjects of Scott #383.

The collectible position of Scott #383 is a pane of 160 stamps with a plate number ONLY over the top left stamp and a plate number ONLY under the bottom left stamp. We surmise that most of these panes have been broken up; if anyone has one please notify the Editor.

The plate numbers that have been reported for the above variations are:

5603	5604	5605	5607	5620
5622	5639	5640	5643	5644
5647	5651	5672	5673	

APPENDIX C

EARLY IMPERFORATE PLATE NUMBERS

Although the following items were not issued in the normal manner by the Post Office Department, they have been given catalog status. For the record we list the plate numbers that have been reported for each of the stamps involved.

#252a 2¢ WASHINGTON
Imperforate Vertically
152

#253a 3¢ JACKSON
Imperforate
47

#254a 4¢ LINCOLN
Imperforate
50

#255b 5¢ GRANT
Imperforate
53

#255c 5¢ GRANT
Imperforate Horizontally
130

#256a 6¢ GARFIELD
Imperforate Horizontally
28

#258a 10¢ WEBSTER
63

#264b 1¢ FRANKLIN
Imperforate Vertically
24

#264c 1¢ FRANKLIN
Imperforate
314 334 336

#267a 2¢ WASHINGTON
Imperforate
319 340

#268a 3¢ JACKSON
Imperforate
103 107

#269a 4¢ LINCOLN
Imperforate
94 106

#270b 5¢ GRANT
Imperforate
251 351

#271b 6¢ GARFIELD
Imperforate
373

#272b 8¢ SHERMAN
Imperforate
249

#273a 10¢ WEBSTER
Imperforate
305

#274a 15¢ CLAY
Imperforate
52

#275b 50¢ JEFFERSON
Imperforate
75

#276b $1 PERRY
Imperforate
76

#277b $2 MADISON
Imperforate
84

#278a $5 MARSHALL
Imperforate
85

#E5a 10¢ SPECIAL DELIVERY
Imperforate
257

#J31a 1¢ POSTAGE DUE
Imperforate
57

Other stamps in these issues have also been reported imperforate. However, there is no report of the plate number for any of the stamps.

APPENDIX D

ROTARY PRESS COIL PLATE NUMBERS

The stamps produced by the Stickney rotary presses of the 1911 Series of postage stamps for use as coil stamps have now been listed in the front section of this catalog. As an aid in determining the possible plate number to be deciphered from the partial plate number on the stamp, we will list all of the known plate numbers that were sent to press to produce the rotary press coils. The Scott Catalog numbers of 448, 449, 450, 452, 453, 454, 455, 456, 457, 458, 459, 486, 487, 488, 489, 490, 491, 492, 493, 494, 495, 496 and 497 were produced from these plates. Due to the procedure used to manufacture these coil stamps in rolls of 500, large quantities of printed paper that was perforated 10 in one direction were left over. Rather than destroy this surplus of printed paper, a decision was made to perforate at right angles to the existing perforations and produce sheets of 170 subjects which could be sold at the post offices. A complete description may be found in The United States Specialist. This product is known as the coil waste stamps and is listed under Scott Catalog numbers 538, 539, 540, 541, 545 and 546. All of the coil waste issues are on unwatermarked paper so not all of the early plate numbers were used. Almost all of the known rotary press coil plate numbers from the 170 subject plates are from the coil waste issues. The extremely few known plate numbers on the coils produced from the 150 and 170 subject plates are partial numbers existing on off-centered stamps. To furnish the reader with a means for checking the partial plate numbers we will list all of the plates used for printing. We will list the different marginal inscriptions that exist and then will break down the listing by the face value and the arrangement. We will not list the plates that were known not to be used and those that were not completed.

The changes in the listing are the result of the examination of all proof sheets by Dr. Cleland.

The following is a description of the marginal markings of the various arrangements that were used on the finished plates:

ARRANGEMENT #1 used on 150 subject plates has one plate number located to the left of stamp #71.

ARRANGEMENT #2 used on 170 subject plates has one plate number located above stamp #9.

ARRANGEMENT #3 used on 170 subject plates has a plate number located above stamp #9 plus the symbol S20 above stamp #10.

ARRANGEMENT #4 used on 170 subject plates has a plate number located above stamp #9 plus the symbol S40 above stamp #10.

ARRANGEMENT #5 used on 170 subject piates has a plate number located above stamp #9 plus the symbol S30 above stamp #10.

ARRANGEMENT #6 used on 150 subject plates has the symbol S30 located to the left of stamp #61 and the plate number to the left of stamp #71.

ARRANGEMENT #7 used on 150 subject plates has the symbol S30 located to the left of stamp #61, the plate number to the left of stamp #71 and a star to the left of stamp #141.

ARRANGEMENT #7a used on 150 subject plates has the symbol S30 located to the left of stamp #51, the plate number to the left of stamp #61 and a star to the left of stamp #141.

ARRANGEMENT #8 used on 170 subject plates has a star located above stamp #1 and the plate number above stamp #9.

ARRANGEMENT #9 used on 150 subject plates has the plate number located to the left of stamp #71 and a star to the left of stamp #141.

ARRANGEMENT #10 used on 170 subject plates has a star located above stamp #1, the plate number above stamp #9 and the symbol S30 above stamp #10.

ARRANGEMENT #11 used on 170 subject plates has both a star and a plate number located above stamp #1.

ARRANGEMENT #12 used on 150 subject plates has both a star and a plate number located to the left of stamp #141.

The 170 subject plates print sideways coils and the 150 subject plates print endwise coils.

1¢ Rotary Press Coil Plates

170 Subject

ARRANGEMENT #2

7170	7171	7182	7183	7506
7507	7508			

ARRANGEMENT #5

7552	7553	7558	7559	7565
7566	7567	7619	7626	7627
7690	7691	7744	7745	7763

ARRANGEMENT #8

13445	13446	13447	13448	13491
13492	13575	13576	13611	13612
13615	13616			

ARRANGEMENT #10

7766	7767	7957	7958	7963
7964	7978	7979	8081	8082
8336	8337	8339	8340	9099
9111	9112	9113	9114	9141

APPENDIX D

1¢ Rotary Press Coil Plates

170 Subject

ARRANGEMENT #10 **Cont.**

9142	9151	9152	9450	9451
9452	9453	9463	9464	9467
9468	10087	10088	10089	10090
10103	10104	10184	10185	10202
10203	10345	10346	10347	10348
10349	10350	10361	10640	10641
10642	10643	10686	10687	10688
10689	10690	10691	10692	10693
10694	10695	11740	11741	11742
11743	11764	11765	11766	11767
13312	13313	13314	13315	

ARRANGEMENT #11

13810	13811	13812	13813	13820
13821	13826	13827	13828	13829
13856	13857	13872	13873	13896
13897	13906	13907	13910	13911
13930	13931	13942	13943	13968
13969	13976	14104		

1¢ Rotary Press Coil Plates

150 Subject

ARRANGEMENT #1

7433 7434

ARRANGEMENT #7

7563	7564	8079	8080	10081
10408	10409	10410	10411	

ARRANGEMENT #7a

10082

ARRANGEMENT #12

13928 13929

2¢ Rotary Press Coil Plates

170 Subject

ARRANGEMENT #2 **Type I**

6856	6857	7174	7175	7230
7231	7270	7271	7408	7409
7417	7418	7422	7423	

ARRANGEMENT #2 **Type II**

7425	7426	7427	7428	7429
7430	7437	7438	7443	7444
7445	7446			

ARRANGEMENT #3 **Type II**

7457 7458 7462 7463

2¢ Rotary Press Coil Plates

170 Subject

ARRANGEMENT #4 **Type II**

7467	7468	7469	7470	7482
7483	7489	7490	7496	7497
7502	7503			

ARRANGEMENT #5 **Type III**

7510	7511	7512	7513	7521
7522	7523	7524	7617	7621
7624	7625	7630	7631	7636
7637	7661	7662	7672	7673
7677	7678	7679	7680	7686
7687	7688	7689	7738	7739
7746	7747	7751	7752	7782
7803	7804	7813	7814	7826
7827	7829	7830	7835	7836
7909	7910	7915	7916	

ARRANGEMENT #8 **Type III**

13397	13398	13399	13400	13401
13402	13413	13414	13417	13418
13425	13426	13427	13428	13505
13506	13507	13508	13509	13510
13511	13512	13514	13583	13584
13585	13586	13595	13596	13597
13598	13599	13600	13601	13602
13603	13604	13605	13606	13607
13608	13637	13638	13641	13642
13647	13648	13651	13652	13657
13658	13677	13678	13692	13693
13694	13695	13718	13719	13720
13721	13740	13764		

ARRANGEMENT #10 **Type III**

7852	7853	7939	7940	7953
7961	7962	7965	7967	7976
8049	8050	8051	8052	8056
8057	8061	8062	8071	8072
8073	8074	8075	8076	8169
8170	8171	8172	8326	8327
8328	8329	8928	8939	8940
9103	9104	9105	9106	9153
9154	9233	9234	9235	9236
9237	9457	9458	9465	9466
9469	9470	10097	10098	10115
10116	10175	10176	10177	10178
10183	10295	10296	10297	10306
10307	10308	10315	10316	10317
10318	10384	10386	10387	10388
10389	10444	10445	10446	10447
10448	10449	10450	10451	10452
10453	10466	10467	10468	10469
10470	10471**N**	10478	10479	10480

N The S30 is inverted with respect to the plate number.

APPENDIX D

2¢ Rotary Press Coil Plates

170 Subject

ARRANGEMENT #10 Type III Cont.

10485	10486	10487	10488	10489
10491	10492	10648	10649	10650
10651	10652	10670	10671	10680
10681	10723	10724	10725	10726
10727	10728	10729	10730	10731
10732	10733	10738	10739	10740
10741	10750	11718	11719	11724
11725	11726	11727	11730	11731
11732	11733	11734	11735	11736
11737	11769	11770	11771	11772
11797	11798	11799	11800	11808
11809	11810	11811	12464	12465
12466	12469	12470	12471	12472
12473	12474	12475	12476	12483
12484	12485	12486	12513	12514
12515	12516	12517	12518	12519
12520	12529	12530	12531	12532
12601	12602	12603	12604	12918
12919	12920	12921	12922	12927
12928	12929	12970	12971	12972
12973	13002	13004	13005	13239
13240	13253	13254	13286	13287
13288	13289	13290	13291	13292
13293	13294	13295	13386	13387
13388	13536	13537	13538	13539

ARRANGEMENT #11 Type III

13741	13742	13743	13765	13766
13767	13776	13777	13778	13779
13786	13787	13788	13789	13800
13801	13802	13803	13804	13805
13807	13809	13814	13815	13830
13831	13840	13841	13842	13843
13874	13875	13894	13895	13938
13939	13958	13959	13960	13961
13970	13971	13984	13985	14030
14031	14032	14033	14038	14039
14040	14041	14050	14051	14052
14053	14054	14055	14056	14057

2¢ Rotary Press Coil Plates

150 Subject

ARRANGEMENT #1 Type I

6279 6280

ARRANGEMENT #1 Type II

7431 7432

ARRANGEMENT #6 Type III

7561 7562 7628 7629

ARRANGEMENT #7 Type III

8077 8078 10767 10768

2¢ Rotary Press Coil Plates

150 Subject

ARRANGEMENT #9 Type III

13629 13630 13631 13632

3¢ Rotary Press Coil Plates

170 Subject

ARRANGEMENT #2 Type I

7441 7442

ARRANGEMENT #8 Type I

8107	8108	8109	8110	8124
8125	8151	8152	8153	8154
8155	8201	8202	8203	8216
8217	8218	8219	8226	8227
8228	8229	8233	8234	8237
8238	8239	8240	8244	8245
8247	8248	8250	8251	

ARRANGEMENT #8 Type II

8269	8270	8275	8276	8281
8282	8402	8408	8409	8428
8429	8442	8454	8455	8458
8459	8463	8464	8467	8468
8469	8470	8471	8472	8474
8475	8482	8483	8923	8924
8949	8950	8951	9107	9108
9109	9110	9133	9134	9135
9136	9143	9144	9145	9146
9181	9182			

150 Subject

ARRANGEMENT #9 Type I

7634 7635 8111 8112

4¢ Rotary Press Coil Plates

170 Subject

ARRANGEMENT #2

7440 7452

ARRANGEMENT #8

7675 7676

5¢ Rotary Press Coil Plates

170 Subject

ARRANGEMENT #2

7435 7436

ARRANGEMENT #8

13633 13634

10¢ Rotary Press Coil Plates

170 Subject

ARRANGEMENT #8

13625 13626

APPENDIX E

COLLECTING PLATE NUMBERS FROM BEP ROTARY PRESSES

The Bureau of Engraving and Printing (BEP) produces United States postage stamps on high speed web-fed rotary presses. Multicolored stamps are currently printed in a variety of ways such as intaglio, gravure, offset, and combination intaglio and offset. As of December 1996, there are five web-fed presses in operation at the BEP for the production of postage stamps: the Andreotti Gravure Press, the Goebel C & D Presses, the Giori F Press, and the Goebel Optiforma Offset Press. In the following we use the term "plate" as a generic term, and point out the cases when the printing plate takes the special form of a cylinder or sleeve.

Stickney Press

The first intaglio rotary presses used at the BEP were the Stickney Presses. These presses were designed by Bureau employee, Benjamin R. Stickney, and were in use from 1914 until 1962. The Stickney Presses used the so called "wet" printing process. These presses produced sheet stamps with a plate number in one corner (UL, UR, LL, or LR) of a post office pane. Two semicircular plates were used at a time. Since a guillotine was used to separate the web into press sheets, a normal post office pad of panes consisted of a single position of two alternating plate numbers. Plate numbers for booklet stamps were entered in the four corners of the plate (UL, UR, LL, or LR) and were normally trimmed off. Miscut booklet panes of 6 stamps (e.g. Scott #807a) may show partial plate numbers to the left of stamp 1 or 5, or to the right of stamp 2 or 6 in the pane. The production of coil stamps was from two semicircular plates each 10 stamps wide by 15 or 17 stamps around. The actual plate number was entered on the plate above the first stamp of the first row and below the last stamp in the last row of stamps and was intended to be cut off in the slitting operation. Misslit join line strips from these rows may show a partial plate number. Only one partial plate number will appear near the join line. For side coils (vertically perforated, e.g. Scott #842) a partial plate number may appear over the stamp to the right of the join line, or below the stamp to the left of the join line. For end coils (horizontally perforated, e.g. Scott #851), a partial plate number may appear to the right of the stamp below the join line, or to the left of the stamp above the join line. Partial plate numbers coils from the Stickney Press are usually collected in strips of 5 with the partial plate number on the center stamp.

Cottrell and Huck Presses

The next intaglio rotary press used at the BEP was developed by the Huck Company. The first stamp printed was the 1952 International Red Cross commemorative (Scott #1016). The cross in the stamp design was added by a letter press attachment to the Huck Press. These presses used the so called "dry" printing process. Refinements were made to the Huck Model and new presses were supplied by Cottrell. The first stamp printed on these presses was the 3¢ Statue of Liberty of 1954 (Scott #1035). The first commemorative stamp printed was the Wheatland issue of 1956 (Scott #1081). For the next 30 years, the Huck prototype and the Cottrells printed the bulk of the regular issues, including sheets, coils, and booklets plus most of the single color commemoratives. The last Cottrell Press was retired on November 20, 1985. These presses produced sheet stamps with a plate number in one corner (UL, UR, LL, or LR) of a post office pane. Since two plates were used at a time a normal post office pad of panes consisted of a single position of two alternating plate numbers. Prior to the use of representative plate numbers (USPS "suffix numbers"), the actual plate numbers for booklet plates were trimmed off. Representative plate numbers for booklet stamps appear on the binding tab of the booklet pane. The production of coil stamps used two engraved plates at a time. Initial production of coils used plates that contained 384 subjects (16 stamps wide by 24 stamps around). The plate was divided into two halves each containing 8 rows. The plate numbers were entered above the first stamp of the first row and below the last stamp in the last row of stamps in each half. The plate numbers were intended to be cut off in the slitting operation. Misslit join line strips from these rows may show a partial plate number. Only one partial plate number will appear near the join line. For side coils (vertically perforated, e.g. Scott #1054) a partial plate number may appear over the stamp to the right of the join line, or below the stamp to the left of the join line. Partial plate numbers coils from the 384 subject plates are usually collected in strips of 5 with the partial plate number on the center stamp. Later production of coils used plates that contained 432 subjects (18 stamps wide by 24 stamps around). Prior to the use of representative plate numbers, the actual plate numbers were entered below the first and last stamp in the last row of stamps. The plate numbers were intended to be cut off in the slitting operation. Misslit join line strips from this row may show partial plate

APPENDIX E

numbers. Two partial plate numbers may appear, one on each side of the join line. For side coils (vertically perforated, e.g. Scott #1054) partial plate number may only appear at the bottom. Partial plate numbers coils from the 432-subject plates are usually collected in strips of 6 with the join line in the center. The representative plate number on coils, e.g. on the Transportation Series, appears in the design of the last stamp in each row. Plate number coils are usually collected in strips of 5 with the plate number on the center stamp.

Giori and I-8 Presses

New presses were developed that were capable of printing in more than one color from a single intaglio plate. The sheet-fed Giori Press (and later models designated I-8) printed up to three colors from a single plate. These presses were often used in conjunction with offset lithographic presses. The actual offset plate numbers were regularly trimmed off until 1981. After the introduction of representative plate numbers, both intaglio and offset plate numbers appeared in the selvege. The Giori Press was first used to print the 1957 4¢ Flag Stamp (Scott #1094). Sheet stamps produced by these presses have post office panes with plate numbers in one corner (UL, UR, LL, or LR). A normal pad consists of two or four different plate numbers repeated in groups of four throughout the pad.

Huck 9-color Press

A short-lived 9-color Press designed to Bureau specifications by the Huck Company was intended to be the most advanced stamp press in the world. It printed stamps from up to 3 Giori-type stations each with a cylinder of 30 small plates giving it the capability of printing nine colors (three from each cylinder). The first stamp printed by this press was the 1968 Christmas issue (Scott #1363). Since the press could only be used economically for very long press runs, the only stamps printed on it were the 1968 Christmas, the 1969 Christmas (Scott #1384), and the sheet and coil versions of the Flag stamps: 6¢ (Scott #1338D and Scott #1338A), 8¢ (Scott #1338F and Scott #1338G), 10¢ (Scott #1509 and Scott #1519) and 13¢ (Scott #1622 and Scott #1625). The press produced an extremely high rate of spoilage and was scrapped in 1978. When printing sheet stamps, the press used plates 20 stamps wide and either 2 commemorative size stamps around (40 subjects) or 4 ordinary size stamps around (80 subjects). Plate blocks are usually collected in complete strips of 10 or 20 with the selvege on one side (T and B, or L and R). When printing coil stamps, the press used 72-subject plates, 18 stamps wide and 4 stamps around. Very few partial plate numbers have been found.

Andreotti Gravure Press

The Andreotti Gravure Press was acquired from Andreotti S.P.A. in 1969 to print aerogrammes and stamps. The first stamp produced was the Missouri Statehood (Scott #1426) stamp of 1970. This press uses one cylindrical plate per color and has the capability of simultaneously printing up to seven colors (normally six colors and the tagging compound). Sheet stamps produced by this press have post office panes with plate numbers in one corner (UL, UR, LL, or LR). Each pane in a normal post office pad has the same plate number combination. When actual plate numbers were used, each plate number appeared in the selvege of a different stamp. Plate blocks showed three, four, five or six plate numbers on adjacent stamps. When representative numbers are used, they are all grouped together on the selvege of the corner stamp. For the production of coils, the press used plates 18 stamps wide by either 24 stamps around (432 subjects) or 38 stamps around (684 subjects). The representative plate number appears in the design of all stamps in one column of the plate. Plate number coils are usually collected in strips of 5 with the plate number on the center stamp. There is no join line on issues produced on this press. Bureau precancels are produced on this press by using a separate gravure cylinder which may be indicated by an additional black plate number, as on the 18¢ George Washington and Washington Monument coil stamp (Scott #2149a) or by changing the black line cylinder as was done with the 21.1¢ Letters coil (Scott #2150a). Although both unprecanceled and precanceled coil plate number stamps show apparently identical numbers (11111), the last digit (black) was printed by different cylinders. NOTE: Some plate cylinders were interchangeable for use on either the Andreotti Press or the gravure section of the A Press.

A Press (Intaglio/Gravure)

The combination gravure/intaglio press designated as the A Press was obtained in 1973 and scrapped in 1993. The first stamp produced was the 13¢ Christmas issue (Scott #1703). The early production from this press used only the gravure section by itself or the intaglio section by itself. The first combined use of the gravure and intaglio sections was the Touro Synagogue issue of 1982 (Scott #2017). The press printed up to five gravure colors (one from each gravure plate) and up to three intaglio

APPENDIX E

colors (from one intaglio plate). The press with an Andreotti gravure section was built by Koenig and Bauer with Giori as the prime contractor. The first stamps from this press had a distinctive characteristic, namely that the plate numbers moved or "floated" instead of being in one fixed location. The numbers were located either in the top and bottom margins in the left and right margins. The gravure section plates were 23 stamps around by either 10 commemorative or 20 ordinary stamps wide. The intaglio section plates were 46 stamps around by either 10 commemorative or 20 ordinary stamps wide. When using actual plate numbers, each of the plate numbers (for illustration: A, B, C, D and E) was entered three times on the printing cylinder with either two or three blanks filling out the 23 available spaces around the cylinder.

1 2 3 4 5 6 7 8 9 10 11 12 13 14 15 16 17 18 19 20 21 22 23 1 ...
A B C D E x x x A B C D E x x x A B C D E x x A ...

The web was cut every 10 stamps into sheets. Because the number of stamps around the plate was not a multiple of 10 each cut occurred at a different relative location. It is possible to collect 23 different positions of plate numbers in complete strips. When the changeover was made to representative plate numbers, a change was also made in the layout of the plate numbers on the cylinder. Where previously each gravure plate number appeared adjacent to a separate stamp, now all gravure plate numbers appeared adjacent to a single stamp. This rearrangement produced three distinct types of plate blocks: gravure plate numbers only, intaglio plate numbers only, and with both intaglio and gravure plate numbers. Stamps having only gravure or only intaglio plate numbers are usually collected in plate blocks of 6 stamps with the plate numbers adjacent to the center stamp. Stamps having both gravure and intaglio plate numbers are usually collected in plate blocks of 4 stamps. Later production from this press utilized a change in cylinder layout which resulted in the plate numbers being located in the standard four corners of the sheet. Each sheet in a normal post office pad has the same plate number.

B Press

The 3-color intaglio press designated as the B Press was obtained in 1973 to print multicolor coil and booklet stamps. The B Press was scrapped in 1993. The first 3-color product was the $1.20 booklet pane (Scott #1892-93). The press was built by Koenig and Bauer with Giori as the prime contractor. When printing coil stamps this press utilizes sleeves (cylinders tapered to fit the press mandrel) that are 18 stamps wide by 52 stamps around. There is no join line on coil stamps produced by this press. The same digit is entered on all eighteen stamps in one column of the plate. Therefore the same plate number is found 52 stamps apart in each roll of coil stamps. When printing booklet stamps, the plate number appears on the tab of each booklet pane over the left stamp. All panes in a booklet regularly have the same plate number.

C Press

The 3-color intaglio press designated as the C Press was obtained in 1982 for coil and booklet production. In addition, the press is capable of printing single or multicolor regular or commemorative sheet stamps. The first product was the 20¢ Flag booklet (Scott #1896a). The prime contractor was Goebel. When printing coil stamps this press utilizes seamless printing sleeves that are 20 stamps wide by 48 stamps around. There is no join line on coil stamps produced by this press. A representative plate number is entered on all twenty stamps in one column of the plate. Therefore the same plate number is found 48 stamps apart in each roll of coil stamps. When printing booklet stamps, the plate number will appear in the tab of each booklet pane over the left stamp. All panes in a booklet will have the same plate number. When printing sheet stamps on this press, all post office panes will have one number in one corner (UL, UR, LL, or LR) in a normal pad.

D Press

The combination offset/intaglio press designated as the D Press was obtained in 1984. The press has the capability of printing 6 offset colors (one from each offset plate) plus 3 intaglio colors from one intaglio sleeve. The first stamp produced was the Smoky Bear Commemorative of 1984 (Scott #2096). Since no acceptance run had been made prior to the production of the stamp, the rate of spoilage of this issue was extremely high. Goebel was the prime contractor. When used to print sheet stamps, the offset plate numbers appear in the selvege of one stamp and the intaglio number appears in the selvege of an adjacent stamp. A normal post office pad will have a single combination of offset and intaglio numbers in one corner (UL, UR, LL, or LR). When used to print multicolor booklet stamps, the offset plate numbers are trimmed off and only the intaglio number is available to collectors.

F Press

The F Press is a 4-color offset, 3-color intaglio combination press. The prime contractor is Giori. The first stamp printed was the 1993 World Columbian Stamp Exposition stamp (Scott #2616).

APPENDIX F

Guide to Use of Asterisks to Indicate Scarcity

The use of an asterisk to indicate scarcity is based on:
1) The number of reports in the BIA Plate Number Survey. The exact number of reports for each plate is listed in the BIA Plate Number Checklist, Plates 1-20,000, and serious plate number collectors should obtain a copy of this publication, which lists all of the information known about each plate. The survey reports should be taken as a guide to relative scarcity; the number of copies in existence will usually be considerably greater than the number of reports. The reports did not specify the Scott number, the size of the item (single, block), or the number of examples of the plate number held by the reporter. That is, the number of reports is the number of people reporting that plate number.

The following table indicates the criterion used for each issue. Thus on an issue where the average number of reports is large, plates with 9-11 reports will be considered rare, while on an issue where no plate has more than 4 reports, only single report plates will be given an asterisk. Unreported plates are marked with a †. In most cases, we consider a plate rare only when it has less than half the reports of the average for non-rare plates.
2) When a plate was used for more than one issue, we have marked some plates rare on a given issue on the basis of our experience of their rarity.

Scott #	range of reports	range of reports for plates with *	lowest reports of non-rare plates	average reports of non-rare plates
255	9-26	9-11	19	23
267, impt V	9-28	9-11	12	21
268	8-29	8-11	17	23
270	9-26	9-11	14	21
271	9-27	9	13	18
272	6-32	6-8	11	19
279	1-35	1-4	5	8 (note 1)
279B	2-27	2-7	8	17 (note 2)
279e	1-4	1	2	2.7
280	4-17	4-7	8	13
281	5-24	4-8	9	15
282C	4-24	4-8	11	17
283	4-13	4-6	11	12
285	16-35	16-18	21	28
286	7-31	7-10	13	19
287	14-29	14	25	27
294 frame	14-28	14	18	23
294 vignette	1-18	1-3	6	10
295 frame	9-25	9-10	15	21
295 vignette	6-14	6-7	8	10
300	0-20	1-2	3	6.3
300b	0-6	1-2	4	5
301	3-17	3-5	6	10
301c	1-4	1	2	2.4
302	4-13	4-6	7	11
303	3-17	3-5	6	10
304	4-12	4-5	6	8
305	2-15	2-4	13	14
319	1-16	1-3	4	7
319f	1-13	1-3	4	7
319g	0-7	1	2	2.6
319h	1-4	1	2	2.6
323	3-18	3	7	12

Note 1: Plates above 950 are much more difficult than the earlier ones.
Note 2: Average is 24 for plates below 1000, 12 for plates above 1000.

APPENDIX F
Guide to Use of Asterisks to Indicate Scarcity

Scott #	range of reports	range of reports for plates with *	lowest reports of non-rare plates	average reports of non-rare plates
324	3-18	3-5	6	9
328	4-22	4	15	18
329	5-16	5-6	7	11
331	3-20	3-7	8	13
331a	6-15	6-7	10	13.5
332	5-24	5-7	8	14
332a	2-20	2-5	7	12
334	6-16	6-7	8	11
374	5-19	5	8	14
374a	0-18	1	14	15
375	4-24	4-8	10	15
375a	0-20	3	9	14
405	5-28	5-7	8	15
406	5-25	5-7	8	14
406a	6-16	6	7	10
424d	6-25	6-8	11	18
425e	6-19	6	7	12
463	9-28	9	12	21
498	5-27	5-9	10	18
498e	9-27	9	10	15
499	1-32	1-10	11	20
499e	7-26	7-9	10	16
501	5-25	5-7	12	18
502	0-20	1-7	8	14
504	7-26	7	10	18
507	7-23	7-9	10	15
509	6-28	6	15	21
510	7-29	7	10	20
511	5-28	5-8	17	24
514	6-23	6-9	13	16
525	0-21	1-7	8	13
526	1-19	1-5	6	10
527	0-20	1-5	6	10
528	0-21	1-5	6	11.5
528A	0-19	1-4	6	12
528B	0-24	1-5	6	12
529	0-20	1-7	8	13
530	0-22	1-7	8	14
538	1-15	1-2	3	5.4
540	1-12	1-2	3	4.75
541	3-10	3	4	6.6
552	0-33	1-10	11	20
553	3-32	3-12	14	23
554	0-32	3-11	12	21
554c	2-24	2-7	8	14
555	4-29	4-7	11	20
556	1-30	1-12	18	25
557	2-30	2-9	12	24
559	6-29	6	9	17
561	12-33	12-13	20	27
562	3-29	3-10	11	19
566	6-34	6-12	18	26
567	2-30	2-12	14	22

APPENDIX F
Guide to Use of Asterisks to Indicate Scarcity

Scott #	range of reports	range of reports for plates with *	lowest reports of non-rare plates	average reports of non-rare plates
569	10-36	10-11	17	24
578	1-12	1-3	4	7.4
579	0-11	1-2	3	5.5
581§	1-24	1-7	8	14
582§	2-20	2-7	8	12
583§	0-26	2-7	8	15
583a§	0-5	1	4	5
584§	2-16	2-7	9	12
586§	7-20	7-9	10	13
587§	9-24	9-11	19	23
591§	7-21	7-9	11	16
595	1-11	1-2	3	5.6
597*	0-20	1-2	3	note 3
598	0-14	1-2	3	5.5
599*	0-24	1-2	3	note 4
599A	0-7	1-2	3	4.3
600	0-23	1-4	8	15
601	1-8	1-3	6	7
602	0-13	3-5	10	11
603	0-14	1-2	9	11
604	1-13	l-4	6	9.5
606	0-11	1-3	4	6.4
632a	7-21	7	10	16
634d	0-28	1-7	8	15
656	4-17	4	6	10
720b	3-22	3	10	16
721	0-20	1-6	7	13
804b	1-27	1	19	22
806b	8-23	8-9	15	21
807a	0-30	1-9	14	21
839	0-20	5-7	8	13
840	0-21	3-7	13	17
841	7-21	7-10	13	16
842	0-19	3-7	8	13
843	0-17	1-3	11	13
845	2-14	2	12	13
847	0-15	1	13	14
C10a	3-10	3	9	9.5
C11 center	11-32†	11-12†	14	23
C11 border	12-27	12	14	20
C25a	0-20	1-10	15	18
C39a(wet)	2-21	2	11	16

§ Plates used on perf 10 only.
* Plates not used for coil waste
† Except single known copy of 19639.

Note 3: For plates up to 16827, only 3 not used for coil waste had over 4 reports, and the majority had 0 or 1. Plates in the 19000 and 20000 series had an average of 12 reports.

Note 4: For plates up to 19823, only two not used for coil waste had over 5 reports, and the majority had 0 or 1. From 19833 to 20354 the range was 8-24, with an average of 16 reports. From 20363 to 20799 the range was 1-13 reports, with an average of 7.

APPENDIX F

Guide to Use of Asterisks to Indicate Scarcity

Scott #	range of reports	range of reports for plates with *	lowest reports of non-rare plates	average reports of non-rare plates
E5	4-20	4-9	12	16
E11	7-26	7-9	10	15
E12	2-27	2-9	10	18
E13	13-34	13	20	28
E14	5-32	5-9	17	25
J38	4-25	4-6	10	19
J39	2-23	2-5	9	17
J40	4-23	4-8	13	18
J41	4-21	4-9	16	18
J42	4-21	4-5	11	16
J61,impt IX	8-27	8-14	20	25
J62,impt IX	8-33	8-15	18	26
J63,impt IX	7-27	7-13	18	23
J64,impt IX	8-27	8-9	14	22
J65,impt IX	3-32	3-4	16	22
J66,impt IX	4-15	4-8	11	13
J67,impt IX	7-29	7-10	27	28
Q1	9-23	9-12	15	19
Q2	9-20	9-10	12	15
Q4	9-21	9-11	13	17
Q5	7-19	7-9	12	15
Q9	6-15	6-7	13	14
Q12	3-13	3-5	13	13
JQ3	5-17	5-8	16	17

APPENDIX G
ROTARY PRESS BOOKLET PANE PERCENTAGES

Over the years many devices and/or methods have been used to attempt a determination of the percentage of the partial plate number that may appear on either rotary press printed coil stamps or rotary press printed booklet panes. Virtually all have required a "guesstimate," involving 10% of the number.

Finally, the gauge shown in the adjacent column evolved. The following is taken directly from the included instructions.

DIRECT READING PARTIAL PLATE NUMBER GAUGE

This plate number gauge is usable on plate numbers 17700 and up. (H.M. Southgate, Bureau Specialist, Oct. 1936, p145)

Each black bar in the outside rows is 50% of the plate number. The inner rows are labeled as to the % of the plate number. Thus at the 100% position it is possible to measure 100%, 150% (100 + 50) or 200% (100 + 50 + 50). Also for example, at the 30% position 30%, 80%, and 130% may be measured. A word of caution: we have enlarged many plate numbers up to 30X and have found small variations in the heights of the digits within any number. Check one or more digits within each plate number for an average height.

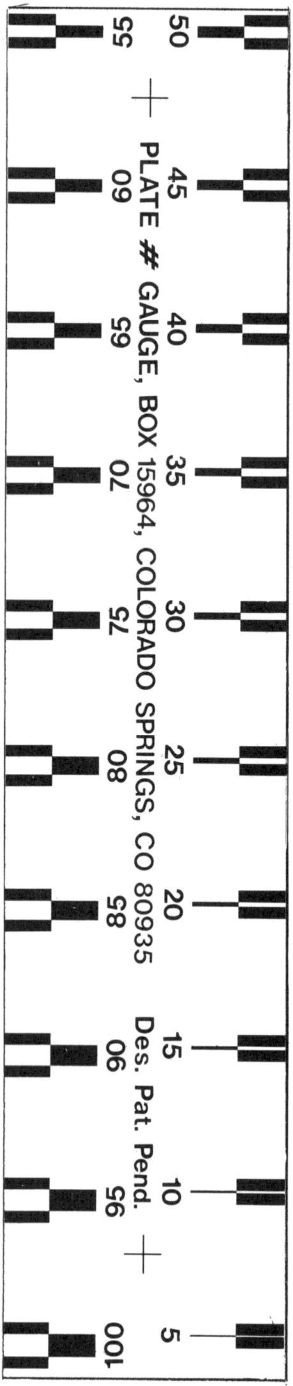

The following pages list all of the 360 subject rotary press booklet pane plate numbers that were printed and issued from Scott #583a through the last use of the 5 digit plate numbers that appeared alongside of the stamps in the UL, LL, UR, and LR positions. Only those numbers which have been reported on 320 and 400 subject plates are listed. The intent in the manufacturing process was that all of the plate numbers would be removed in the trimming operation. This was the case until the new plate numbering system started which shows the suffix number in the margin similar to the old flat plate press printing.

The percentages of plate numbers listed were measured using this gauge. **Positions are determined by orienting all panes with the tab at the top, except for 320 and 400 subject plates were the tab is held at the left.**

If you have any booklet panes showing a larger percentage of plate number, please report them to the editor at:

P.O. Box 2641
Reston, VA 20195

APPENDIX G
ROTARY PRESS BOOKLET PANE PERCENTAGES

#583a 2¢ WASHINGTON

	UL	LL	UR	LR
17450		60		
17451		65		
18550		45		
18551		35		
18662	22.5			
18663	25	30		
†18695				
18696	30			
18697	40	50		
18698	40	55		
18705	45	70		
18706	30	30		
18708	40			
18710	40			

#632a 1¢ FRANKLIN

	UL	LL	UR	LR
18915	80	60		
18916	65	75		
18917	40	70		
18918	50	50		
19529	30	30		
19530	40	40		
19531	65	65		
19532	70	60		
19561	80	85	10	35
19562	80	55	15	45
19563	80	80	T	20
19564	80	70		20
19921	50	50		
19922	30	45		

#634d 2¢ WASHINGTON

	UL	LL	UR	LR
18662	30	45		
18663		35		
18697	85	70		
18698	75	75		
18705	35	35		
18706	20	40		
18707		15		
18708	70	20		
18709	25			
18710	70	25		
†18711				
18712	25	10		
18716		35		
18717		15		
18718	65	55		
18719	35			
18720	80	100		
18721	40	30		
18842	30	75		
18843	40	60		
18844	90	40		
18845	85			
19183	25N			

N Plate single

634d 2¢ WASHINGTON Cont.

	UL	LL	UR	LR
19184		35		
19193	35	55		
19194	40	60		
19199	55	65		
19200	60	50		
19274	65	55		
19275	70	55		
19276	60			
19277	60			
19278	60	50		
19279	90			
19314	35	65		
19315	60	55		
19316	60	75		
19317	30			
19357	80	70		
19358	65	55		
19359				
19360				
19361	45	20		
19362	30	15		
19404	30			
19405	60	40		
19406	75	35		
19407		40		
19408	45	40		
19409	60	55		
19760	80	20		
19761	45	55		
19762	40	45		
19763	60			
19834	100	100		
19835	90	90		
19844	70	100		
19845	67.5	95		
19846	70	100		
19847	65	100		
19848	100	100		
19849	100	100		
19850	100	100		
19851	100	100		
19962	55	100		
19963	65	100		10
19972	40			
19973	100	100	T	10
19990	100	90		
19991	100	95		
20041	40	95		10
20042	45	50		20
20096	100	100		5
20097	100	100		5
20100	65	60		10
20101	70	60	45	15
20106	40	100	20	20
20107	55	65		

APPENDIX G

ROTARY PRESS BOOKLET PANE PERCENTAGES

#720b 3¢ WASHINGTON

	UL	LL	UR	LR
20900	100	50		10
20901	90	30		
20902	60	60		
20903	50	45	70	
20904	80	100	37.5	T
20905	60	45	20	10
21010	100	80		T
21011	100	60		30
21012	60	75		30
21013	45	70		10
21489	45	95	27.5	27.5
21490	30	90	27.5	27.5
21515	50	60		T
21516	40	60		5
21519	20	80	10	5
21520	75	50		

#804b 1¢ WASHINGTON

	UL	LL	UR	LR
Pre-Eye Plates				
22007	25	15	10	10
22008	10	15	20	3
22009	100	100	45	40
22010	100	100	35	35
22234	95	100	20	35
22235	95	100	20	10
Eye Plates				
22389	95	50	15	T
22390	70	80	20	10
22402	100	100	10	10
22403	100	100	10	10
22930	100	85	25	30
22931	100	75	25	20
22977	100	95	35	15
22978	100	90	40	15

#806b 2¢ ADAMS

	UL	LL	UR	LR
Pre-Eye Plates				
22011	100	80	20	20
22012	100	100	85	25
Eye Plates				
22392	90	70	15	5
22404	95	95		
22405	65	95		
22461	80	90	20	10
24298	30	35	50	
24299	35	75	50	

#807a 3¢ JEFFERSON

	UL	LL	UR	LR
Pre-Eye Plates				
21995	100	100	60	40
21996	100	100	55	35
21997	100	100	50	25
21998	100	100	55	35
22170	100	100	45	40
22171	100	100	30	50

807a 3¢ JEFFERSON Cont.

Eye Plates	UL	LL	UR	LR
22434	100	100	35	25
22435	100	100	40	15
22436	100	100	30	25
22437	100	100	35	25
22886	100	100	10	25
22887	100	100	20	10
22932	100	100	20	15
22933	100	100	25	10
22973	100	100	20	5
22974	100	100	20	10
22975	100	100	15	20
22976	100	100	20	22.5
23158	100	100		
23159	100	100		
23160	100	70	25	15
23161	70	50	15	15
23283	100	100	T	10
23284	100	100	T	10
23291	80	100	T	10
23292	70	70		10
23412	95	90	25	15
23413	90	80		T
23422	100	80	5	20
23423	100	90	15	25
23573	80	90	T	
23574	85	100	30	T
23594	80	80	20	30
23595	80	100	15	25
23758	90	85		25
23759	100	85		10
23770	70	100	15	25
23771	85	70	25	10
23847	70			
23848	70			
24089	80	100	20	25
24090	85	90	20	25
24255	100	95	10	20
24256	100	100	5	35
24257	100	100		10
24258	70	95		30
24412	100	95	20	T
24413	100	90	10	
24418	90	100	5	20
24419	75	90		
24420	95	100	20	15
24421	95	100	20	10
24422	60	30		
24423	100	100	25	5
24424	70	80	25	30
24425	80	80	25	25
24426	70	60	20	
24427	60	80	25	
24428	70	20		
24429	60	T		
24443	60	95		
†24739				
†24740				

APPENDIX G
ROTARY PRESS BOOKLET PANE PERCENTAGES

#C64c 8¢ CAPITOL

TAGGED	UL	LL	UR	LR
Slogan 3	"Always Use ZIP"			
27646	37.5	57.5		
27673	25	40		
27674	25	100		
27677	40	50		
27697	10	75		
27698	15	75		
28030	70	85		
28031	40	20		
28032	70	80		
28050	35	40		
28115	95	95		
28116	90	90		
28317	55	70		
28403	65	65		
28404	77.5	85		
28405	80	80		
28469	75	60		
28470	75	60		
28480	85	100		
28481	85	100		
28496	90	90		
28497	85	90		
28575	35	55		
28576		60		

#C72b 10¢ STAR RUNWAY

320 and 400 Subject Plates

No reported numbers

#C72c 10¢ STAR RUNWAY

	UL	LL	UR	LR
Slogan 4	"Mail Early"			
29564	45	60		
29568	25			
Slogan 5	"Use ZIP Code"			
29563	50	50		
29567		45		

#C78a 11¢ JET AIRLINER

	UL	LL	UR	LR
32964	100	100	10	10
32965	100	100	15	
32994	100	75		
32995	100	75		
33485	75	100		
33486	75	100		

#C79a 13¢ WINGED ENVELOPE

	UL	LL	UR	LR
34795	100	100		
34796	100	85		
34843		100		
34844		20		
35338				
35339				

APPENDIX H
"KANSAS CITY ROULETTES"

Imperforate sheets of the 1912 issue were shipped to Kansas City, MO for sale to the vending and affixing machine company in operation at the time. When the demand for the imperforate sheets ceased, the postmaster had a large quantity on hand. He purchased 15 standard "tracing wheels" for use by his clerks to provide a means of separating the stamps for sale to patrons of the office. His unoffical action of providing rouletted stamps was approved on Jan. 15, 1915 by the P.O. Department.

#408 1¢ WASHINGTON

		T	L	R	B
6011	$150	I	I	I	I
6012	$150	I	I	I	I
6013	$150	I	I	I	I
6018	$150	I	I	I	I
6020	$150	I	I	I	I
6041	$150	I	I	I	I
6042	$150	I	I	I	I

#409 2¢ WASHINGTON

6343	$150	I	I	I	I
6358	$150	I	I	I	I
6436	$150	I	I	I	I
6464	$150	I	I	I	I
6490	$150	I	I	I	I
6491	$150	I	I	I	I

APPENDIX J
ALLIED MILITARY POSTAGE STAMPS

The initial plates prepared by the Bureau of Engraving and Printing for use by the Allied Military Government occupation forces consisted of ornamental frames with the wording "ALLIED MILITARY POSTAGE" in white roman letters plus a center ornament with white Gothic numerals.

The plate numbers assigned for the various denominations were as follows:

PLATE NO.	DENOMINATION	COLOR
44460	30	Grey
44462	60	Yellow
44463	2	Red
44464	1	Green
44465	5	Blue
44466	10	Brown
44467	50	Purple
44687	15	Orange
44688	25	Olive

The intent was to prepare an additional plate for overprinting showing the country name above the denomination and the monetary unit below the denomination for each country requiring stamps for AMG usage.

The following overprinting plates were prepared and used; printed in black.

PLATE NO.	COUNTRY	MONETARY UNIT
44620	Italy	Centesimi
44621	Italy	Lira
44622	Italy	Lire

FOR USE IN ITALY

By combining the basic plate printing and the proper overprinting plate the following stamps were prepared for use in Italy.

SCOTT CAT. NO.	FRAME PLATE NO.	VALUE PLATE NO	FACE VALUE
1N1	44687	44620	15 centesimi
1N2	44688	44620	25 centesimi
1N3	44460	44620	30 centesimi
1N4	44467	44620	50 centesimi
1N5	44462	44620	60 centesimi
1N6	44464	44621	1 Lira
1N7	44463	44622	2 Lire
1N8	44465	44622	5 Lire
1N9	44466	44622	10 Lire

FOR USE IN FRANCE

These issues had the country name and the face value as part of the basic design.

SCOTT CAT. NO.	PLATE NO.	FACE VALUE	BASIC COLOR
2N1	45440	5 centimes	Maroon
2N2	45472,45474	10 centimes	Grey
2N3	45442	25 centimes	Brown
2N4	45437	50 centimes	Olive
2N5	45443	1 Franc	Green
2N6	45444	1.50 Francs	Red
2N7	45445	2.50 Francs	Purple
2N8	45568	4 Francs	Blue
2N9	45446	5 Francs	Black
2N10	45475	10 Francs	Orange

These issues utilized one basic frame plate for all denominations showing country name. The frame plate was number 45891. This plate was printed in various colors and the denomination was then applied by an overprinting plate.

SCOTT CAT. NO.	BASIC PLATE NO.	COLOR	OVERPRINTING PLATE NO.	FACE VALUE (Black).
2N11	45891	Orange	45965	30 centimes
2N12	45891	Grey	45966	40 centimes
2N13	45891	Olive	45967	50 centimes
2N14	45891	Purple	45968	60 centimes
2N15	45891	Yellow Green	45923	80 centimes

APPENDIX J
ALLIED MILITARY POSTAGE STAMPS

FOR USE IN FRANCE

Cont.

SCOTT CAT. NO.	BASIC PLATE NO.	COLOR	OVERPRINTING PLATE NO.	FACE VALUE (Black).
2N16	45891	Brown	45931	1.20 franc
2N17	45891	Light Red	45924	1.50 franc
2N18	45891	Yellow	45962	2 francs
2N19	45891	Rose Carmine	45925	2.40 francs
2N20	45891	Maroon	45963	3 francs

FOR USE IN GERMANY

These issues were printed from separate plates for each value of an identical design.

SCOTT CAT. NO.	PLATE NO.	COLOR	FACE VALUE
3N2a	45865	Purple	3 pfennig
3N3a	45866	Grey	4 pfennig
3N4a	45867	Green	5 pfennig
3N5a	45868	Yellow	6 pfennig
3N6a	45869	Orange	8 pfennig
3N7a	45870	Brown	10 pfennig
3N8a	45871	Purple	12 pfennig
3N8a	45882	Purple	12 pfennig
3N8a	45883	Purple	12 pfennig
3N9a	45872	Red	15 pfennig
3N13a	45873	Blue	25 pfennig

FOR USE IN AUSTRIA

SCOTT CAT. NO.	PLATE NO.	COLOR	FACE VALUE
4N1	46506	Orange	3 groschen
4N2	46508	Light Brown	4 groschen
4N3	46509	Green	5 groschen
4N3	46517	Green	5 groschen
4N4	46510	Maroon	6 groschen
4N5	46511	Claret	8 groschen
4N6	46494	Grey	10 groschen
4N7	46495	Brown	12 groschen
4N8	46496	Red	15 groschen
4N9	46499	Bistre	20 groschen
4N10	46497	Blue	25 groschen
4N11	46500	Magenta	30 groschen
4N12	46501	Slate Blue	40 groschen
4N13	46505	Olive Green	60 groschen
4N14	46512	Purple	1 schilling
4N15	46513	Yellow	2 schilling
4N16	46514	Indigo	5 schilling
4N17	46916	Blue	1 groschen

The AMG stamps printed by the Bureau of Engraving and Printing were converted to use as postage due stamps by locally applying the overprint "PORTO".

SCOTT CAT. NO.	PLATE NO.	COLOR	FACE VALUE
J189	46506	Orange	3 groschen
J190	46517	Green	5 groschen
J191	46510	Maroon	6 groschen
J192	46511	Claret	8 groschen
J193	46494	Grey	10 groschen
J194	46495	Brown	12 groschen
J195	46496	Red	15 groschen

APPENDIX J
ALLIED MILITARY POSTAGE STAMPS

FOR USE IN AUSTRIA **Cont.**

SCOTT CAT. NO.	PLATE NO.	COLOR	FACE VALUE
J196	46499	Bistre	20 groschen
J197	46497	Blue	25 groschen
J198	46500	Magenta	30 groschen
J199	46501	Slate Blue	40 groschen
J200	46505	Olive Green	60 groschen
J201	46512	Purple	1 schilling
J202	46513	Yellow	2 schilling
J203	46514	Indigo	5 schilling

APPENDIX K
BLUE COVER "MDI" BOOKLETS

During 1996 several issues appeared in handmade "booklets" produced by Minnesota Diversified Industries. Some of these booklets simply contain blocks of 15 stamps torn from normal sheet stamp production while others were made from stock intended for sheetlets of 20 self adhesive stamps. These later panes are unique to these booklets, but contain no plate numbers as the strip normally containing the number was removed in the manufacturing process.

Panes unique to "MDI" booklets

in both $4.80 and $9.60 booklets

32¢ PINK ROSE

#2492b pane of 15 + 1 label
#2492e pane of 14
#2492f pane of 16
#???? pane of 16 + 1 stamp removed

32¢ MIDNIGHT ANGEL

#3012c pane of 15 + 1 label
#???? pane of 16 + 1 stamp removed

32¢ LOVE CHERUB

#3030b pane of 15 + 1 label

32¢ FLAG OVER PORCH

#2920f pane of 15 + 1 label
#???? pane of 16+1 stamp removed

Panes from sheet stamp stock

$4.80 booklets except #3090

#3024 32¢ UTAH
BK245
P11111 P22222 UL, UR

#3065 32¢ FULBRIGHT SCHOLARSHIP
BK246
1111-1 UL, LL

#3069 32¢ GEORGIA O'KEEFFE
BK247
S1111 UL, UR, LL, LR

#3070 32¢ TENNESSEE STATEHOOD
BK248
S11111 UL, UR, LL, LR

#3072-76 32¢ INDIAN DANCES
BK249
P1111 P2222 P3333
UL, UR, LL, LR

#3082 32¢ JAMES DEAN
BK250
S1111111 UL, LL

#3083-86 32¢ FOLK HEROES
BK251
no plate numbers

#3087 32¢ DISCUS THROWER
BK252
P1 UL, UR

#3088 32¢ IOWA STATEHOOD
BK253
P1111 P2222 LL, LR

#3090 32¢ RURAL FREE DELIVERY
BK254
1111-1 1112-1 1122-1
1123-1 2235-1

#3091-95 32¢ RIVERBOATS SELF ADHESIVE
BK255
no plate numbers

#3105 32¢ ENDANGERED SPECIES
BK256
no plate numbers

#3107 32¢ MADONNA
BK257
1111-1 2222-1 UL, UR

#3118 32¢ HANUKKAH SELF ADHESIVE
BK258
V11111 LL

For a more detailed description of these booklets please see Research Paper #2.
Order form: W. Cleland, 1710 University Ave., Madison, WI 53705 (write for current price)

APPENDIX L
UNREPORTED PLATE NUMBERS

The numbers listed in this Appendix were sent to press but have not been reported for ANY Scott Catalog Number. In the days of the flat plate printings, the same plate was used to produce many different Scott numbered stamps including sheet stamps with various perforations and/or watermarks in addition to side and end coils. A similar situation exists for the early rotary press printed stamps where the plates used for the production of coils, later had the stock used to produce the sheet stamps known as the coil waste issues. If the plate number has been reported as ANY Scott number it is not listed here. We are also not listing the numbers used for lithographic plates or offset plates that were used in conjunction with multi-colored issues. The only reported example is shown on page 352. We have also omitted the nine-color Huck coil plates for the 6, 8, 10, and 13 cent values. Should you have any examples of numbers specifically listed here or any of the nine-color Huck coil numbers not listed in the proper place in the catalog, please send a report plus a clear xerox so that your stamp may be listed in the next edition.

Flat plates - Booklets

1323	1846	1847	1848	2234
2605	3215	3216	3235	3236
3237	3240	3405	3406	3413
3414	3421	3422	3450	3464
3474	3475	3479	3531	3637
3638	3639	3666	3667	3670
3756	4003	4004	4007	4008
4057	4062	4107	4109	4223
4275	4357	4544	5455	5457
5469				

Flat plates - End coils

6566	6567	6569	6573

Flat plates - Sheets

8866	8867	8903	13390	15433
16562	19636	19637	19638	

Offset plates - Sheets

8617	8717	8720	8725	8814
8969	9718	9720	9791	9840
9979	9992	10031	10924	10978
10981	11051	11145	11221	11264
11310	11480	11500	11562	11563
11690	11707	11841	11889	11922
12127	12148	12149	12161	12188
12240	12344	12348	12361	12397
12405	12626	12646	12656	12700
12731	12738	12770	12794	12795
12796	12804	12848	13162	

Rotary plates - Sheets

17284	18124	18125

Back numbers

34080	34086	35715	35721	35727
35751				

Huck plates - Sheets

29923	30428	30491	32169	32839
32900	33663	33664	33670	33677
33680	33681	33720	33721	33722
33723	33724	33725	33867	33868
33870	33871	33872	33875	33876
33877	33878	33879	34951	35010
35020	35181	35451	35464	35469
35478	35479	35480	35481	35970
35981	36252	37786	37803	

Rotary plates - Booklets

18695	18711	24739	24740	29397
29398	29440	29441	29444	29445
29455	29456	29463	29464	29465
29466	29469	29470	29477	29478
29485	29486	29498	29499	29521
29522	29523	29524	29528	29529
29538	29539	29540	29541	29550
29551	29596	29597	29644	29645
29646	29647	29675	29676	29677
29680	29681	29698	29699	29703
29704	29710	29711	29713	29714
29732	29733	29739	29740	30109
30110	30113	30114	30115	30136
30307	30308	30309	30310	30324
30325	30330	30331	30335	30336
30409	30410	30566	30567	30570
30571	30641	30642	30652	30653
30657	30666	30667	30682	30683
30699	30700	30776	30777	30784
30785	30792	30813	30814	30823
30824	30834	30848	30849	30911
30912	31014	31015	31244	31743
31744	31745	31746	31774	31795
31872	31917	31918	31925	31926
31933	31961	31962	32010	32170
32171	32761	32770	32771	32772
32773	33293	33294	33295	33296
33297	33298	33299	33300	33301

APPENDIX L
UNREPORTED PLATE NUMBERS

33302	33338	33339	33401	33402
33414	33419	33420	33425	33426
33763	33764	33765	33766	33796
33797	33821	33822	34100	34234
34402	34403	34482	34483	34499
34500	34526	34527	34534	34535
34536	34537	34730	34957	35212
35293	35294	35674	35675	35682
35764	35765	35785	35786	35787
35788	36005	36006	36068	36074
36097	36098	36121	36122	36142
36281	36282	36502	36503	36504
36505	36517	36650	36724	36772
36773	36774	36775	36885	36902
36903	36904	36905	36910	36911
36917	36918	36944	36945	37151
37253	37258	37321	37377	37572
37573	37574	37575	37699	37706
37824	37825	37826	37827	37829
37850	37851	37852	37853	37854
37855	37856	37970	37971	37972
37973	37975	37986	37987	38042
38043	38045	38046	38047	38048
38049	38050	38055	38056	38233
38657	38658	38659	38660	38661
38674	38675	38681	38682	38683
38684	38724	38745	38746	38827
38828	38829	38830	38831	38846
38847	38848	38849	38878	38879
38908	38970	38971	38983	39002
39003	39004	39005	39045	39046
39059	39060	39067	39068	39200
39201	39202	39203	39212	39214
39215	39216	39217	39218	39225
39227	39228	39230	39240	39251
39252	39253	39254	39255	39256
39257	39469	39471	39472	39476
39477	39483	39484	39493	39494
39496	39497	39581	39582	

Rotary plates - Coils

6279	6280	6856	6857	7171
7174	7175	7182	7183	7230
7231	7270	7271	7408	7409
7417	7418	7422	7423	7425
7426	7427	7428	7429	7431
7432	7433	7434	7435	7436
7440	7441	7442	7443	7444
7445	7446	7458	7467	7468
7469	7470	7482	7483	7489
7497	7502	7503	7506	7507
7508	7510	7511	7512	7513
7521	7522	7523	7552	7553
7561	7562	7563	7564	7565
7566	7567	7617	7619	7621
7626	7627	7628	7629	7630
7634	7635	7636	7637	7661
7662	7672	7673	7675	7676
7677	7678	7679	7680	7686
7689	7690	7691	7738	7739
7744	7745	7746	7747	7751
7752	7763	7766	7767	7782
7803	7804	7813	7814	7826
7827	7829	7830	7835	7836
7852	7853	7909	7910	7915
7916	7939	7940	7953	7957
7958	7961	7962	7963	7964
7965	7967	7976	7978	7979
8049	8050	8051	8052	8056
8057	8061	8062	8071	8072
8073	8074	8075	8076	8077
8078	8079	8080	8081	8082
8107	8108	8109	8110	8111
8112	8124	8125	8151	8152
8153	8154	8155	8169	8170
8201	8202	8203	8218	8219
8226	8228	8229	8233	8237
8238	8239	8240	8244	8245
8247	8248	8250	8251	8269
8270	8275	8276	8326	8337
8402	8408	8409	8428	8429
8442	8455	8458	8459	8464
8467	8468	8469	8470	8471
8472	8475	9181	9182	9457
10081	10088	10345	10346	10349
10408	10409	10411	10487	10767
10768	11718	11719	11725	13401
13402	13413	13417	13425	13426
13427	13428	13505	13506	13507
13509	13510	13605	13606	13607
13608	13625	13626	13629	13630
13631	13632	13633	13634	13637
13638	13641	13642	13776	13800
13804	13805	13821	13828	13829
13830	13928	13961	14155	14156
14660	14721	14980	15244	15280
15322	15340	15371	15406	15407
15418	15442	15444	15450	15541
15543	15565	15590	15617	15618
15638	15665	15666	15706	15707
15808	15824	15825	15838	15839
15846	15870	15909	15916	15918
15928	15929	15930	15931	15936
15937	15938	15939	15973	15975
16015	16022	16039	16054	16063
16109	16110	16161	16162	16164
16204	16220	16265	16284	16285
16339	16340	16396	16397	16422
16423	16424	16425	16435	16436
16437	16457	16458	16459	16461
16462	16480	16481	16482	16483

APPENDIX L
UNREPORTED PLATE NUMBERS

16485	16486	16509	16510	16512
16513	16516	16517	16522	16523
16524	16525	16542	16543	16544
16545	16676	16683	16685	16696
16729	16730	16731	16736	16779
16809	16810	16822	16854	16883
16945	16995	16998	17027	17028
17069	17271	17272	17275	17276
17277	17278	17279	17280	17281
17282	17283	17290	17306	17307
17323	17324	17434	17435	17502
17503	17504	17505	17510	17517
17518	17563	17571	17573	17574
17575	17600	17633	17635	17636
17662	17663	17664	17665	17674
17675	17691	17776	17777	17800
17801	17806	17827	17846	17847
17859	17872	17873	17879	17902
17903	17904	17905	17907	17963
17973	17974	17976	17981	17982
17985	17991	17992	17996	17999
18014	18015	18046	18048	18049
18050	18051	18052	18053	18067
18069	18071	18073	18074	18075
18077	18078	18090	18100	18101
18102	18128	18129	18147	18174
18254	18271	18293	18306	18315
18324	18339	18353	18354	18366
18393	18427	18447	18448	18514
19052	19177	19178	19179	19180
19219	19224	19356	19367	19386
19450	19471	19491	19492	19499
19516	19524	19533	19535	19536
19683	19684	19751	19817	21592
21593	21596	21597	21639	21640
21641	21642	21643	21644	21646
21647	21702	21703	21704	21791
21792	21800	21803	21804	21979
22103	22208	22209	22223	22224
23394	24052	25167	25171	25172
25433	25434	25435	25436	25443
25444	25479	25480	25575	25576
25577	25578	25617	25618	25629
25630	25663	25666	25899	25900
25975	25976	26034	26035	26193
26194	26211	26212	26213	26214
26360	26361	26374	26375	26381
26382	26436	26437	26449	26450
26455	26456	26478	26479	26484
26485	26505	26506	26513	26514
26538	26539	26547	26548	26585
26586	26656	26657	26703	26704
26732	26733	26748	26749	26812
26813	26835	26836	26839	26840
26857	26861	26862	26872	26876
26877	26879	26880	26881	26882
26891	26892	26893	26894	26902
26903	26918	26919	26922	26923
26924	26925	26933	26934	26941
26942	26947	26948	26949	26950
26953	26954	26957	26958	26962
26963	26968	26969	26973	26974
26984	26985	27012	27013	27018
27019	27022	27023	27030	27031
27043	27044	27069	27070	27077
27078	27084	27085	27094	27095
27097	27098	27100	27101	27123
27124	27133	27135	27136	27139
27140	27141	27143	27144	27158
27183	27208	27209	27234	27235
27240	27241	27244	27245	27256
27257	27258	27259	27269	27270
27284	27285	27287	27288	27291
27292	27302	27303	27309	27310
27319	27320	27321	27322	27334
27336	27367	27368	27385	27394
27395	27396	27397	27399	27400
27404	27405	27406	27407	27419
27420	27421	27422	27423	27424
27429	27430	27440	27441	27442
27443	27444	27445	27448	27449
27451	27452	27470	27471	27480
27481	27495	27496	27531	27532
27533	27534	27536	27537	27538
27539	27542	27543	27544	27545
27549	27551	27552	27580	27581
27582	27583	27617	27618	27619
27620	27628	27629	27631	27632
27633	27634	27635	27648	27665
27666	27667	27668	27690	27691
27699	27700	27708	27709	27710
27711	27712	27713	27729	27730
27752	27753	27755	27756	27757
27758	27759	27760	27761	27762
27767	27768	27769	27770	27781
27782	27783	27810	27817	27835
27837	27907	27908	27963	27964
27978	28045	28052	28053	28120
28121	28199	28200	28280	28288
28289	28446	28447	28451	28452
28454	28455	28464	28465	28477
28489	28490	28502	28503	28504
28534	28535	28546	28547	28551
28552	28555	28556	28563	28566
28583	28584	28585	28586	28596
28597	28811	28812	28886	28887
28891	28892	28901	28907	28913
28916	28924	28926	28928	28932
28933	28934	28935	28936	28937
28939	28950	28952	28953	28959

APPENDIX L
UNREPORTED PLATE NUMBERS

28965	28974	29082	29138	29139
29150	29151	29156	29157	29171
29172	29175	29176	29178	29179
29188	29219	29220	29238	29273
29274	29285	29286	29290	29291
29302	29303	29338	29339	29360
29361	29386	29387	29410	29411
29554	29555	29577	29578	29584
29585	29606	29607	29626	29628
29724	29725	29747	29748	29770
29771	29776	29777	29783	29784
29788	29789	29797	29798	29804
29812	29813	29815	29853	29856
29866	29960	29981	29982	30030
30038	30053	30054	30067	30090
30091	30107	30108	30118	30119
30149	30158	30159	30197	30361
30391	30429	30430	30501	30519
30538	30539	30549	30569	30584
30585	30639	30640	30661	30674
30860	30878	30890	30891	30902
30903	30919	30920	30959	30960
30971	30972	31243	31427	31428
31438	31439	31450	31451	31471
31477	31543	31544	31573	31574
31908	31909	31936	31937	31953
31954	31966	31967	32037	32129
32130	32288	32289	32339	32372
32373	32395	32396	32470	32471
32860	32884	32885	33455	33539
33873	33889	33962	33963	34038
34039	34150	34353	34354	34657
34658	34659	35504	35505	35506
35507	35547	35548	35549	35560
35570	35575	35624	35625	35626
35627	35670	35671	35695	35696
35697	35698	35699	35700	35701
35702	35705	35706	35758	35877
36012	36014	36088	36119	36206
36207	36359	36360	36817	36849
36853	36854	37149	37169	37304
37536	37537	37549	37550	37551
37576	37577	37595	37602	37603
37607	37608	37609	37612	37613
37654	37655	37715	37716	37717
37718	37948	37949	37976	37977
37988	37989	38116	38117	38118
38119	38148	38182	38183	38184
38185	38215	38216	38230	38231
38261	38262	38263	38264	38342
38343	38345	38351	38352	38396
38397	38420	38423	38456	38457
38458	38483	38492	38529	38532
38563	38692	38747	38768	38785
38819	38850	38877	38894	38914
38923	38932	38933	38934	38935
38963	38964	38996	39021	39028
39029	39030	39048	39061	39062
39065	39066	39071	39073	39074
39165	39183	39184	39199	39283
39288	39289	39291	39292	39300
39315	39344	39345	39346	39347
39366	39367	39373	39374	39399
39414	39415	39433	39434	39435
39436	39449	39450	39451	39452
39455	39456	39473	39474	39481
39482	39491	39492	39510	39511
39552	39553	39573	39943	39955
40011	40167	40168	40222	40223

APPENDIX M
PLATE POSITION DIAGRAMS

The following issues appeared with plate position diagrams in the margin indicating the position which each post office pane occupied on the uncut press sheet. All positions have been reported for each plate number except for those indicated at the end of this Appendix.

Style 1

1	2
3	4

#2477	1¢	Kestral (revised)
#2587	32¢	James K. Polk
#2812	29¢	Edward R. Murrow
#2816	29¢	Allison Davis
#2819-28	29¢	Silent Screen Stars
#2839	29¢	Norman Rockwell
#2848	29¢	George Meany
#2862	29¢	James Thurber
#2897	32¢	Flag over Porch
#2933	32¢	Milton S. Hershey
#2934	32¢	Cal Farley
#2938	46¢	Ruth Benedict
#2940	55¢	Alice Hamilton
#2943	78¢	Alice Paul
#2955	32¢	Richard Nixon
#2956	32¢	Bessie Coleman
#2980	32¢	Women's Suffrage
#2999	32¢	Palau
#3004-07	32¢	Santa and Children
#3024	32¢	Utah
#3032	2¢	Woodpecker
#3033	3¢	Bluebird
#3065	32¢	Fulbrihgt Scholarship
#3070	32¢	Tennessee
#3087	32¢	Discus Thrower
#3088	32¢	Iowa
#3104	32¢	F. Scott Fitzgerald
#3106	32¢	Computer Technology
#3108-11	32¢	Family Scenes

Style 2

1	2
3	4
5	6

#2544	$3.00	Challenger Shuttle
#2544A	$10.75	Endeavor Shuttle
#2590	$1.00	Saratoga
#2592	$5.00	Washington & Jackson
#2749	29¢	Grace Kelly
#2755	29¢	Dean Acheson
#2807-11	29¢	Winter Olympics
#2814¢	29¢	Love
#2842	$9.95	Moon Landing
#2867-68	29¢	Whooping Cranes
#2871	29¢	Traditional Christmas
#2948	(32¢)	Love Cherub
#2957	32¢	Love Cherub
#2967	32¢	Marilyn Monroe
#2968	32¢	Texas
#2998	60¢	Eddie Richenbacker
#3003	32¢	Madonna
#3061-64	32¢	Communications
#3069	32¢	Georgia O'Keefe
#3077-80	32¢	Prehistoric Animals
#3082	32¢	James Dean
#3090	32¢	Rural Free Delivery
#3107	32¢	Madonna

Style 3

1	2	3
4	5	6

#2750-53	29¢	Circus
#2815	52¢	Love
#2854-61	29¢	Blues and Jazz Singers
#2869	29¢	L. of the West (revised)
#2870	29¢	L. of the West (recalled)
#2951-54	32¢	Kids Care
#2958	55¢	Love Cherub
#2961-65	32¢	Recreational Sports
#2975	32¢	Civil War
#2982	32¢	Louis Armstrong
#2983-92	32¢	Jazz Musicians
#3000	32¢	Comic Strips
#3066	50¢	Jacqueline Cochrane
#3068	32¢	Olympic Games
#3072-76	32¢	Indian Dances
#3081	32¢	Breast Cancer
#3083-86	32¢	Folk Heroes
#3096-99	32¢	Big Band Leaders
#3100-03	32¢	Songwriters
#3105	32¢	Endangered Species

Style 4

1	2	3	4
5	6	7	8

#2872	29¢	Christmas Stocking
#2950	32¢	Florida
#2966	32¢	POW/MIA
#2976-79	32¢	Carousel Horses
#3001	32¢	U.S. Naval Academy
#3002	32¢	Tennessee Williams
#3058	32¢	Ernest E. Just
#3059	32¢	Smithsonian
#3067	32¢	Marathon

APPENDIX M
PLATE POSITION DIAGRAMS

Style 5

1	2
3	4
5	6
7	8

#3019-23	32¢	Antique Automobiles

Style 6

1	2	3
4	5	6
7	8	9

#2817	29¢	Year of the Dog
#2818	29¢	Buffalo Soldiers
#2834	29¢	World Cup Soccer
#2835	40¢	World Cup Soccer
#2836	50¢	World Cup Soccer
#2849-53	29¢	Popular Singers
#2863-66	29¢	Wonders of the Sea
#2876	29¢	Year of the Boar
#2974	32¢	United Nations
#3060	32¢	Year fo the Rat

Style 7

1	2
3	4
5	6
7	8
9	10

#3091-95	32¢	Riverboats
#3118	32¢	Hanukkah

The following positions are unreported:

Style 1

#2477	1¢	Kestral (revised)
1112	1	
3333	1, 3, 4	

Style 2

#2544A	$10.75	Endeavor Shuttle
P2222-1	5	
#2842	$9.95	Moon Landing
B2222-1	1, 6	
#3090	32¢	Rural Free Delivery
1112-1	6	
2235-1	2	
#3107	32¢	Madonna
1212-1	4, 5	

Style 3

#2815	52¢	Love
2222-1	1, 2, 5	
#2951-54	32¢	Kids Care
P55555	2	
#3066	50¢	Jacqueline Cochrane
2212-1	1, 2, 3, 5, 6	

All other positions have been reported.

NOTES